D1478683

Furrows in a Field

ADVANCE PRAISE FOR THE BOOK

'This meticulous and detailed account of H.D. Deve Gowda's very full life that spans nearly nine decades, provides a rich treasury of insights into the politics of India since Independence. Sugata Srinivasaraju has produced a powerful and resonant book. His writing is vigorous and expressive. This is a work of scholarly exactitude, critical sympathy and warm humanity' —Jeremy Seabrook, author and columnist

'A vivid and textured biography showing how Deve Gowda's agrarian roots and regional moorings shaped his brief stint at the apex of national power. Srinivasaraju illuminates a long life of struggle, with key insights into the complexities of caste, class and religion in Karnataka, and the contributions of the south to all-India politics. *Furrows in a Field* uncovers the green shoots of a generous federal alternative to the bigotry of religious majoritarianism and the dead end of secular uniformity'—Sugata Bose, Gardiner Professor of Oceanic History and Affairs, Harvard University, and author of *His Majesty's Opponent: Subhas Chandra Bose and India's Struggle against Empire*

'H.D. Deve Gowda's short tenure as prime minister was not inconsequential. As chief minister of, and as a minister in, Karnataka, he made several contributions that have endured. As a public figure living for and breathing politics for almost six decades, he has carved out and occupied a distinctive niche. His commitment to the cause of farmers, particularly, has been legendary. It is only fitting that this remarkable man has at last found a biographer who does full justice to his life story. Through this extensively researched work, Sugata Srinivasaraju has made a major contribution to contemporary Indian history'—Jairam Ramesh, member of Parliament, and author of *A Chequered Brilliance: The Many Lives of V.K. Krishna Menon*

'H.D. Deve Gowda is one of the tallest leaders of India. I came in contact with him when there was extreme turmoil in Jammu and Kashmir, and he was prime minister. He had the courage and dedication to save the situation from going from bad to worse. He conducted fair elections, through which I came to government . . . Gowda is a committed secularist and stands by the ideals and principles on which our founding fathers based this country'—Farooq Abdullah, former chief minister of Jammu and Kashmir

'This fascinating biography of former prime minister H.D. Deve Gowda demonstrates that outsiders could rise to power in twentieth-century

India's democracy—and not by default, but because *kisan* politics was still meaningful then. This book does not only tell the life story of the most improbable prime minister of India, it also narrates the trajectory of the country over several key decades—with special references to Karnataka, a state whose rural countryside, too often obliterated by the shine of Bangalore, is apprehended here through one of its sons'—Christophe Jaffrelot, research director, CERI–Sciences Po, Paris, and professor, King's India Institute, London

'This richly illustrated biography captures the triumph of an unpretentious prime minister who had more grassroots experience than many of our more celebrated prime ministers. It is unfortunate that he did not survive long in the chair. Indian democracy would have been reassured and deepened if he had'—Saeed Naqvi, author and journalist

Furrows in a Field

THE UNEXPLORED LIFE OF
H.D. DEVE GOWDA

SUGATA SRINIVASARAJU

VINTAGE
An imprint of Penguin Random House

VINTAGE

USA | Canada | UK | Ireland | Australia
New Zealand | India | South Africa | China

Vintage is part of the Penguin Random House group of companies
whose addresses can be found at global.penguinrandomhouse.com

Published by Penguin Random House India Pvt. Ltd
4th Floor, Capital Tower 1, MG Road,
Gurugram 122 002, Haryana, India

Penguin
Random House
India

First published in Vintage by Penguin Random House India 2021

ISBN 9780670093434

Typeset in Adobe Garamond Pro by Manipal Technologies Limited, Manipal
Printed at Thomson Press India Ltd, New Delhi

www.penguin.co.in

MIX
Paper
FSC FSC® C010615

For Rosy D'Souza,
song of a hundred stars

'For, I remember very well, in a discourse one day with the King, when I happened to say there were several thousand books among us written upon the *Art of Government*, it gave him (directly contrary to my intention) a very mean opinion of our understandings. He professed both to abominate and despise all *mystery, refinement*, and *intrigue*, either in a prince or a minister. He could not tell what I meant by *Secrets of State*, where an enemy or some rival nation were not in the case. He confined the knowledge of governing within very *narrow bounds*; to common sense and reason, to justice and lenity, to the speedy determination of civil and criminal causes; with some other obvious topics which are not worth considering. And, he gave it for his opinion, that whoever could make two ears of corn, or two blades of grass to grow, upon a spot of ground where only one grew before, would deserve better of mankind, and do more essential service to his country, than the whole race of politicians put together.'

—From 'A Voyage to Brobdingnag' in *Gulliver's Travels* by Jonathan Swift, Penguin Books, 1967 (first published in 1726); emphasis as found in the original text

* * *

'So, apply, apply as much perfume as you want, sandal scent and musk. Indulge in as many epicurean delights. Let's see how long you do this, I'll watch intently.

Those who apply vermilion marks, sandal paste and ash on their foreheads and think they are better than those who work like donkeys in the field; those who think they are better than those who sweat profusely, and whose bodies are smeared with mud and manure; do not worry, this thinking is soon going to turn on its head.

The plough will displace the king's sword, pearls will fall off the crown, and pearls will be ploughed to grow glistening paddy. That finest hour comes packed closer and closer.'

—A loose translation of the last few lines of the poem 'Gobbara', written in old Kannada by Kannada writer Kuvempu (K.V. Puttappa) in January 1935

* * *

'Probability theory is nothing but common sense reduced to calculation.'

—Pierre-Simon Laplace, eighteenth-century French mathematician and astronomer. The quote was found painted without attribution in January 2021 on the wall of the Holenarasipur Municipal High School in the Hassan district of Karnataka, where H.D. Deve Gowda completed his matriculation.

Contents

Introduction

In the Kannada language, the phrase *doddajeeva*, roughly meaning a big life, would be culturally associated with a person who has led a long life and whose breadth and depth of experience is both exhaustive and expansive. This unassuming phrase has great pertinence to the life of the nearly nonagenarian H.D. Deve Gowda. His political life to date has spanned seventy years, that is if one takes into account the year he became a primary member of the Congress party. He became a legislator sixty years ago, but that was not his first election. Right from when he joined politics, around 1952, to becoming the eleventh prime minister of India, in 1996, and for twenty-five years thereafter, Deve Gowda has learnt to carry the mixed bag of victory and defeat, adulation and humiliation by shifting them with ease between his shoulders.

Despite a long and eventful innings in politics—which has, in significant ways, shaped not just post-Independence power shifts in India, but also offered correctives to our indigenous imagination of democracy—there has quite literally been no serious literature to understand the man and his work. There is no appraisal that helps us understand his personality, his personal transformation from a small-time grassroots operative to chief minister and prime minister, his political stamina and resilience, or his Machiavellian instincts and skullduggery. What is available now is an impatient, uninformed, and prejudiced media construct, which flatly portrays him as a shrewd arbiter of power, as a philistine and as being clannish, dynastic and vindictive. He is put in the same category as some other Indian political patriarchs and painted with the same broad brushstrokes of ignorance. This is not just unfair to Deve Gowda, but also to us and our understanding of history and democracy. This biography is a small effort to offer a corrective and fill the gap.

Deve Gowda is a very early model of a politician who tried to combine caste identity politics with legal battles, legislative interventions and big development ideas to play the electoral game. This makes him a very interesting, and at the same time, a very complex, multidimensional subject of study. Once, H.Y. Sharada Prasad, well-known as Indira Gandhi's confidante and information adviser, said that if only his boss had Gowda's understanding of the law, which came from the practical experience of litigating at all levels of the Indian judiciary, she would have never imposed the Emergency. This, he said around 2004, and that is when I started looking at Gowda differently, with a curiosity that went beyond drawing-room chatter. Sharada Prasad and Deve Gowda came from the same hometown—Holenarasipur. As I began to look at him closely, I came across similar assessments by rival politicians, top attorneys and bureaucrats about Gowda's deep understanding of water disputes, irrigation issues and agriculture policy; his appetite for technological change; his embrace of modernity; his administrative acumen, and a firm commitment to the plural inheritance of India. I always wondered why all of this had never been put together.

Not many people would be aware that a paddy variety in Punjab was named after Deve Gowda by the peasants there. This was not an honour bestowed by a sitting government but was an ungazetted intervention on the part of the people who were informally acknowledging his focus on agriculture and an empathetic approach to farmers' issues during his short tenure as prime minister. Gowda's popularity and goodwill similarly extended to the North-east. He enjoyed goodwill in Kashmir. As prime minister, he restored the democratic process there. He also made a name in Bangladesh. The book discusses how in an unconventional manner he got himself into the centre of so much.

It is not that the pan-India narrative about Gowda is truncated. Even in his home state of Karnataka, his legacy is measured by the myopia of caste identity politics. The fact that he is the patriarch of the Vokkaligas, a powerful peasant community that controls the electoral destiny of south Karnataka, has subsumed every other aspect of his political journey. Also, a reference to Gowda invariably brings up a reference to his rivalry with Ramakrishna Hegde. These references are not without an undercurrent of Brahmin–Shudra narratives, prejudices and perceptions. In the process, his fight for water rights of major rivers like Cauvery and Krishna and their tributaries is not adequately highlighted. Similarly, his efforts to ensure communal peace are underrated. He had peacefully resolved the Idgah Maidan issue as chief minister. Bangalore as a metropolis was his modernity project too, and that has never found mention anywhere. If Bangalore as an IT services and technological innovations hub today commands over 60 per cent of the state's revenue and has become the back office of the world, his policy initiatives in the 1990s cannot be ignored. In fact, even for a city like Delhi, the fruition of the metro rail project began with Deve Gowda, who gave it a financial closure.

All through his career, Deve Gowda demonstrated a knack for picking the right people for the right job and working with some of the most credible bureaucrats in the country. It was he who picked J.M. Lyngdoh as election commissioner of India (he later became chief election commissioner) and brought in credible people like T.R. Satishchandran, T.S.R. Subramanian, B.N. Yugandhar and S.S. Meenakshisundaram to work with him. He retained A.P.J. Abdul Kalam in an advisory role despite opposition from the scientific community. Arguably, if Kalam had not been given an extension by Gowda, he would have been out of sight and out of the system for

the Vajpayee regime to pick him as President of India later. Even
in the political arena in Karnataka, the many people he groomed
developed the ability to govern the state with some efficiency.
Alongside Devaraj Urs and Ramakrishna Hegde, Gowda is seen as
one of the finest talent scouts in Karnataka politics.

Perhaps Gowda could not assert his legacy because his stints
in power have always been short-lived or rather cut short. As we
understand, documenting of legacies often happen with some
kind of invisible scaffolding that executive power erects around
personalities. The irony is, despite his long years in politics, Gowda
has never completed a term in office. He resigned as a minister in
the Ramakrishna Hegde government over differences in 1988, he
came close to becoming chief minister a few times, but when he
did become in 1994, his term was cut short as he was catapulted to
the prime minister's chair in 1996, which again was over in under a
year. In his entire six decades as a politician, he has held the reins of
power for less than eight years. In fact, his only unbroken stint has
been that of leader of the Opposition in the 1970s for seven years. If
Gowda has remained relevant in electoral politics even without long,
unbroken stints in power, that should certainly be one of the big
curiosities to hold this book together.

Post-Independence Indian political history with a regional
perspective forms a gentle backdrop to this biography. The Janata
Party papers that I was able to access at the Nehru Memorial Museum
and Library were particularly helpful to illustrate the story of Gowda's
political life in the 1970s. Gowda shared some papers from his private
collection too, especially those concerning Ramakrishna Hegde and
Atal Bihari Vajpayee, but that was only a minuscule portion of what
I understand lies scattered and undocumented. His interventions
in the assembly and Parliament are public documents, but some
interesting tour reports he submitted to the Speaker of the Karnataka
Assembly in the 1970s—after solitary trips to different corners of
the world to study irrigation, agriculture and urban infrastructure—
could not be traced.

All through his life, Deve Gowda has shown an enormous appetite for hard work and risk-taking. Gowda never chose the winning side. He always joined the struggling ones—the Congress (Organisation) in the 1960s, the Janata Party in the 70s, the Samajawadi Janata Party in the 80s, the Janata Dal in the 1990s and finally, the Janata Dal (Secular) at the end of the millennium. The struggling side gave him an identity that a winning side could never have. If he had joined the winning side—in this case, the Congress led by the Nehru–Gandhi dynasty, and later the Bharatiya Janata Party (BJP)—he would have soon been relegated to a corner like many of his contemporaries. Gowda was wooed by Indira Gandhi but never joined her; he had a good relationship with Atal Bihari Vajpayee but never accepted his support. On the contrary, Veerendra Patil joined Indira Gandhi soon after he lost to her in the Chikmagalur by-election in 1978. Ramakrishna Hegde joined hands with the BJP in Karnataka in 1999 to contest elections and become a minister in Vajpayee's cabinet. The same year, J.H. Patel joined his friend George Fernandes and became part of an alliance led by the BJP. S. Bangarappa, who was a Congress chief minister, joined the BJP, and finally, S.M. Krishna meekly surrendered to Narendra Modi's BJP after decades in the Congress.

It was Ramakrishna Hegde and J.H. Patel who strengthened the electoral possibilities and vote share of the BJP in Karnataka, seven years before Gowda's son H.D. Kumaraswamy gave the saffron party its first taste of power. Gowda had, however, aborted the son's enterprise within twenty months when he ensured power was not transferred to them. The dilemma that Gowda faced at this point could be a classic question in moral philosophy: was reneging on the son's promise of power to B.S. Yediyurappa a bigger mistake, or allowing his uncompromising secular credentials to further wane a greater crime? He chose the former and put his party into a path of struggle for ten years when he rejigged its orientation. Many regional political parties like the Dravida Munnetra Kazhagam (DMK), the Annna Dravida Munnetra Kazhagam (AIADMK), the Janata Dal

(United) [JD(U)], the National Conference (NC), the Bahujan
Samaj Party (BSP) and the Telugu Desam Party (TDP), etc., have
aligned with a secular alliance [United Front or United Progressive
Alliance (UPA)] or a nationalist alliance [National Democratic
Alliance (NDA)] in Delhi, alternatively. Gowda has never allowed
such a swing, except for a twenty-month 'indiscretion' of his son.
The troika of Deve Gowda, Lalu Prasad Yadav and Mulayam Singh
Yadav never joined the BJP-led nationalist alliance at the Centre.
Gowda's ideological steadfastness has been with the Left parties, and
his party has been part of the Left Democratic Front (LDF) in Kerala.

For the devout and temple-hopping Gowda, secularism is not a
result of an academic engagement or learning, or imbibed through
travel and exposure to a cosmopolitan ethos. It is a default setting like
it is for most Indians whose common sense and humanity teach them
to coexist and empathize with others. He has never romanticized his
secularism. Gowda took tough and unpopular positions that were
politically expensive on the Ram Temple movement in Ayodhya,
and later, when he waged a battle against Vajpayee's government
when communal riots broke out in Gujarat's Godhra in 2002. He
did not make blistering speeches in 2002 but quietly went and visited
Muslims in camps they were pushed into and wrote angry letters to
Vajpayee. He called out the hate that had spilled over to the streets.
He appealed to Vajpayee's reason in the Parliament. I have discussed
the letters and the speeches in the chapter on Vajpayee.

I once asked Gowda what made him secular? He did not have
a ready answer for that. After some thought, he said, 'The Muslim
man who my father accommodated in our fields when I was growing
up was very decent and kind. He would show me how to write Urdu.
The Muslim household which rented me a room in their outhouse
when I was studying in Hassan saw me as their son. They were
generous. In fact, Bettaiah, my right-hand man when I became a
contractor, who I could trust to get my wife's jewels safely, was a
Dalit. My unlettered father and mother never discriminated against
people on the basis of their caste or religion. It never occurred to

them that it could be otherwise too. That is how most people I grew up with in Hardanahalli, Holenarasipur and Hassan were. We had our local quarrels, but it never had a communal undertone. Perhaps this made my politics inclusive.' He had personalized the answer.

Gowda has constantly wrestled with the world, conspired against it, bent it to suit his needs, and also surrendered to its overwhelming power. It is banal to say his is, and has been, one big life of struggle. Life is a struggle for millions of others too, but each life and each struggle are woven differently and they hide a fascinating story. In this biography, I endeavour to learn what brick and mortar constructed this man's struggle, who started his life as a civil works contractor in the rather boring plains of Hassan in Karnataka. It is not just his life as a politician that has been important to this biography. His vulnerabilities as a human being find sufficient focus as well.

Deve Gowda has led such an enormous life that I could easily write another volume of this size from the material I was able to gather and interviews I was able to conduct for nearly three years. But since this is not a journal of record, I have tried to offer a perspective to his life, which others may agree, partially agree, partially disagree or totally dispute. I have worked on this biography always aware that I am not the last word, and there can be more than one perspective of the man. Gowda, who gave me long interviews, and did not once ask to preview the manuscript of this book, may himself be surprised with my reading of his life at certain points. But I count on the democratic blank cheque he gave when he cheerfully agreed to be interviewed for the book. He had told me plainly that he would answer my questions truthfully, and I could make whatever I wanted of his responses. It is rare for a politician of his standing, anywhere in the world, to be so carefree and detached about his biography. All through his career, he has never lost sleep over how people perceived him or portrayed him, many a time with outright prejudice. But he never spent a penny on public relations or image management firms like his contemporaries or younger colleagues. He always believed in fighting it out politically.

This book stops being particular and specific around 2004, that is at the end of Prime Minister Atal Bihari Vajpayee's term in office. However, I have discussed the near-death encounter Gowda had in 2006, when his son, H.D. Kumaraswamy, defied him to become chief minister by joining hands with the BJP in Karnataka. The epilogue offers a glimpse of the last fifteen years, when Gowda continued to contest elections, built his party, and also faced accusations of allowing it to be converted into a family firm. But I have deferred a closer examination of it since it is too proximate in time to read, and I thought it prudent to give it some more years when a clear distance is established.

This biography, to an extent, is also a marvel of Gowda's phenomenal memory. He remembers the texture, length and colour of the shirt he wore as a three-year-old. He remembers the names of lawyers who were present in court on a particular day in the 1950s in Hassan. The name of the judge who pronounced the judgment and what his family background was. The kind of glass in which he was served juice when he went to see someone in Bangalore as a student. The names of constables who stood guard at his door in the 1980s. The kind of slippers Ramakrishna Hegde was wearing when he met him in a guest house. The date and time of the day he stood up to speak in the assembly or the Parliament, and who was present when he spoke, etc. 'You can crosscheck in the records, sir,' he would say if I looked bewildered.

Heaps and heaps of facts intertwined with strands and strands of memory are compactly stored in some part of his brain that offers an epic narrative of the times he has lived. Gowda spoke without embellishments in Kannada, and how many ever times he repeated a story, he would not misplace or twist a single detail, and the sequence of facts would never change. I should confess that I have used this to cross-check the veracity of the narrative at times—waiting to catch a deviation from the previous time he had mentioned the incident, but he never gave me an opportunity to catch him on the wrong foot. He simply replayed the track from his mind with the same emotional angst, same sighs, and sometimes, the same abuse. What was committed to his memory was what he believed to be the truth and remained unchanged when circumstances and contexts changed.

Gowda is a great raconteur. His narrative is like the oral epics. It begins somewhere but soon the subplots consume the main plot. After a long detour spanning a few sittings, he comes back without fail to the main story and to the exact point from where he had digressed. The narrative is never linear; it is concentric. Gowda never kept a diary and did not preserve photographs. But his not keeping a diary has been compensated by his phenomenal memory. When it comes to photographs, he once quipped, 'I did not collect them because there was hardly any glamour in them.'

I struggled for a long time with the title of the book. Finally, I settled with the current one–*Furrows in a Field*. I thought it offered a rich mix of metaphors. There are furrows and ridges in a field, and the plough could be thought of to be commanded by destiny, which Gowda greatly believes in. This agricultural metaphor mirrors the ups and downs of life as well as that of politics. There are green shoots, and there are big harvests. There can be a complete failure when pests raid, or there could be a course correction with manure and medicine. Destiny or plain uncertainty could come to play in the form of clouds, through sufficient or insufficient rains, through sunlight and mist. At the end of it all, there are stubbles to be burnt to once again ready the field for another season of ploughs, ridges and furrows. Another season of sowing and reaping. Another season of uncertainty. Furrows create a pattern on a field, like they would on the forehead or the face, with age, learning, unlearning and experience. That has been the life of Deve Gowda—a peasant's son who became prime minister without pelf, patronage or pedigree. He just ploughed the field with local knowledge, native wisdom, common sense and extraordinary perseverance, and saw the world in a grain of sand.

'The Unpredicted' could have very well been the title of this book. Nobody predicted that a Shudra boy from Hardanahalli would one day hold the highest office in India. He dabbled with astrological charts much later, but his birth did not predetermine his success. It was unpredicted. Nobody predicted that he would last this long in politics. His decennial political obituaries were promptly written. Nobody could ever predict the limits of his stubbornness, skulduggery and shrewdness that would outwit some of the sharpest in the land. Nobody predicted that beneath a lifelong activist for the fair distribution of river water, there was a river basin planner par excellence, and beneath an indefatigable litigator, there was a counsel of counsels. Nobody predicted that beneath the rustic exterior there was a rooted cosmopolitan individual who, in his idiosyncratic way, rejoiced in the diversity of this nation, embraced constitutional values and argued that it should stand on reason, and not religion. Forget others predicting him, he could not predict himself.

Gowda was the ultimate outsider to every pattern and structure that existed in politics in India till he became prime minister. Manmohan Singh and Narendra Modi who came later had similar backgrounds, but Singh, who was self-made, had received the finest education and was a technocrat. He was not a political man. In fact, he was defeated in the only election he contested. In the case of Modi, he was made by one of the world's largest non-governmental organizations with committed cadres and fellow travellers—the Rashtriya Swayamsevak Sangh (RSS), the ideological parent of the BJP. The organization had put him in the groove right at the beginning, and he, too, the first time, had been nominated as chief minister without ever having won a popular contest. With Gowda, that was not the case. He had to literally cycle his way up. Before he became a legislator in 1962, he was known as a 'bicycle man' in Holenarasipur. After he was denied a ticket by the Congress, he had contested as an independent with the bicycle as his election symbol and had to wait for 21 long years to become a minister for the first time.

Gowda always thought he was a work in progress. He never thought he was complete like Modi, who gave the impression that he became prime minister to share his enlightenment. Gowda was not privileged like Nehru or Indira. He did not have the academic learning of Singh. He perhaps had the cunningness of P.V. Narasimha Rao, but certainly not his network, experience and cultural capital. He was not from within the Congress system or had a privileged caste background like Lal Bahadur Shastri. He was not a maharaja like V.P. Singh. He was not Chandra Shekhar with wide exposure to national politics. He was not entrenched in Lutyens' Delhi like Gujral. He did not have the verbal sophistication of a Vajpayee. He, however, absorbed the elements of Morarji to speak one's mind with brutal nakedness. Even though he did not verbalize his ideological positions, he had an abiding relationship with the Left parties. It was pragmatism and the liberal values distilled through religion, by living a hard life, by living on the fringes of the caste system, and by living in a pastoral setting that propelled him. He never traded self-esteem for power.

The year 2021 marks a quarter-century since Deve Gowda became prime minister. India has transformed beyond imagination in these twenty-five years. There were seven people from Karnataka who played in the Indian cricket team when Gowda was prime minister. That number came down later, but enormous talent from the hinterlands took over Indian cricket. The mobile phone service was in an experimental phase in 1996. Internet and email were nascent and expensive. Google and social media were nowhere on the horizon, and the most popular car brand was the Ambassador. Gowda, as prime minister, went around in a white bullet-proofed Ambassador. Not only has India transformed in the last twenty-five years, the perception about the country has also undergone a sea change. When Gowda met Bill Gates on his first-ever visit to India in 1997, nobody ever thought that Satya Nadella, the brilliant son of one of his secretaries, B.N. Yugandhar, would take over Microsoft as CEO in a couple of decades. Gowda was at the cusp of India's transition from an old order to the new. He had loosened the foundation on which the old elite stood. He accidentally became a symbol of aspiration in a newly aware democratic India. If Gowda could be prime minister, anybody could in a free and democratic country.

There are two sections to the book. The first is the phase that deals with his life and work before he became prime minister. The second deals with the time after he became prime minister. The chapter plan is tell-tale. It progresses chronologically, but each chapter can be read independently too. One of the longest chapters in the book is on the Gowda and Hegde relationship, because that was an epic battle he fought, and it has still not ended in his mind. This biography has also been an excuse for me to explore the local, the non-English, non-Hindi knowledge systems and thinking patterns. Finally, this biography is an exploration of a life and not an excavation.

In November 2018, I was invited by the Government of Karnataka's Department of Kannada and Culture, to introduce H.D. Deve Gowda to a large audience, with whom he was to later interact and answer questions on his life. At the end of that speech, I borrowed from a column written on Jawaharlal Nehru by academic Pratap Bhanu Mehta. He had said that Nehru was 'bigger than the sum of his imperfections'. This was in the context of the virulent attacks and unfair blame that India's first prime minister has had to retrospectively suffer at the hands of right-wing trolls. I concluded by saying Deve Gowda, too, was more than the sum of his imperfections, and much more than the sum of all perceptions and prejudices about him. This biography endeavours to take a comprehensive view. Happy reading.

SECTION ONE

1

The Beginnings and the Background

Haradanahalli Dodde Gowda Deve Gowda's birth on 18 May 1933 meant one thing to his father and another to his mother. For the father, Dodde Gowda, it was reconciliation and renegotiation with life. It was the divine signalling of peace on the cruel and excruciating pathways he had trudged along. For Lakshmi Devamma, the mother, it was the arrival of her first child. It was an uneventful graduation to the experience of motherhood. Something not uncommon to young women of her age at the time, either in Haradanahalli village[1] or in the wider Hassan district, or elsewhere in the princely Mysore state. Girls were married off between the ages of 16 and 18.

In 1928, Dodde Gowda's entire family had been wiped out by the influenza epidemic. He had lost his wife, Eeramma, and all his children—three boys aged eight, four and two—in a span of ten days. His spirits had been crushed by this extraordinary blow of fate. He had resisted the advice of remarriage from his father Appe Gowda and uncle Putte Gowda for over two years but had finally relented in 1931. He married Lakshmi Devamma from the neighbouring village of Mosale Hosalli. The uncle, Putte Gowda, played an important role in convincing Dodde Gowda because he had no children and had raised his nephew as his own child.

3

The influenza or H1N1 flu, which had been a raging pandemic in 1918–19, fourteen years prior to the birth of Deve Gowda, had taken a total of 22,741 lives in his native Hassan district alone. It accounted for 4.4 per cent of all deaths in the Mysore state. The neighbouring Tumkur district had topped the death charts with 4.7 per cent of the total 1,66,391 people who had succumbed to the pandemic.[2] What had not touched the Gowda household then had arrived a decade later. Although described as a regional epidemic of lesser virulence in 1928-29, it had a devastating effect on the large, undivided peasant family of patriarch Dyavale Gowda, the great grandfather of Deve Gowda.

This tragedy of his father's previous family had no direct play on Deve Gowda's mind, but perhaps he came to terms with it indirectly through his father's lifelong anxieties and fears, accentuated and reconfigured by the tragedy. Nobody discussed the misfortune repeatedly because they knew it would rekindle pain for Dodde Gowda as they allowed it to be a memory quietly buried in the unwritten genealogy of the family.

Many men in Haradanahalli and neighbouring villages had remarried like Dodde Gowda after influenza had crippled their emotional structures. It had also affected the local agrarian economy because it had taken away hands that either worked on the fields or took care of livestock. It scarred the minds of those left behind. The enthusiasm for life was absent even long after the recovery and remarriages had happened as it was gloom on which lives had been rebuilt. Memories had always remained mixed. Dodde Gowda carried on with his life and raised Deve Gowda with the haunting spectre of his humungous loss. His melancholy never fully escaped him. Therefore, when Deve Gowda was born, it was a small reassurance that life could be fair, and God could be kind to him too.

Ever since Dodde Gowda and Devamma had married, they had propitiated Lord Eshwara (Shiva) at the temple,[3] which was about twenty steps from their home in Haradanahalli. They had pleaded for a healthy male child. Basavaradhya, who was the temple priest, had nurtured their devotion. Devamma, every single day, had cleaned the courtyards of the temple and drawn rangolis (huge geometrical floor decorations drawn with rice flour). On Mondays, it was special. The parents took a bath, lit an incense stick to the deity, and the father made an offering of rice, jaggery and curds.

There was an Anjaneya (Hanuman) temple on another street in the village, and the priest there, Kulla Iyengar[4] would tell Dodde Gowda that 'Anjaneya can make anything possible, pray to him'. That became a Saturday ritual for the father. Deve Gowda was seen as an answer to all the prayers. He was the firstborn, and it was injected very early into his mind that he was the gift of the gods, and being devout was a sacred obligation. The mountain that formed the backdrop, or rather a halo, to their house had a Ranganatha (Vishnu) temple, also known as the Mavinakere Ranganatha temple. The parents read the perceived shadow of the mountain as a direct blessing of the lord who occupied it. On every Saturday of the Shraavana[5] month, Gowda rode to this temple on the shoulders of his father and made special sweet offerings to Ranganatha.[6] The priests who managed this temple were also from Kulla Iyengar's family. Within a decade, Gowda had three siblings—brother Basave Gowda, and two sisters, Akkayyamma and Puttamma.

When Deve Gowda was born, his parents had no intimation or visions of his future glory, political genius, and an impending rise to power. They were simple, straightforward, hardworking, unlettered folks without social, cultural, or even real capital. They could not weave a conception myth even retrospectively after they saw their son emerge.[7] With all the uncertainty that existed, the only thing the Shudra couple did was sell two sheep to fund the writing of his horoscope by a Brahmin priest. The cost of one sheep those days was two or three rupees.[8] Even then, nothing unusual was detected. Perhaps the price of two sheep was not enough to predict the future chief minister and prime minister. The priest who first wrote the horoscope of Deve Gowda is said to be Bandihole Ramanuja Iyengar, a relative of Kulla Iyengar.[9]

Interestingly, Deve Gowda's very first memory, recollected at the age of 87, was that of a fortune teller with a tiny rattle drum (*Budubudike*) held between his index finger and thumb. 'It was around seven in the morning. My mother was cleaning the cowshed with a broom made from coconut frond and my aunt was shelling *avarekai* (hyacinth beans, botanical name *lablab purpureus*) in the front yard. I was sitting on a stone slab swinging my legs. The handloom shirt I was wearing, the texture of which my fingers can still feel, was so long that I didn't need shorts. I must have been a two- or three-year-old. The fortune teller said that I would be "king" (*dore* was the Kannada word) one day. My mother stopped cleaning and stared at him. She was bewildered. But my aunt shouted at me and asked me to move inside. "Yes, yes, with such thick mucus running down your nose, you will surely be a king," she taunted me. It was not about belief or disbelief in his prediction that provoked this reaction in her. She thought the fortune teller was pulling a fast one to collect alms.'[10] The rattle drum fortune tellers have a reputation of playing on peoples' fears and anxieties. They also swing to the other extreme at times to make outlandish predictions to ensure that people are generous with their offerings. They mostly came at the break of dawn to catch peoples' attention at a pristine moment when they were transitioning from slumber to awakening. They rattled out their predictions, which they claimed to have heard from the *halakki* bird (owl) at the dead of night in a graveyard. Anyway, one is not sure here that if a nearly nonagenarian Gowda is accessing memory via a retrospective vision that is searching for signals and signs from the past to illustrate his destiny's fait accompli.

The first death that registered in Deve Gowda's mind is that of his paternal grandfather, Appe Gowda. He remembers him as a man who ate last after checking on the itinerant traders and salesmen who occupied the front yard of his house after sunset. Itinerant guests were a regular feature those days when there were no motels for people walking cross country for business.

The name Deve Gowda that his parents gave him was also the most ordinary and the most common among the Vokkaliga community into which he was born. In the 1930s, and roughly till about the 1960s, popular Vokkaliga names were not Sanskritized.[11] They did not commonly borrow from the epics—the Ramayana, the Mahabharata or the Puranas. Even if they did, they were clipped and localized. Their imagination and position in the *varna* hierarchy did not allow them to appropriate names that the upper castes used freely. Therefore, they named their kids, without deliberation or very casually—after their physical attributes like skin colour, height or seniority among other children in the family, or after family elders, in which case the name repeated every second generation. Deve Gowda was also the name of Deve Gowda's maternal great-grandfather. Deve could just mean a generic, common noun for God in Kannada (*Dyavaru* or *Devaru* in Kannada means God. Deve is an inflexion of the word *Deva*), and Gowda was the Vokkaliga affiliation.

The Tenant of the Soil

The term Vokkaliga quite simply means people who are engaged in agriculture—'a farmer, a husbandman or a tenant of the soil'.[12] Interestingly, when Gowda was delivering his farewell address as prime minister in the Parliament on 11 April 1997, he had said: 'I come from that community, and it is not a caste.'[13] That was a very liberal interpretation. But as identity politics had heated up in Karnataka after the linguistic reorganization of the state, the Vokkaligas, who were in direct competition with Lingayats for power, began to organize themselves as a tight-knit community. The exclusionary and inclusionary ideas of caste and sub-castes became sharp. When the Kannada-speaking districts in the former Madras and Bombay presidencies, as well as Nizam's Hyderabad, joined to become a unified linguistic state in 1956, the demographics of the state were turned on its head. The Lingayats became dominant, controlled many more assembly segments, and therefore decided who should be the chief minister of the state. After Kadidal Manjappa, a Vokkaliga, was displaced as chief minister in 1956, it took nearly four decades for another Vokkaliga to occupy the seat of power. It was Deve Gowda who had broken the jinx in 1994. For nearly a decade between 1972 and 1980, the Devaraj Urs experiment had ensured that both the dominant communities in Karnataka—the Vokkaligas in the south and the Lingayats in the central and northern parts of Karnataka—were kept at bay by his singular brand of backward class politics.

The Vokkaligas were Shudras who were at the bottom of the varna hierarchy. Their initial drive to organize themselves in the erstwhile princely Mysore state was to end the domination of Brahmins in education and employment. The numerical size of Lingayats did not threaten Vokkaliga aspirations at that point in the Mysore state, which was ruled by the Wadiyar family. This aspirational flame in Mysore was an extension of the awareness that had spread in the neighbouring Tamil country where the non-Brahmin Justice Party movement had begun to establish itself.[14]

The Justice Leslie C. Miller Commission was set up in 1918 by Krishna Raja Wadiyar IV, the Maharaja of Mysore, to study the imbalances in access to education and employment in the state among various communities. Miller was the chief justice of the Mysore High Court and a line in the terms of reference for the commission read: 'There is a preponderance of the Brahmin community in the services, and that it is the desire of the government that the other communities in the state should be adequately represented therein.'[15] To get an idea of what Brahmin dominance meant, it would be instructive to look at the annexures of the report, which was submitted in 1919. The total population of Brahmins was 1,93,137. Employed in 'superior positions' of government were 9712; those who earned Rs 100 and below were 9110; those earning between Rs 100 and Rs 250 were 362; those who earned a salary above Rs 250 were 240. When it came to education, 80,409 among them were literates and 15,455 were literate in English.[16]

Compare this with the Vokkaligas (spelt as 'Vakkaliga' in the report) whose total population size was 13,28,237. The literate population among them was 42,206, and those who were literate in English were only 737. The total number from the community in 'superior positions' of the government were 338; those who earned Rs 100 and below were 330; those earning between Rs 100 and Rs 250 were only four, and those earning a salary above Rs 250 were also just four. The numbers clearly explain the skewed social and economic condition of the Vokkaligas compared with the Brahmins. According to the report, although the Lingayats were nearly half the population size of Vokkaligas in Mysore, their progress in both education and employment far superseded the Vokkaliga numbers. In fact, the position of Muslims (referred to as 'Mahomedans' in the report) was better than the Vokkaligas and Lingayats—their population size was 2,91,708, and 1708 members occupied 'superior positions' in the government.[17]

Even in the face of this data that so eloquently explained the imbalance, there was huge opposition to the implementation of the report and at the forefront was Sir M. Visvesvaraya, the diwan (equivalent to a prime minister) himself, who eventually quit. Even outside the government, all the newspapers painted scenarios of doom. But there was much at stake for the kingdom of Mysore to entertain partisan voices. The social milieu was bordering on the radical not just inside the state but around it too. The report was swiftly accepted and representation to various communities was given in a seven-year timeframe.[18]

In the backdrop of this situation, the Vokkaligas had started organizing themselves. In 1906, they had started the Vokkaliga Sangha, an association to lobby for the interests of the community. A year before, in 1905, the Lingayats had organized themselves under the banner of Mysore Lingayata Vidya Shreyobivruddi Sangha (Lingayat Educational Improvement Association). In 1907, the Vokkaligas started a progressive Kannada weekly called the *Vokkaligara Patrike*.[19]

The Vokkaliga assertion was complete when in the 1980s the Adichunchanagiri Math's (seminary) identity concerns started overriding its spiritual concerns. It soon became a prosperous institution to protect and determine not just the educational and employment interests of the Vokkaligas but also the community's political interests. The seventy-first pontiff of this Nath Pantha[20] seminary, Sri Balagangadharanath, offered a leadership that ensured a never seen before flourish for the community. Once the Adichunchanagiri Math had become a power centre in the 1980s, the other backward castes were also inspired to create seminaries and pontiffs. It became a unique sociological phenomenon in Karnataka, which permanently altered the way politics was conducted in the state. To organize one's caste, sub-caste through caste seminaries was an idea borrowed from the Lingayats, who had organized themselves through hundreds of such seminaries across Karnataka for more than a century.[21]

If one sees photographs of the small group of Vokkaliga elite in the early- to the mid-twentieth century, we see them mostly dressed in a turban made with elegant golden-threaded lace on silk—the Mysore *zari peta*. The most iconic ambassador for the Mysore zari peta was Sir M. Visvesvaraya. This peta stood out against the khadi white cap of Gandhi's freedom movement. So did a similar but stiffer black cap of ordinary people in the still-unformed north Karnataka districts, as well as the silk *roomal* (cloth) turbans of their own elite.[22] The station in life of Deve Gowda's family when he was born in 1933 could be determined through what they wore on their heads. The fact was that neither his father or grandfather, nor his other elders and ancestors ever wore a Mysore zari peta. They did not even wear the Gandhi cap and they were not aware of the existence of other turbans and caps signifying a host of things. They were poor peasants, unlettered and unconnected with the assertion of their community identity, or any of the ideological debates or the freedom movement. When they tilled the fields, and if the sun was harsh, they covered their heads and faces with a plain white cloth. By the time Gowda became a legislator in 1962, the Mysore zari peta was anachronistic. Not that he had designs of using them. All through his political life, he remained loyal to the plain white cloth.

The power that Gowda's elders or the ordinary members of the Vokkaliga community in general enjoyed in Hassan district or in any part of Mysore state, lay within the village structure. Their hold over land and food production put them in alliance with Brahmins, who controlled knowledge and revenue records. This was a convenient arrangement of the physical and the abstract, but still, the Gowda was a Shudra who had limited social and cultural capital. The big landlords among Vokkaligas may have been feudal in their behaviour, but in the case of the Gowda family, his father, with four ragged acres of ancestral share, and a small dairy farming enterprise, led a hand-to-mouth existence. His situation grew tight as his family grew. Till the 1970s, they remained the poor country cousins of the educated and landed elite among the Vokkaligas.

Even when it came to the Vokkaliga seminary, Deve Gowda and his family maintained their distance. In fact, at one point in the 1990s, Gowda got into conflict with its seventy-first pontiff. He did not approve of his playing a non-spiritual role. Once, he had even told the pontiff to take his 'saffron robes off and come to politics.'[23] Interestingly though, he remained loyal to the Sringeri Math or the Sringeri Sharada Peetham established by Advaita philosopher Adi Sankaracharya in the eighth century—to which the Mysore Wadiyar rulers and Tipu Sultan also remained loyal. Gowda's political guru A.G. Ramachandra Rao, a Brahmin and a Congress politician, had in the late 1950s introduced Gowda to the Sringeri Math,[24] which was just about four hours away from Hassan, by road.

The Swish of the Cane

Returning to Deve Gowda's childhood, there was nothing particularly unusual about it. He went to primary school in Hardanahalli, and there was a teacher named K.M. Mariyappa from the nearby

Kinarhalli village, who made an early impression on him. He taught him numbers and alphabets, and more than anything else, the value of education. After school, like all the other peasant kids, he had to help his father in the fields or take out cattle for grazing. After completing his primary school, he was admitted to a middle school in the neighbouring Halekote village, about 3–4 kilometres away.[25]

By the time Gowda joined middle school, his family had managed to acquire a few buffaloes and two cows. They also reared sheep. Along with his school bag, he regularly carried milk, butter and curds for his teacher's family, which was a normal arrangement in a village economy.[26] Besides the teacher, he supplied milk and curds to other Brahmin households in Haradanahalli and Halekote. The people who received them were kind to him, occasionally giving him something to munch on, but there was one ritual that did not make sense to him till much later in life. When Gowda left the dairy supplies at their doorstep, the Brahmins would sprinkle water on them before they took them in. In a couple of generous houses, they would make him sit near the door and serve him what they had cooked. After eating, he had to clean up the area he sat on with cow dung. Even in the bathing area at the river, there was clear segregation. The upper end of the stream was meant for the Brahmins and the lower end for Shudras. Everything had been normalized over the centuries. There was a wonderfully 'arranged cordiality' in the village.[27] Gowda, all through his political career, neither claimed to be a victim of caste bias nor did he use a caste slur against anybody. One is not sure if it was a value system he had cultivated, or the respect his Brahmin gurus and guides had earned or if he feared the retribution of the gods and their priestly managers or if it was the effect of severe social conditioning since childhood.

Another early memory from his Halekote middle school days has to do with a two-anna party. One day, during lunchtime, when he was picking up his lunch box, he saw two annas lying on the floor. He took the money, went to the nearby shop and bought boiled groundnuts and jaggery-peanut cubes (chikkis), and had a feast with a bunch of his classmates. When he returned to the class, the boy who had lost the two annas had complained to the teacher and the teacher enquired if anybody had found it. Gowda put his hand up and innocently recounted the feast he just had. The teacher summoned him before the class and thrashed his backside. That was his first experience of insult. He wept. After the class was dismissed, the teacher who had thrashed him called him again, and in an apologetic tone, said he felt very bad to have used the cane. He repeatedly asked, 'Does it pain, does it pain very badly, my dear fellow?' He also mumbled, 'You had made a mistake, and you claimed it with glee. You left me with no option before the other boys. I got very angry. I should have controlled my anger.' The insult aside, he had been acquainted with the teacher's empathy, reflection and regret. 'I can still hear the swish of my teacher's cane as it forcefully landed on my backside many times. The meaning of that moment has never ended for me,' Gowda recalled.[28]

The Halekote government school is up and running to this day with over fifty students, but the room in which Gowda sat for his classes has been converted into the local Home Guards office. In the school principal's room, on the wall, there were pictures of Jawaharlal Nehru, Indira Gandhi and Lal Bahadur Shastri among prime ministers. Among presidents, there were Sarvepalli Radhakrishnan and A.P.J. Abdul Kalam. There were also pictures of Mahatma Gandhi, Netaji Subhas Chandra Bose, B.R. Ambedkar and Jagjivan Ram. However, the largest picture was of Mother Teresa, printed as a flex banner that subsumed every other picture in the room. When the headmistress was asked if she knew that Kalam had worked as an adviser under Gowda, their school's distinguished alumnus, and that he had given him an extension to continue in government service, she was more shocked than surprised. Recovering herself with quiet pride, she shared the information with her two other colleagues and a dozen children the information she had just received. That was the newest addition to the school and the village's Gowda lore.[29]

2

The Local World

Deve Gowda's father, Dodde Gowda, was keen to educate his son beyond middle school. After all, the son had done well at the Halekote school and his grades were promising. But the father's financial resources were stagnant. In fact, three of his cousins had become his responsibility after their parents passed away. The ten acres of ancestral land, of which Dodde Gowda's share was just over four acres, was not enough to support a family where children were growing up fast.[1] The perpetual uncertainties of agriculture made their life more uncertain. For a short period, while Deve Gowda was in primary and middle school, it appeared they could manage the family with the extra income dairy farming gave them. That was not so accurate a projection. Also, Dodde Gowda had got into trouble with his village panchayat because of a scuffle he had got into with some of his fellow villagers. At the panchayat meeting, he had lost his temper during an argument, and the incident had left him isolated in the village.[2]

Despite these pressures, Dodde Gowda thought his son should have an English-medium education. At that time, it was quite a fancy idea for a poor farmer to have. How such an idea came to him in the isolation of his village cannot be traced. Being himself unlettered, he had no reference points. Nevertheless, he was pretty determined on this count. If Deve Gowda had to access high school education, he had to go to Holenarasipur town. That was the taluk centre and was 35 kms away from Haradanahalli. One day, Dodde Gowda went to Kamaksha Shetty, a trader who had a shop on Holenarasipur's main street. Shetty had two sons, and one of them, Janardhan, was a graduate. Dodde Gowda asked Shetty if he could send Janardhan along with him to speak to the Municipal High School headmaster, Pitchamuthu, a Christian. Shetty was kind. He sent his son along. Seeing Deve Gowda's middle school grades, the headmaster was happy to admit him.[3] The English education of Deve Gowda had begun.

The Holenarasipur Municipal High School had been inaugurated in September 1934, a year after Gowda's birth, by Mirza Ismail. This fact is elegantly engraved on a black marble stone and is prominently embedded into the school wall. It reads: 'OPENED BY AMIN-UL-MULK SIR MIRZA M ISMAIL, KT., C.I.E., O.B.E., DEWAN OF MYSORE ON 18th SEPTEMBER 1934.'[4] Whoever got this engraved had paid enormous attention to punctuations, line breaks and type sizes.

Since Deve Gowda could not travel between his village and town every day, he took a small room in Holenarasipur. He would wash his own clothes, take bath in the Hemavathi river and cook for himself. He would get his twenty shares of ragi grains from his home every month for his sustenance. On the twenty-sixth of every month, he had to pay four annas as school fees, which his father would give him when he went home to the village. Once, he lost the fees money, and fearing his father's reaction, Deve Gowda sold twelve shares of ragi for four annas and paid the fees. This forced him to skip a meal every day for an entire month. A month or two after this, he lost the key to his room. When he went searching for it by the river where he had had a bath, he found a two rupee note lying on the riverbed. He picked it up, spent 13 annas on getting a duplicate key made, and the remaining money was spent at a local eatery, Venkatesha Bhawan, with his friends.[5] That was some retrospective compensation for the meals he had skipped for an entire month.

In high school, Deve Gowda was very good at mathematics. He always scored in the range of 85 to 90 per cent. But, his history marks were below average. That was essentially because his English language skills could not stand up to narratives across centuries. Facts were not a problem, memory was never a problem, but to recount the narrative in English was. His history teacher, Ramakrishna Iyengar would often taunt Gowda: 'Would you like to be A.C. Deve Gowda or Haradanahalli Deve Gowda?' By A.C. Deve Gowda he meant Gowda's namesake, with different initials though, who had become director of education for Hassan district.[6] The history teacher did not live long enough to see Haradanahalli Deve Gowda make history.

Hassan was a predominantly Kannada-speaking district around the time Gowda was in high school. In 1951, of the total 7,15,135 people in the district, 6,14,079 had recorded Kannada as their mother tongue. The next largest linguistic population was of those who spoke Hindustani. They were around 31,290. Tamil speakers were 20,863 and Telugu 17,904. There were only seventy-four native English speakers in the entire district, and surprisingly, there were four native French speakers and one each of Italian and Portuguese.[7] In such a near monolingual ecosystem, English was perhaps confined to classrooms and was taught by teachers whose experience with the language was circumscribed. English was not spoken in the streets or in the marketplace for the young Gowda to get acquainted with its twists, turns and real context of use. It remained hidden in his textbooks.

In 1947, while in high school, Gowda also sauntered into history. It was not about the Independence Day celebrations, when they had all taken out a celebratory march, but had to do with the 'Mysore Chalo' agitation. The maharaja of Mysore, Jayachamarajendra Wadiyar, had delayed his decision to join the Indian Union by a few months, and in the intervening months, people across the princely Mysore state, led by prominent Congressmen, had given a call to march towards the capital city and occupy it. This was to pressure the maharaja to accede quickly and fully. Finally, when the maharaja gave up meekly, a peoples' government was inaugurated on 29 October 1947, and K. Chengalaraya Reddy became the chief minister.[8]

In Holenarasipur, just 80 km away from Mysore, the 'Mysore Chalo' movement had created sufficient heat. Although Deve Gowda, as a young man did not have clarity about it, he joined the Congress crowd to protest. On a particular day, when he was with other boys shouting slogans, he saw a lawyer on a bicycle coming towards him. He stopped the cycle by holding its handle. The lawyer was irked. He slapped Deve Gowda. Not familiar with the ways of Gandhian non-violent agitation, Gowda did not show his other cheek but slapped him back forcefully. It threw the Mysore zari peta off the lawyer's head. The knot that held the turban together unfolded. For any Mysorean at the time, getting his turban knocked off, that too in public, was the gravest of insults. The lawyer, Narasimha Iyengar, got Gowda arrested for assault.[9]

Since the magistrate's court in Hassan was the jurisdictional court, the police took Gowda there and produced him before a judge, whose name Gowda remembers was Mallikarjunaiah. He was from the neighbouring Tumkur district. The judge made Gowda stand in a corner all day until the court rose in the evening. Just before he left for his chambers, the judge called Gowda and advised him not to be a Congress *pudhari* (meaning, a petty politician) but to focus on his studies. The judge also instructed the police to drop him back at the exact same spot where they had picked him up.[10] When this happened, Gowda was all of fifteen years.

The judge's remark about the Congress party is interesting. Although he may have meant it innocuously, or in a personal context, by 1947, Congressmen in princely Mysore had lost a bit of their halo. They had become familiar with power politics. Like elsewhere in the country, there were two types of Congressmen. Those who were true adherents of Gandhi's philosophy, and those who used the organization to seek access to power and build an influential network. H.Y. Sharada Prasad, who was jailed during the Quit India Movement in Mysore, wrote in his prison diary with 'disgust' about his fellow 'Congress truth and justice seekers' (*Satyagrahis*) who were in jail with him. In a 14 April 1943 entry, he wrote: 'The way in which the so-called Congressmen and self-sacrificing patriots and freedom battlers mix in the vices of criminals—the supposed scum of the society; the vices they are so inseparably addicted to disgust me by their nauseating grotesqueness.'[11] Sharada Prasad, like Gowda, was also from Holenarasipur and was nineteen when he wrote this. Sharada Prasad later became information adviser to Prime Minister Indira Gandhi. In 1947, however, Gowda was only a bystander who had become an accidental agitator. He had, at that point in his life, nothing to do with the Congressmen of his town.

When Deve Gowda completed his secondary school, he was around seventeen. He decided to get himself a schoolteacher's job, which was not difficult those days. He went to the Hassan district education officer, submitted an application, and the same day he had an appointment order in his hand. He was posted to a village called Jodigubbi in Holenarasipur taluk. He taught middle school children and received a fixed monthly salary of Rs 30. While he taught at the school, he stayed in Kuppe village, about three kilometres away, in the house of Patel Bhadrappa (Patel was a title given to the village head. Similarly, a village accountant was called *shanubhoga*). Gowda remembers the village being dominated by Lingayats. Later, as a politician, he would internalize each village in Holenarasipur taluk on the basis of its caste demographics. He stayed at the Patel's house because the village head had three children who were his students at the Gubbi school but needed additional tutorials in the evening. His free stay and food were a compensation for tutoring them. He saved almost his entire salary and put it to good use soon.[12]

After four months as a teacher, Gowda started feeling that teaching was not his calling. He learnt that the admission season at the Lakshmamma Venkataswamy Occupational Institute or the L.V. Polytechnic in Hassan, the district centre, had begun. He decided to join a diploma course there. It was a government-aided institution, and the land for the institute had been donated by an excise contractor in the name of his wife. Gowda did not seek his father's approval to join this institution. He just walked in and got himself admitted.[13]

The most common thing for young people of the time was to go to Mysore to seek higher education. The city had been the capital of princely Mysore state and had one of the oldest universities in the country. It was around 180 kilometres and was connected by road. The other option was Bangalore, which was equidistant, and took about four hours to reach by road. The other big city that could be accessed from Hassan, but in the exact opposite direction, was Mangalore. It was also like Mysore and Bangalore about 180 km from Hassan but took a little longer to reach due to the poor and precarious roads via the Western Ghats. However, the essential difference between the choice of Mysore and Bangalore over Mangalore for someone in Hassan was culture. The culture 'below the ghats' (known popularly in Kannada as *ghattada kelage*) was entirely unfamiliar to people 'above the ghats' (*ghattada mele*). The climate, food, language, caste relations, religious exposure and agricultural practices were all very different in Mangalore, a quasi-cosmopolitan city due to its location by the sea. Also, politically, in 1949, it was not part of Mysore but the Madras Presidency. The linguistic reorganization of the state happened in 1956, but to this day, there is neither cultural nor emotional connect between the two regions.

Gowda's salary as a schoolteacher, which had remained unspent, was invested wisely for his higher education. He was a 1949–50 batch student of a course titled Civil Draughtsmanship and Estimating. In other words, civil engineering. There were other branches of engineering that the polytechnic offered, but Gowda picked this. Again, there was no particular reason for picking this course. As a farmer's son, he had not dreamt of becoming a public works contractor or a professional who would build houses. He chose without a clear ambition or understanding. The pragmatic consideration was perhaps that if he earned a diploma, that would get him a government job, and the family's economic pressures would ease.

The foundation stone for a proper building to house the polytechnic that Gowda attended was laid only in September 1951 by Sir A. Ramaswami Mudaliar, the retired diwan of Mysore. His long title is meticulously inscribed on the foundation stone—Diwan Bahadur Rajamantrachintamani. When the building was completed in November 1957, S. Nijalingappa, the chief minister of an expanded and democratic Mysore state, had inaugurated it. There are no ornamental titles for him on the inauguration stone. He is just called 'honourable chief minister'. In six years, the culture of the state had changed, and the perception of government and public personalities had altered. The Mysore palace gave fancy, pedantic titles for life, like Rajamantrapravina, Rajasevasakta, etc., which democratic Mysore had naturally discontinued.

There were sixteen boys in Deve Gowda's diploma class, and he was the youngest at seventeen. The oldest, Satyanarayana Dikshit, son of Krishna Dikshit, had studied at the Municipal High School in Nyamathi. Of the total sixteen in the class, there were nine Brahmins, four Vokkaligas, one Christian and one Muslim. One Vokkaliga student, K. Kenche Gowda, had been transferred to the electrical engineering course midway. Caste, community, date of birth, father's name, native village and the school where SSLC was obtained are all part of the institute's dogeared admissions register.[14] The lone Muslim in the class was Abdul Munoof, the son of H.D. Mohammed Ghouse of Hassan town. The lone Christian was Sadhu Sunder Raj, son of C. Eliappa of the Evangelical Church in Holenarasipur town. Deve Gowda wrote his name as H.D. Dyave Gowda, phonetically closer to the subaltern dialect of Mysore Kannada he spoke. He passed out from the polytechnic in 1952. His graduation ceremony picture also does not show him in a Mysore zari peta. That meant he was clearly outside the circle of the Mysore elite or the aspirational elite of the time.

Once Gowda had admitted himself to the polytechnic, he had wondered where to stay in Hassan. The institute did not have a hostel. He approached the warden, Rangappa, at his Vokkaliga community hostel. He gave him provisional admission but told him that he had to meet the hostel's governing council members and get his admission ratified. Gowda met the members, but nobody seemed to take his request seriously, and he did not know anybody in his community who was influential. Finally, when the list appeared, his name was not there. Warden Rangappa pleaded helplessness and gave him forty-eight hours to vacate. Gowda found a small outhouse room in a property owned by a Muslim. He agreed to pay a monthly rent of six rupees, and as he had done in Holenarasipur while studying high school, he got food grains from home and cooked for himself.[15]

The six rupees house rent in Hassan was becoming a burden for Deve Gowda. Luckily for him, one day, G.A. Thimappa Gowda, a lawyer who passed by his lane to go to court each day, stopped him. He enquired who he was and mentioned that he had seen him walk in and out of the Muslim household with a drawing board and books in hand. He must have got curious because Deve Gowda did not look like he was part of the setting. The moment Thimappa Gowda asked, the young Gowda unburdened his economic misery. Only later did Gowda come to know that Thimappa Gowda was a former member of the Mysore constituent assembly. He helped Deve Gowda get a reasonably generous annual scholarship and eased his burden.[16]

Gowda's accidental entry into politics also happened while he was pursuing his three-year diploma course in the midst of simmering caste rivalry in the institute's student association. It was not that Gowda intended to be part of it. In his words, he was only following the track that destiny had laid for him. One day, Gowda, who played as a centre-half-back in the institute's hockey team, was returning after the evening practice session. He overheard Neelakanta Rao, his fellow student, a Brahmin, and son of the district medical officer, brag to his gang of friends that no 'son of a bitch' would dare contest

against him in the association election. Gowda got so worked up
when he heard this, he instinctually swung the hockey stick in his
hand that it landed on Rao's calf muscles. Perhaps a couple of more
blows landed around the same area and the impact was so strong that
the hockey stick cracked.

Rao and his gang of friends were so shocked that they did not
instantly retaliate. Gowda, however, quickly left the scene, unable
to process what he had done. He took a bullock cart and reached
the house of Y. Dharmappa, an MLC and lawyer who belonged to
his community. He stayed near the railway station. Dharmappa
had just then returned from the court and was seated on his
reclining chair. Gowda confessed what he had done in a moment
of anger and sought help. The lawyer-politician made a call to the
superintendent of police, Kempaiah, and told him not to book a
case against Gowda in case the polytechnic's principal complained
to him. Luckily, for Gowda, Neelakanta Rao had not suffered a
fracture or any other grievous injury but only had a swelling that
subsided in a few days.[17]

The institute's principal, Narasimhan, a relative of Neelakanta
Rao, summoned Gowda the next day and gave him a stern warning
but did not pursue the matter. Gowda assumed that this was
because he had learnt of Dharmappa's intervention. Anyway, this
incident made Gowda a hero among non-Brahmin students, and
he won the association election that he reluctantly contested by an
overwhelming majority.

The inauguration of the student's association that year was
to witness more politics. Gowda invited the education minister
and Holenarasipur legislator, A.G. Ramachandra Rao, as the chief
guest. Ramachandra Rao, also a Brahmin, was to mentor Gowda
and initiate him into electoral politics later. However, the choice of
Ramachandra Rao did not go down well with Gowda's rivals. They
went around saying that he could not convince a top professional,
and therefore had got a Congress *pudhari* as the chief guest. By the
time the valedictory function was due, Gowda was determined to do

two things—one was to deliver a welcome speech in English, and then get a top engineer from Bangalore to be the chief guest.[18]

The head of the department of civil engineering, Gopalakrishna, a backward class person was either from the fisherman community (*besta*) or the salt-making community (*uppara*), had taken to Gowda. He organized mock sessions for Gowda to practise his English speech. He would gather a small group of students after class, and get Gowda to address them, while he corrected him. He also prepared a shortlist of chief guests for the valedictory function. That included Ganesh Iyer, who was a chief engineer with the state government; Chandy, who was the chairman of the electricity board; an American, Zampolin who held a top position at Hindustan Aeronautics Limited; the head of the Chamarajendra Polytechnic in Bangalore; and finally, R. Natarajan of the Indian Telephone Industries.[19]

Gowda went on a mission to Bangalore for two days to approach all these men. Nearly all of them expressed regret. Their excuse was simple—the roads to Hassan were not asphalted and the journey up and down would take up the whole day. He was terribly disappointed and sat near a bus stand and wept. Finally, Gowda went to see R. Natarajan in his office. The security guard advised that it would be best to approach him at his residence in Malleswaram. Gowda went there and stood at the gate, waiting for Natarajan to get back from office. As he drove in, he noticed Gowda but did not roll down the window. However, he soon sent his driver to bring him in. Natarajan asked Gowda who he was and why was he at the gate. Gowda explained. Before he responded, he seated Gowda and asked his daughter to give him some juice, and also make some uppitu (a semolina preparation). This was one of Gowda's earliest encounters with graciousness in the wider world. Nobody till then had called him in, seated him on a sofa, enquired if he was hungry and served him food. Initially, Natarajan too said it was a difficult journey to make to Hassan, but finally succumbed to Gowda's pleading and persuasion. Gowda went back the same evening to Hassan. This had given him a sense of accomplishment. He had gone outside the comfort zone of his village, taluk and district and persuaded someone professionally important to accept his invitation. 'Besides my persuasion, we should not forget that Natarajan was a good human being. He did not look at my caste, which was obvious from my name,' Gowda said.[20]

When Natarajan came to the institute for the valedictory function, Gowda gave him a rousing welcome. He had ensured that his path from the gate to the stage was decorated with flowers and festoons. On the stage, he welcomed him in English for five minutes. The hall was packed with over a thousand people. As a mark of gratitude, Gowda had invited Dharmappa, the legislator and lawyer who had saved him, to preside over the function. While Natarajan spoke for about twenty minutes, Dharmappa spoke for forty-five minutes and praised Gowda's enterprise and organizing skills.[21]

As soon as Gowda successfully completed his diploma, he decided to take a job. He had applied for a Western Railways position that had been advertised, and he got an appointment letter in no time. He was placed somewhere in Gujarat. As soon as Gowda's father, Dodde Gowda, heard of the son's job offer, he staged a dharna at home. He slept across the threshold and told his son to cross over him if he wanted to take up the assignment. That meant he could only go over his dead body.[22] He could not bear sending his son far away to a place they did not even know existed. He wanted him to remain in front of his eyes, straddling the worlds of Haradanahalli, Holenarasipur and Hassan. Even Bangalore and Mysore were foreign to the father. Gowda had no option but to begin his professional life as a civil contractor in Holenarasipur taluk.

Dodde Gowda's fear of losing his son continued till the very end. The psychological impact of having lost three sons in a span of ten days in his previous marriage was perhaps so immense that he never stopped reading threats to his first-born from the second marriage. During the Emergency in 1975, when Deve Gowda was imprisoned, the father thought his son would never come back. The villagers had also fuelled his fears by saying that Indira Gandhi would not let his son out of jail: 'Doddanna, Indramma will never let your son out. She'll finish him off there. It's all over,' they would offer cruel commentary in uninformed idleness. The fear had engulfed the father so much that he had lost his sanity. He passed away in 1977, still not fully cognizant that his son was free. Gowda recalled his father's last days: 'He would loudly shout "my son, my son." They had taken him to Dr. Bhimappa in Hassan, and when he advised that he be shifted to Bangalore, they had taken him to Nimhans. I had called Dr Rame Gowda at Nimhans from jail and requested him to keep my father in a special ward.

'When I was released, I took him back to Hassan as doctors said there was very little they could do. While he was drifting further away from reality, I went to the Anjaneya (Hanuman) temple in Haradanahalli and made a strange prayer. I said, "If I am my father's son, he should die on my lap." Later, I suffered from enormous guilt that I had used this phrase before God, which put a question mark on my mother's integrity. I got into a spiral on this indiscretion and suffered for a few days. Since my work in the legislature was getting affected, after a few months, I thought I would keep him with me in my Bangalore home. I hired a car. My mother sat in the front seat next to the driver with a brass water jar. I sat at the back, and my father's head was on my lap. I noticed his body had shrunk. As we reached Kunigal in Tumkur district, he spoke a few words, and within seconds he had breathed his last. On my lap.'[23]

3

The Grassroots Game

After he had been forced to give up his railways job, Deve Gowda began his professional life as a contractor. Initially, he joined friends Dyavanna and Suttige Gowda to take up odd civil jobs. He bought a bicycle and cycled each morning from Haradanahalli to Holenarasipur. Once he felt a little confident, he started taking jobs on his own with his dedicated team of masons and construction workers. He also developed a band of friends with whom he spent time mostly discussing local politics over coffee.

As a contractor, he became quite well known in Holenarasipur taluk after a particular incident, which also kind of brightened his political options. There was a top railway contractor called Sadiq Ali in Hassan district. He rode around on a horse, smoked cigars and had a fair grip over government officials. He had undertaken many contracts between Arsikere in Hassan and Mysore. He was also contracted to maintaining the Amani tank (Amani Doddakere) near Halekote village, which was the biggest tank at the end of a line of tanks where surplus water of the Hemavathi river accumulated. It invariably breached during monsoon causing floods. Sadiq Ali— who was related to a well-known judge of the time in Mysore, and also the former diwan of the Mysore state, Mirza Ismail—had a clever accounting practice of keeping a balance bill to ensure that the contract came back to him every year.[1]

Deve Gowda, with his newly earned diploma, approached assistant engineer B.N. Srinivas and convinced him that he could do a better job in fortifying the tank. He spoke of new engineering methods. This was in 1953. Srinivas was impressed with Gowda's presentation and gave him the repairs and maintenance contract. Naturally, this upset Sadiq Ali, and when he saw Gowda at the town fair, he insinuated him. He called him a petty 'bicycle man,' and cursed that he would not go far. Gowda was twenty at the time and would not take an insult lying down. He raised his voice and asked Ali to get off his horse if he wanted to talk. Even as he engaged Ali, Gowda sent one of his workers to get a Wills brand cigarette packet, which cost three rupees and two annas. As soon as the cigarette was handed over to him, he put it between his lips and lit it up to imitate the cigar at the edge of Ali's lips. Nobody had stood before Ali and spoken, let alone smoke. When Gowda challenged him, he meekly rode away. Gowda was not a smoker but lighting up before Ali had made him a hero of sorts in the taluk.[2] People who had gathered around raised slogans as if Gowda had won a battle. With the tank bund, Gowda did such a neat job that the villagers of Halekote take pride in certifying that it has not given away to this day, save for small repairs.[3]

With his newly minted fame, and accolades from Holenarasipur MLA, A.G. Ramachandra Rao, Gowda felt encouraged to join the Congress party. He had developed a loose association, but he now formalized it in 1953, and became a mentee of Rao. After the first democratic elections in 1952, Rao had been made the education and law minister in the Kengal Hanumanthaiah-led Congress government. Gowda had wisely chosen his guru.

In 1954, Gowda turned 21, and his parents found Chennamma, a seventeen-year-old bride for him from the Muttige Hirehalli village of the same taluk. Her parents Patel Deve Gowda and Kaalamma were relatively better off than Deve Gowda's family in Haradanahalli.

Her father not only had a lot of influence in his village, of which he was the headman but also in the surrounding villages. Kaalamma was the third wife of Patel Gowda. His first two wives had passed away. Like Deve Gowda, Chennamma was also the firstborn to her parents. It is not that Gowda was entirely unaware of Chennamma's existence until the marriage was fixed. He had seen her because her maternal grandparents lived in his village, and she would come there for festivals and school holidays. Her maternal grandfather Subbe Gowda was a much bigger personality than Chennamma's father. He was a big landlord and was considered rich. He also lent money and had apparently hired Muslim men, an indication of a higher social status in Holenarasipur taluk, to collect his interest and principal amounts. There were times when he had also helped Deve Gowda's father to sustain his son's education. Although Chennamma was Deve Gowda's mother Lakshmi Devamma's choice, Gowda's English education and diploma had made him the most eligible bachelor in the surrounding villages.[4] The bride-to-be had also passed her lower secondary grade exams with decent marks, but that was the maximum a girl would be allowed to pursue education in conservative households of the Mysore state. The marriage took place in the girl's house in Muttige Hirehalli village on 25 May 1954.

The young couple started off well in the sense that Chennamma was supportive of Gowda's business exigencies. In a year or so after their marriage, he fell short of a thousand rupees to pay a tender deposit for a particular civil work that he was bidding. The deadline was drawing close, and Chennamma was at her mother's place in Mosale Hirehalli. Gowda sent a chit through one of his trusted workers, Bettaiah, and without hesitation, and without telling her parents, she quietly sent her marriage jewellery to be pawned. When Gowda had got the jewellery released a couple of months later, she had said that he could make use of it whenever he wanted because she had decided not to wear them until he would not need them to carry on with his work.[5] It took Gowda a few years not to require his wife's ornaments for emergencies.

This understanding and trust between the couple deepened over the years. Right through his career as a contractor, and later as a politician, it appears Gowda never had surplus money. He only rotated it from one project to another and one election to another. He was perpetually in debt. Amidst such glorious uncertainties, the role played by Chennamma to offer a reasonably stable family life to Gowda and their six children was stellar. She was always homebound and saw the world through her husband. She gradually developed an independent judgement of people around her. Her social circuit was confined to her extended family, especially in Holenarasipur and Hassan. Big outings meant attending weddings or going on short pilgrimages. While Gowda always carried a worried look, the calm of the prayer settled better on Chennamma. She was deeply ritualistic in her worship and innovated on an elaborate prayer and fasting regimen for herself by watching women of upper caste households in her neighbourhood in Holenarasipur town.[6]

First Steps in Politics

Getting back to the 1950s, Gowda took his first political steps in 1954, the same year he got married. He was nominated to the Holenarasipur Taluk Industrial Cooperative Society as its secretary. The next year, he was elected president of the Primary Agricultural Cooperative Society. This was the first election he had contested after his college. He got a little ambitious, and the same year, 1955, he aspired for a seat on the Taluk Primary Land Development Bank. In that election, he was snubbed badly. He got just four votes.[7] He decided to take it a little slow after that. His political guru, A.G. Ramachandra Rao, was also defeated in the 1957 assembly elections, and this cut his clout to an extent.

In a couple of years, Y. Veerappa, the Praja Socialist Party (PSP) member who had defeated Rao, went after Deve Gowda and the other young followers of Rao. He got an anonymous letter written to the local authorities that Gowda was submitting fake bills for the civil works

he was undertaking in the taluk. The matter was promptly referred
to the anti-corruption bureau. A local MLC, Suryanarayana Shetty,
decided to intervene on Gowda's behalf. He took Gowda to Public
Works Minister H.M. Channabasappa in Bangalore, and said Gowda
was a very good Congress party worker, and the allegation against
him was a hoax.[8] The state government was a Congress government
led by S. Nijalingappa, and Channabasappa casually remarked that
people wearing khadi were perfectly capable of submitting false bills.
Gowda, who did not like the insinuation, retorted sharply: 'Perhaps
you would have treated me better had I come wearing *kaavi* (saffron
clothes) instead of khadi.' Channabasappa was furious. He got up,
pushed the chair aside, and warned Gowda: 'I will neck you out.'
Gowda was not intimidated: 'This is not your house to neck me out.
This is the people's house. Let elections come; people will chase you
out,' he said, and walked out of the meeting.[9] After Gowda calmed
down, he worried about the Rs 42,000 pending bills and a loan of Rs
33,000. The worry soon turned to determination, which could also
be a euphemism for revenge here. He decided to defeat Y. Veerappa
in the forthcoming assembly elections.[10]

As a preparation, in 1960, Gowda contested the Taluk Board
elections. This was the first big challenge, and he had to woo an
electorate of 38,000 people. Friends pooled in money and A.G.
Ramachandra Rao gave his blessings. He also received the backing
of another prominent Congress leader in the taluk, Patel Huchche
Gowda. He won convincingly. His platform and playfield had
suddenly expanded.

After Gowda became a Taluk Board member, people started
gauging his ambition and tried to make life difficult for him. He
had a loyal following, but he realized that his ring of enemies had
also grown. Not all of them directly confronted him but would
quietly provoke others. One of the most absurd things that he
would encounter was drunk people abusing him. He soon saw a
pattern and learnt that they were being sponsored to do so. He
tried out a counterstrategy. He would pay the same drunkard

double the money to abuse his original sponsor. It worked. People stepped back.[11]

His decision to defeat Y. Veerappa did not mean he wanted to contest the assembly elections himself in 1962. It so happened, A.G. Ramachandra Rao was growing old and decided not to contest the polls. Since Rao had watched Gowda closely for a decade and was familiar with his enterprise, he decided to canvass for a Congress ticket for his *shishya* (protégé). His name was recommended at the taluk and district levels, and at the state level too there was some confirmation that he was the unanimous choice of the party. But things changed when the list went to Delhi. A mysterious hand had knocked off Deve Gowda's name and replaced it with H.D. Dodde Gowda (incidentally, he was Deve Gowda's father's namesake). The Congress then was faction-ridden and Gowda suspected the hand of S. Nijalingappa who had a powerful rival in B.D. Jatti. It is possible that Gowda was perceived to be in the Jatti camp because of his proximity to Ramachandra Rao, but as always, nothing official surfaced within the Congress party.[12]

Gowda, who was by then popularly known in Holenarasipur taluk as 'bicycle man', decided to contest as an independent with the bicycle as his symbol. He first made the decision and then worried about funds. But since his friends and people around thought he had been deceived by the Congress, they decided to crowdsource funds. Gowda also borrowed small sums to print posters and pamphlets.[13] Elections were not as expensive then, but it still demanded a tidy investment for an individual contesting as an independent. Though Ramachandra Rao, a loyal Congressman and Gowda's mentor, could not campaign for him, he gave his blessings to Gowda to pursue his course. This also became a talking point during the election. People realized that Rao's heart was not with the official party candidate. Gowda's campaign strategy was simple—to go on his cycle from village to village, develop for them a micro manifesto, eat with them and ask for votes.

Before he filed his nomination papers, Ramachandra Rao asked Gowda to visit one Achyuta Shastry, his trusted astrologer, in

Mysore. Gowda went to see him and showed his horoscope. Shastry was unambiguous. He said there was no way Gowda would lose, and if he did, he would take his sacred thread (*janivara* or *janeu*) off as a Brahmin. A happy and doubly confident Gowda reported back to Rao and filed his nomination. This practice of seeing astrologers before he did anything became a lifelong habit for Gowda.[14]

After 1956, Karnataka's caste politics had taken a sharp turn, with a division right in the middle between Lingayats and Vokkaligas. There was a sense of victimhood among Vokkaligas that they had lost the seat of power in Bangalore to Lingayats after the linguistic reorganization of the state. In November 1956, S. Nijalingappa had replaced Kadidal Manjappa, and Kengal Hanumanthaiah had quit three months before the reorganization of the state in August 1956. But that was not helping in Holenarasipur because Gowda's principal rival was a Vokkaliga, so his principal task was to garner as many votes from other communities as possible.

On the linguistic reorganization of the state, A.G. Ramachandra Rao had opposed the bill in the assembly and spoken for nearly two hours. He had reasoned that there was no cultural alignment between Mysore and the new parts that were being integrated into it. The food was different and so was the language, he had said. He had also warned that if the linguistic reorganization was allowed, the Lingayats would dominate the state. Gowda had watched his guru speak from the gallery in the assembly.[15] Rao had also addressed the Vokkaliga Maha Sammelana in Mandya to oppose the reorganization, and Gowda had accompanied him there too. Later, Rao was part of the delegation that met Nehru to oppose the reorganization.[16] When this debate was happening, Gowda was just 23 years old and was only emotionally invested in Rao. He had no independent opinion. But later, by the time he became a legislator in 1962, he had accepted the reality of a reorganized state, and in a 1973 debate on the renaming of the Mysore state as Karnataka, he had questioned the loyalty of Chief Minister Devaraj Urs to the idea of linguistic reorganization of the state.[17]

In the 1962 election, Gowda's aim was to defeat Y. Veerappa of the PSP, but H.D. Dodde Gowda from within the Congress had suddenly cropped up to offer a challenge. But Deve Gowda's hard work paid off. He carried the emotion of the electorate by presenting himself as a victim of the Congress party intrigue. He won by a margin of 5284 votes. In that election 63.55 per cent had cast their votes in the Holenarasipur assembly segment, that is 31,920 voters. This was less than the number of people who had voted in the Taluk Board elections in 1960, which Gowda had won. Gowda had got more than double the votes Y. Veerappa had secured, the man who had tried to ruin him. Veerappa had secured only 6052 votes, while Gowda had got 12,622 votes.[18] Gowda entered the state assembly as an independent candidate, and since he had rebelled, he was expelled from the Congress party for six years. From this time on, for the next half-century, Holenarasipur and Hassan have remained a bastion of the Deve Gowda family.

The 1962 election was full of surprises, not just for Holenarasipur, but also for the entire Mysore state. S. Nijalingappa, chief minister, lost his seat from Hosadurga to G.T. Rangappa, a PSP candidate. S.R. Kanthi, the Hungund legislator, was made chief minister to keep the chair warm for Nijalingappa till he got re-elected from Bagalkot after forcing an election, thereby seeking the resignation of B.T. Muranal. B.D. Jatti, the Jamakhandi legislator, had staked claim to the chief minister's chair but was outmanoeuvred by the S. Nijalingappa camp. Lal Bahadur Shastri, the then Union home minister, was sent as an observer to Bangalore.[19] As long as Kanthi was chief minister, Jatti did not join the state cabinet but returned as finance minister after Nijalingappa took charge three months later. He had 'deferred to the wishes' of Shastri.[20] Jatti had already been chief minister of Mysore between 1958 and 1962 when Nijalingappa had lost power due to dissensions within the Congress party.

Jatti had the unique distinction of serving two states—Bombay and Mysore. Since Jamakhandi was part of the Bombay Presidency in British India, and then, between 1948 and 1956, part of the Bombay state, he was first elected to the Bombay Assembly. In 1949, he was made parliamentary secretary by Chief Minister Balasaheb Kher, and then joined the Morarji Desai cabinet as a deputy minister. He too, like Gowda, had risen from humble beginnings as a Jamakhandi municipality member.[21] His father was first a daily wager and then a grocer. Gowda developed an affinity for him over the years. Like Jatti, Gowda too came to be mentored by Morarji Desai in the 1970s.

The composition of the assembly in 1962 was also interesting. If the Congress had a majority of 138 members in the 208-member house (a decade later, the strength of the assembly went up to 224), there were twenty PSP members (the party of Jayaprakash Narayan or JP, J.B. Kripalani and Narendra Dev). They were the biggest political group after the Congress, followed by the C. Rajagopalachari-led Swatantra Party. There were nine Swatantra Party members and they mainly had won from the Hyderabad-Karnataka region, formerly the Nizam's territory. The Jan Sangh had been wiped out. However, the largest contingent was that of the independents: they were 27 in number, and Gowda was one of them.

The other independent member from Maddur who had made his debut was S.M. Krishna. He was also a Vokkaliga but was branded in the following decades as 'English Gowda' or 'Texas Gowda'[22] (he had studied in Dallas, Texas and Washington DC for a law degree as a Fulbright scholar). He won and lost elections later and held prominent positions but could never be the 'son of the soil' like Deve Gowda. He was always the suited–booted, tennis-playing elite for members of his community. He remained atypical of a rustic, dhoti-clad Mandya Vokkaliga who wore emotion on his sleeve. In 1967, Krishna had contested from the same Maddur seat as a PSP candidate but had been defeated. Besides Gowda and Krishna, who had debuted in 1962, the other prominent names in the Legislative Assembly who made a name in the coming decades were Veerendra Patil from Chincholi, D. Devaraj Urs from Hunsur, B. Rachaiah from Santhemaranahalli and M.Y. Ghorpade from Sandur. Former chief minister, Kadidal Manjappa, had also been elected from

Sringeri and firebrand socialist Shantaveri Gopala Gowda from the
Socialist Party was a legislator from Thirthahalli. Vaikunta Baliga
from Belthangady was elected the Speaker.[23]

The State Assembly

H.D. Deve Gowda was administered the oath as a legislator on 12
March 1962 by V. Masiyappa the protem Speaker. The last king of
Mysore, Jayachamarajendra Wadiyar, was the Governor of the state.
After his joint address to the Mysore state legislature, Gowda got his
first opportunity to speak. It was on the morning of 3 April 1962
during the motion of thanks to the governor's address. He spoke
about his experience of corruption in the system. He also made a plea
to implement the Harangi project on the Cauvery. He said it would
irrigate an additional 10,000 acres if done so. He also emphasized the
need for the Hassan–Mangalore railway line.[24]

Soon, the harnessing of the Cauvery for irrigational needs was to
become his cause. The finest moment in his first term was when he
created history by moving the first-ever private member resolution in
the assembly on Cauvery (see the chapter on Cauvery and Krishna).
This made him a leader of the entire Cauvery basin, and not just
Holenarasipur. If he was the 'bicycle man' in his constituency, in the
state assembly, he became the 'water man.'

Another project he fought for during his first term was the Gorur
Hemavathi Dam. There was resistance from the surrounding villages
as they feared they would be submerged, but he spent time with the
villagers and convinced them by retelling the story of the Krishnaraj
Sagar Dam, which despite being resisted by the British, was pushed
through by the Mysore Maharaja and Sir M. Visvesvaraya. They had
built a dam with 35 TMC (thousand million cubic feet) storage,
which irrigated 90,000 acres of paddy and 30,000 acres of sugarcane.[25]

Gowda was taking his first firm steps. Whenever the assembly
was in session, he never missed a single day and never stayed outside.
He attended the house with the discipline of a clerk from 10 a.m.

to 5 p.m., only breaking for lunch. He spent time observing how the assembly was conducted and how speeches and interventions were made. He familiarized himself with parliamentary rules and procedures. He also spent a lot of time in the legislature library, and even after the assembly got over, he went straight back to his room and continued with his study. The fact that Gowda was a teetotaller, non-smoker and nearly friendless in Bangalore helped him concentrate on his primary task—of being a legislator. He did not play cards, a familiar pastime with many legislators, nor did he seek any other entertainment late in the evening.[26] He used the rickety red government transport bus to travel back and forth from his constituency. The only privilege he had was the front row seats in the bus were reserved for him.[27]

As soon as Gowda was sworn in as a legislator, he was allotted room number 135 in the legislators' hostel right next to the Vidhana Soudha. He had to share the room with Hoskote legislator B. Channabyre Gowda, who would walk in and out of the assembly with a Mysore zari peta and a dhoti tied in a traditional style (*kachche panche* in Kannada). Gowda never wore a turban, and the cotton or khadi dhoti for him was a simple wrap-around. There were twin beds in room number 135 with an attached bath and toilet. Channabyre Gowda would gather some friends and play cards all evening, sometimes during the day too. The room was always hosting mini parties with non-vegetarian food in generous supply. When Gowda returned from the assembly at 6 p.m., he hardly had space to rest or room for privacy. It started irritating him. He wanted to move out.

After a week, he went to the speaker, Vaikunta Baliga, and explained his situation. Baliga, who was sympathetic to Gowda, told him that there were no single rooms available in the legislator's home, but if he insisted, he could be allotted a single room in the general hostel, a little distance away. But there was a catch. It had common toilets and a common bathing area with only a single telephone at the reception. 'If you can adjust, I can give you a room there right away,' Baliga told Gowda. Gowda happily consented and was allotted room number six, which Gowda retained till he became a minister in 1983. However, in 1972, when he had become leader of the Opposition, he had taken a house in the Jayanagar locality on a rent of Rs 200, and shifted there with his family: 'That house had a single room, and my children slept in the car shed,' Gowda recalled.[28] When he shifted to the Jayanagar house, he made C.M. Ibrahim, a young party worker from Bhadravati town in Davangere, its caretaker. Ibrahim vacated the room in 1977 when Gowda came back from jail. (See the chapter on Devaraj Urs for Gowda's jail stint during the Emergency.)

After he became a legislator, Gowda also bought twelve acres of land, uncultivated for years, in a nearby village called Paduvalahippe. He had taken a loan and pledged his wife's ornaments again. This was to be his security as well as a retirement plan.[29] He was giving up being a contractor, an independent means of earning and embracing the uncertainty of politics. He had young children and did not know how they would fare in life. He got the land registered in his wife's name. He had by then decided to leave the small parcel of ancestral land in Haradanahalli to his brother and uncles. Gowda went back to till this land in 1978 when he became disenchanted with politics.

In 1967, Gowda again contested as an independent and won the Holenarasipur assembly seat. He defeated the same H.D. Dodde Gowda by an even bigger margin of 8403 votes.[30] The man who had originally pushed him to think of an assembly contest, Y. Veerappa, was not in the fray. In 1968, when S. Nijalingappa became the All India Congress Committee president, he gave up the chief minister's chair. Nijalingappa had made young Veerendra Patil chief minister, after B.D. Jatti was outsmarted again.[31] In an effort to appease Jatti, Indira Gandhi sent him to Pondicherry as lieutenant governor, and a year before the Emergency was clamped in June 1975, he became the Vice President of India.

In 1968, Jatti instigated a group of Congress MLAs to vote against the budget presented by the Veerendra Patil government. At that juncture, Patil had pleaded with Gowda to rejoin the party. Gowda had acquiesced.[32] When the Congress split in 1969,

Gowda remained with Nijalingappa and Chief Minister Patil in the Congress (Organisation). Devaraj Urs had approached him at the time to join Indira Gandhi's Congress or Congress (Requisitionists), but he had politely declined. He had argued that Indira Gandhi had behaved 'unethically and spread indiscipline' in the party by propping up V.V. Giri against Neelam Sanjiva Reddy during the election for the President of India.[33] Gowda had never thought that in 1972 he would end up being leader of the Opposition to Chief Minister Devaraj Urs.

During his first term as a legislator, Deve Gowda was deeply impressed by Shantaveri Gopala Gowda, the sole Socialist Party legislator from Thirthahalli in Shimoga district.[34] Gopala Gowda's irreverence, fearlessness, verbal flamboyance, forceful rhetoric and abiding commitment to the cause of the poor and landless peasants attracted Gowda. Once Gowda was stunned by the way Gopala Gowda addressed Chief Minister Nijalingappa as he was walking into the assembly: 'Come in, come in. We'll slay you today and hang your torn ego at the entrance of the Vidhana Soudha.'[35] Nobody shouted down Gopal Gowda because he carried moral authority. Gopala Gowda did not return to the assembly in 1967 and died in 1972 when he was only forty-nine. His habits had got the better of him as much as the frustrations caused by the limits of electoral democracy. Just before he passed away, Deve Gowda had gone to see him at the Victoria Hospital. He looked fragile and his voice was feeble, but he tried to speak: 'My time has passed. You will make it big one day. Don't ever give up the fight.'[36] Gopala Gowda was a tragic hero who inspired the Kannada novel *Avasthe* by U.R. Ananthamurthy, which was seen as a romanticization of defeat.[37] Poet Gopalakrishna Adiga in a poetic tribute said: 'You were born to be a great leader, but you chose the role of a martyr.'[38]

Deve Gowda as a politician was made from a very different mould, but when he became leader of the Opposition, he endeavoured to blend the fearlessness of Gopala Gowda with his own method of ambushing with a pile of facts. In June 1972, when Gopala Gowda passed away, in his obituary speech, Deve Gowda said that his family was in fragile economic health, and as colleagues, they had a duty towards the family. Devaraj Urs, the chief minister, also a mentee of Gopala Gowda, responded positively.[39]

4

Devaraj Urs, Emergency and a Stormy Decade

The 1970s was the most crucial decade in the political life of Deve Gowda. It propelled him into the limelight, made him a skilled parliamentary player, helped him fine-tune his political method, taught him to punch above his weight, prepared him for roles that would come later, built his pan-India network, packed disappointment and humiliation in heaps and taught him to bide his time until destiny's moment arrived.

The 1970s made Gowda what he finally became. After being a mildly fluttering independent legislator for two terms in the 1960s, he came back to a broken faction of the Congress. The Congress soon became the Congress (Organisation) led by S. Nijalingappa, the stalwart Karnataka politician who had been chief minister and national president of the Congress. The party had split under his watch, nationally, in 1969. The mid-1970s also saw the Emergency being clamped; Gowda went to jail and later witnessed the birth of the Janata Party. He had the chance of becoming Karnataka's first non-Congress chief minister in 1978 but tripped at the threshold.

The most productive years of the decade were when Gowda functioned as the Opposition leader in the Karnataka Legislative Assembly. He was chosen to lead a motley, assorted group of forty-one legislators who had strangely survived the electoral assault of Devaraj Urs in 1972. Urs had broken the electoral dominance of the Lingayats and Vokkaligas in the state by galvanizing the backward classes and minorities as well as the poorer and oppressed sections of society.[1] An empathetic aristocrat from Mysore, Urs was the first non-Lingayat, non-Vokkaliga chief minister in twenty-five years since Independence. The dynamics that he had unleashed with his victory in 1972 had permanently altered Karnataka's politics, and Gowda was one of its closest witnesses.

While the Urs-led Indian National Congress (INC), popularly known as the Congress (R), had an overwhelming majority of 165 seats in a house of 216[2] with an unprecedented vote share of 52.17 per cent, the Congress (O) had twenty-four seats with a 26.22 per cent vote share.[3] There were three legislators each from the Communist Party of India and the Samyukta Socialist Party, one from Janata Paksha and twenty independents. The Swatantra Party and the Bharatiya Jan Sangh had drawn a blank. Gowda was made the Opposition leader since all the senior leaders opposed to Indira Gandhi and Urs had either lost or not contested. His choice as an Opposition leader was a quirk of circumstance. Both Veerendra Patil, who was chief minister till 1971, and Ramakrishna Hegde, his finance minister, both senior Congress (O) leaders, had stayed away from the assembly contest.

It was not easy for Gowda to stand up and face Urs, who had developed a halo. He was a political giant and a master strategist. The effect of his social and caste engineering was such that he created at least half-dozen future and potential chief ministers in the early 1970s.[4] Although he was from a Mysore aristocratic community (Arasu) with strong links to the Wadiyars, he was a practising agriculturist. He was well read in both the humanities and social sciences. He was handsome, charismatic and had wide legislative experience. The smoking pipe at the edge of his mouth complimented his personality. He never compromised on his Royal Salute whisky. His appreciation of Charles Dickens and Carnatic music was wholesome.[5] In spite of his regal bearing, the poor instantly connected with his compassion. Against Urs, Gowda, who had no pedigree, pizzazz or great professional qualification, was fielded in the assembly. All that Gowda, a humble farmer from Holenarasipur, had in his arsenal was extraordinary drive, dedication and determination to succeed and unflinching faith in his destiny.

When Urs heard that Gowda had been picked as leader of the Opposition, he had apparently laughed it off. He is said to have deployed a dismissive expression. This was reported to Gowda by his journalist-friend H.S. Ramprasad: 'I now wonder as to what had given me the confidence at that time to be leader of the Opposition. When Ramprasad, who was at Urs's press conference, told me about his dismissiveness, I was disturbed. I was out of depth as to how to face the mighty Urs. Ramprasad asked me not to worry. We both sat down under the banyan tree at the Airlines Hotel near the Vidhana Soudha and worked out a rough strategy. Ramprasad and I met there many times to fine-tune our method and way forward. My first speech in the assembly was on Cauvery. I had prepared well and spoke for over an hour. That gave me some confidence. But for six months, I was still groping in the dark. Ramprasad was of immense help.'[6]

But after the initial hiccups, and as the Urs government started rolling and ministers in his cabinet, most of whom had unexpectedly, and for the first time landed in positions of power, started behaving erratically, Gowda girded his loins. 'By then, with the help of Ramprasad, I had created a method for myself. I used to read all the newspapers, started clipping and filing reports department-wise and kept a notebook on what each minister was saying and doing. Since I was the chairman of the Public Accounts Committee (PAC) of the legislature, I got audit reports, which I started reading and making margin notes. Ramprasad and I would discuss how to pick an issue and how to present it effectively. It was a lot of hard work. Those days, the Opposition leader did not have facilities like he has now. I had no secretarial assistance. I had to do everything myself.'[7] Gowda as Opposition leader often used public transport and walked from his room in the general hostel to the Vidhana Soudha.

To make his presence felt and attract the attention of the media, Gowda decided on an interesting strategy. Whenever the house was in session, he decided to put out a scandal, big or small, every day, against the Urs government. It was an ant-like effort against an elephant-like personality, but it worked. Gowda managed to chip off a bit of Urs's halo. It was not so much the disagreement with Urs's policies but missteps, maladministration, nepotism and corruption that he focused on. The high-handedness of Urs's son-in-law, M.D. Nataraj, who had formed the Indira Brigade, was one other frequent area of confrontation between the two (for more, see the chapter on Morarji Desai). Nataraj was from a backward class community and had married Urs's second daughter, Nagaratna. It was a love match. It is an entirely different story that Urs's daughter died at the age of 28 under mysterious circumstances.

P.G.R. Sindhia, who was with the Rashtriya Swayamsevak Sangh (RSS) and Akhil Bharatiya Vidyarthi Parishad (ABVP) then but would later join the Janata Party to become a minister in the Hegde cabinet, said: 'I have known Gowda since 1974. He was a top-class debater with a ringing voice, which he of course lost later due to a throat condition. I used to get a pass to sit in the visitors' gallery of the assembly just to listen to Gowda's speeches, which was quite an event in the media. There was a lot of publicity to the encounters between Urs and Gowda on the floor of the house. In a very short period, he became an extraordinary Opposition leader. When there was a flood or a drought or any other public distress, Gowda became the voice of the people. K.S. Nagaratnamma, the Speaker, did not have a great relationship with Urs, so she encouraged Gowda to speak. I have seen Ramprasad of *Kannada Prabha*, who was also from Holenarasipur, helping Gowda. He would guide him. Gowda would sit down and work on his speeches in the general hostel, and it soon became familiar to everybody that he was very thorough with his homework. He never entered the house without documents. Urs was a great democrat. He allowed Gowda to speak for hours and was always present when he spoke.'[8]

Sindhia recounted further on those times: 'During those days, student unions were a breeding ground for political lumpenism. Gowda never encouraged student leaders who were the disruptive and muscled type. He would have benefited by encouraging them but he took a principled position against mainstreaming such elements. But Urs, through his son-in-law Nataraj and his associates F.M. Khan and Gundu Rao, would cultivate such youngsters. The other defining memory of Gowda from the time was his poverty. He did not take the salary or perks of an Opposition leader; he made do with what he got as an MLA. He was entitled to a government house, but he chose to stay in the government hostel. After a few years, the farmers of Hassan gifted him a car—a blue Ambassador (MEQ 6087). He toured the state in that car. He was so popular with the people that if he went to a play, there would be additional collection that night. In the RSS and ABVP, we used to admire the organizational skills and discipline of Gowda. There were a series of by polls at that time. Gowda would be the principal strategist. Veerendra Patil, with an all-Karnataka presence, would come to deliver speeches, and Hegde would organize resources. That was the distribution of labour between them. In the popular imagination, these three were seen as a trio taking on Devaraj Urs.'[9]

Although Gowda did not concede an inch to Urs on the floor of the house, he had otherwise a cordial relationship with him. There was also an age difference of nearly twenty years between the two that made Gowda think of him as an 'elder brother.'[10] Urs was not without affection for Gowda. In fact, in 1969, when the Congress spilt nationally, Urs came to see Gowda: 'I was at the government hostel. He came in his Fiat car. He drove me to the Cubbon Park nearby, bought peanuts for two rupees, made me sit down under a tree and counselled me, "See Gowda, I will make you Hassan district president. If Indira Congress comes to power in the state, I will make you a minister. Join me." He spoke in a tone that an elder brother would employ for his younger sibling. I refused. I did not like what Indira Gandhi had done to Sanjiva Reddy in the presidential polls. She had put up V.V. Giri and called for a conscience vote. I felt she had sowed the seeds of indiscipline in the party. To my refusal to join, Urs reacted in his typical way. He used stories and circumstances from the Mahabharata to convince me. When I did not budge, he did not force me, nor did he hold it against me. He was a good, large-hearted man,' Gowda recalled.[11]

During the 1960s, when Devaraj Urs was the transport minister in Nijalingappa's ministry, Gowda used to often go to him to get new bus routes sanctioned to his constituency or seek employment for his constituents as conductors and drivers. Urs and S. Nijalingappa did not have a great relationship and since Gowda had rebelled against Nijalingappa and had been elected as an independent in 1962 and 1967, Urs had admired his grit and saw potential in him. Their friendship developed, and whenever Urs was to go to Kallahalli, his village near Mysore, he would go via Holenarasipur, Gowda's hometown. 'He would tell me, "Hey Gowda, I'll come for lunch, get some special chicken dish made." He would enjoy his food, relax for a while, smoke his pipe and also offer a packet of Dunhill cigarettes to me. I was a non-smoker, but he would still insist.'[12] This relationship was put on trial many times on the floor of the assembly after Urs became chief minister and Gowda, his Opposition's leader. However harsh the exchange of words, it did not affect the core of their relationship, insists Gowda.[13]

One wonders if it is a retrospective sentiment because battles that Gowda waged at the time and the charges he levelled against Urs could not have been just clockwork dispassion. The archives of newspapers and legislative assembly debates certainly reflect relentless verbal assault by Gowda against Urs. People like Chiranjiv Singh, who was deputy secretary to Urs, confirm that this could be a retrospective and reflective reconfiguration of a relationship that has been left far behind in time: 'We have seen Gowda get very angry at Devaraj Urs in the assembly on many occasions. He wouldn't concede an inch. He was the most effective Opposition leader I have seen. Ramakrishna Hegde in the legislative council too was extremely sharp, and Urs found it relatively easier to handle Gowda's shrillness over Hegde's shrewdness. It was my job to work on Urs's replies to Hegde's queries in the council,' Singh recalled.[14]

When Urs was a couple of years into his term, the Iyengar community and Sarvodaya leaders of Holenarasipur, which was Gowda's constituency, wanted to felicitate the chief minister and the Opposition leader together. They invited Gowda. He was naturally hesitant. He said, 'I have been attacking the chief minister daily, and it would not make for good optics to be felicitated with him.' Since the organizers insisted, he asked them to check with Urs first. Urs, when contacted, was charming. He picked up the phone instantly, called Gowda, and asked him why he was hesitant about the joint felicitation proposal: 'You are my Opposition leader only on the floor of the house,' he chided him.[15] When Urs went to Holenarasipur for the felicitation, it upset his own party men. They held a black flag demonstration. He asked the police to detain them and carried on with the function and also inaugurated development works. In the speech he made that day, he again drew from the Mahabharata, and said that Gowda was like King Shalya in the epic. He should have been with him but had been tricked to fight on the other side.[16]

As the battle between Urs and Gowda intensified, and Gowda with great fanfare was releasing documents against ministers in the Urs cabinet, Urs realized that it had begun to dent his image. He telephoned Gowda one day around 6.30 a.m., and said, 'I'll send my car. You come over. Let's walk and talk.' They went to a corner of the Bangalore Palace Grounds and started walking. Gowda recounted the words of Urs: 'Hey Gowda (he always addressed him in the first person), you have gone to the extent of certifying me as a "corrupt" person. Let me tell you one thing, I am not corrupt. I have nothing other than this ring that the Mysore maharaja gifted me. I had a site in Bangalore, which I have divided into three parts and have given away to my three daughters. You think the Mysore maharaja rolls around in luxury, but he too has a loan of a few crores.'[17]

What Urs meant was that perception and reality could be different. They walked a small distance and then stopped at a cafeteria run by a Malayali in the palace compound. Urs took out his pipe, packed tobacco and lit it. After a while, when the mood had lightened, Gowda further recounted what Urs said: 'See Gowda, I have got reports on you from the police intelligence, your Hassan deputy commissioner and the Corps of Detectives. I wanted to fix you, but honestly, there is nothing really that I can lay my hands on. On the contrary, the reports say that you have a loan of Rs 1,30,000. You have six children. Do you intend to feed mud to those children? Does Indira Gandhi bring money from her father's house to do politics? Does your Veerendra Patil bring money from his grandfather's house? Do you have any sense? Why do you pledge your personal belongings to do politics? Take this briefcase (packed with money), repay your loans and educate your children.' Gowda gently refused: 'He was not trying to bribe me. On the contrary, he was moved by my plight and financial condition. I said, "accepting this money would be like pledging myself, sir."'[18]

Urs's son-in-law, M.D. Nataraj, continued to put his father-in-law in embarrassing situations. Once, an army officer had come on leave to see his wife and their newborn. He was taking a stroll with his sister-in-law on the Sankey Tank bridge. Nataraj and his friends, who were passing by, stopped to rag them. As tension flared up, both parties landed up in the police station and asked for an FIR to be registered against each other. This obviously reached the newspapers and they splashed it as yet another 'hooligan act' by the chief minister's son-in-law. The house was in session and the Opposition did not lose time in attacking the chief minister. Gowda sat quietly, listening to the debate. He also saw that Urs's face had dropped. He was crestfallen by the heap of humiliation. At

that point, the Speaker of the house, K.S. Nagaratnamma, turned
towards Gowda and asked why he was sitting quiet. It was more
a provocation to attack Urs. Gowda stood up: 'Urs is the chief
minister for five crore people. He has respect for all the women in
the state and is fully aware that he has to protect their honour. He
too has three daughters. This incident has given him a lot of pain
and he has no direct role in it. Please have faith in him to solve the
problem and end this debate forthwith. I appeal to all of you.'[19]
Gowda never believed in personally humiliating Urs. He was harsh
but kept it professional.

As the house adjourned for lunch, Urs sent for Gowda through
his secretary J.C. Lynn. When Gowda reached his chambers,
Urs's eyes grew moist. He hugged him. Gowda became emotional
too. Urs thanked Gowda for his sensitivity and blessed him that
he would make it big one day.[20] Whenever Urs complimented
or said a nice thing to Gowda, he would suffix or prefix it with a
warning that Gowda's colleagues in the Congress (O) were adept
at exploiting his raw energy but would never actually allow him
to be chief minister when the time came. But on this occasion,
it was an unconditional blessing. 'Urs was a great man. I was a
small-time Opposition leader with no background or support. If
he wanted to silence me, he could have shut me up. But he did
not do that. He was thoroughly democratic in his approach. He
allowed debate, discussion, and wild allegations too. He never got
the house adjourned without responding to debates and charges. I
have also not seen another politician in my life who would frankly
admit to his mistakes if he had committed any. He never stood on
ego. Among all the politicians I have seen in my life, I would give
him the highest marks,' Gowda said.[21]

Over forty-five years after these exchanges took place, Gowda's
acknowledgment of Urs's magnanimity and large-heartedness may
be retrospective, yet genuine, as Chiranjiv Singh confirmed earlier.
After all, life's experiences and progress spread a reflective parasol in
his mind and offered corrections. In Gowda's mind now, Urs was a

fine human being with flaws necessitated only by circumstance, but as a forty-year-old Opposition leader, he never made such a concession. Even on occasions when Urs was plain and honest, he was unrelenting and unsparing. For instance, when the state of Mysore was being renamed Karnataka, Urs had made an emotional sacrifice. He was not only from the Mysore region but also an aristocrat from there. He had been vociferous in his opposition to the name change in the past but was now 'bowing to the will of the majority'. Naturally, he was being complimented in the house by nearly everybody. One of Urs's party legislators compared him to Abhimanyu who had fought his own people in a *chakra vyooha* to change the name of the state. Urs initiating the debate had spoken with candour about his past opposition, not just to the name change, but also the linguistic reorganization of the state. He had said that as the 'wheel of time moves', ideas, individuals and institutions undergo transformation. Quoting the Bard of Avon, he rationalized the shift: 'I am personally of the opinion that a name change is not going to alter our material conditions. As Shakespeare said, what is there in a name? A rose will smell as sweet as it is even if you call it by some other name . . . but a human's world is not made up of just the material, it has creative and emotional components too, and this name change will satisfy the emotional urge.'

In spite of Urs's long, erudite speech, Gowda had sprung up to object Urs being called Abhimanyu. He displayed an anxiousness to play the textbook role of an Opposition leader. He was also anxious to demonstrate all the reading he was doing in the legislature library, which many of his colleagues admit none have used as extensively as him. 'When I heard Sri Gatti Chandrashekar (Gubbi legislator) compare Urs to Abhimanyu, I felt I should mention if there has been a delay in the name change, Urs has also been responsible. There is enough proof for this. You should read what he spoke when a private resolution on the state's reorganization committee report was discussed in this house in 1968. As the wheel of time has moved, he is suiting himself to its demands. We will welcome the name change resolution he has brought and also his personal transformation, but there is no need to call him Abhimanyu,' Gowda said.[22]

In a debate on the transfer and retirement of certain 'honest' officers, and rewarding the 'corrupt' ones, and creation of outlandish new posts like 'super chief engineer', Gowda got very harsh and combative. Sample his sarcasm: 'I'll make a few suggestions to the officers of this state. Many of them have suffered because they are honest and straightforward. Such officers need to be given special training and orientation. They have to be taught to function after understanding the needs and desires of their bosses. If their bosses are greedy for money, they should learn to arrange it. If they are in the habit of drinking foreign whisky, they should learn to procure it. If they have a sexual appetite, they should learn to satisfy that. If an officer does all this, he will be hailed as an efficient officer and make progress in this state.'[23]

On a 'good officer' who had been given an extension after superannuation by the previous government, which was abruptly cancelled when the Urs regime took over, Gowda said: 'He actually wept.' An irritated Urs asked Gowda: 'Did he weep before you?' Gowda replied: 'He is weeping before everybody.' Urs retorted: 'Is he not getting his pension?' Gowda countered: 'He may be getting his pension for having served the state for thirty-five years. He is getting the pension as a matter of right but not as a matter of charity.'[24]

In the same debate, the transfer of certain other senior 'able' officers comes up. Urs asks: 'Why are you so much interested in him?' Gowda replies: 'I am not interested in anyone. I am only interested in a clean administration.' Urs: 'Yes, the responsibility is ours. It is not yours.' Gowda does not let go: 'How can you discharge your responsibility unless we bring to your notice these things. I am also equally interested in the integrity of the administration.'[25]

Gowda turned out to be an investigative journalist too as a PAC chairman, the default role he played as Opposition leader. He used the PAC position diligently from day one to embarrass the government and erode its credibility. In one instance, special permission had been granted by the agriculture department to transport fertilizer by lorries from the Madras harbour. Usually, fertilizer was transported as freight on goods train. When he saw the audit report and the use of lorries, he grew suspicious. He called the agriculture secretary to the PAC meeting and asked him to submit records of lorries used for transportation. Once the records were submitted, he called the transport commissioner and asked him to check the register which recorded the movement of lorries at the toll gate. He randomly picked a few registration numbers of lorries in the documents and asked him to check if they had really passed the toll gate. A couple of weeks later, his hunch was confirmed. The registration numbers were not that of lorries but that of mopeds, cars and some government vehicles. The officials who had fudged the records had also included the registration number of the assembly Speaker's car. This kicked up a row in the assembly.[26]

As mentioned earlier, Gowda did not have too many quarrels with Urs's big policy, be it water disputes (the 21 August 1974 speech in the assembly by Gowda on boycotting the Krishna River water tribunal could be an instructive read), land reforms, or backward class reservations. His objections would be minor and when it came to water issues, he wisely understood the need to put up a unified front (see chapter on Cauvery and Krishna). Urs's policy disposition too was to create advantage for the disadvantaged majority. He was seen as a kind of messiah of the poor, of neglected and disadvantaged smaller castes and communities, and to speak against such an agenda, Gowda understood, would be politically incorrect, if not suicidal. Therefore, he largely focused on corruption and issues related to poor governance.

The land reforms legislation that came to effect in March 1974 was a major challenge for Gowda because he belonged to the land-owning peasant caste. But to his credit, he sought concessions and clarifications but did not oppose it. The land reforms legislation was the most revolutionary piece of legislation, by which 'all tenanted land was to pass on to the government which, in turn, was to transfer it to the tenants after an examination of claims by specially constituted, powerful tribunals. The amended act also barred the leasing of land, abolished sharecropping and prescribed ceilings for various categories of land.'[27] The erstwhile Mysore state had passed a land reform legislation in 1961, but its scope was very limited.[28] 'Land to the Tiller' became a popular slogan during the Urs years. The impact of this legislation was such that by 1979, when Urs's time at the helm was coming to an end, about 8,00,000 applications from tenants had come before tribunals, and they had disposed 5,00,000, and '60 per cent of it went in the favour of tenants who received ownership of over 12,50,000 acres'.[29] It is not to be made out here that Vokkaligas, Gowda's community, lost out as a result of the land reforms. In fact, a good majority of them, who were poor, benefited. This perhaps explains Gowda's policy neutrality better.

The chief concession that Gowda asked from Urs's land reform bill was, strangely, related to widows: 'I urged Urs to offer a concession to widows in the bill. I told him personally and also in the assembly. I wrote letters to him. I said if widows shed tears, it would not help him. In the Holenarasipur tribunal, in which by virtue of being an MLA I was a member, an Idiga (toddy-tapping community) widow made an application to spare her eight acres, which she had let out when her husband had died, and her children were still legal minors. She was set to lose her land and said, "Give me nectar or give me poison". There were many such cases across the state. I had no problem with big landlords being jolted, but the bill was affecting a lot of people from small communities, whose cause Urs was championing. For example, *dhobis* (washermen and women), barbers and those who traditionally were into other professions, were poor and had informal tenant arrangements on their tiny patches of land. They were affected too. I wanted Urs to understand this, but he was overenthusiastic. He was being cheered by socialists from Shimoga and elsewhere, and he was deaf to any pragmatic suggestion. Therefore, I said, at least spare widows. I went to the extent of saying that their curse will affect your family, but he was reckless. However,

I agreed with the man's larger intent and nobility of idea. When the bill was being passed, I voted in its favour.'[30]

The Emergency and After

By 1974, nationally, politics was heating up. JP had begun a mass movement, Sampoorna Kranti, to oppose the authoritarian and corrupt ways of the Indira Gandhi-led Congress government. The slow descent to the suspension of the Indian Constitution, the infamous Emergency, had begun.

The anti-Congress activists and politicians of the time in Karnataka, including J.H. Patel, P.G.R. Sindhia, Prof. Nanjundaswamy, P. Mallesh, Kadri Shamanna, Sardar Venkataramaiah, Ramachandre Gowda and P. Venkoba Rao, came together under the guidance of Kadidal Manjappa, the former chief minister, to invite JP to tour Karnataka: 'Some of us went to Patna, and then to Delhi to invite JP. We formed the Sangharsh Samiti to host his meetings. He came to Karnataka on 23 June 1975 from Kerala. He reached Mangalore first, then went to Belgaum, Davangere, Mysore and Bangalore. He toured for four days and flew to Calcutta from Bangalore. The next day he was arrested,' Sindhia recalled. He also said that Ramakrishna Hegde and Veerendra Patil were not convinced with the idea of JP's *Sampoorna Kranti* (Total Revolution): 'When we went to invite these two for the meetings they asked us to be pragmatic. 'Is Sampoorna Kranti possible in this country?' they asked rhetorically. They told us that the focus should be on winning elections and keeping power. Gowda remained neutral. He did not say anything publicly or privately in support or against the JP movement.'[31]

After the Emergency was clamped, the central prison in Bangalore became the focus of national attention because important Opposition leaders like Atal Bihari Vajpayee, L.K. Advani, Madhu Dandavate and S.N. Mishra were arrested when they were visiting Bangalore on 26 June 1975. Ramakrishna Hegde and Gowda were arrested a few days after this. Gowda was in Delhi to go to Jammu and Kashmir for a political meet. But he had returned to Bangalore with Veerendra Patil after the Emergency was declared on 25 June 1975. Gowda was released three months later after the court took a dim view of his arrest under the Maintenance of Internal Security Act (MISA). However, he was picked up again within hours when he was having dinner at home. N. Santosh Hegde (later a judge of the Supreme Court of India) was Gowda's lawyer. There was a sinister plan to pressure Gowda to join the Congress. There were already rumours floating around that Veerendra Patil had met Hitendra Desai in Coimbatore and would join Indira Gandhi. Since Gowda did not succumb to pressure, he was arrested. Sindhia recalled: 'I was picked up on 4 July under MISA, and was a B-class detenu in the Bangalore jail along with our senior leaders. It was Hegde who confirmed the rumours on Patil's hobnobbing with the Congress and that there was a lot of pressure on Gowda too. When they could not crack Gowda, they put him in jail. Patil and S.R. Bommai were never arrested. All the senior leaders, including Gowda, were A-class detenus. We all became very close in the jail.'[32]

As an A-class detenu, Gowda got a cot and proper bedding to sleep. He would get a mosquito net too. He had one roommate. He never asked for food and clothes from home. All B-class detenus were put in groups of twenty to twenty-five and made to sleep on the floor in a large hall. There was not much difference in the food that was served to A- and B-class detenus. The only privilege that Gowda enjoyed was that there was no restriction on the number of visitors he could receive. Large groups of people would come to see him almost every day, especially from Hassan district: 'Urs had a soft corner for Gowda, and perhaps had instructed the then Inspector General of Prisons, C.S. Mallaiah, not to restrict Gowda's visitors. He was the only one among all the leaders who enjoyed this liberty.' Sindhia also remembers the frequent visits of Gowda's father: 'His father, a typical farmer from the plains, in a crumpled dhoti and a black coat with a stick in hand would get very emotional seeing his son. He would weep. Gowda would be seen consoling him.'[33] The father's mental condition deteriorated seeing his son in jail. He was overcome by fear that Indira Gandhi would never let him out and had to be offered professional help. When Urs learnt about Gowda's father, he said he would allow an unconditional release provided Gowda joins his cabinet. Gowda did not respond, and the father got into a spiral of fear from which he could never recover.[34] (For more on Gowda's father, refer to Chapter 2.)

While Advani and Hegde were involved in poetry and yoga, and Advani would be seen teaching the Urdu language to Hegde, Gowda would get involved in serious conversations on provisions of the Constitution, agricultural practices, the plight of rural India and of course, Indira Gandhi and her politics: 'He educated us youngsters. He kept himself informed through an RSS newsletter, which would get circulated clandestinely. It was Gowda who told us about the torture of George Fernandes' brother, Lawrence Fernandes. His ambition was apparent. He wanted to defeat Urs and become chief minister. He would speak about the volumes of corruption in the Urs government. He would get very passionate about Cauvery water not being put to proper use and allocation of meagre resources to build distributary canals for the Hemavathi river.'[35]

When Gowda was in jail, there was nobody to either checkmate or question Urs inside the assembly. In a short biography of Urs, senior journalist Vaddarase Raghurama Shetty wrote: 'Urs became bloated with arrogance during the Emergency. He had put all his political opponents in jail. There was a visible change in his disposition during assembly sessions. It hurt me to see him that way. H.D. Deve Gowda, the Opposition leader who had made Urs watch each step he took, and would often tie him up in his tracks, was put in jail. His replacement as Opposition leader, Nagamangala legislator H.T. Krishnappa, did not have the political wherewithal to handle Urs. He would get dismissed and ridiculed. There was nobody in the Congress (O) who could challenge Urs. The three communists in the assembly found new ways each time to defend the Emergency, but the socialists—Kagodu

Thimappa, S. Bangarappa and Konandur Lingappa—raised their voice against it.'[36]

After the Emergency, Veerendra Patil was made Karnataka president of the newly formed Janata Party. Ramakrishna Hegde became the national general secretary, and Gowda went back to become the Opposition leader in the assembly. But Morarji, who disliked Patil, wanted someone else as the state party president, and his preference was Gowda, whom he described as a 'fighter' in party forums.[37] Chandra Shekhar too openly sided with Gowda and Hegde secretly wanted Gowda as president. But Nijalingappa, the grand old man of Karnataka politics, was neither for Gowda or Patil, but would have gone with Hegde (see chapters on Hegde and Morarji for more details). 'All this had to do with the 1978 assembly elections. Patil and Gowda were contenders for the chief minister's chair, and Hegde was a secret aspirant. I was in the election committee. Hegde, who was by then powerful in Delhi, altered the list of candidates finalized in Bangalore. A robust, winnable list of candidates that Gowda had put together was altered without an explanation at the very last minute. Hegde even gave the Ankola seat to his loyalist Anasuya Gajanana Sharma so that he could get her to stand down in case he needed a seat to contest after becoming chief minister. Due to this manipulation, the election was lost. But Gowda had to unfairly bear the brunt of it all. He was buried in a heap of insults. He was accused of selling tickets, which was completely untrue. In fact, Jeevaraj Alva, Hegde's close associate, and I had given party funds to people Hegde had indicated. In those days, party candidates were given Rs 5000. It was all decided in Hegde's house. But after the election loss, Gowda was villanized. Hegde and Patil worked independently to sully Gowda's image, and they had indirect blessings of Nijalingappa. Devaraj Urs made use of this opportunity to pour ghee into the fire that had been lit. He was, anyway, a master player. For over a year, Gowda could not face the public,' Sindhia recalled.[38]

During the 1977 general election, the Janata Party in Karnataka performed badly when it had vanquished Indira Gandhi's Congress across the nation. Veerendra Patil was party president (state unit) and they had won only two out of the 28 seats. One was Justice K.S. Hegde (father of Justice Santosh Hegde) from Bangalore South who went on to be the Speaker in the Lok Sabha, the other was S. Nanjesh Gowda from the Hassan parliamentary seat. The Hassan victory was Gowda's personal triumph. Nanjesh Gowda was a little-known president of the taluk development board whom Gowda had fielded and ensured victory. Electorally he had never failed, so they made him president by the time the 1978 assembly elections came, but it was sabotaged (Nijalingappa too had a role in this): 'If Gowda had had his way in 1978, he would have become chief minister,' Sindhia said.[39] However, on the insistence of Morarji and Chandra Shekhar, Gowda continued as state president till 1980. S.R. Bommai replaced him after that.

In the final moments of the 1978 assembly election, Nijalingappa, who was also a prominent Lingayat leader, unhappy with the distribution of tickets, said he was quitting politics altogether. Not only did Nijalingappa resign, but he also received Gowda's principal opponent, Devaraj Urs, at his Chitradurga home. The Nijalingappa–Urs meeting splashed all over in the media had sent a signal to the Lingayats. They voted against the Janata Party (more in the chapter on Hegde). Chandra Shekhar rushed to meet Nijalingappa and tried to pacify and clarify but the damage had been done.[40]

Nijalingappa in his letter dated 30 January 1978 to Chandra Shekhar offered a fierce moral argument for his withdrawal from public life: 'I had written to you more than once and urged that in setting up candidates to the legislature two main considerations should weigh. No defector should be set up as a candidate and in Bangalore on the 21st of this month when I emphatically pleaded that defectors should not be given tickets for the Assembly elections you were pleased to say that defectors from Congress after the Lok Sabha polls should not be preferred and that some considerations may be given to defectors in Andhra Pradesh . . . The present atmosphere has been such that loyalty, sacrifice, suffering and integrity are at a

discount and the opposite characters are at a premium. Janata has
not escaped from it . . . But the most distressing and intolerable fact
is that persons who did everything against our party and supported
Indira Gandhi till a few weeks and even days back have been largely
accepted as Janata candidates, some of them having the worst
reputation . . . One cannot be in a party and decline to work for
its candidates. That would be acting against the discipline. I have
believed in it all through. I therefore feel bound to get out of the
party. I am going to issue a statement in this behalf.'[41] Nijalingappa's
press statement on the same day, also attached to the letter, read:
'After due consideration I have decided that I should retire from
politics and should not be a member of any political party. Apart
from politics, there are several avenues of service to the country and
the people. I hope I will be able to devote myself to that service.'[42]

But after taking such a principled position and speaking out
against Indira Gandhi's Congress and defectors from her party, it
is quite mysterious as to why Nijalingappa received the Congress
chief minister Urs and posed for media photographs with him. It
had animated the Vokkaliga–Lingayat rivalries that had been in place
since the reorganization of the state in 1956 when Vokkaligas had
lost power to the Lingayats.

But before Nijalingappa took to writing letters, Gowda had
written to Chandra Shekhar on 5 January 1978. He was caustic
about Nijalingappa: 'I have received a copy of the letter dated 30th
December 1977 appending also a note with it by Shri S. Nijalingappa.
So far as the letter is concerned, it is for you to consider and take
such action as you deem fit. But the note appended to the letter
has terribly annoyed me beyond measure. As you are fully aware,
with your blessings and continued solicitude, I assumed this onerous
responsibility of the presidentship of the Karnataka Pradesh Janata
Party. Ever since I took up this responsibility I have put forth my
best efforts and am working ceaselessly to build up the edifice of
our organization . . . For all this hard and sustained work in the best
interests of the party, I am agonized and annoyed to receive from

Shri. S Nijalingappa this kind of certificate. It is apparent that Shri Nijalingappa is under the mistaken notion that barring himself and his sycophants all others working in the political arena are corrupt, dishonest and men with no probity or rectitude . . . Regarding the constitution of the Selection Committee and also of the selection of candidates to the ensuing Assembly elections, he is going through with the presumption that the proposed Committee may not consist of men of character, integrity etc., and the committee may recommend candidates without any sense of responsibility. He has jumped to the hasty conclusion that the Selection Committee would pick out unreliable, dishonest candidates on the basis of groupism. Although he has not said in so many words one can safely infer from the verbiage used in the note that all his venom and fulminations are directed against me and my colleagues in the party. I hasten to apprise you that almost every second day, he writes letters to me, giving directions to do this or that. Such sermons are for specific purposes to remove some District Janata Party Presidents and other office bearers on the strength of some representations sent to him. Unfortunately, after the Lok Sabha election in March 1977, a small coterie or group has emerged in the state and Shri Nijalingappa has willing provided leadership to this group . . . It is amazing that at this age (he is now 75) instead of bidding good bye to politics, he wants to be more active by projecting his unwanted interference in the party affairs . . .'[43]

Gowda continued: 'I may also press the point and categorically deny with utmost candour and sincerity that I have any wish to become chief minister or hold any other high office. The note and the contents has a disguised and hidden presumption that I am after the loaves and fishes of office. I strongly disapprove of this baseless, frivolous, and mean allegation levelled against me by Shri S. Nijalingappa. On the contrary he is having some of his own people in his mind. That is why he is making all this unhealthy and unsavoury exercises . . .' Gowda wrote another letter around this time to Ramakrishna Hegde, the national general secretary, to complain that

Nijalingappa was 'leaving no stone unturned to scuttle and demolish
the recently constituted State Election Committee'.[44] This letter was
endorsed by other colleagues of Gowda, namely, Kagodu Thimappa,
M. Chandrashekar, P.G.R. Sindhia, A.K. Subbaiah, Baburao
Deshpande, B. Satyanarayan Singh and Lakshmidevi Ramanna.
Gowda stuck to the choice of candidates, which was unanimously
endorsed by the election committee, but the list was tampered with
in New Delhi. When the election was lost, except for Morarji and
Chandra Shekhar, nobody came to Gowda's rescue.

Sindhia recalled: 'During the elections, as party president, let
alone Gowda making money out of selling tickets, he even hesitated
to use an old Plymouth car that the party had borrowed from RSS
leader Gopinath. He never collected money. People like Dr. C. Vittal
and M. Chandrashekar gathered whatever money they could and
gave it to him during the polls. He became very bitter and depressed
after the electoral loss. He was so upset that he packed his bags and
went back to till the soil in his village. The six or seven times I went
to see him there, he used to be in his vest and shorts working in the
fields. I have seen him plant paddy. He had also got potato seeds
from Haryana and Punjab and was anxious about that crop. He came
for assembly sessions but remained quiet. Till he became a minister
in 1983, Gowda remained a committed farmer.'[45] At the beginning
of the 1960s, Nijalingappa had expelled Gowda from the undivided
Congress party, and at the end of the 1970s, he had forced him into
a partial self-exile.

The End of the Urs Era

A few months after the Morarji Desai-led Janata Party government
was established in 1977, Hegde and Patil got together and pressured
Gowda to move a no-confidence motion against Urs in the assembly.
Gowda said the motion would be defeated because they did not
have numbers and he would not indulge in symbolic measures. He
reminded them that he had brought out a scandal a day against Urs

till he was sent to prison.[46] Hegde and Patil, however, pressured the Central government to set up the Justice Grover Commission of inquiry to probe allegations of corruption against Devaraj Urs.[47] Both Morarji and Deve Gowda were not keen on setting up this commission; they thought it would backfire because Urs was very popular among the poor, and it had been proven during the March 1977 parliamentary polls when only two Janata Party candidates had won against the Congress' twenty-six.[48] Indira Gandhi had failed electorally across India in 1977, but Urs had succeeded in Karnataka. Nevertheless, the commission was set up and also the Urs government was dismissed in January 1978. Gowda was taken into confidence by Charan Singh before the government was dismissed.[49] He did not oppose it this time, but in fact, smelled an opportunity.

After Urs won the polls and returned to power, the Justice Grover Commission indicted Urs, but the Central government was in complete disarray and on the verge of implosion. Strangely, in May 1979, the indictment report was sent to the state government for further action against its own chief minister. The *Indian Express* reported on its front page: 'Despite two years of work put in by the Grover Commission, the Karnataka Chief Minister Devaraj Urs, it appears, has got away. The commission in its final report has indicted Urs on charges of favouritism and abuse of power. The Union government has accepted the findings of the Grover Commission, but finds itself helpless in taking action against Urs, who was the main target of the inquiry by the former Supreme Court judge. After studying the Grover Commission report for two months, the Union government has merely passed it on to the government of Karnataka for what it describes as 'follow-up action'. This has led to the peculiar situation when the Centre expects that the state government will take action against the chief minister and two of his former colleagues. Early last year, the Grover Commission submitted its first report indicting Urs on four charges relating to nepotism, favouritism and misuse of official position. Devaraj Urs appeared unperturbed over the findings of the Grover Commission. In reply to a question if he would oblige the Opposition by conceding their demand for his immediate resignation, he said that it was only a report not a judgment.'[50] Gowda, whose spirits were down at that point, did not make a fuss. He let it be.

Soon after this, in a political twist, Urs developed serious differences with Indira Gandhi and quit the party. He could run the government until legislators defected to the Indira camp. But he had done one big favour to Indira Gandhi before this. He had given her political rebirth by necessitating a by poll in Chikmagalur in 1978. When Urs moved away from Indira Gandhi, ironically, Gowda was asked to speak to Urs by Morarji and Vajpayee to work out an alliance with him.[51] Even prior to this, during the 1978 Chikmagalur by poll, Morarji had sent Ramnath Goenka of the *Indian Express* to Gowda to work out a secret pact with Urs to defeat Indira Gandhi. By then, the Grover Commission had been appointed, and one of the offers made to Urs was that the commission would be withdrawn if he helped defeat Indira Gandhi. By then Urs had fallen out with her, and it was no secret in political circles. But Urs told Goenka and Gowda who went to see him: 'I know she will remove me as me chief minister. I know she is working closely with Gundu Rao and F.M. Khan. I know she thinks I will stab her in the back. But it is not my dharma to stab her in the back. I will ensure she wins. I am sorry I can't help you.'[52] After the Janata Party lost the by-poll Gowda wrote to Goenka: 'It is really unfortunate that we lost in the bye-election in spite of the best efforts put forth by all of us. Particularly the State Janata Party is grateful to you[r] good self for the co-operation extended by you. In spite of your old age, you evinced keen interest and toiled day and night to secure success for the Janata candidate and your help will be ever remembered. We are not disheartened by the election result. We will continue our fight against Fascist forces represented by Smt Indira Gandhi and we are confident that we will always have your blessings in this behalf.'[53]

By the end of the 1970s logic, politics, and life too was standing on their head for Gowda. After the 1978 defeat of the Janata Party in the state assembly polls, Gowda had made a strange promise to himself: 'I decided I will never raise issues related to corruption in the assembly. I would rather focus on development issues. Despite my relentless onslaught against Urs government's corruption, people had voted him back to power. Urs was not personally corrupt. He left nothing behind for his children. During this period, corruption got institutionalized in Karnataka politics; there was no alternative, and it was a question of political survival. He did not come from a caste with big numbers, and he had to keep the assortment of backward class communities he had forged into an alliance together. He needed money for that. When people he had groomed and given power deserted him, I met him. He was full of regrets about the people he had promoted and also about Indira Gandhi who had backstabbed him.'[54] Urs had similarly expressed regrets to his former deputy secretary Chiranjiv Singh a month before he had passed away in June 1982. On Indira Gandhi, he had said: 'How many crores have I not given her? I have not seen any other person with that kind of hunger for money. How much blame did I not take for her sake? I did all the work and gave her the credit, see where it has landed me today.'[55]

On corruption in the Urs-led government, senior journalist Vaddarase Raghurama Shetty recalled an off-the-record conversation that Urs had with a bunch of journalists: 'Urs had fever. He was reclining on his bed and speaking to us who were seated around his cot. When the topic of corruption was raised by our association president, H.A. Muniyappa, Urs became emotional. He agreed to the charge and described the progressive reforms he had swiftly brought about to Karnataka's social landscape and asked, "Don't I need power to do all this? To be in power in our country, we either need the support of caste tradition or the blessings of business houses. If you have neither, then you need the backing of caste. I have to continue in power without any of these. How would it be possible? You tell me . . . I have neither tradition nor caste on my side. If I keep philosophizing and theorizing like your Lohia, you think the MLAs would have stuck around and allowed me to continue in power? The

MLAs are not behind me because they want the backward classes to prosper. They want to individually prosper. They are all very hungry people. Each time they come to me, they want something. I don't have my father's property to share with them. I have to snatch it from somewhere else and pass it on to them. I don't have to do any of these to fill my stomach, but I am compelled to do this for the sake of retaining power to bring about social progress.'"[56]

Urs's conversation with the journalists was around 1974. But after he had stepped down in 1980, Urs's lament in loneliness about the new social and political base he had built was as insightful. He had realized that the backward castes he had limitlessly empowered at best functioned as a class grouping that came together to enjoy economic benefits but would not stick together like a caste to offer consistent political support to their benefactor. Gowda, who came from the dominant Vokkaliga community, commanded caste loyalty. On this solid foundation of caste support, he had worked on a bigger arithmetic of castes and built a political coalition to stay perennially relevant in Karnataka politics. Interestingly, after the exit of Urs from the Congress, Indira Gandhi sent senior leader Kamalapati Tripathi to woo Gowda to join the party. He was promised the chief ministership, but he did not succumb (see the chapter on Congress dynasty).[57]

The Gundu Rao Blip

In a surprise, Indira Gandhi loyalist Gundu Rao replaced Devaraj Urs. Rao was a minister in Urs's cabinet. For a state that had seen Urs, this was a rude shock. Rao could not match Urs in stature or vision, and the contrast was obvious from day one. Also, as a Brahmin, he being catapulted to the top was an affront and challenge to the social justice agenda that Urs had pursued diligently for eight years. As soon as Rao came to power, Gowda suffered a setback because twenty-five MLAs, out of the fifty-eight under his watch, crossed over to the Indira Congress. Gowda's arch-rival H.C. Srikantaiah had mobilized them.

Initially, Gowda struck a cordial relationship with Rao. He came out of his self-imposed hibernation, but the cordiality did not last long.[58] A police-firing incident during a foundation laying ceremony for a drinking water project on 26 September 1982, in Doddahalli village of his Holenarasipur constituency, led to the death of two persons and left several injured.[59] Congress and Janata Party workers had clashed when Srikantaiah, who was also a minister in the Rao cabinet, had organized the function in Gowda's constituency without involving him. This offered political capital to Gowda. He tendered his resignation as a legislator and sat on a fast for nine days in front of the Vidhana Soudha, protesting the deaths and demanding a judicial inquiry. When his health deteriorated, he had to be shifted to the hospital. He broke his fast on the insistence of Ramakrishna Hegde and S.R. Bommai.[60] Ironically, the two had earlier told party workers that this fast was a personal battle and had nothing to do with the party. They had revised their stance after they saw the crowd surge. General secretary of the state unit of the Janata Party, B.L. Shankar, in his report to the central party on the working of the state unit between 1981 and 1983 wrote: 'The [Gowda] hunger strike continued for one week and it was supported by hunger strikes in all the districts of the state in support of Sri Deve Gowda's hunger strike. On the eighth day of the hunger strike Sri Deve Gowda was arrested and was forcibly removed to the hospital on the grounds of health. This course of action of Sri H.D. Deve Gowda was a tremendous morale booster to the party and its workers throughout the state.'[61]

The fast by Gowda only hastened the decline of the Rao government. It had already been mauled between 1980 and 1982 by various popular movements like the Nargund farmers' uprising in 1980; the language movement led by matinee idol Rajkumar, the Dalit movement and the farmers' movement led by M.D. Nanjundaswamy. The net result of all this was the establishment of the first non-Congress regime in Karnataka.

5

Morarji: The Mentor and the Mantle

H.D. Deve Gowda had many formative influences, but they were all local in some sense until he found Morarji Desai, India's first non-Congress prime minister. Typically, for someone steadfastly loyal to anti-Congress politics of his time, that is the 1970s, Jayaprakash Narayan, or JP, would have served as a greater inspirational figure, and the Emergency would have defined his politics, but not so in the case of Gowda. The turbulent phase of modern Indian politics when democracy was suspended did, of course, have an impact on him. He did look up to JP. He was also a political prisoner at the time but was not swept off the ground by its hysterical force. The Emergency victimhood did not become persistent political rhetoric for him like it became for many of his colleagues through their careers. The unusual choice of Morarji as a mentor perhaps suggests that Gowda was more a man of individual loyalties than ideological currents.

The emphasis on Gowda's individualistic approach is essential because Karnataka was a playfield of socialist politics at the time and was intellectually inspired by an assortment of figures such as Ram Manohar Lohia, M.N. Roy and Narendra Dev, besides JP. If Gowda's contemporaries and comrades like J.H. Patel thought of themselves as Lohiaites, and S.R. Bommai was a Royist, Gowda never chose to give himself any of those labels. He was always an independent-minded Vokkaliga leader who took up people's causes. That his caste identity had a greater grip over him is a fact. However, the record of his assembly debates and an inventory of issues that he picked to fight in his long career would put many of his socialist mates to shame. They appear like theoreticians and he the practitioner. He primarily answered divinity and destiny, not any ideology. His politics was pragmatic with a vague, self-constructed idealism, but then he was emotionally attached to those who put their hand around his shoulders, nurtured his interests and gave him confidence. That is how Morarji Desai became important to Gowda. Morarji too was stubborn about his individual beliefs and principles than ideological matters.

Morarji writes in his autobiography:[1] 'The reason for the decisions I made and the risks I took so easily was that from my childhood I had an unshakeable faith in God . . . The things that happen to one are results of one's past actions. A man has to undergo what has been determined by his past actions . . . A man who faces this task gladly should not make any attempt to escape difficulties. If a man has faith in God, he can remain cheerful and peaceful even in the most difficult circumstances.' This voice has a resonance in the life of Gowda. His faith in God, determinism, destiny, and karma have been unshakeable. Morarji was not ritualistic,[2] but Gowda is more ritualistic than spiritual in his expression.

Once, Gowda narrated Morarji's life like a bedtime tale:[3] 'He was very young when his father passed away and he too came from a farming family like me. His was a big family with many brothers and sisters and he studied with the help of scholarships. The family was in such dire financial condition that he had to share even his scholarship money to ensure its sustenance. He studied hard and became a deputy collector. There came a time in his career when his integrity was put to the test. There was a farm crisis in the Bombay Presidency. The British resident commissioner told him to obfuscate reality in his report. They didn't want him to get too factual as it would make lives difficult for officials with their higher ups. He did not agree. He was obstinate. He wrote the report as it should be. Then he went to Gandhiji to seek his advice. He wanted to resign from service. Gandhiji suggested that he should take care of his family first. But he argued that if God had created them, he would also devise a way to feed them. "I will leave it to you then," Gandhiji replied. That is when he jumped into the freedom struggle.'

Morarji was not as poor as Gowda imagined him to be. After his father, a headmaster of an English middle school, suffering from melancholia, committed suicide, Morarji had the larger family, as well as the Brahmin network, to fall back on. Morarji wrote:[4] 'I used to get a scholarship of Rs 10 per month from the Bhavnagar State and take tuitions. I used to send this money to my mother, and she managed the household within that amount . . . we were nine in all. A small house and four bighas of land were all that he (father) had left us. The income from the land was just Rs 10 per year and even that did not come regularly. But we had the support of the family of my maternal grandfather.'

Also, unlike Gowda's narration of events, Morarji had not quit government service on the farm crisis report, but it was about communal riots in Godhra.[5] This was in April–May 1930:

Within few months of going to Ahmedabad, I had received a notice from the commissioner saying that the Collector of Panchmahals had asked for an inquiry in the riots of Godhra. The burden of the issues framed by the commissioner was that I was a communalist and that I supported the Hindu against the Muslims. Within six or seven days of my receiving the notice I sent a detailed reply and requested the commissioner in person . . . The commissioner replied at that time, 'I am quite satisfied with what you have said and I do not consider any further investigation necessary.' In spite of this, he sent an altogether different report to Government . . . I was held guilty of acting in a partisan way on account of communal bias. No reasons were given for this conclusion, but Government also said that it did not think it necessary to take any action against me in view of my good record of twelve years of service. I was degraded by four places in the list of seniority . . . Since the time that Mahatma Gandhi opened a new chapter of non-violence and satyagraha, many British Civil Service officers were engaged in inciting Muslims against the Congress and the Hindus. On getting the arbitrary and unjust decision of the Government, I made up my mind to resign from service.

Gowda continued the Morarji story in puranic style:[6] 'Why do I adore him? That is because they treated him just like they treat me now. They always tried to make a villain out of him. When he was Bombay CM, the labour unions created unrest. They chose a destructive path and Morarji took a position against them. Nehru passed uncharitable remarks against him. He asked him not to take a hard position. But Morarji was again adamant. He said, "If I concede to the unions, our industries will be destroyed and investments will dry up." At that point he was taken off as chief minister and moved to Delhi. He thought Nehru had developed a secret desire to groom his daughter, so he was cleverly eliminating him.'

The words 'intransigent,' 'stubborn', 'adamant', 'uncompromising', 'obstinate' peppered Gowda's story of Morarji. He clearly wished those words reflect his personality too: 'I like him because they deliberately projected him in poor light. I used to sit in the Parliament gallery and watch the debates. People like Madhu Limaye made him look like a terrible administrator and an even terrible human being simply because he stood steadfastly by the truth. He was not into gimmicks. When sugar was Rs 12 a kg he brought it down to Rs 2 a kg within a year. He opposed bank nationalization. He was uncompromising. He had a daughter and a son. His daughter immolated herself. Kanti was his son, and he was afraid that he may lose him too, so kept him close. When Morarji became prime minister, naturally the son was very visible to his opponents. They said he had a house in London, here, there and everywhere. They said he had kept money here, there and everywhere.

But the fact was that Morarji lived in a rented house on Marine Drive in Mumbai. When the court issued orders to vacate it, his daughter-in-law, Kanti's wife, was so devastated that she jumped from atop the building and committed suicide. It was very tragic. But they did not stop manufacturing lies against an honest man. It was all propaganda. I have the highest regard for Morarji. I tried to model myself after him.'[7] As is evident from Gowda's narrative of Morarji's life, chronology, and in places fact, have been suspended. Morarji had two daughters and a son. In Gowda's mind, it had become one epic tale to empathize with his own political trials and tribulations.

There was one other sudden recall when this story was being narrated. Gowda said Morarji's life was vaguely like that of the protagonist in a story he had read in his school textbook.[8] He was referring to Guy de Maupassant's short story Piece of String. The story is about Maitre Hauchecome spotting a string on the road and picking it up with the hope it would be of some use in the future. But suddenly, he notices that his enemy Maitre Malandain is watching. He is terribly embarrassed and does not want Malandain to think he was picking up an insignificant piece of string. So, Hauchecome pretends he is searching for something else. But one day, news came that someone in the town had lost their wallet. Malandain loses no time in accusing Hauchecome of stealing the wallet. The town of Goderville believes the accusation falsely made. Hauchecome argues his innocence, but no one trusts him. The disbelief continues even after the wallet is found with the francs intact. Trapped in an unfair accusation, Hauchecome dies disgusted and lonely.

The Three Incidents

Deve Gowda came in close contact with Morarji as Karnataka's Opposition leader. Whenever he visited the state, first as deputy prime minister and then prime minister, Gowda took care of him like an ardent follower would. He served him food. He ensured goat's milk and newspapers were delivered by 6 a.m., watched him do yoga and read the Bhagavad Gita. He also travelled with him for public programmes and saw how Morarji was a stickler for time. He would never allow Gowda to alter what was already on his tour chart, and never ever made an unscheduled stop for a waiting crowd.[9] Once, when Morarji as prime minister came to Mandya district, the hotbed of Gowda/Vokkaliga politics, his office had asked the district collector to arrange a lunch of nuts like almonds and pistachios, a glass of milk and alphonso mango if it was seasonal and available. When a ladder was kept ready for him to alight from the chopper, the over eighty-year-old Morarji had hopped down the chopper, skipping the last couple of steps.[10] Gowda grew up admiring his spartan habits, forthrightness, physical agility and discipline.

In the Janata Party papers, there is one letter dated 25 April 1979 addressed to Gowda from Morarji's office.[11] It reads: 'Morarjibhai would be free between 1230 hours and 1800 hours on the 4th June for any programmes you may like to have for him in Bangalore. Kindly send the draft programme for his approval immediately.' Gowda was at that time the Karnataka president of the Janata Party. He was not bothered with gossip mills at the time constantly spinning tales around Morarji's urine therapy. 'I had not seen him consume his urine. He never suggested it to me. He never spoke about it ever. How can such a tall leader, who sacrificed so much for this country, be reduced to something as silly as that? Indira Gandhi's men had a way of character assassinating anybody who questioned or opposed the dynasty. They joined hands with a pliant media to caricature him,' Gowda said.[12]

There are three specific incidents that gave Gowda a feeling that Morarji was an elder who cared for him and wanted him to do well in life. Once, at a public function, near Belgaum, Gowda made a fiery speech in the presence of Morarji. When travelling back, Morarji asked Gowda why he was shouting despite there being a microphone to amplify his voice. 'You'll damage your vocal chords,' he had warned, and it did get damaged as predicted.[13] Gowda had to seek the help of the Mumbai surgeon Dr L.H. Hiranandani to get it fixed.

The second incident had to do with the removal of Veerendra Patil as the president of the Janata Party in Karnataka in early 1978. Patil's one-time mentor, S. Nijalingappa or SN, wanted him out. Patil had succeeded SN as chief minister in 1968 when the latter became national president of the Congress party. After the Congress split in 1969, SN had controlled Congress (Organisation), which had later become part of the Janata Party. Patil had journeyed with him all through. But by 1978, the distrust between the two had deepened. When this incident took place, the Chikmagalur by election had not taken place. Patil in that poll which revived Indira Gandhi's political career, reluctantly became the Janata Party candidate.

The distrust between the mentor and mentee had to do with a hand loan that SN had taken from a medical college trust,[14] which he had helped establish. Apparently, he came under pressure to repay the loan because Siddaveerappa, the medical education minister in the Devaraj Urs-led Congress government, had threatened an inquiry for misusing the provisions of the trust. It became very embarrassing for SN and he sought help from Patil. It is said that Patil, at that point, asked his mentor to sign a promissory note to lend money from the Janata Party coffers. This enraged the grand old man of Karnataka politics. SN and Patil came from the same Lingayat sub-caste, and SN had, after all, groomed Patil, who wanted to be a government official, into an influential politician. He had inducted him as a junior minister with Ramakrishna Hegde in 1957 and had acknowledged the duo as Lava and Kusha (the twin children of Rama and Sita in the Ramayana). They were seen as young, bright administrative twins in his government.

Given SN's seniority, he put pressure on Morarji to replace Patil as the president of the state unit. In a bid to save Patil, Gowda with his colleagues Hegde, J.H. Patel, S.R. Bommai and a couple of others, went in a delegation to Morarji in Delhi, and presented their case. Morarji being the stubborn man he was, did not relent. He said SN was adamant and wanted Patil out. The delegation tried to impress Morarji but seeing they were making no headway, Gowda went a step ahead and made a casual remark. He told Morarji: 'Sir, you have been brainwashed by SN.'[15] The moment he heard it, Morarji flew into a rage. He stood up, kicked the chair, and asked loudly: 'What do you mean?' He kept repeating the phrase until tears started rolling down Gowda's cheeks. Hegde, standing next to Gowda, tried to console him while Morarji continued to badger: 'Do you know Patil is another Hitendra Desai (a former Gujarat chief minister who had crossed over to the Indira Gandhi camp). Has he not already met D.K. Baruah, president of the Indira Congress?' The entire delegation went quiet. Morarji gained his composure, patted Gowda on his head, put his hands on his shoulder and said: 'Control your emotions young man, you have a bright future.'[16] That touch and the phrase remained forever in the folds of Gowda's memory. It was like destiny's indication of things to unfold before him, and each time he climbed the power ladder, he recalled this line of Morarji. Of course, two months after the incident, Gowda took over from Patil as president of the Janata Party in Karnataka. Patil, within a short period, crossed over to Indira Gandhi's Congress just as Morarji had predicted.

The third incident was in the aftermath of a by poll debacle to the Karnataka assembly. Gowda was president of the Janata Party. He picked a candidate, but he lost by 300 votes. At that point a legislator, allegedly a Hegde confidante, wrote a letter to Morarji accusing Gowda of being in the habit of selling poll tickets. During the national executive meeting of the Janata Party in Delhi, Morarji sent for Gowda during the lunch hour. He gave him the envelope with the letter and asked him to read its content. Gowda lost his cool: 'Do you believe this, sir. Tell me. Do you seriously believe this?' He asked. 'If you do, then I'll not continue as party president for a single minute,' he grew emotional.[17] This time Morarji consoled him: 'Don't I know Karnataka politics? Don't I know what Hegde is trying to do? Don't I know how many times he goes to London? Don't I know with whom he walks around in London's Hyde Park. You are a blunt person and that does not suit them. Do you think I believed the contents of the letter? If I had believed the accusation, would I have called you and spoken about it confidentially? You should control your emotions. You have a bright future.'[18] The phrase about the future was repeated. Gowda started to believe that his destiny was speaking through Morarji Desai.

The letter[19] that Morarji showed Gowda is available in the Janata Party papers, as a copy of it was also sent to Chandra Shekhar, the party president. There are initials of Hegde, the national general secretary, on the letter with instructions to place it in the Karnataka file. The letter marked 'Confidential', and dated 7 January 1979, is written by A. Ramachandra, the Sullia MLA. Making only a cursory reference to the assembly by poll debacle, it makes far wider accusations related to the parliamentary elections of 1977, and the Chikmagalur by poll of 1978: 'Shri H.D. Deve Gowda, President of Karnataka Janatha [sic] Party is solely responsible for the defeat of our party in Karnataka . . . So far as the by election of Chamarajpet (it was actually Chamaraja constituency in Mysore, not Chamarajpet in Bangalore) is concerned, the failure of our party was due to the lack of efficiency in leadership and there are reasons to believe that Shri Devegowda has played his own part by a corruptive method. The Congress (I) members have raised questions in the assembly to the effect that Shri Devegowda was given Rs 25,000 by each of the members of his party to get a ticket . . . I beg to submit that I am not placing these facts before you out of personal enimity [sic] on Shri Devegowda . . . Shri Devegowda has played all these acts at the instigation of Shri Devaraj Urs . . . necessary enquiries may be made as against the mischiefs done by Shri H.D. Devegowda as it is an urgent need of the day.' The letter does another thing throughout, which is lobby for the restoration of Veerendra Patil as president of the party: 'Shri Veerendra Patil is the only person to lead the party in the state . . . Shri Veerendra Patil is a man of anticorrupt [sic] and the people of Karnataka have great regards on him.' Ironically, by then, Patil had lost the Chikmagalur by poll against Indira Gandhi and was ready to join her party. After all, 1978 was the worst year for him. He lost the Rajya Sabha seat to Ramakrishna Hegde, state party presidentship to Gowda, and lost the by poll to Indira Gandhi. So, the letter could have been written either to genuinely back Patil, or to mislead the party against Gowda. There were more letters of complaint, marked 'personal' and 'confidential' reaching Morarji on Gowda and the way he ran the state unit of the party, but Morarji did not offer them credence.

Interestingly, the Sullia MLA wrote another letter[20] to Morarji, quoting yet another confidential letter he had written on 19 February 1979. He says, in the earlier letter he had asked him to make Patil a minister in the Union cabinet: 'I had mentioned to you the name of Shri Veerendra Patil, ex-chief minister of Karnataka, but now I came to know that he is no more the Member of Parliament . . . I request you to take any Member of Parliament from our State as your cabinet colleague.' Hegde by then had become a Rajya Sabha member and Patil had firmed up his plan to join the Indira Congress.

Anyway, on the specific subject of the assembly by poll to the Chamaraja constituency, there is a letter[21] by Gowda to Hegde dated 11 September 1978, just before the polls on 24 September 1978. In this letter, Gowda is explaining the charge that he had unduly delayed the submission of the candidate's name to the party's parliamentary board for approval:

> I would like to state the factual position in the matter so that you can draw proper inference therefrom. On receipt of your letter (dated 28 August 1978) I contacted you again in person to clear the misunderstandings and you were good enough to tell me that the Hon'ble Prime Minister (Morarji Desai) was not quite happy about the undue delay caused in sending the recommendation by the state unit . . . I had fixed up my pilgrimage tour from 9th August 1978 to some of the North Indian Pilgrim centres like, Prayag, Benares etc to perform the first death anniversary of my father. In fact, before proceeding on the tour, I did enquire with the

office of the chief electoral officer regarding the programme
for Bye-election to 115-Chamaraja Assembly Constituency,
Mysore, but I was not told anything definitely about the
programme till the date of the commencement of my tour.
After finishing my tour-programme in some of the Northern
parts, I visited New Delhi on 19th August 1978 where I got
a letter from one of our secretaries Shri. M. Chandrashekar,
forwarding the programme for the bye-election . . . the
observers M. Chandrashekar, Bhaurao [sic] [Baburao]
Deshpande and S. Venkat Ram visited Mysore and met the
workers on 24th August 1978 and submitted their report on
27th August 1978. The Election Committee met on 28th
August 1978 and selected Sri H. Kempegowda to contest
the bye-election and this decision was communicated to
you on the same day by telegram . . . I can assure you that I
am the last man to hustle such matters with an intention of
manipulating or manoeuvring in the selection of candidates.
If the Parliamentary Board feels that the delay in sending
the recommendations on my part is intentional, I own the
mistake because it was unavoidable under the circumstances
explained and not in any case intentional.

There are some episodes in the Morarji autobiography where he
tries to resolve his disagreement and differences with Nehru, first,
and then Indira Gandhi, in a manner Gowda had resolved it with
Morarji. But in the case of Morarji, there was no surrender to their
judgement, or total trust in their fairness. On the other side too,
there was little or no affection. About Nehru, Morarji resented his
sympathy for socialists and found him to be 'not so transparent'.[22]
However, with Indira Gandhi, the power game was of an altogether
different proportion. The settlement that came about between
them was always strategic and thoroughly negotiated. Sample this,
when charges were being hurled against his son Kanti's business
associations:[23] 'When Sri Madhu Limaye demanded my resignation

in Parliament, I said that if the Prime Minister had any doubts in
any of these matters and if she felt that there was some substance
in the allegations, I would immediately resign from the cabinet . . .
The Prime Minister said publicly and also in Parliament that she did
not have any doubts whatsoever about my integrity and accepted my
contentions fully.'

While we speak of alignments and affection between Morarji
and Gowda, it is also important to emphasize a key difference.
Morarji had the habit of constantly painting himself into an
intransigent moral corner. He judged people on a harsh moral
scale and often sounded self-righteous. Gowda is emotional
and his idealism has a conservative ring, but his refined skills of
political wrestling is an altogether different game from Morarji's
moral upmanship. Perhaps it has to do with caste. Morarji was
a Brahmin and Gowda was a Shudra. Traditionally, it was the
Brahmin who canonized, codified and stratified what was morally
acceptable for the rest.

On most occasions, Morarji comes across as black and white, but
Gowda is grey. He would never borrow his mentor's moral absolutism
(Morarji's life story is strewn with absolutist statements. Example:[24]
'It was a principle with me not to entertain malice against anyone
and not to speak falsehood for any reason whatsoever.' Also, this:[25]
'From the very beginning I was of the firm principle not to flatter
anyone, not to speak a falsehood or do something that was wrong or
to be afraid of anyone.') Morarji artlessly spoke naked truth, Gowda
artfully deployed it. The guru made enemies naturally, the *shagird*
chose his enemies carefully. But then, Morarji was perceived to be
an obstructionist by Indira Gandhi, so was Gowda by Hegde. Their
discipline, doggedness and unflinching faith in God and destiny
created a bond between them.

The bond between the two had even prompted a question from
Chandra Shekhar, Gowda's party boss in Delhi, and later prime
minister. He had asked: 'How is it that Morarji does not believe any
allegations against you?'[26]

Garland of Slippers

Gowda's first meeting with Morarji happened around 1968 when
he was deputy prime minister. Gowda, as an Opposition MLA, was
part of a legislature panel that was visiting steel plants across India, to
study them and rectify operational problems in the Bhadravati iron
and steel plant. The panel was led by M.Y. Ghorpade, the erstwhile
ruler of Sandur, and a minister in the state government. At the end
of the tour, the panel reached Delhi, and met both Prime Minister
Indira Gandhi and Morarji, her deputy. While Indira posed for a
photograph with the panel and went away without engaging them,
Morarji engaged them in a brief conversation, but it was not exactly
an exchange of customary pleasantries. In the few minutes the panel
was with him, he suspected them of having had an excursion at
government expense. His reasoning was that the problems in the
Bhadravati plant did not warrant such an elaborate examination
of plants across India. He gave them a quick lecture about being
judicious with public money. The panel was thoroughly embarrassed,
and when it sought permission to leave, he asked Ghorpade to count
the flock as they moved out. 'No one should go missing, it will
become a problem for you,' he twisted the knife of sarcasm.[27]

Ghorpade recorded this travel in his autobiography,[28] but left out
the Morarji episode that is etched in Gowda's memory. Ghorpade
said: 'There were fourteen other members in the (assembly) Estimates
Committee including H.D. Deve Gowda, who later became prime
minister and K.S. Nagaratnamma, who later became the Speaker
of the state assembly. The Estimates Committee undertook a study
in response to the concern expressed in the Mysore Legislative
Assembly about MISL (Mysore Iron and Steel Ltd), Bhadravati. The
committee decided to visit other steel plants in the country, both
in public and private sector, such as those in Bhilai, Rourkela and
Durgapur . . . The committee met Indira Gandhi at her residence in
Delhi after completing the study tour.' Ghorpade and Gowda, each
had retained only what they cherished in their memory.

There is one other episode that cannot go unrecounted in this chapter. It was sometime around December 1978 when Indira Gandhi had been sent to jail. Morarji apparently was hesitant to imprison her. He had argued against it. He thought it would create sympathy for her and would harm the Janata Party government but his colleagues like George Fernandes were insistent on action. The Parliament also moved a privilege motion. The Shah Commission inquiry against Emergency excesses had just then begun. Morarji did not wish to pursue a vindictive path, and there is an interesting incident from 1977 which supports this. Indira Gandhi's adviser G. Parthasarathy[29] went to the new prime minister to discuss if the defeated PM could get a house from the government pool. Morarji impatiently enquired about the palatial farmhouse Gandhi was said to possess. Parthasarathy invited him to come and see for himself, thereby gently countering the propaganda. A magnanimous Morarji allotted 12 Willingdon Crescent to her amidst all the bitterness that existed at the time.

Returning to the Gowda story, on a December 1978 afternoon, Gowda was getting back from his hometown in Hassan district. At the Nataraja Talkies in Bangalore's Sheshadripuram locality, there was a huge procession blocking the road. He was driving his car and was continuously honking for space to move ahead, but the crowd wasn't relenting. There was his wife in the car. There was a huge presence of policemen. Somehow, he made way for himself, and as he moved ahead, he saw that the procession had a huge photograph of Morarji with a garland of slippers around it. He became furious. He dropped off his wife at home and immediately rushed to the legislators' hostel where he kept a room. He called up chief minister Devaraj Urs and asked if he could come and see him immediately.[30]

He collected colleagues who were available, prominently A.K. Subbaiah, Krishna Iyer, S.R. Bommai and T.R. Shammana, and reached Balabrooie, the official residence of the chief minister. A few days back, shops had been vandalized in the city following Indira Gandhi's arrest, and it was largely believed that Urs's son-in-law,

M.D. Nataraj, had instigated the mobs. Gowda had accessed the transcript of a phone intercept by the intelligence in which the father-in-law visiting Delhi and the son-in-law in Bangalore had apparently exchanged a word on ending the protest. This had made them the managers of the violence. When they stood in front of Urs, Bommai began by saying that things were limping back to normal in the city. Gowda was provoked by the statement. Recalling the episode in 2019, he said, he did not know what came over him that day. Rage had overtaken, the chappal had come into his hand, and his tongue lashed out at Urs's son-in-law. He also mentioned the phone transcript in his possession. Urs's face apparently turned ashen, and the state police chief T. Albert Manoraj, who was in the room, came and stood in between Urs and Gowda. There was also J.C. Lynn, Urs's principal secretary. Gowda challenged Manoraj to arrest him. 'What can the court do? It'll impose a fine of ten rupees and let me out on bail. Then, I'll go to the people and explain what happened. Let's see how they react. A prime minister's portrait is garlanded with chappals and a procession is taken out, and the police offer protection to such a gathering,' he burst forth.[31] Seeing things going out of control, Urs and Gowda's colleagues pacified him. Recalling this episode, Gowda tried to offer evidence of his emotional attachment. One does not know if this incident was reported back to Morarji and if any political benefit accrued to him, but the proximity between Morarji and Gowda had raised eyebrows.

Gowda did not leave it at that. He planned a larger, structured action against the Urs government, and it is reflected in the letter[32] that his colleague and leader of the Opposition in the legislative assembly, S.R. Bommai, wrote to Morarji:

Myself and Sri H.D. Devegowda, President of our Party have already submitted a memorandum to you on 27th Decr [sic] 1978 giving all the details about the incidents that took place on 19th and 20th December 1978 throughout the State, immediately after the Lok Sabha decision to convict and expel

Smt Gandhi . . . On 18th January 1979 the Janata Legislature
Party met and the deliberation went on for four hours to
consider the future course of action . . . It was unanimously
decided that until and unless the Government agrees in
principle for a judicial probe into the incidents of 19th and
20th December and for payment of compensation, we should
not co-operate with the Government inside the Legislature . . .
In pursuance of this decision I made a move and requested
the Speaker of Karnataka Legislative Assembly on 19th January
1979 to postpone the Question hour and to take up discussion
regarding the incidents referred to above.

Gowda not only edited the draft of this letter but also ensured that
Bommai delivered a strong statement in the assembly. He wanted the
inadvertent 'limping back to normal' message to be totally erased.
A copy of the four-page long statement was also sent to Morarji. The
written statement filled with rage appeared breathless with minimal
punctuation. The harshest parts of the statement read as follows:

Following the expulsion of Smt Indira Gandhi from the
Lok Sabha and her imprisonment on the privilege issue an
unprecedented and virulent wave of violence, arson, hooliganism
destruction and looting of public and private property was let
loose by some of the ruling Congress (I) Party Leaders and
anti-social hirelings on the innocent and peace loving citizens
of our State on 19th December 1978 and subsequent days
resulting in wanton distruction [sic] of property and loss of
innocent lives and the Police administration completely failed
or refused to take preventive and protective steps to maintain
law and order and protect the lives, property and honour of
the people . . . This was no spontaneous people's 'upsurge' as
is being claimed by some apologists of the Congress (I) Party
and the State government. For days before these incidents some
of the Congress (I) Leaders in the State had been holding out

threats of 'blood flowing' and 'mass upsurge' in the event of
Smt Gandhi being punished by the Lok Sabha. What actually
happened after the expulsion and imprisonment of Smt
Gandhi was not political protest by any stretch of imagination
but a pre-planned reign of terror by the anti-social elements
organised and financed by some so the State Congress(I)
leaders and allowed by the police . . . Further the most sinister
aspect of these disturbances was the instructions to the police
that they should not take action against the anti-social elements
but only to watch and report. It is this game of immobilising
the Police and mobilising the anti-social elements to terrorise
the people in general and the political opponents in particular
which marked out this government as fascist regime. By this act
of bringing about a police-goonda gang up for partisan ends,
this Government has forfeited all democratic credentials, if it
ever had any.

The Memorial

One of the first things that crossed Gowda's mind in April 1995,
when Morarji passed away, was to erect his statue in the premises
of the Vidhana Soudha, the seat of power in Karnataka. Gowda was
chief minister then. But he was advised against the statue. The fear
was that a Congress government may get it removed later. Therefore,
Gowda came up with the idea of setting up residential schools
for underprivileged children across the state in Morarji's name.[33]
Morarji Desai Residential Schools in Karnataka have maintained a
good record and reputation to this day.

A few weeks after he had become chief minister, Gowda decided
to seek the blessings of his mentor. He visited him at his son Kanti
Desai's apartment, in Mumbai. He had grown weak and was lying on
a reclining chair in a balcony overlooking the Marine Drive. Gowda
grew emotional and touched his feet. Morarji spoke softly but with
clarity: 'At last, you have become chief minister. I am happy,' he said

and cautioned his shagird: 'Be careful about that fox Hegde. He is bound to play games.' Gowda did not say anything.[34] He just nodded his head. P.G.R. Sindhia, Gowda's home minister, was a witness.

By the time Gowda became prime minister, Morarji's memory had slipped into national oblivion, but the loyal follower was determined to resurrect it. On 28 February 1997, he inaugurated the Morarji memorial, Abhay Ghat, near the Sabarmati Ashram in Ahmedabad. That day also marked the conclusion of Morarji's birth centenary year. He spoke from his heart:[35] 'A few months ago, when I was paying homage at Sri Morarji Desai's Samadhi, my mind went back to what this great soul had said in 1977 on being asked how he had passed all his days in prison alone. Morarji Desai had answered how anybody could keep him and his spirit in solitary confinement when he was able to strive all the while in a prayerful mood to realize his dream of total surrender to God. His detention, he had said, had reinforced his faith in God. He was indeed a remarkable man.' During the Emergency, Indira Gandhi had imprisoned Morarji Desai and kept him in solitary confinement for eighteen months without access to newspapers or the radio. What Gowda meant was that someone without the spiritual wherewithal of a Morarji would have gone 'insane'. There was no reference to politics in Gowda's speech, but only his mentor's character, discipline and moral purpose. It reiterated how he had viewed his connection with Morarji—it was not merely through politics but as a knot of destiny. After all, Morarji's prediction had come true. Gowda's career had sparkled beyond anybody's imagination.

6

The Epic Battle with Ramakrishna Hegde

To say Deve Gowda and Ramakrishna Hegde are two very complex individuals is a surrender to banality. The two, for a stretch of time, appeared to be dependent on each other and were also defined by each other in Karnataka politics. Yet, even as they progressed as comrades for decades, they remained fiercely competitive. The intensity of their friendship or rancour was central to the fortunes of non-Congress politics in Karnataka for nearly three decades, starting from the early 1970s. There were always quiet and loud jealousies, suspicions and intrigues between them. They are another interesting pair in contemporary Indian politics who facilitate a fine study in contrast. We have seen Jawaharlal Nehru and Sardar Vallabhbhai Patel, Indira Gandhi and Morarji Desai, VP Singh and Devi Lal, Vajpayee and Advani being presented as personalities in contrast. To that fascinating list, however limited and binary it is in its imagination, Gowda and Hegde would be a worthy addition. In a blood sport called politics, they waged many battles to destroy each other, leaving both their purpose and personalities roiled. Gowda may have won eventually, but his victory is sometimes described as pyrrhic. Even seventeen years after Hegde's death (2004), if there is anything that animates Gowda's conversations, monologues and victimhood, navigates his impulses and judgements and is a touchstone to reckon his life's good and bad moments, it is the memory of Hegde.

When it comes to contrasts, Hegde was a Brahmin from Siddapur in Uttara Kannada district, nestled in the Western Ghats. Gowda was a Shudra from the boring plains of Holenarasipur in Hassan. One was suave and had cultivated refinement and people; the other thought if anybody had to be cultivated, it was the gods. Hegde enjoyed his Black Label whisky, Dunhill cigarettes, and fish, fowl and meat delicacies.[1] Gowda was a teetotaler and a non-smoker and had given up meat around 1978. He occasionally lit up a cigarette to take a few noxious puffs in his early days when only Devaraj Urs or S.R. Bommai tantalizingly held a packet of 555 before him.[2] It was always to rejoice either a winning idea or a happy compromise or a hopeful alliance. A cigarette was never an idle rumination for him.

Hegde liked to be in a silk robe at home that made him look like a dandy ascetic, Gowda was always a political baba in his cotton dhoti, which he wrapped a few inches above his waist when indoors, and at the waist when outdoors. The consensus is Hegde had a roving eye, but Gowda is deeply attached to his wife. Hegde had a liberal arts education, while Gowda was a technical man. One had a life beyond politics; for the other, life was politics. Hegde spoke of 'value-based politics' and Gowda believed in 'naked truths'. Hegde evolved as a manager of mass leaders, and Gowda was a mass leader himself. Hegde, by virtue of his birth, had enormous social and cultural capital, while Gowda had none. He had no pedigree or reference point. When Hegde was vindictive and petty, nobody would know but when the other indulged in it, the entire world would take aim. However, both were deeply calculative and manipulative in their own ways. They would wrestle with their ideas for nights before they wrestled with others during the day. In a sharp profile of the two that journalist and writer P. Lankesh wrote in 1996, he called them Karataka and Dhamanaka, alluding to the two jackals in the Panchatantra story: 'Hegde is a fair complexioned Havyak Brahmin with soft lips that have a sheen of red lipstick. He has a soft voice, and his grey hair

and delicate wrinkles match his 68 years. He has all the qualities of a
senior actor steeped in epicurean delights . . . Gowda goes around as
a great believer of God and portrays himself as a brother of Bhakta
Kabir, but is as petty and deceptive as Hegde.'[3] In fact, Lankesh had
popular nicknames for top politicians and always referred to Hegde
as the cunning fox (*gullenari* in Kannada) in his eponymous weekly
tabloid. While Gowda was referred to as 'Gowda', his caste name
which in itself evoked feudal connotations in the local context,
chief ministers Bangarappa and Gundu Rao were called 'Bum' and
'Gum' (the first syllable of their names). The coinage 'Yeddy' for
Yediyurappa also happened in the 1990s in Lankesh's tabloid.

The epic battle between Gowda and Hegde is part of Karnataka's
political folklore. How, and in what context, did they collaborate?
Why did they fall out? Why does Gowda think Hegde constantly
undermined and finally betrayed him? How did they try to reconcile?
All these questions will be dealt with in this chapter. Hegde was senior
to Gowda both in age and the political game and had acquired an early
pan-India network. He was educated at the Kashi Vidyapeeth, aka
Banaras Hindu University, and had therefore a good grip over Hindi,
which was a major handicap for Gowda to operate in the north of
India. When it came to English, Gowda's knowledge was decent, while
Hegde could deploy it with flourish. As Karnataka's chief minister in
the 1980s, Hegde's latent national ambition acquired new feathers.
Anglophone intellectuals and the media, predominantly controlled by
the upper castes, spoke about him as a prime ministerial candidate and
a secular alternative to Rajiv Gandhi. The 'Mr. Clean' image spin for
Gandhi saw a counter, and competition, in Hegde's coinage of 'value-
based politics'. In fact, writer Salman Rushdie in a 1988 essay had said
that people like Rajiv Gandhi will have to 'reckon' with leaders like
Hegde.[4] All this build-up had happened without realizing that Hegde
had not even nurtured a parliamentary seat to contest in Karnataka,
and if he did, he needed Gowda to ensure his victory. In 1991, when
he had fallen out with Gowda and had contested from Bagalkot, a
relatively safe parliamentary seat, he was handsomely defeated by a

rookie Congress politician called Siddu Nyamagouda. That was his last popular election. He did not contest the Karnataka assembly elections in 1994 or the general (Lok Sabha) elections in 1996, but Gowda as chief minister sent him to the Rajya Sabha (upper house) in April that year. But in June 1996, when Gowda pipped Hegde to the prime minister's post, he was completely distraught. He was never the same person again; the ugliness that Gowda had argued was inherent in Hegde manifested in his words and actions, so did Gowda's vindictiveness. Hegde had always felt entitled to national glory, and now, when it had rudely changed hands, he could not come to terms with it. He entered into a series of compromises with the BJP that jolted his legacy as a prominent leader of India's secular third front.

Let us begin from where it all began—in the 1970s, when Urs was chief minister and Gowda the Opposition leader in the assembly. The Emergency had not been imposed and the Janata Party was yet to be formed.

The First Deception

Within a couple of months of Devaraj Urs becoming chief minister in 1972 after sweeping the polls for Indira Gandhi or the Congress (R), Veerendra Patil, a former chief minister and Gowda's senior colleague in the Congress (O), was sent to the Rajya Sabha. His going to the Rajya Sabha was nothing short of magic because in 1972, the party had only 24 MLAs, and they needed double the number to win. Gowda, who was elected as an independent, had been chosen leader of the Opposition in the assembly. He had worked hard and maneouevered the 'conscience' vote of many to secure a win for Patil. Urs, who knew what Gowda was up to, had, in fact, asked him to let it be that one time and that he would help Patil when the opportunity opened up again in the next couple of years, but Gowda's adamancy had prevailed.[5] He wanted to prove his newly earned position and refused to drive the 'last nail in the coffin of the Congress (O)'.

After Patil's political future had been secured, Gowda turned to Ramakrishna Hegde, who had not contested the 1972 assembly polls. Hegde was not doing much. S.R. Bommai had lost the polls. Gowda, Patil, Bommai and Hegde were slowly appearing like an influential political quartet in Karnataka. Gowda teamed up with Patil, met Hegde and convinced him to come to the upper house of the Karnataka legislature and become the Opposition leader: 'He said, "I will not enter the Vidhana Soudha as long as Urs is there." I argued that it was a silly vow to make. He finally agreed,' Gowda remembered.[6]

In Gowda's mind, that was one of his early acts of kindness towards Hegde and the blossoming of their political camaraderie. He is unable to explain though as to why he felt drawn to Hegde. Perhaps he saw Hegde as charismatic, experienced and also learned. It also perhaps was a latent Shudra complex to align and appease someone at the pinnacle of caste hierarchy. In the language of social anthropology, it could be read as 'Sanskritization'.[7] There is no forgetting that Gowda believed in the Vedic worldview. Hegde, who had been elected to the state assembly for the first time in 1957, five years before Gowda, had made an impression as a young and efficient minister in S. Nijalingappa's cabinet. While Gowda and Patil represented two dominant castes, Vokkaliga and Lingayat, respectively, Hegde, a Brahmin, brought influence and goodwill to the new circle Gowda was cultivating and expanding. Bommai was also a Lingayat.

But soon after Hegde became leader of the Opposition in the legislative council, he launched sharp attacks on Urs. His personal animosity found expression at times and that irked Urs, a chief minister with a brute majority. One day, Urs sent for Gowda and said that he had decided to humiliate Hegde. He said he had definite information about a certain activity going on in his close circle, which also involved a family member. When that family member is caught red-handed, Urs threatened, Hegde's image and political career would nosedive. He added that the Raj Bhavan too was being misused for the activity: 'I was shocked. I tried to assuage Urs by saying that it was beneath his stature to act in such a manner. I said people saw him as a large-hearted person, and that he should not stoop to a level that would disappoint them. Urs cooled down a bit and said he would take criticism on issues, but would not tolerate relentless personal jibes. He expected me to communicate that to Hegde. I would attack Urs on matters of policy and corruption, and he seemed to be fine with that,' Gowda said.[8] Soon after this, the national scene started heating up, and Hegde's focus shifted, and Bommai replaced him as the Opposition leader in the council. Urs did not pursue the matter about Hegde, and Gowda had every reason to believe that his intervention had stopped him.

After the Emergency, when the Janata Party was formed, Gowda and friends thought it would be good if Hegde became a general secretary of the party, but there was a hurdle. Prime Minister Morarji Desai did not like Hegde. There was a serious trust issue between them. Morarji similarly disliked Veerendra Patil. Anyway, a delegation comprising Gowda, A.K. Subbaiah, Baburao Deshpande and S.R. Bommai went to Delhi to plead Hegde's case with senior Janata Party leaders, and Gowda was chosen to place the argument before Morarji. When Gowda made his case, Morarji did not relent. Instead, he offered a technical reason and said the party constitution did not allow one more general secretary: 'I was not the one to give up so easily. I went to Neelam Sanjiva Reddy, who was the Speaker of the Lok Sabha. He liked me as much as Morarji. I said that Hegde should be considered as it would immensely benefit the party. I also said that I won't remain the Opposition leader if he was not made general secretary. Reddy called up Morarji in my presence and mentioned that I was being stubborn. He also said: "Morarjibhai, let's accommodate an extra general secretary and ratify it later." Morarji knew my ways, he relented. That's how Hegde became general secretary of the Janata Party.'[9]

Once he was settled in Delhi at the Jantar Mantar Road office of the Janata Party, Hegde's network naturally expanded. He came in

direct contact with leaders from across the nation. He was Gowda's
boss in the party hierarchy and was writing stern, formal letters to
Gowda with instructions and punctuations in their perfect place.[10] In
contrast to Hegde's letters, party president Chandra Shekhar's letters
to Gowda come across as warmer and friendlier.[11] In 1978, there
was a toss-up between Hegde and Veerendra Patil to go to the Rajya
Sabha from Karnataka. Chandra Shekhar preferred Hegde over
Patil, who had suffered during the Emergency. Patil was suspected of
hobnobbing with the Indira Gandhi regime. Patil had also famously
been described by Morarji as the 'Hitendra Desai of Karnataka' and
ensured that Gowda replaced him as the state Janata Party president
before the assembly elections in 1978 (more details in the Morarji
Desai chapter).

It was in the buildup to the 1978 Karnataka assembly elections
that Gowda had his first bitter experience with Hegde. The Morarji
government at the Centre dismissed the Urs government in the state
with Governor Govind Narain taking over the reins of administration.
Gowda was euphoric because he saw himself as next chief minister of
the state. For six years as the Opposition leader, he was at the centre
of exposing the administrative overreach, goondaism and corruption
of the Urs government. His performance as an Opposition leader
had earned the admiration of the Janata Party leaders as well as Urs's
rivals inside the Congress. In his years as an Opposition leader, he
had acquired a pan-Karnataka appeal and was seen by the people as
a 'fearless, dedicated fighter'.[12] The impression was that bit by bit,
nearly single-handedly, he had chipped away the halo built around the
phenomenal personality of Urs, and it was not a small achievement.[13]
It was like making a road in the middle of a mountain. There was
no other leader in the state who looked as much in command and
promising as Gowda at that point.

In this context, the selection of candidates happened in Bangalore
at the guest house of a steel company on Nelamangala Road. All
senior leaders, except Veerendra Patil, were present. Nearly 215–216
seats were cleared unanimously, and for the remaining 8–9 seats,

a choice was offered to the party's parliamentary board.[14] Gowda went to Delhi with the list of candidates that had been finalized and submitted it to Hegde to be placed before the parliamentary board. By then, Hegde had tried to introduce 'value-based' conditionalities by saying that those who were not elected could not become chief minister. In the same breath, he had suggested that Gowda and Patil should not contest polls because they had to take charge of the campaign across the state.[15] If they contested, the Congress would willy-nilly tie them down to their constituencies. Patil was very upset about this idea: 'He telephoned Hegde from Bangalore and bluntly asked "What is your game? Why are you denying me a ticket?" I was present when this conversation happened. Hegde tried to convince him by saying that "everything is in our hands", and that the parliamentary board would reverse its decision later,' Gowda recalled.[16] In reality, Gowda and Patil were the two senior leaders who were clearly in the running for chief ministership, and Hegde had now put a clever barrier for either of them to achieve it after the polls without jostling and lobbying. All this was not an issue for Gowda. He knew with Morarji, Charan Singh and Chandra Shekhar on his side, Patil would not be in the reckoning for the chief minister's chair, but something unforeseen hit him. When the list of candidates was published in the newspapers (a letter from Hegde to Gowda says the list was officially approved by the parliamentary board on 29 January 1979[17]), Gowda was jolted. He saw Hegde had altered around seventy names, mostly in the north, central and coastal regions of Karnataka. Gowda's party colleague S. Venkatram, who had gone out for a walk early in the morning, had hurried back to Karnataka Bhavan in Delhi, where Gowda was staying, with the newspapers: 'I quickly got ready and rushed to Hegde's house. The only thing he said was: "Don't worry, we will do well. You don't understand those regions as much as I do." I was the party's state president, and he had not shown even the courtesy to discuss the changes with me. I read deception in this but could do nothing. The list was out. I was crestfallen. When I returned to Bangalore the same day, upset party workers were waiting at the Bangalore airport with slippers, stones and sticks for me. They were naturally angry, and accused me of selling tickets for money. They insinuated that I was the kind who would even sell my wife to make money. There was so much commotion that the police transported me incognito, in an escort van, to my house. The area around had been cordoned off. How could I convince people that it was Hegde who had changed the list? I was the face to the crowds, not Hegde. I swallowed the insults and did not campaign with Hegde that election. I also confined my campaigning to the Mysore region and my constituency (the party had cleared his candidature later). Hegde's game was clear. He first wanted me confined to a region and a caste, and not emerge as a chief ministerial choice.'[18]

Party president Chandra Shekhar did try to salvage the situation for Gowda in between, but it was too late. In the middle of the election, S. Nijalingappa, a key Janata Party and anti-Indira Gandhi figure plus a prominent Lingayat leader in Karnataka, also announced his retirement from politics over the poor selection of candidates.[19] His timing had a direct implication for Gowda. Chandra Shekhar, before leaving for Delhi, summoned Gowda and tried to instil confidence: 'As I was driving him to the airport, he advised that I concentrate on my seat and the Mysore region. He kept Rs 2,00,000 in the dashboard drawer of the car for election expenses. I won my seat and decided to resign as party's state president. Even at that point, Chandra Shekhar told me on the phone, "It is not you who should resign, I should. It is the parliamentary board that has let you down." When I went to Delhi to the national executive, I returned the money he had given in the presence of Morarji, Charan Singh, Advani and Jagajivan Ram. Morarji complimented me for returning the money.'[20]

The Janata Party lost the assembly election even in the middle of an anti-Indira Gandhi wave across the nation. The results were a repeat of the 1977 general elections in Karnataka. People had not voted against Gandhi but voted for Devaraj Urs and his progressive policies for the poor. The infighting in the Janata party had also spread a negative sentiment among the voters. It should have otherwise done much better given the way Gowda had cornered Urs at every bend, but the party managed only fifty-nine seats. Hegde's sabotage had worked. Not once during or after the election did Hegde own up to the loss caused by his manipulation. 'He behaved as if nothing had happened. I felt helpless,' Gowda said.[21] According to his former associates, after the results, Gowda went into a sort of depression.[22] He did write a report on the election results to the central office, but that report was misplaced. There is a letter[23] asking Gowda to resend the report, but one is not sure if he sent it again.

Oddly, despite the party's serious drubbing at the polls, Hegde wrote congratulatory letters to local party operatives in his home district of North Kanara (now Uttara Kannada). One such letter to Shri Bisalhop Timmappa Hegde of Sirsi read as follows: 'I have to congratulate you on our party's success in Sirsi. The manner in which you organised the election campaign, with the help of our friends and party workers, is really praiseworthy… I am sure the team spirit with which our party workers worked during the elections will continue.'[24] Similar letters went to party heads of Yellapur and Ankola taluk in the same district.[25] He was also provoking leaders like K.S. Nagaratnamma, the Speaker of the outgoing assembly, who had lost in the Gundlupet seat in Chamarajanagar district: 'I hope the fact of the Taluk unit Janata Party workers not working wholeheartedly for you has been brought to the notice of Shri Deve Gowda for enquiry and necessary action' (although Nagaratnamma was in the Congress, there was an effort made in 1978 to establish a healthy convention that the Speaker's seat should not be contested by an organized party).[26]

Other leaders in Hegde's camp, like legislator Y. Ramakrishna, were writing long 'personal' letters, to Morarji and Chandra Shekhar asking for Gowda's sacking. Ramakrishna wrote: 'Our party workers have become disillusioned on account of the party's debacle under Sri Deve Gowda. Most of the senior leaders of the party are not co-operating with him.'[27] There was a flood of letters actually to the office-bearers in Delhi, including Hegde, offering unsolicited analysis on why the elections were lost, and most of them spoke about the poor selection of candidates besides other reasons.[28] But there is one letter in the stack, written by G.S. Kulkarni of Indi Taluk in Bijapur to Advani, then the minister for information and broadcasting, which says: 'Sri HD Deve Gowda who is honest worker of the party did not get any valuable voice while distributing the tickets. Some other persons like Veerendra Patil and others got valuable voice. For this Sri Deve Gowda is not at all responsible and he is having joint responsibility with all.'[29] Why this person wrote in defence of Gowda and sent his letter to Advani is a difficult guess (it could be because Advani along with Rabi Ray had attended the state election committee meetings to help the selection of candidates[30]), but Advani responded by saying he was forwarding the letter to the party's central office.[31] There is also one letter by Veerendra Patil to one I.C. Nagathan of Bijapur who was denied a party ticket to contest, in which he says: 'In a situation like this you have to appreciate the inter-play of inner party democracy.'[32] Hegde had lit the fire, but mass leaders like Gowda and Patil had to face its consequences and battle to douse it.

After the Janata Party government fell in Delhi and the general elections were called in 1980, a split Janata Party had decided to fight the elections under Jagajivan Ram. Hegde, who needed a workhorse again, warmed up to Gowda and said Ram will be prime minister, and even if the Janata Party did not get a clear majority, it would be the single-largest party. A Rs 6,00,000 campaign budget was planned for Karnataka in Hegde's house. Jagajivan Ram called Gowda from Dum Dum airport in Calcutta and told Gowda not to hate or attack 'gentleman' Urs.[33] By then, Urs had fallen out with Indira Gandhi and formed his own party, the Karnataka Kranti Ranga. However, in that election, both, the Janata Party and Urs, were rejected by the people.

Making Hegde Chief Minister

In 1982, the Congress party under R. Gundu Rao collapsed in the polls, and Chief Minister Rao himself lost. This paved the way for the first non-Congress government in Karnataka, with the Janata Party as the single largest party. Urs had suddenly passed away in June 1982 and members of his Karnataka Kranti Ranga, with socialists and progressives like S. Bangarappa, J.H. Patel and Abdul Nazir Sab, came together and merged with the Janata Party. There were a few Left MLAs and about 18 BJP legislators who decided to back a non-Congress government from the outside. S. Bangarappa from the Kranti Ranga, Deve Gowda and Bommai were widely discussed as possible chief ministers to head the coalition,[34] but out of nowhere, Ramakrishna Hegde emerged for the top job. That he had worked his Delhi connections was obvious. Also, since there was such a mélange of parties, Hegde seemed to have the skill and patience to work through the divisions and hold the coalition together. But Hegde had not contested the polls, and he had no constituency to contest either.

B.L. Shankar, who was the Janata Party's general secretary then (he joined the Congress later when S.M. Krishna became chief minister in 1999 and became the chairman of the Legislative Council), and received a crucial phone call from party national president Chandra Shekhar, gives a ringside view of how Hegde's name was manoeuvred to the top: 'The legislature party meeting happened. I was part of it. It was not decided who should be chief minister in that meeting. S. Bangarappa, S.R. Bommai and Gowda had a strong claim. Party national president Chandra Shekhar, who was on Bharat Yatra, was walking somewhere in Tamil Nadu. After the meeting was over, the office telephone rang, I received the call. Chandra Shekhar was on the line. I briefed him about the discussions in the meeting. The next question he asked was "where is Deve Gowda?" I said he was still around in the office. He said, "call him." They spoke for only two minutes. He said you have to propose Hegde's name for chief minister. Gowda tried to say something, but Chandra Shekhar simply said from the other side, "Go to Hegde's place and convince him." The call was over in three minutes. Gowda was very close to Chandra Shekhar, and his word was final for him. Almost immediately, Gowda led a small group of colleagues to Hegde's house. That included Bommai, M. Chandrashekar, Jeevaraj Alva, P.G.R. Sindhia and myself. We went to 229 Krutika, Hegde's house in Sadashivanagar. Until then, Hegde's name had not been discussed. He was surprised to see us all troop in. Gowda did the talking.'[35]

As Gowda spoke, Hegde tried to tell him that it was a mission that would not succeed because Bangarappa would never agree. At that point, Gowda said, 'Leave that to me.'[36] Straight from Hegde's house, they headed to Bangarappa's house. There was a milling crowd and chaos all over. They banged the bonnet of Gowda's car, and as he tried to get out, he was roughed up. They tore his kurta too. Bangarappa came out, shouted at his supporters, and took Gowda and others in. Bangarappa was clear from the outset. He said, 'Gowda, you become the chief minister, I have no problem. Bommai, if you want to take the chair, I will not object. But I will not support Hegde.'[37] Bangarappa's chief objection was that Hegde had not contested the election and that as a leader of the backward classes, he could not put his lot behind a Brahmin. Also, Gundu Rao, another Brahmin, had just then been defeated, and one Brahmin could not be replaced by another when they were a micro minority community in the state.[38] Bangarappa was the leader of the Kranti Ranga, a party set up by Devaraj Urs when he split from the Congress and Urs, in the 1970s, and had successfully engineered the emergence of the backward classes in state politics. 'If you follow this line, your path and my path may never meet again,' Bangarappa warned.[39] Although the Janata Party and the Kranti Ranga had fought the polls together, and on the Janata Party symbol, it was important to convince Bangarappa because he had a sizeable number of followers among the newly-elected legislators and could easily wreck the already delicate numbers for the non-Congress front. How this hurdle was finally overcome is recorded in some detail in a book by E. Raghavan and James Manor.[40]

From Bangarappa's house, Gowda headed back to Hegde's house and told him that he should get ready for a contest in the legislature party. Gowda called a secret meeting of Vokkaliga legislators under a tree in the Cubbon Park in Bangalore.[41] The Vokkaliga legislators refused to endorse Hegde. They repeated what Bangarappa had said. Gowda knew he would always outshine Bommai any day, but Hegde's name was a huge surprise for him too. It was most unexpected. When Chandrashekar had called, he gave his word, and now, he wanted to stick to it. 'Gowda looks stubborn, but on certain matters, he yields easily. That is his nature. That was how he was until he went to the Parliament in 1991,' Shankar recalled.[42] He took a couple of hours, but Gowda finally convinced Vokkaliga MLAs. The next day, at the legislature party meeting, there was a contest but, Hegde sailed through with Gowda's manoeuvring. Other leaders like Bommai, Gurupadaswamy and Lakshmisagar did not make the cut. The BJP, whose 18 MLAs were crucial for forming the government, also preferred Hegde over Bangarappa, who remained unrelenting for a while. When a majority of the leaders like J.H. Patel, Abdul Nazir Sab and Chandre Gowda broke away from the Kranti Ranga camp, totalling 36, Bangarappa's rebellion and numbers did not threaten the government. In the hope of becoming chief minister, Bangarappa had declared the merger of Kranti Ranga with the Janata Party after the results, but that did not alter the situation for him.[43] Gowda made efforts to keep Bangarappa inside the ruling coalition by offering him the deputy chief minister's post, but that did not work. Bangarappa had to wait till 1990 to become chief minister after he had returned to the Congress.

Hegde was certainly not the face of the 1983 election, nor was he in the frontline campaigning, but he was in the background. Shankar remembers that he would stay back in the office till late in the night sorting out problems: 'The party's situation was so bad that when Morarji Desai's campaign tour was fixed in the Bombay-Karnataka region, and he was to land the next day in Belgaum, there was no decent car to pick him up from the airport. Hegde, in my presence, called at least ten of his industrialist friends, pleading them to lend their car for a former prime minister. Many of them did not come on

the line. Those who took the call offered a lame excuse or another.
Finally, he called his friend, who had a Benz car, in the Dandeli paper
mills. He obliged. That night, he sent Sarojini Mahishi, by bus, to
receive Morarji. To that extent, he was involved in the campaign,'
Shankar remembered.[44]

The next big task for Gowda was to get Hegde elected to the
assembly within six months because he was not a member of either
house of the Karnataka legislature. The tough part was that Hegde
did not have a constituency to call his own. Gowda first checked with
R.V. Deshpande if they could find a constituency in Hegde's home
district of Uttara Kannada. Deshpande reported back that it would be
very risky to put him up there for contest.[45] Then Gowda spoke to his
protégé P.G.R. Sindhia and asked him to give up Kanakapura in the
outskirts of Bangalore, a quasi-rural constituency with a Vokkaliga
domination. Gowda camped there for four weeks, led the campaign,
and ensured Hegde was elected. He even flew in a reluctant Morarji
Desai to campaign.[46] Morarji had deep reservations about Hegde,
but Gowda was his favourite. Hegde openly acknowledged Gowda's
role, and Gowda basked in Hegde's indebtedness. Their relationship
was the finest between 1983 and 1985: 'Gowda was a pillar in
Hegde's government, and they were pretty close. It was a period of
great camaraderie. For our generation of leaders and the party, it was
a golden period,' Shankar remembered.[47]

Sindhia remembers how Gowda broached the subject of
Kanakapura for Hegde:

One afternoon we were having lunch in Gowda's office in
the Vidhana Soudha. I was the minister for health and family
welfare in the Hegde cabinet, and we had set a routine to meet
for lunch every day. Gowda would get lunch from home and I
too would carry my lunch box. That day he said, 'Hegde has got
intelligence report from twenty-two potential constituencies,
and it is not looking good. There is a tough fight from wherever
he contests in the Lingayat or coastal belt. Bommai is scared to

sponsor him from north Karnataka. What do we do?' I pre-empted him and asked, 'Sir, what is on your mind?' He said he wanted to offer a constituency in South Karnataka where he could pull off a victory for Hegde. Then I asked if he wanted me to vacate Kanakapura? Without batting his eyelid, he said, 'Yes.' It was not a story of great sacrifice for me to give up the seat. In fact, I benefitted immensely from it. I became known in all circles that Hegde was known across India. People like L.C. Jain[48] complimented me. The Delhi Janata Party leaders praised me. Whoever may say whatever today, Gowda was the architect of that campaign and victory. Without Gowda, there was no chance that Hegde could have entered the state assembly.[49]

During the campaign, Gowda had injured his leg while walking eight miles to reach a hamlet called Doddabettahalli. He had taken a heavy dose of medicine to quickly recover and had returned to the campaign within thirty-six hours.[50] Interestingly, Sindhia defeated his leader Gowda when he contested from the same Kanakapura constituency in 1989 after the Janata Party in Karnataka had melted down. 'It was in the knowledge of all ministers in 1983 that the stability of the Hegde government was in the hands of three people: Gowda, S.R. Bommai and J.H. Patel. Gowda's task was to manage not just Vokkaliga MLAs but also the chief minister. Bommai managed the Lingayats, and Patel had influence in the group that came from Kranti Ranga. Hegde indulged Gowda, he listened to him,' Sindhia remembered.[51]

Doubts and Differences Catch Up

In 1983, when the cabinet was being formed, Gowda suggested to Hegde that he should keep it small. In terms of strength of MLAs and social justice distribution, he said give three posts to Vokkaligas, four to Lingayats, two to scheduled castes and one to a Muslim. He said don't go beyond this for the time being. His advice was to proceed carefully. He also suggested that he would stay out of the government to 'protect' it but said cabinet berths should be given from among Vokkaligas to the three he would suggest from its three sub-castes: Dr Thimme Gowda, M Chandrashekar and B.L. Gowda. S.R. Bommai would help with Lingayat berths and that would include himself and J.H. Patel. Abdul Nazir Sab would be the obvious Muslim choice and B. Rachaiah would be one of the Dalit ministers.[52]

Hegde was not willing to accept Gowda's suggestion. He insisted that Gowda, who had worked for twenty-one years, should be in the cabinet. Hegde perhaps intuitively understood that Gowda staying outside may not offer stability to the government. Gowda relented and became the minister of irrigation and public works (PWD) minister, a powerful portfolio: 'Bommai demanded industries. Hegde asked me what I wanted? I said, "I won't ask for anything particular. But once you give me a certain portfolio, you should not change it or interfere. I need independence. Of course, if I do not produce results, you can remove me. If you decide to give me agriculture, then horticulture and animal husbandry departments should also be with me." He then offered irrigation and PWD. I again said that I would accept it if it is offered as a consolidated department where minor and major irrigation departments are not split. He agreed,' Gowda remembered.[53]

As soon as Gowda took over, there were nine posts of chief engineers vacant in the irrigation department. He studied the dossiers and annual reports of prospective candidates and found that the Lingayat engineers were rated in superlative terms, and the rest fell into the 'good' or 'satisfactory' category. He decided to redistribute the post on a social justice formula. He went to Hegde and told him how the candidates were graded by the previous regimes and said, that he should be permitted to issue the orders and not the department of personnel (DPR). The reason was that if it went to the DPR, the information would get leaked, and some aspirant or the other would get a stay. The appointments could be made public after the engineers took charge. Hegde understood and gave him the go-ahead. But in the cabinet meeting, Chief Secretary R.A. Naik took up the matter: 'Naik was an upright officer whom I respected. But, he said that never in the history of the state's administration such a thing had happened where the DPR had been bypassed. Hegde quietly placed the file before me. I saw the remarks and got a little irritated, "Hegde-*avare* [a Kannada honorific], let me tell this to your Chief Secretary. If an engineer does not work to the target I set, will he respond in the assembly? If the Chief Secretary agrees to respond to attacks in the assembly, then I will appoint those he suggests. You have given me a department to run. If something goes wrong, I will take full responsibility. I will not shift the blame to you. I know the rules and procedure too, and I did not become a minister overnight." Hegde grasped my mood and moved to the next subject on the agenda. From that moment, I have a feeling, that it got into Hegde's head that I was a hard nut to crack.'[54]

In August 1984, a little before she was assassinated, Indira Gandhi destabilized the N.T. Rama Rao led Telugu Desam government in Andhra Pradesh which enjoyed a full majority. When this happened, Hegde, Bommai and Gowda were in Belgaum and they had a long chat. Gowda told Hegde that he had often referred to 'vultures coming from Delhi' in his speeches, and now, after Andhra Pradesh, they may actually descend on Karnataka. The Hegde government was far easier to destabilize because it was a fragile coalition, and the Congress had already begun snapping at its heels. The Veerappa Moily tape scandal had exploded in November 1983. As the Congress' leader in the assembly, Moily was caught on tape allegedly wooing independent MLAs like C. Byre Gowda, who were supporting the Hegde government, to switch loyalties for a tidy sum.[55] Therefore, the dismissal of the NTR government sent ominous signals. Gowda had a plan. He suggested to Hegde that it would be best if he reshuffled and expanded his cabinet with senior ministers like himself, J.H. Patel and fourteen others stepping out to strengthen the party and get ready for the parliamentary polls scheduled for January 1985,

and also perhaps a possible midterm assembly poll if things went out
of hand. The vacancies created by the exit of seniors could be used
to mollify aspirants in the party. Hegde went ahead with the plan,
and the presidentship of the party returned to Gowda. J.H. Patel
became state general secretary, Bommai continued in the cabinet.
Unexpectedly, Indira Gandhi was assassinated in October 1984,
and Rajiv Gandhi who took over advanced the general elections to
December 1984.

During this stint as party president when Hegde was heading the
government, Gowda started realizing that Hegde's slogan of pursuing
'value-based' politics was an 'image management trick'. Earlier in the
year, when Gowda was still part of the cabinet, he was not happy
with the casual manner in which Hegde had dismissed a serious
complaint about a junior cabinet colleague's midnight outing with a
bunch of college girls in Bangalore. Gowda was informed about this
by B.N. Garudachar, the Bangalore city police commissioner: 'The
commissioner had come to my house at 6 a.m. in the morning to
tell me what had transpired the previous night. I was worried that
it may reach the media. When I spoke to Hegde about this, instead
of feeling alarmed, he said such things were common in politics.
I was shocked. I had been long enough in politics to understand what
was acceptable and what was not,' Gowda recalled.[56] The minister in
question was Hegde's close associate and troubleshooter.

Two other episodes from this period have remain etched in
Gowda's mind. The first had to do with the extension of certain
concessions to the Dolphin car manufacturing company. An agent
for the promoters of the car company came to Gowda and said
that they were struggling and needed a five-year extension to the
concessions that the state government had offered them: 'They
promised to contribute Rs 5,00,000 to our election fund. We had
to fight parliament elections and the party coffers were empty.
I called Hegde about the proposal before me. He lectured me about
'value-based politics' and said doing something like that would give
the government a bad name. I kept quiet.'[57] But after a few days,

the same agent came to Gowda and showed him the certificate of extension. When asked how he had managed it, he said he had got it done through Hegde's secretary Ramappa. In a second similar incident, the federation of housing societies offered a huge donation to the election fund against a few pending clearances: 'Again, I called Hegde. He said such a thing would be contentious. But within a month, he set up a cabinet sub-committee and got it cleared. None of that money got credited to the party account. I stopped sending people to Hegde to raise resources for the party.'[58]

The December 1984 Lok Sabha election was a washout for the Janata Party. B.L. Shankar says that the Congress adopted a simple but emotionally effective campaign strategy. They organized hyperlocal death rituals (*thiti*, as they say in Kannada) for Indira Gandhi who had been assassinated and that included feeding the poor. Like elsewhere in the country, in Karnataka too the Congress swept the seat tally with twenty-four seats out of twenty-eight. Of the four seats that the Janata Party won, three were in the south of Karnataka, which was Gowda's stronghold. Following the results, the threat to the already fragile Hegde government became imminent. The ground reports on MLAs planning to desert the ruling coalition was reaching Hegde and Gowda. At that point, Hegde did what he was most comfortable doing: he said he would take 'moral responsibility' for the defeat and seek a fresh mandate to continue as chief minister. He recommended the dissolution of the assembly. Gowda, the state party president, had to now shoulder the responsibility of another election.

The Janata Party swept the assembly polls and came to power on its own. The Karnataka electorate in a gap of just four months had sent a clear message that they wanted the Congress at the Centre but the Janata Party to continue in the state. That tactical wisdom of the Karnataka voter was subjected to a lot of analysis. The Janata Party got 139 seats out of 224 with an unprecedented 43.6 per cent vote share. The Congress was reduced to sixty-five seats and the BJP to just two. Hegde made the mistake of reading this victory as his personal achievement. One could not discount his contribution to the victory, but in reality, he neither commanded a caste base, nor a region in the state nor the minorities. For all of this, he was solely dependent on people like Gowda, Bommai, Nazir Sab and Dalit leaders like B. Rachaiah. The mainstream press, dominated by Brahmins, which was seen as Hegde's true and only constituency by the Kannada tabloid press, went overboard in showering praise on him.[59] This did not go down well with Gowda: 'When we were defeated in the parliament polls held four months back, the press squarely blamed me as party president, although Hegde was chief minister. Now, when we swept the assembly polls, the press gave the entire credit to Hegde, while I and many others had slogged. I asked my colleagues and myself, how is it that defeat is always attributed to me and success to Hegde. In all fairness, both defeat and victory had to be equally shared. I was naturally upset. I made a statement that this was not an individual's victory but that of the Janata Party workers.'[60]

On the mainstream press and Hegde's hold over them, senior journalist Vaddarase Raghurama Shetty wrote, albeit in a different context: 'Hegde had a great relationship with all senior correspondents of national newspapers and the chief reporters of local newspapers. He would often call them in small groups and have secret strategy sessions with them. People like me who were not privileged to get an invitation, would ridicule these reporters as 'five-star reporters' in Vidhana Soudha's press room.' He also describes how most newspapers lacked diversity and were staffed with people who mostly came from the Brahmin community.[61]

Sindhia and Shankar, who were both eyewitnesses and participants in the cabinet and party proceedings, say that the 1985 election was a result of the stellar work that Gowda and Nazir Sab had done in Hegde's cabinet. The good name that the government earned in rural areas was largely because of the schemes that these two men drew up: 'Gowda used to work for eighteen hours a day. He was possessed. From Kollegal in the south of Karnataka to Aurad in the north, he took up minor and major irrigation works and also built a fine road network across the state. He did not discriminate between the different regions. Nazir Sab as rural development and panchayati raj minister made potable water accessible across the state with borewells and conceived the decentralization of governance, which later inspired the seventy-third amendment to the Constitution. Nazirsab became very popular as 'Neersab' ['neer' in Kannada meaning water],' Sindhia said.[62]

Shankar added: 'If the Hegde government got a pro-development image that was largely due to Gowda and Nazir Sab. This coupled with Hegde's brilliant image and data management worked wonders. Five days before the polls, Hegde felt the party needed an extra two per cent vote swing to get a majority. In consultation with Gowda and other seniors, he released an additional manifesto. The party promised rice for rupees two per kg and a pair of clothes (dhoti and saree) for Rs 25. I was asked to make that announcement in Mangalore. It seemed to have a magical effect on the voter. After the elections, Hegde's popularity reached its peak, and expectedly, he started asserting himself. He also thought it was his leadership that had brought the party to power. Some journalists also wrote on those lines. Hegde also cultivated youngsters in the party, gave them key positions, and kept them on his side. I was made the youth services minister and could see Hegde and Gowda slowly drifting apart. By 1987, the differences between the two became very sharp.'[63]

Gowda got back his irrigation and PWD portfolio and he started making demands for budgetary allocation to complete projects. On one occasion, sometime in 1986, when he had sent a detailed note on how much money would be necessary to complete irrigation projects within the deadlines set by river water tribunals, M. Shankarnarayanan, the finance secretary, had responded 'arrogantly' (see the chapter on irrigation) by saying that the finance department is not a 'Akshaya Patra (an inexhaustible vessel)'. On another occasion, he had said that 'money does not grow on trees'.[64] Gowda had offered to quit the cabinet refusing to be 'taught' by bureaucrats, but Hegde had assuaged him, and a showdown had been narrowly averted. Gowda soon started developing a feeling that Hegde who addressed bureaucrats in their first name (something that Gowda never did however junior they were) was cleverly playing them against him. That he was trying to provoke him through them. But Gowda wrote his long remarks on officers who disregarded him and insisted in cabinet meetings that they should get into their confidential assessment reports.[65]

Gowda also became impatient with Hegde's anglophone think tank, called the 'Economic and Planning Council', which assembled in Bangalore for long 'hot air' sessions from Delhi and Mumbai to delve on aspects of rural governance without an inkling of the ground situation. Hegde primarily created this elite group of experts, intellectuals and friends to expand his influence and national imprint. It was like a 'super cabinet'. The national magazine, *Sunday*, reported: 'The think tank has the ears of the chief minister, who is said to listen avidly and faithfully to its prolonged debates, and of course, he in turn, has the collective ear of the cabinet. That is how many of the think tank's recommendations have found their way into state policy.'[66] In fact, in one such ideation session, the secretary in-charge of rural development wrote a limerick and passed it on to his colleague. If Gowda had read the limerick then, he would be glad that he was not the only one to feel that the think tank was wasting everybody's time: 'The great think tank/Has breached its bank/With a nonstop torrent of words/The little fish cry/As the tank goes dry/And in the sky above circle hungry birds.'[67]

The Personal Attack

Between 1987 and 1988, two incidents—which Gowda thought were targeted personal attacks led by Hegde—deepened the distrust and bitterness between them.

The Hemavathi bridge was being constructed. The iron rods were being welded and cement concrete was being poured. The executive engineer went for an inspection and his junior followed him. The welder, by mistake, had not switched off the power connection. The junior engineer was electrocuted. G. Puttaswamy Gowda, Deve Gowda's arch-rival from his constituency of Holenarasipur, made a wild allegation that Gowda's son Revanna had an illicit relationship with the wife of the junior engineer who had lost his life.

Gowda recalled:

They wanted to arrest my son and finish me politically. They sent a police officer close to the Hegde camp to build up a case against Revanna. R. Jalappa was the home minister. He spoke to labourers on the site; they spoke in the negative. He went to the family, they asked not to 'insult' them with such queries. The investigating officer spoke to the Hassan superintendent of police. He too said he did not smell anything foul. They were hellbent to fix Revanna but were unable to progress because there was no evidence. Then, I called a top intelligence officer. I had helped a few months ago in getting his transfer cancelled. He did not pick my calls. I wanted to understand what was happening. Then I decided to meet Hegde. I called Ramappa, his loyal secretary. He asked me to come to a guest house on Bellary Road where Hegde used to meet his acolytes and friends. As I alighted from my car, I saw the intelligence officer whom I was trying to reach. He was getting into his car. I stopped him. I said, 'I did so much for you and now you don't even pick my calls?' His eyes became moist. 'Is this it or are they trying to do anything else?' I asked. He whispered, 'Keep an eye on the horticulture department labourers who come to clean your garden.' I asked him for more details. He said the plan is to place Rs 25,00,000 in the car garage and then arrest you. I returned without going through with the meeting. Three security people were on duty at my official residence. I told them not to allow any horticulture department labourers inside without thoroughly checking their bags. A couple of days later, I called up Hegde's secretary Ramappa, who was not a Brahmin but came from a backward class community, again, and told him about the plot I had discovered. I said, 'You think I don't get to know the dirty games that your boss plays?' Ramappa heard me out. He was fiercely loyal to Hegde, but was not unsympathetic to me. The murder allegation against Revanna did not take the wings they expected it to take.[68]

Gowda later went to confront Hegde in a room at the government's Kumara Krupa guest house. He was sitting with one leg across the other in 'durbar style'. He was shaking his feet and the slippers were tapping the legs of the table before him. Gowda thought it was not an involuntary action but a deliberate one to communicate his confidence. It was that sound that spoke to Gowda first before they actually exchanged words. Tears welled up in Gowda's eyes: 'I said, I will resign and go back to till my lands in Paduvalahippe. You can tap my phone there. I will keep away from this wretched politics. I also asked why he was trying to do this to me? "I have always stood by you. When nobody was willing to support you in 1983, I mobilized numbers. I antagonized a lot of people for your sake. I gave up my claim to the chief minister's chair just because Chandra Shekhar asked me to stay away. I ran the state unit of the party to my best ability because Morarji trusted it to my care. Now, I am done. You run the government and also save the party," I said,' Gowda recalled.[69]

After some silence, Hegde spoke. Gowda recalled his words: 'He asked if I had understood my enemy. He said my words were my biggest enemy. "You not only try to tell the truth but you try to tell the naked truth. That is your problem. That creates enemies for you," he said. I said I cannot change myself at this stage. I have been brought up in a certain way. I cannot speak one thing in the front, and another behind your back. Resignation is the only solution. Tears were running down my eyes. He said, "No, no. Change your attitude. I will not accept your resignation." I got up and left.'[70]

Just before this, another incident which gave Gowda anxious moments and also scarred him happened early in Hegde's second term. Gowda had got a site allotted in Mysore for his sister-in-law Savitramma, a widow. This was to apparently because he had sold her house to repay loans he had incurred during the assembly elections in 1978:

> There was one Puttaiah, a backward class person. He was my loyalist. He was the chairman of the Mysore City Improvement Trust Board (it became Mysore Urban Development Authority in 1988) and wanted to be an MLC. Since the relationship between Hegde and me had soured, I said my recommendation may not carry any weight. Before he left, he said he was allotting sites in Mysore and that I should take one for myself and reiterated that there was very little demand. Mysore, in the late 1970s, was still a sleepy town. It had not acquired the real estate value it has in the last two decades. I said I don't need one, but if he could, he should help my sister-in-law. He asked for a formal application, which she gave, and in no time the site was allotted. It was one of the 500 sites that he had allotted. There were many politicians too who had got it allotted to themselves, their relatives, friends and followers. The Hegde camp, which was on the prowl, picked this issue up.[71]

The allegation of corruption and nepotism was raised by Gowda's one-time protégé, G. Puttaswamy Gowda, backed by the Hegde camp. To amplify the effect, Puttaswamy Gowda charged that Deve Gowda had got fifty sites allocated. By then, Puttaiah had been replaced by Made Gowda, another Gowda loyalist. He informed Gowda that the Hegde camp had explored the issue six months before it was made public, and they had taken all the relevant files. A. Lakshmisagar was the urban development minister at the time. When the issue came up in the assembly, Gowda did not think twice. He admitted that he had got one site allocated to his sister-in-law and did not know anything about the other forty-nine. He also said that if there was any illegality, they should withdraw the allocation. Until Kadidal Manjappa, the former chief minister and a fellow Vokkaliga elder, read Gowda's statement in the newspapers and called him, he did not realize that Hegde was up to something bigger. Kadidal said: 'What is wrong with you. Why did you make such an admission? That is exactly what Hegde wants. He will destroy you.'[72] As predicted by Kadidal, a complaint was filed before the Lokayukta, which had been newly formed under a retired Supreme Court judge, A.D. Koshal. After conducting a probe, Gowda was indicted for showing favouritism in the allotment of one site and dismissed the charge that he had got forty-nine others allotted[73] (an RTI application in September 2020 to get the original Lokayukta indictment report did not yield results[74]). Finally, when the matter went to Karnataka Governor, P. Venkatasubbaiah, he did not give sanction to prosecute Gowda.

K.A. Thippeswamy, who was Gowda's personal secretary at the time, recalled the trying times. He said those days, people sought letters from elected representatives for allocation of sites in Mysore and in Bangalore. Like any other politician, Deve Gowda too had given recommendation letters:

> They did not bother about the letters that others wrote but targeted only him. The irony was that it was not the Opposition that was attacking Gowda but his own colleagues and chief minister. It was not just on the sites that Puttaswamy Gowda wrote letters; he raised other issues too and alleged corruption. It was a witch-hunt. For instance, Gowda had been compensated, like anybody else, for the land he lost when the main canal of the Hemavathi river was being built. He brought that under scrutiny, although he himself had received such compensation from me as the tahsildar in charge. He made similar allegations against Gowda's cousins. He raised questions about a movie theatre that Gowda's son had built in

Holenarasipur. Hegde's game was clear. He wanted Gowda to
run around defending himself. He wanted to destroy the image
that Gowda had built up as an anti-corruption crusader against
the Devaraj Urs government. This made Gowda very bitter.
I was a witness as to how these charges depressed him. He would
sit up till 2 a.m. to build his defence before the Lokayukta. His
elder son, H.D. Balakrishna, and I would be with him. When
Gowda appeared before Justice Koshal, who was a gentleman,
he was treated with respect. Justice Koshal, in his observations
said politics in Karnataka has become 'murky'. Gowda first did
not understand the word murky. It was a new word for him.
He came home and looked up the dictionary.[75]

The Hegde camp was very unhappy that the Governor had let Gowda
off the hook. They did something mischievous. They apparently got
Bommai to influence B.B. Shivappa of the BJP to raise the issue
again. He charged that the inquiry had not been done properly
and demanded reinvestigation. The moment Hegde received
such a petition, he handed over the investigation to the Corps of
Detectives, the state's investigative agency. This was in the first week
of November 1987:

> I returned home from the Vidhana Soudha at 9.30 p.m. My
> daughters were crying. They told me that the matter had been
> reopened again, and Hegde had announced a fresh inquiry.
> I could not take it anymore. That was the last straw. There was
> a defence guest house near Hegde's house, 229 Krutika, which
> he used for his various activities. I went there at 8 a.m. the next
> day. A boy from my community, Gidde Gowda, used to keep
> watch there. He said, 'sahebru is still sleeping'. I shouted loud
> and said, 'I know what time your saheba slept last night. Go
> wake him up.' When Hegde heard the commotion, he came
> out. He did not sit, neither did I. I asked him point-blank:
> 'Are you trying to finish me? You parachuted from Delhi,

and I made you CM just because of the word I gave Chandra Shekhar. I helped you survive on the chair. You don't seem to have any gratitude. I am your colleague. You should have called and asked me about the charges. You never did. You were waiting to receive the petition from Shivappa and wasted no time in ordering an inquiry. What have I done to you to deserve this humiliation?' I also warned him, 'Beware of Deve Gowda. From now on, it is a dharma *yuddha*. I will never suppress my feelings like I did so far.' Our relationship was quite civilized till then. This was the breaking point.[76]

Gowda sent in his resignation in March 1988. By August 1988, Hegde had to step down as chief minister.

Raghavan and Manor commenting on Hegde agreeing to a second inquiry against Gowda, wrote: 'The political significance of this episode lies in Deve Gowda's anger over what he saw as a conspiracy to finish him politically. He suspected Hegde's involvement. He knew he was not the first or last politician to have done what he was accused of. The issue refused to die down. A BJP legislator raised it again and challenged the chief minister to hold an inquiry. Hegde agreed and promptly turned the evidence over to the Corps of Detectives. This further incensed Deve Gowda who, like anyone else in his position, decided to strike back. His moves were meticulously planned.'[77]

The Long Letters

Gowda had become cautious and watchful of Hegde long before this encounter. He also created anxiety for Hegde on many occasions, and the election of Ram Jethmalani, Hegde's controversial lawyer-friend, to the Rajya Sabha was one such moment in March 1988. This was just before he threw in his resignation. Gowda's fifty loyalist legislators had refused to support the choice of Jethmalani, who those days was actively pursuing the Bofors case against Rajiv

Gandhi. There were many technical and moral questions around his candidature. He was neither a resident nor a registered voter in Karnataka. He had hurriedly registered himself as a voter days before filing his nomination and declared that he was a permanent resident at the Bangalore guest house of the *Indian Express*. Earlier, when Indira Gandhi had contested from Chikmagalur in November 1978, the Janata Party, and Hegde himself, had questioned the fielding of 'outsiders'. Gowda relented only after Madhu Dandavate, who was the observer for the election, placated him, and Chandra Shekhar as national president intervened. Chandra Shekhar had developed antipathy for Hegde by then since Hegde's well-oiled media network had repeatedly projected him as a potential prime minister since 1985. The belief at the time was that Gowda was very close to Chandra Shekhar, and had also established contact with Rajiv Gandhi (see the chapter on the Congress dynasty).[78]

The resignation letter that Gowda wrote on 28 March 1988 was a couple of thousand words.[79] The core of the letter was not a diatribe against Hegde, but he had smartly converted it into a major policy difference between the two. In other words, he spelt out differences in approach and ideas, if not ideology. Speaking about the Cauvery and Krishna water river projects, he charged Hegde with promising funds but deliberately withholding them, and thereby withholding the development of the state. He presented a blow-by-blow account of how Hegde had deceived and dodged him in this regard. Gowda knew that if he made the personal fight public, it would descend into an ugly altercation that the tabloids would fight on their behalf in the gutters. Gowda had always believed that the urgency he had demonstrated to harvest the state's rivers was more useful to the people than Hegde's passion for decentralization of governance through the Panchayat Raj legislation. Gowda had expected his irrigation projects to be the focus of Hegde's administration. This difference and heartburn were genuine, and he used it strategically to camouflage his personal anguish and anger in the resignation letter. The letter, besides serving its original intent, is a fine document on the state's river water projects and disputes.

Hegde spun this resignation letter differently in the media. He said Gowda did not want to resign as a cabinet minister but actually wanted a change in portfolio, which he had agreed to and made a recommendation to the Governor. Gowda was furious with this spin that Hegde had offered. He wrote a short second letter on 29 March 1988 clarifying his intent to get out entirely from the cabinet, and this time simultaneously released it to the media. The last line read: 'I have written this clarificatory letter to inform the people of the state that I have no obsession to be a minister, I am not attached to the chair, and I have no desire to continue in the role.'[80]

After his resignation had been accepted, Gowda wrote another letter dated 19 April 1988. This was longer than his original resignation letter, a few thousand words more, twenty-six pages in all.[81] He attempted to appeal to Hegde's conscience through it. In its original Kannada form, it reads like a great psychological ploy to create a loop of guilt inside Hegde. The letter offered a devastating character sketch of the man and how he was an untrustworthy individual whose private and public personas could not be bridged. The letter opens this way: 'I have wondered about the utility of this letter for many nights, staring emptily at the roof. I did not want to write bitter words, but it is not in my nature to ignore and brush things aside. Therefore, I am writing to get the weight off my chest.' He lists all political favours Hegde had received from him, and yet how ungrateful he had turned out to be: 'To construct your public image you will spend any amount of money from the exchequer. Soon, a day will come when we will have to publicly debate this. But even more wretched is the ease with which you stoop to any level to character assassinate your opponent. . . but be sure that to destroy my personality is not within your capabilities . . . I have total belief in God. My life is not dependent or built on injustices or deceptions like yours. Yet, in the last few months using some of your intimate journalists, courtiers and gossip mongers you have got things written and spread about me. If you do not eschew from this activity to malign me, you should know that my patience too has a limit.'[82]

Gowda continued to mix sarcasm, which comes naturally to him, in the letter: 'I am not highly learned or intelligent like you, but you have subtly painted me as a man with devilish instincts. I am not bothered about that. To your high learning and intelligence, all that I perceived with my limited capabilities as just must have appeared unjust to you. In my behaviour too, you must have seen the absence of refinement and perfection. Even as I reflect on aspects that have harmed the dharma of our friendship, I will benefit hugely if you can tell me the wrongs that I have inflicted on you.'[83]

Then, he begins to recall from their political journey together: 'In 1969, despite all the enticement I did not abandon our democratic mission against the Congress. When nobody agreed to be opposition leader in 1972, when the opposition had only 24 MLAs, I shouldered the responsibility. Although I had not enjoyed power in previous dispensations, I bore the fury and ridicule of the [Devaraj Urs] government. You cannot deny the fact that from 1968 to 1976 Veerendra Patil, you, Bommai and I worked together, and in harmony, to build the party. In 1975, I supported your line of thinking and joined you in prison. You are aware of the pressure I was subjected to, first shockingly by Veerendra Patil, and then by Om Mehta not to be on your side. You also probably remember the efforts I put to make you general secretary of the Janata Party in 1978. Then the stand I took helped you get the Rajya Sabha ticket against Veerendra Patil's claim. You are aware of the personal consequences I had to face as a result of the stand I took, and how I was defamed as "intolerant" by him [Patil].'[84]

All through the letter, there is an attempt to place things on record. He reminds Hegde of the events of 1983 and his selection as chief minister: 'You know there was a contest between Bangarappa, Bommai and me for the chief minister's chair. But on the instructions given by Chandrashekar via a telephone call from Nagercoil [Tamil Nadu], I gave up my claim. When I came to your house that day you were alone. When I asked if you want to be CM, you said I will throw my hat in the ring only if "I have your complete support". Then I asked you to get ready for the next day's battle.'[85]

He plucks out more from his memory: 'When you had a back problem, and you had to go to the US for treatment, I came and told you that you should not have any worry while away, and that I would ensure that there is no threat to the government. During the 1984 Lok Sabha polls, though I was party president you did not keep me informed as to how you collected money for the election. But when the issue came up in the legislative party meeting, you told our colleagues that only yourself, me as president and treasurer were privy to it. How does your conscience permit you to speak like this? The stench of the illegal money you had collected stalked me when opponents in my home district attacked me. Did you take it as my weakness that I did not confront you about this?'[86]

Then Gowda's ire turns towards how Hegde used friendly media to plant rumours and falsehoods to destroy his credibility. How he cleverly sowed the seeds of suspicion between friends to 'divide and rule'. Then he discusses the cases that were foisted against him by his own government and how Hegde had used the inquiry to boost his image as an impartial, value-based administrator.

Finally, he says: 'If it is deeply imprinted in your mind that you can rise and rule by assassinating the character of a person who helped you in your political rebirth, then please continue with it. But I would suggest that you do not shadow-box me, fight me directly if you want to. It would be best and conclusive. . . There shall be no temporary truce between us. That will solve nothing. We have to decide if we have to continue as friends or break the shackles of its traditions. In this regard, whatever is acceptable to you is acceptable to me.'[87]

For Gowda's twenty-six-page letter, Hegde wrote a ten-line response and dispatched it to his Crescent Road bungalow the very next day, that is 20 April 1988. He never specifically addressed the charges Gowda made or his recall of events, but treated them with a general dismissal, which Gowda perceived as arrogance and *niruttara* (an empty response): 'Your 26-page letter has just reached me. I am not sure that if I write a letter as long as the one you have written the knots in your head would dissolve. Sometimes when old knots dissolve they create new ones. I have no knots in my head. That should be evident to you from the manner in which I have treated you in the last five years. A person in whom a devil of doubt has built a nest, such a person will not trust anybody. The biggest tragedy of my life is that the person in whom I had placed trust, and in whose future, competence, character I had great faith, has turned out to be like any other. You have spoken about your immense faith in God repeatedly. Please do what your God asks you to do.'[88]

Gowda's letter-writing skills are well-known in political circles. He writes them first and foremost to petition on something, then to place things on record, and finally, to vent his emotion. This April letter to Hegde had the last two elements on display. He never wrote such a long letter before or after this one. Neither Gowda nor Hegde had made public this letter. In Gowda's six decades in politics, his epistolary literature perhaps extends to thousands of pages.

Hegde's Scams Tumble Out

A little before the Gowda resignation saga started playing out, Hegde had gotten into a spiral of scams and controversies. The 'value-based' politics that he had professed and the morality card he had routinely advanced in the media stood exposed in the courts, but mainstream media was still in love with him. They downplayed the details, shifting the blame on to others, and sometimes suggesting that people around Hegde may be corrupt, but Hegde personally was not. Ravindra Reshme, a botany professor and independent journalist who exposed many of Hegde's scams in the *Lankesh Patrike* then, said:

Within three months of Hegde returning to power in 1985, we exposed the arrack bottling scandal. Excise contractors who

were eligible to get the licences but were denied had filed a
writ petition in the High Court. The contracts had gone to
surrogates of those politically powerful. There were two PILs
also filed. Although we exposed it, not a word appeared in the
mainstream press. It came to light only during the monsoon
session of the Karnataka legislature when A.K. Subbaiah, an
independent MLA and an expelled former president of the state
BJP, created furore. That too did not receive great display in the
newspapers. People who were defending Hegde's government
were top lawyers like Shanti Bhushan and K.K. Venugopal.
Even when the most intense hearings were happening in the
court, the newspapers buried the story. In January 1986,
when the judgment was delivered, the division bench of N.D.
Venkatesh and M. Rama Jois, described the government's
action in strong terms. People who did not read the *Lankesh
Patrike* but only followed the mainstream papers were shocked
as to what this scam was because of which Hegde resigned.[89]

When Hegde resigned, there was talk that Gowda may take over, but
the resignation played out differently in the legislature party meeting.
Some senior ministers in the Hegde camp manufactured melodrama.
There were scenes where some legislators grabbed Hegde's shoes and
put them into their kurta pockets, saying they would return them
only if he promised to withdraw his resignation.[90] Gowda did not go
against the mood of the meeting but instead offered a stellar defence
of the government on the floor of the house, holding forth for a
couple of hours. The opposition Congress praised Gowda on record
for defending Hegde better than his battery of senior lawyers. Hegde
had got back his political power but had lost his moral authority
around that time.[91]

Reshme, recalling the Lokayukta case against Gowda, said: 'After
the complaint in the Lokayukta against Gowda was filed, a complaint
was registered against Hegde's son, Bharat Hegde, in the postgraduate
medical seat scam. That was too much of a coincidence. Everybody

suspected that Gowda was behind it. Bharat Hegde was charged with taking money from an Andhra Pradesh student to facilitate a seat in a private medical college. The commencement of the Lokayukta Act was from 15 January 1986 and these were almost the first two cases. Interestingly, the original Act had the chief minister too under its purview, but after the arrack bottling case surfaced, Hegde quietly amended the act and excluded the chief minister from it. This deserved to be condemned, but those days nobody wrote anything against Hegde.'[92]

Besides the bottling scam and the medical seat scam, the four-acre Revajeetu land scam threw the spotlight on Hegde's son-in-law and daughter. Also, the names of Hegde's family members propped up in the 110-acre NRI housing society scam (popularly known as the Lokhandwala scam). Subramanian Swamy held a press conference in Bangalore and demanded a judicial inquiry into the scams of the Hegde government. The Rajiv Gandhi government responded by setting up the Justice Kuldip Singh Commission of Inquiry.[93] Both Swamy and Gowda had a fine relationship with Rajiv Gandhi (see the chapter on the Congress dynasty). The findings of the Commission were severe and blew the lid off Hegde's carefully cultivated image. It wrote: 'That the decision of the BDA [Bangalore Development Authority] dated July 3, 1987 approving the allotment of 110 acres of land in the name NRIHA (K) [NRI Housing Association (Karnataka)] was to the knowledge of Hegde. That it was further to the knowledge of Hegde that the NRIHA (K) was a non-existent body and it was a false front set up by Lokhandwala to grab the multi-crore NRI housing project. That in spite of Hegde's knowledge that the NRIHA(K) was a false front behind which Lokhandwala was operating, he did not take any action to stop the fraud from being perpetuated. By deliberate in-action on his part Hegde abetted the commission of the fraud by Lokhandwala.'[94] On Hegde's son-in-law, Manohar Lal Nichani, the commission said: 'Nichani used his influence as son-in-law of the chief minister to help Lokhandwala procure the 110 acres NRI housing project from the BDA.'[95]

What role did Gowda play in setting up this commission? Did he, with his wide network and experience, pull out facts and files related to Hegde's misdeeds? There is total silence, but the general perception is that since Hegde went after Gowda, and got personal too, he was left with little choice but to fix him. Gowda's role is acknowledged in the memoirs of Roxna Swamy, Swamy's wife, where she says: 'Swamy proceeded to rub salt in Hegde's wounds. Through his Gowda [Vokkaliga] contacts in the Bangalore land department, Deve Gowda already at the receiving end of Hegde's intrigues, obtained and handed over to Swamy reams of documents on land scams in which Hegde appeared to have specialized, thereby enabling his son-in-law to corner Government land at dirt cheap price and then sell them to builders at a huge profit. From this mountain of documents Swamy selected the two most promising and well documented, which later became notorious as the "NRI land deal" involving prime Government land in Bangalore and Mysore, practically gifted to an NRI Co-operative Society.'[96]

In the mid-1980s the camp followers of Hegde and Gowda had spun many jokes around them. Some of them have survived and mutated, but many have been forgotten. One of them went like this: 'Once Hegde invites Gowda to play chess. Gowda agrees. Hegde goes in to get a glass of scotch whisky for himself. Meanwhile, party workers gathered there advise Gowda not to play the game because his defeat at the game of chess with Hegde was imminent. They quickly tell him to invite Hegde for a game of football. When Hegde returns, Gowda suggests a football game, but Hegde backs out.'[97] If chess symbolized Hegde's sophistication and polish in playing the mind game, football suggested the physical stamina and rough edges of Gowda. But by 1988, Hegde had been checkmated by Gowda. Not only did Gowda play football well but had convinced everybody around that he had mastered the chess game too.

Even as scams and inquiries were gathering steam against Hegde, it was the telephone-tapping scandal that finally put him at the precipice of his political career. On 10 July 1988, the *Indian*

Express published a full-page telephone conversation between Gowda and Ajit Singh, the son of Chaudhary Charan Singh and then the president of the Janata Party. It was not so much the conversation that stirred people but the fact that the administration systematically monitors and hears calls. For nearly a month, Hegde was in denial mode until the issue came up in the Parliament and dramatically turned against him. Gowda and Hegde's colleagues, Prof. Madhu Dandavate and C. Madhava Reddy, raised it with the hope that it would put the Rajiv Gandhi government in the dock, but it boomeranged. They asked on 9 August 1988: 'Will the Minister of Communications be pleased to state: (a) whether Government have seen recent press report regarding tapping of the telephonic talks held between political leaders; (b) if so, the facts thereof; (c) whether such talks are tapped by the Telephone Department and if so, under whose instructions; and (d) if not, whether Government propose to get this investigated through an independent agency as to why the talks were tapped and at whose instance?'[98]

Bir Bahadhur Singh, the Union minister for communications, responded:

Yes, sir. Government has seen a report in the *Indian Express* dated 10 July 1988 regarding the tapping of a telephonic conversation between Shri Ajit Singh and Shri Deve Gowda. (b) and (c). numbers 73835, 77611 and 77175 at Bangalore stood in the name of Shri Deve Gowda, then Minister in the Government of Karnataka. By an order dated 30th August, 1985, the DIG of Police, Intelligence, Government of Karnataka directed that telephone messages passing through telephone Nos. 73835 and 77611 should be intercepted. By order dated 30th June, 1986, the said DIG of Police directed that interception in respect of telephone No. 73835 may be cancelled. By order dated 6th January, 1988, the Special IG of Police Intelligence, Government of Karnataka, directed interception in respect of telephone No. 77175. By order

dated 11th July, 1988, the said Special IG of Police directed
that interception may be cancelled in respect of telephone No.
77611. By order dated 27th July, 1988, the said Special IG of
Police, directed that interception in respect of telephone No.
77175 be cancelled.[99]

The response was a bombshell. When there was a commotion in
the house as members tried to ascertain if it was the Centre or the
state that had ordered the tapping, Prime Minister Rajiv Gandhi
intervened and said: 'Let me assure the hon. member that no
telephone of any politician has been tapped by us at the Centre. Let
me assure the member . . . what has happened in Karnataka, as far as
I believe, is outside the purview of the Act, of the law. He [Hegde]
could not have asked for the telephones of politicians to be tapped
but he has asked for it to be done. Karnataka has violated the rules
under that Act. We will definitely look into what has happened. Not
only that, sir; we will amend the rules, if required, to see that such
violations cannot take place again.'[100]

The minister elaborated on his earlier response: 'Sir, I want to
tell the hon. member that a number of telephones, about 51 to be
exact, were being tapped out of which some telephones belonged to
members of Parliament.'[101] In the names he read out, besides Gowda,
it had the name of Gowda's eldest son H.D. Balakrishna, the leader
of Opposition Veerappa Moily, former chief minister R. Gundu Rao,
P. Lankesh, the editor of *Lankesh Patrike* that was exposing scams
against Hegde, A.K. Subbaiah who was vocal against Hegde, B.L.
Shankar, the Congress (I) legislature office and the RSS office among
others. Hegde had no option but to resign the next day. The vow
that Gowda had made in March had been fulfilled. S.R. Bommai
replaced Hegde, but he did not last long. Gowda had a major role in
his exit too (see chapter on the Congress dynasty).

The 1989 assembly elections were a disaster for both the Janata
Party and Gowda, who lost the assembly polls for the first time in
nearly thirty years as people were fed up with the infighting in the

Janata Party. Gowda and Hegde's old friend, Veerendra Patil, became chief minister with an overwhelming majority. Hegde went ahead and made Bangalore the launchpad for the Janata Dal experiment nationally with V.P. Singh as its face. However, Gowda and Chandra Shekhar stayed away. The Janata Party split again.

The Reconciliation That Did Not Last

After the defeat, and by 1991, it had dawned on both Hegde and Gowda that they need to come together to bring the party back to power. B.L. Shankar recalled the reconciliation process:

In 1991, just before the parliamentary polls, Jeevaraj Alva from Hegde's side and I on Gowda's behalf decided that we should do something to bring the two leaders together. Hegde liked me but was also upset because I had gone with Gowda and had contested against him in the 1989 assembly polls in Bangalore's Basavangudi constituency. When we spoke to Hegde, he was not stubborn. Since everybody had lost, there was a willingness to compromise. He said he had only one condition, that he would meet Gowda at a neutral venue, and not his home, 229 Kruthika. He was personally hurt as much as Gowda was but would not display it. His face would turn red at the mention of Gowda and he would quietly light up a cigarette. We had a common astrologer-friend Ravinarayan, who ran a software company. He was close to Gopal, Hegde's son-in-law (married to his second daughter Samata). We planned to bring the two together at Gopal's house. There was Hegde, Gowda, Ravinarayan, Alva and I. Gowda was very quiet. He is very quiet in the presence of those he has fought bitterly with. He needs somebody to speak on his behalf. Hegde was naturally reticent. We broke the ice. Then they spoke. Gowda, in his typical style, chose to blame the planetary movements. In Kannada, he used words like 'vidhi, vishaghalige, kettaghalige'

(meaning destiny, bad time, inauspicious moment), and in the
interest of party workers the two should forget their differences.
After that, there were two or three more meetings. Finally, it
was agreed that the Janata Dal would have an alliance with the
newly formed party of Gowda, and offer it five seats to contest.
After the polls, the party would merge with the Janata Dal.[102]

In the 1994 assembly polls, the Janata Dal led by Gowda swept the
polls, and he became chief minister. Hegde was sent to the Rajya
Sabha since he had lost the 1991 parliamentary polls from Bagalkot
when Gowda had made his parliamentary debut from Hassan.
Nobody expected the events of 1996, which catapulted Gowda to the
prime minister's chair (see the chapter on Gowda becoming prime
minister). Hegde was left very bitter by the development. Shankar,
who became the all-powerful parliamentary secretary to Gowda as
prime minister, recalled:

> Hegde made a statement as soon as Gowda was declared prime
> minister by the United Front. He said he could not bear to see
> someone like Gowda occupy Jawaharlal Nehru's chair. That
> statement implied a lot of things to someone like Gowda.
> He was very badly hurt. He wondered why Hegde made the
> statement when he knew his work for decades. It haunted him.
> Nehru had caste, dynasty, foreign education, right associations
> in history, and also had his own capacity and charm. Gowda
> had none. He was an ordinary man, had worked hard, had a
> sharp mind, and his elevation was the beauty and triumph of
> democracy. Hegde, who had fought the Congress till then,
> had belittled himself. In Nehru's chair, others too had sat—
> Morarji, Charan Singh, V.P. Singh, Chandra Shekhar and
> Vajpayee (for thirteen days). By making the statement, Hegde
> portrayed Gowda as the poorest choice among them all. He
> was a Shudra; he had seen poverty; he was a small farmer;
> the implications of the statement were very big on his mind.

Mentally, I would say, for a few days, he slipped into the Babu Jagjivan Ram state of mind. He, too, was extremely bright and deserved to be prime minister but had been discriminated against because he was a Dalit. He was in limbo because he was neither acceptable to the Ambedkarites nor the Congress. Gowda thought he was being meted out the same treatment. He went into depression. He went into a loop repeating Hegde's statement to his colleagues and repeatedly asking if it was fair. Hegde had destroyed the joy of the moment when he had become chief minister and now when he had become prime minister. He kept saying, 'This is very cruel.' It was also true. Many of us who knew Hegde were surprised. It was not his true nature or character to issue a statement like that. He was sophisticated in his use of language and was refined in his tastes. Within the national Janata Dal and among coalition partners, nobody liked what Hegde had said. They saw it as a statement against the majority of India that was rural, poor and non-English. When democracy should have been celebrated, Hegde had played for the dynasty and that was a wrong move. Gowda did not have media on his side to offer this spin. He was an outsider for them, although he was a true mass leader. It is another thing that this statement of Hegde drove Gowda to do exemplary work as prime minister. The thought that Hegde can be expelled first came to Gowda. S.R. Bommai, Lalu Prasad Yadav and others stood by him.[103]

A letter was prepared recounting Hegde's anti-party activities before and after the election. The one who complained was C.M. Ibrahim, who was a minister in Gowda's cabinet and also the Karnataka president of the Janata Dal. According to Shankar, the letter was typed in the prime minister's residence in the presence of another close Gowda aide and Shankar. At 2 am, Ibrahim carried the letter to Bihar Bhavan to get it endorsed by Lalu Yadav, the national president of the party. He woke up and signed the letter. Hegde went out, formed his own front, and then aligned with the BJP, making it a prominent player in Karnataka, which it was not until then.[104]

'Ibrahim, who had an early morning flight to Kochi, woke up J.H. Patel, chief minister of Karnataka, at 5.30 am. Patel was camping in Delhi. He heard the news from Ibrahim and went back to sleep, telling his attender not to wake him up. He was otherwise scheduled to take a flight back to Bangalore early in the morning. Bommai had developed differences with Hegde at that point. Gowda knew that Patel would not be on his side, so he took Bommai into confidence. If the two had not agreed, Hegde could not have been expelled,' Shankar remembered. Apparently, Bommai was upset with Hegde because he had planted a news item on his money transactions after he had welcomed Gowda's elevation as prime minister and joined the central cabinet.[105]

The expulsion drew the curtains permanently on the Gowda–Hegde relationship, which had had a roller-coaster ride for nearly three decades. The Janata Dal was an idea, and a party, that Hegde had nurtured by bringing together anti-Congress leaders and Congress rebels like V.P. Singh. He had thought it would one day make him prime minister, but in Gowda's language, it was destined otherwise. Interestingly, before Hegde, Devaraj Urs was spoken of as a potential prime minister who could replace Indira Gandhi. People thought Hegde may replace Rajiv Gandhi. Though Gowda had been in a formal and informal opposition role to both Urs and Hegde, he was never ever spoken of as prime minister. But eventually, it was he who had emerged as a dark horse, or was that a destiny's horse?

Immediately after his expulsion, in October 1996, Hegde tried to blow up Gowda's image yet again by getting an expelled former BJP MP, and a maverick professor of economics, K. Venkatagiri Gowda, to release a scurrilous booklet titled *H.D. Deve Gowda: The King of Corruption and the Unmaking of India*. He attempted to play two men from the same caste (Vokkaliga) against each other. According to Gowda, he had an intelligence report that a booklet with a litany of unsubstantiated charges was being 'manufactured' in Hegde's house.

He remained alert.[106] He knew that the booklet was being typed by a person called Nagaraju, and that Jeevaraj Alva, Hegde's confidante, was handling the professor, besides arranging for the booklet to be printed in Chennai. As soon as they released it, Gowda's son moved the court in Bangalore, which restrained 'republishing and distribution' of the copies.[107] However, it made national news and was an unnecessary distraction in Gowda's finest hour.

This professor had been a friend of Gowda and they had fallen out over a petty matter.[108] He had been expelled by the BJP in 1995 for his outbursts against L.K. Advani. Interestingly, or rather funnily, the book was dedicated to two South Korean dictators, Chun Doo Hwan and Roh Tae Woo. The dedication read: 'The two South Korean corrupt dictators who were awarded death sentence and life sentence respectively by a Seoul Court and whose fate — death and disgrace — it is hoped, will serve as a stern warning to the predatory political fatcats of India like Deve Gowdas, Sukh Ramsd [sic], Laloos, Satish Sharmas. Hawala tainted heroes and others of their detested tribe against unbridled black money and black asset accumulation with impunity.' The self-published booklet's central argument was that Gowda who had only 'three acres of dry land and an old house in a state of dilapidation in Hardanahalli village' at the beginning of his political career had become a 'multi-crore monster', and that he held his properties *benami* (through surrogates). The narrative was incoherent without actually identifying who the surrogates were. It made cheap and defamatory remarks against Gowda's wife, Channamma [sic], and called Gowda 'henpecked': 'She rules supreme in the household and her word is "Magna Carta" . . . Is she Lady Macbeth? Yes, in a sense, she is,' he wrote.[109] Amidst all the serious matters supposedly discussed in the booklet, the professor gets excited that the word 'prime minister' has thirteen letters 'each representing a coalition partner'. Gowda's United Front government had thirteen alliance partners. Along with this book, Professor Gowda published another thin volume, titled *From Order to Anarchy: Politics and Economics of the United Front Government*.

Hegde's Last Days and Death

After the United Front government fell in 1998, and Vajpayee became prime minister for thirteen months after his thirteen-day stint before Gowda, Hegde, who had partnered with BJP in Karnataka, became commerce minister. He did not contest the February 1998 election, but was in the third year of his six-year Rajya Sabha term. Even then Gowda had full information on Hegde and his activities. Hegde used to go to the US via Singapore to see his new partner who had delivered twins there. 'When Vajpayee's government fell by one vote in 1999, Hegde attempted to prop up an alternate government by approaching the Left and other regional parties. Vajpayee came to know of this and was terribly disappointed with Hegde. He immediately recommended the dissolution of the Parliament and went for fresh elections. After he came back to power in April 1999, he did not entertain Hegde. That was the end of Hegde's political career. He was loyal to nobody,' Gowda recalled.[110]

There is one interesting anecdote from the time that Hegde was commerce minister. Gowda accidentally was seated next to him in an Air India flight between Bangalore and Delhi. The airlines 'unthinkingly' had allocated seats next to each other. Gowda, who had SPG (special protection group) security as former prime minister, was the last to board, and since there was no seat vacant, he had to sit next to Hegde. They were meeting each other for the first time after the expulsion episode, and it was embarrassing for both of them: 'I said, "*namaskara, saar.*" He did not respond. During the entire duration of the flight, he kept himself busy with magazines and newspapers. At one point, I tried to start a conversation, but he turned his face. I left it at that.'[111] Even if they had spoken, one wonders what they would have spoken!

After 2000, Hegde's health started deteriorating rapidly. When he was on his death bed, sometime in December 2003, Gowda went to see him in the hospital. Hegde's wife Shakuntala Hegde was present. The boy who typed the noxious booklet by Venkatagiri

Gowda was also in the room. He did not sit on the chair meant for visitors but sat at the edge of Hegde's bed, at his feet: 'I spoke about facing death. I spoke about karma. I said, "You may be the one to go now, I too will have to follow soon." He heard everything but did not respond. As I was leaving the hospital, M.P. Prakash, our party colleague, told me that media waiting outside was keen to have my comments. I left without uttering a word.'[112]

When Hegde passed away a month later, on 12 January 2004, Gowda checked with Mrs Hegde if he could come to pay his last respects: 'Shakuntala Hegde started crying on the phone. I said I have not stepped into your house after our showdown. I don't want to hurt you and your children by coming there. She said, "Don't speak like that, please come." I went. I paid my respects. Sat alone in a corner for forty-five minutes. Nobody, not even my past party colleagues, spoke to me. I told whatever I had to tell the media and came home. I again sought permission from the family to attend the cremation the next day. I sat with common people. My political colleagues were in an enclosure opposite me. Hegde's face had blackened. When the rituals were drawing to a close, Mrs Hegde sent for me. I was the last to perform the ritual of putting rice into his mouth.[113] Then, the body was kept on the pyre. They all left; I stayed back as the flames went up. I had tears in my eyes. How badly he had hurt me and how bitterly we had fought. Only death had put an end to everything.'[114] Death did not put an end to everything. The memories of his many clashes with Hegde still rankle Gowda's guts.

7

A Lonely Phase, Unpredicted

In the previous chapter, we discussed the reconciliation between Deve Gowda and Ramakrishna Hegde after the defeat of 1989. In some ways, it was inevitable to go ahead of the story to ensure that there was no rupture to the dramatic flow of an epic tale. But it is important to go back a bit to look closely at the defeat itself, and what it did to Gowda, and how his emotional and electoral rebirth was constructed.

Gowda had not joined the Janata Dal formed in October 1988 but had contested on the Janata Party ticket (in the Election Commission records, a variant of the original party). Out of the 224 seats, the party had put up candidates in 217 constituencies. A couple of days before the poll results were announced, Gowda was in New Delhi and a close aide recalled that Subramanian Swamy was repeatedly assuring him that he would be next chief minister of Karnataka. Gowda, who was far more aware of the reality, had demonstrated visible signs of tension.[1] On the day before the results, without informing anybody in Delhi, forgetting his spectacles and briefcase behind, he just flew to Bangalore to confront the devastating results the next day. He had contested from two seats (Kanakapura in Bangalore rural district and Holenarasipur) and had been defeated by his one-time protégés—P.G.R. Sindhia and G. Puttaswamy Gowda. Sindhia had moved over to the Hegde camp, and Puttaswamy had been given a Congress ticket.

The election strategy of the two former protégés was simple. If Sindhia argued before the people that Gowda was sure to give up Kanakapura for Holenarasipur after he wins both seats, Puttaswamy argued in Holenarasipur that since Gowda is likely to win Kanakapura, they should elect him this one time.[2] The result was that Gowda lost both seats. In Kanakapura, he went to third place with only 22.48 per cent vote share, while Sindhia got nearly double — 40.70 per cent. In his home constituency, he had come second, but the margin of victory was over 8000 votes.[3] This was Gowda's first electoral defeat since 1962. In 1978, when the Janata Party had done badly against Devaraj Urs's Congress, he had still retained his seat. But now, after the showdown with Hegde, he had lost. Interestingly, Hegde, who had needed the Gowda crutches to electorally survive, had retained the Basavanagudi seat in the heart of Bangalore, which he had adopted in 1985. That was some consolation for a former chief minister, but the Janata Dal he had forged with V.P. Singh five months back had lost badly. It had only got twenty-four of the 224 seats, making way for a massive 178-seat victory for the Congress. Only two of Gowda's Janata Party colleagues won—C. Byre Gowda from Vemgal, and M.P. Venkatesh from the reserved Heggadevanakote seat. The BJP got only four seats in that election. While Gowda had been clearly defeated, Hegde could not claim victory.

After the 1978 defeat of the Janata Party, Gowda had withdrawn and packed himself off to till the lands in Paduvalahippe village, but this time he lived an isolated life in a house in Bangalore's Lower Palace Orchards, near the Mahalakshmi temple. Isolation meant that his wife and children too stayed away from him. The children had grown up by now, they were independent, and the wife went to live with their elder daughter in a different locality of Bangalore. There was nobody to even cook a meal for him, nor could he afford to appoint a help. Family was Gowda's only support and now he was aloof. He had no other diversions or indulgences like business, racing, club-hopping, cricket, concubines, travel or alcohol. There was no concept of reading or music purely as a pastime. He was never part of the leisure society. He was like a blinded horse on the political turf, but now politics had vaporized. The only association he had was the party, and that was broken. He suddenly felt cleaned out of his existence than lonely. All the purpose that surrounded him had vanished. Each morning, he bundled his loneliness and placed it at the feet of the goddess next door. He stood before the deity and mumbled his woes, without even hoping that the constellations will align again. He just needed to unburden the weight on his head, not seek deliverance because he thought there was no deliverance. People were quick to write Gowda's political obituary, but only a couple of them who interacted with him during that phase knew the situation was far graver.[4]

Why did Gowda choose to live a solitary existence? That is a question that has not been answered convincingly or conclusively by either Gowda or his associates. Gowda was in the habit of borrowing money to fund his elections. It was a kind of gamble that had paid off till then. During the 1989 election, too, apparently, he had borrowed heavily because he was operating on his own. According to a version, the family was not willing to share the responsibility of repayment or the consequences of non-payment. The one thing about Gowda and loans was that he was a stickler who believed in repaying the last paisa. There was a religious belief behind this. He was afraid that the burden of the unpaid loan would affect his karmic cycle.

B.L. Shankar, who was with him during those difficult days, recalled: 'The two-bedroom house that Gowda stayed near the Mahalakshmi temple belonged to a Mandya contractor. He was staying all alone. His wife was with their elder daughter. His food had to come either from well-wishers or from a nearby restaurant. Many nights he would just eat curd-rice and sleep. He did not have a telephone. If he had to make a trunk call or an STD call, he had to go to the house of J.P. Narayanswamy, a businessman. At times, he would sit there from morning till evening and make calls, which naturally annoyed them. There was one L.R. Srinivas, a Vijaya Bank employee, who would drop in to check on him occasionally. I, too, would occasionally take him to Chit-Chat, a restaurant on MG Road. We would have sandwiches and a single scoop of ice-cream. When he seemed to have normalized his loneliness after nearly a year, I would pull him out to see action movies at the Rex and the Galaxy. If at all Gowda had a weakness for something, and if it could be called so, it was Chinese food and action movies. It pepped him up in a limited way. Chinese food was what Hegde had introduced him to at the Mandarin restaurant in Delhi.'[5] K.A. Thippeswamy, who had been Gowda private secretary, had found a new government posting, but he too used to check on him: 'Those were very, very hard times,' Thippeswamy emphasized.[6]

Gowda recalled how God came to his 'rescue' one day during that phase of his life: 'I was completely drained out. I still had to pay a rent of Rs. 3200 for the two-bedroom house. Each morning I would be the first worshipper at the Mahalakshmi temple next door. I would ask the goddess as to why she was putting me through this test. Once, when I returned from the temple, and the constable at the door, Bore Gowda, had gone to get breakfast from a nearby restaurant, an old friend whom I had helped in the early 1970s walked in. He said he'll give me some money every month to rebuild the party and my political career. I felt he was God's messenger. This friend was a Tamilian, and he had set up a professional college in the outskirts of Bangalore when Devaraj Urs was chief minister. He was being harassed by a minister to pay a monthly donation (*hafta*). I had spoken to Urs and threatened to move a censure motion against the minister. Urs had ensured that the harassment was stopped. Nearly fifteen years later, when this friend learnt that I was in difficulty, he had been sent by God to help me. I had no option but to accept the help.'[7]

When Gowda was in political wilderness, V.P. Singh had become prime minister, and Hegde the deputy chairman of the

Planning Commission. That political experiment did not last long as Chandra Shekhar and Devi Lal splintered to rework their faction of the old Janata Party in 1990. They formed a government with outside support of the Congress party. Both wanted Gowda to join the Union cabinet, but he was not enthusiastic.[8] However, with no other option, he merged his faction of the Janata Party with that of Chandra Shekhar. By then, B.L. Shankar and Jeevaraj Alva had initiated a reconciliation process with Hegde (read the Hegde chapter). When the 1991 general elections came, Gowda was reluctant, yet desperate for a political rebirth. He decided to contest the Hassan parliamentary seat because the assembly polls were over three years away. State politics was still an unfinished business for him, but he had no option but wait. When Gowda contested the Hassan parliamentary seat as a Janata Party candidate with an electoral alliance with the Janata Dal, Hegde too decided to contest the Bagalkot parliamentary seat. This time, Gowda won and Hegde lost. But Gowda's victory was not easy. He had to sweat it out. Rajiv Gandhi's assassination postponed the polling day for a fortnight and the situation became complicated.

There was sympathy for the Congress everywhere, and Gowda was caught in a whirlpool. The Congress, by way of campaigning, had started performing death rituals with accompanying feasts (what is called *tithi* in Kannada) for Rajiv Gandhi. It was a repeat of their campaign strategy in 1984 when Indira Gandhi had been assassinated. Gowda was aghast. For twelve to thirteen days, he did not put his head on a pillow. He slept in his car. He was pitted against H.C. Srikantaiah, a formidable Congress rival and a fellow Vokkaliga. He would take a bath and get into the car, and go from village to village. He would hold small street-corner meetings. He had no resources for big rallies. If it was late in the evening, he would literally wake people up and seek their support. His supplication for votes had an anxious ring, and people responded well to this anxiousness. They saw their own selves, their own perennial condition in him. He knew that the battle was very close, and he knew it was his last chance. It was not just about his revival as a politician; it was about life and death. If he lost that election, it would all be over. Wherever he was when the day broke, he would get into somebody's house, take a bath, have a little to eat, and then get into the car again. He had no designated halting place.[9] He had two drivers travelling with him. It was a struggle. On the day of counting, as anticipated, the suspense would not end soon. The results took a while to come out.

B.L. Shankar explained what happened on the counting day in Hassan:

The margin became very narrow. It came down to 3191 votes. Counting was happening at the Hassan engineering college. Congress leaders were sure of their victory. In Channarayapatna taluk, there is a Dandidganahalli hobli, part of the Holenarasipur assembly constituency. In that hobli, there were about ten to eleven booths, and nearly 100 per cent voting had taken place. When those votes were counted, more than 90 per cent went in Gowda's favour. If those votes were counted, Gowda was certain to win. If they were kept out, he was sure to lose. IAS officer N. Sivasailam was the returning officer. He followed the rule book. He said according to the election manual, if in a particular booth more than 90 per cent voting had happened, and if 90 per cent of that vote had gone to one candidate, and if that eventually turned out to be the margin of victory, then those votes cannot be counted. It was 2 a.m.

Gowda was crestfallen. He did not understand why God was testing him in this fashion. Sivasailam was in the mood to declare the poll and wind up the process. We wanted it to be delayed. We wanted to find an excuse to stop him from declaring the results and buy ourselves time to think. As a returning officer, Sivasailam had used students of the Malnad engineering college for the tabulation of votes. They were not authorized by the Election Commission. We raised objection and started fighting. Chandra Shekhar was the caretaker prime minister. I told Gowda that this will not get solved until we spoke to Chandra Shekhar. Gowda asked who could possibly speak to him at that hour. I was close to Chandra Shekhar and I volunteered to do so. Two to three km away from the counting centre, there was a house with a telephone. It was that of the brother of Malleshanna, a close friend of Gowda, who was in the horticulture department. I reached there around 2.30 a.m. and called Chandra Shekhar. Durga Singh, his personal assistant, answered the call. He knew me. I told him I need to speak to Chandra Shekharji urgently. He said he was resting. I said it is very urgent. Durga Singh did me a favour. He woke up Chandra Shekhar. I briefed the prime minister on what had happened. I said if all votes polled were not counted, Gowda was sure to lose. I suggested he may have to speak to T.N. Seshan, the chief election commissioner. He asked me to be on the line. He called Seshan on the hotline (what was known as the rack system), but the call was not answered. Then he called a senior cabinet colleague. I overheard him instruct that colleague to drive down to Seshan's place, wake him up, and ask him to quickly examine the issue and instruct the Hassan returning officer. The prime minister asked for my contact number. He said, 'Don't move from that place, I will call you.' He called back in forty minutes, and said that Seshan will instruct the returning officer shortly but asked me to ensure that the results are not declared by then. I went back to the counting centre and as assured, the instruction came. The returning officer was asked to count all the votes. Sivasailam said, 'Mr Shankar, I have to obey instructions, but I will leave a detailed note behind on these developments. Your boss' election may be challenged in court.' I said, 'Please do what you have to but declare the results.' Sivasailam was an upright officer. He wrote his report and declared the results around 4 a.m. Gowda smiled for the first time after 1989. He had got 26,07,61 votes and his Congress rival was close behind at 25,75,70. It was nothing short of a rebirth.[10]

The election was not challenged as feared.

What if Gowda had lost that election would remain a classic 'what if' question. But once Gowda entered the Parliament, he acquired a new stride and confidence. His exposure widened. He was back in mainstream politics again, and became a nationally known state leader. Until that point, whatever his political achievements and experience were, he was confined to the state. This election also revived hope of his chief ministerial dreams. In Delhi too, as a first-time MP, he did not have it easy for the first eight months. He used to be alone. He did not have friends. He stayed at the Karnataka Bhavan until the 5, Safdarjung Lane residence was allotted. When that happened, Haranahalli Ramaswamy, a senior Congressman and legislator, who was visiting Delhi, insisted Gowda should throw a party. For both Gowda and Ramaswamy, a party would mean only a grand vegetarian meal. Gowda himself went to the market and bought vegetables and ghee. His wife made ash gourd curry, puliyogare (rice made with tamarind paste and south Indian spices) and onion fritters, among other dishes that day.[11] A semblance of normalcy had come back into his life.

Before shifting into his new home, Gowda had a surprise visitor at the Karnataka Bhavan—Gujarat chief minister Chimanbhai Patel. He had come to say he will commit regular funds to rebuild a strong political third force in Karnataka. He also offered help during the assembly elections: 'I said, "Sir, you should have sent word for me, and I would have come. You are a chief minister. You should not have taken the trouble to come here." It was all God's play.'[12]

In 1993, a year before the assembly polls, Gowda merged his party with the Janata Dal and became the state president, yet again. With Congress in total disarray—it had seen three chief ministers in four years—the countdown for Gowda to become chief minister had begun. After the 1991 victory, the family came together again. In fact, he had reached out to them before the polls and told them that this would be his very last gamble. Gowda kept the house where he had isolated himself in Lower Palace Orchards as a grim reminder of the hard times till he became chief minister in 1994.[13]

After 1989, defeat came to Gowda mostly in a decennial cycle. He lost the parliamentary polls in 1999. Again, he lost one seat of the two Parliament seats he contested in 2004. In 2019, when he vacated the Hassan seat for his grandson and contested from Tumkur, he lost. To put it in a Tolstoyian idiom, each defeat had its own reason, but all his victories were alike. But there was no defeat like 1989. After 1989, all defeats for Gowda were akin to losing a kabaddi match. He did not lose sleep. He knew he will win the next round and bounce back. It is perhaps this 1989 moment that gave him the confidence in 1997, when he lost the prime ministership, to say that he will rise from the ashes again like a phoenix. For him, everything seemed to be a preparation for an event that the Gods had planned and the planets had sewn into the fabric of his life.

Planets And Predictions

It is no secret that Gowda has faith in astrology and cultivates astrologers. The only difference between him and other politicians is that he does not hide his indulgence, while others wear a mask of reason. Indira Gandhi, Morarji Desai, Chandra Shekhar and P.V. Narasimha Rao, all had their favourite astrologers and spent hours reading planetary movements to plan political moves. For their uncertain and stressful existence, astrology is perhaps a therapeutic concession. It builds a simple inventory of good and bad time, and helps rationalize victory and defeat. It also helps construct hope outside the limits of human reason and a cushion for an imminent fall. It is also like a gamble and a lottery, when you are always drawn one last time and think, it may be true this one time.

One is not sure if Gowda's 1989 crisis was predicted, but P.G.R. Sindhia speaks of two experiences from 1978, the first time Gowda was politically down, and later in 1993, when he was unsure what the 1994 assembly polls had in store for him. In 1978, the year the Janata Party had lost the assembly polls in Karnataka, Srinivas Prasad, a prominent Dalit politician, was getting married in Mysore. He invited Gowda, the party president, and Sindhia, his good friend. Gowda and Sindhia drove in a Plymouth car that had been at the party's disposal to Mysore. The wedding was over by 11 a.m. After that, Gowda went into a house in a Mysore locality, asking Sindhia to wait outside: 'I waited outside smoking. Gowda did not come out of the house for a good three hours. When he finally emerged, I was feeling hungry, so we went to Dasaprakash restaurant and had lunch. On our way back to Bangalore, somewhere near Srirangapatna, the car broke down. While our resourceful driver was trying to fix it, Gowda and I were stuck under a tree for two hours. I mustered the courage to ask Gowda, 'Where did you go? Why did you take so long?' He revealed it was the house of one Achyuta Shastry, and he knew him since 1962. I asked, "What did he say?" Gowda swore me to confidence and said, "Devaraj Urs may not last long as chief minister and he may also not live long." Shastry had advised Gowda to stay quiet and do nothing politically while the cosmos was plotting his revival. He had asked him to come back in September for more planetary readings. This conversation happened in April. In September, Gowda went to Kashi (Varanasi) to perform his father's death rituals. He could not come back in time to meet Shastry as the airport was shut down due to heavy rains. Shastry passed away in September. But, like he had predicted, Urs lost power in 1980 and died in 1982.[14] Achyuta Shastry was the one who had predicted Gowda's victory in his first assembly election. His guru A.G. Ramachandra Rao had initially put him in touch with Shastry.

Sindhia recounted another incident from their trip to Chennai. This was for the wedding of a businessman's son, who had contributed to party funds at a crucial time. It was in 1993 after Gowda had merged his new Janata Party with the Janata Dal. Hegde, Gowda and party colleagues Jeevaraj Alva and R.V. Deshpande were with Sindhia. While Hegde was put up at a three-star hotel, the rest of them stayed at the Woodlands. Alva said that there was a famous

astrologer named Balan Nair, who they could visit after the wedding.
Hegde said he had another engagement, but the rest of them went.
Nair took their dates of birth and asked them to come back after a
few hours. When they returned, he looked at Gowda and said, 'You
will be chief minister in six months, you will not last in that position
for long and will go to a higher position. You will have a long, healthy
life, and you will be in power till the end.' He made other predictions
to the others, all of which Sindhia claimed were accurate.[15]

Another Ahmedabad-based chemical engineer with a PhD, Gitesh
Shah, who had been practising astrology as a hobby, casually walked
into Gowda's home in New Delhi in 1991, and told him he would
be chief and prime minister. Gowda had laughed it off, apparently.
Shah continued his relationship with Gowda, and in October 2019,
he said: 'When I made the prediction sitting in Gowdaji's lawn
nearly thirty years ago with my spiritual intuition and astrological
calculations, he did not believe me. He said, "I am not born in the
Nehru–Gandhi family to be prime minister, but with my hard work I
can become chief minister of Karnataka." The day he was designated
prime minister, I met him in Karnataka Bhavan and observed his face.
He had a placid look. I looked carefully at his face when he lost power
in 1997; the expression had not changed. For me, he is a *stitha pragna
purush* (a contented, calm and wise person).'[16]

In the chapter on Gowda as chief minister, we will read that
Gowda had himself shared a prediction with his principal secretary
that he will have a stint in Delhi but had not guessed that he could
be prime minister. In the chapter on the PMO, we will see the SPG
chief recall that Gowda, as prime minister-elect, wanted to visit Satya
Sai Baba because he had addressed him twice as 'prime minister'
even while he was chief minister. Gowda's reading was that Baba's
vision had reached the future. In the chapter on Kashmir, we see
the appearance of astrologer Devendra Mishra. There have been
many more astrologers who tried to predict the future and course
correct for Gowda, like Jnana Chakravarthy, S. Ravinarayan, a tech
entrepreneur in Bangalore, and S.S. Pandey, among others. In fact, a

close aide said Pandey had predicted Gowda will be prime minister the second time. They thought that moment had chosen itself in 2019, but that was not to be. On the contrary, Gowda was defeated when he contested the Tumkur parliamentary seat. But the question to ask here is: In 1989, when Gowda was alone and devastated, would he have believed if someone had told him that he will be chief minister five years later and prime minister two years after that? He was, at that point, a man without family, friends, party and a constituency. In the first place, did anybody predict his 1989 slump? Perhaps there were more mispredictions than accurate ones. It is only natural that the accurate ones are remembered, while the inaccurate ones recede from memory's shores.

8

Finally, in the Fifth Attempt, Mr Chief Minister

When Deve Gowda entered politics in 1962, as an independent, his imagination did not have the resources to think that he could be chief minister one day. Forget chief minister, to even imagine becoming a minister in the future would have been outrageous at that point. There were too many stalwarts in the political field at the time who blocked his vision beyond the immediate, and also, he felt terribly inadequate, both in terms of his exposure and education. His only ambition at the time was to cultivate Holenarasipur as his political *karmabhoomi*. He wanted to strike his roots deep there. He did not wish to look beyond the taluk. When Hassan district itself was outside the perimeter of his mind, to think of the entire old princely Mysore region and the larger state that had just then been linguistically reorganized was an impossible calculus.

The absence of a good bus or rail connectivity between Holenarasipur and Bangalore in the early 1960s also limited his ambition.[1] As the connectivity and contact improved, his ambition found roads and highways to run on. However, it is important to clarify that in Gowda's terminology, there was nothing called 'ambition'.

There was only a destiny to be lived out, a pre-determined path to tread. When he got where he got, individuals were important. He acknowledged their role, but deep within, he knew they had merely acted out their part. They were instruments of a larger design. If he had to be truly indebted, it was only to the divine.

It was only in the 1970s when Devaraj Urs became chief minister, and Gowda his accidental Opposition leader, that purpose was created beyond Holenarasipur for him. When his performance as the Opposition leader began to be acknowledged, and his popularity was on the rise around 1974–75, a surge of confidence must have made him think he had it in him to be chief minister. After the Janata Party had been formed, when his organizational genius, and his ability to work hard had admirers in Morarji Desai, Charan Singh and also Chandra Shekhar, there was a layer of certainty added to the ambition. All of this led him to think that the 1978 assembly polls would catapult him to the chief minister's chair, but that was not to be. Again in 1983, he had the brightest chance, which too slipped out when he was assigned the role of a kingmaker by Chandra Shekhar. There was a small window of opportunity in 1986 when Hegde abruptly resigned,[2] but that too passed. In 1988, when S.R. Bommai became chief minister, he felt cheated by circumstances. With this history of missed opportunities, he was extremely alert in 1994, when his claim to the chair was as legitimate as the previous four times. He had led his party to victory, and he was not underprepared for the executive role. On all four previous occasions, Ramakrishna Hegde had scuttled his path. In 1994 too, Hegde tried to derail his elevation, but there was a backlash.

The Crowds and the Chaos

As soon as the assembly election results were declared in December 1994, Biju Patnaik came to Bangalore as an observer of the central Janata Dal to the state party legislators meeting to select the chief minister. After the election had been fought under the leadership of Deve Gowda, it was a foregone conclusion in the minds of a majority of party workers and the people of the state that Gowda will be made chief minister. This was said when Gowda's party had formally merged with the Janata Dal in August 1993, and later, Hegde had himself declared during the campaign that if the party won, Gowda would be chief minister. V.P. Singh had also reiterated this in his campaign speeches. Hegde had also dilly-dallied re-contesting his Basavanagudi seat because the prospects were grim. Therefore, at the airport, when media persons asked Patnaik who will be picked as chief minister on 10 December 1994, he stated what was obvious to everybody that day: 'Deve Gowda is our natural choice.'[3] But Patnaik's statement irked Hegde, and he made his displeasure known rather brusquely when he met Patnaik later at the Windsor Manor Hotel.[4]

The next day, 11 December 1994, a sea of supporters surrounded the Vidhana Soudha where the legislators meeting was to be held. They had gathered there, part in the excitement that Gowda could become chief minister, and part in anxiety if a familiar old trick would be played to keep him out. There are many versions as to who had transported the crowds from Vokkaliga dominant districts around Bangalore to nearly lay siege to the Vidhana Soudha that day. But, many from the Janata Dal of those days point out that it was not a crowd Gowda had dictated to be assembled.[5] There was a bunch of enthusiastic party legislators, drunk in victory, who had decided to demonstrate support for their leader. Gowda had won that election from Ramanagara, then part of the Bangalore Rural district, leaving the Holenarasipur seat to his son, H.D. Revanna.

During the Janata Dal legislators meeting in the Vidhana Soudha, in what was understood by most as only a formal gathering to endorse the elevation of Gowda, Hegde sprang a surprise. He forced a contest. When Gowda directly confronted him and challenged him to contest, he offered a proxy in J.H. Patel.[6] The count of support delayed the meeting and tested the patience of the crowd outside. Gowda won the contest with an overwhelming majority, and as a compromise, accepted Patel as his deputy. The word got out that Hegde had not been supportive of his candidature. It was not a signal that should have gone out to a charged, impatient crowd. They became restless and the police lost control. As soon as the meeting concluded, Gowda left in a hurried fashion to Raj Bhavan. Biju Patnaik, too, had left the meeting similarly. The crowd misread their exits. They thought some last-minute hurdle had been placed before Gowda and that he was rushing out upset.[7] There was nobody to brief the crowds either. They went on a rampage. When they saw Hegde and Patel come down the lift, the crowds that had surged asked who they had made chief minister. When they did not answer, a boy from Chennapatna town caught Hegde by his kurta and pulled him around. When Patel, the deputy chief minister-elect, tried to get away, they chased him and landed a few blows on him. When R.V. Deshpande, later to be the industry minister in Gowda's cabinet, came to pacify the crowds, they pushed him into a bathroom close by and assaulted him.[8] The police had a tough time extricating the leaders from the crowd, putting them into a car, and packing them away. Later, a furious Hegde spoke of 'betrayal'. He said they were hired crowds and alleged that Gowda's son, Revanna, had a hand in the chaos.[9]

Meanwhile, Gowda was sworn in as the fourteenth chief minister of Karnataka at Raj Bhavan, on 11 December 1994 evening, by Governor Khursheed Alam Khan. What was to be a celebratory event in the forecourts of the Vidhana Soudha had become a ruptured, low-key event hidden away from the eyes of the adulatory crowds and in the absence of his family. For a mass leader like Gowda, there was no greater disappointment than that. Immediately after the event, Gowda met Hegde and pacified him. He put out a public statement distancing himself from the chaos and the crowds. He apologized for all that his colleagues had to go through at the hands of an 'angry, misguided' crowd.[10] A little later, Hegde too issued a statement that there were no differences between him and Gowda, and that they were 'like brothers'.[11] Curtains had been drawn on

the incident and as Hegde withdrew from the public eye, Gowda
began his work. He constructed a cabinet that was a mix of young
and old, competent and virtuous. It also ensured regional, caste and
factional balance. It included people like J.H. Patel, Siddaramaiah,
P.G.R. Sindhia, R.L. Jalappa, C. Byre Gowda, R.V. Deshpande,
D. Manjunath, H.G. Govinde Gowda, Ramesh Jigajinagi and
Jayaprakash Hegde among others. 'We went to the guest house of
the Devaraj Urs Medical College in Kolar to finalize the cabinet.
There were just three of us with Gowda—Siddaramaiah, Jalappa
and myself,' Sindhia, who became home minister, recalled.[12] He also
added that Gowda established a routine from day one: 'Five or six of
us, that included police and intelligence chiefs, would meet around
6 a.m. We would review the previous day's happenings and anticipate
what would unfold during the day that would begin. Planning done,
we would disperse by 7 a.m. Those were days when you neither had
computers, internet or mobile phones. This kind of diligent planning
by Gowda helped him be on the top of things and have total control
over the administration.'[13]

Settling Down

The first task on the desk for Gowda was the panchayat elections. His
colleagues in the cabinet were not very keen that they get ready for
another poll while they were just about settling down to govern the
state. They wanted the polls to be held six months later. But Gowda
thought the panchayat polls would be an excellent opportunity to
cement his position as chief minister. He thought the tailwinds of the
assembly victory would help sweep the panchayat polls too. He called
S.S. Meenakshisundaram, the secretary of the Rural Development
and Panchayat Raj Department, from Israel where he had been
to study agricultural practices with limited irrigation facilities. He
said: 'My party does not want an election, but I have decided to
go ahead with it. Why don't you sit down with the state election
commissioner and pick a date between mid-February and March first

week.' Gowda was very particular that this time window be adhered to because it was astrologically favourable to him. 'They will argue. They will create hurdles. But ignore all that and go ahead. If need be, ignore your minister [M.P. Prakash] too. Just follow the rule book, which says elections have to happen within six months.'[14]

Meenakshisundaram was happy with the decision but was also surprised. The surprise was because he had watched Gowda in Hegde's cabinet not being very enthusiastic about the panchayat legislation. Although he was not demonstratively opposed like R.L. Jalappa, his cabinet colleague, he was indifferent. Jalappa did not like the devolution of power, but Gowda was unable to decide if it was a good or bad piece of legislation. He had kept his reservations, whatever he may have had, private, though. He had not thrown a spanner into Hegde's enthusiasm.[15] Anyway, the panchayat elections were held smoothly and as Gowda had predicted, rather his astrologers had, the Janata Dal swept the polls.

A fortnight after the panchayat polls, Meenakshisundaram was picked as Gowda's principal secretary. He was a Tamilian IAS officer of the Karnataka cadre and had just finished a stint in Delhi. It was an unusual choice. Gowda volunteered an explanation when he called Meenakshisundaram: 'There is a lot of caste politics in the state. There is a lot of pressure from my community too. Devaraj Urs never allowed a minister and a Secretary to be from the same caste. I want to follow the same tradition.'[16] A few months later, after Meenakshisundaram was firmly established in his role, Gowda had reasoned his choice further during a casual conversation: You see a politician needs someone who tells him what is good and what is bad, although it is a politician's karma that he cannot always go by merit. He will often have to succumb to politics. But I need someone to constantly make an impartial assessment and tell me when I go wrong.'[17] He had applied the same logic later when he became prime minister.

Gowda's choice of chief secretary also generated a lot of curiosity. He went strictly by seniority and next on the list to take over after J.C. Lynn retired, less than a month after he took over as chief minister, was S.B. Muddappa. There was no problem with Muddappa. As an officer, he had a fine reputation and was known as a gentleman, but he was a Lingayat, and also the son-in-law of S. Nijalingappa with who Gowda had a bitter history. Everybody in government circles expected Gowda to bypass Muddappa, but he did not do that. Muddappa was himself surprised.[18] He was left with exactly one year of service and he became invaluable to Gowda's administration. After Muddappa retired, Gowda picked Cecil Noronha, a Goan Christian, as his chief secretary. This again was viewed as a surprise choice. Noronha as health secretary in the 1970s had not given an appointment to Gowda when he wanted to follow up on a public health centre in his constituency. He had made Gowda wait for forty-five minutes and sent him back without seeing him.[19]

In his earlier avatar in the government, as irrigation and PWD minister in Hegde's cabinet, Gowda was distrustful of IAS officers. He did not want them to be anywhere close to the departments he was heading. He had even gone to the extent of appointing engineering professionals as secretaries to the two departments in his charge. But as chief minister, his views had altered. He once told Meenakshisundaram: 'Engineers work hard, but they do not know how to express themselves or present things cogently in a meeting. But IAS officers seem to have mastered it.'[20] This appeared to be some kind of realization about himself than the contrast that existed between professionals and officers. Gowda always knew that he had fine technical command of a subject, any subject that he had applied his mind to, but could never put it across in an impressive fashion to an audience before him. He could always get heaps of information, marry his uncommon insight and deep memory, but could not develop a cogent narrative out of them or spin it to great effect. As he meandered with his narrative, the anxiety that he is not able to place everything that he knows on the table would at a certain bend ambush him, and derail the presentation. Nobody prepared like him, but he had limited ability to prioritize the material before him. His colleagues Ramakrishna Hegde, J.H. Patel and M.P. Prakash could mix information, insight, poetry and wit brilliantly, but could not always compete with Gowda's genius grasp and understanding. Therefore, when he made this comment to Meenakshisundaram, he knew the limitations of his own technical education.

Even otherwise, Gowda was not disrespectful to any officer but only distrustful, and that distrust was always couched in a different language. He never lost patience with his staff or the secretaries. He never displayed anger. If they were not effective, he would work around them or quietly get them changed but would 'never harass'.[21] There are examples of ministers and chief ministers throwing files and tantrums at officers, but there has been no such single allegation against Gowda. On the contrary, he would go out of the way to help them. The story of IAS officer J. Vasudevan, serving then as urban development secretary in Karnataka, is a case in point. The Supreme Court had sent him to jail for contempt of court in a matter unconnected with him personally or with the Gowda administration. The case was from an earlier period and was related to the promotion of an engineer working in the Bangalore City Corporation. It is just that Gowda and Vasudevan were in charge when the contempt petition was heard. Gowda camped in New Delhi for almost a week to secure a reprieve for his officer. 'His pleas to the Supreme Court— and even to the President—went unheeded; the state legislature was paralysed for several days as opposition parties demanded an inquiry into how an "honest" bureaucrat had been imprisoned,' the *India Today* reported.[22] Brushing their service rules aside, seventy-five IAS officers had sat in a day-long protest in Bangalore expressing solidarity with Vasudevan, detained at the Bangalore Central Jail.

K. Padmanabhaiah, the Union home secretary then, who obviously did not imagine that he would be serving Gowda as prime minister less than a year later, recalled Gowda calling on him in Delhi: 'Chief Minister Gowda came to see me seeking a presidential pardon for the IAS officer. Gowda's argument was that he was outstanding with a brilliant record, and the matter was held against him on purely technical grounds, and that an imprisonment would completely demoralize the entire bureaucracy. There was merit in Gowda's arguments and I was impressed that the political head of a state government thought fit to personally plead an officer's case.'[23]

Fali Nariman also mentions this case in his autobiography (*Before Memory Fades*) and says that he and his wife found Gowda 'to be a caring person': 'When an honest officer (Vasudevan) was sent to jail for six months for contempt of court – wrongly in my view – by a bench consisting of Justice K. Ramaswami and Justice Hansaria, Deve Gowda felt that he must help this officer from his state. He flew over to Delhi on three evenings in succession (from Bangalore) to consult with me as to whether the president could not exercise his power of pardon.'

With his vast experience as an MLA, the Opposition leader and minister, Gowda had the administration under control from day one. He knew more than any officer how the wheels moved in the government. Officers, too, knew that he was sharp, shrewd, and would not let any sloppy advice go unchallenged. Within a short period, Gowda was being applauded for his administrative acumen. 'There was no chief minister as accessible as him and as travelled to the corners of the state like him. No other chief minister had pushed a development agenda to the fore as quickly as he did. He had no distractions (of the wine and women variety). It was either work or home. He worked for nineteen hours a day. That way, Gowda was boring compared to Hegde and his deputy, Patel. He had become chief minister at the right age—sixty-two, when he was administratively and politically mature. The bureaucracy was on its toes,' B.L. Shankar, who was made Gowda's political secretary to be a bridge between the party and government, recalled.[24]

Besides making decisive strides with the Upper Krishna Project (see the chapter on irrigation), Gowda focused on investments, industries and infrastructure. One of the first things he negotiated was a new international airport for Bangalore to be located at

Devanahalli with a consortium led by the Tatas. A memorandum of understanding was signed in December 1995. This was a major decision as the old Hindustan Aeronautics Limited airport in Bangalore was congested. Worse, the old airport was five kilometers from the city centre, and perennially contributed to traffic jams on Bangalore's main thoroughfares. Thinking of a new airport for Gowda was thinking of a new Bangalore, which was slowly gaining a reputation of being India's own Silicon Valley. Unfortunately, like a few other infrastructure projects he had negotiated, this too developed a snag after he stepped down as chief minister and prime minister. Politics had come into play. In June 1998, the consortium pulled out owing to delays in getting government approvals. New arrangements came up later with a new consortium when S.M. Krishna became chief minister, which Gowda thought was a 'terrible let down' to the city. He wanted Ratan Tata to build the airport. It was also Ratan Tata's early years as chairman of the Tata Group, and Gowda's staff remember a cordial relationship between the two in 1995. For one of the meetings, Tata had arrived a few minutes early, and was found unassumingly sitting alone in the Vidhana Soudha's conference room on the third floor.[25] Gowda recalled: 'The Tatas wanted 4000 acres of land for the airport project, although my initial offer was 2000 acres. They had wanted ownership of a certain portion of land to develop a golf course and hotel, but I had offered it on lease for ninety-nine years. It had all been worked out to our mutual satisfaction.'[26] Finally, the new airport, after inordinate delays, was inaugurated a decade later in 2008 with an altogether different consortium.

The other landmark during Gowda's term as chief minister was his inauguration of the international technology park at Whitefield, which had been mooted by the prime ministers of India and Singapore in 1992. This ensured that the nascent information technology ecosystem in Bangalore was better supported. Gowda did a good job of physical connectivity between the information technology hubs in Bangalore by planning the intermediate ring road and also the first flyover at Sirsi Circle to reduce congestion in the city. The determined manner in which he secured approvals for the flyover and fixed the alignment within a short period is legendary in bureaucratic circles.[27] He laid the foundation stone for the flyover on 31 May 1996, a day before he took oath as prime minister. After he took over as prime minister, he facilitated the clearing of legal hurdles in acquiring defence land for the outer ring road project. As compensation for the defence land, a certain number of flats were given to defence personnel at the Asian Games Village that was being built in the Koramangala locality of Bangalore.[28] As Bangalore was at the threshold of becoming the back office of the world and was being crowned as the 'Silicon Valley of India', Gowda was one of those administrators who was helping the city brace up for international arch lights. In fact, it can be argued that if Ramakrishna Hegde created intellectual capital for the technology industry by promoting engineering education in Karnataka; Veerappa Moily created easy access to technical education for the middle classes, rural talent and backward class communities by designing and implementing the Common Entrance Test; while Gowda planned physical infrastructure for the city as chief minister and as prime minister, and also thereafter when he mentored the J.H. Patel-led Janata Dal government. Gowda's effort to bring Cauvery river water to meet Bangalore city's drinking water needs is among the stellar contributions not remembered.

After the Nehruvian era of mega investments in public sector companies and scientific institutions, the 1980s and 1990s offered a new dimension and potential to the city. It was in 1985 that Texas Instruments had set up its first overseas development centre in Bangalore. The year Gowda became chief minister, in 1994, Infosys had moved its headquarters to the Electronic City. However, it is a travesty that S.M. Krishna, who became chief minister between 1999 and 2004, became the poster boy of the Information Technology (IT) industry in the media while his predecessors had collectively contributed to creating infrastructure for its development. He had pulled off a successful public relations trick by engaging the IT elite in Bangalore and had also endeavoured to make them the city's quasi-bureaucracy. Krishna had made Nandan Nilekani the chairman of the Bangalore Task Force, and N.R. Narayana Murthy the chairman of the Bangalore International Airport Limited. Both were founders of the IT bell-weather company Infosys. The fact that Krishna's son-in-law, V.G. Siddhartha (who died by suicide in 2019) was an early and big investor in IT stocks, especially Infosys, further propelled his indulgence.[29]

None of Krishna's predecessors or successors were able to build this cosy network with Bangalore's technology elite and the English language media. Anyway, the hallmark of the Gowda administration was to ensure land, water and power availability as well as concessions to industries that had already existed and to those that promised to set up shop. The Toyotas, in a joint venture with the Kirloskar company, decided to set up a manufacturing unit in Bidadi, just outside Bangalore, during his time as chief minister. Bidadi was part of Ramanagara, Gowda's constituency as chief minister. He was largely responsible for Bidadi to develop as a manufacturing hub, which now hosts Bosch, Britannia, Coca-Cola, a clutch of Tata and Aditya Birla companies, besides Toyota–Kirloskar.

Gowda also sanctioned the Bangalore–Mysore Infrastructure Corridor (BMIC) project, which was ahead of its time. It was not only to reduce travel time to Mysore with an express highway and make the heritage city a development satellite of Bangalore, but five new townships had also been sanctioned along the expressway. This project was envisioned to create an investment and economic vibrancy in the entire southern Karnataka region. But as soon as Gowda lost power, this project got into protracted legal battles, which reached the Supreme Court of India. The story of this project's incubation and incompleteness would by itself make for a separate study. It had all begun as a partnership between the State of Massachusetts and the Government of Karnataka in February 1995. In 2008, the legal cell of the Janata Dal (S), Gowda's party, published a booklet titled

Bangalore–Mysore Infrastructure Corridor Project: A case study in fraud and collusion to defeat the ends of justice and defraud courts. Gowda, in his foreword, alleged that the infrastructure project he had sanctioned had been converted into 'a real estate project'.[30]

Unfortunately, Gowda's political branding as a farmers' leader and being from a rural background never allowed recognition of his urban planning skills. Like for instance, it is never mentioned that it was Gowda who gave financial closure to the Delhi Metro Rail Project in September 1996 as prime minister and also as in-charge of the ministry for urban development. He had cleared the 55.3 km long phase one of the metro project, which included eleven kilometres of underground line, at a cost of Rs 4860 crores despite strong opposition from his finance minister P. Chidambaram.[31] It is said that in the cabinet meeting, Chidambaram expressed reservations to the project on the grounds that it had a low rate of financial return (IRR) and consequent lack of commercial viability. But Gowda argued that Delhi urgently required a rail-based mass transit system to handle its fast-increasing volumes of traffic and that the losses during the operational phase could be shared by the Centre and the local Delhi government.[32]

As chief minister, Gowda had an excellent relationship with prime minister P.V. Narasimha Rao and that made things easy for him. 'Rao had respect for Gowda because of his grassroots links. He also knew he was brighter than projected in the media. It is also possible that they consulted the same astrologer,' Shankar chuckled as he recalled.[33] Soon after he was sworn in as chief minister, Rao insisted that Gowda go to Davos to the World Economic Forum as part of the Indian delegation.[34] He returned from Davos and amended the land reforms act to ensure that industry could access land easily. There was a committee formed under the chief secretary to offer single-window, timebound clearances to investors. That was his first Davos trip. The second time he went there was when he was prime minister. Rao also sent US commerce secretary Ron Brown to meet Gowda in Bangalore to discuss US investments. Brown was so impressed that he gave a glowing picture of Gowda's administration to the national press. He said Gowda was 'determined' to earn a special spot for Karnataka in the emerging story of India.[35] Sadly, Brown died in an air crash in Croatia in 1996, a couple of months before Gowda became prime minister. 'When investors came calling, Gowda never met them alone. He would always insist that his senior cabinet colleagues should be present. His logic was that it would give confidence to the investors when they saw that the administration had depth and coherence,' K.A. Thippeswamy, his longtime private secretary, recalled.[36]

When Gowda was discussing investments, he realized that Karnataka had a severe power shortage. But when he learnt that Maharashtra had surplus power, he decided to meet Shiv Sena chief Bal Thackeray in Mumbai.[37] Amar Singh, who had just then been sanctioned a mini hydel project in Karnataka, arranged the meeting at Amitabh Bachchan's house. When Gowda requested for 500 MW of power, Thackeray immediately called Chief Minister Manohar Joshi and asked him to help Gowda.[38] N.K.P. Salve, the Union power minister, similarly helped with 250 MW of power from Orissa, which was kept on standby in case of an emergency.[39] It is around the same time that the 1000 MW Cogentrix thermal power project in the ecologically sensitive Dakshina Kannada district became one of the big-ticket items before the Gowda government. He pursued the project as chief minister (MoU for which had been signed in 1992 by the S. Bangarappa government), but when he decided to fast track it as prime minster, George Fernandes accused him of having received kickbacks for the deal. Maneka Gandhi, who was later expelled from the Janata Dal, also hinted at kickbacks, besides alleging that the project had violated environmental norms. *India Today* had reported in August 1996: 'To make matters worse, the prime minister told Parliament on July 17 that the Centre hadn't yet cleared Cogentrix. Actually, the crucial environmental clearance was granted 36 days before his statement to Parliament. So did he mislead the House? The Opposition thought so, and moved for breach of privilege, which is

still pending with the deputy speaker of the Lok Sabha.'[40] Neither
the corruption allegations nor the privilege motion took wings.

Sindhia and Shankar, who were Gowda's colleagues then but
later branched out, insist that Gowda never cut deals to award
contracts. 'I may have developed political differences with Gowda
later but I can tell you in the name of Goddess Mookambika I trust,
Gowda never sold government orders either for awarding contracts
or for official transfers as a minister or chief minister. People who
benefitted from the policies of the government would donate to the
party fund during elections. That was the standard thing,' Sindhia
remembered.[41] Meenakshisundaram also said: 'There was no quid
pro quo in the Gowda administration.'[42]

Social Justice Agenda

It is not all industry and investment that Gowda was pre-occupied
with as chief minister. He also re-examined the social justice agenda.
He constituted a cabinet sub-committee under M.P. Prakash, a
senior minister, which internally redistributed reservation quotas for
backward classes in education and jobs. Muslims were given a 4 per
cent quota. This earned him enormous political capital. The previous
Moily government had been considering this proposal, but when
Gowda came to power, he rejigged it and swiftly implemented it.
'He also introduced political and gender-based reservations to local
bodies as chief minister. This altogether changed the way politics was
done in Karnataka,' recalled C.S. Dwarakanath, the former chairman
of the Karnataka Backward Classes Commission. Dwarakanath
added: 'In Karnataka, Muslims and all religious minorities are given
reservation under the backward classes category. There is no separate
reservation category for religious communities. This ensured that it
was not legally challenged like it was done elsewhere in India.'[43]

Gowda's relationship with reservations in Karnataka has been
complicated. His position was mostly dictated by political exigencies
than social justice ideals. In the 1970s, when Devaraj Urs constituted

the Havanur Commission to give reservation to backward classes, Gowda's response was nondescript. This was because Urs accommodated, or rather did not antagonize, Gowda's Vokkaliga community. It was the Lingayat elite who felt targeted by Urs. However, in 1983, when the Venkataswamy Commission dropped Vokkaligas from the OBC list, Gowda protested. He ensured that the Hegde government, of which he was part, rejected the report. At the end of the 1980s, when V.P. Singh implemented the Mandal Commission report, Gowda had left the Janata Dal, and was in political wilderness. He was mostly silent about it. Again, when his predecessor chief minister, Veerappa Moily, accepted the report of the Justice O. Chinnappa Reddy Commission for backward class reservations, which again did not favour the dominant communities, Gowda was out on the streets to demand its rollback. 'Chief Minister Moily, who came from a micro-minority backward class community, was left with little option politically but to issue a fresh government order re-accommodating the Vokkaligas and Lingayats,' Dwarakanath remembered.[44]

The singular contribution of Deve Gowda to the social justice debate in Karnataka has been the idea of 'internal reservations'.[45] He mooted this after he had stepped down as prime minister to ensure that the majority within the scheduled castes, that is, the Madigas, get political identity. This idea also had an implication for dominant backward class communities like Kurubas and Idigas, who were walking away with a bulk of the benefits. By floating the idea of internal reservation, Gowda was actually doing two things at a time, or as the proverbial saying goes—striking two birds with one stone. He was dividing the scheduled caste vote of the Congress and also trying to cut to size Kuruba leaders like Siddaramaiah, who had fallen out with him. 'Devaraj Urs and Deve Gowda were masters of social engineering. They knew how to align and realign communities and keep their political capital intact. They had exhaustively worked on nuancing the social justice debate much before politicians in north India had even woken up to it,' remarked Dwarakanath.[46]

Gowda's idea of internal reservation found echo two decades later when the Supreme Court passed an order in August 2020 allowing internal reservations among the scheduled castes, the scheduled tribes and the socially and economically backward classes. Gowda reacted enthusiastically: 'This will be a game-changer across the nation. . . We often assume that the scheduled castes, the scheduled tribes and the backwards are a homogenous group, while in reality, they are very vibrant and diverse. Inequalities within the groups with regard to affirmative action had become apparent in recent decades. It had to be corrected. Now that it has happened, I wholeheartedly welcome this judgment . . . I urge state legislatures across the nation to take steps to implement this judgment and ensure that the idea of reservations and justice are deepened and broadened.'[47]

When Chandra Shekhar was prime minister in 1991, Gowda had used his proximity to get an ordinance promulgated to give Valmikis or Nayakas in Karnataka the scheduled tribe tag. The demand had been pending since 1978. Gowda referred to his efforts while speaking in the Parliament in August 1991 when Sitaram Kesri, the social welfare minister in the Narasimha Rao cabinet, presented it as a Bill before the Parliament. Kesri made it clear in his response to the debate on the Bill that this was a legacy of the Chandra Shekhar government, and he was pursuing it because he agreed with the 'objective'.[48] The Scheduled Tribe tag empowered the Valmiki community to such an extent that by 2000, they had started emerging as a political force in Karnataka. If the Reddy Brothers, the notorious Bellary miners, captured power in a handful of districts of the state for the BJP and helped Y.S. Rajasekhara Reddy of the Congress across the border in Andhra Pradesh, among their secret weapons was the support of the Valmiki community. The close association and alliance of the mining Reddys with B. Sriramulu, a former MP and a powerful minister in all BJP governments in Karnataka, was crucial to their progress. Sriramulu, in turn, had made use of the monetary clout of the Reddy Brothers to capture the leadership of the community. Gowda had thought the Valmikis would remain loyal to his party for the efforts he had put in, but the project got somewhat derailed.

As chief minister, Gowda looked at gender justice too. He perhaps wanted to shape it as an autonomous political constituency in Karnataka where rules that usually defined caste identity politics would not apply. His government passed an order to ensure that 33 per cent of jobs in all government departments would be reserved for women. This was the first time that any state government in India had made a specific reservation policy for women. He followed this up with another order to ensure that 50 per cent of jobs in all educational institutions were reserved for women. He extended the reservation to elected positions in local bodies. To complete the circle, he wrote to Prime Minister Narasimha Rao to bring a constitutional amendment to provide reservation for women in the state assemblies and the Parliament.[49] He also sent a delegation to meet leaders across party lines to canvass support for this agenda. The fact that Gowda attempted this progressive measure, in such a decisive manner, never got spoken about for two reasons: One, Gowda did not know how to arrange communication or publicity around it, a deficiency of his political life. Two, he did not speak the language of anglophone liberals or ideologues when he did this. He was not familiar with it at all. He may have thought of women as an independent political constituency but the collateral social benefits this could potentially unleash were enormous, and more significant than a political advantage it could accrue for a political leader or his party.

Gowda did not give this up when he quit as chief minister, he was so personally invested in the gender justice agenda that he took it along with him to the prime minister's office. Within three months of being sworn in, on 28 August 1996, he ensured that the cabinet discussed the Women's Reservation Bill.[50] It was thereafter introduced in the Lok Sabha as the Eighty-First Constitutional Amendment Bill on 9 September 1996. But discussions on it were blocked on technical grounds. It was 'a pattern that was to become familiar later', wrote T.S.R. Subramanian, the then cabinet secretary. Nearly fifteen years later, in March 2010, when the Women's Reservation Bill was passed by the Rajya Sabha as the 108th Constitution Amendment Bill, there was a lot of hype and excitement created, even though its passage through Lok Sabha remained a challenge. The Congress-led UPA government was in power. Nobody remembered Gowda. However, Subramanian wrote: 'History will record that the Women's Reservation Bill was first moved in the Lok Sabha by the Deve Gowda government.'[51] The Bill has still not become law in 2021, twenty-five year after Gowda first thought of it.

The Idgah Maidan Controversy

It was not just investments, development, and social justice that Gowda focused on as chief minister, communal peace was one of his top priorities. He had the goodwill of the Muslim community and wanted to leverage it to resolve the festering communal problem that the Idgah Maidan issue had become. In 1992, when BJP leader Murli Manohar Joshi tried to hoist the national flag in Srinagar, local RSS and BJP activists in Hubli tried to do the same at the Idgah Maidan, a Muslim prayer ground. They were, however, prevented from doing so. Just before Gowda took over as chief minister, Uma Bharati, in 1994, had tried to hoist the national flag at the maidan leading to rioting and protests and the death of five people. Matters died down when members of the Anjuman-e-Islami themselves hoisted the national flag when Gowda was chief minister.

Gowda recalled:

> When I tried to address the issue, some local Congress leaders did not want me to take up the issue. In Hubli, there was an RSS sympathizer from a particular backward class community who had become a legislator with the support of Lingayats. He was in the excise business. There were around sixty households belonging to the backward community in Hubli city. As far as

this issue was concerned, boys belonging to that community were the most militant. I got many of them arrested. It was under preventive custody. The moment these arrests happened, the legislator came running to me. He came alone. He did not come with B.S. Yediyurappa, his leader. He pleaded with me to let the boys out. I said, 'I will release them one hour after the flag is hoisted on Independence Day.' I also assured him that I will not get them chargesheeted. 'I only expect you to behave,' I warned him. He agreed and left. Then Yediyurappa charged into my room and accused me of behaving like a dictator. I told him that I only intended to solve the problem. I also said, 'I know how you guys operate. You will try to mobilize support from Mangalore, but I have ordered they be stopped en route to Hubli. You will try to mobilize support from Belgaum, I will again block your vehicles on the highway. None of them will enter Hubli. I will also get you and your colleagues arrested.' He shouted, 'What do you think of yourself?' I countered, 'Don't I know that you use your caste as a shield and collaborate with the RSS?' He walked out of the room. I didn't stop him. There was a pontiff who was also instigating the crisis because he had an eye on the Idgah Maidan property. Intelligence officers had briefed me about all this. I called and confronted him. I said I had no choice but to detain him because he was disturbing communal peace. The pontiff was so scared that he ran away to Pune for a month. To give confidence to Muslims, I sought the help of a low-profile Muslim leader. He was not very educated, but my officers told me he was respected in his community. I summoned him. I asked if he can arrange mohalla meetings and that I could address those meetings myself. I promised him that I'll make him an MLC if he handled this successfully for me. He agreed. I went to the mohallas and heard the problems of the Muslim community. I was surprised that they were not big problems. I immediately ordered that they be sorted out, but before that, I extracted a promise that they will cooperate with

the flag hoisting on August 15. I came to Bangalore and asked
Sindhia to take charge of the situation. He did his job sincerely.
C.M. Ibrahim, who was the Janata Dal state president then,
also played a part. He managed high-profile Muslim leaders
and organizations. I kept all my moves under wraps without
giving them any publicity. Nobody knew what was happening.
At 9 a.m., on 15 August 1995, I hoisted the flag in Bangalore
and it also simultaneously went up at the Idgah Maidan.[52]

Exactly a year ago, in 1994, *India Today* had reported on how Idgah
Maidan, Hubli, and the neighbouring districts had been converted
into a charged communal zone:

> For the BJP in Karnataka, starved of an election plank, the
> Hubli Idgah Maidan dispute couldn't have come at a more
> opportune time. The controversy stems from a dispute over
> the ownership of the 1.5-acre plot, with the Anjuman-e-Islam
> laying claim to it and the BJP saying it is municipal property.
> Actually, its current status, determined after prolonged legal
> action, is that the land has been licensed to the Anjuman,
> and that it is permitted to hold only prayer meetings there,
> twice a year. The right of anybody to use the maidan for
> public purposes is still under consideration by the Supreme
> Court. But the BJP planned to hoist the tri-colour there on
> Independence Day—its sixth attempt to do so. On August 14
> (1994), Hubli was sealed, a curfew clamped and police and
> Rapid Action Force personnel deployed. Said Chief Minister
> Veerappa Moily: 'I'm not Kalyan Singh to close my eyes and
> allow violence to carry on.' (referring to the Babri Masjid that
> had been demolished under the watch of Uttar Pradesh chief
> minister Kalyan Singh in 1992). But although BJP leader
> Sikander Bakht was arrested in Bangalore, Uma Bharati, MP,
> managed to sneak into Hubli and declared that 'the flag will be
> unfurled at any cost'. On August 15, violence erupted as BJP

supporters tried to march to the Idgah Maidan, defying curfew orders, to hoist the flag. State BJP leader B.S. Yediyurappa and Uma Bharati were arrested, and the mob ran amuck. The police opened fire, killing five people and injuring about a hundred. Four days later, the BJP organised 'Moily Hatao' meetings all over Hubli. Violence broke out again when the police over reacted and opened fire, killing a woman. Moily, seeing that his administration's image was taking a beating, threatened to invoke the dreaded TADA if the violence was not curbed. Tension spread to the communally-sensitive town of Bhadravati nearby, which witnessed group clashes a week later. Meanwhile, BJP leader LK Advani predicted: 'Moily's fate was sealed when his administration ordered firing on innocent patriots in Hubli.' He also likened the incident to the Naragund police firing at a farmers' rally a decade ago during the Gundu Rao administration, which ultimately led to the Congress (I) losing power in the state.[53]

This report from the previous year should explain why Gowda kept everything under wraps, and deployed a strategy that was far removed from confronting the communal crowd on the streets. This was a trademark style of Gowda in approaching and solving a problem, which he had tried out earlier and employed in good measure as prime minister too.

Gowda took great pride, and justifiably so, in the manner in which he had resolved the Idgah Maidan issue. Speaking in Parliament, in April 2002, in the aftermath of the Godhra riots, he said: 'Sir, I was the chief minister of my state for eighteen months. My friend Jaffer Sharief is here and the hon. home minister [L.K. Advani] also knows the Hubli Idgah Maidan issue. It was an issue created by the BJP. Every year, more than 5000 policemen, drawn from all districts of the state, used to be deployed there to maintain security. When I became chief minister, I made a Muslim leader hoist the national flag in that place. Since that day, there has not been a single instance of communal violence in that place . . . during my time (as chief minister) I had given 4 per cent reservation exclusively for Muslims. The Hindus or even the other minority communities did not have any objection to that. It was not only job reservations for Muslims but I also opened residential schools for students belonging to the Muslim community . . . (reservation for Muslims) was not part of the Mandal Commission recommendation where only some small benefits were proposed . . . These are some steps that I took as chief minister irrespective of the fact whether it would have fetched me political benefits or not. It is not the issue of the vote bank. It is an issue that needs to be solved. We should not give them a step-motherly treatment. The question today is as to how we can bring them into the mainstream of our life. Those who wanted to go to Pakistan have gone.'[54]

The Parliament Polls and the Surprise

Even as Gowda's work as chief minister picked up pace, the Parliament elections had arrived. He was determined to put up the best show possible. The planning was diligent, and for the first time, resources were not an issue. Senior ministers in his cabinet were assigned specific election duties and constituencies. Mentally too, Gowda felt free this time. There were no challenges and no conspiracies being hatched behind his back. He was totally in control. His popularity as chief minister had reached a height when deciphering positive vote swings had become easy. B.L. Shankar, who contested the Chikmagalur seat that election and won, recalled: 'There was no dearth of resources. People in the Congress and the BJP were stunned by our campaign style. Gowda never promised specific resources when he gave us tickets, but he distributed it as it arrived. He would never touch election money, which was his long-held principle. He would only indicate where it should reach.'[55] Shankar also gave an example of how Gowda was shrewd and ruthless in his deployment of resources: 'Although S.M. Krishna was in the Congress, his son-in-law,

V.G. Siddhartha, wanted to donate to the Janata Dal election funds during the 1994 assembly polls. I asked him if he was sure. He said, "I want to do it as a businessman. I have contributed to all parties. I want to give it to your party too." When the money came, Gowda asked it to be handed over to a leader who was in charge of the Maddur seat where Krishna was contesting. He used the son-in-law's money to defeat Krishna in that seat.'[56]

Right from the start of campaigning Gowda was sure that he will get eighteen out of twenty-eight seats.[57] He had his intelligence inputs and astrological calculations in place. The party won sixteen seats, and lost two seats (Mysore and Bellary) by very narrow margins. That was the biggest haul for the Janata Party or the Janata Dal ever in Karnataka. And before Gowda could begin savouring the victory, he had become prime minister-elect. Meenakshisundaram, Gowda's principal secretary, who had gone to Washington DC for a World Bank conference on decentralization of governance, heard of his boss' elevation from the British academic James Manor. He recalled: 'I did not believe it at first. During a trip to Delhi, Gowda had told me that he would like to be the Jyoti Basu of Karnataka, ruling the state for 15–20 years. Had he continued as chief minister, he would have done a great job. His heart was in the right place, and he knew the state and its specific requirements like nobody else. Soon after I had heard the news from Manor, I got a call asking me to return early to Bangalore.'[58] Gowda's astrologers had apparently alerted him about a stint in Delhi, but he thought he would be the vice president of India, much later, like B.D. Jatti, whose camp-follower he had been in the Congress of the 1960s.[59]

Long, multiple tenures as chief minister looked assured in 1996 to Gowda because politically, the challenges inside his party had dissolved. The Congress was weak, the BJP had not risen and Gowda was on a song when it came to administration, policies, investment and welfare. But it was an irony of sorts that Jyoti Basu, whom he admired, had passed on his 'Himalayan' opportunity to Gowda.[60] That was seemingly in the DNA of his destiny.

9

The Krishna and the Cauvery

Gowda's approach to rivers has not been that of a naturalist or an ecologist but that of an engineer. It is in the tradition of Sir M. Visvesvaraya whom he grew up admiring. In popular history, it is Visvesvaraya's engineering vision that had overseen the construction of the Krishnaraja Sagar Dam across the Cauvery, which helped irrigate large hectares of land in South Karnataka, from where Gowda came. The narrative over the decades has been built in such a way that Visvesvaraya is more deified than the Mysore maharaja, Nalvadi Krishnaraja Wodeyar, who commissioned the project at great personal stake.[1] The rivers are sacred to Gowda, no doubt, but they are also the gift of God to be harnessed for humankind's development. This is not his stated position, but that is what can be deduced. Gowda's development or irrigation politics started with the Cauvery, which made him the politician that he eventually became. He then extended his expertise to the Krishna, and later it encompassed the Narmada and the Ganga.

We will first start by examining his contribution to the Krishna, where his innovation and creativity have largely gone unrecorded. When Gowda started out in politics, Cauvery was essentially a water-sharing dispute between Karnataka and Tamil Nadu. The development of the basin had been done to a large extent by the maharaja. Therefore, legal battles assumed centre stage. One could not build a new dam over the Cauvery because the Mysore state, later Karnataka, was saddled with agreements of 1892 and 1924. Under these agreements, the princely Mysore state had lost its freedom to build new dams across the Cauvery without the consent of the Madras government. A kind of veto power had been granted to Madras, which was a British presidency. What was possible was to plan new canals, modernize existing canal systems, build reservoirs, and fill up tanks to efficiently utilize Karnataka's share of the water. But there were no such obstacles to utilizing the Krishna water. It needed an administrative vision and engineering acumen that Gowda provided. In fact, the Krishna could be his greater legacy than Cauvery.

The Upper Krishna Revolution

The Upper Krishna Project (UKP) in Karnataka was planned in 1962 to irrigate the drought-prone districts of Bijapur, Bagalkot, Gulbarga, Yadgir and Raichur in north Karnataka. It was a project that was inordinately sluggish with huge cost overruns ever since it was started by Chief Minister S. Nijalingappa. Between 1962, and 1994, when Deve Gowda took charge as chief minister, that is for a good three decades, only 10 per cent of the project had been completed.[2] The project was envisioned to irrigate over 15,00,000 acres of land. The Naryanapura Dam, as part of the project, had been built during stage one, but that was only a diversion dam and not a reservoir. The full storage was to happen at the Almatti dam, which was to be the largest in Karnataka, and one of the largest in the country. It was under construction. In the Krishna valley, the Almatti dam was to be the second biggest after the Nagarjuna Sagar dam in Andhra Pradesh.

Although the Naryanapura Dam was completed in 1982, and 1,00,000 acre was declared irrigated, when Gowda became chief minister, it did not take long for him to realize that in reality, only a little over 50,000 acres of land was being served.[3] He had to also deal with something else—an ensnaring deadline set by the Krishna Water Disputes Tribunal. It had awarded Karnataka's share of water in 1976 (also known as the Bachawat award) and expected it to utilize it fully by 31 May 2000. Deve Gowda's role in innovating upon, accelerating and enabling the UKP project should be seen in the backdrop of this deadline. He became chief minister in December 1994 and had just about six years to harness the state's share of the Krishna.

Four months into Gowda's term as chief minister, Congress leader Mallikarjun Kharge, who was leader of Opposition then, spoke in the state assembly on UKP.[4] His accusation was that the government had not yet woken up on UKP although the deadline of the Bachawat award was hanging on the state. He also accused the Gowda government of not making necessary budgetary provisions for the project. Gowda was intrigued by Kharge's attack and wondered why he was suddenly getting so impatient without fully understanding how the government had begun to approach the issue. In his typical manner, he examined the assembly records and found that there had been no debate on UKP in the assembly between 1989 and 1994.[5] For the five years that the Congress was in power, there was no debate on UKP. He sternly asked them not to question his commitment to cover up their apathy.

UKP also meant confronting the humungous issue of resettlement and rehabilitation (R&R) of people displaced by the project. This had remained largely unattended. The number of villages fully affected by the Narayanapura Dam were around thirty, another fifteen were partially affected. But in 1994, the partially affected ones were still living on what had become the project site, and although the fully affected thirty villages had been shifted, the conditions at the temporary camps were sub-human. The displaced were in a kind of limbo.[6] R&R required large sums of money and the previous state governments had no idea as to where that would come from. Around the time, there was a lot of emphasis nationally on

R&R since activists like Medha Patkar had drawn attention to those who were displaced by big dams. UKP was bigger than the Sardar Sarovar Dam built over the Narmada that she was fighting against. To complicate matters further, the World Bank had suspended funding UKP the second time because its conditionalities had not been met. Gowda took over from here.

The first thing that he did was to spot, and appoint, S.M. Jaamdar, a 1980-batch IAS officer who had just then returned from the United Kingdom after his higher education leave. Jaamdar had a doctoral degree in criminology from the United States, and by then, had earned a reputation for being forthright and efficient. He had given up a teaching career in the US and had also opted out of a United Nations job to get into the IAS. Politicians knew he brooked no nonsense. He had felicity with big data and would never deviate from the rule book. Gowda created a new position for him as commissioner and ex-officio Secretary to the government, vested special powers and sent him to the UKP site to sort out the R&R mess because he knew that was the first step towards getting the World Bank to lift its suspension.

Jaamdar was surprised that Gowda had picked him because the only meeting he had had with him until that point was when he was irrigation minister, and that was not in very pleasant circumstances. However, as soon as he became chief minister, Gowda had summoned Jaamdar, personally briefed him on the task ahead, and promised full administrative support. 'When I landed at the UKP site, there was literally no infrastructure. I occupied an old government circuit house and began my work with a rickety jeep, a driver and a peon. On the top of my mind was to get the World Bank suspension lifted, and at the same time, there was the Bachawat deadline to complete the project by 2000. This was the biggest irrigation project in Karnataka. All its beneficiaries were in north Karnataka, although Gowda came from the Cauvery basin in the south,' Jaamdar recalled.[7] The emphasis here on north and south Karnataka is important because the south is the richer erstwhile Mysore princely state, and the north was integrated after the linguistic reorganization in 1956. Until then, the Kannada dominant areas of the north were either part of Bombay or Madras Presidency or Nizam's Hyderabad. Emotional, cultural and developmental asymmetries between the two regions have lingered on to this day. Therefore, Gowda, a Vokkaliga leader from the south, making a decisive intervention in a project that needed huge resources in the Lingayat belt of the north assumes enormous political significance. The fact that Lingayats and Vokkaligas have been on politically opposite sides since 1956 made this a major non-partisan initiative.

For the completion of the UKP 3,34,000 acres of land had to be acquired, but until 1994–95, during the first phase, only 1,40,000 acres had been acquired. That meant acquiring 2,00,000 acres of land in the second phase, and this would result in displacing 179 villages as well as the Bagalkot town.[8] Expectedly, there was a lot of chaos and a lot of adverse publicity. There were already 40,000 court cases related to land acquisition that were pending. There were seventeen special courts to deal with them. Gowda knew what he was taking on, and felt strangely inspired by the magnitude of the problem. The money that was being offered as compensation to the villagers was a pittance. The government till then was offering Rs 2000 or Rs 3000 per acre, but the courts were enhancing it four or five times and passing orders.[9] On day one, when Jaamdar went out for a morning walk at the break of dawn, his eyes surveyed the 4000 acres where the new Bagalkot town was to be built, and there was a standing jowar crop on it. He had to build infrastructure for the new town on those green fields.

'Due to land disputes, lawyers were making hay. The mood was anti-establishment, anti-government, anti-everything. It was gloomy. The only solution was to have huge staff, computers, offices and vehicles. I went to Gowda. He said, "I want work done. Go ahead and send the proposal." There were six rehabilitation officers, I raised them to seventeen. There were only two special deputy commissioners for the division, I added two more. I suggested a total of eighty officers, 120 jeeps and 120 computers that had just then started coming to the market. He approved without batting an eyelid. Funds flowed. In the first year, my budget was Rs 40 crore. Then I enhanced it to Rs 100 crore and sent a proposal. I was given the power of issuing letters of credit (LoC). I went on issuing credit notes and at the end of the year, I had issued up to Rs 80 crore worth. This is what Gowda could do and others would not. That is spending beyond budgetary limits and rectifying it retrospectively. Giving the power of LoC to a field officer was itself a huge thing. And allowing a field officer to buy computers and increase staff is not a joke in the government. He had an enormous appetite for risk-taking. By God's grace, not even a single voice was raised against my recruitment of the new staff,' Jaamdar remembered.[10]

After six months, when work was going on in full swing, a World Bank team came for an inspection. They were impressed with the new energy they saw on the ground. They also recognized the new work culture. They went back and gave a positive report. Their first report just noted that things were improving, but the second report was a clearer endorsement of the progress. At that point, the World Bank invited Gowda's government to Washington, DC for further negotiations to lift the suspension. Gowda sent Jaamdar. He spent eleven working days there. The decision was taken to lift the ban, and by the time Jaamdar reached India, Gowda had a copy of the order lifting the suspension in his hand.[11]

After the suspension order was lifted, money started flowing, restrictions went away and things started moving rapidly. In one straight year, Gowda had changed the impression about the project not just in the World Bank but in Karnataka as well. 'This would not have happened without the farsightedness of Gowda. He knew all the project details. No engineer, secretary or officer could compete with his knowledge. Gowda's mastery of the subject, whichever subject he picks up to deal with, has always amazed IAS officers. How he does it, only God knows,' Jaamdar said.[12]

Rehabilitation was going on smoothly at the UKP, but when it came to land acquisition, the biggest hurdle was litigation. The quantum of compensation given to farmers neither covered their trauma of displacement nor their poverty and hardship. The Gowda government decided to tackle this. An additional legal adviser, of the rank of senior civil judge, was appointed to study the pattern of judgments that the courts were giving. His findings were an eye-opener. For dry land, courts were awarding four times more compensation to the litigants than what the government was offering, and in the case of irrigated land, they were giving three times the government rate. These awards were being made after five to seven years of litigation. The delay defeated the purpose of the compensation. First, it was a Rs 4000 per acre, then after five years they got four times for dry lands, that is Rs 20,000. On the extra Rs 16,000 they also got 16 per cent interest for five years, plus 12 per cent cess. All this put together, they received Rs 40,000 per acre, out of which lawyer's knocked off one-third. That would leave them with around Rs 25,000 per acre.[13]

The government studied all this and decided to enhance the compensation four times more. The thinking was that why should the lawyers be allowed to benefit? Why not put money directly in the hands of displaced farmers, and save them the hassles of litigation? The Gowda government decided to go for what was termed the 'consent award'. The Land Acquisition Act was a central act and could not be amended to the state's desire. There were only a few provisions that could be interpreted to suit the state's goals. 'Under the Land Acquisition Act there was a liberal clause, which was deleted later. It said " . . . whatever is agreed between the district collector and the landowner that would be the final compensation". We decided to apply that. When the idea was presented to Deve Gowda, he readily accepted it. It was unimaginable. The cost would shoot up by four times for the government. It was a one-time action— one cheque, no middlemen, no court, no lawyers. The farmer would sign an agreement that they will not go to court after they accept the compensation. I tell you, Rs 4000 became Rs 40,000. It caught on like wildfire. Farmers were very happy. When we started giving these consent awards, lawyers were up against the government. They held a huge strike and led protest marches in Bangalore, but nothing really happened,' Jaamdar recollected.[14]

The Gowda government decided yet another thing. It said farmers need not make trips to government offices to collect compensation. Instead, the government would reach their doorstep. It was decided that the compensation money would be distributed in gram sabhas. The dates of gram sabhas were announced in advance, and local MLAs would be present when cheques were distributed. Officials from three to four banks were also invited to open new accounts for villagers and ensure that money did not go to wrong hands. All the gram sabha events were videographed. 'In a day, we would distribute anywhere between Rs 3 crore to Rs 20 crore. Services were offered at the doorstep. They were affected people. They had sacrificed their land for the greater good. They were not beggars waiting for government dole. They had to be treated with respect, and they were. Since the entire village was present at the gram sabha, there was no question of fraudulent claims. People would dispute and shout out. Farmers could not imagine that deputy commissioners, assistant commissioners and tahsildars were reaching their doorstep to offer compensation. Thanks to Gowda, these were extraordinary decisions. It had never happened before,' Jaamdar remembered.[15] Gowda had ensured that with the consent award, the vicious circle of low compensation, litigation, corruption and delays were removed in one stroke. This created a halo for the Gowda government in the World Bank. They were so excited with the 'Gowda R&R model' that they recommended it to other Asian countries. Jaamdar would get regularly invited to train officers in Nepal, Sri Lanka, Thailand and other countries where they had to deal with R&R issues. He also delivered lectures on this model on behalf of the World Bank at international seminars.[16]

Money to complete the project was still a huge problem. The World Bank loan was not sufficient; therefore, Gowda made a bold decision to issue public bonds and raise money from the market. The idea to raise money from the market for irrigation projects existed as an idea before Gowda, but Krishna Jala Bhagya Nigam as an entity had not taken off. Gowda pursued it diligently. The SEBI clearance for the bonds came in mid-January 1996 and the Reserve Bank of India cleared it in the third week of February 1996. The bonds were such a hit that they were oversubscribed. Around Rs 650 crore was raised.[17] Initially, people were hesitant about the bonds. It was unfamiliar to them. Assessing the public mood, Gowda and his wife picked up bonds for around Rs 1 lakh each and advertised it.[18] Soon, it started flying off the shelf. Like the R&R model, the irrigation bonds too became a model for other states. Soon, Maharashtra followed in the footsteps of Karnataka to issue Krishna valley bonds, then other states experimented with the idea.

Since the government was racing against time on UKP, an entrustment panel was created to award small contracts for short lengths of canal work to a number of small contractors bypassing the usual tender process of the government. A technical oversight committee was also created for this purpose. Although this was cleared by the cabinet and the government order[19] clearly said that contract should be given to those who can acquire land directly from the farmers, it led to a controversy and Gowda had to face allegations of corruption. An inquiry was ordered, and a legislative house committee also gave its report much later, but nothing came of it. In Gowda's mind, small contracts, in small parcels, was the only way to progress fast and achieve the deadline. He had not violated the law but had worked within it. It was also not his personal decision but the decision of the cabinet. 'But for Deve Gowda, UKP would not have been completed. No other chief minister would have dared to do it the way he did it. Subsequently, everybody got on to the wagon he had set in motion. He was an original,' Jaamdar said.[20]

The northern canal (NRBC) of the UKP was to be done in stage two, much later. But, Deve Gowda knew that if he did not complete it, the state could not utilize its share of water before the deadline. He decided to take it up immediately. The law department was against it. It said this would give rise to legal complications, and the central government would be upset too. 'When the objection was raised, in the presence of all officials, Gowda said if they want to dismiss my government, they can go ahead and do so. He sanctioned the work on the 175-km-long canal. But when it was finally inaugurated, S.M. Krishna was chief minister. At the inaugural function, Gowda, the man who risked his own government's dismissal, was not remembered. I reminded S.M. Krishna, and Gowda's own Janata Dal MLA, Amregouda Byyapur, to mention his name, but they conveniently ignored my advice. I was at the function and on the dais. I whispered into Krishna's ears, but he did not respond. Pettiness and ingratitude that I witnessed hurt me,' Jaamdar remembered.[21] NRBC canal goes to the most undeveloped areas like Lingsagur, Devdurga and Kustagi taluks of Raichur and Koppal districts of Karnataka.

Meanwhile, Andhra Pradesh was worried that Karnataka was creating extra capacity and an oversized Almatti dam. Within a few weeks of Gowda becoming prime minister, the Krishna controversy erupted. A public interest litigation (PIL) was filed with a prayer that Karnataka should be directed to stop the construction of the Almatti Dam. When Gowda took over as chief minister, the dam had reached 507 metres height. A question arose at that point whether Karnataka should construct Almatti Dam up to its full height and store water up to 524.256 metres or should store only up to 519.6 metres as the Krishna Water Disputes Tribunal had awarded only 173 TMC to Karnataka against its demand of 445 TMC. Gowda decided to go up to 519.6 metres for irrigation uses and up to 524.256 metres for hydro power generation. Gowda also understood that if Karnataka did not push for 524.256 metres, Andhra Pradesh would commit surplus water under Telugu Ganga Project. This kicked up a row a little over a month after Gowda became prime minister. It was a delicate issue because the Telugu Desam Party was part of his United Front coalition government, and N. Chandrababu Naidu was under pressure to defend his state's interest.

Gowda, who was now 'head of the family' as prime minister, could not argue for Karnataka's case alone. He sagaciously decided to solve this dispute outside the court through mediation by setting up a technical committee of five states where United Front constituents had governments. He involved West Bengal chief minister Jyoti Basu to work out a compromise solution, and the technical committee was led by West Bengal's chief engineer. The chief engineers of Uttar Pradesh, Bihar, Tamil Nadu and Assam were also on the panel besides lawyers. Senior advocate Mohan V. Katarki, who was on Karnataka's Cauvery legal team, was part of it too. Justice N.V. Ramana who was then a lawyer with a hotline to Naidu was part of the Andhra team.[22] The panel toured Karnataka and Andhra Pradesh for eight days and gave a report. It fixed the height at 519.6 metres as against the earlier 514 metres. Therefore, as chief minister, Gowda boldly triggered the Almatti Dam storage up to 524.256 metres and later as prime minister, laid the foundation for its eventual resolution by appointing a mediation committee.

The Constitution Bench of the Supreme Court in its judgment of 25 April 2000 relied on the suggestion of mediation panel and upheld Karnataka's claim to store up to 519.6 metres at Almatti. The Supreme Court also noted that the question of further raising storage up to 524.256 metres at Almatti will be considered by the next Krishna Water Disputes Tribunal. The second Krishna tribunal permitted Karnataka to store up to 524.256 metres at Almatti in its award of 2010. It revisited and confirmed the award in 2013. The total allocation of water to Karnataka under the UKP increased from 173 TMC as awarded by the first Krishna Tribunal to 302 TMC under the second one.

The full capacity at Almatti has not been reached to this day, which means Gowda had fully exploited the storage potential while he was in power. Also, Karnataka and UKP were the principal beneficiaries for the first decade of the Accelerated Irrigation Development Programme that he started as prime minister. Gowda started this scheme because as irrigation minister and chief minister, he had realized how difficult it was for states to raise resources to complete irrigation projects that had been started ambitiously. But Naidu, who was Andhra Pradesh chief minister and convenor of the steering committee of the United Front government, suspected that Gowda was bringing this scheme only to complete UKP. Gowda recalled:

Naidu attacked me in the steering panel meeting. He said it was a mistake to have made me prime minister because I was cheating his state. Karunanidhi, Jyoti Basu, Mulayam Singh and Lalu Yadav were all present. Tamil Nadu did not have major dams, so Karunanidhi kept quiet. I said I have common sense and gave a list of projects that had remained unfinished in all states due to lack of funds. I also spoke about incomplete irrigation canals of the Bhakra Nangal Dam too, which had been inaugurated in Nehru's time. I told them about my struggles in the past to raise money. I argued that this scheme was true co-operative federalism. Jyoti Basu understood. He stood up for me. He asked Naidu not to raise objections. The proof of the scheme's utility is the fact that no prime minister after me discontinued it. UKP alone has got Rs 18,000 crore from this scheme over the years. Not a single penny was spent on the Cauvery River projects from this fund since there was a water-sharing dispute. In short, this scheme did not help south Karnataka where I hailed from.[23]

Jaamdar said that he was not a Janata Dal man, nor was he a great fan of Deve Gowda, but 'one cannot, and should not, forget the monumental work Gowda has done'.[24] The UKP was completed and inaugurated by President Abdul Kalam in August 2006; even in that function, there was not a word of appreciation for Gowda. However, the World Bank reports, which record the roller-coaster ride of the project, identify Gowda's tenure as chief minister as the period when a dramatic turnaround happened. They also acknowledge his political will. The Staff Appraisal Report of the World Bank in 1989, five years before Gowda took over as chief minister, had said: 'The lessons learned from the past experience clearly indicate that a coherent, well planned and designed resettlement plan should be formulated and implemented.' It had also said: 'A common denominator of many of the deficiencies encountered during the implementation of the irrigation components of UKP's first phase was the project's weak institutional base; lack of effective project management; lack of accountability at all levels and lack of a properly trained, properly supervised and motivated staff.'[25]

In contrast, a World Bank paper in June 1998, after Gowda's intervention, spoke about the dramatic turnaround: '(With the) Appointment of a new secretary for Rehabilitation and Land Acquisition (Jaamdar), Upper Krishna Project, the situation began to change substantially. The secretary has a keen grasp of the situation, has energy and managerial capability, and is personally responsible for many of the improvements in this project since October 1995. During his tenure resettlement staffing increased from 150 to 900, tens of thousands of families started construction on their homes, thousands of ex-gratias and grants were paid, the consent award system was introduced, land compensation rates finally caught up to market prices, corrupt resettlement officers were fired, beneficiary participation is reaching reasonable levels, and much other work has been accomplished. The adoption of the consent award system in January 1996 was a key turning point in moving beyond the excessively adversarial approach previously followed. In fact, more was accomplished at Almatti between October 1995 and June 1997 than in the entire UKP up to 1995.'[26]

The paper also said: 'The resettlement operation at Upper Krishna has made one of the most dramatic turnarounds of any resettlement operation in a Bank-assisted project, from crisis and two suspensions to approaching satisfactory performance. More remains to be done, but for the first time in a sad 20-year history the fundamental building blocks of an acceptable resettlement program —political will, a legal framework, institutional capacity, adequate budget, comprehensive planning, a development program, and participation of the affected population—appear to be in place.'[27]

Gowda's focus on harnessing Krishna water for irrigation had a long-term socio-economic effect in the region. The north Karnataka districts were drought-prone areas where seasonal migration had been inevitable for hundreds of years. The poor, small and marginal landowners all migrated. They went to either Maharashtra or Goa. Without irrigation, they had only one crop and could not stay in their homes for more than six months of the year. The poverty level was high and the wage level was low. After UKP, this migration came down by 95 per cent. On the contrary, there was migration into these areas from Maharashtra and Andhra Pradesh. Agriculture labour income shot up. Minimum wages went up too. Round the year employment was guaranteed. Poverty level dropped in north Karnataka, and this led to the overall reduction in the poverty level of the state.[28] 'Gowda was a son of a small farmer and had seen acute poverty. He converted his exposure to rural life and poverty into big ideas,' Jaamdar said.[29]

In fact, even in 1976, as leader of the Opposition, Gowda had fought for a higher share of the Krishna water. When the Bachawat award came, Gowda felt that maximum benefit had been given to Andhra Pradesh. He thought this had happened because K.L. Rao was a very influential figure. (Rao was irrigation minister under Nehru and Indira Gandhi. He had helped design the Nagarjuna Sagar Dam across the Krishna River. During a debate on the Krishna tribunal in the state assembly, in August 1974, Gowda had said, 'The decision of this body [tribunal] is based on the parochial attitude under the influence of Mr K.L. Rao.'[30]) Gowda recalled: 'Chief Minister Devaraj Urs came directly to my residence from Delhi. He explained the award to me. I took the papers from him and went straight to chief engineer S.G. Balekundry's house. He studied the papers and said there was an injustice and that we should get more water. He advised me to refuse the award. I communicated this to Urs. Without any hesitation, Urs said if it is going to help our state let us reject it. That was his greatness. 'It may be our own party's government at the Centre, but I cannot

sacrifice the state's interests,' he said. Following this, I moved a
resolution in the assembly, and the house unanimously rejected
the award. Later, in 1979, the share was revised to 734 TMC from
700 TMC.'[31]

The Cauvery and the Beginning of It All

As mentioned at the beginning of this chapter, the Cauvery was
essentially a water-sharing dispute and did not expect a developmental
vision like the Krishna did. It was a 200-year-old dispute, and it had
started with the fall of Tipu Sultan in 1799. The dispute persisted
across centuries between Mysore (later Karnataka), an upper riparian
state, and Madras (later Tamil Nadu), a lower riparian state. There
were brilliant legal minds on both sides making a case against each
other. At the beginning of the twentieth century, if M.C. Setalvad
was the counsel for the Mysore maharaja, representing Madras was
Alladi Krishnaswamy. C.P. Ramaswamy Iyer, who was a member of
the executive council of the Madras Governor, had played a crucial
role in the negotiation of the 1924 agreement. Iyer went to England
in the last leg of his life to write a book, tentatively titled 'A History
of My Times' that included a long chapter on the Cauvery dispute,[32]
but died before he had completed his research at the India Office
library. In more recent times, the dispute has seen the involvement
of legal luminaries like Fali Nariman.

Deve Gowda's role in forwarding the case of Cauvery and wanting
to harness it fully by taking a relook at the projects that existed in
the river basin started in his very first term as a legislator in 1962.
He had been elected as an independent after being expelled by the
Congress, and within two years into his term, he sponsored the first-
ever private member resolution in the history of Karnataka's lower
house. He was thirty-one years old. Gowda presented his resolution
on 31 March 1964. It read as follows: 'That this House recommends
to the Government to take all necessary steps to utilize the full extent
the potential resources of Cauvery waters and also to implement all

the schemes necessary in this behalf within the Fourth Five-Year plan period.' In his 45-minutes speech that followed, he had passionately argued that the river was the lifeline to people in Hassan, Coorg, Mysore, Mandya, Tumkur, Chitradurga and Bangalore districts, and the state's share of water should be constructively utilized for the development of the people of this region, failing which the 'future generations may not condone us'.[33]

This looked like an innocuous resolution, but it created a flutter in the assembly and outside, because it suddenly painted the government as unthinking towards the people of the south, which was dominated by Gowda's Vokkaliga community. The chief minister at the time was S. Nijalingappa, and Veerendra Patil was public works minister. Both were from the Lingayat community that controlled the politics of north Karnataka. It stoked the latent fire of regional power imbalances. In one stroke, Gowda had appropriated the politics of Cauvery, and that too as an independent member from a constituency in the corner of Hassan. He had also suddenly attracted the attention of the pan-Mysore region and had come into reckoning overnight. Cauvery became Gowda's life mission and the cornerstone of his politics. It took him to heights that he did not anticipate he would reach in 1964. 'Do you think when I presented this private resolution, I was doing it with the aim of becoming chief minister and prime minister? As an expelled member of the Congress, I was in a situation where I could not even dream of becoming a minister. When I spoke in the house that day, senior legislators like Shantaveri Gopal Gowda congratulated me. It gave me an identity,' Gowda said.[34]

After Gowda had presented the resolution, Nijalingappa and Veerendra Patil spoke to him and requested him to withdraw it. They assured him that they would focus on Cauvery, draw up projects, and implement them. They gave an assurance in the house too. But when Gowda saw that they had not followed through on their assurance, two years later (in 1966), he presented the resolution again with a firm resolve that he will not withdraw it this time.

He was adamant about getting the resolution passed unanimously. It was passed. In the history of the Karnataka legislature so far, this is the first and only private member resolution that has been passed unanimously. It forced the government to urgently lay the foundation stone for the Harangi and Hemavathi reservoirs. This move had introduced the people of Karnataka to the intransigence of Gowda, which they would encounter many times in the next half century.

What had provoked Gowda to think of a resolution in the first place was a speech that S. Nijalingappa had made at the birthday celebrations of his Tamil Nadu counterpart, K. Kamaraj, in July 1963: 'Nijalingappa said, "I will give you any amount of Cauvery water, give me paddy". I was taken aback. I wondered how could he commit our water like this, especially when we ourselves were facing a shortage? I decided to study the issue. I first went to S.G. Balekundry. He was then joint secretary in the irrigation department. He asked me to meet Aminbhavi, an engineer in charge of investigations for irrigation projects. He provided me with all the details related to Cauvery. I also met the son-in-law of my political guru, A.G. Ramachandra Rao, who was also an irrigation engineer in Mysore. He offered insights too. Then, I mobilized legislators from the Cauvery basin and sought time with Nijalingappa. In the meeting, Nijalingappa was indifferent. He used a Kannada proverb, *"Hole neer kudiyokke donnappan icche na"* (roughly meaning, does one need the approval of the village headman to drink water from the stream). As we made our case, he grew impatient and said he was getting late for his next appointment. At that point, Balekundry, who was a fearless man, said, if the chief minister did not have the time, he should ask Veerendra Patil to sit in for him. There was another reason for Nijalingappa's impatience. He saw me as being aligned with B.D. Jatti, his rival in the Congress party. It is for the same reason that he had denied Congress tickets to nine Vokkaligas, including me, in 1962. It was after this meeting that I gave a notice for the resolution. Speaker Vaikunta Baligar said I had only fifteen minutes to present it. I demanded an hour and went ahead,' Gowda recalled.[35]

Gowda's role in building a political movement around Cauvery, indirectly led to the revival of the Vokkaligas' urge for political dominance. The community had lost its pride of place with the reorganization of Karnataka in 1956. Kadidal Manjappa was unseated and Nijalingappa had become chief minister. Though the two communities shared political power, the chief ministership invariably went to the Lingayats. The Vokkaligas had to wait till 1994 when Gowda became chief minister. That was nearly a four-decade wait. Even when Gowda became chief minister, it was not a smooth anointment. He had to literally grab it from a crafty Ramakrishna Hegde. After Gowda, Karnataka has seen two other Vokkaliga chief minsters: S.M. Krishna and Gowda's son H.D. Kumaraswamy.

Cauvery was about litigation and it needed a shrewd litigator like Gowda. Mohan V. Katarki, senior advocate in the Supreme Court and part of Karnataka's Cauvery legal team led by Fali Nariman, said Gowda is basically a tough and an obstinate litigant: 'His mastery of litigation is superb. Even after decades, he can tell you who the judge was in the 1950s in a particular lower court in Karnataka and which lawyer argued what on which day. In the Hassan district court there was a time when he knew every lawyer, similarly in the Karnataka High Court. And any politically sensitive PIL filed in the Karnataka High Court until ten years ago (that is, up to 2010), would not escape Gowda's attention. His best friends are lawyers. He can't start or end his day without a lawyer.'[36] This interest and understanding of litigation by Gowda helped him navigate the complex Cauvery terrain. In the courts, he was virtually Karnataka's lawyer without the black robes.

When the Cauvery Water Disputes Tribunal gave its interim order in 1991, the Karnataka government passed an ordinance against it and the President of India referred it to the Supreme Court. At this point, Gowda did not erupt immediately. He studied and watched. He had anyway opposed the formation of the tribunal. He revolted once the tribunal reiterated its interim order of 25 June 1991 on

2 April 1992. He organized a massive rally of over 1,00,000 people
in Mysore. That revolt shook the state government. S. Bangarappa,
a backward class leader, was chief minister, and it was not easy for
him to survive the ire of a major community like the Vokkaligas. At
that time, he got a PIL filed in the high court, which basically argued
that when the tribunal's judges went on an inspection tour of Tamil
Nadu, they accepted gifts and local hospitality. 'The PIL was not in
good taste,' Katarki remarked.[37] It presented a video that showed the
tribunal's judges being felicitated in different towns of Tamil Nadu.
It also showed how in every nook and corner of Tanjore district,
there were posters put up by political parties welcoming the judges.[38]
Like other Vokkaliga leaders in the Cauvery belt, Gowda never easily
resorted to the politics of agitation. His preferred method always
was litigation. 'Governments in Karnataka have always watched
Gowda closely on the Cauvery issue. Either they wanted to please
him or checkmate him. The ordinance passed by the Bangarappa
government in 1991 refusing to release water to Tamil Nadu was
an act of constitutional belligerence. However, it came in handy for
Bangarappa to placate Gowda politically,' said Katarki, who has been
on the Cauvery legal team since 1991.[39]

The elaborate speeches Gowda made in the parliament as a
first-time member, in July and December of 1991, on the Cauvery
tribunal's interim order was more a lawyer's argument with facts,
figures, history of judgments, hidden clauses, legal precedence, logic
and reason than an emotional plea or empty rhetoric of a politician.
Gowda argued: 'An atmosphere is being created that the people of
Karnataka are not law-abiding citizens . . . after the Presidential
reference was made to it (the Supreme Court has said) that the state
of Karnataka has passed an ordinance which will ultimately lead
to lawlessness and also forebodes evil consequences to the federal
structure of the Constitution . . . If this impression has been created,
then it is the responsibility of the central government or the other
forum, that is the Parliament, that we are representing, to clarify how
did such a situation arise?'[40]

After putting various legal arguments and tons of data on the table, he alluded to the history of the Cauvery dispute:

> Sir, about the political background, I want to say one thing. In the nineteenth century, the state of Mysore was a princely vassal state, whereas Madras was a province in the British Presidency. This political set-up and the advantage of being a lower riparian were fully made use of by the then Madras state to develop large areas of irrigation by putting restrictions on the upper riparian Mysore. They forced the restrictions in the form of 1892 rules and 1924 agreement by which the Mysore state was forced to take the permission of Madras whenever they had to take a new work in the Cauvery basin, whereas Madras did not have any corresponding obligation to take the permission of Mysore. I would like to ask one thing from my Tamil Nadu friends. In 1914 Justice H.D. Griffins arbitrated in the matter and gave his final award. Madras did not respect that award. Today they want to blame us that we are disrespecting the award.[41]

During Gowda's tenure as chief minister, the Cauvery crisis broke in September 1995. He spoke to the Cauvery legal team directly. The team wrote to him saying that there was a deficit of 15 TMC, and if Karnataka did not release water, Tamil Nadu was sure to knock at the Supreme Court's door. 'I advised that it will complicate matters if the court passed an order. Karnataka was already viewed as the one that violated the interim order. He understood that the state could not afford negative publicity. "We will release the water," he assured but asked me to write another letter on what the legal team thinks is the minimum that should be released to escape the court's wrath. I consulted Nariman and wrote a letter saying that 5 TMC should be released immediately to ward off a crisis. We said that would help the state to put up an arguable face before the court. He released the water and all hell broke out in the state assembly. They accused him of having compromised,' Katarki recalled.[42] But to Gowda's good luck, when the debate started in the assembly, there was a heavy downpour in the state. The issue was put on the backburner.

However, by December 1995, Jayalalitha revived her claim in the Supreme Court. She said Karnataka had not released water, and the standing crops were withering. It came up before a bench headed by Justice A.M. Ahmadi. He said the issue should be resolved by the Cauvery tribunal. The tribunal passed an order on 19 December, holding Karnataka liable for 11 TMC. 'Gowda requested me to stay in Delhi since it was winter vacation. We knew Tamil Nadu would approach the court. Nariman was not there. He had in fact gone to Karnataka for a lawyers' conference. The matter came up before the court on 28 December 1995. Senior advocate Anil Divan, who had just then joined the legal team, led the arguments for Karnataka. Justice K. Ramaswamy was presiding over the vacation bench. Everybody expected that the court would direct Karnataka to release water, the state would refuse and invariably President's rule would be imposed. Gowda was very tense. He asked me to do something and get the matter referred to the Government of India (GoI). "If the central government directs, we will release water because that will be a political decision," he said. It was a Congress government at the Centre and the principal Opposition in the state was the Congress. That was smart thinking on his part. If the court issued directions, then it would be between the court and Gowda, and Gowda would be cornered and villainized. If the Centre directed, then the political blame was shared. We had a tough time in the court,' Katarki recalled.[43]

The argument built up before the court was that the Gowda government was ready to release the water, but it could not be done forthwith as the tribunal had ordered. The state needed some time as consensus was being built in the state with all political parties. The likelihood of a law and order problem was also emphasized. Then the lawyers produced the resolution of the Congress party, which had asked the government not to release water and not to honour the tribunal's order. The party meeting had been attended by two central ministers too. 'The moment we read that out, Justice Ramaswamy understood. He said "All right, we will direct the prime minister to work out a solution." That is exactly what Gowda wanted. He was thrilled. He said, "Let the prime minister do whatever he likes. I will simply follow his orders." Immediately, he called the prime minister and regular trips to his residence began,' Katarki said.[44] The meeting of Cauvery basin chief ministers with the prime minister took place on 6 January 1996. As per the prime minister's direction, 6 TMC was released, and for the second tranche of 5 TMC, a committee was constituted under the chairmanship of Y.K. Alagh. When the Alagh panel toured Karnataka, Gowda did the technical briefing himself. They were impressed. They even made a public statement that they had not met a chief minister who was so thorough with technical aspects. It is at this point that Alagh came in contact with Gowda, and he later became a minister in the Union cabinet under Gowda.[45]

According to Mohan Katarki, the Cauvery litigation took Gowda to P.V. Narasimha Rao and finally to the prime minister's chair. The regular meetings between Rao and Gowda between January and May 1996 built a rapport between the two, which helped Gowda later. Gowda honouring Rao's decision to allow the release of water to Tamil Nadu when the Supreme Court had shifted the onus on the prime minister's office, impressed Rao. Gowda ensured Rao's writ ran and that he was not embarrassed. When the prime minister gave a direction in the meeting of chief ministers, in which Gowda and Jayalalitha were principal players, an upset Jayalalitha walked out, but Gowda went back and followed Rao's direction despite opposition at home. 'If Gowda had refused, it would have created a federal crisis. This created trust between the two and a personal bond. Later, in 1996, when the United Front coalition with outside support of the Congress had to pick a prime minister, Rao was the Congress president, and he did not object to Gowda's candidature. He was reportedly pleased,' Katarki said.[46]

Meenakshisundaram, who was Gowda's principal secretary then, remembers attending the prime minister's arbitration meeting:

> Jayalalitha herself argued Tamil Nadu's case. She did not allow her Secretaries and engineers to explain. She was very thorough. Gowda listened carefully. In a piece of paper, he noted down the points that were being misrepresented. He passed on the slip to me. I thought he was just keeping me informed. But after she had completed, he said, 'My principal secretary will present our case.' I was from Tamil Nadu, my name unmistakably revealed it, but Jayalalitha was Tamil Nadu chief minister who hailed from Karnataka. To get me to represent Karnataka's case was a politically shrewd move. When I started explaining, he was very attentive, and if I made an error, he would gently touch my hand and correct me in Kannada. Only in the end he spoke to summarize all the arguments and explained why Karnataka found it difficult to release the quantum of water that was being demanded. But, he added, that he was very keen to help 'our neighbours'. He told the prime minister that, 'if you give a reasonable direction, I will persuade my party and the Opposition to release water'. Finally, Rao gave an order. Jayalalitha did not like it. She walked out. Gowda immediately said he will obey the prime minister.[47]

When Gowda was prime minister, in 1997, the question came up in the Supreme Court on a suit filed by Tamil Nadu that the interim order of the Cauvery tribunal should be implemented by forming the Cauvery River Authority. The Karnataka government was opposed to it, but the legal team felt that the state should agree to an authority because that would become an alternate redressal forum, or else the Supreme Court could directly intervene, which was not so desirable. Gowda called up, asking Karnataka's view. Gowda spent a couple of days discussing it, and then Ashok Desai, the attorney general, told the court that the central government was ready to frame the Cauvery scheme. 'That was a Gowda masterstroke. Everybody was surprised, including Tamil Nadu. Within weeks of that announcement, Gowda lost power. Then the matter came up in 1998 again when Vajpayee was prime minister. The court asked what had happened to the assurance given by the Gowda government. It passed an order saying it will not give more than eight days. There was a lot of confusion in Karnataka. Chief Minister J.H. Patel was not sure how it would turn out. Everybody was thinking of their own survival. Gowda was tense too. He called us every single day and requested us to speak to certain people and convince them about the scheme. The then irrigation minister H.N. Nanje Gowda was appointed interlocutor from Karnataka's side. Finally, the Cauvery River Authority was formed. Tamil Nadu insisted that the prime minister should head it. That is how Vajpayee became its first chairman,' Katarki recalled.[48]

After he stepped down as prime minister, Gowda could not directly be involved with the Cauvery legal issue, but he always remained in the background. The difficulty came in 2005, when Gowda's party, the Janata Dal, was in a coalition arrangement with the Congress, and Dharam Singh was chief minister. The Cauvery tribunal decided to tour basin areas for the second time. When the tribunal had toured Tamil Nadu the first time, a massive human chain of 200 km was organized to create sympathy. With this in mind, Karnataka opposed the second tour as unnecessary. It also argued that distorted impressions gained during the tour may prejudice the case. The chairman of the tribunal agreed with Karnataka, but two fellow judges dissented. The disagreement between the judges became so apparent in court that the tribunal members started openly airing dissent between each other. Even senior advocate Parasaran, who was arguing Tamil Nadu's case before the tribunal, asked the judges to settle differences in their chambers. 'The press reported it as "the broken tribunal". Everyone was exasperated. Karnataka wondered if it should ask for the reconstitution of the tribunal. The legal team realized that it was not possible legally. The Supreme Court would say people dissent and differ all the time and that could not be grounds to change the tribunal. Gowda did not agree. A PIL was filed. Then the crucial question arose as to how the government, which Gowda's party was supporting, should react to the PIL. Gowda suggested that the Karnataka government should file a reply supporting the petition. However, the legal team disagreed,' Katarki said.[49]

The government took Gowda's line and said they will support the petition. The Cauvery legal team said the team under Nariman would not wish to represent the state in the PIL. If the team appeared in the case, and if the plea to reconstitute the tribunal was rejected by the Supreme Court, it would be difficult for the team to appear before the tribunal's judges whose dismissal they had sought. The team's argument was that the PIL would cast a shadow on Karnataka's main Cauvery case. 'Gowda was upset, and we said we are equally upset. Finally, what we predicted happened, the petition was dismissed.' Thereafter, for a few years the relationship between Gowda and the Nariman-led legal team was rather cold,' Katarki said.[50]

In 2012 and 2013, the Cauvery crisis erupted again over the implementation of the interim order. 'Irrigation Minister Basavaraj Bommai telephoned and said, Gowda would like to speak. We had a long chat. The relationship revived. In 2018, when the final order came, the legal team immediately announced that Karnataka had won the case. We asserted because each time we did well in the court, Karnataka would still present itself as a victim. I came out and told the media that this is a balanced judgment and we are satisfied at present with the share of Karnataka, since the state's burden had been reduced by 14.5 TMC. After parting 177.25 TMC with Tamil Nadu, Karnataka would get its share of 284.5 TMC, and also the right to use available surplus water which is another 30 TMC. I thanked the judges and said this brings justice not only to Karnataka but also to Tamil Nadu's farmers. I did not ask the government before making the statement. In a couple of hours, Chief Minister Siddaramaiah took the same line. Gowda, however, was not entirely satisfied with the judgment. Of course, Gowda had good reasons to expect more.

He had toiled for decades. But can everybody be satisfied entirely in the allocation of water in an inter-state dispute?' Katarki asked.[51]

The Cauvery legal team and Gowda enjoyed a special relationship. The team realized that Gowda, besides being a shrewd litigator, was a master in water-planning who combined his engineering skills and practical experience. 'We relied on Gowda's advice on hydrology more than any other engineer's advice. Gowda is the one who cracked the complex theory of pro-rata sharing of distress and demonstrated its unjustness to Karnataka. On his advice, Karnataka had to change its stand in 1995–1996. Later, we found that the US Supreme Court, too, has taken the same view against pro-rata sharing of distress,' said Katarki.[52]

In the Cauvery legal battle, there were two patriarchs, so to say. One was Nariman, the patriarch of Indian law ('patriarch' is used here in a benign sense to indicate that he is an elder or 'a venerable old man'), and the other was Deve Gowda, who had emerged as the patriarch of the Cauvery basin. The relationship between Nariman and Gowda was one of warmth and respect. As prime minister, Gowda wanted Nariman to be his attorney general, but Nariman had refused not just Gowda, but also Vajpayee later. Although the two differed over the PIL in 2005, that did not in the slightest affect their personal relationship. Whatever differences arose on legal matters, at whichever point, Gowda would call on Nariman to clarify. He described one such meeting. There is confusion over its date, but it must have taken place after 2005, that is, after the dust over the PIL had settled: 'I had not gone to see Nariman as long as S.M. Krishna was chief minister (Krishna stepped down in 2004). I sought an appointment and went to his house in Delhi at 9 a.m. The sun was not very harsh, so we sat in the lawn. His wife also came out to greet me and served tea and biscuits. She was always a very good host. I gently brought up the points about which I had a different opinion. He listened patiently and said that he would look into it. Then he said, "I never got a chief minister like you from Karnataka who could brief me properly on Cauvery matters." I felt happy.'[53]

When Nariman's wife, Bapsi Nariman, passed away, Gowda wrote a letter, which was not just warm but also reflective: 'One of the obituaries I read described Mrs. Nariman as a large-hearted person. I am sure she was because I have always experienced your generosity and magnanimity. Without our knowing, over the decades of living together, our companions transfer a lot of their good to us. It is they who hold everything together.'[54] Nariman responded: 'Yes, Bapsi not only warmly greeted you whenever we met, but was very fond of you as well. She always chided me for not accepting your gracious offer as Prime Minister to be the Attorney General! With fond and respectful regards.'[55] The exchange between the two suggests there has been a special ring to their relationship.

The Cauvery journey that began for Gowda when he introduced the resolution in the Karnataka assembly as a first-time legislator will perhaps never end. Once, he emotionally said that when he is gone, his ashes would be distributed equally between the Cauvery and Krishna rivers.[56] What people even in south Karnataka, the ground zero of his politics, do not remember is that it was Gowda who was responsible for completing projects in the Cauvery River basin. Kabini, Harangi and Hemavathi projects and twenty-three other smaller ones were all completed during his tenure as irrigation minister for six years, then nearly two years as chief minister, and eleven months as prime minister.[57] Even as prime minister, his local interest did not disappear; his supervision was constant and continuous. He always brought new ideas to the table. The Cauvery projects were not started by him, but completing them was his achievement, or was it his karma?

Years of Learning and a World Tour

In the 1980s, for over six years, Gowda held two portfolios of irrigation and public works (PWD) in the Janata Dal governments of Ramakrishna Hegde and S.R. Bommai. Once, he asked Rajan, his irrigation secretary and K.C. Reddy, his PWD secretary, to prepare a financial projection as to how much it would cost the government to complete projects in the Krishna and Cauvery basins within deadlines handed down by tribunals, and how many years it would take to complete the projects if they continue with existing allocations. They prepared a document, which said that in the current year alone, that is 1986–87, Rs 500–600 crore was needed over and above the Rs 300 crore that had been set aside. Gowda sent the file to the finance department. Finance Secretary M. Shankarnarayanan perused the file and wrote that 'the finance department was not an Akshaya Patra' to provide the kind of money that was being demanded. What he meant was he did not have a magical bowl to produce infinite resources on demand. Gowda was upset.[58] He wrote a letter to Hegde saying if this was the attitude towards his department, he would quit the cabinet. Hegde panicked and assuaged Gowda with an assurance that he would try to increase the allocation. In a couple of years, when he still did not get the resources he was looking for, he quit the cabinet. By then, there was a mountain of political ill-will, too, between Gowda and Hegde. While Hegde was trying to build his legacy with the panchayat raj legislation and the decentralization of governance, Gowda was competing to build his legacy by focusing on irrigation.

Before dealing with the World Bank as chief minister in the 1990s, Gowda dealt with the bank even as irrigation minister in the 1980s. This was just before the second suspension of the loan. Since the bank's conditionalities with regard to rehabilitation had not been met, they had not released the money. By then, Hegde had stepped down and S.R. Bommai had become chief minister. Karnataka chief secretary A.B. Datar, Irrigation Secretary Chikkanna and a GoI representative went to Washington to negotiate. The GoI, which was to offer a sovereign guarantee, did not accept certain loan conditions, and the negotiations fell through. 'Gowda was informed of the development. He asked the officers to stay back and immediately left for Washington DC via Mumbai at his own expense. He helped reopen the negotiations sitting in a hotel room, pushed GoI to accept a few things they were earlier rigid about, and got the loan and project agreement cleared,'

Thippeswamy, his longtime associate and private secretary, said.[59] Unfortunately, soon after his return, the Bommai government fell. Due to inaction, the World Bank suspended its loan for the second time, and it was revived only when Gowda became chief minister. We have read that story earlier in this chapter.

Now, the question arises as to where did Gowda develop the passion for irrigation? How did he acquire knowledge without any formal education in the subject? The diploma in civil engineering he had studied did not deal with basin planning, dam construction, hydrology, water resources and water laws or any such advanced knowledge. Whenever the question is asked, Gowda is unable to give a clear answer, essentially because there is no one source, or a formal institutional exposure through which he picked up this knowledge: 'I learnt it by getting immersed in it. My interest drove me. A lot of learning happened when I became the Opposition leader in 1972. By default, I was also the Public Accounts Committee chairman, and all reports came to me. I read them carefully. I also used the legislature library well. I read newspapers diligently. I went to experts and asked them to explain something I did not understand. I did not want to be a fool when I spoke in the house. So, I prepared myself well,' Gowda said.[60]

Before Deve Gowda came to the limelight, among politicians in Karnataka, H.M. Chennabasappa was seen as an irrigation expert who was well versed in interstate water disputes. He was a cabinet colleague of Devaraj Urs. Gowda surpassed him with his irrigation knowledge because he had a fine technical grasp as well. 'Other irrigation ministers and chief ministers knew as much as they were briefed by their Secretaries. They knew as much as they needed to clear a particular file or take a call with regard to a dispute. But people like Chennabasappa and Deve Gowda knew the 100-year legal history of water disputes and its intricacies at their fingertips. They knew which agreement or decision would clash with which one from the previous years. The manner in which Gowda briefed top lawyers like Fali Nariman has been widely acknowledged,' Thippeswamy said.[61]

After Gowda became a legislator in 1962, the Hemavathi project became part and parcel of his constituency. It perhaps began in his mind as a constituency interest, and as his politics grew, it became a south Karnataka and Vokkaliga interest and finally, it became an all-Karnataka interest. He kept expanding the scope of his irrigation interest. When he became prime minister, he took this interest with him to Delhi. Therefore, he picked up the Narmada, Tehri and the Farakka problems to solve. He grew in each of the roles he came to play.

'All three main canals of Hemavathi passed through his constituency. There was one Srirangadevaru Annekattu (reservoir) in his constituency built by Tipu Sultan. As a young man, Gowda knew every technical detail about it. It all began there. He was born and brought up on the irrigation bank. It was natural for him to develop interest in harnessing water,' Thippeswamy said.[62] During the final year of his diploma course, his polytechnic college had arranged an educational tour to the Bhakra Nangal Dam, and he got a chance to see its canal system.[63] Around the same time, the Tungabhadra dam was being built in Karnataka. This was probably the only exposure he had to big dams before he started developing a deep interest in them in the 1960s and 70s.

Gowda also learnt from engineers like S.G. Balekundry, who had worked with Nijalingappa and Devaraj Urs. Balekundry had been instrumental in initiating the Malaprabha, Ghataprabha and UKP projects under Nijalingappa. He had studied in Edinburgh and was a thorough professional. He did not believe in pleasing politicians. Engineers like K.C. Reddy, who worked with Gowda closely, also filled him in continuously.[64] In the case of Nijalingappa and Urs, they respected what their engineers told them. But in the case of Gowda, he was both chief minister and chief engineer of the state.

In 1973–74 as the Opposition leader, Gowda went on a world tour to study agricultural practices and engineering projects. He was selected for a sixty-day tour of the US by the Speaker of the Karnataka assembly, and was offered first-class air travel and a five-star hotel stay. He wrote to speaker K.S. Nagarathnamma saying that he would travel economy and stay in budget hotels but would utilize the money that he would be saving to go around the world. The Speaker agreed. Gowda went to many states in the US, and studied a variety of dams. He visited the Hoover Dam, Roosevelt Dam and some other engineering projects around Las Vegas, but the one that interested him the most was the Oroville Earthen Dam over the Feather River in California: 'I walked the entire distance of the drainage gallery of the earthen dam,' he remembers. 'I also studied how water was priced in many states. They had a three-tier structure, and the highest cost per litre was for drinking water, the second highest was for industries, and the least was for agriculture. Near San Francisco, I went to a vineyard. The owner was so kind that he took me around his farm in a jeep for two hours and explained everything. In the end, he gave two bottles of vintage wine to take back. When I returned to Bangalore, I gave a bottle each to Ramakrishna Hegde and J.H. Patel since I am a teetotaler. I also studied America's highway infrastructure. I spent every minute constructively and did not waste my time going to topless bars and restaurants. Later, I went to Australia, Russia, South Korea and Japan. I studied the underground rail network in Russia and Tokyo. In Australia, I was fascinated by the Snowy Mountain Project. I presented a report of my learnings to the Speaker after my return from the tour. I had also kept a diary of my travel, but that was lost when we moved homes,' Gowda recalled.[65] All this passion, preparation and learning of years came in handy when Gowda became a minister in 1983 and held him in good stead all through his career.

This chapter began by mentioning the greater deification of Sir M. Visvesvaraya over the progressive Mysore king, Nalvadi Krishna Raja Wodeyar, who actually envisioned and commissioned the Krishnaraja Sagar Dam over the Cauvery at great personal stake. A certain social and cultural dynamic at play has ensured Visvesvaraya is better commemorated than Wodeyar. This works as an analogy for Deve Gowda too. He planned irrigation projects, litigated madly, invested his passion and doggedly pursued their completion. But, he has not been remembered or celebrated as much as the people he partnered with, deployed and sought help from to execute his vision. The larger social, cultural and political prejudice that surrounds him has not allowed credit to accrue on the riverbank of his public life. In abject dejection, he once said: 'They will remember me when I am gone.'[66]

SECTION TWO

10

Becoming Prime Minister and the Left Connection

As soon as S.S. Meenakshisundaram, Gowda's principal secretary as chief minister, returned to Bangalore from Washington DC, he got a call from Anugraha, the chief minister's official residence. He thought it was a farewell dinner by the prime minister-elect for senior officers who had worked with him in the state. But when Sundaram reached Anugraha, he realized that it was Gowda's wife Chennamma who was waiting to meet him, and there was no other official invited. Sundaram had never interacted with Gowda's wife before, and when she spoke, her anxiety was palpable. She had still not come to terms with the fact that her husband was now to rule the nation. She also did not look terribly pleased that he had accepted the job: 'He had become chief minister after long years of struggle and was doing a good job. We were happy here. Why did he have to accept this responsibility? I am afraid and the family is afraid too. We don't know what awaits us in Delhi. We do not know anybody there, nor do we know the language. Whoever I talk to about Delhi scares me about the place. Now that he has made up his mind, my request is that you should go with him,' Meenakshisundaram recalled the conversation.[1]

After the two of them had spent talking for twenty minutes,
it was announced that the prime minister-elect had arrived. They
shifted to the dining room. Chennamma served food to Sundaram
and her husband. Gowda presciently told Sundaram: 'Sundaram-
avare ("avare" is an honorific in the Kannada language), you please
join the PMO. Our tenure will not be long. Don't bring your family.
I too will not shift mine. We will go with just one suitcase.'[2]

The events in Delhi that had preceded this conversation for
over a fortnight had been edgy and dramatic. A.B. Vajpayee had
been prime minister from mid-May 1996 for thirteen days. He
had been called to form a government by President Shankar Dayal
Sharma because he was the leader of the largest political party, albeit
without a majority, and also because the United Front, a coalition of
thirteen parties, had taken time to assemble its majority. It eventually
happened with the outside support of the Congress, but after that,
it took time to pick its prime ministerial candidate. When President
Sharma invited Vajpayee to form the government, the leaders of the
secular coalition were jolted. They went to the President to protest
his hurry and betrayal of sorts. Harkishan Singh Surjeet, who was
the general-secretary of the Communist Party of India (Marxist) and
the architect of the United Front government, was furious: 'There
was a heated argument between the United Front delegation and the
President. Comrade Surjeet became very angry. He asked Sharma,
"Is this why we made you President, to bring an RSS (Rashtriya
Swayamsevak Sangh, the ideological parent of the BJP) government
to power?" He refused to accept tea and snacks that were served
at the Rashtrapati Bhavan,' Sitaram Yechury, who was present in
the delegation, recalled the words and action of his party elder and
predecessor as general-secretary.[3]

He also explained why Surjeet made such a statement in the
meeting with the President: 'Sharma had been elected President with
the support of the Left parties. Surjeet had agreed to the elevation of
Sharma, who was then vice president, with the condition that K.R.
Narayanan is made the new vice president. Comrade A.B. Bardhan

and I met P.V. Narasimha Rao with this proposal. I was also later despatched to meet Narayanan, who was the former vice-chancellor of my alma mater, the Jawaharlal Nehru University. Although the presidential polls came before the vice presidential polls, Surjeet strategized in such a way that he insisted that both the names be announced together. If the Left parties had not supported, the Congress would not have had the numbers to make Sharma the president. This was the background to Comrade Surjeet's anger.[4] After Vajpayee was sworn in, there was fear that United Front parties may not stick together with the 'secular alternative', but they surprised everybody, and knocked off cynicism when not a single member of Parliament in their coalition defected. They ensured H.D. Deve Gowda became the eleventh prime minister of India.

The selection of H.D. Deve Gowda was even more dramatic compared to scenes witnessed in the Rashtrapati Bhavan. Although Gowda was an entrenched player in India's political system for four decades, he was labelled a 'dark horse' because he was a rank outsider to the Delhi–Lutyens establishment. However, within the secular front, the Left parties infused perfect reasoning for his selection. Arguably, it was one of the finest moments of democratic India when a poor peasant's son without pedigree, pelf or patronage was given charge of the nation. He was also from the bottom of the varna pyramid—he was a Shudra who had often been trapped in the prejudices and stratagems of upper caste politics (there are multitudes below the Shudras and outside the varna classification of the Indian caste system—the Dalits, who have faced greater discrimination and segregation for centuries. Ironically, even among the Dalits, there is further stratification). Until then, there had been no prime minister who had been a Shudra other than Chaudhary Charan Singh, who was prime minister for only twenty-three days and had not been confirmed by the Parliament. Although Gowda has never discussed his 'Shudrahood' openly, he was arguably India's first full-fledged prime minister from the bottom rungs of the pernicious Indian caste system.[5] What the Left parties, who mostly dealt with class issues instead of caste structures, had achieved from the point of view of social justice, was incredible. They had proposed K.R. Narayanan, as India's first vice president from the Dalit community (later President), and H.D. Deve Gowda, a Shudra, as prime minister. This may not have been a deliberate effort, but Narayanan and Gowda were present at the right time and at the right bend in history, and the Left parties did not circumvent them but instead performed a historic role in recognizing them.

The role of the Left parties becomes apparent when one understands how Harkishan Singh Surjeet collaborated with Jyoti Basu, who commanded a veto, besides seniority and stature, in picking a prime minister after his party had rejected his own candidature. Gowda recalled the turn of events: 'The first choice of the coalition partners of the United Front was V.P. Singh. When I discussed Singh's name with Jyoti Basu, he was not very excited. He said, "You still admire him. Do you recall he had called the 1989 government he headed as a political experiment? Is he serious about politics? Anyway, try convincing him." After this, Karunanidhi, Chandrababu Naidu, Murasoli Maran and myself, with a couple of other friends, went to see Singh at his 1, Rajaji Marg residence. We sat in the lawn. Coffee, tea and biscuits were served. Singh came, greeted us and went inside the residence, and did not come out for a long time. We later learnt that he had left by the back entrance to some unknown place. After nearly two hours, his wife came out and told us that he had asked her to communicate that we should not wait and that he would not agree to our proposal to be prime minister. We did not know how to react. We just left the place.'[6]

From there, they came straight back to Basu and Surjeet and told them that there was no option but Jyoti Basu. The longest-serving chief minister of any Indian state should take over. Gowda remembered:

There was not just unanimity for his name, but there was genuine celebration in the coalition that it had come up. Basu happily consented too but said he would like his party to formally ratify his choice. The rest is well-documented history. His party rejected the offer not once but twice. The first time it was rejected, I argued with Surjeet that they should go back to the Central Committee. But the Communists committed a 'Himalayan blunder' by not approving Basu for prime minister. They were principled people with whom we could not argue.

Immediately after this, Basu summoned me. Lalu Yadav, the Janata Dal national president, and Surjeet were present when we met. He straight away said, 'Mr Gowda, you should take over.' I was shocked. I said, 'There are others in my party, sir.' He got a little angry, 'Don't I know your party leaders,' he retorted. He turned to Lalu Yadav, 'Mr. Lalu, make an announcement immediately. The press is waiting outside.' Lalu consented with the choice but said that he would like to go and inform his party leaders waiting in Bihar Bhavan. Basu cut him short, 'You can inform them on the telephone too,' he said. Meanwhile, I recovered a bit to plead, 'Sir, I have been chief minister for less than two years. My career will end abruptly. The Congress party will not let us run the government for long. I want to be like you, sir. I want to rule Karnataka for many years. Don't we all know what the Congress did to Charan Singh, V.P. Singh and Chandra Shekhar. Will they spare me? Please sir, change your mind. I also have no felicity in Hindi and have not travelled the length and breadth of this country. You are our elder, I beg you.' [In terms of age, Basu was nearly two decades older than Gowda.] When I saw he was unwilling to listen, I touched his feet and requested him to accept my argument. He was moved. He reasoned with me further, 'Mr Gowda, do I go out and tell the people of India that we have no secular alternative to Vajpayee? Can we put out an advertisement in the newspaper for a secular prime minister? Please understand, we will have no face to show people if you do not accept this offer, and we do not have time.' It appeared

Basu and Surjeet had made up their mind. I was left with
no choice. Lalu and I went to Bihar Bhavan to formalize the
arrangement. By the time we reached there, our party leaders
had all the information. Surjeet and Jyoti Basu had made it
clear that they would like to see me as prime minister.[7]

Basu spoke in an oral archives interview in 2001:

> There was nobody. As I told you, when all this trouble was
> going on, it seems some persons went to V.P. Singh's house
> but he was not in a fit condition. He was having dialysis
> every alternate day. At that time, the Karnataka (former)
> chief minister Ramakrishna Hegde was also there. So, I told
> him jokingly, of course: 'Why don't you become the prime
> minister?' He kept quiet. But then Deve Gowda was agreeable
> and, of course, he was also a good person. We presented him
> to the President. After that, once M.J. Akbar of *Asian Age*
> asked me: 'What do you feel personally?' I said—I have not
> said this anytime publicly in my life about party differences
> though I have differed with my party on many occasions. We
> Communists don't talk that way, but on this decision of the
> majority I think it was a historic blunder because history does
> not give such opportunity to the Communists . . . I said: 'In
> a Parliamentary democracy, never in the world has such a
> situation arisen.' Again, I say, this is a historic blunder. Historic,
> why, because such opportunity does not come, history does not
> present you with such opportunities . . .[8]

In the same interview, when asked if he was offered the prime
ministership earlier too, that is before 1996, Basu said: 'I cannot
remember; there was a crisis in the Congress in 1990. For some work,
I had gone to Delhi. Then the present finance minister, Yashwant
Sinha, came to see me—I was staying in 2, Circular Road. He said:
"As you know there is a crisis in the Congress. But a government has

to be formed and you head it." I said: How suddenly [can] I become the prime minister? . . . So, he left and then came our Chander [sic] Shekhar—he was a good friend of mine and I used to meet him earlier also. He said: "You become the prime minister. We will all be there to help you." I said, "I told your friend (Yashwant was with Chander [sic] Shekhar at that time, later he was with the BJP)." Then he said: "Then I [will] become [PM]." I said: Very good. You have all my support, but how long will you last? How many people do you have?"[9] From this, it is clear that Basu had passed on the opportunity to be prime minister twice, once in 1990 and the second time in 1996, and both times it had gone to men he liked or preferred. On both occasions, in popular parlance, he was the kingmaker.

If Basu was making a sacrifice by giving up the prime minister's post in 1996, Gowda was making a sacrifice by giving up his secure, hard-earned chief minister's chair for a clearly short-lived prime minister's position and an uncertain future. If he lost power as prime minister, he could hold no other executive office. He could not go back to becoming a chief minister like C. Rajagopalachari, who, after being the Governor-General of India between 1948 and 1950, had become the chief minister of the Madras state between 1952 and 1954. Those were exceptions that iconic Congress leaders of the freedom movement could create for themselves. Any such thing in the 1990s, or later, could be construed as impropriety and avarice. Therefore, Gowda's retirement date from executive power was nearly fixed the day he was caught in the cross-currents of history and succumbed to the persuasion of Basu and Surjeet.

Yechury agreed with Basu's reading that there was 'nobody' else after V.P. Singh had refused. The fodder case was brewing against Lalu Prasad Yadav and he was out of contention. Also, the two Yadavs—Lalu and Mulayam Singh Yadav—would have cancelled each other out if there was a contest. They would not have allowed one among them to get ahead of the other. Chandrababu Naidu, the then Andhra Pradesh chief minister, was relatively young. He was all of forty-six years and stayed out. The Tamil Nadu contingent was

big with thirty-seven seats. G.K. Moopanar's Tamil Manila Congress
and M. Karunanidhi's DMK had swept the state with twenty and
seventeen seats, respectively, but here again, the two Tamil leaders
were not only disinterested in a Delhi stint, but they cancelled each
other out in the power game. Also, the Congress would have never
accepted Moopanar, who had rebelled against the party to form his
own outfit on the eve of the Parliament elections. He had electorally
decimated the Congress party in Tamil Nadu, in 1996. Besides,
the Janata Dal was the single biggest party inside the United Front
coalition with forty-six seats. Out of these, Gowda had delivered
the largest chunk, sixteen, from Karnataka. The Janata Dal had a
pre-poll alliance with Mulayam Singh's Samajwadi Party, Naidu's
Telugu Desam and a few smaller parties. As an alliance, they had
won a total of seventy-nine seats. Above all, Surjeet and Basu took
a liking for Deve Gowda. They saw him as a diligent administrator.

Gowda had never met Jyoti Basu or Harkishan Singh Surjeet
before 1995, that is a year before he became prime minister:

> Their party had organized a central committee meeting
> in Bangalore for three days, and I was chief minister. The
> Karnataka state secretary of the CPM, S. Suryanarayana Rao,
> whom we called 'Suri', was a very dear friend. He came to me
> one day and asked if I could help bear a day's expenses of the
> meeting? It was a very small thing. I said that I would be happy
> to help. At the end of their three-day meeting, I hosted a dinner
> for Surjeet and Basu. That day we spoke a lot. I was surprised
> how they had kept track of the work I was doing in Karnataka.
> That was the first time I had met them. The first time I saw
> Basu was in the early 1970s. It was at a conference of the Public
> Accounts Committee (PAC) chairmen of state legislatures in
> Guwahati. I had only seen him but had not interacted with him.
> He was still not a chief minister but had already been deputy
> chief minister. In the conference, Jyotirmoy Basu, the firebrand
> Communist party parliamentarian, who used to openly accuse

Indira Gandhi of being a 'fountainhead of corruption', had applauded my work as PAC chairman in his opening remarks. He had said Karnataka had done 'a wonderful job' of digging out many scams against the state government.[10]

The other secret admirer of Gowda was P.V. Narasimha Rao, who was Congress party president at the time and had committed the party's outside support to the United Front coalition. Rao and Gowda's personal equation was exemplary. They shared a similar interest in astrology and planetary movements and also had a history. In 1991, when Rao was trying to settle his minority government, the Samajwadi Janata Party of Chandra Shekhar and Gowda had won five seats. While Chandra Shekhar had indicated that they should vote against Rao's confidence motion in the Parliament, Gowda had argued against it and stood by Rao. This had forced Chandra Shekhar to abstain from voting.[11] Immediately after that, Gowda had started visiting Rao's 7, Race Course Road residence often. He had such access to Rao that he even became a powerful conduit for Rao's own Congressmen. For instance, he pushed a 'reluctant' Rao to agree to S.M. Krishna's nomination to the Rajya Sabha in April 1996. Krishna had been defeated in the 1994 assembly polls and was down. The Congress, with only thirty-four legislators, did not have the numbers to send Krishna to the upper house of the Parliament, and Gowda was chief minister.[12]

Srikant Kumar Jena, who had become the leader of the Janata Dal parliamentary party after the resignation of Sharad Yadav, confirmed the relationship between Rao and Gowda: 'Their personal equation was excellent. Right at the beginning, Rao had said that he would like to see Gowda as prime minister for all five years.' Meanwhile, he recalled the events at the Bihar Bhavan where Gowda's name was officially accepted: 'In the meeting, Biju Patnaik stood up and proposed Gowda's name. Nobody had asked him to do so. He just stood up and did it. I was at the meeting and Ramakrishna Hegde was sitting right next to me. He quietly walked out as the name was proposed. Nobody objected. As a floor leader, I did whatever had to be done technically. Sharad Pawar was the Congress parliamentary party leader. With all the letters of support in a file, we all went to meet President Shankar Dayal Sharma.'[13] Interestingly or providentially, Biju Patnaik had played a role in Gowda's selection as both chief minister and prime minister.

Gowda accepted the nomination as prime minister with the 'grain of sand' principle in mind. He had worked in Karnataka until then, and now, he began to imagine the nation through that grain of sand called Karnataka. The pains, problems and developmental challenges across the country were different but not entirely different. That was one way of building inner confidence and a method to govern a large and diverse nation. The laws were similar, the bureaucracy was similar, and his long experience had devised a method to approach them.

There was one last task that Gowda had to do before he became prime minister. He had to put a new chief minister in place for Karnataka. There should have been little confusion because J.H. Patel was a senior in both politics and the party; he was from the demographically large Lingayat community besides already being deputy chief minister. But Siddaramaiah, finance minister in Gowda's cabinet, challenged his automatic elevation. The fight became so bitter that in Gowda's Delhi Karnataka Bhavan suite a furious Patel took slippers to his hand to settle an argument with Siddaramaiah. Gowda had to intervene to calm them down. Siddaramaiah was told that his actions may threaten the survival of the state government, and also cast a shadow on the elevation of Gowda. If he pursued his ambition, in no time Patel could walk away with enough Lingayat legislators and others sympathetic to Hegde. The matter was settled after Siddaramaiah was convinced to be deputy chief minister.[14]

Amidst the melee, Gowda's colleagues, who were busy wrangling for bigger positions in the changed political scenario, did not think of a civic reception or a farewell function for Gowda. There was not even a high tea organized at the Banquet Hall of the Vidhana

Soudha for the outgoing chief minister and prime minister-elect. Gowda himself had always been a gracious host, but his colleagues had behaved gracelessly in his finest hour. Hegde, who had still not been expelled from the Janata Dal, had done his bit to spike the celebrations. However, nobody could stop ordinary people of the state from erupting in joy. Gowda had risen to the highest point in India's political pyramid, but he felt lonely and unacknowledged from day one. His mother, Devamma, was alive when he became prime minister. He sought her blessings when he left for Delhi to take oath. Swaddled in innocence, she asked, 'What is the meaning of prime minister, son?' Gowda could think of no other way to explain but to tell her that he was going to occupy the chair that Indiramma (Indira Gandhi) had once occupied.[15] That animated her, momentarily. Gowda was inaugurated as prime minister on 1 June 1996. As Gowda took oath, Chennamma, his wife, sat next to Sonia Gandhi, Indiramma's daughter-in-law. Ironically, Gowda's father had lost his mind during the Emergency in 1977, fearing that the very same Indiramma would harm his son in jail.

11

Prime Minister's Office and the Circle of Trust

India Today, the national news magazine, did a cover story[1] in August 1996 on the prime minister's office (PMO) that was just about settling down. Deve Gowda was barely one-and-a-half-month old in the chair when the story appeared, but there was already an element of surprise, as well as awe, in bureaucratic circles about the manner in which he had put his office together and the talent he had infused. He had brought in officers known for their integrity, efficiency, and decades of administrative experience to assist him. It indirectly spoke about Gowda's intent[2] to govern well and leave behind a good name.

Gowda as a chief minister and a minister in Karnataka had always preferred credible and competent officers with diverse caste, religious and linguistic backgrounds. Almost as a rule, he never packed his office with people from his own caste. He had always placed enormous trust in his officers, fought for them and never humiliated them. He never demanded their loyalty but expected only professionalism and dedication. But since such expectations were so rare in any political milieu, he commanded loyalty of the best too. However, he never verbalized his work ethic or flaunted them as

precious beads in his value necklace. When asked why he had never
spoken of these things, Gowda sarcastically said: 'I left all such things
to my friend Ramakrishna Hegde. It was he who always claimed a
patent to "value-based politics". It suited his image.'³ All this was
familiar in Karnataka, but in Delhi, where he was seen as a 'dark
horse', they were blind to his governance record. They projected him
as someone picked up by the wayside and made prime minister, as
someone who could neither trot nor gallop.

In this backdrop, the *India Today* cover story was a fair piece
of reporting. The copy said: 'Helping him (Gowda) are a team of
handpicked bureaucrats who he has worked with in Karnataka . . .
with whom he has a steady rapport. Heading the trio that has moved
from Bangalore to New Delhi is Satish Chandran, the former chief
secretary, Karnataka . . . Respected for his integrity and honesty . . .
Chandran is now Deve Gowda's key official, vetting all the files before
they reach him. And, as a political aide of Deve Gowda says, "He
occupies the seat mainly because he will not become a power broker."
A problem that (P.V. Narasimha) Rao's senior cabinet ministers
faced with (A.N.) Verma (Rao's principal secretary), considered the
most powerful man after the prime minister, was clearing of Rao's
political appointments; keeping even Governors waiting for three
days and returning without meeting Rao. Deve Gowda too has built
up a parallel team, but unlike his predecessor, there was a strong
separation between the bureaucratic and the political turfs.'

Further, the copy said: 'By his side is another trusted aide,
S.S. Meenakshisundaram, who was principal secretary when Deve
Gowda was chief minister. Moving into South Block as an officer on
special duty, he is now a joint secretary, but has both Deve Gowda's
eyes and ears. His reputation of being an upright rulebook bureaucrat
has made him the second-most important man in the PMO, and
according to his colleagues, "Deve Gowda trusts him enough to know
that his notings on any file will be the right advice." When it comes
to backtracking or changing an opinion, it is normally Deve Gowda
who has to do it rather than he. Like he did, one month into prime

ministership. A 1983 batch IAS officer, who was on deputation to the
Centre as the private secretary to a minister in Rao's cabinet, wanted
to stay on in Delhi and he approached Balwant Singh Ramoowalia,
minister in Deve Gowda's team, to take over as his private secretary.
Ramoowalia spoke to the prime minister, who agreed. But when the
file arrived, Meenakshisundaram advised that the officer be deputed
back to the state as his five-year deputation period was over. It would
set a bad precedent, he advised, and Deve Gowda demurred, aware,
as one bureaucrat put it, that Meenakshisundaram would rather
change the rule than break it. The officer returned to Karnataka.'

On Deve Gowda's choice of private secretaries, *India Today*
wrote: 'Gowda picked Mahendra Jain to be his private secretary.
An MBA from the Indian Institute of Management, Ahmedabad,
Jain was the collector in Hassan—Deve Gowda's home district—
before occupying a chair made notorious by the likes of R.K.
Dhawan and Vincent George. But quite unlike them, Jain is a quiet,
in-the-shadows man, shuttling with the prime minister between
South Block, Parliament and Race Course Road, organizing his
appointments and meetings in assistance with Thippe Swamy, the
prime minister's additional private secretary, who has also come in
from Bangalore, where he had been with Deve Gowda since 1983.
And it's not just trustworthiness and integrity that have seen them
cross the borders. Both Chandran and Meenakshisundaram are
known for their expertise in rural development and Panchayati Raj,
and fit Deve Gowda's publicly proclaimed bias towards the poor.'
The copy quoted Meenakshisundaram, who had said: 'I respect the
rules, but where there is scope for interpretation, I'll do it in favour
of the poor.'

So that was the core team of Karnataka origin. T.R. Satish
Chandran was made principal secretary to the prime minister, he
was energy secretary to the government of India earlier and was chief
secretary to the government of Karnataka for three years between
1983 and 1987 when Ramakrishna Hegde was chief minister,
Gowda was then the PWD and irrigation minister in the state

cabinet. It was nine years since Satish Chandran had retired when he was brought into the PMO. S.S. Meenakshisundaram was the senior-most among joint secretaries in the PMO; he had a masters in mathematics and a doctoral degree in economics. Private Secretary Mahendra Jain was not Gowda's choice. He was Holenarasipur MLA and Gowda's second son, H.D. Revanna's pick. Gowda was not exactly happy about this, therefore to counterbalance, he brought in K.A. Thippeswamy, a Karnataka Administrative Service officer in the assistant commissioner grade at the time, as his additional private secretary. Thippeswamy had seen Gowda since his days as the Opposition leader in the 1970s when he was a young tahsildar in Hassan.

To complement this team from home was B.N. Yugandhar, another fine 1962 batch IAS officer from the Andhra Pradesh cadre with thoughts leaning left and heart in the right place. He was Meenakshisundaram's mentor earlier in the ministry of rural development. The duo had worked with P.V. Narasimha Rao to ensure the passage of the seventy-third and seventy-fourth amendments to the Constitution that decentralized governance by introducing the panchayat raj system. Rao had brought Yugandhar to the PMO, and Gowda was more than happy to ensure his continuation. He had superannuated but was given an extension. Yugandhar is today remembered as Microsoft CEO Satya Nadella's father, but when Bill Gates called on Deve Gowda in March 1997, his first-ever visit to India, he could have hardly imagined that his son, around twenty-eight then, would one day take over the leadership of Microsoft from Gates.

Satish Chandran was arguably the first engineer-IAS officer in the country and an alumnus of the Indian Institute of Science and the London School of Economics. His father, T. Ramaiah, was also a senior civil servant in the princely Mysore State. His elder sister, T. Sunandamma, whose daughter Chandran had married, was a well-regarded literary figure in the Kannada language. Officers who worked with and under Satish Chandran remember him as gentle and incorruptible with an understated sense of efficiency and righteousness. His absence of flamboyance and reticence could be mistaken for reclusiveness, but his warmth and involvement were always complete and palpable to those dealing with him.

Chiranjiv Singh, his fellow Karnataka IAS officer, recalled:[4] 'He was so unassuming that as chief secretary of Karnataka, in 1986, he stood outside a packed auditorium, to listen to M.S. Subbulakshmi's Carnatic music concert when he could have demanded a front row chair. After all, the concert was a government-sponsored event, and he was the government's top-most bureaucrat. I came to know he was at the event only when he congratulated me for organizing it well, when I perchance met him the next day. Satish Chandran's sense of right and wrong was so intact and intuitive that as a practising Sikh, when I protested the army's entry to the premises of the Golden Temple in 1984 and the riots thereafter, he protected me when the Central government wanted stern action initiated.' Gowda respected Satish Chandran who was about five years older to him so much that at times he would 'feel embarrassed', recalled Shyamal Datta,[5] who was the chief of the Special Protection Group (SPG) that was responsible for the prime minister's security. Gowda's finance minister P. Chidambaram said he found Satish Chandran to be a 'very wise man'.[6]

If this was the nature of professionals that Gowda assembled in the PMO, he picked another remarkable officer, T.S.R. Subramanian, as cabinet secretary. He was chief secretary of Uttar Pradesh, and Gowda's defence minister, Mulayam Singh Yadav, had spoken highly of him. Gowda's son and first-time MP, H.D. Kumaraswamy, too had heard good things about him. Subramanian had been to Calcutta University, Imperial College and also Harvard University. Since the 1970s, there always existed an undercurrent of tension between the cabinet secretariat and the PMO,[7] but Gowda as the boss of both institutions became a seamless bridge and offered balance. His men of choice with great experience, learning and character were not prone to politics or pettiness.

Subramanian wrote: 'I held the post of Cabinet Secretary for two years. My elevation to this post, the highest in the bureaucracy, may seem a contradiction of all that has been said. The repeated assertion has been that honest, bold and independent officers are filtered out of the system. The reader could well wonder if I am as lily-white after all. Anyway, all I can say is that the government's decision had something to do with the coalition politics of that particular period. Perhaps my being apolitical with no patron helped in that coalition situation. The new prime minister was not steeped in the Delhi system. He had no vested interest or axe to grind, not during this period at any rate. He had a principal secretary who was straightforward, not prone to playing games. So, it was a quirk of circumstance.'[8]

On Chandran, Subramanian said: 'Blessed with transparent honesty and highly intelligent, he is one of the morally upright persons I have come across. Chandran probably represented an ideal civil servant. His analysis was brilliant, based on a sound command of his facts, and he could, in any forum, express his views calmly and cogently, without fear or favour . . . As a principal secretary, he had enough confidence in his own position and himself that he did not have to score brownie points against the cabinet secretary.'[9]

On any issue, when both Chandran and Subramanian agreed, Gowda would agree 'instantly without a second thought'. When Chandran and Subramanian disagreed, Gowda would apply his own mind. Even after applying his mind, if he was in doubt, he would take Chandran's side. When Gowda had to overrule both of them due to political compulsions, he would 'apologetically' explain. Rao, before Gowda, was known for playing one top officer against the other and supporting each by turns.[10]

Getting Started

The question as to who will run the PM's office came up as soon as Gowda reached Bangalore as a designate to the chair. He called

Meenakshisundaram, his principal secretary as chief minister, and asked him to make a shortlist. Someone from the Karnataka cadre would make it easy for him to relate. Meenakshisundaram knew that it was a tradition to pick a retired officer to head the PMO. Within a couple of hours, he went back with two names he knew Gowda respected: T.R. Satish Chandran and J.C. Lynn. Both had experience in Delhi, and both were former chief secretaries of Karnataka. Chandran was older to Lynn. Gowda was delighted. Either choice would not have made a difference to him. He wanted Satish Chandran to be sounded first: 'If Satish Chandran *sahebru* agrees, I will be happy. He was our chief secretary. We should not now call him secretary, it is too small for his stature. We should give him a higher designation. Perhaps we should call him senior adviser,' Sundaram recalled Gowda telling him.[11]

Chandran those days was with M.Y. Ghorpade, a former finance minister of Karnataka and the erstwhile maharaja of Sandur. He had been inducted to the board of the Sandur Manganese Company. Meenakshisundaram went and spoke to Chandran. His first reaction was that he should consult Ghorpade and it would not be fair to take a decision without consulting him. 'I don't want to do anything behind his back. I am sure Mr Ghorpade will agree because it is a great honour that a Kannadiga is going to be the prime minister of this country, and we should all stand by him.' Chandran also added: 'I am willing to come and work. But please tell the PM-designate that in the government of India nobody will bother about an adviser. I would prefer to be called principal secretary to the prime minister.'[12]

By then, officers had started lobbying. Some approached Thippeswamy to express their interest because they knew he had access to the big man. There was one particular additional chief secretary-rank officer from Karnataka who even prepared a full list, totally unsolicited, of officers who Gowda should pick from the IAS pool across the country. He had specifically spoken against Chandran and Lynn.[13] Thippeswamy was himself reluctant to go to Delhi because he thought as a non-IAS officer, he may not exactly fit into the PMO structure, plus his family was against his relocation. But he had already become indispensable. He had started handling the temporary hotlines that the SPG had set up in Anugraha, Gowda's chief ministerial residence in Bangalore. There was a call nearly every minute from Delhi and he had temporarily been designated as the liaison officer. He was being continuously briefed on what was being planned and how things would be taken forward. His job was to convey the information to Gowda and take his consent. Thippeswamy was practically given no choice. He had to relocate.[14] Satish Chandran took charge on 11 June, the day Gowda sought the vote of confidence in the Parliament. For eleven days, from the day he was sworn in as PM till the day he was confirmed, many senior officers met Gowda and lobbied for PMO jobs, including the top job of principal secretary. Gowda had listened to all of them, was unfailingly courteous, but had not committed anything.

The first big task for the PMO, before Chandran arrived in Delhi, was the ministry formation. The PM was very particular that the entire cabinet should take charge in one go. He thought it would avoid unnecessary confusion and competition for portfolios. The senior cabinet ministers would anyway be picked in consultation with party bosses, and in some cases, the party bosses themselves would be joining the cabinet. That was being personally dealt with by the PM, but when it came to ministers of state, Gowda told Meenakshisundaram that his coalition colleagues would submit names, and he should sit with Yugandhar and fit them into different ministries given their backgrounds and suitability. Once the list was complete, he would scrutinize and clear the names. The only guideline that Gowda gave was that he wanted a Muslim as a junior minister in the home ministry. Since Yugandhar had been in the PMO, he sifted and matched names and ministries, and the list got ready before the deadline. They had proposed a Muslim name from Bihar as junior home minister but soon realized that it was an error because he had criminal cases pending against him. His name was replaced later with that of Maqbool Dar, the MP from Kashmir.[15]

The next question before the PMO was, how does one run a government with an assortment of thirteen political parties with different manifestos and divergent world views. Gowda wanted to create a unity of purpose and wanted an agenda for governance with a clear policy focus. He called for a meeting of senior coalition partners at South Block. Attending it were Moopanar, P. Chidambaram, Harkishan Singh Surjeet and a few others, including a Congress representative. Yugandhar and Meenakshisundaram were also present in the meeting, and the idea of the common approach to major policy matters and a minimum programme or what popularly came to be known as the Common Minimum Programme (CMP) was born. Chidambaram was authorized to work on a draft.[16]

Central to the CMP was the idea of Basic Minimum Services (BMS) that Gowda formulated. It was about identifying some development areas for the government to work on, which no political party could object to. Gowda involved Sundaram and Yugandhar to finetune this. He also passed it by his communist friend Surjeet, who added further polish. He wanted to involve chief ministers of states to take the BMS idea forward. He hoped it would signal his commitment to federalism.[17] It got into the CMP and finally the first budget. The logic behind the CMP and BMS was to ensure that the governance agenda was clearly defined and also to signal its precedence over politics. Although Chandran came eleven days after the PM was sworn in, Meenakshisundaram had ensured that he was kept informed on everything that was being planned.[18] The day he took over, he was familiar with every single file on his table.

As soon as Chandran had settled down, Gowda insisted that a meeting of all chief ministers be called to explain the BMS concept. It was decided that there would be a lump sum allocation to the states, and they could spend it on the seven or eight items listed in the document. This was important because most of the basic minimum services identified were on the state list, and Gowda was very keen that in a federal structure, the states should have the autonomy to spend funds in a manner they deemed fit, but the Centre could draw broad parameters. He got the Planning Commission on board this idea, and while talking to the CMs, he took charge. He said if they wanted to construct a road to the market, they could use this allocation; if they wanted to set up a primary health centre for every 5000 population, they could do that as well; they could use the funds for housing too, but it would be prudent to decide in advance how much they wanted to allocate for each of these seven or eight items. 'Chief ministers present were amazed by Gowda's attention to detail. They realized he was hands-on and approachable. In that meeting, he promised that with development funds, he would neither play politics nor discriminate between states,' recalls Thippeswamy.[19]

In hindsight, Sundaram thinks they made a mistake: 'People like Lalu Prasad Yadav spent these allocations to get votes. They mostly spent it on housing. If you give somebody a house, you capture their vote for life. If you put a road to the market that may not personally benefit voters. What is done for the community is not seen as a personal favour. The focus here was to provide infrastructure in rural India—primary education, health centres, roads, houses, girl child enrollment to schools, etc. Some politicians converted this into a vote-catching programme, and some used them wisely. But these things do happen in big democracies. But the PM's intent was very honourable. Gowda would have surely identified and corrected the gaps if he were to stay longer in the chair.'[20]

Diversity Design

Within a fortnight in the chair, the prime minister's attention had shifted towards the North-east and Kashmir. He said people in the two regions feel neglected and it is important to erase their neglect. He told his officers that he would like to visit the North-east first. 'But there was a problem. We were told that by the end of July, it would start pouring in the North-east, and to land and move around there would be tough,' Meenakshisundaram remembered.[21] When this was mentioned to Gowda, he surprised the officers by saying that he would like to go right away before the rains started. There was a sense of urgency in his voice. 'That urgency was also because he had this one-year phobia. He thought he would not be allowed to stay in power for long and therefore had to quickly make a mark,' Meenakshisundaram recalled.[22]

Finally, the PMO organized a weeklong trip in October 1996 after there was a bit of a let-up with the rains. Gowda asked Yugandhar and Meenakshisundaram to join him on this trip. An informal agreement in the PMO was that for all international trips, Chandran would go, but in India, if there was a need, the Secretary would travel, otherwise, it is always the joint secretary dealing with that state who would accompany the PM. Home Secretary K. Padmanabhaiah was also part of the team. 'Yugandhar and Padmanabaiah were from Andhra Pradesh and they got along famously. I played the role of a person listening and taking notes and ensuring that everything was fine before it went to the PM,' Meenakshisundaram said.[23] The PM toured the North-east states for seven continuous days. He was the first prime minister to spend a night at each of the seven state capitals. None before him had devoted such time. Although Gowda wanted to go to the North-east before Kashmir, the weather pushed him to take up the Kashmir agenda first. The PMO's logic was that he should visit the North-east after the rains and go to Kashmir before the cold sets in.

In the PMO core team, Satish Chandran was a Kannada person, Meenakshisundaram was a Tamil with a functional knowledge of Kannada, and Yugandhar was of course Telugu. The PMO's lingua franca was English, but with Gowda, Chandran and Sundaram always conversed in Kannada. Even as the policy was shaping up, Gowda had a specific diversity design for his office. He wanted representation from every region and every religion in the PMO. But positions in the PMO at the senior level barely touched twenty, and that did not allow the following of this principle to the last dot. Meenakshisundaram recalled being told: 'The PM said this is a diverse country I need an officer from every corner, and I also need a Hindu, a Jain, a Muslim, a Christian, a Sikh and also representation from the scheduled castes and tribes. No region should have more than one person. No religion can be similarly over-represented. 'You and Chandran have come here that was my choice. With the rest, I have no specific choice. Pick the best.'[24]

They picked some very good people. Some had never thought they will ever get into the PMO, but they got in under Gowda. For example, Javed Usmani was picked as director in the PMO. He later became chief secretary of Uttar Pradesh. Jarnail Singh came in. He was a sardar, his wife was from Manipur, and he was also from the Manipur cadre. He too became chief secretary of Manipur later. An SC officer each from Haryana and Maharashtra were picked. Many officers working with P.V. Narasimha Rao were completing their terms. Whoever was going was replaced by applying the merit-cum-representation guideline of the prime minister. Jarnail Singh wrote about his entry to the PMO: 'When all efforts, including meeting the establishment officer yielded nothing, I reconciled to my fate of serving in Manipur much longer and possibly, for all remaining years of my service period. Then as luck would have it, on 9 August 1996, I got a telephone call from B.N. Yugandhar, secretary to Prime Minister H.D. Deve Gowda. He rang up to ask if I would like to join the Prime Minister's Office as joint secretary. I conveyed my willingness and joined the PMO on 16 August 1996 and was there till 6 August 2004.'[25] Prior to Yugandhar's call, Jarnail Singh's efforts to become the development commissioner for handicrafts in the ministry of textiles had been unsuccessful, and his appointment order as deputy election commissioner had been cancelled.

Gowda had explained the advantage with such a setup pretty lucidly: 'If there was any problem in any state across the nation, we will have an officer in the PMO ready to offer insight, perspective, scrutinize information, and get feedback. In crises, we will not lose time.'[26] After all, the Internet and mobile services in India were in their infancy those days. In fact, they were not even a year old.

Google was nearly a decade away. Social media was not even on the horizon. Things were organized differently, and Gowda did so in this manner.

Gowda wanted H.Y. Sharada Prasad, Indira Gandhi's trusted man, as his information adviser, but he had grown old and was unwell. Sharada Prasad hailed from Holenarasipur, Gowda's assembly constituency that he represented till he came to the Parliament in 1991. Gowda had great admiration for Sharada Prasad's integrity and intellectual capacity. Prasad, too, admired Gowda's tenacity, hard work, and administrative capabilities. When Prasad could not join him, H.K. Dua was brought in. Gowda said Dua was not his choice and believes he did not serve him well. 'Sharada Prasad suggested his name in good faith and I accepted it, but it did not turn out well. He let me down,' Gowda said.[27]

Meenakshisundaram recalled this slightly differently: 'Dua came to interview the PM, and someone indicated that he could be considered for the press adviser's role; since the PM did not have anybody particular in mind after Prasad had declined, Dua was inducted.'[28] After Gowda stepped down, the Vajpayee government gave Dua a Padma Bhushan in 1998 and sent him to Denmark in 2001 as ambassador, and much later, in 2009, the Congress-led regime nominated him to the Rajya Sabha. Perhaps Dua's steep rise under Vajpayee had sown a seed of suspicion in Gowda's mind retrospectively. While Dua had been feted and promoted by the Vajpayee regime, Chandran was unceremoniously removed as Governor of Goa, three months after he had taken charge.

There were also one or two appointments that Gowda regretted later, and one of them was certainly that of Joginder Singh as CBI chief.[29] Here again, there is confusion as to who recommended him to Gowda. If one version says that he was Harkishan Singh Surjeet's recommendation, Gowda remembers him to be P.G.R. Sindhia's candidate. Sindhia was a senior party colleague in Karnataka and was home minister when Gowda was chief minister. Sindhia also admitted to recommending Joginder Singh, an IPS officer of the

Karnataka cadre.[30] Singh had never done serious policing duties, nor had he worked in the investigation or intelligence wings. For a very short duration, he was Bidar district's superintendent of police, but he had spent the rest of the time in unrelated departments like youth services, commerce ministry, etc.

As CBI director, Joginder Singh became more loyal than the king (see chapter titled 'City of Intrigues and the September Shifts'). According to Meenakshisundaram, the prime minister had not directed him to do so: 'The PM was not petty, and he was experienced enough to know which pot to stir and when. Joginder just went out of control. Satish Chandran had advised the PM against his appointment. Gowda regretted the decision later. He admitted it to Chandran and me. Joginder did not do any harm by design. He was not a corrupt person. He was, in fact, a good, warm fellow. But he was very talkative, liked being in the news, was inexperienced, and a bad fit into the CBI director's job. He went on creating casualties and consequences for Gowda and the government. Things unfolded so rapidly that there was very little time for corrective action.'[31]

Gowda was very keen that G.V.K. Rao, a bureaucrat originally from the Mysore civil service, be associated with his administration. He offered him the chairmanship of a commission to study the linking of rivers. Rao had produced a seminal report for the Planning Commission on panchayat raj institutions in 1985, and Gowda was familiar with it. But Rao, like Sharada Prasad, expressed regrets. He wrote to the PM saying that his mind was willing, but his body was not cooperating.[32] Gowda also wanted eminent jurist Fali Nariman to be the Attorney General of India. But he was unable to accept it too. Nariman recalled this episode when he thanked Gowda for the letter[33] of condolence he had sent when his wife, Bapsi Nariman, passed away in June 2020.[34]

Overall, the Gowda PMO was harmonious, but there were minor clashes, which obviously never got escalated to Gowda. The man who knew Gowda for the longest period, Thippeswamy, said he did not enjoy his Delhi stint. In his view, he suffered because he was a non-IAS officer amidst glorious IAS officers. Although people like Vincent George and R.K. Dhawan, who were also non-IAS people with Indira Gandhi and Rajiv Gandhi in the PMO, advised him to assert himself, he was mild-mannered and could not do so. They would say he enjoys the confidence of the prime minister and that is his power, and between a private secretary and a prime minister, they reminded, it was always a different sort of a relationship.[35]

Thippeswamy recalled that some IAS officers even asked what grade he was with their nose up in the air. When he said he was an assistant commissioner-level officer, they would condescendingly equate him to an Undersecretary in the Union government. After a period, Swamy learned not to respond to their personal queries. In some cases, he would bluntly ask why they were so curious? 'Once, I sent a note to Mr. Yugandhar. He called and asked me why I had sent the note. I said that I had sent it in my capacity as an additional private secretary to the PM. He said, "No you should not write like this. You cannot issue a direction." I said I had not given a direction but only suggested appropriate action. He insisted that I should alter the wording. I said fine. He called me again and said I could not be there on the first floor (where the PM sits). He said, "You seem to be everywhere, at the PMO, at Race Course Road and the Parliament office." I got upset. Never in my life had I spoken to anyone like that. I asked who had asked him to question me. I said, if he was close to the PM, he should ask him to relieve me. I would happily go back to Karnataka. Or, if he had the power to relieve me, he should do so; I was not there on my own. He countered by saying, "You should have a job description." I said, "If you have the power, please notify my work and schedule. I will do whatever you ask me to do." I reminded him that I had worked with the boss for over twenty years, and he had never questioned me. After this episode, suddenly everybody became alert. The work culture in Delhi is very different. Egos were big.'[36]

Thippeswamy further spoke of the emotional hurt he had suffered and how the CM's office and the PM's office were very different experiences: 'Psychologically, I felt the PMO job was a demotion. As private secretary to chief minister, I was there for everything. I was the key facilitator. But in the PMO, I had to plead with others to sort things out. All party-related work was dumped on me. People came seeking help. I had to attend to them. Sometimes very senior politicians and officers from Karnataka would come just to see the room the PM occupies. You could not lose patience with them either. You had to give them a quick tour. There was enormous curiosity about the high office that their own man had come to occupy. They had no access when Indira Gandhi or Rajiv Gandhi were there, but with Gowda they thought they could walk in. In the CM's office, the culture was to attend to everybody who came seeking help. Many people had helped Gowda at different points of his political career and came seeking help. It was important to satisfy them and maintain those relationships. That was my job. But the PMO officers would not readily oblige. Their gaze was fixed on big things. I had to slowly work out a system to function with some officers, like P.P. Shukla and Sujata Mehta, who were more helpful. I feel bad about the way I spoke to Mr Yugandhar. He was an excellent officer of the chief secretary grade, and the PM liked him very much, but he had a problem with me. Satish Chandran was too big to be dragged into these matters. He never ever got involved in office politics. I reached a stage when I wanted to return to Karnataka, and I did even before Gowda stepped down.'[37]

Thippeswamy could not have run the PMO like the CMO, but he was naïve to the difference, well-intentioned and had only his boss' interest in mind. He never actually left Gowda, and Gowda never stopped caring for him. After Thippeswamy retired from government service, Gowda ensured he was made Karnataka's information commissioner between 2005 and 2010, and in 2019, he was nominated to the upper house of the Karnataka legislature.

On both occasions, Gowda's son, H.D. Kumaraswamy, was chief minister.

Files and Secret Files

Besides these little tussles that remained hidden to the outside world, there were other secrets being stacked away in the PMO's almirahs. Gowda had a great relationship with P.V. Narasimha Rao. He would visit him regularly and had accepted him as the elder who would offer the correct advice.

Meenakshisundaram recalled one interesting episode between Rao and Gowda in which he was willy-nilly involved: 'Rao kept some secret files on political personalities who could create trouble. Files that could be used in case they misbehaved or double-crossed. One day, Rao told Gowda that since he was not returning as PM, he should take the files from him. He asked Gowda to nominate an officer he trusted to hand over the files. Gowda sent me to Rao and also told me that I need not show him the files but would only like to be briefed on its contents. The files were like an atom bomb. Rao gave me more than a dozen files on very important people who were inside and outside his cabinet. If I remember correctly, there were files on Mulayam Singh Yadav, J. Jayalalitha, S. Bangarappa, Sharad Pawar and others. These files were with me as long as I was in the PMO. I handed them over to Ashok Saikia when Vajpayee took over. Ashok was a joint secretary like me. We knew each other, and whatever I was to Gowda, he was to Vajpayee. When I.K. Gujral became PM in between, I had told him about the files. He had asked me to continue holding them as he did not have anybody he could trust. When Vajpayee came, I told Brajesh Mishra about the files. He asked me to keep them too. But when my term at the PMO was coming to an end, I said I would like to hand them over. That's when Ashok came into the picture. Whether Ashok gave them to someone else after Vajpayee stepped down, I have no knowledge.'[38]

Meenakshisundaram had worked closely with P.V. Narasimha Rao as a rural development ministry officer between 1992 and 1994. He came to the PMO under Gowda, continued with Gujral, and stayed with Vajpayee till March 1999.

To continue with the topic of files, and since governments are all about files, to understand Gowda's file disposal system would be very instructive. He had evolved this as a minister and a chief minister, but in the PMO, Satish Chandran and Meenakshisundaram finetuned it and helped him further indulge in his diligence.

When Gowda was chief minister, getting him to dispose of files was a tough task for Meenakshisundaram. He would often ask him away to a location where nobody would disturb them and get the job done. In Delhi, his seclusion was never a problem because the PM's office was like a fort, and one had to pass through the SPG. There were no hangers-on like in the CM's office. It was comparatively easy to get him to be involved with files: 'Getting near the PM is an extremely difficult thing, while getting near the CM is very easy. But as CM, he had his information up to date. He would have all the details too. Before the police intelligence would tell him, people would have told him either in person or by phone. In the PM's office, that was not the case. IB, RAW and others were trying to grab his attention. Still, I found him to be extremely well-informed as a PM. His network was incredible and sometimes he would work the phones himself to get to the heart of the matter he was occupied with,' Meenakshisundaram said.[39]

Gowda made a simple rule in the beginning. He said that files that necessarily need the PM's attention should enter the PMO, and routine decision-making should be decentralized. Earlier, even the appointment of deputy secretaries and directors would come to the PMO for approval. Gowda asked his trusted aides if that system could be unentangled. Therefore, it was decided that only appointments of joint secretaries and above would come to the PMO, rest the ministers and their secretaries could sort out. This automatically reduced the file pile. Second, he asked Meenakshisundaram to go through each file and give him a quick summary of its contents and implications. Based on it, he would approve or reject: 'On a sheet of paper, I would create three columns. I would write the file number, subject of the file, and orders of the PM. Orders of the PM, too, would be in my handwriting. At the end of the sheet, the PM would put a single signature. As a result of this method, we would get the formal approval of the PM on 100 files in a matter of five minutes by taking some twenty signatures. Most files did not need the fine attention of the PM. Everybody at the ministry level would have gone through it, Satish Chandran would have gone through it, and I would have gone through it. The PM insisted that files always came through proper channels, and this was a blessing,' recalled Meenakshisundaram.[40]

The routing of the files was as follows: All important and sensitive subjects, postings, atomic energy, defence and matters related to external affairs came through Satish Chandran. Then rural development, urban development, social welfare, health, education, and other files from related departments came through Yugandhar. 'All these files landed up on my table. I had to simply go through these files to brief the PM, just in case he wanted more clarity. But the most important aspect was each file, whoever had seen it, on its return journey would pass through Satish Chandran's desk. In case we had made any mistake, he would hold it back and get it corrected. Suppose Yugandhar had recommended, I had put it up before PM, and the PM had approved, even then Satish Chandran would have the final say. The sheet I had devised would also go with the stack of files,' Meenakshisundaram explained.[41] Gowda had bestowed these powers on Satish Chandran, the powers to intervene and correct even the PM's orders. That was the trust he had in the man. Once the minister of state for power had been accorded approval by the PM to travel to the US for a conference, but when the file came before Chandran he saw that the conference was meant for officials and not ministers. He went by the rule book and cancelled the approval. The minister who had booked his tickets was very angry. He called up Joint Secretary Jarnail Singh: 'He asked me, "Who is the prime minister in the PMO? I have a photocopy of his approval with me. Who has cancelled the approval given by him?" . . . So much for the firmness of Chandran that a proposal approved by the prime minister, albeit based on incomplete information, could not escape the rule book.'[42]

Even on files that Chandran had himself originally sent to the PM, he would apply his mind again during its return journey. Chandran had told the PM that one person should be accountable for all files. There should be no opportunity for escape or shifting of blame. He had insisted that the PM should have one person who would see all files before they leave the PMO. Chandran never let him down. Even after twenty-five years, nobody has spoken about a single scam from Gowda's time as PM. Gowda said: 'Whenever politically the situation heated up, people looked for files they could use against me, but they could not find even a single one. I know what happened in and around 2002, and then after 2015. I did not get into a mess like some other prime ministers whom I do not want to name. I had the finest officers, and they took care of me.'[43]

Gowda's file disposal system was excellent. Incidentally, when Gujral became PM, Sundaram was not managing the files. He was only handling his subject. Gujral followed the method that Gowda had created but only up to the point that they landed on his table. He would not sign. The files would get stuck. Gujral did not trust his officers. He wanted to pore over every file. He lacked the administrative experience, acumen and grasp of Gowda. Gowda knew the system from the gram panchayat level to the office of the chief minister. He had handled the system every single day for decades as a legislator, as an Opposition leader, as a Public Accounts Committee chairman, and of course as chief minister.

T.S.R. Subramanian wrote: 'Those prime ministers who have had a stint as chief ministers would tend to have a much better grip over the administrative machinery. The example of Narasimha Rao, arguably one of the more effective prime ministers we have had, comes to mind. Deve Gowda was in this category too and brought tremendous politico-administrative acumen to his work as prime minister for the short while that he was there. It is my belief that in a short period, he made a major impact on Indian administration . . . Morarji Desai and Charan Singh had also become prime ministers after serving as chief ministers. Perhaps Morarji lends support to my thesis. Any rule needs to have an exception, and in this case, it was Charan Singh. The converse is also true. Those who do not have experience of state politics and administration, especially at the chief minister level, would rarely be effective as prime ministers. Gujral and Vajpayee come in this category. The failure of Rajiv Gandhi was due to inexperience at both the state and central levels. But then, Indira, seemingly an exception, was quite effective. This was because of her long association with state politics in the shadow of Nehru's political career.'[44]

Gujral thought that he was leaving an imprint on history each time he put his signature. But that was not how it was with files. Once Gujral told Meenakshisundaram that at the external affairs ministry where he was earlier, after every round of discussions, the most important thing they decided was when to meet next, and where. 'He told me in a lighter vein that the date and place of the next meeting was all that he had to settle for until he became PM. He never had the opportunity to take any major decisions that would affect the lives and livelihoods of millions. He was a well-read man. People thought he was an intellectual prime minister, but there is a saying in Tamil: *Pala maram kanda tachan oru marateyum vettamatan*. That means, 'A carpenter who has seen many trees will never be able to cut a single one.' This was told about Narasimha Rao, but it applied more to Gujral,' Meenakshisundaram said.[45] Rao did it as a strategy. Gujral was plain clueless. 'He was so knowledgeable that he always thought of ten alternatives to every problem, but by the time you took the decision, the problem would have either vanished, changed shape, or gone beyond your control,' Meenakshisundaram added. Deve Gowda had no such problems. He would listen to his officers with his eyes shut, ask a few pointed questions after the briefing, and quickly made his position known. If he had further doubts, he would call up experts himself.

N.N. Vohra was principal secretary to Gujral. He later became Governor of Jammu and Kashmir. Vohra once asked Sundaram: 'People say in Gowda's time files moved very fast, how did you do it? Why are we not able to do it? I was still in the PMO. I explained Gowda's method. I said the trust was central. Vohra sighed.'[46]

Gujral's trust problem persisted till the end. 'In the case of Vajpayee, he had 100 per cent faith in Brajesh Mishra. I never got any approval from Vajpayee. I always got my files cleared by Brajesh Mishra. Once Mishra has given his approval, I would do it because I knew nothing further would happen. There were areas where he did not have expertise, and he would let us decide. He once told me that he was from a different service and didn't know the nuances of rural development and urban development. "You decide. You put it up to me, I will approve." Once Mishra approved, things would get implemented. He took decisions on behalf of the PM. In the case of Gowda, not even one decision was taken on his behalf by either Chandran, Yugandhar or me. It was always the PM. He would clearly say what he wanted,' Meenakshisundaram recalled.[47]

Somnolence Strategy

Gowda had his quirks. He gave too many appointments in a day, and maintaining the schedule became very difficult. He was a workaholic. He almost never slept. He was like that even as CM. As a result, in most meetings, he would get into a somnolent state. He would not exactly sleep, but to the rest of the world, he looked drowsy and disengaged. Officers could never figure out what this phenomenon was because at the end of the meeting, he would be on top of all facts and opinions expressed when he was seemingly away. Subramanian mentions this: 'Deve Gowda was much misunderstood—in conferences and seminars, he would be portrayed as yawning prodigiously, and ever pictured in the midst

of forty winks. Having been with him on so many occasions, I can
vouch for the fact that he was fully alert and alive to the issues under
discussion.'[48] In general, his officers thought his attention span
was about twenty minutes. Beyond twenty minutes, unless it was
politics or meeting of the coordination committee of supporting
parties, it was difficult to keep him engaged. The officers had to
work around this problem. Meenakshisundaram narrated a story
on this:[49]

> The army people wanted to make a presentation. They asked
> for a half-day appointment. The army chief sent one of
> his deputies to meet me. I told him frankly that the PM's
> attention span does not exceed half an hour. Whatever
> important points you want to make, make it in the first half-
> hour. That gentleman took it amiss. He said, 'IAS officers
> always block us, they never allow us to speak to the PM,
> we want to explain our problems. We need a minimum of
> two hours; half an hour is not acceptable.' I said, 'Fine, it is
> your choice. We will give you half day. I went to Chandran
> and told him the problem. I wondered what would happen
> if the PM sleeps with the army people around. Chandran
> was unperturbed. He said he would attend the meeting and
> asked me to inform the defence secretary, and through him,
> ensure that the defence minister was present too. He added
> it was not prudent for the PMO to directly deal with defence
> issues. He said "You and I will sit with the PM. I will take
> care of all the subjects. If in between the PM dozes off, do
> not panic. At the end of the meeting, you get up and tell him
> our principal secretary wants to make a few points. The PM
> will not object.' So, we came to an understanding as to how
> to handle the meeting.
>   On the appointed day, the meeting began, and as expected,
> the army fellows started from 1952. By the time they finished
> history and reached Rajiv Gandhi, PM was disengaged. The

gentleman who had sought appointment came and said, 'The PM is not listening.' I said, I cannot do anything, and he could try waking him up if he wanted. However, I pacified him by saying, 'Don't worry, the PM, when he wants to listen attentively, closes his eyes. You continue with the presentation. Your problems will be dealt with.' At the appropriate time, the PM opened his eyes. The last fifteen minutes he was very alert. As per plan, at the end, I told them that Chandran will summarize. PM too said the principal secretary should react first to the presentation. Chandran did a brilliant job. He said whatever the army had said fell into three categories and offered some possible solutions. Then he asked the PM to address the gathering. The PM brilliantly picked up not only from what Chandran had said but also from where Chandran had stopped. He added his perspective and assured all that was agreed would be done in a timebound manner. He also politely asked the defence minister and the defence secretary for their views. They agreed with the PM and his principal secretary. Then the PM got up, broke protocol, and went around shaking hands with everyone in the room irrespective of their rank and seniority. The army delegation went back happy. Gujral's attention span was longer, but it was not helpful. Vajpayee, too, like Gowda, did not have a great attention span. It was less than half hour. Like we covered for Gowda, most of the time Jaswant Singh and Brajesh Mishra covered for Vajpayee. They were very dedicated to him, and he trusted them fully.

On the sleep issue, Gowda picked a story to tell from his mentor Morarji's autobiography, not so much to defend himself but to point out that it was a very human thing to happen. Morarji had recounted[50] how Pandit Nehru had fallen asleep in a meeting with John Foster Dulles, the US secretary of state. Dulles had apparently felt so offended that he went to Pakistan and made a deal to supply military equipment: 'Panditji was a great man, but he too felt tired and exhausted at times. Can we hold it against him? I had a serious problem. I could not take light directly falling on my eyes, but invariably there would be a lot of light falling on me when I sat on the dais or in a meeting. Most of the time, I kept my eyes shut and listened carefully, and sometimes I did feel exhausted. I always had this anxiety that I had very little time on the PM's chair, so I worked till late in the night against the advice of my family and doctors. I would see files till late in the night, and it had its implications. I may have kept my eyes shut at times, but God ensured I did not make blunders.'[51]

Gowda's cabinet colleagues like P. Chidambaram said that although the popular story was that he dozed off, he never actually did: 'I don't think he dozed off, he was quite alert. That was his style. The head would drop, but the moment his subject came, he would perk up.'[52] Montek Singh Ahluwalia, who was finance secretary then, also endorsed this: 'He had this habit of looking very sleepy. But I think he was always attentive. He appeared to be in that somnolent kind of state, but one ear was always open. Whenever something needed to be said, he would say it, and then one realized he had not missed anything.'[53]

Returning to the trust issue, Meenakshisundaram had a story to tell:[54]

One day, I came to my office in the PMO around 9.30 a.m. My assistant said Chandran wanted to see me urgently. I rushed to his room. He said, 'This is a difficult file. An Ordinance has to be issued by the President by evening. The home ministry has slept over this and sent it at the last minute. The submission note is ready, and it has to be signed by the PM. First, you explain the problem to the PM, take his approval on the file, go to the President, take his approval and bring the file back to me by evening.' The file, if I remember correctly, was about prisoners on death row. The PM was at his home office. I went there. Thippeswamy said the PM was with fifteen politicians in a coordination committee meeting. Mulayam Singh Yadav, P. Chidambaram were all there. When a party meeting is on, officers usually do not get in, but this was an emergency. I saw the India Coffee House fellow moving towards the room with his tray. I went behind him. When he opened the door, luckily, the PM was sitting directly at the other end and saw me. He gave a smile. I quickly went in. He asked, 'What's the matter?' I said, I need your signature, and we need to get an Ordinance out by evening. He took the file and just signed and asked me to take care of the rest. I met President Shankar Dayal Sharma and briefed him. He understood the urgency and signed immediately. Everything was done in half an hour. By lunchtime, I met Chandran again and told him what had transpired. He said, 'What you did was wrong.' I was taken aback. He said, 'How could you take the PM's signature without briefing him.' I said you please get the orders issued, I will brief the PM before the issue hits the press. He agreed, but still said, 'What you did was wrong.'

That was Chandran's value system. He was a stickler for rules. Again, I went to the PM's residence. Thippeswamy said the meeting was winding down. The PM got out in ten minutes and was looking very tired. He ordered coffee and snacks for himself and me. I briefed him about the file and asked him if he had been misled? He countered, 'You have said all this, but did you notice what I did with the file? My eyes looked for Chandran's signature. He had signed. You have personally brought the file. I have great faith in my officers. If I do not trust you and Chandran, how do I govern? I know you are not the one who will barge into a party meeting? If you got in, I realized, it must be urgent.' He added, 'When I select a person, I apply my mind. I believe in God. I know Chandran follows his dharma. He will never betray me.' That was a moving episode.

Kalam and Lyngdoh

It is not always that Gowda went by the advice of his PMO officers or his cabinet secretary. A case in point was the extension file of A.P.J. Abdul Kalam who was then the principal scientific adviser to the defence minister. When Gowda took charge, Kalam's term came up for renewal. The recommendation on the file was that he had got a few extensions already and should be allowed to retire. He was sixty-six at the time. Gowda thought it would not be fair to retire a person from a minority community as soon as he took office. He gave him a further extension of three years. All hell broke loose as soon as he did that. Gowda recalled: 'Satish Chandran and Subramanian came and said, "Sir there are really tall scientists and technologists in the department, taller than Kalam, why did you do this?" I said, I have taken a decision and written on the file, let us not reverse it. They tried to convince me, but when they saw that I was unlikely to change my mind, they let it be.'[55]

Sundaram also remembers that there was an uproar when the extension was given. Kalam was seen as blocking others down the line. They hoped that a line of ambiguity in standard officialese, such as 'until further orders', would replace the definite three-year extension, but that did not happen. Kalam came to the PMO every month: 'He would come straight to my room and say in Tamil, "*Periyavara Pakonome*" (Can I see the big man?). Until Thippeswamy came and accompanied him to the PM's room, he would keep speaking about Tamil literature, in which we shared a common interest. Incidentally, Kalam and I hailed from the erstwhile Ramanathapuram district in Tamil Nadu,' Sundaram recalled.[56]

Thippeswamy said: 'When Kalam was with the PM, nobody would be allowed inside. The principal secretary would be there of course. That was an established protocol. Sometimes Kalam wanted to talk to the PM alone, then Satish Chandran would come out and wait in my room. When we got emergency calls, we would connect them to the PM, Kalam would get a hint. He was very sensitive. He would get up and leave. Kalam and Gowda had an excellent rapport.'[57]

A 'what if' history question could be, had Gowda not given Kalam an extension, and if he was not around in the system when the Vajpayee government came to power, would he have become India's eleventh President? Gowda said: 'His destiny and good karma took him to the heights. I was only an instrument in God's hand. Kalam came from a humble background like me. Why should anyone grudge his rise? He was a good man.'[58]

Another surprise appointment that happened during Gowda's time was that of J.M. Lyngdoh as election commissioner. He went on to be the chief election commissioner later and is remembered as a shining example of probity and public service. One day Gowda gave a very tight deadline to Sundaram to suggest a top-class name for the vacant election commissioner's post. He was wondering if he should appoint J.C. Lynn, the former Karnataka chief secretary, who was a Christian, or someone from the North-east, but he wanted a couple of names before he could take a final call. Sundaram called Chiranjiv Singh to discuss. James Michael Lyngdoh's name emerged. He was both a Christian by birth (although an atheist by practice) and was from the North-eastern corner of Meghalaya. His name more than met the PM's criterion.[59] Gowda made mandatory checks, recommended his name to the President, and got the orders issued the same day. By giving Kalam an extension, if he wanted to send a message to the minorities, by picking Lyngdoh he wanted to tell the people of the North-east that he had their interests at heart.

The Nuclear Tests

While on the subject of Abdul Kalam, there is one other issue associated with him that came up during Gowda's prime ministership, and which continues to have resonance to this day. It had to do with the testing of the atomic bomb, what came to be known later as the Pokhran-2 tests. In February 1997, the chairman of India's Atomic

Energy Commission, Rajagopala Chidambaram, Abdul Kalam and Satish Chandran assembled in Gowda's office for a meeting. It was not one of those routine briefing sessions but a classified exchange. The file seeking approval for nuclear tests was before Gowda, and he was not inclined to give it a go ahead. He had discreetly studied the economic implications there may be if the tests were approved and made notes in a notepad that was not a letterhead. Since it was a top-secret file, he could not engage in open consultation nor could he leave traces of his study.[60]

By then, the Gowda government had decided not to succumb to American pressure and sign the Comprehensive Test Ban Treaty (CTBT). Gowda was due to visit Moscow and earlier, in November 1996, he had broken protocol to receive the Chinese President Jiang Zemin at the airport for a historic visit. Besides, he had initiated measures to improve relationship with neighbouring countries. The Ganga water treaty with Bangladesh had been signed, the Mahakali treaty had been inked with the Bhutan king, and he was working the back channels with Pakistan. He was also concerned about the prevalent economic situation. But the scientists sitting across his desk had fixed a date for the tests. It was to happen on a Sunday. If he approved the tests, everything that Gowda was trying to achieve diplomatically, and for the economy, would be thrown out of gear. The scientists tried to convince him for an hour.

But Gowda carefully illustrated his position without sounding as either disapproving or discouraging their decision. He said: 'I will give you permission. I will give you more money, but please wait for a year. There is a lot of pressure on me with regard to the CTBT. I am also trying to improve relationships with all our neighbours, including Pakistan. The tests will throw everything we are doing out of gear. Plus, we need some more time to stabilize the economic situation. The master control facility of the Indian Space Research Organisation (ISRO) is located in Hassan, my constituency, I have been there many times, and I am aware of the dedication with which all scientists work. I am not afraid of sanctions, but I need time.'

Gowda added: 'Even as I spoke, I could see they were disappointed. They told me how this would demonstrate to the world that India was powerful. I repeated that I knew they were capable of blasting it the next day and that I was not against the tests. I had great pride too in the work they had done, but I had to get my priorities right, and they had to give me time for at least a year.'[61]

Gowda, whose political problems with the Congress were mounting by then did not think of the tests as a convenient ploy to survive and secure his premiership, which is what he thought Vajpayee did when he sanctioned the tests eventually in May 1998. Gowda remembered:

Vajpayee gave a go-ahead to the tests within three months of coming to power in 1998. He knew the political uncertainty that was enveloping him with Jayalalitha's AIADMK being an unreliable coalition partner. He converted the tests into a nationalist slogan, which was unfortunate. When the tests happened, in an emotional outburst, Jagmohan, who was a minister in Vajpayee's cabinet, called the previous prime ministers 'impotent'. He was targeting Narasimha Rao, I.K. Gujral and me. Gujral wanted to counter that remark. But I thought he would not be effective because he had not seen the file or written on it. Also, he was too soft to do a political hit back. Therefore, I stood up and said, 'none of us was impotent'. I asked Vajpayee to place the entire file in the House so that everybody could read what I had written and determine for themselves who was potent or impotent. I knew they could not table the file in the House. Vajpayee suddenly became alert. He signalled peace. Even as I was speaking, the news came that Pakistan had carried out similar nuclear tests. Everybody rushed to the Central Hall to watch television news. That day five crore Pakistanis and ninety crore Indians had been equated. India had lost its strategic advantage. Nothing that Vajpayee did worked later. The Agra summit also failed,

and we had to bear the brunt of sanctions. The bomb did not
stop Jayalalitha from withdrawing support to his government
nine months later.[62]

In a lengthy intervention in the Lok Sabha, a fortnight after the
blasts, Gowda said:

> Senior Member Shri Jagmohan has mentioned that previous
> prime ministers had not shown courage to take a decision.
> I would like to just mention courage and conviction are not the
> issues alone when we are going to take a decision of this type . . .
> When we were heading a coalition with thirteen political parties,
> on an important issue like CTBT—the question was signing
> CTBT—the then minister of external affairs, Shri I.K. Gujral
> approached Shri Vajpayee, Shri Narasimha Rao, Shri Chandra
> Shekhar and a senior member Shri Somnath Chatterjee who is
> sitting here. All these four or five leaders were consulted before
> we took a decision. I am only mentioning how we tried to take
> the House or every political party into confidence when we
> decided not to sign the CTBT in 1996 . . . [The Bill Clinton
> administration had also sent Henry Kissinger, the former
> secretary of state, to persuade Gowda to sign the CTBT.[63]] Sir,
> what was the threat perception? The dispute between India
> and Pakistan over Kashmir and the border dispute between
> India and China, as you have quoted in your letter, have been
> there since the last fifty years. There is nothing new about it.
> The hon. home minister cited the reasons of militancy and
> insurgency. They are also not new . . . Sir, during 1997–98, our
> trade with China had gone up by $1.75 billion, if I am correct.
> Our trade with China had improved last year and our bilateral
> talks were going on. In such a situation, can you cite security
> threat as one of the major reasons for taking this courageous
> decision? Yesterday, the hon. minister tried to enlighten this
> House by saying that the government wanted to put an end to

insurgency activities which are encouraged by our neighbouring country, Pakistan. If they are going to achieve that by showing the bomb today, we welcome that . . . How was this Pokharan-II test conducted? It was a hidden capability. I can only say that nobody has doubted India's capability. Otherwise, where was the need for a superpower to force us to sign the CTBT? If they had considered that this country is not capable, they would not have put pressure on us . . . Mr Prime Minister, by showing your bomb, whether it is a big bomb or small bomb, you cannot solve the boundary problem in Kashmir or the problem in the North-eastern states.[64]

The issue rankled Gowda for a long time. He wanted to prove that it was nothing but a vanity bomb to improve the BJP's political prospects. In the Motion of Confidence debate in April 1999, he tried to puncture Vajpayee's argument, again: 'Some people have said that there were impotent prime ministers and the potent prime minister had taken a decision to have the nuclear tests as if in thirty days, they had manufactured the bomb. We took the decision at that time not to allow them when we were running the government because of the economic situation. Now, I do not want to again dilate particularly on that issue. What has happened? Pakistan has also conducted two tests. They have a population of about six or seven crore people. We have a population of about 100 crore, but we have now come to an equal level in the eyes of the entire world. That is all what they (BJP and Vajpayee) have achieved.'[65]

The Farewell

Returning to the discussion on the PMO, Satish Chandran, who had contributed immensely to Gowda's prime ministership and with whom Gowda had assumed a kinship, moved out as principal secretary immediately after Gowda stepped down. The Gujral government made him the Governor of Goa. He was in office for a very short period. As soon as Vajpayee took over as prime minister, he had to resign. True to his self, the rest of his years were passed outside of public glare, which he never sought in the first place throughout his long and distinguished career.

Chandran passed away in the early hours of 12 September 2009 in his Bangalore home. The family planned for a quiet cremation as per his wish. But the word got around, and it reached Gowda. An officer informed him over the phone.[66] He started out immediately. As soon as he reached Chandran's home, he took over the funeral arrangements. He told Chandran's wife and two sons that he had lost an elder brother and could not allow an uneventful cremation at an electric crematorium. He ensured Chandran got befitting police honours. He also arranged sandalwood for the pyre and lent his shoulder to the bier. As he did this, tears were rolling down his cheeks.[67] Top bureaucrats like J.C. Lynn, Chiranjiv Singh and Meenakshisundaram were witnesses. Singh recalled: 'No one else would have done something like that, and he would have done it for no one else.'

12

SPG and the Incognito Dream

The story of Deve Gowda's PMO would be incomplete without looking at Gowda through the eyes of the Special Protection Group (SPG), an organization largely in the mould of the Intelligence Bureau, which keeps a low profile and offers 'proximate security' to the prime minister from his time of waking, till he goes to bed. According to the SPG Act, 1988, 'proximate security' would mean, 'protection provided from close quarters, during journey by road, rail, aircraft, watercraft or on foot or any other means of transport and shall include the places of functions, engagements, residence or halt and shall comprise ring round teams, isolation cordons, the sterile zone around, and the rostrum and access control to the person or members of his immediate family.' [1]

The day Gowda became PM-designate, the SPG was already operating from five locations. They were protecting Sonia Gandhi, a former PM's wife, and former PMs V.P. Singh, Chandra Shekhar, and P.V. Narasimha Rao, besides the outgoing PM Vajpayee. Gowda became the sixth person to come under their protection. The proliferation of SPG locations at the dawn of a coalition era in Indian politics did worry the elite organization, and it knew that additional resources may not be available straight away.[2] As an individual, there was not much threat to Gowda. But as an institution of Indian democracy, to the PM's office, there was threat from terrorists, insurgent and extremist groups, plus subversive elements. His threat assessment was lesser than that of P.V. Narasimha Rao and Vajpayee, but as an institution the threat was similar, and the SPG was guided by that.[3]

As soon as Gowda was designated PM, the SPG rushed to Karnataka Bhavan where he was staying. Shyamal Datta, the director of SPG, called on him, and it appeared not much of that meeting registered in Gowda's mind. He was still coming to terms with the fact that he had become PM, and there was a palpable air of reluctance. Expectedly, there was a lot of confusion, but swiftly the SPG positioned itself and took over his security.[4] The PM-designate was leaving for Bangalore late in the evening. They ensured the PM's Air Force One was put on the tarmac, and for the first time, they accompanied him.

After a thunderous crowd giving him a glowing reception at the Bangalore airport, Gowda was driven to Anugraha, the chief minister's residence. Perhaps for the SPG, this was a new experience. With the others they had protected or were protecting, there was no home crowd that constituted an entire state. None of them were sitting chief ministers, and more importantly, none of them were seen as sons/daughters of the soil. In a sense, the others were tagged 'national', and the local roots they may have had was limited to their parliamentary constituencies. That too was incidental. They had all become New Delhi residents for decades and did not evoke a mass eruption or exuberance in any specific local or community pocket.

At Anugraha, Shyamal Datta had a meeting with the chief secretary and the director general of police, and retired for the night at the Ashoka Hotel, next door. But he was woken up in the middle of the night by the assistant director in charge of the SPG's close protection team (ADCPT), K.V. Madhusudanan. He said the PM-designate wanted to visit certain places the next day morning, but the state government was clueless as to how to go about it since the SPG had taken over the security. Gowda, who was free to travel where he wanted to, at short notice, till the previous day, was amused that he could not now decide unilaterally. That was a kind of first awakening for Gowda—being PM was different from being a CM. Datta sat up the whole night and worked out the arrangements. The first visit was to Satya Sai Baba's ashram in Whitefield, outside Bangalore. Then to the temple on Chamundi Hills, near Mysore, and finally, the wedding of a party worker in Mysore city.

Gowda had reasoned it out with the SPG as to why he wanted to visit these places. For instance, he had said that Satya Sai Baba had addressed him as 'prime minister', not once but twice when he was still chief minister, and there was not even a glint of such a development in the distant horizon. According to Gowda's belief, it was not a slip of the tongue but the Baba's divine vision. Therefore, he thought it was his duty to pay his respects before he took charge as PM.

Within days after being sworn in, Gowda got used to SPG protocols. 'There was not another prime minister who was so overtly and expressively courteous. He made all the adjustments, accommodations and adaptations with such ease that it made our job easy. At times, I would feel bad for raising reservations. As a PM, he could have conveyed, "I will go where I want to go, it is for you to protect me the way you want" but he never did that,' recalled Datta.[5]

This does not mean that Gowda did not make demands on the SPG, but they were placed in such a manner that there would always be ample space to negotiate. There are two specific instances that Datta remembers: 'One day, we were walking from his home–office, the 7 Race Course Road (RCR) bungalow to his residence at 5 RCR. He struck a conversation like he would normally do. There was never an awkward silence with him: "Mr Datta, how would you react if I say I want to go to Jama Masjid area incognito, no convoy, no ADCPT, just you and I. We will move around, I will get a feel of the Masjid area and we can come back. I can put a shawl around my face so that I am not recognized by anybody." I was shocked by

248 Furrows in a Field

the nature of the request. I gently said, "Sir, pardon me, I will have to raise objections." He asked, "Why?" I said, "First of all, I will be violating the security drill laid down as well as the security blue book." He responded like a child, "*Arrey baba*, I will protect you." I told him, "Sir you will surely protect me if you are destined to do so, but what if something untoward happens?" His face became glum. He never spoke of walking around incognito ever again."[6] (The prime minister's residential complex at RCR currently has six bungalows, but in Gowda's time, there were four. Under P.V. Narasimha Rao, 3 RCR was the private zone, but Gowda designated 5 RCR as the private zone, subscribing to the rules of vaastu. However, 7 RCR has always been the home–office of the prime minister. (RCR was renamed Lok Kalyan Marg in 2016.)

One wonders where this idea of moving around incognito came to Gowda. Perhaps it was from sufficiently mythologized folk narratives of kings travelling incognito to understand their subjects. The request he made to Datta was either out of plain innocence or a one-off flight of fancy. Gowda was sufficiently rooted and pragmatic to not imagine himself as a king. He was always aware of the democratic context he was in, and more than understood that he led a thirteen-party coalition with its growing pulls and pressures, which kings would certainly not be circumscribed by.

The very next episode that Datta recounted points to the indirect pressure of accountability in a democratic system:

He had to file his Rajya Sabha nomination in Bangalore. He said, 'I will not use Air Force One.' The blue book does permit the prime minister to make use of the resources at his disposal, even for something that could be strictly construed as personal. But, he said, filing of nomination is not official. It is personal. The secretary, security in the cabinet secretariat, B.K. Ratnakar Rao, tried to convince him, but the PM appeared adamant. He kept saying, 'No, I will not use Air Force One. You can take me by a public carrier, why don't you try.' Then

I explained the dislocations and inconvenience it would cause
to the public. But he looked at Rao and me beseechingly. We
had to decide before we took leave of him. We said, 'Okay sir,
we will do it.' That turned out to be the first-ever visit of a PM
in a public carrier. We took all precautions and went through
the entire drill that goes with aviation security. The PM flew
Indian Airlines, filed his nomination and returned to Delhi the
same evening. One should have seen the child-like joy on his
face when we landed back in Delhi. He was humble, preferred
to negotiate than to order around. I always found him to be
transparent.[7]

But with Gowda, there was one shortcoming, and that had to do with
time. He had grown used to the idea of auspicious and inauspicious
hours in a day, as described in the Hindu calendar. The inauspicious
hours would be vacant for Gowda. He would not so much as lift his
pen to sign on an important file, nor would he sign off on a new
idea. Many politicians, including former prime ministers, followed
this, but in Gowda's case, it was a little more pronounced because
he was guileless on certain matters. What he was beholden to could
easily be dismissed as superstitious, but it was a belief system that was
not easy to shake, especially given the scary fickleness of fortune he
had experienced. In the language of science, it perhaps offered him a
limited psychological relief.

Anyway, the SPG was often stumped by *Rahu Kalam*. Datta said:

Suddenly, we found Rahu Kalam was being talked about in
the PMO. I asked Ratnakar Rao what this was. He explained
it to me. I learnt it was considered an inauspicious part of the
day, and a lot of complex calculations were involved in its
determination. We found the PM's schedule was not being
adhered to as a result of this. Say, it was written that he will leave
at 1200 hours. That would never happen if Rahu Kalam was
on the wane at the time. There would be an invariable delay.

When the schedule was not followed, there was a cascading effect for not just security personnel but also traffic managers. We could not share what the reason behind the delay was with Delhi police, who were managing traffic, but traffic got halted for a longer duration and this inconvenienced the public. On the day Gowda had to attend the 15 August ceremony at Red Fort, he was running behind schedule by a few minutes. Madhusudanan, the ADCPT, was with him. He was one PM who would chat up security people in the car. PMs usually don't talk. So, Madhusudanan took the liberty of telling him, 'Sir, we are late. We have to visit Rajghat, Shantivan and then reach Red Fort.' He became so apologetic that immediately after we reached Rajghat, he almost ran to save time. He assured the ADCPT that he will manage it, and lo and behold, he was on the dot at Red Fort. He managed. So, this Rahu Kalam we had to deal with as long as he was there. We did take Delhi Police into confidence later, but we could not do much.[8]

Datta felt Gowda was very sensitive in his interactions with people and his staff. He had never seen him being discourteous to anybody or talking down. He recalled an incident when they visited Vaishno Devi temple: 'We landed at the helipad. Governor of Jammu and Kashmir, General K.V. Krishna Rao was very imposing. He usually monopolized dignitaries who visited his state. He told the PM: "I would advise you to walk the distance to the main shrine." I expressed my reservations to the PM about walking all the way. The terrain was tough. But the PM got carried away by the Governor's suggestion. We had arranged for a palanquin. He wanted to avoid that optic of sitting in a palanquin, but that we could have managed. When returning from the shrine, out of mischief, I went and asked him, "Sir, will you walk back?" He said, "*Na baba, na baba* (no, no)." I looked at the Governor. Gowda was a very decent man. He did not look at the Governor. He did not want to give him a feeling that he was responsible for the blisters and pain on his feet. He quietly got into the palanquin. He was sensitive about personal relationships, and in this case, did not want to embarrass his host.'[9] Apparently, the next day, Gowda had to keep his feet in lukewarm water the whole day to relieve himself of the pain.

Datta travelled with Gowda across the country and found it surprising that in sensitive regions like Jammu and Kashmir, people came of their own volition to listen to him. They did not have to be goaded. 'They said let's listen to the new man. The fear that had overshadowed the region dissipated for a while. The future looked more promising with him at the helm. In the North-east too, people straight away loved him. They loved his transparency and humility. They felt there was nothing between him and them, no hurdles, no obstructions. He could create that feeling in people.' Datta recalled.[10]

Gowda had similarly landed in Lutyens's Delhi as an object of surprise. But in Delhi, with his *panche* (or dhoti, the wrap around) and *jubba* (kurta), people were unable to comprehend as to what was happening. They were not used to it. He did not look smart enough to fit into the clients and operators of Lutyens Delhi. It was an unsettling moment for him as well as for them. But that was not the case in the rest of India. He was flocked around, welcomed and loved. The ordinary people saw themselves in him. If someone with his humble background could reach the pinnacle of political power, they thought hope was, after all, not a mirage. He became somewhat of a phenomenon. In politics, they started believing that one need not be connected with dynasty, need not have a parliamentary majority, and need not be servile to money bags to get to the top. 'It was Gowda's elevation as PM that ignited an ambition in the political class that they too could reach where Gowda had reached. It was palpable as we toured across the country. Nothing better could have happened to parliamentary democracy in India,' remembered Datta.[11]

Shyamal Datta returned to the Intelligence Bureau a month before Gowda stepped down: 'We got down from the airplane in Lucknow. The prime minister was introduced to people in the line

to receive him. After that suddenly, there was a pat on my shoulder.
It was the PM. He said, "Dattaji I have cleared your file." "Which
file, sir?" I asked. "Your transfer file, it was in the bag of files in the
aircraft. I don't know why you are going back, you shouldn't have.
But anyway, all the best," he replied. That was his personal touch. At
times, he disarmed you with his affection.'[12] Datta soon became the
head of the Intelligence Bureau and post retirement, between 2002
and 2007, became the Governor of Nagaland.

13

Mission Kashmir and a Bullet-Proof Birth Chart

H.D. Deve Gowda had never been to the Kashmir valley. Not only had he not been there, he had neither the need nor inclination to apply his mind to its peculiar history and problematic existence on the Indian map. Sitting in southern India, he had gaped at newspaper headlines of violence in the Valley for years, but without dwelling on them had moved on to local issues.

In fact, it was not just Gowda, but most politicians and people in the south were only remote witnesses to events in the north. Be it the trauma of Partition, the wars with Pakistan and China, terrorism in Punjab and Kashmir, or insurgency in the North-east, they were all distant happenings in cultures and languages that were not entirely familiar. The south was a different country.

Specifically, in the Kannada popular imagination, Kashmir either had connotations of romance or religion even as late as 2000. In *Shabdhavedhi*,[1] the final acting enterprise of Kannada cultural icon Rajkumar, there is a song titled *Prema Kashmira* (Love Nest Kashmir). In this, a nearly seventy-one-year-old Rajkumar, made to look thirty-five something, romances Jayaprada on the snowcapped slopes and touristy spots of the Valley. It's a duet and the lyrics circle around these lines:

> In Kashmir a beauty from Belur
> In Kailasa a jasmine from Mysore . . .
> The river of joy is the Ganga that Lord Shiva spills.

Beauty from Belur in the song is a reference to the twelfth-century curvy Hoysala figurines in the Chennakeshava temple of Belur, incidentally in Gowda's home district of Hassan.

When Gowda visited Kashmir for the first time, as prime minister, and as the cavalcade passed the Dal Lake to reach the Nehru Guest House, a romantic thought wafted through his head: 'It's so beautiful. I should have brought my wife along,'[2] he thought. Kashmir had plucked a forgotten string in Gowda's heart, who was not known to be a romantic but often characterized as emotional. It was an unexpected beginning.

Gowda always wanted to go on a pilgrimage to the Amarnath cave in the Valley to have a darshan of the stalagmite Shivalinga, but that has not materialized to this day. However, he had visited the Vaishno Devi shrine in Katra, near Jammu, once before he became prime minister and a few times after he stepped down.[3] But, the shrine has been independent without the affiliation of a state in his mind. Pilgrim centres are perhaps stateless in the mind of a believer. They are sovereignties of gods they trust.

Given this background of distance and indifference, it is astonishing as to how quickly Gowda developed a grasp of issues that tormented the Valley. He earned the trust of Kashmiris when everyone and everything was being viewed with cynicism and he endeavoured to make this engagement one of the central missions of his prime ministership. His agenda was not just to restore political normalcy in the state, which he did, but to ambitiously aim for a pragmatic solution to the vexing international issue it had become since Independence. In nearly eleven months that he lasted at the helm, he visited the state of Jammu and Kashmir four times. No prime minister had visited the Valley in nearly a decade, during which militancy was in its ascendancy. The state assembly elections, too, had been deferred in the state for seven years. The parliamentary polls that had just been held, which the National Conference had boycotted, was not exactly a crowning achievement. It had just about maintained a low decibel of democracy in what was referred to as a 'militarized zone'.

In retrospect, it was incredible and brave that Gowda chose to address one of the biggest uncertainties that shadowed India in his short tenure. His lack of national-level political experience, and lack of a policy baggage, became his biggest advantage because he deployed earnestness instead. Interestingly, he was deeply involved in the conduct of the state assembly elections but neither campaigned during the polls nor tried to score political points after the new government was installed. Kashmir for Gowda was beyond politics. It was a surprise passion and an exploration of his own statesmanship.

The First Visit

During his first week as prime minister, Gowda tried to give a broad focus and direction to himself. He quickly resolved that internal security issues would be his priority.[4] He did not want to accept tour programmes abroad, except those inevitable. He thought they would devour a lot of his time. The seasoned politician that he was, he knew his time at the desk may be limited. Focusing on big issues within India would help him make a mark, besides mobilizing political constituencies and popular support that he needed to finally be his own man. Until the day he became prime minister, Gowda was a regional leader; it was now imperative for him to gain currency as prime minister and become somewhat acceptable beyond his fiefdom of Karnataka.

Gowda had wondered when policymakers and fellow politicians had offered a staid defence and a phrase to the disquiet in the Valley

by saying it was an 'integral part of India'. In a commonsensical way,
he thought, if it truly became emotionally aligned with India there
would be no need for such platitudinal reiterations. That was the
beginning in his mind. He read up as much as he could and sought
thorough briefings. He also decided he should visit the state to get a
first-hand idea. When he mentioned it to bureaucrats, he was made
aware that he would be the first head of state to be doing so in nearly
a decade. It sounded more like a warning. But Gowda put forward
a disarming argument that as a head of state, he was only visiting a
corner of his own country.[5]

As a first step, he fixed a date to visit the Valley. Intelligence
and security officials met with the cabinet secretary and the prime
minister's principal secretary to make an assessment. It did not
take them much time to conclude that the situation in the Valley
was bad, and the threat to the prime minister's life was high. They
communicated that it would be difficult for them to permit a visit.
He accepted their view. But within a few days, he fixed another
date and sought a reassessment. The officials came back with a
similar response. He asked: 'If Kashmir is an integral part of India,
why should a prime minister be afraid to go there?' That was a
rhetorical question.[6]

Gowda decided to get a different kind of assessment done,
outside of the officialdom. He summoned an astrologer-friend,
Devendra Mishra. He had faith in such things and was unabashed
about it. He was not like other politicians who consulted their birth
charts all the time but wore a mask of reason and rationality. Gowda
asked if there was any unnatural death predicted in his chart? The
astrologer-friend was categorical: 'I have studied your horoscope
many times. You don't have to go by what your officials say. You
don't have to fear for your life.' After Gowda heard what he wanted
to hear, he gave him an additional task of fixing an auspicious day for
his maiden visit. Once it was decided that he would travel on 6 July
1996, he simply communicated the date to the officials and asked
them to work on the logistics.[7]

Simultaneously, he called up General K.V. Krishna Rao, who was Governor of Jammu and Kashmir, and asked him to extend an open invitation to all political parties, all manner of Kashmiri organizations, including secessionist groups, to come and make their case before him. He also said he would go straight to the meeting from the airport, where he was scheduled to land at 8.30 a.m. He added that the Governor should not worry about organizing breakfast as he would take care of it before the plane touched down. Breakfast and such formalities would consume time, he thought, and wanted to convey a certain urgency to his visit. 'Anybody can come and see me. Whoever wants to talk to me can walk in,' he said.[8] This was something unheard of inside and outside of Kashmir. Free access to India's prime minister, that too in a troubled territory, instantly created an impression about Gowda. From a little-known politician, who had accidentally become prime minister, he had suddenly acquired a character. The plan worked pretty well. He met a wide range of leaders who had been advocating different destinies for Kashmir and had different affiliations.

Interestingly, Prime Minister P.V. Narasimha Rao, in his capacity as the president of the Congress Party, had made a two-hour stop in Jammu two months ago, strictly for purposes of electioneering. The Valley, however, was not on his itinerary. The fleeting visit was so ill-organized by his party, let alone the public and the media, even Governor Rao was not aware that the prime minister was visiting Jammu, and he was not very pleased: 'I was told by a subordinate police officer that the prime minister was visiting Jammu on 5 May for an election meeting being organized by the Congress party. I was rather surprised, as nobody had mentioned this to me. I was always keen that the prime minister of India visit the state as the PM and not just as party president . . . Of course, I received him and saw him off with due courtesy.'[9] This made Gowda's visit the first real prime-ministerial visit to the state in nearly a decade, and the administration was delighted to cater to his diligence.

Earlier, in the airplane, the security officials had continued to fret about Gowda's visit. When they were putting the bullet-proof jacket on him, Shyamal Datta, the chief of the elite Special Protection Group (SPG) that protects prime ministers, had said: 'Sir, you seem to be taking this very casually. You know what they did to Kennedy in Dallas.' But Gowda pointed his forehead to Datta: 'Whatever is written there will take place. In case something happens, send my body to Holenarasipur (his hometown). In Delhi's dirty politics, they'll not even cremate me properly.' Astounded by the bluntness of the exchange, Datta had gone quiet. Even twenty-five years later, Datta had not forgotten the exchange.[10]

After the first visit, *India Today*[11] wrote: 'The signs of hope are unmistakable. There was silent admiration in the war-weary Valley after the first visit by a Prime Minister in nine years brought about the improbable . . . Schools which admitted children only after parents signed indemnity bonds are now taking them to Gulmarg and Pahalgam for weekend holiday camps . . . In the coming months, Deve Gowda's political acumen will be put to test—by the militants and a people who, with hopes rekindled, are in no mood for another round of games'.

In Gowda's words, people 'trusted his intent'. He said they had also done their homework on his approach towards the Muslim community in Karnataka, as chief minister. After talk of mutual trust, the one thing that all leaders who met him in the Valley spoke about was the severe distress in the local economy. They pointed out tourism had been dead for a decade, there were no employment avenues, there was poverty, and people were deep in debt. They asked if a loan waiver was possible. They also said that if a healthy atmosphere was created, tourists would come in, and the economy could limp back to normal.[12]

Gowda wanted to build on the goodwill and wanted to be seen acting upon their demands. As soon as he reached office the next day in New Delhi, he sent for Montek Singh Ahluwalia, the finance secretary. He discussed the loan waiver and asked him to start working on it immediately. His office communicated to the Governor, before noon, about the government's intention to underwrite the loans. The news was flashed across the Valley. It had not even taken a day since his return.[13] People were surprised. They wondered how a prime minister heading a thirteen-party coalition had acted so decisively. 'It was my administrative style to take decisions then and there, not procrastinate. In this particular case, it had helped create tremendous confidence among people in the Valley,' Gowda recalled.[14]

Ahluwalia does not remember the exact conversation on the loan waiver but said the finance ministry was aware about the exceptional circumstances in Kashmir: 'Every state claims its circumstances are exceptional, but Kashmir's was really exceptional. The PM was very informal. Often, he spoke to me directly, but any order in the government would take time, and would have to go through the process. Loan waiver was an easy thing to do but if the government had stayed longer there would have been many positive outcomes.'[15]

Three days before his second visit to the state, on 2 August 1996, Gowda made a mention of the loan waiver in the Parliament,[16] and his logic was impeccable: 'Tourist arrivals in the Valley declined from a peak figure of 700,000 in 1986–87 to almost a trickle during the last few years. This affected the livelihood of thousands of families deriving sustenance from tourism and related activities. The affected units and individuals who had taken commercial loans from banks have not been able to repay the loans since there was no cash flow and have fallen into a debt trap. The state government has identified that 31,000 borrowers from the sectors of small-scale trade and industry, transport, hotel and houseboat businesses took loans to the extent of Rs 181.87 crore. During the last six years, there has been hardly any repayment and the interest on these loans itself amounts for another Rs 212.79 crore . . . Government, therefore, proposes to write off the outstanding loan and interest of all borrowers whose original borrowing is less than or up to Rs 50,000. This would enable these small borrowers to get fresh loans from the banking sector to restart their businesses. As regards borrowers above

Rs 50,000, an inter-ministerial committee is being constituted to look into the questions of moratorium and rescheduling of repayments of their loans, reduction in interest rates and any other reliefs that could be given.'

In an earlier statement in the Parliament,[17] Gowda had shared his government's other initiatives for the Valley to resurrect the economy and generate employment. Among them was the revival of two major power projects: 'Hon'ble members are aware that work on the Dulhasti Hydro Electric Project (3x130 MW) came to a halt in 1992 with the withdrawal of the French civil contractors. An amendment to the overall agreement with the French consortium has been finalized in July 1995. As a result of this, while the machinery is being supplied by the French consortium, the remaining civil works could be taken up by other contractors . . . Government would ensure that the civil works are commenced at the earliest and would also see that the funds for the balance civil works would be mobilized through various sources including government assistance and market borrowings . . . another major hydro-electric project, namely, the Uri Hydro Electric Project (4X120 MW), is under construction in the state. The work on this is going on according to schedule and the first unit is likely to be commissioned during this year itself beginning December 1996.'

While in the Valley, Gowda had visited the Uri power project area. They had dug a tunnel and the debris was all over. He inspected the tunnel as the security forces kept warning that the ground beneath may cave in. He walked around wearing a helmet like a civil engineer, fearlessly. His astrologer had anyway assured him of his life. As soon as he had returned to Delhi, he had asked officers to tell the French consortium that the new government was keen to see the power projects completed.[18]

During the first visit, his intuition had prodded him to check if there was a railway connection between the mainland and the Valley. Gowda has a lot to say about his intuition, sometimes he attributes it to a divine voice speaking to him, and at other times, he is more rational to see it as a skill honed through experience. Anyway, the response to the query on the railway line was a 'no'. This spurred him to act on developing a plan to connect Baramulla in the Kashmir valley to the rest of the country. A part of this rail line between Jammu and Udhampur had been conceived in 1983 under Indira Gandhi, but Gowda expanded its scope and gave it more resources. He not only asked his railway minister, Ram Vilas Paswan to lay the foundation stone, but also declared it as a national project. Until then, no project in the rail ministry had been declared a national project. This was the first. He spoke about this too in the Parliament:[19] 'Government would be taking up the construction of a 290-km railway line from Udhampur to Baramulla as a national project to be financed by Government of India outside the Railway's plan. The project is estimated to cost Rs 2500 crore and would be a great factor in integrating Kashmir with the rest of the country. The survey work from Udhampur to Banihal has already been completed and survey work up to Baramulla will be over by March 1997. The line would pass via Katra-Riasi-Banihal-Qazigund-Srinagar,' he announced.

The second visit to the state happened within a month on 5 August 1996. He visited Leh, Kargil, and Jammu and addressed a public meeting in Rajouri. During this trip, Gowda created some drama. From Rajouri airport to the town where he was to address a public meeting, he wanted to be taken in an open jeep so that he could wave at people assembled on either side of the road. The distance to be covered was over two kilometres. The area commander, Lt Gen. J.S. Dhillon, shuddered when he heard the idea. 'If I do something like this, the country will hang me, sir,' Gowda recalls Lt Gen. Dhillon telling him. 'Nothing will happen, don't worry. You drive and I'll sit next to you. Assume somebody lobs a grenade; both of us will die. Where is the question of you being hanged?' He reasoned wickedly. Soldiers with automatic rifles sat around. There were motorcycle outriders, the general drove the prime minister in an open jeep. Perhaps the astrologer's assurance that his life was absolutely secure gave him the audacity to venture into something like this.[20]

On the day Gowda recalled this incident, in August 2019, he said with his trademark smile that bordered on a smirk: 'Both of us are alive to this day. I knew nothing would go wrong.' Gowda, when he speaks, especially in Kannada, does not do it straight and to the point. His narration loiters to construct ironies. They juxtapose a series of events, emotions and reflections from the past and present, often icing it with a smile that takes the shape of a smirk, indicating transient joy of vindication or an excruciating defeat by destiny. His communication is very complex.[21]

When Lt Gen. Dhillon[22] recalled the open jeep drive nearly twenty-four years later, he said: 'Naturally, I was anxious. Prior to his arrival, I had sent a message across to the opposite side that if you interfere with our PM's visit, do a ceasefire violation, we'll blast you and we have every weapon system ready to do so. We had taken necessary precautions, but I hadn't expected a request for an open jeep ride. I was frankly very surprised. Prime ministers don't do this. They want to be protected all the time. Vehicles are flown in for them. But Gowda-*saab* always moved around with minimal protection. He was a brave chap. The Valley would have changed if he had been around longer.'

Amidst all the trust-building activities, Gowda's mind was constantly preparing for assembly elections in Jammu and Kashmir. On 2 August 1996, he had ended his speech in Parliament[23] by saying: 'I would like to take this opportunity to reiterate the government's commitment to give maximum autonomy to the state. Once an elected government is in place, we would hold consultations with them to arrive at a consensus.' There was a mention of Kashmir and elections in his Independence Day[24] address too: 'I visited Jammu and Kashmir twice and met the people of the state and felt their aspirations. The conditions are changing there . . . We will complete the task of restoration of normalcy and return of a popular government in Jammu and Kashmir.'

Gowda's two trusted aides—Satish Chandran and T.S.R. Subramaniam—had suggested that he should persuade Farooq Abdullah to contest the polls. He, too, thought it was important because a state assembly poll without the National Conference, the main political party participating, would not make sense. As it was in the Gowda scheme of things, there was never a delay. He had spoken to Abdullah, who was in London, as soon as he had heard the suggestion: 'Your father was like a lion. What is wrong with you? Why are you staying away? You should contest. Your party will sweep the polls.' Gowda paraphrased the conversation he had had.[25]

In the parliamentary polls that had just been held, the National Conference had declined to participate in the elections. Since the P.V. Narasimha Rao-led Congress government had not committed itself to the autonomy issue, Farooq Abdullah had decided against participation. The Governor, General K.V. Krishna Rao, writes in his book[26] of reminiscences: 'I met Prime Minister (P.V. Narasimha Rao) on 25 March and he was keen that the National Conference first participate in the elections and the autonomy issue could be resolved after the elections.' But obviously, Farooq Abdullah did not want to move ahead without some resolution on the issue.

But once Gowda took oath after Vajpayee's thirteen-day government fell, General Rao had written[27] to the new prime minister emphasizing the need for early holding of assembly elections while the additional forces were still in Jammu and Kashmir. 'He was kind enough to ring me on 4 June, appreciated our efforts and the results achieved, and wanted me to carry on. He assured that he would pursue the matter regarding assembly elections.' The common policy and programme document of the United Front government had also committed itself to holding assembly elections as early as possible, respecting Article 370, and had assured maximum autonomy to the region. The working committee of the National Conference, which had met in the second week of June, had 'noted with satisfaction'[28] the idea of the Gowda government to grant maximum autonomy but wanted a speedy implementation.

The Polls

Even as poll preparations began, the big question on everybody's mind was if they would be free and fair. There was some history to this. During the parliamentary elections, some sections of the foreign media said that people were coerced to vote. Gowda came up with an idea to make the process credible. He called ambassadors of a few countries for a breakfast meeting and asked them if they would act as observers and dispatch independent reports to their respective countries and international agencies? They agreed. The National Conference, in its discussions with Delhi leaders, had also insisted that elections to the state assembly be held in the presence of independent observers. Gowda took another major decision, which was to allow international media to freely travel anywhere in Jammu and Kashmir and report. 'I had nothing to hide, I had nothing to fear,' he recalled.[29]

The *Washington Post*[30] wrote: 'After almost seven years of separatist rebellion, at least 14,500 deaths and the destruction of a thriving tourism industry, Indian officials hope the election of a new state government here will restore democracy and normalcy to the disputed Himalayan state of Jammu and Kashmir.'

Lt Gen. Dhillon played an important role during the polls. When Delhi decided to hold elections, they asked him for his views on the security situation. He had responded positively. The Election Commission on 7 August, two days after the PM's second visit, announced elections in four phases in the month of September. Lt Gen. Dhillon[31] recalled:

Anantnag was the most difficult area, and the day the elections were being held there, I got a call suddenly, around mid-day. They said on the other side that the PM wants to talk to you. The general protocol is the PM speaks to the defence minister, he to the army chief, and then it comes to us. But he called directly. Look at his involvement. He asked, how is it going?

H.D. Deve Gowda's parents, Lakshmidevamma
and Dodde Gowda.

The primary school Deve Gowda went to in Haradanahalli.

The municipal high school Deve Gowda went to in
Holenarasipur.

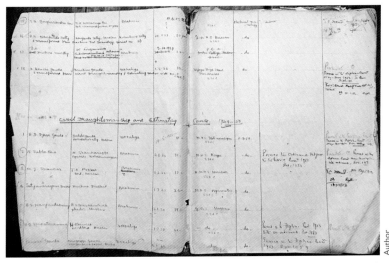

Author

The polytechnic college admission register. First name in the list for the Civil Draughtsmanship and Estimating course is that of Deve Gowda.

HDD office

The earliest available picture of Deve Gowda, from 1954, as a public works contractor.

HDD office

A picture from 1960, when his involvement in politics was getting serious.

A picture taken in 1962 for a handbill, when he contested for the Mysore Legislative Assembly for the first time, as an independent candidate.

HDD office

Devaraj Urs, the chief minister
with his Opposition leader,
H.D. Deve Gowda, circa 1973.
The Urs era was when Gowda
matured as a politician.

As president of the Janata Party,
Karnataka unit, 1977.

With Morarji Desai, 1977. Also seen here: C.M. Ibrahim
(third from right) and Veerendra Patil (second from right).

With Morarji Desai, 1978. Also seen here: Governor Govind
Narain (right edge).

With Babu Jagajivan Ram, 1980.

With Charan Singh, circa 1978.

With former President of India Neelam Sanjiva Reddy. Also seen here: Chandra Shekhar (third from right), S. Bangarappa (second from right) and V.C. Shukla (first from left).

The car in which Deve Gowda went around across Karnataka in the 1970s to build the Janata Party. It has now been refurbished.

Being sworn in as a minister for the first time in 1983. Flanked by J.H. Patel and S.R. Bommai. Ashoknath Banerji was the Governor.

At a farmers rally in the late 1980s. Also seen here (from
left) are Mahendra Singh Tikait, Devi Lal, Kanshi Ram
and Chandra Shekhar.

In front of an election
campaign vehicle
in 1989, when he
split from the Janata
Dal and started his
own outfit.

With Ramakrishna Hegde, early 1994.

Being sworn in as chief minister by Khursheed Alam Khan,
December 1994.

With former Congress president and Karnataka chief
minister S. Nijalingappa.

With his wife, Chennamma Gowda, circa 1995, when he was
chief minister.

The very devout Chennamma Gowda performing
her morning pooja.

President Shankar Dayal Sharma inviting Deve Gowda to form
the government in 1996.

Being sworn in as prime minister.

HDD office

Meeting P.V. Narasimha Rao in 1996, the then
Congress Party president.

Praveen Jain, *Indian Express*

Meeting Sonia Gandhi in 1996, after being sworn in as prime minister.

Meeting V.P. Singh in 1996, after being sworn in as prime minister.

Meeting A.B. Vajpayee in 1996, after being sworn in as prime minister.

Meeting L.K. Advani in 1996, after being sworn in as prime minister.

With Harkishan Singh Surjeet. A picture that Gowda is very fond of. He got a copy made after he saw it in Surjeet's home.

Shaking hands with Sitaram Kesri, the Congress Party president in 1997, before stepping down as prime minister.

With Lalu Prasad Yadav and
Harkishan Singh Surjeet, when Deve
Gowda was prime minister.

The open-jeep ride as prime minister
in Rajouri, Jammu and Kashmir,
with Lt Gen. Dhillon at the wheel
and Farooq Abdullah at the back.

As prime minister, serving lemon juice to end the protest fast of Sunderlal Bahuguna
against the Tehri Dam project.

With K.R. Narayanan, the then vice
president of India.

The doctor and his patient: Dr L.H.
Hiranandani and Deve Gowda in the 1990s.
Dr Hiranandani was Prime Minister Gowda's
secret special envoy to hold back-channel talks
with Pakistan prime minister Nawaz Sharif.

At the Janata Darshan as
prime minister.

At his desk in the
Prime Minister's Office.

With Kannada matinee idol Rajkumar
and former chief justice of India
M.N. Venkatachalaiah, at a function
in New Delhi when Deve Gowda was
prime minister.

At a ceremony to rename the
Ahmedabad airport as Sardar
Vallabhbhai Patel International Airport.
Also seen here: the then civil aviation
minister C.M. Ibrahim, Gujarat
Governor Krishnapal Singh and Gujarat
chief minister Shankersinh Vaghela.

In a jacket to beat the cold in Moscow,
just before he stepped down as
prime minister.

With M. Karunanidhi, the then chief
minister of Tamil Nadu.

With Biju Patnaik, the senior Janata Dal Leader who proposed Deve Gowda's name for both chief ministership and prime ministership. Also seen here is former Andhra Pradesh chief minister N.T. Rama Rao.

With former prime ministers A.B. Vajpayee, P.V. Narasimha Rao, Chandra Shekhar and I.K. Gujral.

With former West Bengal chief minister Jyoti Basu.

With former prime minister Manmohan Singh.

With Prime Minister Narendra Modi.

In front of a bust of Sardar
Vallabhbhai Patel in the Statue of
Unity complex in Vadodara, 2019.

At the Sardar Sarovar Dam, Vadodara, when
it reached full capacity in 2019.

Speaking to engineers at the Tehri Hydroelectric Project, 2019.

Performing Iyengar-style yoga, 2014.

H.D. Deve Gowda, as both chief minister and prime minister, was in the habit of writing notes in his own hand to his secretaries, on what development works to follow up and what public announcements to make. He duly signed each of these notes at the bottom. This was an unusual practice, given the fact that politicians do not wish to leave paper trails.

Last page of Deve Gowda's seven-page note to his joint secretary, which he wrote while waiting for British prime minister John Major at the Calcutta Raj Bhavan in January 1997.

The first page of Deve Gowda's two-page note on the letterhead of Hotel Imperial in Singapore, to the principal secretary in the chief minister's office, during their official tour of Singapore in August 1995.

Deve Gowda's note to the principal secretary, Social Welfare, and Women and Child Welfare, written when he was chief minister, in July 1995.

I remember he said his worry was this election was not just for India but also for the world. They have to see that the population of that area is voting. It has to be a success. I said it will be a success. He went into details. 'What is your estimate of polling?' he asked. I said, we should be able to achieve 55 per cent to 60 per cent. His worry was if the turnout was any less, it would send a bad message to the world and the rest of the country. The prime minister's office was involved in ensuring that we succeed. The very fact that the PM expressed his views directly and said the image of the nation was involved, and it was not about routine politics meant a lot.

The press had asked Lt Gen. Dhillon[32] many times if the army would interfere in the polling process: 'I had said we will not interfere, but if militants threaten people not to vote then it is our duty to neutralize the militants. We want people to vote, but we are not interested in who the people vote for. I will give the people a free environment to vote. We won't influence even 1 per cent. We are looking for a fair election.'

The general had another story[33] to tell from the elections:

Once Mufti Mohammad Sayeed came to see me in my Badami Bagh office. He was in the Congress those days. He said his daughter, Mehbooba, and his wife, were both contesting from the Anantnag area, and wished that they both won. I said, 'Mufti saab, I don't know about winning, but you take it from me, voting will take place there. Militants may be in any number, but voting will take place. Beyond that, if you think we will assist your daughter and wife to win, that won't happen.' He was a little taken back. His daughter won. She was a small girl those days. His wife lost. That area saw a turnout of 55 per cent. Farooq saab became CM. I was to move out. Farooq saab went to Delhi and met the defence minister and said, 'I want to have Dhillon with me.' He asked me to be his security adviser.

I said I have been in uniform throughout my life, and I won't leave my uniform. He said, 'You can have the powers of a home minister.' I said the government can extend my tenure in the Valley. If you want me to advise you officially, I'll do so, but I won't leave the army. That was accepted. Gowda saab was also involved in my extension. The system of unified command that you hear now was started then. We started it.

Senior journalist Ajith Pillai had an eloquent account of how prime minister Gowda was perceived in the Valley and the impact of his poll announcement in 1996:[34] 'I was a frequent flyer between Delhi and Srinagar those days reporting for the *Outlook* magazine. Srinagar resembled a ghost town with virtual curfew from sunset to sunrise. The one functional hotel (Ahdoos) ran half empty. Tourism was at a low point and the boatmen on the Dal Lake complained of dwindling business. The public mood was a mix of frustration and despondency. Everyone you met had something ill to say about the "government in Delhi," and the high handedness of the army and the paramilitary forces stationed in the Valley.'

Pillai wrote[35] that the new United Front government headed by Gowda had to put the discredited Parliamentary elections in Kashmir behind them and ensure the credible conduct of the forthcoming assembly elections. 'Gowda went about the task without resorting to any theatrics. He refrained from invoking any catch phrases like *"jamhooriyat, insaaniyat* and *kashmiriyat"* to woo the people. Neither did he resort to chanting mantras of *"vikas* and *vishwas"* while promising a better future for Kashmiris. Instead, the prime minister put it across in plain terms that they promised a free and fair election. At the end of the day, it was Deve Gowda's down-to-earth approach that struck a chord with the people in the Valley.'

Pillai also mentions[36] the sharp contrast in the perception of this exercise in Delhi and Srinagar: 'In sharp contrast to the Delhi media, I recall ordinary folk and journalists in Srinagar telling me that their own assessment was that the new prime minister was sincere and had his heart in the right place. He was someone who could be trusted and was not given to making tall claims that he could solve the Kashmir problem overnight. All he was promising for a start was to hold a credible election in a strife-torn state.'

Pillai concluded[37] by saying Gowda's low-key Kashmir initiative did meet with more than reasonable success: 'Deve Gowda did prove a point that a good-natured, reasonable and sincere effort does reap dividends. The humble farmer from Hassan managed to fleetingly win back the trust of the Kashmiri people lost during his predecessor Narasimha Rao's tenure, which also witnessed the horrific Babri Masjid demolition.'

Anyway, prior to the election, Gowda had promised 'maximum autonomy' to the state. He had already had five rounds of talks with the stakeholders. Even as early as June 1996, the assurance of 'maximum autonomy' had generated hope and discussion in the Valley. He recalled: 'I remember the Hurriyat leaders were stubborn. They said let the Centre keep railways, highways, currency, defence, foreign affairs and let us manage the rest. I never discussed 370; I discussed only autonomy. I did five rounds of talks but did not give any publicity. My strategy was to solve it like I had solved the Idgah Maidan issue in Hubli: quietly. One of my conditions to the Hurriyat was you should not discuss anything with the media, and I too will not speak to them.'[38]

Outlook had reported the mood that was developing:[39] 'The winter of political deadlock in Kashmir is not quite over but the first signs of the ice thawing are visible. The promise by the United Front (UF) Government that it will give "maximum autonomy" to Kashmir is being widely seen as a positive signal that could end the strife in the Valley and restore peace. Suddenly everyone—from the All Party Hurriyat Conference (APHC) to Farooq Abdullah's National Conference (NC) is ready to talk and though the different political groupings may differ on the modalities to resolve the crisis, they are all agreed that the new Government in Delhi does hold out hope.' Shabir Shah, a senior Hurriyat leader, was quoted as saying in the magazine: 'We have great faith in Deve Gowdaji. We have never said no to talks but I think this is the most opportune moment to initiate talks.' Other Hurriyat leaders, including its chairman, Moulvi Omar Farooq, were reported to have echoed a similar sentiment. The APHC wanted a tripartite meeting that would include the governments in New Delhi and Islamabad but wanted to begin with the United Front Government first and bring in Pakistan later. The National Conference was keen to be seen in the valley as the party that was negotiating with Gowda's ministry to draw up the parameters for the implementation of the promised 'maximum autonomy'.

In a column, *Outlook*'s editor-in-chief, Vinod Mehta[40] had written: 'I understand the Americans have told the Hurriyat not to waste time in rhetoric or posturing: The United Front, Ambassador Frank Wisner is believed to have reminded the Hurriyat, represents their best bet—take your maximum autonomy and run. The militants have also been reminded of the United Front's limited life thus giving further urgency to early initiatives.' The *Washington Post*[41] had said: 'Prime Minister H.D. Deve Gowda's promises of "maximum autonomy" for Kashmir and an easing of tensions between India and Pakistan have raised hopes of resolution of their territorial dispute that has triggered two wars.'

The National Conference swept the polls as predicted and Farooq Abdullah was sworn in as chief minister on 9 October 1996. General Krishna Rao who administered the oath of office, noted:[42] 'A democratic government was coming to power after seven years. Farooq Abdullah broke down while taking oath.' On 2 October 1996, Gowda congratulated the people of Jammu and Kashmir by saying: '(They) have not only elected a government of their choice but have also shown where their heart lies.'

The only thing that had dampened the enthusiasm of the polls during its run-up was the Amarnath Yatra tragedy, in which 214 people died. The devout annually trek to the holy Amarnath cave, nestled at 12,729 ft in a glacial gorge in Kashmir, to worship a naturally formed '*ice lingam*'. Around August 22, for three days, freezing rain and snow plunged temperatures below zero. 'The cold burst blood vessels and sent hundreds into shock. More than 214 died on the road to Amarnath. For the record number of 1,25,000 pilgrims, the holy 47 km trek from Pahalgam turned into a seemingly endless march of death.'[43] But anyway, this was outside the purview of Deve Gowda's political manoeuvring. It was a natural disaster.

Flying Over the LoC

Four months after the polls, Gowda visited the state once again. This was on 13 February 1997. The timing was impeccable. General elections in Pakistan had given a landslide mandate to Nawaz Sharif. He was to be sworn in as Pakistan's prime minister on 17 February 1997. Gowda now wanted to work on a permanent peace settlement in the Valley and that clearly meant involving Pakistan.

During this visit, Gowda expressed his wish to see the Line of Control (LoC) between India and Pakistan. He was not just curious but also wanted to send a signal across the border. But the request to see the LoC again put Lt Gen. Dhillon in a dilemma. It portended a greater misadventure for him. He resisted like he resisted the open jeep ride in Rajouri, but he also had some idea of Gowda's stubbornness. 'I can't go back without seeing the LoC. You must cooperate,' the prime minister was stern.[44] Lt Gen. Dhillon was soon left without a choice. The audacity of the armed forces is clearly different from the audacity and risk-taking of the political class. With the former, it is structured and institutionalized, while in the case of the latter, it is either instinctual or an intentional act. An army man goes prepared to die, but a politician seeks the phantasmagoria of death for greater survival. With someone like Gowda there was faith in an extra armoury called the horoscope. 'As we flew over the LoC, we could see soldiers on either side. I realized that we were fighting over a vast parcel of land on which even a blade of grass does not grow, at least ninety per cent of the area.'[45] For a man from Hassan in faraway Karnataka, and for whom land meant lush green irrigated crops, this was a bit of a disappointment. It was a farmer's assessment of the LoC.

There is an untold story in the Kashmir gamble of Gowda. When Deve Gowda developed a major problem with his vocal cords in the mid-1980s, he was treated by Dr L.H. Hiranandani, a renowned ENT surgeon in Bombay (now Mumbai). This Dr Hiranandani became a confidential conduit between the two prime ministers, Gowda and Nawaz Sharif, in 1997. Gowda knew Dr Hiranandani and Sharif's father were friends and thought deploying him would achieve the desired results in the Indo-Pak relationship.[46]

Dr Hiranandani had not just treated Gowda in Bombay, but also Mohamed Ali Jinnah, Sheikh Abdullah and a real long line of VVIPs from politics, films (Hollywood included). He hailed from Thatta in Sindh Province and was born in September 1917. In an interview,[47] he recounts: 'When I came back to Bombay after completing my FRCS from England, I was called by Mohamed Ali Jinnah. He was suffering from an ENT problem, which he had discussed with Dr Charl Putton. He wanted to consult only an FRCS surgeon and luckily, at the time, I was the only FRCS in Bombay. The partition of India was not far away. When I examined him, I was very much impressed with his personality. He was not an ordinary man . . . Many international political bigwigs used to consult me. Ministers from Burma and China were my regular patients.'

About his relationship with Sheikh Abdullah, he says: '(He) too, was a regular visitor . . . A boy of 15 was to be hanged. I saved his life, pleaded with Sheikh Abdullah, who initially commuted it to life imprisonment, and later he was acquitted. I arranged for his employment with the government. His name was Rashid and presently he is an inspector general of police.'

In the interview, Dr Hiranandani refers to Gowda as an 'old time friend'. Then he speaks about the back-channel role he played: 'When he was the prime minister, he phoned me and said he wanted to meet me. He had been a regular patient of mine. I asked him when he would be coming to Bombay. He said that he had some other work and I better meet him in Delhi. I went to Delhi and met him. He said that he wanted to settle India-Pakistan dispute, once and for all. I asked him what role could I play in it. He said that I was regarded in high esteem in Pakistan and that he had read some six of my articles, titled *Babus of Pakistan* published in *Blitz* and he wanted my help.'

Dr Hiranandani reached London as the prime minister's personal envoy. He promptly conveyed the message he was entrusted with and ensured that the two prime ministers spoke on the phone subsequently. Surprisingly, Gowda and Sharif hit off quite well. They came to a basic understanding quickly and discussed measures to further build confidence. About 30,000 tons of sugar was exported to meet Pakistan's expediency and boost bilateral discussions. They also agreed that the foreign secretaries of the two countries should meet immediately.[48] Unfortunately, the Congress withdrew support to the government by the time this plan developed definite contours.

This is how Dr Hiranandani describes the mission he was assigned by Gowda: 'He said that I should meet Prime Minister Nawaz Sharif. Initially, I was indicated a schedule to meet him in Islamabad. Then it was cancelled, perhaps because of apprehensions about the military wondering about the purpose of my visit. Subsequently, they directed me to see Nawaz Sharif in London. When I went to London, I was met not by Nawaz Sharif but one of his emissaries whose name I still don't want to disclose. It was decided there that Nawaz Sharif and Deve Gowda would meet and resolve all the issues. A venue, date and time were fixed for their meeting, but alas, it was not to be because in the meantime, Deve Gowda's government fell.' This secret peace mission is also narrated in a private volume[49] on Dr Hiranandani. There is also a warm picture of the doctor hugging his patient—the prime minister—in the book.

When asked about the enthusiasm for better ties with India, Nawaz Sharif in an interview to *Outlook*[50] in February 1997, said: 'We are forty-seven years late, and we can't afford any further delay.

We have to talk. We have to sit at one table.' When asked about
what he thought of Gowda, he said: 'I think he is a gentleman.
I think well of him.' When further probed if there would be talks at
the prime ministerial level, he said: 'Yes, subsequently, yes. Why not?
But initially, we want talks at the foreign secretary, foreign minister
and then the prime ministerial level.' Unfortunately, Gowda did not
last that long as prime minister.

Within a month of Gowda assuming power, Vinod Mehta[51]
had precociously written: 'Let me stick my neck out and predict that
this wobbly government may pleasantly surprise us in two areas of
supreme national worry. One, they could achieve a breakthrough in
Kashmir by persuading a wide variety of political groups including
militants to participate in assembly elections. Two, some progress in
our frozen relations with Pakistan may be on the horizon. I will go
further and assert that in both areas only this fragile Government can
succeed where others have so catastrophically and consistently failed.'

Montek Singh Ahluwalia,[52] who was part of the Gowda
administration, felt similarly: 'To my mind, Gowda's Kashmir
approach rang a very genuine bell. Someone coming from a part of
the country that is very, very, far away from Kashmir, and with very
different circumstances, empathizing with the people of Kashmir fits
in very well with my image of him.'

In the final moments of the Gowda government, on 11 April
1997, Saifuddin Soz participating in the debate on the motion of
confidence, placed on record what Gowda had meant to himself
and to Farooq Abdullah as politicians from Kashmir, and even
more importantly to the people of the Valley: 'I want to tell you
one thing, which only I can tell you. This prime minister created a
situation of hope in Jammu and Kashmir state. He went to Jammu
and Kashmir four times. For six years, nobody went to Kashmir.
You are all the time saying Jammu and Kashmir state is an integral
part of India. Yes. It is. But why did the previous prime ministers
not go there? Shri Narasimha Rao was the prime minister for five
years. Shri Chandra Shekhar got a short stint, and he could not

go, nor could Shri V.P. Singh go. But Shri Deve Gowda went to Jammu and Kashmir state four times and he created a situation of hope and understanding there . . . I have a word of caution for the BJP. Jammu and Kashmir is not an ordinary issue. It is a settled issue. But when you want to put up a bright face, you pilot Shri Jaswant Singh, but when you have to put up a dark face, you tell Kumari Uma Bharati to represent you. This double standard is not acceptable to me because she has run down Dr Farooq Abdullah, who should be rated as a hero. He performed a miracle in Jammu and Kashmir in the assembly elections. (Interruptions) There was an attempt to disrupt elections, but he stood like a rock because he had a friend like Shri Deve Gowda here. Shri Deve Gowda was at his back, and he performed a miracle there. Today the BJP put up Kumari Uma Bharati to denounce Dr Farooq Abdullah. This double standard is not acceptable.'[53]

Intent and Memory

In March 2019, when the BJP government was dithering to hold assembly polls in Jammu and Kashmir, Omar Abdullah[54] tweeted: 'It's worth remembering that since 1995–96 Pakistan, militants & separatists have always tried to ensure elections don't take place in J&K. Successive governments since H.D. Deve Gowda have ensured all attempts at disruption fail.' In the minds of Kashmiris, the Gowda initiative was a benchmark.

In April 2019, four months before the Narendra Modi-led federal government suspended Article 370, which gave special status to the state, and trifurcated the region into three union territories, Deve Gowda opposed any attempt to scrap it. Speaking to reporters at Yaliyur near Channarayapatna taluk in his home district of Hassan, he reasoned:[55] 'The Article took shape when Jammu and Kashmir joined India after the country got Independence. Leaders of that time arrived at a decision after analyzing the situation in a historical context. Why should it be abolished now?' He further said: 'I'm also a Hindu. But I take people of all religions along. We should try to bring harmony among all people.'

While all prime ministers who preceded Gowda had either a historical, emotional or ideological tangent drawn to Kashmir, Gowda, a complete outsider, attempted a political connection with the Valley. Perhaps that was the most ideal approach. For Jawaharlal Nehru, Indira Gandhi and Rajiv Gandhi, Kashmir was always placed in the trough of history and emotion. They were originally from the state. They had a memory received and reconstructed multiple times in their minds. They could never escape that. Their judgement was guided and clouded by this memory. For a prime minister like Vajpayee, there was an overwhelming ideological pressure. There was a rigid ideological construct of his forbearers like Shyama Prasad Mukherjee. He was forced to accept a solution that was predetermined in an inflexible binary. Prime ministers like P.V. Narasimha Rao or Morarji Desai were indifferent. Lal Bahadur Shastri was caught up in a war, V.P. Singh didn't apply himself, and Chandra Shekhar didn't have the time to apply himself. But Gowda had an instinctual political approach. There was pragmatism written all over in his method.

Months before she was assassinated by her Sikh guards, Indira Gandhi toppled a year-old Farooq Abdullah government in July 1984 by propping up his brother-in-law, Gul Mohammed Shah. The Opposition leader and former Uttar Pradesh chief minister, Hemwati Nandan Bahuguna, with others, rushed to Kashmir to lend moral support to Farooq Abdullah. On his way, he remarked on Rajiv Gandhi and his coterie of friends, who had by then begun playing a role in the administration: 'He is a sweet boy. Not very intelligent, but good. The problem is that he is not at all political and it's very difficult to rule India if you are not political.' When asked what he meant by 'not being political', he said: 'Well, for a start, someone with even minimum political sense would never have toppled Farooq's government, especially not now with Punjab in flames. Someone political would never have attacked the Golden Temple because a political person would have found a political solution to Punjab instead of a military one.'[56] Gowda was very political in this sense. As he engaged with the issue, his politics acquired a method, and a purpose too.

In February 2020, speaking at a peace conference in Seoul,[57] Gowda recalled his mission Kashmir: 'To initiate change . . . I have often realized that we need to function with the purest of intent. People have a knack of finding out how genuine and serious we are about what we say. They will cooperate only if they are convinced. As prime minister in 1996, when I went to Kashmir to revive the economy and the electoral process, which had been suspended for a decade, at every step I realized people gauge the honesty of purpose. I could successfully hold elections to the state assembly only because people realized that we meant good. There was no hidden agenda.'

14

Gowdanomics, Kisan Raj and Chidambaram's Debut

It may sound audacious to begin this chapter by asking if Gowda had original macroeconomic ideas? Or, is it necessary to ask a more basic question: Did he understand the nuances of a nation's economic management? When it came to foreign policy, an article in a national newspaper once asked if there was 'A Deve Gowda doctrine?'[1] It had gone on to explore and illustrate the question in a positive manner. In a similar way, can we ask if there was Gowdanomics, and do we have enough to illustrate it? Did he have an economic worldview, and did he demonstrate courage to place it on the table as prime minister, especially because he was surrounded by those who were educated in Harvard, and those who had worked at the World Bank? Or, like any other non-specialist politician, did Gowda just do what his secretaries, advisers and ministers asked him to do? Was it largely his intent, pragmatism and experience that saw him through, or was there a bigger spark?

Since the time that Gowda was the Opposition leader in the Karnataka assembly, his long and grand interventions were on budgets. He sliced the different aspects of it, asked for cuts, clarity or enhancement of allocations. It was known to everybody in the legislature, including chief minister Devaraj Urs, that Gowda would come fully prepared for budget sessions. Urs would jokingly ask, 'Check how long Gowda was in the library?' He never gave an easy time to Urs's Cambridge-educated finance minister, M.Y. Ghorpade.[2] That diligence continued even when he became a member of Parliament in 1991. Like he taught himself many things, he was also self-taught in economics. He sparingly and hesitantly used economic jargon, but had his own way of sorting out basics and large ideas in his head, more than enough to ask the right questions.

Gowda also did something very intelligent. He approached economics through agriculture, his area of expertise. He would evaluate everything through its prism, and since agriculture comprised such a large part of the Indian economy and society, it automatically gave his exposition a fresh insight. That was his vantage point, and he mixed it with the rich–poor, global–local binary very often to give it a political force. He would pile up dry details after dry details before his audience, and like a haystack set afire, he would suddenly ignite his dry pile of facts with passion and combativeness. This would get him attention. This pattern can be noticed in the state assembly debates many times, and in the Parliament ever so often during his first term as MP. Even before he completed his first term, he returned to the state to become chief minister, and after he became prime minister, his confidence on various aspects of the economy, and economic administration was at a different level.

His opposition to reform, foreign direct investment and development in the first decade of liberalization was not dogmatic. He often succumbed to the exigencies of the time. Sometimes, as we will see in this chapter and other chapters, he could even surprise his advisers with a radical choice that went against his personal and political branding. Between 1991 and 1995, 1995 and 1997, and finally, between 1997 and 2004 in three tranches, we see Gowda's approach to large issues undergoing refinement and transformation. He never gave up his politics. His preoccupation with and passion for agriculture and irrigation continued, but intuitively and through study, he learnt to place them in a larger global context. He quickly adjusted and adapted to the India that was rapidly changing.

The beginning of the telecom and internet revolution coincided with his time as prime minster. He was more mindful of reform than P.V. Narasimha Rao, for whom it was an inevitable response to a gargantuan economic crisis. Gowda was also acutely aware that he was inheriting a young nation and job creation was extremely important. The fact that Gowda was trained as an engineer and not a social scientist or philosopher perhaps helped. If Gowda had chosen to remain doctrinaire, dogmatic or plain intransigent, like some of his communist friends were, perhaps he would not have remained relevant for twenty-five years after he stepped down as prime minister. Gowda's greatest skill as an administrator was to balance and reconcile worldviews without creating a rupture. This skill of his has been largely underestimated and unrecounted.

As a first-time MP in the Parliament, and as witness to the historic reforms and liberalization process that Manmohan Singh unleashed in 1991, he practically attacked all of Singh's budgets in his parliamentary speeches. Interestingly, the target of his attack almost all the time was Singh, the finance minister, and never P.V. Narasimha Rao, the prime minister whom Gowda respected. His favourite two phrases against Singh in the Parliament were 'Don't think you are the only intelligent person', and 'Don't fool the nation'. But when it came to Vajpayee's regime after 1998, his focus was not on his regime's economics, but communalism. He did take on Yashwant Sinha, Vajpayee's finance minister, occasionally, but his tone had altered. He was mindful that he was a former prime minister. He was sober, and there was invariably a recollection of his time in office and the measures he had taken. The sobriety also came, as we have noted earlier because he had learned to look at things in a larger context. It was not just the politics of Hassan and Karnataka that he was fixated with, but he saw a larger pan-India position for himself. We will look at the Manmohan Singh–Gowda face off in the Parliament between 1991 and 1994 a little later, but let's first look at his time as prime minister, his economic approach and the two budgets that were presented by his government, the first in July 1996, and the second in February 1997.

First Budget and the Differing World Views

A month after Deve Gowda had sailed through the vote of confidence, he started independently consulting various people that included bankers, businessmen, former RBI governors, economists, former members of the planning commission, former finance ministers of states, and senior business journalists to understand what the impetus of his budget should be. He was candid enough to tell them that he knew very little, and they should help him offer a direction. He was aware of the arguments that were being put forward in the backdrop of economic liberalization that his predecessor had initiated. He did not want to undo in the slightest measure the good that had happened in the past five years and the promise and potential that it had created, nor did he want to look like a blind follower of the previous regime's policies. Retaining his pro-poor, pro-farmer identity was important, yet he could not fathom the populist label. He wanted to strike a middle ground. With his political position on an extremely weak wicket, he had an eye on the budget to strengthen his position just in case he had to lead the United Front government to a snap poll. There was also the Left, which supported his government, and they could not be embarrassed on economic policy.

As he met people, his principal secretary Satish Chandran took copious notes. His finance minister P. Chidambaram was also part of some meetings. At the end of these interactions, the different views of experts were blended with Gowda's thoughts and handed over to Chidambaram to examine while he crafted the budget. Gowda all along knew that Chidambaram had a different economic approach but also knew he would not go beyond a point to impose it because he was all too aware of Gowda's rusticity and raw reaction.[3]

The very fact that Gowda had picked Chidambaram as his
finance minister was an indication that he chose continuity over
disruption. However, for a day, prime minister-elect Gowda was in a
dilemma if he should pick Murasoli Maran as his finance minister or
P. Chidambaram. He had mentioned this to his party colleague and
later parliamentary affairs minister, Srikant Jena, but had quickly
concluded that Chidambaram was a better fit. Maran, whom Gowda
categorized as a 'highly dignified gentleman' was perhaps Gowda's
Plan B in case the Left parties opposed Chidambaram's appointment.[4]

Chidambaram himself had not expected to be named finance
minister. He thought like Rao, Gowda would prefer an expert from
outside. He recalled: 'It was not the decision of the coalition partners
or my party chief to make me finance minister, it was that of the
prime minister. Even before he was sworn in, Gowda made it clear
that I would be his finance minister. We were some eight or nine
people making decisions. From my party, that is the Tamil Maanila
Congress, it was Moopanar and myself. From other parties, there were
Sharad Yadav, Lalu Yadav, A.B. Bardhan, Harkishan Singh Surjeet,
A. Raja, C.M. Ibrahim, Murasoli Maran, T.R. Baalu and others. In
their presence, he made it clear that he had decided to make me the
finance minister. I had thought he would bring in an outside expert
or an academic. When he mentioned my name, nobody opposed it.
The other portfolios were still under discussion at that point. Under
Gowda, people were nominated by parties, and portfolios were decided
thereafter. In coalition set-ups after Gowda, this process was reversed,
portfolios were distributed to parties and parties nominated ministers.'[5]

That was Chidambaram's debut stint as finance minister, and
he was relatively young at fifty. Gowda had watched Chidambaram
closely as a commerce minister under P.V. Narasimha Rao. He had
also watched him resign during the Harshad Mehta securities scam
because of his investments in a Bangalore firm that had come under
investigation. From parliamentary exchanges, it is also apparent that
Gowda had assessed Chidambaram to be closer in spirit to Manmohan
Singh than to Rao. In December 1993, he had remarked sharply in
the Parliament when discussing the securities scam: 'Yesterday the

whole argument of Chidambaramji was only to protect the finance minister and not the government. I could see that.'[6] All this was before Chidambaram quit the Congress in early 1996 to join the Tamil Maanila Congress under G.K. Moopanar, protesting Rao's alliance with J. Jayalalithaa's AIADMK in Tamil Nadu. 'It was uppermost on my mind to signal continuity of policy to industry and investors. I knew the economic situation was not very bright, the oil pool deficit was rising, foreign debt was not looking good either. The World Bank and IMF conditionalities were also rather tight. I had observed all this as a chief minister. Therefore, when I had to pick my finance minister, I knew instinctively that it should be Chidambaram. I was aware his thinking differed from mine, but that was small compared to his ability to handle the situation,'[7] Gowda recalled.

Differences in worldview and approach cropped up early between Gowda and Chidambaram. When Chidambaram brought the draft of the budget for discussion, Gowda was not happy with the slant it had acquired. By then, the finance ministry had put queries and raised objections to some things Gowda had tried to do or had announced in public: 'I was not very happy with the negative approach of the officials. I had not done anything that was not within my purview and powers. Therefore, I told Chidambaram in front of everybody that he should first understand that he was the finance minister of a thirteen-party coalition government and not a Congress finance minister. "Do not get me wrong, but what is the message that you are trying to give through this budget. How does our budget differ from the ones that Manmohan Singh has presented?" I asked. I also told him bluntly that he should have overhauled the finance ministry as soon as he took over because advisers and officers who worked with the previous regime would only perpetuate old ideas and old attitudes. Our government stood for something, and it had a common minimum programme too. I wanted the budget to reflect this and have a new imprint. I wanted it to signal hope to the poor and rural masses. I could see Chidambaram did not take my comments well. He was upset. When he and the officers were speaking, I used to shut my eyes but would be listening carefully. They thought I was drowsy. But when I said I cannot accept this budget, nor can I convince the coalition partners to accept it, they became alert.

'Chidambaram left the meeting without saying anything. The next day he came in the morning and asked my private secretary how my mood was that morning? He was informed that I was sitting with Meenakshisundaram and disposing of files. After a while, the private secretary walked in and said the finance minister was waiting for the past fifteen minutes. I got angry with him, I asked why he hadn't told me before. I got up and went myself to bring him in. "Why are you sitting here? You are one of the senior ministers, you should have just walked in." I took his hand and led him into my room. We had a cordial exchange on all issues that I had raised the previous day. I handed over a document that I had kept typed and ready. I said I would like to see all this covered in the budget. He agreed to include them.'[8] To put it across through an economic platitude, Gowda had ensured that Bharat made space in India's budget. That is rural India had found adequate representation.

Since there was a sword of uncertainty hanging on Gowda's head about the longevity of his government, as soon as he had become prime minister, he had followed a well-calculated strategy of public announcements to ensure that people quickly recognized his welfare intent. He would try to get his announcements formalized retrospectively with the finance ministry. When he made an announcement on fertilizer subsidy on 14 June 1996 a month before the budget session began, his finance secretary, Montek Singh Ahluwalia, cautioned him. He said that Manmohan Singh's vote on account budget had not made a provision for this subsidy, and therefore there was no money available. He suggested that the allocation should be made in the new government's budget that was due. Gowda recalled Ahluwalia's words:

> He said, 'Sir, the budget session is fixed for 19 July, you are making this announcement a month in advance. If somebody moves a cut motion and it is defeated your government will

be in trouble.' I said, I was not worried about the fall of the government. If it does fall, I will go home.

I had the experience of Chandra Shekhar before me, who similarly had outside support of the Congress party. Chandra Shekhar wanted me to be a minister in his government, and Devi Lal was keen to bring me to the Rajya Sabha from Haryana. I did not agree. But at that juncture, when I met Chandra Shekhar at his Bhondsi ashram, I said, 'I don't know how long you will last in office but announce the schemes that you want to announce. You have done Bharat Yatra. You have gone from state to state and understood what the problem is in each one of them. Whatever you think is important just announce. Give emphasis to rural areas and irrigation. Whether Rajiv Gandhi will allow you to pass the budget or not, don't worry, that is secondary. Lay down your vision before the people. They will understand and appreciate what you intend to do.' But he argued that it wouldn't be prudent to do so until the Congress agreed. When I became PM, I followed the advice I gave him. I knew if I kept consulting and asking the Congress or my officials, they will not allow me to do anything. I went on announcing schemes from day one. Therefore, in the first budget, Chidambaram had to say that he is ratifying a few things that the prime minister had already announced.[9]

Gowda's recollection was correct. On 22 July 1996, Chidambaram said in para 13 of his budget speech: 'We have taken a number of decisions that will directly benefit the farmers. Two weeks ago, the prime minister announced increases in the subsidies for phosphatic and potassic fertilizers. Government has decided to extend the subsidy under the Integrated Cereal Development-Rice Programme to power tillers at the rate of Rs 30,000 or 50 per cent of the cost for each power tiller. The subsidy scheme on small tractors at the rate of Rs 30,000 per tractor is presently restricted to small and marginal farmers. I am extending this scheme to all farmers. I am also enhancing the subsidy on sprinkler and drip irrigation from 50 per cent to 70 per cent of the cost of the system and the ceiling is also being raised from Rs 15,000 to Rs 25,000 per hectare. In respect of small and marginal farmers, women and scheduled castes and scheduled tribes, this limit is being raised to 90 per cent of the cost of the system.'[10]

Chidambaram also pledged his commitment to the coalition's common minimum programme: 'When I began work on the CMP (Common Approach to Major Policy Matters and a Minimum Programme), I was not even a minister. When we completed our exercise, I found myself in the office of finance minister. Therefore, my commitment to the CMP goes beyond the office I hold. Hon'ble members will have many opportunities this afternoon to test my commitment and they will find that the CMP has provided the foundation and set the agenda for this budget.'[11]

There was one item that Gowda had asked Chidambaram to include in the budget that finally got dropped. He wanted a 5 per cent tax to be introduced on trust properties. He had calculated that thousands of crore of revenue would accrue to the government: 'There are thousands of trusts in the country. The rich have made trusts even in the name of their dogs. When I wanted this tax proposal in the budget, my principal secretary Satish Chandran came to me. I was in the Rajya Sabha. He sent me a chit asking me to spare five minutes. I went out. There were people. I went to the telephone booth close by and shut the door. Chandran told me that Chidambaram wanted to be sure if the tax on trusts should be part of the budget. He had also cautioned that it may not go down well with political parties, who may block the passage of the budget and destabilize the government. In addition to Chidambaram's apprehension, Chandran tried to convince me on a different line. He said it may not pan out well in Karnataka where there were many educational trusts controlled by powerful caste lobbies. "It may affect your home base, sir," he said. I knew what I was doing and its implications, but I realized that Chandran too was not for it. "If you think so, then delete it," I said. He got it deleted,' Gowda remembered.[12]

This tax on trusts was something that Gowda had spoken about earlier too. In September 1991, participating in the discussions on the Finance Bill, he had told Manmohan Singh: 'There are ways and means to raise our resources . . . You have mentioned in the Finance Bill about the so-called charitable trusts. How many charitable trusts are there? You see the Bombay Charitable Trust Act or the Indian Trust Act, 1856. Whatever money or income is earned, if that is transferred to the trusts, they will totally escape income tax or wealth tax. With your background, Mr Finance Minister, can you not think of some ways and means by which these thousands and thousands of trusts which are making a lot of money and at the same time avoiding income tax and wealth tax totally, are made more accountable?'[13]

Besides the discussions on the budget, at the beginning of his term, Gowda had to face a huge challenge relating to the oil pool deficit. The balance was around Rs 17,800 crore and people like Vijay Kelkar, then petroleum secretary, suggested a steep increase in petrol, diesel and kerosene prices: 'I was rattled by the suggestion. I said people will think that some idiot has taken over as prime minister if I agree to the suggestion. But it was a difficult situation, and our choices were limited. I decided not to increase a single paisa on kerosene because the poor use it. On petrol and diesel, I allowed an increase of rupees two and one respectively, against the three each they had suggested. As regards the repayment, I said, write to Organization of the Petroleum Exporting Countries (OPEC) countries and tell them that a new prime minister has taken over and has requested six months extra time to repay. Fortunately, the OPEC nations instantly agreed. I later came to know through diplomatic channels that Islamic nations in the OPEC had great appreciation for the way I had treated the Muslim community as a chief minister in Karnataka. They appreciated the fact that I had solved the Idgah Maidan issue peacefully and had given educational and job reservations to Muslims under a separate category. They had done their homework.'[14]

Speaking on the 2002–03 budget in Parliament, Gowda recalled his decision not to hike the price of kerosene: 'During my period we were also facing the same problem, about Rs 18,000 crore of oil deficit. When the matter came to me, I said except for kerosene, I am ready to accept the proposal made by the department. I said I am not going to increase even a paisa on kerosene. At that time, the cost of crude oil per barrel was 28 dollars . . . But again, who is going to lobby for the kerosene users. They are all small people living in huts . . .'[15]

The 1997 budget is often referred to as Chidambaram's 'dream budget', but from Gowda's perspective, the 1996 budget, which managed to achieve a balance between the rich and poor, rural and urban, agricultural and non-agricultural sectors, was a dream budget too. Besides subsidies on fertilizers and agricultural implements, there were other elements in the budget, which according to Gowda made the rural folk and agriculturists 'go mad with joy'.[16] The budget proposed to increase the share capital of National Bank for Agriculture and Rural Development (NABARD) from Rs 500 crore to Rs 2000 crore in five years. During 1995–96, NABARD had sanctioned loans aggregating Rs 1984 crore to nineteen states for completing 2489 projects. The budget decided to give an additional Rs 2500 crore for the financial year to finance rural infrastructure through the Rural Infrastructure Development Fund (RIDF).[17]

The other item in the 1996 budget, which has remained a legacy of Gowda to this day, was the introduction of the Accelerated Irrigation Benefit Programme. Chidambaram said: 'In addition to the RIDF, I am proposing an Accelerated Irrigation Benefit Programme (AIBP) under which the Centre will provide, on a matching basis, additional central assistance by way of loans to the states for the timely completion of selected large irrigation and multi-purpose projects. I am making an allocation of Rs 800 crore in 1996–97 to launch this scheme which is designed to accelerate the completion of irrigation projects where the project cost exceeds Rs 1000 crore and is beyond the resource capability of the states. I am also allocating Rs 100 crore in the current financial year for irrigation projects where, with just a little additional resources, the projects could be completed and farmers could get the benefit of assured water supply. 1,00,000 hectares will be brought under irrigation through these schemes, and I have been assured that the first crop will be harvested on these lands during one of the next four agricultural seasons.'[18] As chief minister Gowda had realized that he did not have enough resources to complete the Upper Krishna Project and had to innovate to raise resources. As soon as he became prime minister, he decided to permanently take care of states facing a resource crunch to complete large irrigation projects.

There were many other items in the budget that took care of social justice as well as the poor. Chidambaram referred to the prime minister again while reading out these proposals: 'The prime minister has repeatedly declared that this government is a government of the poor and for the poor. Growth with social justice will be the motto of this government. Unless the country's GDP grows at over 7 per cent per year in the next ten years, we will not be able to abolish poverty and unemployment. However, there is a need to identify vulnerable sections of the people and help them.'[19] One such initiative was a provision of Rs 5 crore for building residential facilities for *hamals*. There was something for the sick, for the old, for widows, for families of lorry and truck drivers, who had met with accidents. Nobody was forgotten or made to feel insignificant. With this budget, Gowda had adopted the approach he had used for decades to craft an inclusive manifesto for his party. It was political yet pragmatic. It built hope and stymied cynicism.

Another of Gowda's life-long passions, federalism, also received sufficient impetus in the budget. He had after all sat down with chief ministers and personally worked out the Basic Minimum Services concept, and it became his government's flagship programme. The budget said: 'One of the first acts of the prime minister, Shri Deve Gowda, was to convene a meeting of chief ministers on Basic Minimum

Services. This reflects the resolve of the United Front to "advance the principles of political, administrative and economic federalism." The chief ministers' conference recommended adoption of seven objectives to be attained by the year 2000. These are 100 per cent coverage of provision of safe drinking water; 100 per cent coverage of primary health centres; universalization of primary education; public housing assistance to all shelter-less poor families; extension of the mid-day meal scheme; road connectivity to all villages and habitations; and streamlining the public distribution system targeted to families below the poverty line. These objectives are now being served by centrally sponsored schemes and schemes in state plans. Hon'ble members will be glad to know that I am providing an additional amount of Rs 2466 crore as central assistance for state and UT plans to significantly increase the availability of funds for these schemes.'[20] Gowda recalled: 'The Inter-State Council and the National Development Council had not met for five years, I revived it. I did not go to those meetings to just deliver a speech like Indira Gandhi. I sat there from morning till evening. We reviewed everything. Among other things, we worked out the modalities of the Basic Minimum Services. All chief ministers sat throughout, including Jyoti Basu.'[21]

Gowda had ensured his imprint on the budget without disturbing the progress that Rao and Singh had done between 1991 and 1996. On the reforms front, he trusted Chidambaram and Montek to take it forward. A five-year tax holiday was also extended to enterprises investing in irrigation, water supply, sanitation and sewerage systems,[22] Until then, it was available to enterprises engaged in developing, maintaining and operating infrastructure facilities such as roads, highways, bridges, new airports, ports and rail systems.

The Coffee Free Sale Quota

During the first budget, there was another interesting argument that developed around the coffee free sale quota. Under P.V. Narasimha Rao, the quota had only been partially liberalized. A hundred per cent coffee free sale quota did not exist, it was a central excise commodity and planters had to operate through the Indian Coffee Board. They had to pool coffee there, and the board would auction the beans and give planters the money. While 70 per cent of what was grown could go to the open market, 30 per cent had to be pooled with the board. Most planters would not do that. As a result, criminal cases were booked for violation of the Central Excise Act. In 1996, many Karnataka coffee planters were about to get arrested and B.L. Shankar, then Chikmagalur MP and Gowda's parliamentary secretary, approached Chidambaram for help. When the finance minister did not help, he approached the prime minister.

Shankar remembered what transpired:

Veerendra Kumar from Kerala, Devdas, MP from Tamil Nadu, Rudresh Gowda, MP from Karnataka, myself and a couple of others from Andhra Pradesh went in a delegation to P. Chidambaram. At that time, criminal cases had been registered against thirty senior and reputed planters in Karnataka like U.K. Lakshmana Gowda, M.D. Narayan, K.S. Malle Gowda, A.C. Shive Gowda, M. Basave Gowda and others. When we explained this to Chidambaram, he said, 'No, I can't do anything.' He said coffee planters are arrogant. They have no respect for law. 'Let them go to court and realize what the law is,' he said. Although P.C. was himself a planter, he responded harshly and unsympathetically. There were three days left for the first budget to be passed. This was nothing but plain harassment.

We went to Deve Gowda and explained the matter threadbare. He knew every planter who was booked personally, and he was shocked. We said, 'If you don't step in, they will be arrested. All that has to be done is that it has to be removed as a central excise commodity. Planters should be allowed to sell wherever they want.' He agreed. It was in the evening. After an hour, he called Chidambaram to his office and also sent for me. I knew if I went alone, Chidambaram would corner me, so I took Veerendra Kumar along. In the meeting, Gowda tried to convince Chidambaram. He said when land reforms were initiated in Karnataka in 1974, coffee plantations were given an exemption because their export earnings were high. Although it was agriculture, he said it was also industry. He said all those booked were good people. 'What will you gain by sending them to jail?' He asked. He argued further that the free-market quota should not have been allowed in the first place, but to have 70:30 distribution quota was a problem and would remain so if not amended. When he saw Chidambaram was unmoved, he said, 'All right, I have given my word to these people, I don't know how you will do it, but do something.' When Chidambaram argued that to do it in flat two days would be difficult, Gowda said it can be done, and to delay it would serve no purpose.

Next day, Gowda followed it up with the commerce ministry. He put Meenakshisundaram on the job to see it was done well in time. In his reply to the budget discussion, P.C. announced 100 per cent free sale quota for coffee. This led to a coffee industry boom. If Café Coffee Day became big, this decision was behind it. Gowda did not benefit personally from this. If Gowda was convinced about something, he would go to any extent to do it.[23]

The Dream Second Budget

By the time the 1997 budget was presented, political uncertainty had set in. The opening lines of Chidambaram's budget speech sounded like a valedictory address coupled with victimhood. It endeavoured to capture the Gowda government's nine-month journey and the perception that existed when it was born: 'Hon'ble members will indulge me for a few minutes while I reflect on those eventful days in May 1996. One national party acknowledged that it had lost its claim to form the government. Another tried but failed. It is in that situation that regional parties, and certain parties with a larger national presence, came together to form the United Front government. These parties, long regarded as children of a lesser God, have demonstrated that given the opportunity, they can form a government not only at the state level but also at the Centre. Inspired by the idea of a truly cooperative federal polity, chief ministers have assembled, more often than ever before, at the Inter-State Council, the National Development Council and at the Special Conferences to formulate national policies . . . our efforts to take decisions by a national consensus, in the fiftieth year of India's Independence, have deepened and broadened Indian democracy.'[24] The phrase 'children of a lesser God' was well chosen.

Chidambaram remarked that the budget was presented in the shadow of defeat hanging over Gowda's head: 'It was passed without a debate. In fact, I presented the second budget, but the day it was passed, I was not finance minister. I became finance minister again after a gap of ten days after my party rejoined the United Front government under Gujral. It was a rather peculiar situation.'[25]

But Gowda did not allow politics and the possible loss of office to bother him. His strategy was to go on relentlessly till the last day. He diligently followed the advice he had given Chandra Shekhar. He wanted his intent to be established. The boldest step that the 1997 budget took was to do a major restructuring of the personal income tax rates. The existing rates of 15, 30 and 40 per cent was replaced by new rates of 10, 20 and 30 per cent. The 10 per cent rate applied to the first slab of Rs 40,000 to Rs 60,000, 20 per cent in the slab of Rs 60,000 to Rs 1,50,000 and 30 per cent for all income above Rs 1,50,000. Chidambaram said: 'The one thing I commend Gowda was he readily agreed to the new tax rates. I gave him two options 10, 20, 30 per cent and 15, 25, 35 per cent as income tax rates. I was pleasantly surprised he chose 10, 20, 30 per cent. It was a steep cut at that time. The department wanted 15, 25, 35, but my personal preference was for 10, 20, 30, he said to go with it. I checked with his principal secretary Satish Chandran if he fully understood the implications of the cut in tax rates. I was assured he did.'[26]

The 1997 budget did more, it identified nine public sector companies and called them *Navratnas* and decided to back them to become global giants. It also assured that it would go ahead with the disinvestment of three companies while examining the other recommendations made in the first report of the Disinvestment Commission it had set up in August 1996. Telecommunications, oil exploration and industrial parks were put under the infrastructure bracket and a five-year tax holiday was announced. For the first time, it took a hard look at information technology policy recognizing it as a 'science that will dominate the twenty-first century'.[27] Chidambaram said in his budget speech that the spread of information technology had radically altered conventional wisdom on growth strategies, and proposed several measures to encourage this industry and to reduce costs, which included full exemption to computer software.

The other contentious announcement in the budget was the Voluntary Disclosure Scheme (VDS). Contentious because the prime minister and his finance minister were not on the same page on it. Gowda wanted it to make good his assurances to tackle the black money issue, and also wanted to use the money that came from it to fund the Basic Minimum Services programme but Chidambaram was not very enthusiastic. Finally, after some prodding, it found a place in the budget: 'I believe that the time is opportune to introduce a Voluntary Disclosure Scheme. This would be a simple scheme where, irrespective of the year or the nature or the source of the funds, the amount disclosed, either as cash, securities or assets, whether held in India or abroad, would be charged at the revised highest rate of tax. Interest and penalty will be waived. Immunity will be granted from any action under the income tax, wealth tax and foreign exchange regulation acts. Of the total resources which can be secured under the scheme, a substantial part—77.5 per cent—will accrue to the state governments . . . The share which becomes available to the Central government will go entirely towards financing the Basic Minimum

Services programme and infrastructure needs,'[28] Chidambaram said in his speech.

Much later, in March 2002, speaking in the Parliament, Gowda had recalled the VDS debate from his time in office: 'I am not an economist, but during my short tenure as prime minister, I told the finance minister that we should introduce the Voluntary Disclosure Scheme. He did not agree with me and said that the government was not able to get even Rs 200 crore in the past when such a scheme was announced during the tenure of Shrimati Indira Gandhi. He said the government could get only about Rs 780 crore or so and that the government had to take the blame from tax payers . . . I persuaded the finance minister by saying that after the introduction of economic reforms, a lot of black money had accrued in the hands of so many people and so, we should try that scheme once again. Then he requested me to talk to our friends from the Left parties. When I spoke to Shri Jyoti Basu, I should be fair to him, he readily agreed . . . Everybody doubted that there would not be much revenue in that. An amount of Rs 33,000 crore was declared. We got revenue of Rs 10,800 crore.'[29]

The figures of the 1997–98 budget spoke eloquently of Gowda's economic management of the previous year, especially agriculture, his thrust area. Not only did the economy grow at 6.8 per cent, but agriculture and allied sectors grew at 3.7 per cent after a disappointing minus 0.1 per cent in 1995–96. What was unprecedented was the rebound in food grains production. The 1997–98 economic survey noted: 'Food grains output in 1996–97 was estimated to have risen to 199 million tonnes. This was 19 million tonnes higher over 1995–96 production, representing an increase of 10.5 per cent. Rice production was estimated at 81.3 million tonnes compared to 77 million tonnes in the preceding year. Wheat production was 69.3 million tonnes as against 62.1 million tonnes in the preceding year. Coarse cereals output in 1996–97 was estimated to be about 5 million tonnes more over the preceding year's output of 29 million tonnes. Thus 1996–97 emerged as one of the best years in respect of food grain production, pushing up the overall growth of agriculture production to a record level of 9.3 per cent.'[30] This was clearly Gowda's finest moment: 'When I saw these figures, I thanked the good lord. Unfortunately, no one in the media highlighted this achievement. In Vajpayee's time, Nitish Kumar was agriculture minister. They fixed a 4 per cent agriculture growth target to achieve but they fell short. They came somewhere close 2.6 or 2.8 per cent. At that point, I studied everything and told them where they went wrong. What we achieved was a record, which neither previous nor successive governments could match. I did not do any magic. I just applied my mind. The farmer will be subject to vagaries of monsoon. You should do what you can to take care of those vagaries,'[31] Gowda remembered.

Chidambaram reminisced: 'Agriculture and irrigation may have been Gowda's thrust areas, but he was not anti-reform. He was a chief minister and understood the role of industry and knew that investments had to come. The popular story in the media was he dozed off in meetings. I don't think he dozed off—he was quite alert. That was his style, the head would drop, but the moment his subject came, he would perk up. The English papers ran him down. That perhaps happened because he was not part of Lutyens Delhi. He was not part of the ruling elite in Delhi, largely English speaking with a bias towards Hindi. He was a shrewd, calculating politician. He was not interested in making English speeches at various gatherings. But he spoke perfect English. During his time, we were hit by the Asian currency crisis. The 1996 budget would have delivered better if not for the Asian crisis. It was a major crisis. In terms of the outcomes, the 1997 budget did not turn out to be as expected but is still considered to be a dream budget because in terms of what it intended to do. It clearly remains a landmark. It clearly said these are the things India has to do. Opening up of the financial sector was announced, security markets reforms were announced, taxation reforms were announced. In 1996–97 we had reasonable growth and 1997–98 would have taken it to a higher notch, but unfortunately, the Asian financial crisis was major. Political stability and minus the Asian crisis, we would have done much better.'[32]

Gowda's joint secretary and trusted aide, S.S. Meenakshisundaram, recalled the relationship between Gowda and Chidambaram: 'He had affection for Chidamabaram, although he was not the kind who would verbalize it. He backed him fully and the gestures sometimes spoke loudly. I sat in cabinet meetings to take notes and used to be right behind the prime minister so that I could explain things in Kannada if someone spoke in Hindi that went beyond him. Once when minister Beni Prasad Verma spoke on some issue, Chidambaram got worked up and became impatient. He countered. He said something like, "How is that possible?" or "How can you say that?" Gowda noticed this but did not say anything. He cleverly took up the next item on the agenda. But after the meeting was over, he called me and said, "I am sure you noticed what I noticed. Chidambaram is young and talented. He has a bright future. He will need all these leaders later. Sometimes one may be correct, but there is no point in antagonizing the other person. You should let it pass. Why don't you go to Chidambaram and tell him in your language (Tamil) what I wish to communicate?" I met Chidambaram, spoke to him in Tamil, and put across what the PM felt. He listened patiently.'[33] Chidambaram did not remember this incident but said, 'Gowda relied on Meenakshisundaram heavily. I don't remember this episode, but if the two of them remember, then it is quite possible it happened.'[34]

The Finance Secretary's Take

Montek Singh Ahluwalia, who was finance secretary when Gowda was prime minister, was a key witness to and participant in all that was happening in economic policy and planning. He, like many others, had no idea as to what kind of person Gowda was because he had not exactly been in national politics, but Ahluwalia felt at the end Gowda 'turned out to be a good prime minister'.[35] Over a period of ten months, he realized that Gowda, who projected himself as a representative of farmers, was not like others who claimed to represent this constituency. 'Many farmer representatives are only interested in sops for farmers. Deve Gowda was not like that. He had a good understanding of how to modernize agriculture.' Whenever issues related to involving private sector in agriculture came up, like agricultural marketing, for instance, Ahluwalia realized that Gowda was not dogmatically anti-market or anti-private sector model. 'That gave me a sense that here is a person who actually understands how a modern economy works. He made a transition from a state chief minister to a prime minister extremely well.'[36]

During the 1997 budget, when Chidambaram was planning to propose a major restructuring of tax rates, Ahluwalia said that in the finance ministry, one got a feeling that the prime minister had empowered his finance minister. Internally within the United Front government, there were diverse constituents, including the communists, and prime minister backing the finance minister meant offering political air cover to reforms. P.V. Narasimha Rao and Manmohan Singh had brought the economy out from the crisis. They had started the process of reforms. Internationally, when governments change, it is very important for investors to know if policy has changed or remains the same. Ahluwalia felt that Gowda ran his government 'in a way that those who felt positive about India had a feeling that whatever is positive about the policy will continue. A sense of continuity'.[37]

Ahluwalia offered an example. Manmohan Singh had clearly signaled that custom duties should be brought down. He had said that custom duties must come down to levels comparable to other developing countries.

> We had persuaded Chidambaram when he crafted the budget that you should make this more specific. He said in his budget speech that the Gowda government will bring duties down to East Asian levels within three years. Singh had said duties must be comparable with developing countries but had set no

timeline. Chidambaram, however, said East Asian countries and set a timeframe. Timeframe really meant we will get there by 2000. Whatever the finance minister says, it is the prime minister who carries the responsibility, and he backed that. That was a bold decision. Singh had done that from very high levels of duty. By the time Rao's period as prime minister ended, we had brought duties down to where the Chelliah Committee wanted. Within three years meant 2000, deep down perhaps they knew they may not be around, but a commitment is a commitment. It is something that you defend. I regard that as a very important signal of continuity. If Gowda had been a bit scared and said, 'Why do you want to get into this controversial thing? There are the communists in the government, and even the Congress is ambivalent on these things, let us play safe.' Probably Chidambaram would have agreed not to say it. If Chidambaram said the prime minister is not happy with this statement, we would have said, 'Fine, let's drop it.' But since it was said, it helped us a lot in persuading investors by telling them that policy had not changed with the change in government. It is one thing for a finance minister to say nice things to assure investors in a meeting. Finance minister always says nice things in meetings. But, when he says it in the Parliament, in a budget speech, that is an important signal. That cannot be done without the prime minister's understanding and backing.[38]

Ahluwalia said that Gowda was also very aware of some of the hypocrisies of Indian economic policy: 'You know he had this habit of looking very sleepy. I have noticed that even when he appeared to be in a somnolent kind of state, one ear was always open, and whenever something needed to be said, he would say it without missing anything. My favourite recollection is that on one occasion, we were trying to raise the price of LPG gas as subsidy was building up. So, we said that it is one thing to have targeted subsidy but to keep all cooking gas at low price is not helpful. One minister was arguing that if you raise the price, it will hurt the common man. Immediately, Gowda, who was in his somnolent appearance, disagreed. "You know what is happening in Delhi. Cooking gas is being used by all rich people to cook seekh and tikka kebabs for their parties," he said, and offered to take us around one evening to show how many lavish parties were fueled by subsidized cooking gas. "These guys can afford to pay, why should we subsidize?" That was an earthy response. This would not have been the response of a civil servant.

'A civil servant would have said, "No Mr Minister, NSS survey shows 80 per cent of gas is used by top 20 per cent of people." That is how it would typically go. But if the prime minister gets up and says "you come around one evening, and I will show you", that has a different effect. The point is made very powerfully. This is not a farmer point, this is not an agriculture point, this is a commonsensical point, which practically punctures a lot of our policy hypocrisy, which is ostensibly designed to help the poor but doesn't help them at all. So, he was pretty good at seeing through these things. When there was a proposal to include the private sector in agricultural marketing, there was opposition from a farmers' organization in Karnataka. He did not take them on, but he had a sense they were wrong. He managed to contain the Opposition. Sometimes avoiding damage and defusing something that would otherwise build up is as important as getting the right thing done,' Ahluwalia recalled.[39]

In the case of Chidambaram, although Gowda did not verbalize his affection, when it came to Ahluwalia, he was open: 'I could communicate easily with him. I should say he understood me. Only once, during the budget-making process, I hurt him, but that did not affect our relationship. It was soon forgotten. Even to this day, I consult him,' Gowda said. What was that hurt? He does not remember exactly. He said perhaps it had to do with giving a bonus over the minimum support price (MSP) for wheat to farmers. I wanted to increase yield and wanted to stop importing wheat.

I wanted to take a policy step in this direction; perhaps it had to do with this. I cannot recall.'[40]

In 1996, the price disparity between international price and MSP created a 'strong pressure' on the government to bring price parity between domestic and international prices of wheat. There was a campaign for the increase in MSP of wheat in order to align domestic and international prices 'to provide fair treatment to farmers of India'. Subsequently, during the year 1997–98, the central government raised the MSP by 25 per cent from Rs 380 to Rs 475 per quintal, even though the Commission for Agricultural Costs and Prices (CACP) had recommended hiking MSP by just Rs 25 per quintal.[41] The RBI documents say that wheat prices for 1996–97 included a central bonus of Rs 60 per quintal payable up to 30 June 1997. 'Gowda had a communist representative as his agriculture minister (Chaturanan Mishra). He was a very sensible and straightforward person. I don't know how much he had thought of agriculture, but Gowda knew more about agriculture than anybody else in his cabinet and his political coalition,' Ahluwalia said.[42] Gowda had respect for Chaturanan Mishra, a CPI leader from Madhubani in Bihar. He remembered his stellar role during and after the Andhra Pradesh cyclone of November 1996. Gowda had deputed Mishra to handle the situation.

The Trip to Davos

Deve Gowda's participation in the World Economic Forum in February 1997 was another highlight of his prime ministership. Of course, he had already participated in the Davos deliberations in 1995 as chief minister, at the insistence of P.V. Narasimha Rao. Therefore, he was aware of what transpired in the Swiss ski resort with billionaires and investors in attendance. Before reaching Davos, he had conducted a lot of top-secret business in the shadow of the Alps. He had met the Naga insurgent group, National Socialist Council of Nagaland (NSCN), led by the Isak–Muivah faction, and had negotiated a deal. But since this was under the radar, what the anglophone media picked up was something as trivial as Gowda's dress code. As his SPG chief, Shyamal Datta, recalled: 'It was biting cold in Davos, I asked the prime minister if he will change his dress. He shot back, "Why should I change?" He mentioned K. Kamaraj (the dhoti-clad all India Congress president of the 1960s from Tamil Nadu who manoeuvred to pick Lal Bahadur Shastri and Indira Gandhi as prime ministers) and asked, "You think Kamaraj would have changed if he came here?" We tried to prevail over him and tell him that cold in Davos was an altogether different ball game. He did not give up the dhoti, but agreed to wear a thermal jacket, a woolen pullover and a shawl. He did not change over to a bandhgala or trousers.'[43] In the Kannada media, his second Davos trip created so much curiosity that it also created a new moniker. Instead of Deve Gowda, he became 'Davos Gowda' in the tabloids.

But Montek Singh Ahluwalia who travelled with him and was present in most meetings with Finance Minister P. Chidambaram, put things in perspective twenty-three years later: 'Actually, foreign investors do not care about superficial things. They don't care if you are wearing a suit or if you speak English. After all, the Chinese leadership never spoke English, but the foreigners loved them. Foreigners recognize that you are running your own country. They want to know the bottom line, that is, if you want them. The second is they want to know if you know how to make policy that will make them stay. They are two very different things. When you ask some leaders about foreign investment, they say, "yes, but on our own terms." Others say, "come," and later the fine print is not good. Deve Gowda could not have done the fine print, but in Davos, he came across as a sincere person who wanted foreign investors to come.

'He had a few one-on-one meetings. I was part of them. In each of those meetings although he may have looked different from the usual type of politician, foreign investors got a sense that he was a shrewd politician who knew his country well. They also knew India was a big enough country and even if it takes two or three years, it was worth getting a foot on the ground. They also knew that India was a difficult country to get into, but once you were there, you were there. He conveyed the right kind of message in a few meetings that I attended. His spoken English was pretty good. But that was not important. Investors knew how to read beyond formula. These were important guys. It actually happens this way, when a prime minister says, "Come, we need you," and when they meet him one year later, and say, "Prime Minister, you said come but see what a mess", they know he will probably try and do something to correct that. I think he gave that message.'[44]

Two dispatches from Davos in 1997, in two prominent weeklies, *India Today* and *Outlook*, should also give a fair idea as to what transpired in Davos with Gowda in the lead. The assessment of the two magazines was not very different. *India Today* used Davos to declare to the world that Gowda had finally arrived. The headline said that 'Prime Minister Gowda finally leaves Karnataka behind'. In reality, Gowda had left Karnataka behind a long time back, so this was a moment of realization for the English press, which had grudgingly decided to give Gowda some credit.

Here's an excerpt from the report written by Sudeep Chakravarti:[45]

They wanted him to wear a suit there. 'Are they more interested in what he says and does or what he wears at this time?' fumes a senior official in the prime minister's office (PMO). 'Are they crazy?' No, just plain paranoid . . . After all, the man mumbles. He bobs his head up and down like a tortoise on a spring, in agreement or amusement. He will hold the hand of an executive, journalist, official or head of state and forget that he has, for minutes on end . . . He (usually) takes the family along on state visits. (The joke this time on Air-India 001: Enough seats for everyone in first class as there was no family along, except the Mrs.) If ever, a recipe for a public-relations disaster, on prime time or in front of the prime cut of international business leaders. 'Paranoid?' joked a leading Indian businessman and a Davos regular. 'We were scared shitless.' That was after, when the worrying was over.

Ending February 6, when Deve Gowda wrapped up a five-day tour of Davos and Mauritius, India's increasingly important geopolitical and economic ally in the Indian Ocean area, the verdict was out: the man, mumble, shuffle, ethnic attire and all, handled things—surprise, surprise— better than anyone expected. Better than Narasimha Rao in Davos in 1992, when he blew apart a chance to underscore India's performance and again, two years later, when he opted to answer in-depth queries about economic policy vaguely, arrogantly and impatiently, besides being a tad patronising as well. Deve Gowda took the easier, more sensible way out: sticking to form, he read from a prepared text. But whenever a direct question on policy came along, he just waved it across to finance minister P. Chidambaram (he wore the suit, along with a clipped, measured accent) who answered, if not always very convincingly, then glibly . . .

Here, unlike the time Rao announced his middle path economics, which seemed like India was suddenly applying the brakes, Deve Gowda's speech on emerging economies, which included similar, mixed-economy, bear-with-us stuff seemed to ring true . . . While Chidambaram calmly fielded a wide range of questions . . . Deve Gowda mixed his by now accepted approach of humble farmer with a new one: that of sincere premier. And as senior Indian officials and the Indian business delegation watched aghast (Finance Secretary Montek Singh Ahluwalia tensed visibly, Ranbaxy chairman Parvinder Singh muttered a sotto voce 'Now what?', and Reliance Industries managing director Anil Ambani sat slowly back down), Deve Gowda did something unheard of at the Forum. He called back a departing crowd with a 'Before you leave, I would like to say a few words.' And then launched into a extempore plea and persuasion act. 'We need to accelerate the reform process . . . there is no question of delaying by the bureaucracy . . . Fear should be removed from your minds . . . If the Enron chairman is here, you can ask him, there is justice in India' (Kenneth Lay was present, though people saved the queries till later). What started out with expectations of a total disaster—much the same way as the dress code—unexpectedly turned into a minor victory.

The same evening, at a reception hosted by the Confederation of Indian Industry, Deve Gowda worked the crowds like someone who has passed a difficult examination, relieved, beaming . . . The understatements underscored one thing. At a gathering at which India was competing for attention with Russia, China, South Africa, Indonesia, Eastern Europe and Israel, perhaps for the first time since Rao visited the US in 1994 with a business team in tow, no Indian presence has made a similar impact. Deve Gowda handled himself well during meetings with Russian premier Victor Chernomyrdin and Egyptian President Hosni Mubarak. And ran through a series of personal meetings with some of the world's best-known executives and entrepreneurs: Microsoft's boy–billionaire chairman Bill Gates ('Mr Gates, I'm pleased to meet you before your visit to India'—Bill will, in March), financier George Soros, General Electric chief and India hand Jack Welch.

Vinod Mehta, *Outlook*'s[46] editor-in-chief, used a cricketing metaphor. The headline for his copy read 'Gowda scores for India'. Here's an extract from his dispatch:

En route to the 'most prestigious freebie on the planet,' Indian fourth estaters on the PM's special flight wondered what the Prime Minister would wear. The weather at Davos was freezing, making temperature calculations meaningless.

One other speculation: what would he say to the 1,000-odd
movers and shakers who had gathered at the World Economic
Forum (WEF), which claimed without trace of irony, to have
played a major role in ending apartheid in South Africa, the
reunification of Germany, the Israel-Palestine accords and
the ending of Vietnam's international isolation? On both
counts the scribblers were pleasantly surprised. At Davos
Mr Gowda maintained sartorial consistency. A set of spanking
new *kurtas, lungis* and socks had been acquired, but no
hastily stitched bandgulla or three-button suit. One hurdle
successfully jumped.

The session on India was the PM's first public exposure.
'People are crawling out of the woodwork,' noted the American
moderator failing to add that the crawling was caused by an
overflow of desi industrialists who constituted at least half the
audience. No state secrets are being revealed with the disclosure
that Mr Gowda is not a great public speaker; written speeches
he delivers with even less fluency. His 10-minute presentation
when read in cold text contained useful insights on the Indian
economy, when heard over the microphone it was mumbled
and lofty, 'a typical Indian lecture on how to run the world.'
The PM had not made a promising start at the second hurdle.

P. Chidambaram—suave, erudite, witty—performed the
rescue act. White men set great store by articulation, especially
if it has been acquired at Harvard. The question–answer session
which followed was also dominated by the FM. However, the
routine requires detailing: a question is posed, Chidambaram
defers politely to his chief, the moderator too looks towards
the chief who in turn lazily stretches his left hand indicating
that his finance minister is to give the answer. This double
act, slightly comical, sent out the right signals: the day-to-day
management of the economy was in Chidambaram's hands.

The allotted one hour for the session passed. No clangers
had been thrown, but neither was the session inspirational.

'Workmanlike' seemed the general consensus. As the audience stood up to leave, the moderator suddenly announced, 'Please wait. The Prime Minister wants to say something to you.' Everyone sat down expectantly. 'What is he going to do now? He will make a fool of himself,' said a wizened Mumbaiite sitting next to me. He nearly did. When Mr Gowda speaks extempore, he struggles for the single word, then the next and the next. A sentence can take an eternity. 'Friends, if you have any suspicions just remove them' took nearly 30 seconds to complete. He continued in this vein for over five minutes, rambling, repeating—but coming back to one theme, i.e. he and his Government were totally committed to reforms and speedy clearance of investment proposals. By the time Gowda had finished his unscheduled intervention, the audience was won. 'What he lacked in grammar he made up in sincerity' was the conclusion of a British businessman. An official from the Prime Minister's Office, mindful of Chidambaram's polished performance earlier, observed: 'As you saw, the captain scored the winning run'.

The captain repeated the sincerity at another session where the issue of corruption was raised. Surrounded by the president of Poland, the chief of the World Bank and some leading international CEOs, he assured that dealings with his Government would be 'fully transparent' and while he could not promise to totally remove corruption, his Government had taken 'radical steps' to minimise it. Nothing new, but at a conference widely believed to be about atmospherics, the promise carried conviction.

. . . One discovery this writer made in Davos: you can never please the foreign investor, he will always require reforms to be speeded up. They can never be fast enough for him. Crucially, what is missing is any understanding of Indian democracy and its federal structure. 'If I can get clearances in Singapore in 24 hours, why not India?' is a question bordering

on terminal ignorance. But it is one you frequently hear at
Davos. The Indian response was polite but firm and marks a
welcome attitudinal change. The new approach maintains that
India will determine at what pace reforms should proceed, not
the CEO of General Motors . . . The 'humble farmer' as India's
super-salesman at the WEF? Admittedly, this is an audacious
proposition given his caricatured domestic image. Victims
of that image (this correspondent included) might have had
occasion to change their mind at Davos.

Four months before the Davos visit, the managing director of the
World Economic Forum, Claude Smadja, in his presentation[47] at
the India Economic Forum in New Delhi, had spoken in a tone of
unabashed condescension and patronizing certification. Assessing
the Gowda government's first budget and its openness to economic
reforms, he had said: 'In the first period since the creation of the
United Front government in June, many could have said that
the good news was that the expected bad news proved wrong.
On the whole, the first five months of the new government have
been a rather positive surprise. When this unlikely coalition of
thirteen parties ranging from communists and agrarian populists
to committed reformists came to power last June, many were
concerned that this would mean the continuation, under another
guise, of the paralysis which had marked the last period of the
previous Rao government. But the day before he was sworn in as
prime minister, Deve Gowda was pointing out that India "cannot
give up liberalization". And in selecting Mr Chidambaram, a
forceful advocate of economic reform, as finance minister, he was
sending a clear signal that the process will continue. In fact, for
those who had watched his actions as chief minister of the state
of Karnataka, there were already some indications of his own
orientations: during his mandate of less than two years, Gowda
had promoted foreign investment and tried to rely more on
private industry for the state's development. He was among the

very few chief ministers who had amended land laws in order to facilitate industrial development.' On the increases in the 1996 budget for health and education and on subsidies for food and farmers, Smadja, in a formulaic fashion, had attributed it to the 'leftist component of the coalition'. In reality, it was Gowda who had personally struggled to balance his government's economic approach. He was neither a puppet of the reformists nor the Left.

In 2018, when Narendra Modi went to Davos twenty-one years after Gowda, he usurped all the credit for India's progress. Addressing the plenary session of the World Economic Forum, Modi said that 'when the last Indian prime minister visited Davos in 1997, the country's GDP was just $400 billion. It was now six times that and India's foreign exchange reserves are equal to its 1997 GDP'.[48] Gowda piqued by this claim, countered: 'Modi should realize that the base was prepared by previous governments. He should not forget that starting from Nehru, all prime ministers have contributed to this country, and he definitely should not say he is the only man.'[49]

Tussle with Reforms and Manmohan Singh

As a prime minister, it is clear that Gowda tried to balance his approach towards economic management. He was sometimes adamant about what he wanted, but like always, he was pragmatic enough to adapt to the demands of the times. But for five years before he became prime minister, as a first-time parliamentarian, he was a proximate witness to economic reforms, liberalization and globalization ushered in by the P.V. Narasimha Rao and Manmohan Singh combination. He groped in the dark like everybody else to make sense of it, especially its impact on rural communities and the agricultural sector. His response was varied—there was mild taunt, clear taunt, impatience, outburst and combativeness. Since he had not embraced any particular ideology, his response to economic reforms was not structured or dogmatic but unpredictable and relatively fresh. Sometimes he raised moral and rhetorical questions, and at other times he was alarmist and emotional but never short of passion. He tried to be prescient and prognostic too.

The fact that Manmohan Singh was not a politician but a technocrat made him very suspicious in the eyes of Gowda. His long interventions and arguments to Singh's budget may be naïve in parts, but there was always preparation and study, there was a struggle to express, and above all, there was the sincerity of purpose. When he confronted Manmohan Singh on many occasions, he never for a moment felt he was confronting an Oxbridge economist with a halo. Gowda treated his own worldview and perspective with sanctity, not self-doubt.

There was also a pattern that one sees in his responses. His diatribe and attack were mostly reserved for Manmohan Singh, Narasimha Rao was rarely targeted. His political and personal relationship with Rao was always excellent. Being exposed to Manmohan Singh's years as finance minister turned out to be a great period of learning and preparation for Gowda, the future chief minister and prime minister. He was a good student, and the records speak of it loudly.

Here are samples of exchanges from hundreds of pages between (or directed at) Manmohan Singh, the finance minister, and Gowda, the first-time MP from Hassan. Participating in a discussion on the finance bill in September 1991,[50] he was protesting the cut in subsidy of fertilizers and its dual pricing policy. He refers to the G.V.K. Rao Committee constituted by the Rajiv Gandhi government to make his point. He summons sarcasm here, and in most of his later exchanges too: 'You (Singh) said that the budget is going to be dedicated to the late Prime Minister Rajiv Gandhi. You have got so much loyalty and sincerity for the party and your past leader. This committee was constituted by Shri Rajiv Gandhi's regime and the report was given in 1987 . . . I would like to draw your attention to the recommendations of the committee. The chairman (G.V.K. Rao) is not a farmer . . . (in the report) it has been argued that a dual pricing policy involving concessional prices for small and marginal farmers and higher prices for the medium and larger farmers may help reduce the subsidy burden but is impossible to administer. It is not proper on the part of the government to think of dual pricing policy and also hike price of fertilizers. It will destroy the farming community. So far as production is concerned, they will be discouraged, and this should not be done. This is the recommendation made by him.' Gowda also points out how the report demonstrates that a hike of fertilizer prices would lead to fall in production and how other countries like USA, Japan, EEC (European Economic Community) had tried to help farmers by giving them subsidy.

In November 1992,[51] participating in a debate, again on the implications of the increase in fertilizer prices and the import of wheat, Gowda is angry, but still his logic and command of facts are intact:

Last session on the closing day, the Joint Parliamentary Committee on Fertilizer Prices has submitted its report to the house. The government was anxious to accept that report within about seventy to seventy-two hours of its submission. As a legislator for thirty years, I have never seen any house committee report being accepted so hastily when it is not a unanimous one. It is only a majority opinion report and there are dissenting notes of three members of the committee . . . I had given a categorical dissent note where I have said that decontrol of these items is going to be a disastrous one to the farming community, in particular, and to the rural economy in general . . . Even though the fertilizer price was increased by 30 per cent by this very house, last time, the consumption of the fertilizer went high and that is one of the arguments advanced by the bureaucrats. Let me be very plain (about) how the subsidy amount went high . . .

Saying so, Gowda illustrated how it was actually devaluation of the rupee that had caused Rs 900 crore of additional subsidy burden. Besides, he pointed out that 15 per cent Gulf surcharge, the rise

in railway fare and foreign exchange rate contributed another
Rs 560 crore to the burden. In addition, the market rate of exchange
of phosphoric acid worked out at about Rs 675 crore. While this was
the true reason, the voiceless famer was being erroneously blamed
for increasing the subsidy burden, he had said, turning the entire
argument on its head:

> These are the components where the additional burden has
> been passed on to farmers because of the recent financial or
> fiscal policies . . . One of the things which worries or hurts
> me is when the prime minister addressed about 4000 farmers
> in his official residence . . . he said Rs 9000 crore are going
> to manufacturers and middlemen. The government is unable
> to identify who those people are who have snatched away
> Rs 9000 crore in the name of farmers. The very purpose of
> demanding the Joint Parliamentary Committee during the last
> budget session by me was that this subsidy amount is not at all
> going to farmers; it goes only to industrialists and some corrupt
> politicians. Shri Ashok Gulati, when he gave evidence before
> the committee, said that 52 per cent of the total subsidy is going
> for genuine purpose, and in my opinion, 48 per cent is being
> distributed among corrupt bureaucrats and corrupt politicians.
> He did not want to mention the names of the politicians but I
> knew and I discussed it with him when he gave evidence.

In the same debate, to bring greater attention to his argument,
he made a radical suggestion: 'I would like to suggest one thing.
Nationalize all the land in the country. I am not bothered really.
My family has some acres of land. I say nationalize all the land and
give us the amount equivalent to the salary of a peon or a sweeper
in Indian Airlines. I plead on behalf of the farming community to
nationalize the land because I know the plight of farmers. I have got
every right to say this. The organized sector knows how to exploit
the rural community. That is why I say, take all our land and as

compensation give us the amount just equivalent to the salary of a peon in Indian Airlines.'

In March 1993,[52] debating the Ordinance and Gold Bonds (Immunities and Exemptions) Bill, which had been introduced to mobilize idle gold resources of ordinary citizens to supplement official reserves, Gowda made a case against it, although Vajpayee welcomed it: 'The whole scheme is only to help black money holders to convert it into white money. It is nothing beyond that. Let me be very plain. We have seen in the past several such schemes to attract black money . . . The hon. finance minister is known for his integrity. He is an expert in the field of economy. I do not want either to question his integrity or his efficiency or his knowledge of economics . . . (But) how much money did it generate previously when we announced the Voluntary Disclosure Schemes of 1965 and 1975 or the Special Bearer Bonds in 1981, the Amnesty Scheme in 1985–87, the National Housing Bank Scheme in 1991–92 and earlier to that the Tyagi Disclosure Scheme of 1951? Let me be fair. I do not think much has been generated . . . this Gold Bank Scheme is not at all going to be a major contributing factor . . . Can we not overcome certain defects in our taxation laws to tide over this black money racket in this country?' But interestingly, as prime minister, Gowda favoured a disclosure scheme despite his finance minister's objection. It is another matter that he raised more money than any other such scheme had raised in the past, and as we have seen earlier, his reason for pushing it through was different.

In a discussion related to the general budget in April 1993,[53] and in the backdrop of the securities scam that had come to light, he said he had lost regard for Manmohan Singh and that intelligence alone was not sufficient, but one should have a heart. He was upset that a large sum of money had been set aside to handle the securities scam committed by a handful of individuals, while even a small concession for the farming community had been rejected outright: 'I would like to ask Dr Manmohan Singh one question . . . To make up the financial loss due to swindling by the bank scam, you are going to provide Rs 5700 crore in the current year's budget. What moral right do you have to pay it from the public exchequer which is the money that is given by ninety crore people? But you are not prepared to give Rs 1000 crore for poor farmers at least for a single time benefit of loan abolition. I am ashamed to say this. Let us touch our heart. What sin has the farming community committed? Twenty or thirty handsome people have looted bank funds in the name of shares . . . These people are able to get protection by this very same government . . . You want to pay Rs 5700 crores from the general revenue to make up this fraud that has been committed by few individuals.

'Are poor farmers beggars? In all humility at my command, I would like to say don't treat this community with scant respect. I had got regards for Mr Manmohan Singh. But now I have to say I have lost that regard. Intelligence is not the criterion in this country's administration. I have seen enough intelligent people. We need men with a heart for the poor sections of the society . . . While preparing the budget is there no person who belongs to the farming community in the finance ministry, at least to suggest to the so-called administrators? . . . New maharajas and pseudo-maharajas have come to sit in this house and are running the administration of this country . . . I warn you and your party that if you people adopt a callous attitude towards agriculture and the agricultural sector, a day will come when this country will become another Somalia. Now IMF wants to trap you. Our food production in the next ten years will go down . . . We will not leave you. Tell your government. Tell the prime minister . . . I am asking a simple question. When you have attached the properties of Harshad Mehta and his relatives, why Bhupen Dalal's property has not been attached, even his wife's property has not been attached . . . whatever these looters may do, please do not neglect the farming community which will destroy you and your party.'

In a discussion under Rule 193, in December 1993,[54] he gets under the skin of Manmohan Singh by saying that he was worse than a professional politician:

Yesterday it was advocated by Mr Chidambaram who was the former commerce minister that the scam was due to the failure of the system. I would like to ask one or two points in the form of clarifications from the finance minister. I would like to know whether the scam is due to failure of our system or failure of the administrative machinery and lack of will to take decisions on certain vital matters . . . I know he is not going to go away from the house. The prime minister will not accept his resignation. I have also resigned once from the ministry. But on the day I resigned, I never entered the office. I never signed a paper. My resignation was accepted after one week by the chief minister of Karnataka. I never went to office a single day after I tendered [my] resignation. I know how politicians function. He [Singh] has excelled even a professional politician in dealing with this matter. To the entire world, he has shown that he wants to quit on moral grounds. Again, he left the matter to the prime minister for taking a decision. Now he is functioning in the house as a finance minister. But I have no personal grouse, personal grievance . . . But the way in which he has tried to fool the people of this country, I am sorry to say, is engaging our attention. Having tendered his resignation, whether it is going to be accepted or not, he ought not to have come to this house as a finance minister to discharge his duty . . . The second thing is while giving his evidence before the committee, he took shelter under the Official Secrets Act for some of the documents.

In this debate, Gowda also suggested that Parliament should take over the appointment of the director of the Central Bureau of Investigation, the head of the Enforcement Directorate, the chairmen of nationalized banks, the chief vigilance commissioner, the Governor of Reserve Bank of India and other such top executive functionaries: 'My suggestion is that all sensitive appointments should be made by the Parliament . . . The present system will never improve unless these institutions are made totally free from the clutches of politicians.'

By the time the 1994–95 budget was presented, Gowda's
suspicion of Manmohan Singh had only heightened. The outbursts
continued. He suggested Singh was using his 'intelligence' to hide
his real intent. He also pointed to how he had cleverly shifted his
loyalties within the Congress party:[55]

> In his first speech, Manmohan Singh at least mentioned Rajiv
> Gandhi. But today, there is no such mention. He has quietly
> forgotten him because public memory is very short. Now, he
> has only mentioned the present prime minister because he had
> elevated him to the highest position in the finance ministry . . .
> More than ten top industrialists last year have not paid even
> a rupee worth of tax . . . Yesterday, there was so much debate
> on the Banking Bill. I was watching. All these laws have given
> sufficient scope for those top industrialists or big industrial
> houses as to how to avoid tax. They will engage experts
> outside the country to teach them how to avoid tax. Because
> they are cleverer than Dr Manmohan Singh. Do not be under
> the impression that Dr Manmohan Singh is cleverer. There
> are much more clever people like Mr Palkhivala . . . Please
> understand, for God's sake, do not try to fool the people by
> sitting in this house. We cannot nod our heads to all that you
> are going to say here.

He continues to point out how industrialists have benefitted by
Singh's budgets at the cost of farmers, and his allegations are
accompanied, as always, with numbers:

> In this very house, a decision was taken to abolish loans of
> farmers to the extent of Rs 10,000 crore. Necessary directions
> were issued to the state governments. The guidelines were
> framed by the very finance ministry . . . What is the amount
> that has been released? In the 1991–92 budget, provision of
> Rs 1500 crore was made. But ultimately, the amount released

was Rs 1425 crore. In 1992–93 it was Rs 500 crore. In 1993–94 it was Rs 500 crore, and this year it is Rs 341 crore . . . I am not pleading for myself or Balram Jakhar [then agriculture minister] who is also a farmer . . . So far as the industrial sector is concerned, you have waived the unrecovered bad debts to the tune of Rs 6000 crore . . . I do not expect anything from Mr Manmohan Singh . . . My demand is that 70 per cent of the total income which we are going to spend on development activities should go to rural areas . . . I am not begging here. I am demanding that based on population our resources must be distributed . . .[56]

Just before Gowda quit the Parliament to become chief minister of Karnataka, speaking on the motion of thanks on the President's address[57] in March 1994, he warned that an ugly civil war could break out as a result of the economic policies introduced by Manmohan Singh. He mentioned the frustration of the youth and the violence that it may lead to. In all, it was a precocious, unstructured, unacademic critique of trickle-down economics:

Our friends in the ruling party always try to say that the economic reforms or the structural changes are going to yield the expected results in next three years. Unfortunately, we have already completed three years. My friend, the former commerce minister [P. Chidambaram], in this very same house, instead of three years, has given a lease of life of twenty years for these schemes to achieve the desired goals. That is, poverty will be abolished in twenty years. But in twenty years, the country can become a major economy in the world. I do not know whether I will live up to twenty years to see what this country is going to achieve after these structural changes or economic reforms or whatever they try to propagate day in and out.

'The burning problem today is unemployment. I would like to warn this government that if they do not attend to this burning problem . . . every state will become a ground for militants and all educated, unemployed people will become militants . . . Recently, before the Parliament session, the prices of all the essential items were hiked because IMF conditionalities were to be implemented. Unfortunately, the poor man has to pay more. The government tried to defend the price hike by saying they wanted to give higher remunerative price for agriculture. In Karnataka . . . a quintal of jowar was sold at the rate of Rs 180. However, no government mechanism has come to the rescue of the farmer who is making a distress sale. So, I think, the hon. finance minister is totally anti-farmer and anti-poor. He only tries to appease some industrial houses and some big business houses because they are the opinion builders. He has risen from the status of finance secretary, adviser to the central government, the Reserve Bank governor and now the finance minister. He may even go to the IMF or the World Bank. He may be an honest man. But I am convinced that he is never bothered about rural people. He is never bothered about solving rural problems. I am giving a few figures from his own speech. In 1992–93, the outlay for agriculture was Rs 1050 crore; in 1993–94, it was Rs 1330 crore and in 1994–95 it is Rs 2005 crore . . . Now there is a news item—'Dunkel to hit job opportunities'. The Union commerce minister Shri Pranab Mukherjee has admittedly said that employment opportunities in the organized sector would be drastically reduced . . . You want to mortgage this country. I warn you it is not so simple. People will drag you to the streets, be there any amount of police security. Today some of our Parliament members and politicians are surviving only because of security forces. If I cannot [handle this], I will get out of public life . . . Every state is going to become a place for educated militants or terrorists.

Do not be under the impression that only Punjab had some terrorists and you have completely eradicated the problem . . . An educated boy who applies for a loan gets Rs 1 lakh with all securities. And there are some influential people who get loans without even loan applications, without even any security and surety. In the bank scam, some of the brokers have drawn thousands of crore—800 crore, 600 crore and 500 crore of rupees . . . Have you seen the video cassette *Eyewitness* made by the *Hindustan Times*? They conducted a survey last month in all major cities and they found that more than 80 per cent of the youth want to leave this country. That is the opinion expressed in five major cities by our younger generation . . . They have no confidence in this country.

Gowda came back to these themes on agriculture, industry, economy and the larger good even after he stepped down as prime minister. He asked similar questions to Yashwant Sinha, Vajpayee's finance minister, but his tone or tongue were not as sharp. There was some reconciliation with reforms, but he still insisted that they should be deployed to serve a larger population, the 99 per cent than the 1 per cent. In March 2002, during the budget discussion, he had asked: 'I would urge the minister to not allow them (farmers) to die, commit suicide. Show me one industrialist who has committed suicide?'[58]

In December 2002,[59] participating in a discussion under Rule 193 on 'Problems being faced by farmers in the country', his sobering was evident, but anguish and disappointment had not escaped his voice. The 'Harvard versus hard work' debate that we became familiar with under Narendra Modi's regime appears to have had its origin in Gowda:

Now, we cannot go back from the WTO. We have to improve whatever is possible within the ambit of the Central government. You should take the house into confidence while doing so. One notion, one school of thought is that if you give more emphasis to the industrial sector, the manufacturing sector and the service sector, we will overcome the problem of unemployment; we will overcome the problem of starvation; we will overcome the problem of disparity between the rural and urban population; and the country will flourish. This is the advice given by our economists so far as strengthening of the economy of the country is concerned. We have taken the advice of the economists with all sincerity but what is the situation today? . . . Unless the agricultural sector is going to be given sufficient thrust, there will be no question of any growth in the industrial sector or in the manufacturing sector or in the service sector. Unless money flows, all these sectors are going to fail. Only as an example I would quote what happened to the tractor industry. Today, there is no sale there. There is no sale of power tillers; there is no sale of tractors. There is no money in the hands of farmers, even for household purchases. The farmers have to generate money, then merchants in cities can carry on with their businesses. I am not an economist but it is common sense. We may not be economists; we may not have degrees from Harvard University. That is not required. A person with common sense who knows the rural background can realize this.

Finally, in March 2003,[60] speaking on the budget, Gowda quoted a long passage from Joseph Stiglitz's latest book *Globalization and Its Discontents* to underscore his point on the ill-effects of globalization on the farm sector and poorer sections of society. He demanded course correction and a policy balance. He pointed out how Europe defended its agricultural policy and how it was important to mobilize one's own resources than live on borrowed money. Gowda usually hid his reading to keep up with his rural-farmer image, but this was one of those rare occasions when he quoted from a book publicly. All through his speech, he referred to Stiglitz as Bill Clinton's economic adviser, and the chief economist of the World Bank. Stiglitz had won the Nobel Prize in 2001, but for Gowda, his prize was not important, his experience was more relevant.

In July 2004,[61] when Chidambaram presented his first budget under Manmohan Singh as prime minister, Gowda said in his budget intervention: 'I will conclude with the hope that the demands for grants of the ministry of agriculture will get top priority while we discuss demands for grants in this house . . . The finance minister has quoted from *Thirukkural* in his budget speech. I am very happy for that. I will like to conclude my speech with a quotation from the Father of the Nation, Mahatma Gandhi. I quote: "Remember that dark brown starved man bending under a scorching sun, scratching a little plot of land to eke out a living. Anything you do, do for his benefit."'

Kisan Raj and a Paddy Variety Called Deve Gowda

As a legislator and parliamentarian, Gowda never believed in resorting to protest or slogan-shouting inside the house. He never violated its decorum. There was nothing that he had spoken that had ever been expunged. But only once in his long career did he violate this self-imposed principle, and it was when the welfare of his loyal constituency of farmers was 'threatened'. He recalled this in June 2004[62] when Somnath Chatterjee took over as the Lok Sabha Speaker: 'Sir, in my political career of forty-four years, only once I broke the tradition. You were all there. Late Indrajit Gupta was there. Shri Atal Bihari Vajpayee was sitting this side. On the issue of farmers, on the issue of the World Bank's conditions, I opposed and went to the well [well of the Lok Sabha] breaking all the norms for the first time in my political career.' He had recalled this incident once earlier too in December 1998.[63]

The reference was to the incidents of 31 July 1991 and 1 August 1991. During a heated discussion on Manmohan Singh's first budget, Gowda had rushed to the well of the house to pressure the government to rollback its decision to end subsidies for the farm sector over a three-year period: 'I am a farmer and a tiller's son and I will not allow this. I will sit on a dharna. I will not go out from this house. It is not for publicity's sake that I am doing it,' he had said.[64] He had also taken on comrade Indrajit Gupta, who became his home

minister in 1996, for classifying farmers, and saying they could be
affluent and exploiters too:

> This type of hair-splitting argument is not going to help the
> farming community. I want to humbly submit that a senior
> parliamentarian like Indrajit Guptaji ought not to have gone to
> the extent of saying that the farmers are affluent. After the land
> laws have been introduced in this country, where are affluent
> farmers? I want to say that we are all proud that Karnataka is
> one of the pioneer states with respect to the implementation of
> land reforms. Today, no landlord exists in Karnataka. Nobody
> is holding more than 10 acres of land. When such is the case,
> where is the question of rich farmers? How many farmers today
> live in luxury? . . . I want to draw the attention of my hon.
> friends like Shri Indrajit Gupta who has said that only this time
> fertilizer price has been hiked. It is not so. At least, three or four
> times, the price of fertilizer was hiked . . . I would like to draw
> the attention of the house that the price of wheat in 1977–78
> was Rs 110 per quintal. Now the existing procurement price
> is Rs 215. When the hike in the procurement price during the
> period of ten years is hardly about 100 to 150 per cent, the
> price of fertilizer had gone up by 300 per cent to 350 per cent
> during the same period. This is the fate of the farmers.[65]

In 2002, when farm suicides were being reported in big numbers
from all across India, Gowda took a delegation of nearly 2000
farmers from Karnataka by train to Delhi and got them an audience
with Prime Minister Vajpayee.[66] It was unprecedented, especially for
a former prime minister to protest in this manner. People in Delhi
were bewildered.

As a tribute to Gowda's lifelong commitment to the farmers'
cause, and for his policy initiatives towards the peasant community,
and the stellar pro-farmer budget of 1996–97, the farmers of Punjab
named one of the finest varieties of paddy as 'Dev Gowda' [sic] after

he stepped down as prime minister. It is said the paddy variety was very popular for over two decades. Farmers who could not converse with Gowda in Punjabi, Hindi, Kannada or English had understood and acknowledged the man's intent. Ironically, this tribute too remained little known, and unsung like all other things associated with Gowda. A usually well-informed Gowda was himself not aware of this paddy variety until Karnataka cadre IAS officer from Punjab, Chiranjiv Singh, wrote about it in his Kannada newspaper column in 2014:[67] 'A farmer said, "My crop has not been affected by this rain, I had sown Dev Gowda." Another farmer who heard this asked a third one: "Have you also sown Dev Gowda?" This is a conversation I heard in a village in Gurdaspur district near the Indo-Pakistan border. Again, in a village in Ludhiana district of southern Punjab, a farmer said, "We have not used the Dev Gowda variety this time. We have used another variety. Gowda does not work well with our soil." I picked all this up during my recent Punjab visit. For the work that Deve Gowda did for farmers as prime minister they have named a fine variety of paddy after him. This was not an initiative of any institution or university or a government, the initiative to name the paddy variety was that of the farmers themselves. It was a tribute they were offering a man who they saw as their true representative.'

Singh continued in his column, which has now been collected in his book[68] with his other essays: 'Farmers have forgotten as to what this variety of paddy was called before it was named Dev Gowda. When I asked, they said, "We do not know the original name. Here, all of us call it Dev Gowda." According to the government, this variety is classified as an *avval* or super fine variety. This is a true honour bestowed on Gowda. This tribute that Gowda has received from the people is greater than that any government can offer him. The people of Punjab do not understand the politics of Karnataka or its caste equations, they just evaluated Gowda's work.' The association with paddy, the association with the soil, the association with a staple diet of a people was the most magical and original metaphors that could have been thought of for Deve Gowda.

Interestingly, in 1996, Mahendra Singh Tikait, farmers' leader from the same western Uttar Pradesh belt as Charan Singh, hailed Deve Gowda as the 'Choudhary Charan Singh of the south' at a meeting in Muzaffarnagar.[69] Around that time, Gowda was attempting a pan-India political constituency of farmers and was seeking an alignment with the Jats in Uttar Pradesh and elsewhere. He even wanted Tikait in the Rajya Sabha.[70] V.P. Singh, who was usually reticent about Gowda, chose to compliment him for trying to bring Tikait and Ajit Singh, Charan Singh's son, into the United Front orbit.[71] A hint of this plan was in Gowda's address to farmers at a Meerut rally, in September 1996. He spoke of a 'Kisan Raj':[72] 'Show your strength and political awareness and take a pledge not to allow this government to fall, for this is the first time that Kisan Raj has come to power at the Centre,' he said. The political plan was aborted when his government fell.

15

The Narmada and the Ganga

When a devout Hindu holds water for a ritual bath, there is an ancient chant that is invoked: *Gangge Ca Yamune Cai(a-E)va Godaavari Sarasvati | Narmade Sindhu Kaaveri Jale-(A)smin Sannidhim Kuru*. This translates to: 'O holy rivers Ganga and Yamuna, and also Godavari and Saraswati, O holy rivers Narmada, Sindhu and Cauvery, please be present in this water that I hold and make it sacred'. A deeply religious Deve Gowda must have uttered this chant innumerable times. Besides reaffirming his personal faith, the chant must have also charted the geographical extent of India in his mind, as it has for millions of others.

Gowda's career can be viewed exclusively through his harnessing of the Cauvery and Krishna river waters and their tributaries. But as prime minister, sitting on the banks of the Yamuna, he also got to settle some very knotty, longstanding issues related to the Narmada and the Ganga. The belief that the Saraswati is subterranean has continuously energized his mind. Therefore, rather interestingly, he believes that in his long political life, his destiny connected him with nearly all the rivers mentioned in the ritual chant. 'My bond with this uniquely diverse nation is through its rivers,' he once said but had never expanded on the idea.[1]

The Narmada and an Activist

In October 2019, Deve Gowda decided to go to the Sardar Sarovar Dam built over river Narmada. The primary reason he wanted to be there was because he had read in the newspapers that the reservoir had reached its full capacity of 138.68 metres for the first time since the completion of the dam and installation of the gates in 2017. Prime Minister Narendra Modi had already visited the site on his birthday a fortnight ago to celebrate the milestone.[2] Gowda wanted to be there too. However, his picture before the gigantic Sardar Vallabhbhai Patel's statue made more news than his visit to the dam.[3] Gowda had stood alone, spellbound, at a vantage point on the dam and watched the continuous discharge of water for over ten minutes. When a site engineer asked him why he spent so much time watching the water flow out, he simply said, 'it gives me joy.' After a while, he reflected: 'I had worked really hard and taken a lot of abuse to fix the height of this dam in 1996.' He continued: 'When I met Modi privately in 2015, I had jokingly challenged him, "Look I brought the dam in your state to a certain height, can you increase it by even one foot?" He tried doing it, but his own government in Madhya Pradesh objected. He never proposed the idea again.'[4]

A year before Gowda became prime minister, in 1995, the Supreme Court had stalled the Sardar Sarovar Dam project after the Narmada Bachao Andolan, a movement led by Medha Patkar, had raised serious concerns over rehabilitation and resettlement of people in the project area. The height of the dam was at the centre of the problem. Gowda wanted to make a serious attempt to resolve the issue. He realized that his predecessor, P.V. Narasimha Rao, had skirted around the problem but had never really addressed it.

In July 1996, Gowda decided to assemble the chief ministers of Gujarat, Madhya Pradesh, Maharashtra and Rajasthan, the states involved in or affected by the project. He also invited chief secretaries, irrigation secretaries and chief engineers of the respective states.[5] He asked each one of them to narrate the problem from their respective points of view and suggest a solution if they had one. Most of them stated the problem eloquently. It was like the proverbial blind men describing an elephant. There were many realities and scenarios placed on Gowda's table. In March 1996, months before Gowda became prime minister, the Supreme Court had said it would further hear the petition on the dam only after the states resolved their differences and came to some agreement. But it had not suggested that the prime minister should take the initiative. Therefore, by calling a meeting, Gowda was acting on his own.

At the meeting, Gowda did something unprecedented. He got the entire audio of the meeting officially recorded.[6] This precaution he took because he did not want anybody to go out and twist the points raised and quote the discussions out of context. At the end of the daylong deliberations, he offered a solution. He said the work on the Sardar Sarovar Dam should be allowed to restart by limiting the full reservoir level to 436 feet. Then, he said, the inflow performance of the water should be watched for five years, and a decision can be made later if the dam height should go up to 455 feet. Madhya Pradesh chief minister Digvijay Singh walked out of the meeting although his party was supporting the Gowda government. The *India Today* report,[7] which underestimated Gowda's intervention, said the solution that he had offered was 'almost simplistic'. But Gowda recalled: 'It was a pragmatic decision and not a political decision. I sincerely wanted to solve the problem. Interestingly, the court resumed hearing on the matter in August, and they continued to argue on the height of the dam for years, and finally, when it was decided, the court offered the exact same solution that I had offered. I felt happy and vindicated.'[8] In July 2002, during a Parliament intervention on floods in Bihar, Gowda reiterated the role he had played: 'During my period on Narmada, I had called all the four chief ministers. I worked out an agreeable formula, which ultimately went to the Supreme Court. The Supreme Court gave the same decision based on what we had agreed among the four chief ministers.'[9]

This was the engineering side of the solution. As regards the rehabilitation and resettlement issue, Gowda called a separate meeting with Medha Patkar and her colleagues at his Race Course Road residence. 'I offered to implement rehabilitation and resettlement by following World Bank guidelines like I had done in the Upper Krishna Project (see chapter 'The Krishna and the Cauvery'). Naturally, this would increase the cost of the project, but I decided to absorb that. But Medha Patkar wanted the entire project to be abandoned. When I said that was not on my list, she stormed out of my house shouting slogans. I told the SPG not to stop her but ensure her safe exit. I was not hurt by what she did because she believed in her cause, and I believed in my mission,' recalled Gowda.[10] As we have discussed earlier, Gowda's vision was technological, not ecological. Also, he was not ready to sink the thousands of crores of public money that had already been invested in the project.

Medha Patkar remembered the meeting with Gowda: 'We did not get much time with him to have a conclusive dialogue. When I look back, I feel that he was at least ready to listen to us. I remember that many of us were taken to the prime minister's house. We all sat on the lawn, and he listened to us. His social welfare minister, Balwant Singh Ramoowalia, was also present. We saw that Gowda was sensitive to peoples' movements, which was lacking in other prime ministers. Now, with Modi, there is no dialogue possible. Gowda government's position was that they could only have a dialogue on rehabilitation, they were not willing to reconsider the building of the dam. However, they did not mind our presentation.'[11] She recalled that V.P. Singh, like Gowda, had listened to them when they went along with Sunderlal Bahuguna, Sugata Kumari, Swami Agnivesh and others. V.P. Singh, at one point, decided to get the dam reviewed, but his water resources secretary threw a spanner. Meanwhile, V.P. Singh lost power.

'The Gowda government had a chance to review the project, and we felt it was his duty to review the project. Everything that we said then has come true. People in Gujarat remember us and tell us they made a great mistake. One of the former ministers of Gujarat came to the Narmada valley in 2019 and apologized to the people because the project had not fulfilled the objectives of largescale irrigation. It was much less than what was expected. Also, water is diverted to large cities in Gujarat and industrial estates. Now the focus is not even on completing the canal network or proper distribution of water, but it is on tourism with the Sardar statue. This too is leading to the eviction of seventy-two tribal villages other than those submerged by the dam,' Medha Patakar said and added that even Maharashtra and Madhya Pradesh have not got the power benefit they were promised, but have seen huge displacement.[12] She, however, agreed that Gowda's decision not to review the dam was not his individual position. It was a position taken by the government before him as well. 'There must have been huge pressure from Gujarat government on him. In 1993, V.C. Shukla as water resources minister, had reviewed the project for two days, but he refused to sign the decision taken in the presence of eminent people like V.R. Krishna Iyer, Thakurdas Bang and Upendra Baxi. Gujarat had brought enormous pressure at that time too. At various points, we felt suddenly cheated. That was very sad,' she recalled.[13]

The Ganga and a Gandhian

As prime minister, Gowda's passion for untangling developmental projects stuck due to agitations did not stop with Narmada. He had become prime minister at a time when the anti-big dam movement had acquired momentum, and the Gandhian non-violent conservation movement in the Himalayas had deepened. People like Sunderlal Bahuguna and Medha Patkar were new public heroes who were striving to keep the conscience of governments. Gowda recognized these as mass movements but did not address ideological questions. He was pragmatic. He wanted to give a big push to development projects, but at the same time did not want to ride roughshod over mass movements. As a seasoned politician he understood that it would be counterproductive. Also given the background of mass political mobilization and struggle that he came from, and his mingling with socialists in the Janata Parivar, he instinctually knew that crushing mass movements was not a conscionable act, and that it would erode his political standing.

Therefore, he did the next best thing, which was to negotiate and convince. He had tried and failed with Medha Patkar but did not shy away from trying it with Sunderlal Bahuguna, a Gandhian who was resisting the composite project in Tehri, of a dam and hydro-electric project, to be built over the Bhagirathi, a tributary of the Ganga River in the foothills of the Himalayas. If Gowda found Medha Patkar to be a firebrand activist who could be brusque and irreverent, Bahuguna had a refinement that Gowda found relatively easier to engage with. 'He was a gentle soul, and I had great personal respect for him. He was also a very committed man, and therefore, I had to do a lot of homework before approaching him,' Gowda recalled when he travelled in the Tehri–Garhwal region in October 2019.[14] He wanted to call on Bahuguna to speak about the old times during that visit, but he was misled by his staff. They said the Gandhian conservationist had passed away a couple of years ago (Bahuguna passed away in May 2021).

The Tehri project was not just a development project in Gowda's mind. It was a sacred project. He literally believed that Uttaranchal (later Uttarakhand) was an abode of the gods. As a devout Hindu, he had visited nearly all the holy places in the region except Gangotri (Haridwar, Rishikesh, Badrinath, Kedarnath and Yamunotri), and petitioned for his moksha. In Gowda's worldview, there is no clear segregation of the mythological and the historical. They interact seamlessly in his mind. As his convoy climbed up the hill to reach the Tehri Dam site in 2019, he spoke of Ramayana's geographical connection with the region.[15] Technology and religion could exist in independent compartments in his mind, while history and mythology could be entwined indistinguishably. Yet politically he was wedded to secular values. The monopoly of reason did not flatten his mind or its mindscape. In that sense, he was a typical, complex Indian mind.

When Gowda became prime minister, Bahuguna had been on a prolonged hunger strike protesting the dam and warning ecological damage to the Himalayan region. The fear was that the composite Tehri project would trigger an earthquake and destroy the Himalayas. 'They had created a demon of danger. I had studied the whole thing, and I had also consulted a number of research papers. I had read a book by a geologist, the name of which I forget, who had travelled across the Himalayas and had written how small hydel projects could be created. He had argued that power produced from these hydel projects could not only be used in India, but also in China, Myanmar, Tibet and Pakistan. We had a huge power shortage, and this argument had interested me. I was personally convinced that the Tehri project would not lead to destruction as was being projected.'[16]

Gowda wanted a trusted emissary to reach out to Bahuguna. After a bit of search, he was pleasantly surprised that his close party colleague and deputy chairman of the Planning Commission, Madhu Dandavate, and Bahuguna were friends. Gowda was delighted. He spoke to Dandavate and requested him to meet Bahuguna and bring him to Delhi. He also kept a helicopter at his disposal to fly in the Gandhian. 'When the time is ripe God shows the way. Luckily, Dandavate agreed to take up the mission. When Bahuguna came to Delhi, he spoke frankly. He was a straightforward man. I spoke to him with humility. I assured him that I would develop the region without defeating his cause. I said I would do whatever he asked me to do and find answers for whatever issues he raised.'[17] After patiently listening to Gowda, Bahuguna suggested that Gowda should go to Tehri and try to convince the people himself. Gowda took up the offer.

When he landed there with his team of officers and engineers, Gowda decided to go around the hills in a jeep to meet people who were scattered across. He walked into a few homes and told them that he had come there to improve their lives and not destroy them.

He also invited them for a bigger meeting that he was planning to organize the next day. He asked officials to collect people in one place so that he could address them. They transported people in jeeps from various corners. Around 5000–6000 people assembled. 'I spoke to them sincerely. I did not exaggerate anything with regard to the project or rehabilitation. I only told them that I was a poor farmer's son too and understood their anxiety. I said I didn't intend to create trouble for them. I also said I have gone around and seen that they lived in fragile structures, and I would like to build houses that would last a hundred years. "You should have no doubts about that. You should trust me," I pleaded. I also urged them to speak to me directly without any reservations. They placed their proposals before me, and I agreed,' he said.[18]

As soon as Gowda returned to Delhi, he put all the points that were raised in the meeting and whatever he had promised in writing. 'We immediately issued a government order (GO). It was a slightly unusual GO and pretty exhaustive. We gave wide publicity to it. People, thank God, responded positively. A new township was planned for villages that were getting submerged. Sunderlal Bahuguna also agreed to our decisions. I also got others with him to commit to our plan. Madhu Dandavate had played a very crucial role in connecting Bahuguna and me. Work progressed smoothly. There has not been a single issue till today.'[19]

In 2019, Gowda was visiting Tehri twenty-three years after he had negotiated the deal. Gowda did not forget to mention that when the 2013 floods happened, Rishikesh and Haridwar were saved because of the Tehri dam, while Kedarnath went underwater. V.K. Badoni, the executive director (Tehri Complex) at the THDC India Limited who had come to receive Gowda during the visit, said:

> I belong to this place. My house was also submerged. Now I am heading this project. I was born and brought up in Tehri town. Bahugunaji's son was my classmate. The dam has benefited all of us. You should see houses before the dam and after the dam,

the difference is obvious. Bhagirathipuram is a great symbol of development that has taken place in the last twenty years. When villages were shifted, care was taken to shift them in clusters to maintain the social fabric. It was all done very sensitively. The same names were given to the villages to ensure continuity. The biggest new settlement area is near the Jolly Grant airport. You should see the houses there to believe it.[20]

Gowda had constituted the C.H. Hanumantha Rao Committee in September 1996 [73] to look into the expectations of the local population in Tehri with regard to rehabilitation and resettlement. Based on the panel's recommendations, further modifications were made to the rehabilitation policy. 'Wherever we go now, people ask us to give the Tehri package,' Badoni said. Among the major recommendations of the Hanumantha Rao Committee was the liberal construction of the definition of 'family' of those affected by the project. 'Major sons and daughters' who had attained the age of majority as on 19 July 1990 as well as dependent parents of the 'fully affected entitled landowners' were made eligible for compensation.[21]

Bahuguna also insisted on a technical committee to review the seismic stability of the dam. Gowda readily obliged. He had anyway promised to do all that he was asked to do. A panel of seismologists was formed, and all of them were nominated by Bahuguna. The five-member committee submitted two reports and both found the dam was safe from the seismic point of view. It said the 'the present design of the dam is expected to be structurally safe to withstand the maximum credible earthquake during its economic life'.[22]

Bahuguna tried to recall in November 2019 the events that had taken place twenty-three years ago. 'I have forgotten most of the details, I am ninety-two now, but I remember that Gowda was good to me. He tried to convince me that the Tehri Dam was in the nation's interest. He was a good man but also a prisoner of the establishment. We met because of Madhu Dandavate. Like the dam was in national interest, our agitation too was in national interest to draw the government's attention to the Himalayas.'[23] Bahuguna had no real complaints about rehabilitation but said that 'people who are accustomed to living in open spaces, free from thieves and pollution have been imprisoned in small spaces threatened by thieves and pollution. There is a great difference in the hill surroundings and culture where the highlander's spirit of freedom was their special quality, which is not there in the cities and plains.'[24] When Bahuguna passed away on 21 May 2021, Gowda put out a warm tribute on Twitter the same day. He said the Gandhian giving up his fast in 1996 was 'one of the finest moments of his prime ministership'. It is interesting that Gowda, a man from the plains of Karnataka, had taken so much interest in the Kashmir valley, Narmada valley and the Tehri valley.

The Ganga Seeks Statesmanship

Gowda, who was proactive with water disputes within India, had never imagined that he may get to engage with a transboundary water-sharing problem. The opportunity to look into the sharing of Ganga water with Bangladesh at Farakka presented itself to him when there were monsoon floods in Bihar, in August–September 1996. As per official records, around 67.33 lakh people were affected by this.[25] After 1987, when the recorded numbers were steep (288.62 lakh people affected), it was in 1995 and 1996 that the numbers had again seen an uptick. Floods had become a recurrent annual feature in north Bihar. There were many reasons attributed to the floods, but one of the reasons offered then, like it is argued now by a section of Bihar's politicians, including Nitish Kumar, was that the Farakka Barrage built over the Ganga in the 1970s, in Murshidabad of West Bengal, was causing the floods.[26] Although the barrage was over 400 kilometres downstream from the site of the floods, and eighteen kilometres away from the India–Bangladesh border.

One of the primary purposes of the Farakka barrage was to divert the Ganga to the Hooghly river to flush out sediment deposition from the Kolkata harbour without the need for mechanical dredging. There are many complicated discussions on whether the barrage does serve its purpose and if it is more a hindrance than a help, but they are not relevant for this chapter. When the floods happened in 1996, Gowda did an aerial survey. He saw people perched on trees like birds to escape the fury of the waters. He returned to Delhi and started quietly studying the problem. He held a number of discussions with engineers, water resource experts, and bureaucrats. He realized there was no convergence of views.

When he returned to the drawing board again with all the inputs he needed, he thought it was best to allow the Ganga water to flow into Bangladesh. This would help India and also the lower riparian neighbour. There were short-term agreements between India and Bangladesh with regard to water sharing since the 1970s. He reviewed them. There was a lot of confusion and uncertainty in the language of those agreements. He constructed a rough formula in his mind. If he had to implement the water-sharing formula and bring some permanence and certainty to the arrangement, he knew he had to take his colleague and West Bengal chief minister Jyoti Basu into confidence. He held a closed-door meeting with him without wasting any time, in which he broke down the technical details. He requested him to trust his instinct on this one.[27] Once Basu was convinced, he put the official diplomatic channels to work. 'I first convinced Jyoti Basu on technical issues. I must have spent a couple of hours with him. I assured him that this treaty would not affect West Bengal but, on the other hand, would be beneficial for both countries. Once Basu was convinced, he stood like a rock behind me. He did not allow local politics to intervene. Some politicians from Bihar tried to create mischief (the Kannada word he used to describe the irritation they caused was *tarale*). I realized they were doing it because the flood-damage money that the Centre released had spawned a parallel economy in Bihar. I decided to ignore them. I also did not consult the Congress on this.

When Bangladesh prime minister Sheikh Hasina came to Delhi in December 1996, the water-sharing treaty was the main subject on the agenda. I requested Basu to be in Delhi. I promised him that I would listen to my counterpart carefully, and even if there was an iota of doubt, I will consult him before I sign the treaty. Basu was a great man. He agreed and appreciated my effort to take him into confidence. It is nearly twenty-five years since I signed the treaty and there has been no major trouble,' Gowda recalled in 2020.[28]

Senior advocate Mohan Katarki, who had seen Gowda handle Cauvery and Krishna disputes, said:

> There was a misconception among Indian engineers. At least they were not able to convince political heads that there would be no danger to the Indian share of the water and the Calcutta port. There were complex figures and calculations cited. Actually, if you want to get confused about water treaties, you have to meet engineers. Whenever the Farakka subject came up, bureaucrats would amplify the scare. As a result, everybody would drag their feet. They thought there was an old agreement and that was enough. 'We are getting water by gravity, whatever flows to Bangladesh flows. Why formalize it?' That was their approach. Gowda insisted on putting an end to the uncertainty and gave shape to a treaty. Summer flow was the issue, which he divided judiciously. Planning a dam and the principles of hydrology is one thing, but basin planning demands a larger vision. If you show Gowda any basin map in the world, he can tell you in a day where the fault line is and how it could be resolved. Many of us have wondered where and how he picked up this skill. He resolved Farakka issue overriding the apprehensions of engineers.[29]

Gowda himself is modest about his engineering training: 'I hold a small diploma and that too in civil engineering. I am not an irrigation expert, but God has blessed me with common sense,' he said.[30]

In an interview, Ainun Nishat, a Bangladeshi environmentalist and water resources management expert, offered perspective and chronology on the 1996 Ganga water sharing treaty at Farakka. Nishat was a member of the Indo–Bangladesh Joint River Commission, mentioned in the treaty as a dispute resolution body:

Based on ideas from British times, in 1951 India published its plan to construct the Farakka Barrage along the Bangladesh–India border. The aim of the barrage was to maintain the navigability of the Kolkata port in the state of West Bengal. Between 1960 and 1970, officials of India and Pakistan (when Bangladesh was part of Pakistan) discussed the issues that arose out of building the barrage, but they failed to thrash out an acceptable solution. In December 1971, Bangladesh emerged as an independent country. In April 1975, India formally sought Bangladesh's consent for a test run of the Farakka Barrage—to see if it was constructed properly.

In 1976, India went for total withdrawal of the Ganga waters, causing serious problems in areas of Bangladesh including the southwestern region, which hosts the Sundarbans, the world's largest mangrove forest in the Bay of Bengal. In 1977, Bangladesh and India signed a five-year agreement that stressed that the two governments 'need to cooperate with each other in finding a solution to the long-term problem of augmenting the flow of the Ganga during the dry season'. After the 1977 agreement expired, Bangladesh and India signed a Memorandum of Understanding (MoU) on 7 October 1982 for one year. Another MoU for water sharing between 1986 and 1988 was inked. The second MoU being over, there was no agreement on sharing of the Ganga waters from 1989 to December 1996 when the thirty-year Ganga Water Treaty was signed. The previous deals were for short terms—from one year to five years. When we got thirty years, we thought it a big achievement. You have to understand that

in 1996 we convinced India to sign a treaty—not an MoU
or agreement—on sharing the Ganga waters. A treaty is the
strongest international legal deal between two countries. It was
historic, though the treaty has some limitations.[31]

One of the main limitations of the treaty, Nishat explained, was
that it was only for thirty years (expires in 2026) and that was
'not fair'. He offered an analogy: 'For example, if you and your
brother inherit a piece of land from your father, would you share
it for ten or twenty or thirty years? You will share it forever. What
would happen after thirty years? The time-bound treaty will give
India an upper hand in the negotiation in the long run. So, the
treaty should have stated that it would be in place unless replaced
by another treaty.' There is yet another issue he points out.
Bangladesh is sharing the residual flow at the Farakka point, while
the upper riparian states such as Uttar Pradesh and Bihar were
withdrawing waters in the upper portion. 'Bihar and West Bengal
have been fighting with Bangladesh, but they are not talking about
withdrawal of waters in their upper portion. In the future, I fear
that the Indian Central government may not be in a position to
ensure the minimum 70,000 cusec of water at the Farakka point
for sharing with Bangladesh,' he said.[32]

Whatever problems may exist in the future, in 1996, what
Gowda achieved was a major breakthrough for which he has not
been credited enough. It was his technical workings and personal
equation with Basu that had led to the treaty.[33] As per the treaty,
India's right to withdraw up to 40,000 cusecs of flow at the Farakka
Barrage between 1 January and 31 May every year was agreed. If
availability at Farakka fell below 70,000 cusecs, the flow would be
divided equally between the two countries while guaranteeing a
minimum of 35,000 cusecs to each over alternating ten-day periods
between 11 March and 10 May annually.[34] When Gowda announced
the treaty in Parliament, it was welcomed across party lines.[35] First,
Somnath Chatterjee hailed Gowda, then Vajpayee spoke, and on

behalf of the Congress, P.R. Dasmunsi welcomed the treaty. All of them acknowledged that it was a historic moment in the relationship between the two countries. The treaty made international news too.[36]

Just a month before the treaty was signed, the New Scientist wrote a long piece in which it detailed Bangladesh's woes.[37] Quoting Bangladeshi government statistics, the report said, the minimum Ganges flow in 1996, measured downstream from Farakka at Hardinge Bridge, was 14,691 cusecs compared with almost 73,500 before the diversions began. The flow fell to as little as 9217 cusecs in 1993 and was just 12,819 cusecs in 1995. The decreased water flow in the Ganges led to the drying up of River Gorai, a tributary of the Ganges and the most important source of fresh water to the south-western Khulna division of Bangladesh.

The report further said: 'Bangladesh claims that lack of water and increased salinity across 27,000 square kilometres of its territory caused the loss of 7.5 million tonnes in grain production between 1976 and 1995. Inadequate irrigation means that farmers plant crops later in the rainy season and risk them being damaged by flooding. Fisheries and navigation have also been hurt by increased salinity and decreased river water, while human consumption of water with a high salt concentration has caused outbreaks of diarrhoea and cholera. Overall, Bangladesh claims that damage directly attributed to the Farakka dam affects one-third of the population and has cost the country $3.5 billion.' It also said that in 1976 Bangladesh had taken the dispute to the United Nations and that had resulted in the Ganges Waters Agreement of 1977.[38]

The two countries had not been able to reach an agreement because the endless rounds of talks were always dominated by technical experts, while under Gowda, it was a political initiative. The New Scientist quoted senior journalist B.G. Verghese, who was then a fellow at the Centre for Policy Research in Delhi: 'For twenty years we went around the mulberry bush getting bogged down in technical details and it was all beside the point. This is not an engineering problem, it's a political one.'[39]

Gowda remembered in 2020: 'A few months after I had stepped down as prime minister, I went to Bangladesh to see how the treaty was working. I went to rural areas to meet people. When I went into the home of poor farmers, I saw they had kept my picture with that of Prime Minister Hasina. That was a blessed moment. I just sent up a prayer to God.'[40]

The demonstration of the fact that Bangladesh had not forgotten Gowda's statesmanship in 1996 came in March 2020 when the Sheikh Hasina government invited Gowda along with Prime Minister Narendra Modi and Congress president Sonia Gandhi to the inauguration of the centenary year celebrations of Sheikh Mujibur Rahman, the founding father of Bangladesh. He was overwhelmed. However, the event was postponed due to the COVID-19 pandemic.[41]

16

On the Banks of the Brahmaputra

It was a deep emotional hurt that prompted Deve Gowda to passionately adopt the cause of the North-east. It was a creative response to a 'denigrating' statement by Ramakrishna Hegde. One seldom gets to see such a constructive response pattern in politics, where abuse is often met with either more abuse or violence. One also does not get to hear such a naïve and honest admission from a person who has occupied the highest chair.

When Gowda took over as prime minister, Hegde had said that 'an unworthy person who did not know the geography of this country was being made to sit on Nehru's chair'.[1] That's a paraphrase of the statement indelibly committed to Gowda's memory. As we have seen earlier, Hegde's actions and statements were far harsher and bitter. It cannot be ruled out that this comment, in the mind of Gowda, who was deeply conscious of caste hierarchies, took the shape of an archetypal Brahmin dismissal of a Shudra's ability and merit.

One morning, as Gowda was looking at the newspapers at his residential bungalow in the Race Course Road complex, the North-east came as a brainwave. It was a neglected part of India, and he thought he should work with the people of the region and that they would recognize and appreciate his initiative. As he had to mainstream himself as a national leader, the North-east too had to be mainstreamed was his thinking. It was a modest dream and a perfectly legitimate one to have. Politically too, he thought it would help him because the Asom Gana Parishad had joined the United Front coalition, although their numbers were marginal. Also, Purno Agitok Sangma or P.A. Sangma, a Congress leader and former chief minister of Meghalaya, had been chosen as the Speaker of the eleventh Lok Sabha. Sangma was gregarious, loquacious and was trying to establish a relationship with the new prime minister. In fact, Sangma would routinely drop into Gowda's office in the Parliament, ignoring protocol.[2] The secretaries would have a tough time as he would be blocking the prime minister's scheduled appointments with an unscheduled visit.

Although Gowda wanted to travel to the North-east immediately, that is in July 1996, the PMO decided against it because rains in the region would be an impediment.[3] Therefore, Gowda's diligently planned six-day trip to the North-east came up in October 1996, and it acquired the same priority in his mind as Kashmir, where he had already been a couple of times by then. Before he went, Gowda made it clear to his officers that the visit to the North-east should not end up as a symbolic one but offer a substantial movement forward in terms of policy. He also insisted that all the North-eastern states should be covered, and none should be left out as it would send a wrong message.[4] In six days, he covered seven states, and except Aizawl in Mizoram, he stayed in all the state capitals. Such a long and continuous visit to the North-east, from 22 October 1996 to 27 October 1996, was a first for any Indian prime minister.

'I kept all that Hegde had said in the back of my mind. He had seen me for over three decades, and yet he chose to speak the way he did. I was deeply hurt, but I did not react. God helped me in my resolve to focus on my work. That is when I decided to give special attention to Kashmir and the North-east. The two regions most misunderstood and under-represented. People in these regions had suffered and I decided to do something for them in my own humble way,' Gowda recalled.[5] To Hegde's statement on geography, Gowda's mental response was something like, 'You said I do not know the geography of India, but I will show the rest of India a forgotten piece of its geography.'

Gowda asked K. Padmanabhaiah, the home secretary, to brief him on each of the North-eastern states separately. He then established a protocol similar to the one he had in Kashmir. He decided to meet a broad spectrum of organizations and people without actually worrying about their backgrounds, orientation and disposition towards the Indian state. He asked governors of respective states to send out invitations. 'One day, in one state capital,' was a simple mantra he gave his officers.

I asked three officers to join me. Of course, Padmanabaiah was there. The other two were B.N. Yugandhar and Meenakshisundaram. I requested Montek Singh Ahluwalia to send one senior officer from the finance ministry. He sent an additional secretary-rank person. Sitting from morning till 8 p.m., with just an hour's break for lunch, we listened to various delegations that included local governments and elected representatives.

Each state had a different history, was uniquely diverse with multiple tribal affiliations, and some of them had joined the Indian state at different points after Independence. The whole thing was very complex. The one refrain that I got to hear from people who came to see me was how they felt like 'outsiders' in India and how nobody really understood them. How their language, their culture, their ethnicity and their religion was not sufficiently respected. I knew exactly what they meant because I felt the same way in Delhi. I repeated to all of them that they should not think that way and that I would sincerely try to solve their problems. We started and ended in Guwahati, where I held a press conference and announced a package to develop the region. The Central government was under financial stress, but I wanted to commit money to the region. Padmanabhaiah said, 'Sir, you have to take a bold decision, you know Chidambaram, he'll ask us, Where is the money?' I said all right, I'll announce a package at the Guwahati press meet and that would be binding on the government. I announced a Rs 6100 crore-package. It surprised the people of the North-east. I wanted them to know that I was a man of my word.[6]

Gowda had suspected some resistance or push back to the North-east package within the executive, but to his surprise, he found people cooperating:

We did not take it to the cabinet first. We decided ourselves, that is Chandran, Subramanian, Montek, Meenakshisundaram, Padmanabhaiah and Yugandhar. When there was consensus on the package, we decided Chandran and Subramanian should explain the implications of it to the cabinet. When we took it to the cabinet, to be frank, all ministers agreed. There was no difference of opinion. In fact there was appreciation. Nobody questioned the speed with which I was doing things. They did not think it was *adhika prasangatana* (a Kannada word to mock unnecessary or excessive reaction, as well as hyperactivity). Even Chidambaram said, 'We'll find a way out, sir.'

We started all works immediately. Chidambaram gave a very good suggestion. He said that we should have a monitoring cell for the North-east in the PMO, and one army helicopter should be kept at Guwahati airport so that we would achieve instant connectivity to the entire region for officers to review the progress of works. It was decided that every month, three officers from three departments should go there, review work, and send a detailed report to the PMO. Also, we decided that 5 per cent of funds in the general budget should be earmarked for the North-east exclusively. This was apart from the Rs 6100-crore package, which was a non-lapsable amount.

After I stepped down, Gujral went and increased the package by another hundred crores. Vajpayee, during his thirteen-month stint, added another Rs 500 crore to the package. Both did not tinker with my basic plan. They took it forward admirably.[7]

The Six-Day Sojourn

Gowda's six-day sojourn in the North-east was recorded in some detail by Jarnail Singh,[8] an officer who was part of the PMO under Gowda and three prime ministers who followed. According to him, the six-day tour meant the PM was staying away from Delhi for a week, and that was something unprecedented. Singh with G.K. Pillai, who was joint secretary in charge of the North-east, who later served as India's home secretary, worked on the minute-to-minute details of all meetings and events. They collected information on all ongoing and delayed projects in the states and the issues most likely to come up during the prime minister's meetings. As per Gowda's clear instruction, the tour was designed in such a way that it gave the prime minister adequate time to meet people and listen to them. He had done this earlier in Kashmir too.

Before the tour, there was a preparatory meeting chaired by the prime minister. In the meeting, while discussing matters relating to the increase of bank credit to the agriculture sector, the banking secretary informed the prime minister that banks were reluctant to lend to farmers in the North-east as they had huge unpaid outstanding loans. He quoted a relatively tiny figure of Rs 85 crore as the size of the loan default. 'I was sitting behind the prime minister and saw him getting very angry at the reasons given by the Secretary against increasing credit flow to farmers. In an angry tone, he pointed out that the banks had not stopped lending even after the fiasco of Indian Bank, which lent more than Rs 1200 crore to small corporates and exporters in south India and had already become Non-Performing Assets (NPAs). He turned to Mr Satish Chandran and expressed his unhappiness with the attitude of the

secretary banking towards the people of the North-eastern states
and asked him to be shifted out. However, due to heavy workload
for the preparation of the tour, I forgot to put up a note to the PM
about this and the secretary banking remained,' Singh recalled.[9] It
is unlikely that Gowda would have forgotten his instruction, but
it is very likely that Chandran would have convinced him against
it, and he would have let it be. 'The region has vast agriculture and
horticulture potential and credit flow to the farmers is essential
for expediting the tempo of economic development in rural and
hill areas. Moreover, generation of additional employment was
necessary to wean away the youth from militant activities, which
has plagued the region for decades,'[10] Singh added, justifying
Gowda's anger.

The tour started with Guwahati in Assam, generally referred
to as the gateway to the North-east. The second day, the PM
went to Tripura and stayed at Agartala. The third day was spent
at Aizawl in Mizoram where he had reached by helicopter. For the
seven kilometres from the helipad to the Raj Bhavan, people in
traditional attire were lined up all along the road through which
the prime minister's cavalcade passed. But Manipur, his next stop,
was a contrast. Militant groups there had called for a bandh, which
was usually the case when dignitaries visited from Delhi. Gowda
witnessed deserted roads from Imphal airport to the Raj Bhavan.[11]

Singh recounted an interesting episode from Imphal, which
indicated the nature of work pressure there was during the six-
day trip. The prime minister's accommodation was fixed in Raj
Bhavan, like in other state capitals. But, for others in the entourage,
arrangements were made at a hotel two kilometres away. But the
schedule demanded that senior staff stay back to assist the PM, and
there was little time to go to the hotel to freshen up:

Home Secretary Padmanabhaiah and I sat in the main central
drawing room of Raj Bhawan. We waited for about an hour,
but no one came to enquire if we required anything or even

offer refreshments. I could see the home secretary get very upset at the neglect by the Raj Bhawan personnel. He was sitting on the sofa with his legs crossed on the table in front.

Suddenly, Governor O.N. Srivastava came out of his room into the central waiting room. As soon as the home secretary saw the Governor, he said, 'Who has made you Governor? We are in the prime minister's entourage and there is no place to rest and wash ourselves and no refreshments also.' To this, the Governor replied, 'It is the duty of the state government to make arrangements for the prime minister's party. Raj Bhawan is neither responsible nor in charge of providing boarding and lodging to all persons in the PM's party. Please ask them.' The home secretary did not move his feet from the centre table as the Governor continued to stand. Padmanabhaiah's retort was sharp, 'It is the responsibility of the Governor and his office personnel to look after the prime minister's party as all meetings are scheduled only in the Raj Bhawan. The state government cannot provide refreshments in the Raj Bhawan; the Governor's office must do that. The Governor or his staff should have tied these up before the prime minister's visit rather than cut a sorry figure.'[12]

Next day, Gowda went to Kohima, Nagaland. The prime minister and his entourage kept a punishing schedule. They had to prepare actionable points and convey those to the appropriate government the same day. At the same time, the prime minister had to be briefed about his meetings and programmes for the following day. It was well past midnight when the officers were free.[13] After Kohima, they arrived at Itanagar in Arunachal Pradesh, where besides other meetings, Gowda engaged with engineers who were involved in building bridges and helping in the upgradation of the infrastructure in rural areas. Some of the professionals were from south India.[14] A recurring complaint in all states that Gowda went to was that foundation stones were laid by leaders in the 1980s, but funds had not been released. He visited Meghalaya on the last day of his tour, that was the sixth day. He had visited seven states.

After the Itanagar visit, Yugandhar got Singh and Pillai to work on a draft statement that the prime minister would make at his press conference in Guwahati before he left for Delhi: 'Mr Yugandhar gave us detailed instructions and stated that whatever should be announced at the press meet should be substantial and must be remembered in the coming years as the "Deve Gowda Mantra" for the development of the North-east,' Singh wrote.[15]

A final version of the press statement, which came back with many revisions from the prime minister himself and his top secretaries, Yugandhar and Padmanabhaiah, was handed over to the PM's personal secretary. In the rush, some pages were stapled upside down. This was corrected and stapled again, but unfortunately, the correct copy meant for the prime minister was passed on to railway minister Ram Vilas Paswan, who was part of the team, and Gowda got the one that was stapled wrong. However, Gowda did not lose his cool and read out some portions of the press statement.[16]

At the press conference, Gowda declared that he wanted to bridge the gap in the infrastructure development of the North-east and the rest of India. The PM's statement was titled 'New Initiatives for the North-eastern Region'. The best part was a strict timeframe was put in place for action under each point mentioned in the document. Gowda also spoke about how he intended to follow up on all that he had announced. He spoke of monthly reports from all seven states and a cell in the PMO to monitor it.[17] It was like moving a huge mountain, and Gowda knew where to place the levers.

'The new initiatives laid the foundation for expediting the development of the region. It continued as the guiding principle for development in the later years too, even after the addition of new schemes. The all-important fund called Non-Lapsable Central Pool of Resources (NLCPR), now the main resource available for funding infrastructure projects in the North-east region was created because of the guidelines laid down in the new initiatives even though the population of the North-east was less than 5 per cent of the population of the country, the land area is about 8 per cent of the total area of the country. It was B.N. Yugandhar's suggestion that at least 10 per cent of Central funds should be spent in the North-east to reduce infrastructural deficiencies in the region. Later in 1999, during the tenure of PM Vajpayee, when NLCPR was constituted, the same arguments and concepts as were enunciated by Deve Gowda were used. The then deputy chairman of the Planning Commission, Jaswant Singh, was the one who suggested the NLCPR for the North-east and PM Vajpayee approved the same,' Singh recounted.[18] Vajpayee had taken forward and formalized a plan that Gowda had conceived.

The setting up of a separate ministry of development of North-eastern region under Vajpayee also had its origins in the 27 October 1996 press statement of Gowda at Guwahati. Singh continued to serve in the PMO under not just Gujral, but also Vajpayee and Manmohan Singh. He added: 'Prime Minister Deve Gowda's visit had raised high expectations in the North-east. Former PM Narasimha Rao had visited the region only once, and that too up to Guwahati, during his five-year stint. There were sharp comparisons between the approaches of the two prime ministers towards the North-east . . . It would not be wrong to say that the initiative of PM Deve Gowda opened the door for the accelerated development of the North-east. It really became a "Deve Gowda Mantra" for the development of the North-east, as had been rightly suggested by Mr Yugandhar in Itanagar on 26 October 1996.'[19]

On the follow-up and initiatives, K. Padmanabhaiah wrote[20] that one of the first decisions taken was to upgrade the Guwahati airport, and to station one big helicopter permanently there so that the visiting officers could be ferried to and from various state capitals in the North-east. The visiting officers were merely required to intimate their travel schedule from Guwahati and to send in a request for the helicopter ride. 'A game-changer decision announced was that each of the Central ministries and departments must mandatorily earmark 10 per cent of their budget for spending in the North-east; that any unspent amount would not lapse at the end of the year but would go into a non-lapsable fund. The creation of the department and later the ministry of development of North-east (DONER) owes its origins to this decision . . . In a few days, the prime minister ensured that the Planning Commission appointed the Shukla Commission to identify all the infrastructural gaps, and assess the fund requirements to remove the gaps in a period of ten years, so that the North-east could be brought on par with the rest of the country. This was followed up in quick succession by announcing an industrial policy, an investment policy, and a credit policy for the North-east,' he wrote.[21]

Development over Emotion

Gowda did not play an emotional card of integrating the North-east with the rest of India at the press conference. He was not comfortable using that language. Therefore, his statement was a development action plan. Each state was named, and what his government desired to do was listed, and the statement, later printed by the home ministry and distributed as a booklet in the region, was sixteen pages long. However, Gowda expressed in Guwahati on 27 October 1996 what he felt after the exhausting six-day tour:

> My first visit to the seven states of the North-east has come to an end. To me, this has been a very moving experience. The warmth of the people here will bring me back. I came to the area to know the people, their aspirations, their problems, how they feel and what they think. I came with an open mind. I am going with pleasant memories and with a firm resolve to work with the people to mark a new beginning in the development of this region. Wherever I went, the people from different sections of society came and met me in larger numbers. They were friendly and frank in expressing their views, their desires,

their apprehensions and their hopes. The warmth which they extended throughout my visit has really overwhelmed me. I am fully convinced that the problems can be resolved if all of us work together and look ahead jointly towards a better future. I am thankful to the people for showing so much love and affection for me during the visit.[22]

Gowda also spoke about the range of his consultations during the six days and the potential the region holds:

I have also met at each capital a cross-section of people like leaders of political parties, chiefs of autonomous district councils, representatives of non-governmental organizations, student unions, women's associations, church leaders and the press; in addition to ministers, state government officials and officials of security forces, to get a first-hand account of the conditions in these states. The North-east region is endowed with abundant natural resources. In fact, Assam was at the forefront of the economic development of the country 100–500 years ago. It was a pioneering state and enterprising entrepreneurs invested in the development of tea plantations, oil, coal mining, forestry, railways and inland waterways. However, in recent years, investors have shunned these areas because some of these states turned inward-looking while others have been afflicted by militancy and terrorism. This has set in a vicious circle of terrorism, discouraging investments and economic development, leading to growing unemployment which in turn provided recruits to militancy. Today, there are no major industries or other economic activities which can absorb the educated unemployed. The only avenue for employment in almost all these states is government service. However, government service cannot absorb too many people. Also, too many people in government service only breeds inefficiency. The only way out of unemployment or

militancy is massive all-round economic development leading
to prosperity.[23]

Gowda did not brush aside the ethnic conflicts in the region, he
said: '(There is) the feeling of loss of identity among various ethnic
groups and the feeling that the Centre has been giving step-motherly
treatment to this region. These feelings may or may not be entirely
justified. But the feeling is certainly there. It would be our endeavour
to remove this feeling and to see that the basic infrastructure in this
region is developed to reach the standards in the rest of the country
in a specific time frame.'[24]

In fact, Gowda studied the provisions and the actual working
of the Illegal Immigrants Determination Tribunals Act 1983
(IMDT Act) and felt that it did not solve the problem of illegal
immigration in any way and that it was perhaps unconstitutional.
The All Assam Students' Union had petitioned him. In his press
conference, he announced that he would be taking steps to repeal the
IMDT Act. 'Unfortunately, his government did not last long enough
to do so. Ultimately the Act was repealed in 2005 after the Supreme
Court held that it was unconstitutional,' said Padmanabhaiah.[25]

Interestingly, the issue related to the IMDT Act came up
for discussion during the National Registry of Citizens (NRC)
controversy in 2019. The petitioner before the Supreme Court in
2005 was the same person who had petitioned Gowda—Sarbananda
Sonowal. In 2019, he had become the chief minister of Assam, but in
1996 he was the president of the All Assam Students' Union.

In his public interest litigation (PIL) petition, Sonowal contended
that the IMDT Act was wholly arbitrary and unreasonable and that
it discriminated against citizens in Assam, making it impossible to
detect and deport foreigners from Indian soil. The *Frontline* reported:

He argued that while the Foreigners Act, 1946, applied to all
foreigners throughout India, the IMDT Act, which was enacted
subsequently with the professed aim of making detection and
deportation of illegal migrants in Assam easier, had failed to

meet even the standards prescribed in the Foreigners Act. (In this case) the Supreme Court invoked Article 355 of the Constitution to strike down the IMDT Act that would have placed the burden upon the state in a foreigner's case. The court thus established a constitutional requirement that the burden would always lie on the individual to rebut the allegation that he/she was a foreigner. The court's rationale for doing so was that it would be difficult for the state to give an exact date of entry of a foreign national who had surreptitiously crossed the Indian border and that the court could not remain a mute spectator to the continuing influx of illegal migrants.[26]

The Shukla Commission

As soon as Deve Gowda returned to Delhi, the phrase 'specific time-frame' started playing on his mind. Given the political uncertainty he faced, he wanted works that he had promised to begin right away. He studied status reports regularly and gave his detailed feedback. One such status implementation report,[27] a PMO document, running to twenty-four pages, produced just after he demitted office, said that the new initiatives had seventy-one actionable points, including schemes and projects. The table read as follows:

Points/schemes on which action has been taken and work started and on-going schemes for which adequate funds have been provided for completion in time: 41.

Points/schemes on which action has been initiated and processing is to be completed in 1997–98 and funds provided in 1997–98: 22.

Projects/schemes not found feasible: 2.

Schemes for which feasibility study taken up: 2.

Schemes/points on which action has not been taken up: 4.

Total actionable points: 71.

The status report also said the estimated sum that was required to complete the projects was not Rs 6100 crore that Gowda had assured but Rs 7503.51 crore. This gap was filled up by Gujral and Vajpayee subsequently.

To ensure the long-term development interest of the North-east, Gowda, again, as promised in Guwahati, set up a high-level commission within a couple of weeks of his return under the chairmanship of S.P. Shukla, who was a member of the Planning Commission, and a former commerce and finance secretary to the Central government. Shukla had also been ambassador to General Agreement on Tariffs and Trade (GATT) in Geneva when Manmohan Singh was secretary-general of the South Commission there between 1987 and 1990. If the Guwahati press conference happened on 27 October, the Shukla Commission had its first formal meeting on 28 November 1996. The three members of the commission were also of great experience and eminence. It included B.G. Verghese, senior journalist and fellow of the Centre for Policy Research. He had published a book on the North-east earlier that year.[28] P.U. Sainghaka, the vice-chairman of the Mizoram Planning Board, and Jayanta Madhab, economist and chairman of the North Eastern Development Finance Corporation, were the two others. The team toured all the North-eastern states between 14 December 1996 and 9 February 1997 and produced a 150-page report on 7 March 1997 without a single day's delay over their mandated time. That was the speed at which things had moved under Gowda's watch. He seemed to be a man in a great hurry.

The terms of reference expected the Shukla Commission to critically examine the backlog with respect to Basic Minimum Services (BMS) in the seven North-eastern states, and critically examine the gaps in important sectors of infrastructure development in the North-eastern region, especially, in power, communication, railways, roads, education, agriculture, etc.[29]

The report began by speaking with humility about the complexity and enormity of the task: 'It would be simplistic to believe that development by itself can end insurgency and restore tranquility. Yet, it constitutes the most important element in that task and an effective entry point for dealing with complex problems of historical neglect, rapid transition and social change. The extraordinary ethno-geographic and bio-geographic diversity of the region precludes uniform solutions as different communities are at varying stages of growth . . . The regional economies are simple, heavily deficit and dependent on the rest of the country for many basic needs. All seven units are special category states whose development plans are almost entirely centrally financed on the basis of 90 per cent grant and 10 per cent loan.'[30]

Elucidating its policy frame, the report said that the commission sees its charter to secure elimination of backlogs in BMS, and infrastructure in the North-east not just incrementally but through a quantum leap. 'The prime minister's pronouncements clearly mandate this as a national priority,' it said.[31] Further on BMS, it said that the seven services (drinking water, primary health care, universal primary education, public housing, mid-day meal in primary schools, connectivity to all villages and habitations, streamlining public distribution) adumbrated by the conference of chief ministers in July 1996 lie at the heart of the nation's poverty alleviation programme. 'No surprise, therefore, that the prime minister should make the earliest possible fulfilment of BMS along with infrastructural development the pivot of its North-east Initiative. The promise is to invest with dignity the lives of our countrymen in the North-east,' the report elucidated.[32]

Finally, the Shukla Commission made an indicative outlay of Rs 93,619 crore of investment for various infrastructural development, and recommended Rs 27,391 crore for the seven states under the Ninth Five Year Plan, which included Rs 9396 crore for BMS. The report said: 'The amount may appear very large at first sight. But spread over five years and seen against a proposed Ninth Plan outlay of the order of Rs 8,75,000 crore, this degree of additionality is essentially modest.'[33]

Over twenty-three years after he had submitted the report, S.P. Shukla, then chairman of the commission, reflected. He said Gowda had his feet firmly on the ground: 'He did not put across things in a theoretical framework but knew exactly what India needed, and the problems faced by ordinary people. He conceived the BMS idea and got the Planning Commission to work out its details and allocate resources. He was not great at articulation but had a very refined knack of getting things done. The content of his approach was always sound. It greatly impressed me. Another thing that particularly impressed me was that he thought of geographical areas of India which were not in the mainstream, he was worried about them. Even when he constituted the commission, he was very thoughtful. One of our members, Sainghaka, was a former speaker of the Mizoram assembly, but more importantly, he had fought alongside Laldenga when he revolted against India and lost his son in the battle. Then, of course, Mizoram became a peaceful Indian state. The team was assembled by Gowda with such care, comprising people from inside and outside the region that it instantly reassured people that this would not be just another commission landing from Delhi and submitting a report that would gather dust. Gowda's six-day tour of the North-east had been such a success already. When the commission toured the seven states, ordinary people said that Gowda was the first prime minister who stayed overnight in their capital.'[34]

Shukla recalled his IAS training days: 'Deve Gowda being a man with his feet on the ground knew that going by helicopter or addressing a meeting and coming back to Delhi was different from staying in a place overnight. When we were young IAS officers, tour meant not visiting a place by day and returning by evening. It meant staying two or three nights. Then you know what difficulties people face, and you become part of that. This simple principle of administration Gowda had in his blood and veins. He knew these things instinctively. He had stayed with the people of the North-east for six days. It had not registered on many of us that he had done it, but it was the local people who kept emphasizing it. He had touched their hearts. They had committed it to their memory and underlined and repeated it to whoever spoke to them. That is when I realized that this gentleman had that earthy kind of a sense and knew how to get connected with people.'[35]

During the tenure of the commission, Gowda never once interfered:

He never asked how I was going about my job. He perhaps got an update from his sources. I was known to people like V.P. Singh and perhaps they spoke to him. He never said what I should prepare or put across in the report. When the report was ready, we wanted to present it to the prime minister in person. We asked for time from Satish Chandran, his principal secretary who was four years senior to me. Chandran looked at the schedule, and I don't know what influenced his mind when he said, 'Why do you want to meet him? Send it to me I will place it before him.' May be Gowda was busy. I don't know. I must confess, I felt a little disappointed by that response because we had done a whole lot of hard work. And I had a feeling that members in the commission from the North-east, especially Sainghaka, wanted to meet the prime minister. When Gowda had established a political and personal link with the North-eastern states, this was a small expectation. Instead of pursuing with Chandran, who did not realize what was at stake, I called H.K. Dua, the PM's press adviser. I told him what had transpired. Dua immediately caught the point. He said, 'Don't worry sir, I will organize a meeting.' He called me in half an hour and then said, 'he has given two slots of twenty minutes each, whichever slot you choose he will be available.'[36]

Shukla described the warmth of the meeting with Gowda: 'All of us trooped in and went to the PM's house. He came out immediately, shook hands, was very polite as usual. Like a good host, he made everybody comfortable and got us something to eat and drink. After that, in his own way, he grasped the contents and importance of the report. Again, he spoke not much through words, there was not much of articulation but spoke in a language of gestures and that was more powerful. It was very warm. He made the members feel that he knew them, and they had known him for ages. And then, he told us, "Whatever I can do I will do." He repeated the phrase multiple times. Not that he said much, but the way he said it had a deep impact on the members. The sincerity with which he responded and the body language was most memorable.'[37] One of the reasons Chandran was hesitant to arrange a meeting with the commission was perhaps he knew Gowda was under tremendous political pressure. He resigned at the end of April. The report was submitted in early March.

Shukla remembered what Madhu Dandavate, the deputy chairman of the Planning Commission, had said: 'Dandavate had a good opinion of Gowda. After Gowda was replaced by Gujral, who was suave and like any other bureaucrat, Dandavate always said that Gujral did not have a feel of India that Deve Gowda had. Gowda may not have had a knowledge of macroeconomics like Manmohan Singh, for that you can get any number of professors from Harvard. But Gowda was a good prime minister. He had his feet on the ground and knew how to respond to people and their problems. Our report went so well that in Assam they said it would be a Bible for the region's development.'[38]

The Naga Ceasefire

Gowda's North-east initiative had one other dimension. He not only initiated development and economic measures to erase the neglect of the region, but also honoured one other promise he had made in the October press meet in Guwahati. He had said: 'For too long, senseless violence has prevailed in some of the states of the North-east. For too long, certain misguided elements have been killing their brothers and fellow citizens and resorting to extortion and kidnapping. Violence cannot achieve any political objective. I would like to appeal to all those who have taken to the gun to see the path of reason. I believe that all problems can be solved by mutual discussions. I am giving an open invitation to any group of individuals, including militants, and without any pre-condition, to meet me to discuss their legitimate grievances. I genuinely wish to understand their points of view and what exactly is troubling them.'[39] In February 1997, just before reaching the Davos World Economic Summit, Gowda met Naga separatist leaders Isak Chishi Swu and Thuingaleng Muivah of the dominant National Socialist Council of Nagaland (Isak–Muivah) or NSCN (IM) faction, in the Swiss city of Zurich, 148 km from Davos. It was a top-secret meeting.

After 1991, with the fading away of the Naga National Council (NNC), the parent body, NSCN (IM) had come to be seen as the 'mother of all insurgencies' in the region. They had refused the Shillong Accord with the Indian government in November 1975 under which the NNC had agreed to give up arms and had formed NSCN in 1980. In 1988, they had split into NSCN (IM) and NSCN (K) after a violent clash, and the 'K' faction was led by S.S. Khaplang. The Naga separatists were demanding an independent Nagalim, comprising all contiguous Naga-inhabited areas, along with Nagaland. That included several districts of Assam, Arunachal and Manipur, as also large tracts of Myanmar. The map of Nagalim has about 1,20,000 sq. km., while the state of Nagaland consists of 16,527 sq. km.[40]

Gowda was not the first prime minister meeting Muivah and Swu after they had escaped to Thailand in the early 1990s. P.V. Narasimha Rao met them first in Paris on June 15, 1995, and his cabinet colleague Rajesh Pilot had followed up this meeting in Thailand.[41] Although constructive, these meetings had not produced a definite outcome, and that is where Gowda's meeting became important. The Zurich meeting was arranged by Satish Chandran, Gowda's principal secretary, and the two had travelled incognito in a private vehicle to a house in which the two Naga leaders were waiting.

All that Gowda would say about the meeting, which stretched for over two hours, is that the Naga leaders were willing to trust him and were hugely appreciative of his initiative. Gowda did not want to leave the room without an assurance; finally, they agreed to a ceasefire by the end of the meeting. That was a breakthrough. 'I was frank with them, and they seemed to like it. I said I will do everything in my power to help the Naga people. I also made it clear that I had no mandate to operate outside the Indian Constitution. We went through a lot of arguments back and forth. The fact that they agreed to give peace a chance was a positive step forward to a problem that had plagued us for decades. I did not go to that meeting thinking that I will arrive at a final agreement. I had told Chandran that I sincerely want to engage and talk with the Naga leaders and leave the rest to God. I had an open mind. The full credit of this secret meeting should go to Chandran. He had worked very hard to organize it,' Gowda recalled.[42] The ceasefire agreement that Gowda had negotiated was officially inked in July 1997, a couple of months after Gowda had stepped down as prime minister. It came to effect from 1 August 1997.

The ceasefire held good till March 2015 when NSCN (K) broke the agreement and killed eighteen army personnel in an ambush in Manipur. NSCN (K) had signed a separate ceasefire agreement in 2001. The government immediately declared NSCN (K) faction a terrorist organization under Unlawful Activities (Prevention) Act, 1967, but continued to talk to NSCN (IM).[43] In August 2015, the Narendra Modi government signed a framework agreement with the NSCN (IM). Before this agreement was signed, Gowda was consulted. The draft, too, was shown, but he did not reveal the suggestions he offered. However, he publicly hailed the signing of the agreement as a major achievement: 'This peace accord with Naga insurgent groups is one of the major decisions to bring peace in the North-eastern states in general, particularly Nagaland.'[44] Later, in July 2018, a parliamentary standing committee report quoted R.N. Ravi, the interlocutor for the Naga talks. It said that the agreement was a departure from the earlier position of 'with India, not within India', and that the government had called it a framework agreement and signed it.[45]

In August 2020, a delicate situation arose in the Naga peace talks when the NSCN (IM) demanded the removal of R. N. Ravi, the Indian government's interlocutor and co-author of the 2015 framework agreement. They accused him of having created an 'imbroglio' in the talks.[46] They also alleged that he had made a 'mockery' of the framework agreement. Ravi and NSCN (IM) had exchanged harsh words in Nagaland for a few months before this impasse was created. The Nagas had gone back to saying that Nagas will 'co-exist with India' but will not merge with India. They also said that they cannot give up the Naga flag and constitution.[47]

At this point, Gowda issued a statement, which demonstrated how deeply invested he was in the North-east and the Naga peace process. He spoke sagaciously and pleaded that the progress made in twenty-three years is not forsaken:

Newspaper reports indicate that the Union government's negotiations with NSCN (IM) to resolve the Naga problem has run into rough weather. From recent statements made by those involved in the negotiations, it is apparent that distrust has crept in. The Naga ceasefire agreement in 1997, which followed my meeting with Mr Isak Chishi Swu and Mr Thuingaleng Muivah in Zurich, in February 1997, was a result of constructive diplomacy. We should ensure that the progress made in the last twenty-three years by successive governments is not forsaken now. There is the Constitution and also the 2015 framework agreement, which should help us move towards a solution. I sincerely hope that distrust is put aside, talks continue, and a peace accord is reached at the earliest. The people of the North-east deserve to live in harmony and witness economic progress.[48]

Naga Hoho, the apex tribal body of the Nagas, immediately
welcomed Gowda's statement and acknowledged his statesmanship:
'The Naga Hoho appreciates the wisdom and understanding of
one of our former prime ministers, H.D. Deve Gowda, in his
recent appeal, asking all parties concerned to put aside distrust and
reach a settlement at the earliest. It was, in fact, the magnanimity
of Deve Gowda in reaching out to the Naga leaders in Zurich,
Switzerland in February 1997, which changed the course of the
Naga struggle from war to path of peace.' Naga Hoho president,
H.K. Zhimomi, and general secretary, K. Elu Ndang, had signed the
statement.[49] They also said Gowda's perseverance towards solving
the Indo-Naga political problem had assured once again that their
problem was 'political and not law and order' (that was a tangential
reference to R. N. Ravi's categorization of their struggle).[50] They
said Gowda gave hope to the Nagas and a reason to believe their
years of struggle would not end in vain.

The Bogibeel Bridge

Like Gowda never forgot the North-east, the people of the region
too never forgot him. When the Bogibeel bridge was inaugurated
by Modi in December 2018, locals pointed out that it was Gowda
who had sanctioned it and laid the foundation stone in January
1997. They said he should have been present when the bridge was
inaugurated. The Bogibeel bridge connected the south bank of
river Brahmaputra in Assam's Dibrugarh to Silapathar in Dhemaji
bordering Arunachal Pradesh. The 4.9 km-long bridge is the longest
rail-cum-road bridge in India and is the second-longest in Asia. The
bridge, besides cutting travel time between Assam and Arunachal
Pradesh, was expected to improve defence logistics along Arunachal
Pradesh's border with China and was strong enough to bear the
movement of military tanks.[51] Deve Gowda was 'disappointed' that
he had not been invited to the inauguration of the bridge. He had
impatiently remarked to the media, '*Aiyo rama*, who will remember

me',[52] but nevertheless, he went to see the bridge with an engineer's curiosity two months later, in February 2019. When he was there, he also prayed at the Kamakhya temple with an Assamese *gamosa* around his neck.[53]

That he watched the North-east closely, and that it never slipped away from his memory and prayers, and that he had never forgotten the affection he had received for those six days in October 1996 was evident when he wrote an anxious letter during the Assam floods in July 2020. The media in Delhi, and across the country, had chosen to ignore the natural disaster:

I am deeply disturbed by the reports of floods in Assam. The situation has been steadily worsening in the last few days. The latest reports I could access said that more than sixty people have died, nearly four million have been affected, and about 480 relief camps have already been set up. Large scale damage to public infrastructure has also been recorded. The death of over sixty animals at the Kaziranga National Park is saddening too. It is very unfortunate that the people of Assam have to battle the floods and the deaths and displacement caused by it when the COVID-19 pandemic is raging across the nation. They are fighting on two fronts. I appeal to the prime minister and the Central government to pay urgent attention to the situation emerging in Assam and offer maximum assistance to the state government. The people of Assam, and the people of the North-east in general, had blessed me and showered a lot of affection when I was prime minister, and later too. They will be in my prayers. After the pandemic abates, God willing, I will visit the state.[54]

Chief Minister Sarbananda Sonowal responded instantly, reassured him about the relief measures that had been taken up, and finally said: 'Respected Gowdajee . . . I again thank you for remembering us and for your kind gesture of solidarity towards

the flood affected people of Assam.'[55] Like his becoming prime
minister was accidental, Gowda's engagement with the North-east
was also accidental, but once he encountered his 'destiny', he was
steadfastly loyal to it.

17

City of Intrigues and the September Shifts

New Delhi, the city of intrigues, was as normal as it could be for Deve Gowda in the first few months that he was prime minister. As he had moved into the capital, he had developed a routine for himself. He would go to work at his South Block office in the morning by 10 a.m. and return home late, usually past 9 p.m. He did not party, did not have friends or flings or any other entertainment. That was how he was more or less as a politician for nearly forty years and that did not change after he became prime minister. His staple diet of ragi balls and a curry of lentils and mixed greens reached his office from home around 1.30 p.m. There would also be a small portion of rice and curd and a banana. He would not break for lunch but keep meeting officials and ministerial colleagues as he had his meal. He would get them something to snack or drink and listen to them as he ate. By the end of the meal, he would have developed clarity or arrived at a decision on the issue discussed. That would be considered one job done and one file less.[1]

After he got back to his 7 Race Course Road (RCR) residence in the evening, he would have dinner first and return to his corner to read files. He would just expect one personal assistant to be around to pack and unpack the files and take phone calls. Family issues would be discussed at the dining table when the husband and wife would review news from home—either from Hassan or Bangalore. That was some recharge and relaxation. The dinner appointment with the wife was never usually missed. She, too, had no friends or relatives in Delhi and spent all her time creating new pooja routines for the gods she wished to either pray to or propitiate. All of this was very similar to his time when he was a minister and chief minister. He would invariably wind up past midnight. The mornings began with coffee and newspapers, then bath and prayers. By 7 a.m., his official and political meetings would start. Somedays, he would get up an hour or two early to catch up on a book that he needed to read, and make margin notes, to help an idea circling his mind to take wings.[2] It was never fiction, never reading for leisure, but reading with a specific purpose. This book reading habit for some reason was never publicized. Perhaps it interfered with his carefully cultivated image of a 'humble farmer'.

What seemed to the rest a boring, punishing schedule was not so boring for Gowda because he had long embraced this monotony in his living. It is not that he had given up flamboyance at some stage and become spartan. It is just that he had never lived another life. When his early political life offered modest opportunity, he did not have the means to indulge in them, and his pride prevented him from being a freeloader at parties. There was also an element of conservatism and moral repulsion to the soirees his political friends organized. At one such New Year's Eve party in Delhi, perhaps in the 1970s, where he was accidentally present, a couple of senior colleagues had tried to take him down a certain route that would have caused inside him a permanent moral blemish. He was so shocked that he had upbraided his colleagues and left the party.[3]

Therefore, he knew nothing beyond work, prayer and politics. 'Wives of many political leaders have a problem tracking their husbands after 7 p.m., but there was never such a problem for Mrs Gowda. She knew her husband would go straight to work and come back straight home. In fact, the wife of a very senior Karnataka leader who had stayed back in Bangalore had made it a routine to call the personal assistant in the evening to find out who her husband was with that evening. If she was told that he was at an official meeting or an official reception, she would ask him not to lie, and then remonstrate about her pathetic life,' an aide who was familiar with those calls and enquiries recalled.[4]

Delhi, especially the Lutyens' power circuit, was organized for decades in a certain way, and Gowda, with no networks or media alliances, was a rank outsider.[5] He had almost invaded their habits, comfort and complacency. The established Lutyens elite and power brokers recognized nothing of Gowda—his working style, his dress, his food, his talk, his mannerisms or the reclusiveness of his devout wife. In Karnataka, what was never discussed about Gowda for forty years became news every day in Delhi. Not that Gowda cared much, but he was astonished that nobody was looking at the amount of work he was getting accomplished. He was projected as 'napping' when actually the wheels of the government had picked up pace. He had incorrectly assumed that it was only work that mattered and not appearances and glib talk.

Besides a set personal routine, politically and administratively too, within three months of becoming prime minister, Gowda had developed confidence that he could run the country. His stride had changed, and his tone had nearly drowned out the self-doubt of the initial weeks. He had by then developed his Kashmir agenda and was ready to roll out his North-east initiative. The budget had taken shape, and he had made his move to solve big issues like Narmada and Tehri. He had also stunned the Delhi establishment by putting in place a fine PMO and a committed cabinet. As a leader, he had become fully acceptable to his thirteen-party coalition, and the Left was happy that they had bet on him. As far as the Congress was concerned, P.V. Narasimha Rao still held its reins, and Gowda had an excellent rapport and a personal friendship with him. Everything seemed to have fallen in place quickly.

But things changed suddenly in the last week of September 1996 when Rao was forced out of his party role, and Sitaram Kesri, the treasurer of the party, was elevated as the Congress president. Rao had to step down on 23 September 1996 after a court had summoned him in a corruption case. A London-based pickle tycoon, Lakhubhai Pathak, had testified in court that he had paid a $100,000 bribe to godman Chandraswami to get access to Rao. Kesri was an old conspiratorial Congressman from Bihar who loved backroom games and was more mindful of his Pomeranians than the chair he sat on. He injected an element of uncertainty into the Gowda government as soon as he took over. Although Gowda met Kesri and congratulated him on his elevation, his dislike for the man, Gowda's officers and colleagues felt, was palpable from day one.[6] Kesri, after all, was not an endearing '*chacha*' (he was popularly referred to as 'chacha', meaning 'uncle').

Within four days of Gowda meeting him the first time over lunch for two hours, Kesri told Saifuddin Soz, who was about to join Gowda's cabinet, not to do so because he intended to withdraw support.[7] However, Gowda underestimated Kesri's vanity and recklessness. He could have managed him easily, perhaps, but Gowda's new shoots of confidence did not allow him to entertain such a thought. As soon as Kesri took over, the dynamics in the Congress party also started changing. All those who had left the party under Rao started returning. They included Madhavrao Scindia[8]—who was part of Gowda's United Front coalition till then—and veterans such as Arjun Singh, N.D. Tiwari and S. Bangarappa among others. This further cornered Rao, and he had to also give up the leadership of the Congress parliamentary party. That went to Sharad Pawar.

September Stocktaking

Gowda did not allow the changes in the Congress to consume him. Luckily as a politician, and like most successful politicians, political work, legislative work and executive work were all in different compartments for him. Although not watertight, they allowed him relative peace to pursue each in a different manner. His job at the helm was to achieve perfect synchronicity between the three, and for a small period, it appeared there was.

In the same September month that Congress saw changes, Gowda gave financial closure to the long-pending Delhi Metro project, something for which he has never been credited. He held charge of the urban development portfolio and it was at his insistence, with one half-day session at the 7 RCR and two cabinet meetings, that the project, which eventually changed the face of Delhi, was given financial closure.

The concept of the metro for the capital was first mooted in 1969. In 1989, a techno-economic feasibility study was commissioned. Based on that report, an in-principle approval was given, and also a detailed report was further commissioned. The Delhi Metro Rail Corporation was set up in May 1995 with the federal government and local Delhi government holding 50 per cent equity each, but since high capital costs were involved, and recurring losses in its operation and maintenance were projected, no budgetary allocation was made. It was seen as financially unviable. Gowda took over from there.[9]

At the first cabinet meeting, when the topic came up, the urban development ministry was asked to recheck and update all the figures mentioned in the project report thoroughly. After this, to clear himself of doubts, Gowda organized a session at his 7 RCR home–office, to which the Lieutenant Governor of Delhi, the chief minister of Delhi, cabinet ministers and senior officials were invited. The then urban development secretary, N.P. Singh, made an elaborate presentation, which convinced Gowda that the time for the project had come. He asked for it to be brought before the Union cabinet for clearance. In the cabinet meeting, Finance Minister P. Chidambaram and the expenditure secretary expressed reservations on the grounds that the project had only 3 per cent internal rate of return (IRR) and lacked consequent commercial viability. The finance minister also mentioned that he had reservations regarding the grant of income tax exemption to the proposed Delhi Metro Rail Corporation since such a tax would become payable by the corporation only in years in which that company made profits. But Gowda argued that Delhi urgently required a rail-based mass transit system to handle its fast-increasing volumes of traffic and that the losses during the operational phase could be shared by the Centre and the local Delhi government.[10] He also argued that 'plans of economic viability cannot always be fully imagined in advance as the project would unleash new dynamics. It would expand the economic possibilities of the entire city to such an extent that the investment made in the project would look very small in the years to come'.[11] The 55.3-km-long phase one of the metro rail project, which included 11 km of underground line, at a cost of Rs 4860 crore was cleared.

By September, Gowda had also developed a reputation for dealing with problems directly, however big or small. The farmers started protesting about their unpaid sugarcane minimum support price (MSP) arrears, which had climbed up to Rs 1368 crore. Uttar Pradesh farmers alone were to receive Rs 860 crore. He gathered the representatives of protesting farmers, owners of sugarcane factories and officials in a room. He listened to them for two hours and offered suggestions with a carrot-and-stick policy, where the carrot appeared small, and the stick looked bigger. He set a thirty-day deadline and said, if they do not comply, stringent legal action and penalties would be imposed. That was not a vague threat. He listed all the legal actions and specific sections of the law that he could invoke. He said, 'You can take notes and check with your lawyer friends.' The factory owners scrambled to repay dues when they realized he meant business. For days, officials present in the meeting had regaled their peers and juniors with how the prime minister had handled the factory owners and officials who had stood by them.[12] The fact that he knew the law and that he was somewhat litigious had its advantages in administration. He could not be taken for a ride.

Similarly, in October, there was a serious crisis caused by the outbreak of cerebral malaria in the Nuh sub-division of Mewat district in Haryana. Nearly 18,000 people were affected and 960 were reported dead. The situation had slid out of the control of local officials. When the issue was raised in the Rajya Sabha, Gowda assured that he will attend to it personally. He immediately took an air force helicopter and reached ground zero. The state health minister to chief minister to Governor who had never visited the place were now forced, by protocol, to be there when the prime minister arrived.[13] He walked into the hospital and saw patients, especially women and children, lying all over on the floor. 'Three helicopters landed. There was the prime minister in one of them, and officials in the other two. He held four separate meetings with public health officials, engineers, local media, and the political leadership. In a couple of hours, he absorbed everything, came out and directly announced a step-by-step action plan of the government,' former union health secretary Sailaja Chandra recalled in an interview.[14] He also put a nodal officer of the Union government to coordinate efforts, released funds immediately, and returned to Delhi. The next day, he briefed the house on what he had done.[15]

It was this confidence and control that played out when industrialist Rahul Bajaj led a business delegation to meet Gowda and oppose the minimum alternate tax (MAT) that had been imposed in the first budget of his government. The thinking behind this tax was to ensure that over 1500 companies who paid zero tax begin making a contribution. Some of the nation's top private and public sector companies were astonishingly zero-tax companies, and MAT targeted to raise Rs 1000 crore additional revenue. When the delegation met Gowda, Bajaj in his 'usual brash manner' tried to educate the prime minister. He suggested that Gowda did not understand how the industry works and that he should roll back the tax. Gowda was patient until Bajaj had finished. He then opened the drawer of his table and took out papers of Bajaj's companies, and started pointing out the profits they had made. He argued that MAT would only be a very tiny fraction of that profit. Gowda was never underprepared: 'Perhaps Bajaj did not like what transpired that day, but I have always admired his forthrightness. After that, whenever we ran into each other at social functions, he has avoided me,' Gowda recalled.[16]

The Gowda government was becoming a government of many firsts. As Cabinet Secretary T.S.R. Subramanian pointed out in his book,[17] three progressive legislations—the Right to Information Bill (RTI), the Lok Pal Bill and the Women's Reservation Bill— took significant shape in the Gowda cabinet. While the women's reservation was an idea that Gowda had pursued as a chief minister (see the chapter on Gowda as chief minister), for the RTI, which was promised in the Common Minimum Programme of the ruling coalition, Gowda set up a working group under activist H.D. Shourie and included legal luminary Soli Sorabjee in the group. The Lok Pal (citizen's ombudsman) was an idea mooted by the Santanam Committee in 1962, and Shanti Bhushan had tried to take it forward as law minister in the late 1970s, but Gowda recast it a little. Knowing fully well what Ramakrishna Hegde had done with the Lokayukta Act in Karnataka, where he had first included the chief minister's office under the law and then quietly amended it out, Gowda readily offered to put the prime minister's office for scrutiny in the Bill. The cabinet approved the bill on 9 September 1996. Unfortunately, the Gujral government that came next could not see through any of these progressive legislations. All these three bills came to define the politics of the first fifteen years of the new millennium in India.

The September month also saw Gowda nurture a secret ambition to explore and develop a political constituency. An idea had germinated in his mind that he could consolidate his unique position as a farmers' prime minister to bring the peasant and pastoral communities across India together—the Jats, the Gurjars in north Indian states, the Reddys and the Bunts in south Indian states, the peasants among the Sikhs, and his own Vokkaliga community besides many others.[18] In his very Kannada imagination, it must have been something like 'Vokkaligas of the world unite'. He had already been hailed as the 'Charan Singh of the south' by Mahendra Singh Tikait[19] after he had sorted out the woes of sugarcane farmers, and the farmers of Punjab who were elated with his first budget had named a paddy variety after him (see the chapter on Gowdanomics). At a Meerut rally in September 1996, he had also spoken about a 'Kisan Raj'. He had appealed: 'Show your strength and political awareness and take a pledge not to allow this government to fall, for this is the first time that Kisan Raj has come to power at the Centre.'[20] He had made efforts to bring Tikait to the Rajya Sabha and also Ajit Singh, Charan Singh's son, into the United Front orbit.[21]

Gowda delivering the Independence Day address from the ramparts of the Red Fort, in Hindi, on 15 August 1996, was perhaps part of his Hindi heartland political plan. His efforts to learn Hindi (he had hired Brij Mohan Mishra as his tutor) was not about surrendering to the north Indian hegemony, but to be able to signal and communicate with the peasant class and castes in the north of India. Even when it came to Kannada, Gowda was never a chauvinist. Kannada was the language he had been born into, it was his default language of communication, but it was never central for his political mobilization. In fact, language nationalism in Karnataka is very different from the one in the neighbouring state of Tamil Nadu, but that is a separate discussion.

Gowda knew that English, which had become his link tongue in Delhi, would electorally fetch him nothing, although he had a decent command over it. As P. Chidambaram said (see the chapter on Gowdanomics): 'He was not interested in making English speeches at various gatherings. But he spoke perfect English.' In his book *The Idea of India*, Sunil Khilnani refers to Gowda's Independence Day Hindi moment in the opening lines of his opening chapter and says that Gowda was the 'first Indian prime minister to speak neither Hindi nor English'.[22] That was a half-truth projected by an anglophone intelligentsia[23] not fully conversant with Gowda's political and parliamentary work. He may not have spoken the

English language like the English, but there are many Englishes[24] spoken with reasonable mother tongue influence in the former colonies.[25] Gowda was certainly not a business process outsourcing (BPO) executive handling the phone calls of the world in a tutored standard accent.

The idea or utopia of the political mobilization of peasants did not take any concrete shape because Gowda did not stay long enough at the top to nurture it. For this reason, his Uttar Pradesh political agenda was so close to his heart that it even brought him sometimes in conflict with his home minister, Indrajit Gupta, who was overruled on many issues, including the appointment of Romesh Bhandari as UP Governor.[26] His focus on Uttar Pradesh also made his Defence Minister Mulayam Singh Yadav jittery at times. In his reply to the debate on the confidence vote in the Parliament on 11 April 1997, he said he had held sixty-six meetings as prime minister in connection with Uttar Pradesh. By this he meant, he was either physically present in the state to conduct these meetings or was dealing with an issue connected with the state.

CBI Cases and a Don Quixote

When work was happening at a feverish pace in September, and Gowda was growing in confidence at his job, there was somebody else too who was getting confident. It was the new Central Bureau of Investigations (CBI) director, Joginder Singh. He had been appointed a month ago and had already made headlines for all the wrong reasons. Within three days of his appointment, he had met P.V. Narasimha Rao for thirty minutes at his 9 Motilal Nehru Marg residence. When the media asked why he had met Rao, an accused who was being investigated, he nonchalantly said that he was seeking 'blessings and guidance to run the organization'. That was unbecoming of a head of an autonomous investigating agency who reported directly to the prime minister. When the Supreme Court ticked him off on his meeting with Rao, he said, 'I will be a recluse hereafter.'[27]

Singh was seen at all kinds of places, including at high society parties. The *Sunday* magazine wrote: 'It was the last place you could have expected to find the CBI chief. Publisher Nari Hira's party to launch the *Fashion* magazine was just warming up. Sylph-like maidens were nibbling at carrot sticks. Outrageous outfits drew envious sighs. Society ladies preened as they kissed the air above each other's cheeks while covertly examining their rivals' clothes . . . The CBI's newest chief, Joginder Singh, watched all this entranced. Clutching a glass of Campa Cola, he stared glassily into video cameras, and smiled and nodded at the other celebrities at the party.'[28]

It did not take long for Gowda to realize that he had made a terrible mistake with the appointment of the CBI director. He had overruled the advice from his very wise principal secretary, T.R. Satish Chandran. Gowda, who was usually cautious with appointments, had become casual with this one, or was it really so? Or was it a convenient thing to put in a weaker person to have greater control over the investigating agency? Or was he accepting the recommendation of his party colleague P.G.R. Sindhia, Karnataka's home minister because Joginder Singh was a Sikh IPS officer (Karnataka cadre, 1961 batch) who could converse with him in Kannada? Did Gowda think that a man in a turban would generate the right optics in Delhi circles, yet at the same time would add to his comfort level?

Whatever his calculations may have been, for Gowda's bad luck Joginder Singh turned out to be someone who could be both Cervantes' knight Don Quixote as well as his sidekick Sancho Panza. He could lead a charge and also follow a lead to its ridiculous depths. He could be doubly delusional at times. Therefore, the media kept wondering if he was a supersleuth with an unorthodox working style or a bumbling flatfoot?[29] Singh had not done serious policing duties for a stretch, nor had he worked in the investigation or intelligence wings. For a very short duration, he had been superintendent of police in Karnataka's Bidar district, but the rest of the time had been spent in unrelated departments like youth services, commerce ministry, etc. As Gowda's joint secretary, Meenakshisundaram, recalled in the chapter on the PMO, Joginder Singh was not a corrupt person, but a warm, good fellow. However, he was very talkative, liked being in the news, was inexperienced, and a bad fit for the CBI director's job. He went on creating casualties and consequences for Gowda and the government. Joginder Singh had rebutted the insinuations that he was 'inexperienced'. He had written that none had taken note that he had already worked as a superintendent of police in the CBI in the early 1970s; that he had been posted in Punjab and Kashmir as part of the Central Reserve Police Force and had also served in the Narcotics Control Bureau and the Indo–Tibetan Border Police.[30] Whatever, Gowda admitted that appointing Joginder Singh was the 'gravest mistake' of his premiership.[31]

The CBI at that juncture was handling sensitive cases and it involved people who were central to the survival of the Gowda government. The Lakhubhai Pathak bribery case as well as the Jharkhand Mukti Morcha bribery case against Congress president P.V. Narasimha Rao had become a spectacle. The fodder case against Janata Dal national president Lalu Prasad Yadav was gathering storm, and the Bofors case against Rajiv Gandhi was simmering. To be fair to Joginder Singh, all these cases were being closely monitored by the courts, including the Supreme Court of India. In 1996, the Supreme Court and various High Courts had entrusted 202 cases to the CBI for investigation. Patna High Court was monitoring the investigation of forty-four cases registered in 1996 with regard to the siphoning of Rs 950 crores in Bihar, otherwise referred to as the fodder scam.[32] Joginder Singh could not have strayed too much to please his political masters in any of these cases. His steps and missteps were being watched but it was his method and modus operandi that was louder than his work. However, the one case that nearly sealed the fate of the Gowda government—the re-opening of the murder case against Sitaram Kesri had nothing to do with Joginder Singh. It was handled by the Delhi Police and had its roots in the Congress party's factional rivalry. We will get there in a while.

Gowda had nothing to do with the Narasimha Rao case, it pre-dated him as prime minister. In this case, Gowda's natural instinct would have been to help Rao, but Joginder Singh had suddenly assumed an air of quixotic autonomy. He wrote about the 'urgent summons' he once received from Gowda on 23 March 1997:

Deve Gowda gave me a hand-written slip from Gujral which read, 'Yesterday, I met Mr P.V. Narasimha Rao. He was complaining that the CBI is not helping him in the JMM bribery case.' The burden of Gujral's note and the telephonic conversation, which he had with Mr Deve Gowda in my presence, was that CBI should file an affidavit saying that Shailendra Mahato, a self-confessed accused, who had made a confession before the judicial officer, was an unreliable witness. I explained this could not be done . . . Why should the CBI weaken its case . . . Mr Gowda informed Gujral about my views on telephone in my presence . . . Mr Deve Gowda never crossed the sacred line of *Lakshman Rekha* to save anybody . . . Later, when I met Mr Deve Gowda, in the first week of November 1997 I requested him to give the original or at least a photocopy of the note sent by Gujral for bailing out Narasimha Rao. He did not give it. [By November both Gowda and Singh had stepped down from their respective roles.][33]

Singh wrote of an earlier encounter with Gowda with regard to the JMM case:

When the JMM case was being monitored by Delhi High Court, an allegation had been made that during the no-confidence motion against the Narasimha Rao government, Mr Deve Gowda had voted for the Congress party. It was also alleged that as a consideration, his daughter-in-law was allotted a petrol pump in Bangalore. I felt that it was not good to leave the allegation unverified. So, I broached the topic before him at the first opportunity. Without a hint of anger, Mr Deve Gowda confirmed by citing the Lok Sabha proceedings that he had voted against the government. He said that his daughter-in-law had applied for the petrol pump in 1990 and the allotment came in the normal course only in December 1994. His clarification was in contrast to so many other influential people who refused to be questioned by the CBI . . . As the allegation was not part of the case, so no case dairy [sic] was written, but I apprised the investigating team that I had personally questioned the prime minister on this issue. I also reprimanded them that they should maintain their records well and should know who had voted for the government and who had not.

Singh was factually inaccurate here. According to the Lok Sabha records, Gowda's name was neither on the 'Ayes' list nor on the 'Noes' list, which means he was among the 112 who abstained. The abstentions list is not available.[34]

Gowda had little or no interest in the Bofors case. It had hit the headlines in 1987, but a case had been registered with the CBI only in January 1990 after V.P. Singh had become prime minister. Gowda had good memories of his relationship with Rajiv Gandhi, and Sonia Gandhi was not in the political arena at the time. He had enough political sense to not meddle with it. But in this high-profile case, Joginder Singh planted himself in to possibly make a professional mark. He wrote later that his 'chance' to actively pursue the case came when he had met the Swiss Interpol chief Rudolf Wyss at the sixty-fifth general assembly session of Interpol at Antulya [sic] [Antalya, Turkey]. Wyss had told him that he expected the Switzerland court to issue the necessary orders to hand over the case documents before the end of the year and that he would telephone Singh as soon as he got the orders.

The Swiss chief telephoned him on 22 January 1997, and Singh left for Berne via Zurich. After he received the box of documents at a simple ceremony through the Indian ambassador in Switzerland, K.P. Balakrishnan, he opened the box to find that the Swiss had retained the originals and given only unattested photocopies of the documents. He got each page of the documents attested and then hit upon an idea that could only match the genius of a Quixote: 'I was aware that there was a real danger to me and the documents which I was carrying. So, I did the simple trick of removing the documents from the carton. The documents were given to Mr Dubey, the joint director of the CBI who had accompanied me along with Javed Choudhry . . . He travelled in the club class while in the first class I carried the empty box flaunting the impressive label—Documents of AB Bofors Case.'[35] When they landed in Delhi, Singh dangled the empty box to the waiting media and patiently got himself photographed and videographed. That was his neatly arranged moment under the sun. Gowda was so upset with Singh speaking conclusively and hastily about the Bofors documents to the media, that he gave him a good dressing down.[36]

As regards Lalu Prasad Yadav's fodder case, Joginder Singh wrote that C.P. Verma, a minister in the Deve Gowda government, had been questioned by the CBI:

Mr Deve Gowda had remonstrated and observed that I had not taken his permission for questioning a minister in his government. I told him that the law does not require us to take any permission to question a witness or an accused. None was needed and so none was requested for. He was not very pleased by my reply. But he understood me better than anybody and let the matter rest at that. In the meantime, the draft charge sheet had been received in the office of the director, CBI, for approval. By this time, Gujral had taken over as the prime minister. [The CBI filed the chargesheet in June 1997, and it led to the resignation of Lalu Yadav as chief minister and his arrest.][37]

While all through Joginder Singh gives the benefit of the doubt to
Deve Gowda, he is scathing about Gujral and elaborately lists his
brazen efforts to save Lalu Prasad Yadav. Once, Singh apparently said
that he could not allow himself 'to be used' to save Gujral's chair.
Gujral, however, stealthily effected Singh's transfer in June 1997
while he was away in Lyons, France attending an Interpol meeting.
Singh was very bitter about Gujral, and in his assessment of the two
prime ministers he served, he wrote: 'Anybody can tell there was a
world of difference between the two prime ministers. One was plain
and straightforward. He would encourage you to put your point
of view. He would stand by you and never stab you in the back.
The other was scheming and very shrewd and his sole object was to
survive at any cost, not caring for any damned principle.'[38]

Gowda narrated the pressure there was on him in the
fodder case:

> Some people played on Lalu Yadav's mind, and I suspect it
> was Bommai, Hegde and an additional solicitor-general who
> was close to Hegde. They had convinced him that if the prime
> minister made up his mind, his troubles would go away. He
> once came to my residence past midnight. I had retired for the
> day, but the security woke me up. They had tried to convince
> him to come back in the morning, but he was unrelenting.
> Since he was a senior colleague, I came out to meet him.
> He was agitated but still hugged me and said that I should
> do something about the fodder case. He said the water level
> with the cases had been rising for him, and he could soon be
> drowned. I explained the reality to him. Since the cases were
> being monitored by the Supreme Court, I said, I was powerless.
> I reminded him that Justice J.S. Verma, who was monitoring
> the cases, was very strict and would not brook any interference.
>
> But Lalu would not listen. I pacified him and told him we
> could meet in the morning and discuss the matter with attorney
> general Ashok Desai. In the morning, Desai explained in greater

detail the judicial implications and what would happen if the prime minister intervened. He said the court could even pass strictures against the prime minister. Lalu bargained. He said at least transfer two officials handling the case. I was reluctant because I knew the Supreme Court would stay the order. But my Principal Secretary Satish Chandran said, 'Let us issue it, sir. Let them be told by the court.' As expected, the court stayed the order. I honestly wanted to help Lalu, but my hands were tied. When institutions act independently, even the prime minister with all his powers cannot alter the circumstances. That is what happened in the Lalu case.[39]

After this, Lalu Yadav became so upset with Gowda that he went around telling people that he had done nothing to save his political career while he had made Gowda prime minister. During that period, when he ran into B.L. Shankar, Gowda's parliamentary secretary, he fumed in Hindi: '*Aapka Gowda kisan nahin, kala saanp hain* (Your Gowda is not a peasant, but a poisonous snake).'[40]

The Kesri Blow-Up

The troubles that started in September 1996 for Gowda grew and deepened in the next few months. Sitaram Kesri had only been made the provisional president of the Congress party and plans were afoot for the organizational elections. Gowda and his government got pulled into the ambition of individuals in the Congress, especially people who aspired to contest against Kesri, specifically Rajesh Pilot and Sharad Pawar. With members of the Nehru–Gandhi dynasty sitting out of the elections, senior Congressmen were aligning in different possible ways, and each was trying to see how the Gowda government that they supported could help them capture power. In one such move, Rajesh Pilot, who was familiar with Deve Gowda since Rajiv Gandhi's days, met him at his residence and made a strange request. He spoke about a three-year old murder case against

Kesri and asked if it could be reopened. He was referring to the case related to Surendra Tanwar, a medical officer at a Central government dispensary who was also Kesri's personal physician.

In October 1993, Tanwar was abducted, and a police case was registered. A few days later, his dismembered body was found in a bag in south Delhi. The probe had not yielded any results, and therefore the case had been closed. Pilot did not just orally recount the murder story to Gowda but actually left a written note with him on the case. Gowda claimed he had destroyed the note after Pilot had left as he did not want its toxic content to fall into the wrong hands.[41] But much to Gowda's dismay, a news item appeared in an English daily three to four days later that Gowda had agreed to open the murder case against Kesri. This was pure mischief. (Gowda mentions this letter in his farewell address as prime minister to Parliament in the presence of Rajesh Pilot but stops short of going into details.)

Soon after the news item appeared, a petition was filed in a Delhi court demanding a probe into Kesri's role. The wife of the victim, too, had come out in the open to make statements against Kesri. All this led to the Delhi Police questioning Kesri. The questioning was nothing but heaping humiliation on Kesri in which insinuations were made about Kesri's relationship with the murdered doctor. Although Gowda explains this as an event and investigation unconnected with his government, people who were then in the inner circle of Gowda say that he was not so neutral after all. They point to the sudden change of the Delhi Police commissioner in the dying moments of the Gowda government.[42] Nikhil Kumar, who came from a prominent Bihar political family, was replaced by T.R. Kakkar. Since Kesri was emotionally piqued, no reason and logic could alter the trajectory of his impulsive actions after this. The dismantling of the Gowda government had quietly begun in Kesri's mind with or without allies. The political talk in Delhi was that Kesri could be arrested anytime. 'Fear crept into Kesri. He stopped moving around alone and stopped being easily available out of fear that he may be picked up. Many in the Congress, of course, enjoyed this game and would joke about it,' Shankar recalled.

Meanwhile, there was talk in Delhi's political circles that Gowda was attempting to split the Congress with the help of Sharad Pawar. According to B.L. Shankar, the talk was that Pawar would come out with seventy-three MPs and split the Congress: 'This was a one-sided political game. All the risk was stacked up against Gowda and his government. There was no risk for Pawar. Gowda was, and is, extremely sharp with his political calculations, but one does not know why he allowed these rumours to gain ground and a lopsided situation to develop. We do not know what conversations he had had and what cards he held close to his chest.'[43]

Gowda frequenting P.V. Narasimha Rao was also something that irritated many in the Congress and, more particularly, Kesri. He would openly tell people like Shankar that Gowda was making a mistake. 'I would report this back to Gowda, but he underestimated Kesri. He thought he was not the one who controlled the levers of the party,' Shankar recalled.[44] There was a faction of the Congress party close to the dynasty, meaning Sonia Gandhi, which too did not like Gowda pursuing a warm relationship with Rao. When Kesri did withdraw the Congress party's support to the Gowda government, Congress strategists like Ghulam Nabi Azad openly said: 'The feeling that Deve Gowda was consulting his predecessor irritated Kesriji.'[45] Shankar confirmed that Gowda used to visit Rao almost every week, and this rattled Kesri. 'The Congress, which was slowly distancing itself from Rao, did not like it. It was seen as a south Indian conspiracy to split the Congress,' Shankar remembered. Some people in the Gowda cabinet, like P. Chidambaram, felt that Gowda had made the same mistake as Rao opening cases from L.K. Advani to Madhavrao Scindia. They felt Gowda had been egged on by Joginder Singh.[46]

There was yet another complication related to Kesri in January 1997, and this had to do with Ashok Jain the proprietor of the *Times of India* group who was charged with Foreign Exchange Regulations Act (FERA) violations by the Enforcement Directorate (ED). The ED charge had nothing to do with the Gowda government.

It was based on a judgment by Justice B.M. Mitra of the Calcutta High Court, in October 1996. The case was a twenty-four-year-old dispute between Ashok Jain and N.S. Hoon, an NRI businessman. It was related to the control of Turner Morrison, a formerly British-owned holding company. Hoon had alleged that Jain had illegally grabbed the company and violated FERA provisions in the process.[47]

On 4 January 1997, when Ashok Jain was leaving for a cardiac surgery in Cleveland in the United States, the ED stopped him from boarding the plane. Revenue Secretary N.K. Singh had tried to reason out with the ED director, but by then, Gowda had received a call from one of *Times of India*'s senior editors, M.D. Nalapat, whom he knew from the days he was stationed in Bangalore. Unaware of the court orders and the fact that the ED raids were in progress, in usual style, Gowda picked up the phone, spoke to ED officials, and asked them to allow Jain to proceed for his treatment.[48]

Gowda had felt there was a fuller investigation needed to apprehend him.[49] The next day, N.K. Singh, who met Gowda, said that he should not have intervened as the ED had recorded his intervention, and it may complicate matters in the courts later. Gowda then tried to reverse his order by asking officials to put Jain back into a plane as soon as he touched down in the US. He realized that if he left the airport, it would be difficult to get him back as legal procedures would be lengthy. 'It was only after this incident that I learnt that Sitaram Kesri was a family-retainer of the Jains,' Gowda recalled. He also added that after this incident, the sons of Ashok Jain had met him and spoken harshly. 'I had to stop them and remind them that they were speaking to the prime minister of India.'[50]

In an interview to both *India Today* and *Outlook* in July 1997, Ashok Jain had admitted that 'Kesri knew his parents, who helped him in his early political career. His son, Amarnath Kesri, was employed in one of our companies till November 1991.'[51] He had also admitted in the interview that his family had contacted one of *Times of India*'s senior editors, 'who got in touch with Deve Gowda after which I was allowed to go. The raid was not in progress when

I was stopped at the airport. It was over earlier, at 10.15 p.m.' Later, investigators had unearthed more embarrassing details from Kesri's past. The *Free Press Journal* wrote:[52]

> While *The Times of India*'s owner, Ashok Jain, is facing flak in a couple of hawala cases, his younger brother, Alok, is being investigated for having allegedly salted away a small fortune in secret bank accounts abroad. Investigators hit pay dirt when they found that Alok Jain had opened an account in the name of Kesri in a London branch of a well-known western bank. Worse, the application for the said account was signed by Kesri in his own hand. The initial amount deposited at the time of opening of the account was Sterling Pounds 10,000. Kesri's connections with the Jains go back to the time in the '50s and '60s when the Jain-owned Rohtas Industries was Bihar's largest industrial unit. Kesri was a low-paid factotum of the Jains before he wandered into politics and made "good" for himself and his old masters.

After Gujral had taken over as prime minister, Atal Bihari Vajpayee had alleged that he was shielding Ashok Jain because he was the prime minister's relative. Ashok Jain's daughter was married to Gujral's nephew.[53] The complex web of kinship and business relationships at the time formed political currents that upturned the Gowda government.

More than a year later, in an interview to Prem Panicker of Rediff, George Fernandes wove a candid picture behind Delhi's thick curtains of intrigue: 'Let's not mince words—the Deve Gowda government fell for no reasons other than Sitaram Kesri's 40-year-old relationship with Ashok Jain of *The Times of India*. Kesri, in fact, was on the board of directors of one of the group companies as far back as 1967. Deve Gowda refused to oblige the Kesri–Jain combine on several issues—*hawala,* the receipt of foreign funding by the Congress, the Congress party's funds in foreign countries, Kesri's own funds abroad . . . And, of course, the *chacha–bhatija* relationship between Kesri and Laloo Yadav meant that Kesri sought Deve Gowda's intervention when Laloo was in trouble and Deve Gowda told him (Kesri) to go to hell. So Deve Gowda had to fall. It was that simple.'[54]

On Gujral, who replaced Deve Gowda, he said: 'Well, first, why did Gujral become PM? By virtue of the fact that he is related by marriage to Ashok Jain. Jain's son is married to Gujral's sister's daughter, Gujral's sister's son is married to Jain's daughter. So, it was all nicely in the family. An acceptable candidate for Ashok Jain, so Kesri used his party's muscle to push his candidature through.'[55]

The Endgame

Srikant Kumar Jena, who was a proximate witness to the dismantling of the Gowda government and also the parliamentary affairs minister, offered his diagnosis: 'The great mistake that Gowda made was to appoint a wrong person as CBI director. Gowda was not instructing him, but the CBI director gave an impression that he was acting at the behest of Gowda. He created needless misunderstandings. One day Gowda asked me, "What do we do with this cranky fellow?" The Supreme Court was breathing down the prime minister's neck and it was not possible to change the director within a couple of months of appointment. That would have led to an entirely different controversy. It was beyond everybody in the government and the party as to how Gowda, who had otherwise picked a balanced cabinet and a fine PMO, had erred with Joginder Singh. Then there were people like C.M. Ibrahim, who appeared to be close to the prime minister but did a lot of loose talk. Specifically, in the case of Kesri, he was indiscreet. Ibrahim was a state-level person and had a narrow approach. When Gowda came to know of it, he tried to pacify Kesri, but the damage had been done.' Since Gowda had a handicap with Hindi, he had used Ibrahim as his linguistic crutch in the Hindi states. Ibrahim had used this access to the prime minister to project himself as his 'alter ego'.[56] If anybody knew Chand Mahal Ibrahim better, it was Gowda. He had politically nurtured Ibrahim since the 1970s and had watched him turn against him periodically.[57] Ibrahim had returned to the Janata Dal fold just before Gowda had become chief minister in 1994.

Finally, when Gowda went to Moscow on a state visit between 24 March 1997 and 26 March 1997, Kesri surreptitiously went to meet President Shankar Dayal Sharma with a letter withdrawing support to the United Front government. Sharma is said to have upbraided Kesri and sent him back for attempting to destabilize the government when the prime minister was travelling abroad. A majority of Congress leaders were in the dark about this. In fact, they were in the dark until Kesri went back to the President a second time on 30 March 1997. The charges that were made against the Gowda government were rather flimsy broad strokes, nothing specific. It looked like a whimsical and contrived decision. It was not difficult to punch holes into it, and that was exactly what happened in the Parliament debate later, which we will examine in the next chapter. Some believed that the withdrawal had to do with Kesri's ambition to replace Gowda. But this could also be read as the handiwork of a close group in the Congress, which had egged Kesri on to withdraw support by dangling the carrot of the prime ministership before him. Kesri was to soon realize that he had been tricked. They had played on his insecurities at the time.

The close group of the Congress, according to Pranab Mukherjee, which advised and drafted the letter, included himself, Sharad Pawar, Jitendra Prasada, Arjun Singh and Tariq Anwar. He wrote: 'I drafted a letter addressed to the President informing about the party's decision to withdraw support from the government . . . A few of us, rather than involving the entire CWC (Congress Working Committee), finalized the letter at Kesri's home for taking it to the President. In a bid to maintain secrecy and not allow the reporters waiting outside his residence to get any hint of what was on the anvil, Kesri took me along in his car while mine followed. We took a circuitous route to Rashtrapati Bhavan to throw off any enterprising reporter who might have thought of following us. Close to the destination, I got off Kesri's car, got into mine and headed home, while Kesri went to Rashtrapati Bhavan.'[58] All this explains the surreptitious nature of the operation.

It was Srikant Jena who had called Gowda in Moscow to inform him of Kesri's trip to the Rashtrapati Bhavan. Jena recalled: 'The deputy chairman of the Rajya Sabha, Najma Heptullah, called me around 11 p.m. and said, "Srikant, your government is out. Kesri has met the President." I immediately called Gowda in Moscow. He said, "Okay brother. I am coming tomorrow. Let us see what we can do." He was not perturbed by what I told him.'[59] Gowda remembered an additional detail from Jena's call: 'He also told me that the US ambassador to India, Frank G. Wisner, had met Kesri three times that day though the reason was not known.'[60]

Mukherjee wrote that Joginder Singh's return from Geneva on 22 January 1997, with a box of Bofors papers, was the trigger behind the decision: 'The manner in which the CBI Director showed the box clearly demonstrated the intent to dramatize the entire episode. However, in subsequent investigations or the follow-ups of the case, there was no reference to the "documents on Bofors" brought from abroad by the CBI director himself. It confirmed the suspicion of the Congress members that the Deve Gowda government wanted to discredit the Congress while enjoying its support to rule.'[61] What Mukherjee was implying here was the box that the CBI chief was carrying was empty and they were doing it to instill fear and arm-twist the Congress, and therefore they had decided to call the bluff. Mukherjee also wrote that Kesri had no ambition of becoming prime minister, or was that his way of saying that they would not have allowed him to be prime minister?

During a week of hectic activity that followed, it slowly dawned on Kesri that he had been shortchanged. He sent R.K. Dhawan as an emissary to Gowda on 9 April 1997, just three days before Gowda was to move the motion of confidence in the Parliament: 'Dhawan said Kesri was willing to take back the letter of support withdrawal if I publicly apologized for not consulting him before taking major decisions in the government, and assure that I would henceforth consult him on important matters. I had not done anything wrong, so I said I wouldn't apologize but can publicly assure that I would consult him hereafter. But that was not acceptable to Kesri.'[62] It was too costly an exit route for Gowda to offer Kesri. He went ahead preparing for the showdown in Parliament.

In the meanwhile, Congress MPs rebelled against Kesri and his ad hoc coterie's decision. Nearly 100 of them[63] gathered at Sharad Pawar's house to say that they were not ready to face elections. Pranab Mukherjee also wrote that he rushed there to pacify them. The younger MPs who were particularly happy with the access that Gowda had given them were pressing for his continuation. Mukherjee wrote: 'I rushed to Sharad Pawar's residence and faced the ire of the party MPs congregated there . . . Some members even accused me of being party to the decision since I was in the Rajya Sabha and wouldn't have to worry about losing my parliamentary seat.'[64] In fact, all those who had pushed for the withdrawal—Kesri, Jitendra Prasada, Arjun Singh and Mukherjee—were Rajya Sabha members, except Sharad Pawar, whose role in this political circus was ambiguous. 'Many Congress MPs were happy with Gowda because their work would get done immediately and he gave them access like no other prime minister. Anybody could walk in with a request and talk to him. Other prime ministers till then had behaved like maharajas and maharanis but Gowda had opened the doors of the fortress called the PMO,' Shankar recalled.[65]

When the fall looked almost inevitable, Srikant Jena went to meet Pawar and tried to interest him in taking over the Congress and become prime minister: 'When I went to meet Pawar, he was sitting with P.C. Chacko, Priya Ranjan Dasmunsi and Praful Patel. When I said he should take over, it looked like he was wary of breaking the Congress. I argued that he would actually not be breaking the Congress but saving it. The thinking in the core group of the

United Front coalition at that time was Pawar could be supported as prime minster and Gowda could be made either vice-president or President, since elections to both the chairs were coming up soon.'[66] But since Pawar did not pick up the gauntlet, this idea never took off. P. Chidambaram also said: 'There was some hope that Pawar will split a section of the Congress MPs and shore up the Gowda government, but that never happened.'[67] Or else, in July 1997, Gowda could have been the tenth President of India in the place of K.R. Narayanan, or in August, the tenth vice-president of India in place of Krishna Kant. This is another moment that gets into the 'what ifs' of history.

Whether Gowda built and dismantled his own government or did political circumstances lead to the fall is a question that will remain inconclusive. To political uncertainties, one may also need to add fears and greed of individuals in the game. There were too many twists, turns and complications. Too many insecurities and egos to be handled inside and outside the government. There were too many political permutations and combinations that perhaps needed a sophisticated computer program to manage. There was also Gowda's own political nature and shortcomings, and of course the karma, he so much believed in.

Shankar, who had seen and worked with Gowda for decades captured Gowda's political nature in a witty manner:[68]

> Gowda can build and destroy with equal finesse. Our socialist colleague and former Karnataka chief minister, J.H. Patel, would say, 'Gowda will work very hard to build something in the morning but destroy that in the evening because he does not have any other evening entertainment and engagement. He did not drink, dine or chase women. Out of sheer boredom, he would destroy all that he had built by the day. Again, in the morning, he would strive to build everything again.' That is Gowda. Very accurate. No music, no movies, no drinks and no women. Patel would tease me, 'You were with him for so many years, why didn't you get him on to any of these? Ask him if a

beautiful girl has ever appeared in his dreams? His only dreams have been political nightmares.' Patel was the exact opposite.

Shankar's own witty retort to Patel was that he too had wasted away his youth in the company of Gowda: 'As a young man when I was supposed to be chasing girls, I was chasing Gowda.' Jokes aside, what was considered Gowda's weakness, was his strength too, or what was his strength had become his weakness. That was the paradox of his political life.

18

How Many 'Brutuses', Sir?

Between the withdrawal of support by the Congress and Gowda's confidence vote in the Parliament, there was one final game played in Delhi's portals of power. The rescue formula that Sitaram Kesri had suggested to Gowda through R.K. Dhawan was not acceptable, so the withdrawal letter was confirmed. If one looks at the dateline, until 21 March 1997, the Congress did not look ruffled or restless, but once Gowda boarded Air India One to Moscow, the sly withdrawal game had begun. It was completed in under ten days on 30 March 1997. From then on, it should have been only a dead formality of exit for Gowda, but that was not how it was.

The first instinctual decision among the United Front constituents was to go for elections.[1] They thought it was best to recommend the dissolution of the Lok Sabha and seek a fresh mandate. This decision was firm till 9 April 1997, that is until two days before the confidence vote. There was a dinner meeting of the parliamentary party of the ruling coalition, and there everybody felt confident that a good amount of work had been done in 314 days, and a snap survey had shown that the coalition could improve its tally if it went to polls. But 10 April changed the course of history.

V.P. Singh, who had just vanished when the offer of prime ministership had been made to him in May 1996, met Karunanidhi, Murasoli Maran and Chandrababu Naidu, and planted the idea in their head that there was still fifty months left for the Lok Sabha term to end. He suggested that they should revisit their idea to rush to the polls. He also indicated that they could consider a non-political person like I.K. Gujral to hold things together for a while.[2] This led to cracks in the unity of the United Front constituents that was intact less than twelve hours ago. Naidu, who was the convenor of the Front, grabbed the idea that led to a reversal of the decision. The pressure had built up in the Congress too against the polls and they had offered a compromise formula by saying that they would allow the United Front to carry on if they changed the prime minister. They had proposed it as a face-saving exit route for themselves and also to save the party from an imminent rebellion. Things started changing by the hour. However, Gowda had announced that he will move the confidence motion on 11 April in the Lok Sabha.

When the United Front constituents met towards the evening on April 10 without Gowda, the Left parties insisted that a leader acceptable to the majority had to be chosen in a democratic manner. In an informal count of hands, Mulayam Singh Yadav emerged as front runner with 120 votes, followed by Moopanar with some twenty-odd votes. This was communicated to Harkishan Singh Surjeet around 11 p.m. Surjeet was getting ready to board a flight to Moscow at around 4 a.m. He said, 'Go by the majority decision, make an announcement in the morning.' His flight for Moscow took off in the wee hours of April 11 morning, but between Mulayam emerging and Surjeet taking off, things had changed again. As soon as he touched down in Moscow, Surjeet was told that Gujral had been chosen since Mulayam Singh Yadav was not acceptable to Lalu Prasad Yadav.[3]

Earlier, when the dilemma between going to polls and picking a new prime minister had deepened, Balwant Singh Ramoowalia, the social welfare minister, had met Gowda, and briefed him on the twists and turns of the debate going on inside the United Front. Gowda told Ramoowalia to inform Surjeet who was resting as he had a long journey coming up that night. But still, Surjeet got ready and reached Andhra Bhavan. He saw Jyoti Basu also in attendance at the meeting. He made it clear that whatever it is, the Left parties had decided to stand by Gowda. After that categorical statement, Basu got up and exited the meeting.[4] When circumstances had changed again, within minutes and hours, the Left had little choice but to come around to the idea of an alternate to Gowda as prime minister. That is when the crown started circling over Mulayam Singh for a few hours before it settled on Gujral's head. Gowda naturally felt betrayed.

On the morning of the confidence vote, Srikant Jena as parliamentary affairs minister went to Gowda's 7 RCR residence to accompany him to the Parliament. When they were having breakfast, Gowda received a call informing him that the United Front leaders were coming to see him and that it was 'urgent'. Without betraying his emotion, he said, 'alright'. When they came, they started arguing that Gowda should straight away go to the President and submit his resignation; that he should not face the Parliament. Among the people present were Chandrababu Naidu, Sharad Yadav, Lalu Yadav, Karunanidhi and Jyoti Basu. While Karunanidhi did not speak, Jyoti Basu kept saying in a low voice that it was not a 'decent option' to suggest to the prime minister since he had already announced that he will seek a vote of confidence in the Parliament. However, Naidu and the two Yadavs were relentless. Gowda did not utter a single word. The meeting was suddenly disrupted when Gowda got up, looked at Srikant Jena and said, 'Shall we leave? It is getting late.' Seeing the prime minister move out of the room, the other leaders too hurriedly exited. They were embarrassed.[5]

Just before Gowda was to move the motion of confidence in the Parliament, he was given a slip of paper, which said the United Front leaders were in his Parliament office and wanted to have a quick word. He went out. The leaders, including the ones who were at his residence that morning, said that they had decided to support him during the confidence motion. He impatiently said 'thank you', walked back to his seat in the Parliament and moved the confidence motion.[6]

Barely had he completed moving the motion, Vajpayee's confidante and senior BJP leader Jaswant Singh signalled to Srikant Jena to step out into the lobby. Singh handed over a chit to Jena and asked him to pass it on to Gowda. The note in a cryptic fashion said (not exact words): 'We will save your government. Don't resign. Accept our support.'[7] The offer had been clandestinely suggested a couple of days earlier too. Gowda received calls from Bal Thackeray; Sahib Singh Verma had met him; George Fernandes had pleaded with him, and Ram Jethmalani asked him 'not to be a fool by rejecting Vajpayee's offer'.[8] P. Chidambaram confirmed this offer: 'I had had a private conversation with him. He was very clear that he would not accept BJP's support. He had flatly refused Vajpayee.'[9] Gowda was grateful to Vajpayee. However, in a sea of gloom it was a beacon on an alien shore for Gowda. He would not betray his political beliefs.

The Arguments

Gowda's principal secretary, Satish Chandran, had handed over notes for his reply to the debate on the motion of confidence. Gowda recalled what Chandran had remarked while handing over the notes and supporting documents for his final address: 'Sir, in Julius Caesar there is only one Brutus, but we have seen many "Brutuses" here. I won't stay here for another minute, and I don't want to come and watch the proceedings. I would like to head back to Bangalore by the end of the day.'[10] Gowda had enormous respect for Chandran and saw him as an elder brother. Chandran was not the one to get emotionally carried away, but he looked shaken that day. Gowda said: 'Sir, this is politics. Defeat is victory's best friend. I will come back to this chair again. Don't be disappointed. Please don't be in a hurry to go back to Bangalore.'[11]

Throughout the day in the Parliament some revealing and
passionate speeches[12] were made across the aisle. There were two parts
to Gowda's performance that day. He set the tone in the morning
for the debate by moving the trust motion. In the evening, he was
to reply, at the very end, after the motion had been debated. Then
there would be a vote to seal the fate of the government. In the first
act, he was calm and correct: 'In the last ten months, I have never felt
that there is any instability in the government. I must be fair. The
Congress party or the supporting parties have never interfered in our
taking any decisions. Almost all the decisions which were taken in the
cabinet in the last ten months were unanimous . . . I would like a free
and frank expression, particularly on the omissions and commissions
of this government in the last ten months.' This was an indirect way
of staking claim to all the good work that had been done, and the
'consensus' bit was to signal the acceptance of his leadership.

The entire debate that followed for hours appeared to be an
expedition to find out why, suddenly, the Congress had dropped
Gowda. The Congress speakers, too, did not seem to have answers
to the sharp attacks. Surprisingly, senior Congress leaders P.V.
Narasimha Rao, Sharad Pawar and A.R. Antulay did not speak
during the debate, although their quotes from the confidence debate
when Gowda was inaugurated was on the lips of many speakers. That
exposed the divisions inside the Congress.

When the floor was opened for the debate, senior BJP leader
Jaswant Singh was the first to launch an attack in his deep baritone
and Queen's English:

At the outset, I must comment upon the near-total air of
unreality in which this debate is taking place. Just before
the commencement of the debate, the air was suddenly
thick with rumours about the resignation of the hon. prime
minister, about a last-minute change, and about the partners
in this arrangement having now settled their dispute. I was
very relieved when the hon. prime minister finally arrived,

even though somewhat belatedly, to at least, for the moment, set that rumour to rest . . . The hon. prime minister rather coyly referred to certain new developments that have taken place, which require this debate to take place. I do wish, sir, that the hon. prime minister, who with admirable restraint and ambiguity called them 'certain new developments', had specified what these new developments were. The debate has not been occasioned because we have moved a motion of no confidence. The hon. prime minister has himself sought confidence of the house because, as he explained, there are certain new developments. What are those new developments?

Singh went on to paint a devasting picture of the coalition that Gowda presided over with two big parties as outside supporters. They could well be lines from any of the literary masters carefully reconstructing human treachery, tragedy, envy and unbridled political opportunism and purposelessness:

We are not pretenders. We do not pretend because if anything is to be said explicitly, it is only we that have said it. If at all there is a pretender, the true pretenders in this artificial arrangement are the Congress party and my distinguished friends, the CPM (Communist Party of India [Marxist]). They were the pretenders because they pretended . . . They pretended to wield power. They pretended to no responsibility. They wielded power but without responsibility. They wanted to run this government but without any accountability. They were the pretenders. Therefore, I charge both the defenders and the offenders of bringing about a wholly artificial, spurious and avoidable crisis, a crisis born entirely of mendacity, double-cross, doublespeak, double standards and it is a dishonest crisis . . .

   I do not wish to say much about the kind of rumours that became thick, about all this drama and the charade about talks,

talks about talks, informal talks, then, formal talks of steering
committee and of core group and of yet another core group or
whatever controlling group. We were told when these talks,
double-crosses were going on that those who were entrusted
with actually doing the talking were more interested in ensuring
that the talks failed so that their leaders who were at the helm
could, in turn, be defeated and the second rank could come
forward and take over. The charade, the mendacity of what
we have been subjected to today was entirely avoidable. It is a
crisis born of treachery within parties and it is also the treachery
of arrangements between parties. That is why now when
this debate takes place, the air is befouled with a suspicious
individual conduct.

Gowda would have loved to borrow the lines of Jaswant Singh.

Singh continued: 'They said: "We have objection only to a certain
personality. If the personality changes, then, we will work together
again." Is the legislature to be reduced to an arena for settling personal
disputes between individuals? As a legislature, are we to become the
victim of a certain party's pique against a single individual, however
high the office that he held?' Interruptions broke out at this point:
'After all, we have opposed the hon. prime minister. Our opposition
to him is open, is clear, is categorical and is unambiguous. Mr Prime
Minister, sir, we are your opponents. Your enemies sit behind you
and beside you. We are your political opponents. We make no bones
about it. It is a farce because it is a sad imposition upon a trusting
and unsuspecting nation.'

He termed it 'utterly shameful' the fact that the prime
minster had been called *nikamma* (Hindi word meaning useless or
incompetent) by Sitaram Kesri a few days back. He also asked as
to why the Congress had picked March 30 as the date to withdraw
support. This mystery about March 30 is also referred to by other
speakers, including Somnath Chatterjee and Vajpayee. They are all
perhaps hinting that this was a suggestion made by an astrologer,

or they are trying to indicate that there was some big development to take place after March 30, which would have put the Congress party on the backfoot. Therefore, they had to complete the deed by March 30. Lead speakers from the Congress side, like Priya Ranjan Dasmunsi, refused to bite this bait.

Dasmunsi charged Gowda of ignoring 'the consolidation of the secular forces in this country'. He said: 'Politically, Mr Prime Minister, you are not merely a prime minister of the '50s, '60s, '70s, '80s or even the '90s. You are a prime minister of an era in which the collective wisdom of you people about anti-Congressism has brought the other side of the house to this size. If you go on harping on the score of anti-Congressism again, we may be vanquished but they will cover the whole of that side. That is your desire, Mr Prime Minister.'

Veteran CPM leader Somanth Chatterjee countered Dasmunsi:

[He] was saying that Shri H.D. Deve Gowda is a good man, a nice man, he is a good prime minister, but not a good secularist. Is this the way today that the Congress party will decide? . . . At least, we have felt that there is transparency in the functioning of this government. One of the big achievements of this government is that there has been transparency. But everything seems to have been forgotten when Shri Sitaram Vajpayee comes in [there are interruptions]. I thought you have become fused into one. Really, Shri Sitaram Kesri seems to have become Sitaram Vajpayee. I am sorry. Really, I meant Shri Sitaram Kesri . . . They did not succeed in creating divisions in the United Front. What I can see is that our good friend and Congress leader Shri Sitaram Kesri will not ascend the throne as Ramachandra, but he is assuming the role of 'Atal Bhakta Hanuman' and all my friends in the Congress party, with no disparagement, will be acting like the *vanara sena* [Hanuman's army in the Ramayana].

Railway minister Ram Vilas Paswan, who had stood by Gowda firmly during the crisis, spoke passionately:

> People like us born in poor families had never thought that we can become even a village chief, but this is a democracy where Ram Vilas Paswan, born of poor parents, has become the minister of Railways, and a man like Deve Gowda who was born in a poor peasant family has become the prime minister of the country. It is all because of democracy . . . Therefore, I would like to say that it is a sad day for the country. The post of a prime minister is something very big. It is above party politics. It should not be changed frequently. Deve Gowdaji is our prime minister. He is the leader of the United Front. Rajesh Pilot is present here. Shri Narasimha Rao is also present here. Can anybody raise an accusing finger towards Deve Gowdaji? But still they insist that Deve Gowda be changed, the leader should be changed. But why? . . .
>
> I want to ask you Mr Rajesh Pilot. You are my good friend . . . During the day and night we are in each other's contact. Nobody, even the top leader, knew that letter was being drafted to withdraw support. Everyone was in his constituency. Sharad Pawar was busy in his constituency. He says he knew nothing about the letter. Madhya Pradesh people say that they also did not know anything about the withdrawal of support. Who knew it? Such a big decision was taken but you are defending it. Even, today, if you say that it was a mistake and since it was the order of the high command, and you had to comply with that, then we can understand your helplessness. But instead of saying it, you are defending the same again and again . . . On the very first day, when the constituents of UF met together, we said that 'We are like a rock under the leadership of Shri H.D. Deve Gowda.' Right from the very first day we have been saying that we are like a rock under the leadership of Shri H.D. Deve Gowda . . . Today, as the

leader of the party, I do say that under the leadership of Shri
Deve Gowda, the country has made economic progress and we
have given a clean administration during the last ten months.
No communal riots or caste riots took place during his tenure.
India's reputation in foreign countries and our neighbouring
countries has improved significantly under the leadership
of Shri Deve Gowdaji. Deve Gowdaji is a deserving prime
minister. There seems to be no reason to disown Shri Deve
Gowdaji. We will live and die under his leadership. I want to
make it very clear today that whatever we have to do we will do
that only under the leadership of Deve Gowdaji.

After Paswan's impassioned intervention, there was P. Chidambaram's
reasoned plea. He was also precocious in a way:

This government cannot be wished away. This government's
accomplishments cannot be wished away . . . Those who have
held the scales in a balanced manner and those who have not
done so, will be decided by the deed they leave behind. I believe
this government of Shri H.D. Deve Gowda has left its imprint
on the political and economic history of India. There will be
a time when historians will write about this period. However
brief it may be, and they will say that this government was the
first genuine coalition in India. They tried, they endeavoured,
they did not succeed beyond ten months; yet they have
enshrined in the Constitution of India in a way that can never
be deleted, the principle of cooperative federalism. Historians
will also say that they have written into the economic history
of India certain principles which will make this country one of
the strongest economies in the twenty-first century and that
this government gave an impetus to growth, gave an impetus
to reforms, gave an impetus to social justice programmes which
will make us the fourth-largest economy in the world by the
year 2020. I, therefore, conclude with a sense of achievement,

with a sense of pride, with a sense of humility but also, as I said, with a terrible sense of sadness that an experiment, a promising experiment. should come to an end.

There was a bit of mischief in Nitish Kumar of the Samata Party. He spoke a Bihari–Bengali collusion to bring down Gowda:

> I came to know that, as per the opinion of an astrologer, twenty-fifth was fixed for withdrawal of support and when they were just going to write a letter to the prime minister, someone said that the prime minister is in Moscow. Do you want to make it a banana republic? When the prime minister is in Moscow, it is not justified to talk about withdrawal of support. Then, again, they tried. This time Nelson Mandela was on his visit to India. Thus, Deve Gowdaji's Moscow visit and Nelson Mandela's visit to India gave him five days of respite. When this issue came up again, Indo–Pak talks were being held. Then the conference of foreign ministers of non-aligned countries was to be held. Then it was said that we will not tolerate all this for so long and he went straight to the President . . . there is some 'Bihari' connection in it. Wherever I go, people ask me as to what is this Bihari connection. I get fed up with all this . . . Today a man from Bihar has colluded with a man from Bengal. To ensnare the Bihari gentleman, the Bengali gentleman has made such a draft that there will be blockade in the future as well [not clear what he means by this]. Bihari does have common sense but when it comes to writing a letter, Bengali gentleman stole the show. Till Mr Rao was in power his [Bengali gentleman's] loyalty was to Mr Rao but God knows what happened, maybe it is related to Mr Rao . . .

The Bengali gentleman reference is to Pranab Mukherjee. In plain terms, his charge was that a Bihari had colluded with a Bengali to

withdraw support, but the Bengali who drafted the letter had many more things on his mind. In short, he had fooled the Bihari.

Leader of the Opposition A.B. Vajpayee's speech was pithy but sharp:

> The question asked now by the home minister was very relevant. I was expecting Shri Narasimha Rao to make a speech and so would Shri Sharad Pawar and Shri Antulay. But all are silent. Their silence is more eloquent than their speech . . . I apprehend there may be some mystery behind this date of 'thirty'. The mystery must be unveiled. If the Congress party observes silence, we would request the prime minister to throw some light on the issue as to why the thirtieth date was fixed? . . . Hon'ble Narasimha Raoji is sitting here. If I refer to an incident, I think he will not take it otherwise. We were having lunch somewhere. It was hosted by the government. At that lunch, watermelon was served as a sweet dish. The watermelon was tasteless. Someone sitting nearby Shri Narasimha Raoji complained as to why such tasteless watermelon was served? It is not seasonal. If my perception is not wrong, Narasimha Raoji said that if the support is withdrawn in budget session [as the Congress had done], why [can't] watermelon be served in every season? What are the facts behind this unseasonal decision? What is [the] mystery behind it? . . . Now if the Congress was under apprehension that Deve Gowdaji wants to split the Congress, the step which they took for self-defence was essential to be taken. But I don't think that Deve Gowdaji wanted to split the Congress and if he wanted to do so would you allow your party to be split or were some [of your] members ready to cross the floor.

'I Have Not Betrayed Anybody'

At 10 p.m., Gowda offered a stirring response to the debate that had taken place the entire day. He spoke for over an hour, and there was not a dull moment. He exposed the Congress leadership bit by bit. He was not emotional by any measure, but as he spoke, he gathered a sharp rhetoric and substantial drama. He kept aside a prepared draft and began to innovate. He was anecdotal, too, about the little tales of betrayal. The word 'Brutus' that his principal secretary, Satish Chandran, had used while he was setting out to the parliamentary ring, echoed in his mind. But he did not consciously attempt to offer a Shakespearean tone to his speech. For any politician who has been in the game for decades—plotting, persuading, contesting polls, scoring victories and pyrrhic victories, swallowing defeats and belching defeats, reading and misreading betrayals, waltzing in the company of opportunists and sycophants, the Mark Antony speech in Act 3 Scene 2 of Shakespeare's *Julius Caesar* would anyway come naturally and easily. That was the universality that the Bard had captured. It plays in a politician's mind every day in different cultural contexts, different times, and in diverse languages, but to find a structure and articulation that Gowda found on 11 April was rare. Gowda later saw it as a 'divine rush, when the right words and right ideas rushed at the right time, plucked like ripe fruits from trees'. That speech, spoken with so much conviction and honesty, is arguably the best of his entire political life.

In Shakespeare's Caesar, Mark Antony's immortal lines uses the word 'honourable' to address Brutus to great effect and to mean exactly the opposite. Here Gowda inverts the whole thing and deploys the word 'inefficient' to remarkable dramatic sarcasm: 'Yes, I was an inefficient prime minister, yes I was a useless prime minister, therefore I could do so much in just ten months,' could be read as a one-line summary of the speech. He had turned Sitaram Kesri's insinuation that he was a *nikamma*, meaning 'useless' and 'inefficient' in Hindi on its head. That day, it was not Vajpayee who stole the show with his speech. After Gowda's show was over, Srikant Jena ran into Vajpayee in the Speaker's chamber. Vajpayee did not hide his admiration for Gowda's performance. He said in Hindi: '*Arey Jena saab, is aadmi ko Hindi aati toh hamari dukaan bandh kardeta* (Arey Jena saab, if this man knew Hindi, he would have ensured that we run out of business).'[13]

Here are excerpts from a very long transcript.[14] He begins from the last conversation he had with the Congress president. He reveals that his finance minister had informed him on 29 March, a day before they withdrew support, that the Congress party had not submitted its accounts and if they did not do so before 31 March, penalties were inevitable. Gowda called Kesri and asked for time to discuss 'an important issue'. Kesri promptly said they could catch up on 31 March at 2 p.m. without revealing that he was planning to withdraw support on 30 March: 'I have got some basic ethics in life. I have not come here in search of this office, with any aspiration, with any ambition. I did not aspire to become the prime minister of this country leaving the chief minister's office. There is no need for me to (indulge in) manipulative politics. The people of this country who are politically very much awakened are aware of that. 12.40 p.m. was the time chosen to hand over the withdrawal letter and he gave me the time to meet him at two o'clock.'

On the allegation that he met P.V. Narsimha Rao more times than he met Kesri:

The allegation is that I am meeting only Shri P.V. Narasimha Rao. I am not a person to stab behind the back. Shri P.V. Narasimha Rao was the prime minister of the country . . . Today, those friends who want to [give] sermons and morals in this country, those who want to attribute motives against Shri Narasimha Rao, were they not enjoying office in his government? Today, everybody wants to raise a finger against Shri Narasimha Rao, saying that Deve Gowda is going to safeguard the interests of Shri Narasimha Rao. If he falls ill and is in the hospital and if Deve Gowda goes to see him, he is showing extra regard and respect to him! Just because he has lost the presidentship, lost the CPP (Congress Parliamentary Party) leadership, I am not a person to belittle him. He has done something for the nation. Whether he continued in office by using various political methods or not, I do not want to go into the details of that. He has bailed out this country from the economic crisis. I am not going to make sweeping remarks against everybody, but how some of you, friends, have belittled him, I know that. Even though it is not my concern, even though I know that I am going to lay down the office today, but friendship is not a marketable commodity in this country . . . On the day when he handed over the resignation letter to the CPP leadership, he was alone. I went to his house to know why this had happened.

On how he met everybody as prime minister and not just Rao, he said:

Yes, I respect Shri Chandra Shekhar. My friendship with Shri Chandra Shekhar is very old. I had come in contact with him twenty years back. He is the senior-most leader and I respect him. Whether I was in office or not, I used to go to his house. Going to his house is a sin, going to Shri Narasimha Rao's house is a sin, meeting Shri Sharad Pawar is a sin, but meeting their president [Sitaram Kesri] twelve times is not a sin! I have not neglected anybody in my life. Did I not go to Shri Atal Bihari Vajpayee's house? Did I not go to Shri L.K. Advani's house? We should have some basic manners in public life. It is not a question of wooing anybody or pampering anybody to continue in office. You must try to give respect to your elders. The office which I am holding today for another one hour, is the highest office. Pandit Jawaharlal Nehru, who was one of the tallest leaders in the world, sat here and performed his duties as prime minister.

On his secular character being questioned and on the charge that he was splitting the Congress:

Sir, my secular character was questioned. It is said that the Congress working committee is constrained to note that the United Front has failed to provide the leadership necessary to consolidate the forces of secularism and confront the forces of communalism. Am I responsible for their defeat in Punjab? Am I responsible for their defeat in the corporation elections or the local bodies' elections in Maharashtra? Am I responsible for the defeat of the Congress candidates in all the by-elections except in the by-election of the seat vacated by me in my home state where the BJP lost the deposit and the Congress won? . . . The allegation was that the prime minister was trying to split the Congress party. When Shri Madhavrao Scindia wanted to join the Congress party, he came to me because he was in the United Front at that time. Did I not tell him to go and join and strengthen the Congress party? . . . When Shri N.D. Tiwari and Shri Arjun Singh came to me saying that they were going back to the Congress party since Shri P.V. Narasimha Rao was removed from the presidentship of the Congress party, I said: 'Go, you are most welcome to do that, and I have no objection.' Had I ever tried to split the Congress Party? Let anybody say this.

On being called 'nikamma' by Kesri: 'Sir, I am unable to understand the meaning of the Hindi word, 'nikamma'. He said: "You are foolish, coward and powerless. Just come into open and let us see who is powerful." He (said) in Hindi: "*Yeh vyakti nikamma aur communal hai.*" This man is not only incompetent, but he is also communal. An incompetent prime minister, what he has done in the last ten months, I must apprise this house and through this house the nation.'

Saying so he read from the editorials of *The Hindu* newspaper and the *Washington Post*:

Sir, a foolish and an incompetent prime minister, at least, tried to do something for the nation. I have not kept quiet for ten

months. I would like to recall what I have said on the day when I replied to the confidence motion in this very same house. I know what is going to happen. Whether I remain for five days or five months or five years, it is not my concern. Every minute I am going to use to serve the nation. That is the pledge I have taken. Yes, I did work for eighteen to nineteen hours a day. I am proud of it. There is no regret in vacating this office. There is no regret. I have not wasted a single minute. Whenever I used to get an opportunity, I did my best. There is no need of any certificate from the present president of the Congress (I). I do not need any certificate. I have fought ten elections in my life. Has he fought any direct elections in his life? As long as Shri Narasimha Rao was the president, there was no problem.

On the day when Shri Sitaram Kesri became the president of the Congress party, I called him for lunch. I have not neglected your president. We had two hours discussions in my house. He promised me and he also advised me as an elderly statesman. But on the fourth day, when one of my chief ministers, Dr Farooq Abdullah, whose colleague Prof. Saifuddin Soz, went to see Shri Sitaram Kesri, he was told not to join the United Front government because he was going to withdraw support. This happened within four days . . . I have taken the oath in the name of God, when I came to this house Narasimha Raoji, you may swallow so many wounds (insults) because you are a cultured person. I would now clarify, at least, some of the doubts raised by some Hon. members of the supporting party. The charge levelled against me was that I had neglected Shri Sitaram Kesri after he became the president. It is not based on truth but based on something else. There is a headline which correctly says, "India's old man in a hurry: Now or Never." This was not written by any of the Indian papers. It had appeared in the *London Times*.

It is at this point that he builds on the headline to give one of the most memorable lines for posterity and called Kesri 'an old man in a hurry'. So, it was not entirely Gowda's coinage, it was a headline borrowed to great effect. However, following interruptions, the line was expunged from the records.

Gowda continued on Kesri:

When I was in Russia, I got the message from one of my colleagues, Shri Srikant Jena, the hon. minister of parliamentary affairs that there was likelihood that the Congress might withdraw support. I told him, 'I am coming back. If they withdraw the support, why do you worry? There is nothing to bother. After all, as long as I am in this office, I must do my duty for the sake of my country . . .' I believe in destiny. The late Sanjiva Reddy was thrown out in 1969. He came back in 1978 and he himself administered the oath of office to Madam Indira Gandhi in 1980. Shri Atal Bihari Vajpayee told us about the clock. I am not going to run away from Indian politics. I might not have passed in this house. I have been branded as an inefficient prime minister by the Congress president, but the final judgement is before the 950 million people who are watching us today. An ineffective prime minister would accept this challenge. I will go before the people, and I am not going to run away. Touch your heart and then you vote against the confidence motion. Touch your heart and then take a decision . . .

If I have betrayed the nation, then they can hang me and I would have no objection. You have got every right . . . I have told Shri Narasimha Rao that whenever he feels that his party is uncomfortable, he could tell me, and I would hand over the resignation. I did not want to pick up quarrels. He is also sitting in this very same house now. I told Shri Kesri also not to mention frequently about the withdrawal of support; whenever he feels that his party is comfortable to come to power, he could tell me, and I could hand over the resignation. But why do they make this sort of an allegation against me?

He could have told me, 'Shri Gowda, we have decided to
withdraw the support.' If he had said it very gentlemanly, I
could have told my members not to pursue this matter and
that we would close this chapter. Let us accept—if he has got
the moral courage—to go before the people. They can tell
them [electorate] what they have done. They can tell them
that Deve Gowda's government is not a secular government,
it is an incompetent government. They can go to the people.
Why do they want to search for a new leader? . . . Yes, I
fought in Karnataka to become the chief minister. I am not
a political sanyasi. But I have never, never aspired, had no
ambition to come to this office . . . If the destiny [allows]
me to rise again from the dust of Indian politics, I will come
back with the same force [the often quoted line from Gowda's
farewell speech—'I will rise like the phoenix from the ashes'—
is missing in the transcript]. That is what I want to prove.
I am never afraid of [those] who want to play bullying politics.
I may be a soft man outwardly but if I start fighting then I
have already shown in Karnataka as to what I am . . . I want
to tell this august house and through this august house to the
nation that I have not passed orders about anybody or to hold
an inquiry or to conduct an inquiry by the CBI in the last ten
months. But I have not interfered—I can say this much that
I have not interfered. That is what has been expected by the
house. I have not interfered in any case, including that of my
own chief minister. My own party's prestige is involved here.

Winding up, he says there was 'not a single corruption charge levelled'
against his government, and he had not 'begged any industrialist'
and caused scams in the last ten months: 'I cannot see God. I have
not attained that spiritual power. I am an ordinary human being.
I can see God through my people who are the worst sufferers in
this country. *Janata janardhan* (to see God in people, especially the
poor) is my philosophy. I am going to work for this . . . I was not

such a tall man, but destiny has brought me here. I am satisfied. I have not betrayed my people, my nation or even my friendly partners (coalition partners and supporting parties) in these last ten months.'

Jyoti Basu, in his oral archives interview,[15] briefly mentions what happened after the Congress withdrew support to the Gowda government: 'They all came to my house in Banga Bhawan and then we asked: Who is the leader the Congress wanted as the prime minister? They said Deve Gowda but he is communal. I asked give me one instance. I do not know how he is communal. They could not give me one instance. But they said a face-saving thing: Since we have taken the decision to withdraw support, you make somebody else the PM. They did not name Gujral.' From the debates and from Basu's interview, it is apparent that the withdrawal of support was a freak accident and a conspiracy hatched by a very small group of people within the Congress. But Gowda's exit had invariably strengthened the BJP. Kesri was 'virtually booted out'[16] as party president and Sonia Gandhi was installed in 1998. After the Gujral government fell after being in office for another ten months, a Vajpayee-led government came back for thirteen months, and again in 1999 for nearly a full term. When Sitaram Kesri died in October 2000, Gowda was the first to reach the Congress office to pay his respects. Obituaries said he 'must have been the loneliest of Congressmen' when he died.[17]

The Regret and the Gesture

Gowda gave an interview to Karan Thapar for thirty minutes immediately after he stepped down.[18] He was a former prime minister but had also been designated as the chairman of the ruling United Front coalition. Thapar, a fine professional, set up a gladiatorial ring with his questions. Gowda was not just articulate and patient but equally, or sometimes more combative, in the interview. The confidence and experience came across. Not once did he indicate that he would walk away if tough, uncomfortable questions were posed. It may be instructive to watch this interview for all those in

the media and among the intelligentsia, who heaped ridicule on
Gowda and spread the canard that he didn't speak English or he
mumbles and cannot stitch his thoughts together. The manner in
which he pushes back Thapar, silences him momentarily at regular
intervals by saying 'hear me' and 'listen to me' may also be a lesson
to politicians on how to handle tough professionals. At one point, he
says: 'If you harp on such issues, it won't enhance the prestige of your
programme.' In the same breath, he adds: 'It is not in my nature to
find fault with my critics. They are free to express their opinion. If I
listen to them, I should be able to correct myself. To run a country
of this size, manage the political atmosphere, and take things forward
requires abundant patience.'

In that season, Gowda's encounter with Karan Thapar does not
end with this interview. He gives another one[19] eleven months later
after the Gujral government had collapsed and the preparation had
begun for another general election. Thapar provokes him: 'You don't
like Delhi, do you?' Gowda responds: 'I like Delhi. It is a good city.
(But,) some handsome people who tried to play politics to suit their
own convenience have destroyed the image of this country. In all
parties, there are manipulators, conspirators, including in your own
media.' When Thapar asks if he would like to clean Delhi of these
manipulators, he says, 'My job is to fight against these manipulators,
those people who have brought down the image of the country.'
Finally, when asked if he should become prime minister again?
Gowda, with a straight face, says: 'It is not the question of individual
desire. It is the responsibility of the United Front to democratically
choose a leader.'

As assured on the floor of the Lok Sabha in his farewell speech
as prime minister, Gowda continued to fight on and waited for his
phoenix moment to arrive. He lost the parliamentary polls in 1999.
After the Janata Dal splintered the same year, he formed his own
regional political outfit—the Janata Dal (Secular). He was rejuvenated
after he got re-elected to the Parliament in a by-election in 2002. But
in 2001, he was deep in debt. Running a political party and fighting

elections were never easy, but now all the responsibility was solely on Gowda. During this phase, he met Harkishan Singh Surjeet in his Delhi home.[20] Surjeet was full of regrets and unhappy with what especially Basu and himself had done to Gowda's political career: 'We committed a political murder. I learn you are in debt. How can I help you?' Surjeet grew emotional at this point, held Gowda's hand, and took him to his bedroom to show him a photograph on the mantle. It was a photograph of Surjeet and Gowda in a warm embrace from happier times five years ago: 'You are very dear to me. You are very close to me. Can I arrange money from our party sources?' He asked. Gowda gently refused, but his eyes welled up.

19

Tryst with the Congress Dynasty

For the first insignificant decade of his political life, Deve Gowda, was a member of the Congress party. That is from 1952 till he was elected as an independent to the Karnataka legislative assembly in 1962. He would have perhaps continued in the Congress had he been given a ticket to contest from the Holenarasipur assembly seat in Hassan district. But, when he was shortchanged, he rebelled and won.[1]

For someone not too ideologically worked up, Nehru's Congress was by and large a political default at the time. It was a party of the freedom movement with the halo of power. For the decade he was in the Congress, Gowda was a follower of the local Congress leader, A.H. Ramachandra Rao, whom he regarded as his 'political guru'.[2] Rao had won the Holenarasipur assembly seat since the first election in 1952 and had also been an education minister in the Kengal Hanumanthaiah cabinet. With Rao's blessings, Gowda was elected to the Holenarasipur taluk board as a Congress candidate in 1960.[3] While he was in the Congress or after he walked out, Prime Minister Jawaharlal Nehru did not figure in his taluk-level political peregrinations. He was a distant national icon. In 1962, even God himself could not have convinced Gowda that he would one day occupy the exalted chair in Delhi.

When he did stand near the chair, forty-four years after he had entered politics, he was overcome by emotion. When he entered the prime minister's parliamentary office for the first time and was led to his chair, he saw a tiny metal strip on it with Nehru's name, and the years he had governed India was mentioned. He froze for a few seconds. His eyes welled up. Even as officers began to wonder about his hesitation, he did a quick namaste and sat down. It was not the weight of history that he experienced at that moment, but strangely, the overwhelming burden of blessings.[4]

'Panditji was a giant from an illustrious family, a great scholar, and I was an ordinary person. When I saw his name on the chair, my destiny's path illuminated suddenly in my head. I thought I must have done something right in my past life. Whoever occupies the chair invariably has to work in the great man's shadow. He was such a tall figure. If you accept his stature, you can move ahead and do a lot of good work. On the contrary, if you begin to challenge his place and position in history, you'll only do that all your life. I feel extremely sad and angered the way he has been projected and vilified after Narendra Modi became prime minister,' Gowda said.[5]

When Gowda had initiated the motion of confidence in the Parliament as prime minister in June 1996, he had said: 'I am too small a man. In this very chair, Pandit Jawaharlal Nehru who was one of the tallest men in our history functioned as prime minister.'[6] Again, in his lengthy reply to the debate on the motion of confidence, he had referred to 'statesman' Nehru twice.[7]

Gowda had seen Jawaharlal Nehru only once as a matriculate student. The news that Nehru would be coming to Bangalore to address a rally was in the papers, and he was determined to attend it. He did not have money to buy a bus or train ticket, so he slept on a luggage rack of the Mysore–Bangalore train, which used to pass via Arsikere. He got down at the railway station and walked a few kilometres to the South Parade grounds in Bangalore. He remembers Nehru telling the crowd that we have to build the nation 'brick by brick'. He said the country was passing through a difficult phase, but the Mahatma had shown the way forward. He had also spoken about something related to food scarcity. That's all he remembers from that evening. But this clipped memory and the train journey glided past his mind like a tableau when he took the chair in the prime minister's office. 'I was very conscious I was sitting in Nehru's chair,' he said.[8]

Other than being overwhelmed initially, Gowda does not mention Nehru much during his tenure as prime minister. If one looks at all the speeches he made as prime minister, there is nothing fulsome about Nehru, except one or two minor references. Since he was neither into linguistic flourish nor diligent about quotes that went into his speeches, he ended up using one quote of Nehru twice in a span of ten days. On 28 March 1997, at the civic reception in the honour of Nelson Mandela,[9] he ended his speech with these words of Nehru: 'All nations and people are too closely knit together today for any one of them to imagine that it can live apart. Peace has been said to be indivisible; so is freedom, so is prosperity now; and so also is disaster in this one world.'

On 7 April 1997, at the inauguration of the NAM ministerial conference[10] he read out a fuller version of it: 'We have to labour, and work hard, to give reality to our dreams. Those dreams are for India, but they are also for the world, for all nations and peoples are too closely knit . . . and so also is disaster in this one world that can no longer be split into isolated fragments.' The repetition of the quote perhaps had to do with the lethargy of his speechwriters, but for him, speeches were a ritual to be got over with quickly. They were neither delivered with a demagogue's intent or with an eye on history. For him, speeches did little. It was strategy, planning and action that took precedence over words. He was an engineer prime minister, not a philosopher prime minister like Nehru. However, he was combative in parliamentary debates. Replying to the debate on the motion of confidence, he had said: 'I am not an eloquent speaker in Hindi, or an eloquent speaker in English, a forceful speech in English or Hindi is not going to solve the problems of the poor man of India. I have seen enough.'[11]

The only other time he quoted Nehru was during the golden jubilee celebrations of the constitution of the constituent assembly, and this was the one he adapted: 'A Constitution to be living must be growing; must be adaptable, must be flexible; must be changeable.'[12] But in a short address he made in Moscow when he unveiled Nehru's statue, he gave a full picture of his personality: 'Jawaharlal Nehru's all-encompassing vision and guidance which contributed to strengthening the roots of Indian democracy, charted the path of India's economic development, and evolved a unique foreign policy which was conceptually new, promoted India's national interests, and embraced global causes. I offer my respect to this outstanding Indian statesman, scholar, patriot, and builder of modern India . . . [his] visits moved many Russian citizens to name their children after him and even compose songs about him.'[13] He had chosen to speak these words. 'Speeches are prepared all right, but the prime minister chooses to speak them or reject them. I chose to read them because I respected the man. Would Modi have agreed to speak them? Vajpayee perhaps would have,' Gowda said.[14]

Indira Gandhi's Offer

There was a devotion for Nehru in Gowda, but interestingly, a good part of his politics was shaped in conflict with his daughter, Indira. However, conflict was not the only engagement. He was also in good measure charmed, as well as astounded by her stoic determination amidst mounting odds and personal tragedies. When Karnataka chief minister and longtime associate, Siddaramaiah, lost his son in 2016, he had asked him to bear his loss 'like Indira Gandhi had handled the loss of Sanjay Gandhi by continuing to work and instilling courage in people around her'.[15] Gowda was perhaps charmed the same way Vajpayee was charmed and 'mystified' by her. Vajpayee had called her an 'avatar of Durga' after the war in East Pakistan had ended and Bangladesh was born in 1971. Of course, Vajpayee later denied he had called her so.[16]

Gowda said: 'Indira Gandhi made a lot of mistakes that were avoidable, but whatever differences I had with her were only political. I did not develop a personal hatred for her like many of my colleagues in the Janata Party. Nehru groomed his daughter well, but he cannot be held responsible for all her mistakes. How can I be held responsible for my children's mistakes?' He had unexpectedly made the comparison autobiographical.[17]

As president of the state Janata Party and leader of the Opposition in the Karnataka assembly, Gowda had spoken against her inside the legislative assembly, and outside, an innumerable number of times, but the primary target was always the chief minister and the state Congress leaders. But even with the chief minister, he did not always cross the political limit. This approach was a pragmatic mix of both strategy and principle. Even the Emergency, during which he was jailed, did not make him bitter about Indira Gandhi.

In what little official communication that is available of the period in the Janata Party papers, there are only two letters by Gowda, which refer to Indira Gandhi. The rest are all about party matters and poll reports. In one of the letters, written in April 1978 to his party president, Chandra Shekhar, discussing the fragile unity among national Janata Party leaders, he warns: 'I hope you will leave no stone unturned to bring about understanding and unity among our top leaders. In view of the serious threat posed by Smt. Gandhi, it will be a national tragedy if the Janata Party fails to project a unified leadership at the top. I really hope the situation is not going to be as bad as it sounds and looks to me.'[18]

In another letter, written to the President of India, Neelam Sanjiva Reddy, in December 1978, he endorses the action taken against Indira Gandhi in the Parliament, however, the central focus of the letter is to apprise the President the 'reign of terror' of chief minister Devaraj Urs's son-in-law and founder of the 'notorious' Indira Brigade, Dr M.D. Nataraj: 'You are no doubt aware of the state of complete lawlessness, vandalism, violence and intimidation created by the Congress (I) in many parts of our state, following imprisonment and expulsion of Smt. Indira Gandhi from Lok Sabha. At the outset please permit me to say that our state party wholeheartedly approves the action taken by the Lok Sabha. Nothing less would have met the ends of justice as the former prime minister had shown utter contempt for norms of parliamentary practices and for democratic institutions.'[19] The tone here is certainly measured and civil, and in both the letters, she is not the only concern or target.

Indira Gandhi had perhaps read this sobriety of Gowda or had been told about it. After Urs had deserted Congress (I) to form his own outfit, she sent Kamalapati Tripathi, the former Uttar Pradesh chief minister, as her emissary to urge Gowda to join her. Tripathi sent word to Gowda through R. Gundu Rao. He agreed to meet him with B.M. Patil, the general secretary of the state Janata Party. Legislator K.K. Murthy, a close associate of Rao, was present in the meeting. The chief ministership was offered straightaway. Since Urs, from a tiny princely community in south Karnataka had left Congress (I), Gowda, a leader of the dominant peasant community from the same region as Urs, would have made a perfect replacement. That was at least the thinking: 'Tripathi said madam had kept dossiers on all Opposition leaders and was very impressed with my clean record. He said she had a lot of respect for me and had said so openly in a cabinet meeting,' Gowda recollected.[20] He also paraphrased the response he gave Tripathi: 'I know I will be made CM. I trust madam's word. But how will I come across to the next generation? You are a senior man. You should guide me. It is true I command 15 per cent vote, but all of it is anti-Indira Gandhi vote. It is not Deve Gowda's vote. If I cross over, you'll get only my vote. I have no confidence to say that I will convert that 15 per cent in madam's favour.' Tripathi apparently replied: 'Why do you worry about all that. Madam does not want your vote; she wants your leadership. You can easily fill up the loss created by Urs's exit.'[21]

At that point, B.M. Patil is said to have pulled aside Gundu Rao and said that he would get B.D. Jatti, who had by then completed his term as India's vice president, to speak to Gowda. Gowda was perceived to be part of the Jatti faction while he was in the Congress. Patil wanted to tap the goodwill that existed between Jatti and Gowda.[22] While others broke for lunch and went to K.K. Murthy's home, B.M. Patil and Gowda stayed back. Jatti made the expected call. He gently chided Gowda for being adamant. He asked why he was driving away power that had come to his doorstep: 'You are a fool. You have a big family. How will you repay your loans? Everybody has backstabbed you. Indira Gandhi will give you power and take care of the loans,' Gowda recalled Jatti's persuasion, which came with the authority of a family elder. However, Gowda did not budge. An unsuccessful Jatti did not want to end without some kind of result, so he asked if Gowda would allow his colleague, B.M. Patil, to cross over. Gowda promised not to stop him.[23]

A few months after this episode, and after Gundu Rao had been installed as chief minister, Gowda happened to meet Indira Gandhi in Delhi. She greeted him warmly: 'She said "Gowdaji, you are a tough guy" in front of everybody. I just did a namaste and smiled,' Gowda recalled.[24] He had come in contact with her only two other times. The first was when he went in a delegation with M.Y. Ghorpade (see the chapter on Morarji Desai), and the last time, when he had invited her to preside over the inauguration of the Ghataprabha irrigation project. He was a PWD minister in the Hegde cabinet and she was prime minister.

A Prediction for Rajiv Gandhi

Deve Gowda developed a greater rapport with Indira Gandhi's son, Rajiv Gandhi. The one thing that was common between Rajiv Gandhi and Gowda was that both distrusted if not detested Hegde. One wonders if this was the foundation of their relationship.

Gowda's first meeting with Rajiv Gandhi happened in 1989, in his final months as prime minister. It was in the backdrop of the Cauvery dispute, and he was at the time PWD minister in S.R. Bommai's cabinet. The Supreme Court had ordered that the

Karnataka and Tamil Nadu governments should meet, discuss, and arrive at a temporary water-sharing agreement. Tamil Nadu was under President's rule and P.C. Alexander was the Governor. He came to the home–office of the Karnataka chief minister for discussions, in which Gowda was also present. During the meeting, Gowda felt that Bommai was losing track and he intervened. Alexander stopped him: 'He was very sharp. He said, Mr PWD Minister, I know you are well acquainted in Cauvery matters, but please reserve your arguments before the tribunal.' Immediately after this, Alexander asked if he could speak to the chief minister one on one. Gowda had to leave the room. He returned to his office in Vidhana Soudha and waited. In a short while, they issued a statement saying they discussed at length but could not reach any conclusion and would therefore leave it to the Supreme Court to take a call. Gowda was shocked because invariably, the court would ask Karnataka to release water. He summoned his principal secretary, asked for a copy of the joint statement, and decided to leave for Delhi immediately. In Delhi, he went straight to Rajesh Pilot's house. He was good friends with Pilot, who was the surface transport minister in Rajiv Gandhi's cabinet: 'Rajesh, please help me. My people will be badly affected. Bommai has let me down. Somehow get me an audience with the prime minister,' he pleaded.[25]

Gowda was mildly shocked that he was granted an appointment at 3 a.m. He rested at Pilot's house, and both got up in time to reach the prime minister's residence. Vincent George, private assistant to the PM, ushered Gowda in while Pilot was asked to wait outside: 'The moment he saw me, he walked towards me and hugged me. "You are fighting Hegde alone. I am watching it all. I am with you. This is your house. You can come any time," he told me.' Rajiv thought Gowda would ask for some help for himself, but when he began to explain the Cauvery case, he was surprised. He listened very carefully. When Gowda concluded, he pleaded helplessness. He said he was in no position to intervene as he had to go to the polls in Tamil Nadu within the next two or three months, and his intervention in this very emotional issue would be misconstrued. 'He said it will be a "Waterloo" for him. He used that specific word. So, I said: "Sir, you have been so good to me, I will never mislead you. Karnataka is your state. When your mother lost everything, the people of Chikmagalur gave her a rebirth," Gowda reminded Rajiv his family's debt to the state. 'Tell me what can I do. Tell me what can I do, he repeated twice,' Gowda recalled.[26]

Gowda says at such moments, strangely, God gives him the ability to speak the right thing. He advocated a sort of a temporary solution. It hinged on the fact that Tamil Nadu was under Governor's rule and it would be prudent to wait for a popular government to come in place for the Cauvery discussions to go further: 'The Governor is anyway your nominee, he will agree, and the court too can be convinced on this line. I don't want you to rule in my favour, sir, but let two popular governments discuss the issue.'[27]

Rajiv agreed with Gowda's suggestion and asked his assistant to connect him to B. Shankaranand, who was the water resources minister, incidentally, also from Karnataka but not from the Cauvery belt. 'Rajiv asked: "Shankar, who is the lawyer appearing for the Union government?" When he was told it was Kuldeep Singh, he instructed: "Tell him until a popular government is elected the Cauvery decision should be kept in abeyance." I came to like Rajiv Gandhi instantly, and I felt the proximity,' Gowda said.[28]

The second time that Gowda went to meet Rajiv, Congress was in the process of destabilizing the Chandra Shekhar government on the charge that two constables had been deployed to spy on the Gandhis. Gowda had learnt from his astrologer that there was a threat to Rajiv Gandhi's life and wanted to communicate this to him personally. His astrologer had told him that if Rajiv celebrated his birthday in 1991, then he will be around for another fifteen years. The same astrologer had also made an accurate prediction about Indira Gandhi's vulnerability. He had then communicated it to his friend and the former Speaker of the Karnataka legislative assembly, K.S. Nagaratnamma: 'I don't know if she told her. This time I didn't want to take a chance, so I went myself,' Gowda said.[29]

Right at the beginning, Gowda made it clear to Rajiv Gandhi that he had not come to plead a lease of life for the Chandra Shekhar government. Without wasting much time, he broached the subject: 'It looks like there will be elections. Somehow you must manage to put it off till September. If it happens before that, there is a threat to your life. When he heard me say this, he asked: "Do you believe in all these things?" I continued: "Sir, believe me, this country needs you. If you escape this black spot, nobody can touch you for fifteen years." He hugged me like he had the first time and said I shouldn't be taking this prediction seriously. I insisted that he should not take it lightly. He thanked me and said, "Gowdaji you are a very sensitive man." Our conversation ended there. That was the last.' When he stepped out, he saw Margaret Alva in George's room. He repeated what he had told Rajiv and asked her to speak to Sonia. 'I told her to speak to Sonia Gandhi. I don't really know if she communicated it. What had to happen happened,' he said.[30]

Margaret Alva, who was a Rajya Sabha member at the time, does not recall this particular piece of conversation between her and Gowda.[31] She said: 'I don't recall details from that time. We were all busy, working round the clock. Election work had started internally. This conversation by itself I don't recall, but I must say Deve Gowdaji and I were neighbours and we did have a lot of meetings now and then. I conveyed a lot of messages from him to Rajivji, but I don't recall this message that I was asked to communicate to Soniaji. Whenever he wanted a meeting or wanted something to be conveyed, he would call me over to his house, serve very good coffee, and pour his heart out on what we needed to do, so on and so forth. That I can confirm. Rajivji respected senior people like Deve Gowda. He listened to them very carefully but did not necessarily accept every piece of advice that came from them. He would say: "These people have their own views and we cannot do what everybody wants us to do." That was his attitude.'

Margaret Alva also clarified that during Rajiv Gandhi's time, she had very little interaction with Sonia Gandhi, except when they travelled. She said Sonia 'strictly stayed out' of any kind of involvement or interference in government affairs: 'When I did go to her for one or two things, she would say: "Margaret, I do not interfere in public affairs." She insisted that Rajiv takes his own decisions.' When asked if Sonia Gandhi warmed up to people like Gowda later, after she took over the reins of the party, she said she would not wish to comment on that. Also, when Alva says that she was Gowda's neighbour there is a mix up because they became neighbours only after Rajiv Gandhi's assassination. Gowda entered the Parliament only in June 1991 and became a resident of 5 Safdarjung Lane only towards the end of 1991. Alva was by then in 12 Safdarjung Lane.

There was one final time that Gowda met Rajiv Gandhi. Parliament elections had been declared, and Gowda was in Delhi's Karnataka Bhavan. Rajiv sent for him. The meeting was fixed at 1 a.m. He asked if a seat-sharing arrangement was possible in Karnataka. Gowda, who had stayed away from V.P. Singh-led Janata Dal, was now part of the Samajawadi Janata Party: 'Rajiv said he'll give me five seats, and we could campaign together. The five seats he offered were Tumkur, Gulbarga, Koppal, Hassan and Mandya. I was frank. I said it won't help and gave my reasons. If the pact were to be made so close to the polls that aspirants in other seats would work against me. Hegde and I were on opposite sides, and I wasn't really sure how much I would win. But I gave my word that I'll stand by him if the need arose. We had kind of become close. I really liked him,' Gowda admitted.[32] In a few weeks, Rajiv Gandhi was assassinated. Gowda's astrologer had been proved correct and his faith in the game of predicting the future had deepened.

In Karnataka's political lore, a mysterious episode tries to illustrate the proximity between Rajiv Gandhi and Gowda. This has to do with Gowda's role in the dismissal of the eight-month-old S.R. Bommai government in April 1989. On the night when letters of nineteen legislators withdrawing support to the government reached the Governor's office, Bommai was apparently watching *Zanjeer*, an Amitabh Bachchan movie.[33] The plot to overthrow his government had come as a complete surprise to him. He did not know who was behind it and was rather clueless as to how to save it. Before he could apply his mind and gather support, Governor P. Venkatasubbaiah, without verifying the letters, recommended the dismissal of the government.

The next day when local pressure started mounting and when some legislators started claiming that their letters were being misrepresented, Gowda is said to have offered finishing touches to the toppling game. The paperwork was completed in Delhi within a couple of hours, and directions were issued to the Governor to dismiss the government. Later, of course, this decision was challenged in the Supreme Court, and a bench of nine judges delivered a landmark judgment discussing the provisions of Article 356, which made it constitutionally proper to test the majority of a state government only on the floor of the legislative assembly, and not the Governor's office. It is not clear to this day if the plan to topple Bommai's government was an original Gowda script, or if he was acting at the behest of Rajiv Gandhi, or if the plot was pure conjecture of Gowda's political rivals.

Between Sonia and Rahul Gandhi

Did a similar relationship develop with Rajiv Gandhi's partner, Sonia Gandhi? Gowda's party, the Janata Dal (Secular), shared power with the Congress twice, once in 2004, and again in 2018 in Karnataka, and both times she was at the helm, although in 2018 her son, Rahul Gandhi, was president of the party. There was a working relationship when coalitions were formed. There was constant exchange as long as they ran. There were angry exchanges when they fell, and there were doubts that courtiers on either side plotted all along. More than anything else, there was the growing insecurity of an electorally declining Congress. After 2014, with Modi and the BJP's assault on the Congress, there was an inevitable, strategic congregation of 'secular' political parties from time to time, in which Congress looked like a dinosaur staring at its extinction. Therefore, the answer is that Gowda's relationship with Sonia Gandhi was never warm, but not cold either. Sometimes, she would greet him in Parliament's central hall, and sometimes, she would breeze past without noticing him:

> They never allowed my relationship with her to develop. People like S.M. Krishna spoilt it. He and his minions played it dirty. He became chief minister soon after she took over as president, and she needed money to build the party. Krishna sent money and she listened to him. In 2004, Krishna and his son-in-law, Siddhartha, after losing the assembly polls, came to my doorstep and asked if my party would allow him to continue as chief minister in a coalition arrangement. But finally, Sonia and I picked Dharam Singh.[34]

But much before all this, when Sonia Gandhi was taking her first steps in national politics, she came calling at Gowda's Delhi residence on Safdarjung Lane in 1999. She thought she had cobbled up the numbers to be prime minister after the collapse of Vajpayee's thirteen-month government. People close to Gowda say she had come to seek his support to stake claim to form the government, which he had readily given. In his speech in the Parliament on the motion of confidence sought by the Vajpayee government on 16 April 1996, Gowda had remarked on this without admitting to anything: 'There is all type of gossip going on. Three days back, the media published that Deve Gowda had called all opposition members for dinner and that Soniaji and Jayalalithaji were going to attend the meeting.'[35] Anyway, Sonia's effort ended in a fiasco because Mulayam Singh Yadav, at the instance of George Fernandes, failed to pledge his numbers. The unremarkable relationship between Gowda and Sonia could also be the result of a lot of noise generated about Bofors, courtesy an overzealous CBI chief under Gowda the prime minister.[36]

With Rahul Gandhi, there is the distance of age, and as default, deference takes over. While Gowda went to see his father, the son comes to see Gowda and addresses him with a vague kinship moniker: 'uncle'. Perhaps 2018 and 2019, the two election years was when the two communicated frequently. In 2018, after the Karnataka assembly polls, Congress tied up with Gowda's party to keep the BJP away, but during the campaign, Rahul was accused of insulting Gowda, when he had referred to his party as 'BJP's B Team'.[37] Modi had picked this up in his rally and taunted Rahul: 'Is this your culture [sanskar]? This is arrogance . . . Your life [as Congress chief] has just begun. Deve Gowda is among the tallest leaders of the country. You are insulting him.'[38]

In the 2019 election campaign, however, Gowda said that if Rahul Gandhi became prime minister he would be by his side: 'If Rahul Gandhi becomes the prime minister, I will sit by his side.'[39] By carefully choosing his words, which he is known to do, he gave his statement a warm paternal ring of protection. It was neither patronizing nor surrender. After Gowda was defeated in the May 2019 parliamentary poll, he apparently visited Rahul Gandhi in his Tughlaq Lane residence. He is said to have discussed the sabotage of Congress leaders like Siddaramaiah in Karnataka. But in June 2020, Congress pledged its extra votes to Gowda, who was eleven short of winning a Rajya Sabha seat. Since the BJP too decided to disuse its extra votes and not put a third candidate (perhaps out of deference for Gowda about which there was no public statement though), he was elected unopposed to the upper house with three others. Gowda said Sonia Gandhi had urged him to come to Delhi in a newspaper interview: 'No I am not a consensus candidate as is being made out to be and I'm not politically obligated to either BJP or the Congress. I had not asked them not to field a third candidate against me. I decided to contest the polls on a request from Sonia Gandhi as she chose not to field a candidate against me. She personally called me to say she missed me in the Lok Sabha and she felt my presence in the Parliament was essential under the current circumstances.'[40] One is

Furrows in a Field

not sure if the double and triple negatives that delicately balances this sentence is originally that of Gowda or that of the newspaper reporter, who would have most likely translated Gowda's Kannada sentence or his English–Kannada code-mixed googly.

As is evident, publicly, Gowda never took a harsh line against the Congress dynasty all through his career. Neither did he please them. The record of his speeches as prime minister and leader of the Opposition in the Karnataka assembly validate this. Although his politics was avowedly anti-Congress, ironically, there has been none in the opposition space who has benefitted more from the Congress than him, his family and his party. When Gowda became prime minister, he was supported by the Congress, although at the time it was not headed by a member of the Nehru–Gandhi family. Twice his party shared power with the Congress in Karnataka, and the second time, in 2018, Congress propped up his son Kumaraswamy as chief minister, even though he had just thirty-seven out of 224 seats. Each time, the ghost of BJP had made Congress put power in Gowda's lap without his asking, and interestingly, the same Gowda had been expelled by Nehru's Congress in 1962.

There is a delicious irony in the fact that Gowda who started out in 1962 fighting the Congress, by 2021 had built a political establishment and a family that largely imitated the Congress. The dynasty he built already has three generations in mainstream politics: His two sons, two grandsons, two daughters-in-law and many relatives from the family's first circle.

20

Wrestling with Vajpayee and His Mask

The debate, engagement and sometimes collaboration between H.D. Deve Gowda and Atal Bihari Vajpayee were, arguably, the unlikeliest of it all. The two would not have interacted as much if they had not been prime ministers and former prime ministers, and if one had not preceded and succeeded the other. Gowda succeeded Vajpayee immediately after his first thirteen-day brush with power, and there was the motion of confidence in which the two came face to face for the first time on the floor of the Parliament. The frequency and intensity were never lost till Vajpayee lost power in 2004. Briefly, between 1999 and 2002, there was a hiatus when Gowda was out of Parliament,[1] otherwise, for nearly seven years Gowda never missed an opportunity to engage Vajpayee.

Gowda and Vajpayee were two very different people. Vajpayee was essentially a Hindi person, Gowda used English to communicate, which in reality was notches above Vajpayee's felicity. If Vajpayee was full of rhetoric, flourish, and pregnant silences, Gowda was always about dry details, documents and a kind of drawl. When Vajpayee shifted his stances and positions even on some of the most visible issues of the day, it was seldom noticed and never remembered. But Gowda's consistency was always put under the scanner. If Vajpayee invariably got the benefit of the doubt, Gowda was always placed in doubt. Nothing stuck to Vajpayee, no allegation or diatribe, but everything stuck to Gowda and many a times unfairly. Vajpayee was about grandstanding; Gowda was about trench fights. One was a Brahmin and another a Shudra, and the perception about them, their refinements and commitment invariably had undercurrents of caste, traditions, geography, history and plain old prejudice.

When one reads Gowda's parliamentary speeches and interventions, it is quite revealing as to how many times, both as a sitting and former prime minister, and even earlier as an MP, he resorted to supplication through words like 'request', 'plead', and 'beg' to be ordinarily heard during debates. He often reminded his colleagues that he was from a 'humble' background and was not so highly learned. This, despite a reasonably good engineering diploma coupled with solid political and legislative experience of decades. His grasp of the law and its loopholes were legendary in Karnataka.[2] Yet, Gowda never realized his importance, and he continued to beseech attention for his utterances. The weight of his vast experience, and his learning, mostly self-taught, never added a dimension to his otherwise robust image of a refined political wrestler because there was nobody to package it for him. He perhaps did not even know that it could be packaged. He preferred to be in a groove of his own. He was cerebral in his own way.

Vajpayee never had any of this problem ever. When he stood up to speak, people sat down to listen. There were many to add frills, flowers and put on a pedestal what he had uttered or had not uttered. He was always presented as a representative of a great but suppressed philosophical current; of some glorious ideological value system that had been in chains, and of a gentleness and scholarship that had not received its due. Vajpayee even romanced the victimhood that constructed his political persona. When in the Opposition benches, Vajpayee managed a guilt in people that despite his being such a picture of perfection was not on the treasury benches. When he finally moved to the treasury benches, the guilt was still kept alive.

Gowda and Vajpayee's exchanges in Parliament mostly concerned communalism, the farm economy, water disputes, the economy in general and governance, in the same order of importance. George Fernandes, a minister in Vajpayee's cabinet and a fellow Kannadiga, was also a cause of conflict between the two many a times. On all the topics, Gowda spoke with his own field reports, assessments of experts, legal inputs, data points and common sense. He made thorough use of the Parliament library, but never brandished his reading, or blended it with panache into his arguments. But if somebody questioned him, he would surprise them with his depth of understanding. In his first-ever session, and first-ever speech in Parliament, in July 1991, when the motion of thanks to the President's address was being discussed, Gowda started speaking on the Union government's plan to notify the interim order of the Cauvery Tribunal. Mani Shankar Aiyar, Mayiladuthurai MP, objected: 'Sir, I am on a point of order. Is it in order for a member to devote, as he threatens to do, his entire speech to a subject which has not been mentioned in the President's address?' Gowda responded: 'The President's address makes a mention about the development of irrigation . . . Though I am a new member to this house, I know that anything can be discussed during the debate on the presidential address, within the ambit of rules framed by this very house. I know my limitations. Though I am a new entrant in this house, being a member in the state legislature for more than twenty years (actually, close to thirty years in 1991), I know my limitations.'

What he meant was that he was experienced enough to know the rules. As Gowda continued, Aiyar intervened again: 'May I ask the honourable member a question? Does he or does he not accept that the Supreme Court is the final authority on the law of the land?' Gowda's instantaneous response put his memory, diligence and the grasp of details on display: 'I really want to compliment my friend. This is an Inter-State Disputes Act. A tribunal has been constituted under Sections 3 and 4 of this Act, which has been framed by this very same house, though I was not a member in those days. I am just a new entrant, and I would like to draw your attention to Section 11 of the Inter-State Disputes Act, which says: "Notwithstanding anything contained in any other law neither the Supreme Court nor any other court shall have or exercise jurisdiction in respect of any water dispute which is referred to a tribunal under this Act."[3]

Gowda was extremely sharp and well informed as a parliamentarian, and as a prime minister, he was never underprepared. His collection of books, too, was eclectic. He collected all kinds of reports on subjects of interest to him. He personally clipped articles from magazines and newspapers and placed them in files, which only he knew how to access at the most appropriate time. Knowledge meant one thing to Vajpayee, it could be both emotional and unproductive, like the poetry he wrote. But with Gowda, knowledge was about application. It had no other connotation other than information and data, something he could gainfully deploy either for the good of policy, effective action or to fell his opponents. It could be said that knowledge for him was like soil. It had to be felt, had to be fertile, and finally, give a good yield. The only abstraction he perhaps indulged in was his prayer books and the various editions and exegesis of the two Indian epics—Ramayana and Mahabharata. But that too was not abstract for him. They were scaffolds around his soul.

The Gesture

When Gowda as prime minister had lost the support of the Congress party in April 1997, and his own party men and coalition partners were dithering, Vajpayee offered to save his government. Even when the confidence debate was on in the Parliament, he sent a chit to Gowda and reiterated what he had told him in confidence earlier. There were also others like Balasaheb Thackeray, Sahib Singh Verma, George Fernandes and Ram Jethmalani, who urged him not to resign but instead accept BJP's support and continue as prime minister. However, it was Vajpayee who personally tried to work on Gowda.

'It may have been a strategic move on the part of Vajpayee to save my government, but I also could feel his sincerity,' Gowda recalled.[4]

Gowda never forgot this gesture of Vajpayee. Their interpersonal relationship remained cordial at all times, but that did not stop him from countering and cornering Vajpayee on issues of public, communal and constitutional importance. He had made a tangential mention in the Parliament of this Vajpayee offer twice, but ironically while discussing Vajpayee government's failure to maintain communal peace. In April 2002, when the Godhra riots in Gujarat were being discussed, he had said: 'On 9 April 1997, some of the NDA friends—I do not want to take their names and hurt their feelings—approached me. They tried to persuade me by saying: "Why are you losing this opportunity? The prime minister's office is a big office and it is the first time that a farmer has got this opportunity. Why do you want to quit?" I said: "I do not want to be at the mercy of your friends . . ." I have never bothered about continuing in office with this type of humiliation.'[5] He had mentioned the Vajpayee offer earlier too in December 1998 and had concluded by advising Vajpayee: 'Some people think that the chair is so important in life. My appeal to them is this: Conduct yourself in a dignified manner.'[6]

In fact, the April 2002 reference was even harsher, when for a second time during the debate, he had told Vajpayee: 'You can take out those proceedings and go through it. I (had) said: "I do not care whether I will remain for five days or five months. I want to serve my country to the best of my ability." This was the stand which I took. However, what is going on today? For the sake of continuing in office, you had to compromise with your ideology, your personal ideology, whereas you have been classified as one of the tallest leaders with a moderate, liberal outlook, a man of abundant patience, tolerance, etc.'

Gowda, it appears, keeps a mental list of people who had helped him in difficulty and had been kind to him in crisis. One wonders if he is also in the habit of weighing and counterbalancing every single one of his moves and impending actions by constantly vetting it against this list. There is perhaps another list of those who slighted, insulted and cheated him. Whatever, Vajpayee had certainly gotten on the list of the generous. He genuinely acknowledged Vajpayee's seniority, liberal streak, the stature he commanded among his peers as well as the masses, and his vast parliamentary experience.

The opening encounter between the two, when Gowda sought the confidence vote in June 1996, had unraveled his approach to Vajpayee. There were compliments and concessions, but contradictions were exposed at the same time, and there were vague chastisements too. Initiating the motion of confidence, Gowda had said whether Vajpayee was prime minister for ten days or fifteen days, he had his 'own respect and regard'[7] for the experience and the maturity the latter had in his parliamentary life. Then, after Vajpayee had spoken, Gowda parcelled a taunt while responding to the debate on the motion of confidence: 'I am not an eloquent speaker in Hindi, or an eloquent speaker in English, a forceful speech in English or Hindi is not going to solve the problems of the poor man in India. I have seen enough.'[8]

In the same reply to the confidence debate, he appealed to the liberal side of Vajpayee as well: 'You have advised me on so many issues. I take your advice and guidance for my future administration. You have got some secular face. That is why they named you the future prime minister of this country. You were able to get twenty or thirty seats more because of that, otherwise things would have been totally different . . . Today you must come forward; with your liberal outlook you must come forward,' he had said.[9] And since Vajpayee and his colleagues had held forth on corruption and opportunism in their speeches, it was time to expose the doubletalk with two examples—one from nearly sixteen years ago, and another from the glaring present:

When the government of Shri Morarji Bhai stepped down—
I am not criticizing the role of Shri George Fernandes at that
time—Shri Vajpayee, our senior leader at that time was in the

government . . . Shri Chandra Shekhar was the president of the party (Janata Party). I was also one of the working committee members in the state unit. Shri Vajpayee and Shri Morarji Desai had both contacted me and asked for the support of Shri Devaraj Urs to that government. Shri Devaraj Urs was branded as a corrupt politician and Shri Devaraj Urs was indicted by a commission of inquiry which was appointed by the government of India. Sir, with all sincerity at my command, I am making this. I am not going to make any allegation. Is it not a fact? Is it not a fact—that is all I am going to ask. For political convenience in this country, all political parties have played their own role for a temporary gain, including Deve Gowda. Yes. Let us search our hearts instead of arguing one against the other. At least let us start a new chapter.[10]

Then, Gowda tackled the present:

I will just quote one word of Shri Vajpayee . . . 'The BJP's support to the BSP is tactical (BJP had supported BSP and Mayawati as chief minister for a few months between June and October 1995 in Uttar Pradesh). The Congress' support to the United Front is opportunistic. Deve Gowda's party has hardly forty-five members. The Congress with 136 is supporting Deve Gowda.' It is so only to cover up their sins, according to your allegation. How much strength in the UP assembly had Ms Mayawati got? Sir, for your stature . . . What was the mandate of the people? Was the mandate of the people to support BSP? Tell me, sir, you are a senior-most leader, you can advise me, you can guide me what is right. Day before yesterday, while you were participating in the obituary references, you said one thing—it is still fresh in my memory—that Shri Sanjiva Reddyji was denied the Presidentship and after ten years, he got it. We do not know what is going to happen tomorrow. But for a person of your stature, you should not try to find fault with others when your own party has committed so many mistakes.[11]

In fact, the entire reply had begun by asking why Vajpayee had expressed 'dissatisfaction' and 'dejection' in public life after losing power. Gowda had asked: '(You said) I wanted to retire from politics, but things are not coming in favour of my retirement . . . Why has such a situation happened in this country? A person like Shri Atal Bihari Vajpayee expresses that type of dejection in public life, why?'[12] This should be read in sequence with Gowda's constant assertion in the speech that 'I have no lust for power'; 'I am here for five years or five months that is not a criterion for me'; 'It does not matter if I am here for five days or five years'; 'I am a firm believer in God and that is why I said destiny has brought me here. I never expected that I am going to be the prime minister and that was not my life ambition. There is no excitement for me'.[13] Vajpayee was a favourite to be in the chair. There was always a narrative and expectation around his capabilities, but for Gowda, there was only destiny, so there was nothing called 'dejection' or 'dissatisfaction' for him. As a rhetorical counter for the day, it sounded well crafted, but it could only be half-truth from a man who was to encounter the same dejection and dissatisfaction ten months down the line.

Riots, Letters and Speeches

It was after Gowda stepped down as prime minister in 1997 that he became very combative against Vajpayee and most often, it was on the subject of communalism. There was enormous clarity in his speeches on this subject, and unfailingly, he took the constitutional position without resorting to political point-scoring. Arguably, there was no one as impassioned as Gowda in the Parliament between 1998 and 2004 (of course with a gap of two years between October 1999 and February 2002 when he was not in the Parliament), who could taunt, tease, cajole and tear apart Vajpayee, the individual.

How much it affected Vajpayee is a different question, but Gowda did it relentlessly. By then, he did not have a party to back him with numbers;[14] the Janata Dal had splintered;[15] the many 'secular' parties that were part of the United Front coalition had aligned with the BJP and were part of the NDA government, and the Congress was settling down slowly under its new leader, Sonia Gandhi, who was still unsure and inarticulate.

Gowda put these political transitions to his advantage. He had a near open field in the Parliament to question the government's record on communal peace, and the situation too at the time looked permanently volatile— Ayodhya temple issue, Godhra riots, church attacks, attack on syncretic spaces of worship, Orissa assembly attack, murder of a Christian missionary and the rise of the fringe like Bajrang Dal were happening, as if in an arranged sequence. Being a former prime minister also helped Gowda as his long speeches got a front-row presence, but as usual, there was very little media coverage. Occasionally, Vajpayee would say in his laconic style: 'I would like to listen to my old friend.'[16] Otherwise, he was mostly silent.

Gowda fired the first salvo on 2 December 1998 when the BJP with organizations in its saffron family started a movement in Karnataka to reclaim a Sufi shrine at Baba Budangiri Hills in Chikmagalur. BJP leaders like H.N. Ananth Kumar had vowed to make it the 'Ayodhya of the south'. It was a syncretic place of worship with a long history, and the toxic plan was to generate majoritarian heat to exclusively claim it as Dattatreya Peetha, or the seat of Dattatreya, believed to be an incarnation of the trinity of Hindu gods—Brahma, Vishnu and Shiva.

Gowda directly warned Vajpayee: 'Your party's Karnataka unit should think twice: that this is not going to help them . . . The state government (led by J.H. Patel) will take stern action. It is not going to be afraid of anybody. There is no need of the Central government's help. The Central government's mercy is not necessary now. The state government can deal with the situation with a stern hand. You have expressed fear. I do not agree with you. But it is not

an issue with Karnataka alone. It is an issue concerning the entire
nation. The question is whether we should live together or whether
we should go on with this type of, what is called petty politics. I do
not want to use the words "dirty politics". But it is petty politics . . .
Please tell your party unit not to behave like this. This is not going to
help them if they behave like this. It is not a question of liberation of
that shrine . . . The country will be liberated from the hands of this
people . . . we will not allow such things to happen in Karnataka.'[17]
When Gowda was making this statement, the Patel government was
on its last leg. The Janata Dal was imploding in the state, and Chief
Minister Patel, who was close to George Fernandes and Ramakrishna
Hegde, both in Vajpayee's cabinet, had become inactive. In 1999, a
faction led by Patel and Hegde's Lok Shakti were to merge to become
the Janata Dal (United).

On 16 April 1999, just a day before Vajpayee lost the motion
of confidence in Parliament, Gowda spoke like a journalist about
his field trip to Gujarat to survey communal riots. One could only
imagine the attention he must have drawn as a former prime minister
with his SPG protection still in place. To atone for the communal
riots, Vajpayee, as a sitting prime minister, had gone on a day's fast.
Gowda questioned its intent: 'Why did the prime minister go for a
one-day hunger strike? He went and sat on a dharna for one day.
What made him do that? . . . For what mistake he has to do the
prayashchit? . . . When we were running the government, the BJP
government was there in Gujarat. The same Shri Keshubhai Patel
was chief minister. Why was the Bible not burnt? Why were the
churches not burnt during our period? What is the reason? It is
because of the fact that once they took the responsibility of running
the administration, those people got the inspiration that there is a
government which is going to protect them. That is why this type of
heinous act of attacking one community started . . . '[18]

Then, he narrated bits from his field trip: 'Sir, I personally
travelled 920 kms by road in order to find out what has happened
there because I do not want to believe merely the press version.

I went there. I visited one town, which is a semi-urban area. On the one side, there were the Muslims and on the other side, there were the Hindus, the tribal people. One tribal was killed by stabbing by some Muslim anti-social elements. After the burial, those Hindus were going back. In our custom, while going back, they would touch water and then go home. Some boy shouted that the Muslims are coming with some weapons. The police rushed and shot the person who was inside the house, who was no more connected with these events. I went and saw for myself where the bullet was hit. The bullet hit the door, passed through his chest and hit the mirror . . . This is what happened in Gujarat . . . when the home minister of Gujarat goes to that village with a population of about 10,000 to 12,000, he only visits the houses of Hindus and never bothers to visit those other persons who were killed by the police. When this is the attitude, how can we support this government? If the prime minister wants to have a prayashchit that means there is something wrong.'[19]

Gowda went out of action after this speech when he lost the 1999 general elections. But he returned to the Parliament the same day the riots broke in Godhra on 28 February 2002 and spread quickly to the rest of Gujarat. With a renewed focus and energy, Gowda shot off a letter to Vajpayee on 6 March 2002. He was again blunt:

Kindly permit me to state with heavy heart that what is happening in Gujarat since 27 February is beyond human imagination. The orgy of violence that rocked the state as a reaction to the ghastly Godhra incident and the carnage that shook Gujarat and circumstantial situation there drew all of us to a conclusion, that it is nothing but a state sponsored one.

The chief minister of Gujarat is to be held responsible for all that shameful that has happened there. A proper and impartial inquiry has to take place to evaluate the loss of lives and properties suffered by innocent people. Though law and order is a state subject, the Central government cannot escape the duty and responsibility in a situation like the one

in Gujarat. It is clear that the people who have suffered the
loss of lives and properties cannot get justice at the hands of
the state government. The announcement made by the Gujarat
chief minister instituting an inquiry under the chairmanship of
a retired high court judge is to cover his failures.

You are aware that the Gujarat state civil administration
did not take the assistance of the army in an effective way,
and was also not providing guidance, preventing army to play
its role in curbing and controlling the violence. This clearly
shows the mind of the state government. Compensation to
the innocent people who have suffered and rehabilitation
of the people who are disposed and displaced is a must,
whatever may be the financial burden on the government
of India.

Knowing fully well the attitude of the Gujarat chief
minister and state government, I urge upon you to immediately
constitute a high-powered commission (under Commission
of Inquiry Act) under the chairmanship of a sitting Supreme
Court judge to have a thorough probe into the incidents
that happened in Gujarat. The probe should cover all aspects
leading to ugly communal incidents from the day one when
the kar sevaks who were in a train were attacked and burnt at
Godhra. The terms of reference of the high-power commission
should cover all that happened in Gujarat.[20]

The letter had covered almost everything—a succinct analysis
of the flow of events, the Centre–state laws and relationship,
the rehabilitation, who should pay compensation, who should
conduct the inquiry and under what law, and what the terms of
reference should be. The letter in functional English highlighted
Gowda's experience and solution-seeking approach. He did not
leave it at that. Four days later, on 10 March, he followed it up
with another letter to Vajpayee. This one was very persuasive and
emotional:

The whole purpose behind instituting an enquiry under the Commission of Enquiry Act is to unravel the facts and circumstances leading to the ghastly carnage, the role of the state and the police in quelling it and to evaluate the magnitude of the losses. A true and correct picture that emerges from out of such a meaningful enquiry would not only enable us to undertake purposeful relief measures, but would also help us to arrive at the behind the scene truth. This truth alone would safeguard us from preventing such national shames revisiting us; as and when it revisits, we will be in a state of preparedness to effectively counter it. Otherwise, the institution of enquiry would be another political gimmick, a fraud on the nation.

The merciless massacre of innocent people in the state of Gujarat on a huge scale is a bigger national calamity that has befallen on the nation in the recent years. What pains us most and makes us crestfallen with shame is that this is not a calamity that is brought about by nature or spontaneity, but it is engineered by human follies for ulterior purposes. The recent parliamentary delegation would vouchsafe the fact that the state of victims is worse than that of the Afghan or Bengal refugees, they have become orphans in their own homes living in a continuous state of terror and fear, always haunted by the memories of the brutal violence. This is not a state issue, but an issue that envelopes the whole nation and eats into communal harmony like a devastating fire; destroying the very fabric of our national life like a cancerous disease.

He seemed to be in a flow and one can only imagine him furiously dictating the letter to his secretary. He continued:

This has happened in a country that boasts of giving birth to prophets of non-violence like Buddha, Gandhi and a Vedic heritage, a country that boasts of strong and enduring democracy in the world. Therefore, this calls for a greater introspection.

Hon'ble Atalji, it is with a heavy heart and irretrievable sense
of shame, I appeal to you that we, the politicians owe a duty
to the nation, we can't fail in our duty to reassure the nation
that we are here not just to shed tears and wipe away tears, but
we are here to protect them and govern the country. We have
failed in both . . . Atalji, we have erred, let us not suppress our
efforts, but together we unfold this national shame. Let us not
become the wicked mother who quietens the crying baby by
strangulating it, but a mother who quietens the baby by feeding
it with love and affection.[21]

Next day, 11 March 2002, when a discussion on the riots was
initiated in the Parliament under rule 193, he repeated:

We have also had some experience in running the administration
as chief minister and as the prime minister. I have at least gained
certain experience as to how these things happen. When the
cadre of IAS, IPS had been created, the debate took place in the
very same house. The object of creating the cadres of IAS and
IPS was totally different. Today the whole thing has collapsed.
The IAS and IPS cannot act independently; we know that. We
know how these officers are going to be at the mercy of the
administrators. There has been a serious lapse on the part of the
state administration . . . If the state government is biased about
a particular religion, as has been reported in the press, I do not
want to jump to the conclusion whether the chief minister is
like that or not. But what has been reported in the press makes
us believe so unless it is proved otherwise . . .

 What happened in Gujarat after 1998 when Shri Vajpayee
took over? Nineteen churches were demolished. The Bible was
burnt. Who had instigated it? Did the ISI instigate? I was in
the house at that time . . . I am proud to say that I am also a
Hindu. I go to all the temples. People laugh at times saying
Deve Gowda goes to all temples on pilgrimage . . . The country

is going to disintegrate. If Shri Vajpayee has to take that credit in his life, let him go on with this type of administration. I sincerely appeal to the prime minister that he should not hesitate to appoint a sitting Supreme Court judge and see that all these issues—whether the state government or the chief minister is responsible—are included as terms of reference.[22]

In the first intervention in the Parliament, he was a little more circumspect about the role of the chief minister, but in less than a week, on 16 March 2002, he would make a direct allegation in the Parliament: 'On that day, the chief minister asked his establishment not to go to the rescue of the minorities. It is state-sponsored terrorism, or it is goondaism or by whatever name you may call it.'[23] All this exchange directed at Vajpayee was happening before Vajpayee had counselled 'rajdharma' to Chief Minister Narendra Modi.

Nearly 17 years later Gowda recalled the atmosphere on the day. He said he took oath as an MP on 28 February 2002, shook hands with Vajpayee, went around the Speaker's chair, and sat in the Opposition benches. By the time he settled down, the message was flashed that 90 people had been burnt alive near Godhra. He immediately stood up and pointed out to L.K. Advani, who was deputy prime minister and home minister, that it was happening in his constituency. 'He responded by saying he knows my responsibilities,' Gowda said. He then returned home and spoke to his advocate friends. Each one gave him his own interpretation of the events. The next day, Vajpayee asked Pramod Mahajan to take a delegation to Gujarat. He personally asked Gowda to join the delegation, but Gowda refused. He sent his colleague in the Rajya Sabha, C.M. Ibrahim, instead. Sonia Gandhi was also part of the delegation. However, he decided to go to Gujarat on his own to make an assessment. 'When you go in a delegation, there are limitations. It is like a conducted tour. The tour manager controls your movements. So, I thought if I have to get to the bottom of the truth, I should travel alone. I camped in Ahmedabad. There was no police protection. There was only my local friend, Geetesh

Shah, by my side. I decided to visit all thirteen relief camps. I also planned to visit villages, which had been abandoned by Muslims. Without giving any intimation, I rushed to Hindu camps also. There was no anxiety there at all. People were relaxed and playing cards. The moment they saw me, they tried to cover the cards with a cloth. I observed everything but did not speak to the media. I took the matter to the Parliament.'[24]

On 30 April 2002, he did take it to Parliament, and tried sarcasm with the words *rajdharma* and *tapasya*. He also addressed Vajpayee directly and told him that people do not trust him anymore. It was the liberal mask that Gowda tried to strip. When the motion 'expressing grave concern over failure of administration in ensuring security of minority community in various parts of the country, especially in Gujarat,' was being discussed, Gowda stood up:

Mr Prime Minister, when you went to Gujarat, after seeing all the things, with agony and anguish, you expressed your anger about the state administration. You have visited only two relief camps—one is a Hindu relief camp and another is a Muslim relief camp. But what happened? After you preached *rajdharma*, is there any improvement? Is there any normalcy in Gujarat? That is all what we want to know . . . I believed that Shri Narendra Modi would follow *rajdharma* you have preached. You have described what is *rajdharma*. Has he followed it? Before you went to Gujarat the chief minister had come to Delhi on your direction to see you. He met both you and the home minister. After hearing the whole events, you advised him to go back and win the confidence of the people. This is the advice you have given to the chief minister. Has he followed your advice? Has he followed your *rajdharma*? . . . I do not want to take the name of Shri Narendra Modi. Has he made any sincere attempt? Your concern is whether to keep him or remove him. As long as you enjoy the majority of the house, we cannot put our pressure on you . . .

Why should this happen? Why should any doubt arise in the mind of anybody about your moderation, your tolerance and your liberal outlook, which have been ingrained through your 'tapasya' for fifty years. You used the word 'tapasya' when all these people demanded your resignation on the Tehelka.com issue . . . People had then thought that you are one of the tallest leaders in India but today everybody doubts you. Why the doubt is a big question. When you went to Gujarat, you said something; when you came back from Cambodia and Singapore, you said something else. That is the crux of the problem. That is why the doubt has arisen . . . Nobody expected that Shri Atal Bihari Vajpayee was going to allow such things to happen. There is a startling interview given by the ninety-six year old chairman of the Gujarat unit of the Vishwa Hindu Parishad, Prof. Kashiram Shastri where he has said that the list of shops owned by Muslims in Ahmedabad was prepared on the morning of 28 February itself . . .

I would like to tell you one thing. The few who have tried to go back to their homes in recent days have been forced to return to the relief camps. It is not an admission made by any Tom, Dick or Harry. It is an admission made by Shri K. Srinivas, the collector of Ahmedabad, who admits that at least 5000 Muslims who tried to leave the camps returned back because the conditions were not conducive. How to bring a conducive atmosphere? Please tell this house. We will accept that.[25]

Then, he presented a graphic narrative of what he saw in a relief camp:

When I went to a camp, I saw an eighty-five-year-old lady with sword cuts on her body. When I enquired from her what happened to other members of her family, she was unable to speak. She said somebody came to her house and cut them into pieces. Her son was burnt alive. She is alone. She questioned,

'Why Allah has left me alone in this world?' There were marks
of sword cuts across the chest. Her hand was cut into several
pieces. I do not want to narrate further. I do not want to take
the time of the house with all the information we have collected
at all the thirteen relief camps that we have visited. You may
understand the circumstances. So, even if you give some relief
measures, with the same person at the helm of affairs (Modi)
and with the same establishment, they will not feel secure.
When the district collector says that they cannot go back to
their native places, how can you trust the same person? . . . Mr
Prime Minister, rise up to the expectations of the people of this
country. I will extend my sincere thanks to you, if you rise up
to the occasion and if you prove that you are a moderate and
liberal prime minister.[26]

A year later, on 27 February 2003, he brought up Godhra yet again:
'You may rule, as I said, for another one and half years. Do not be
under the impression that every state has got Narendra Modi and
every state has got Sabarmati-like train incidents. This is a great
country, and it would take all these things in its stride.'[27]

In March 2002, participating in the 'motion of thanks on the
President's address', he had referred to Vajpayee's flip flops and
contradictions:

Sir, I would like to draw the attention of the house to what the
prime minister had said on 28 December 2000. He had said
that the temple issue is a national sentiment. After ten days, he
went to Kerala for a rest. There, he tried to set it right, saying
that he had not said like that. He tried to revive his stand as if
he was committed to secularism and wanted to satisfy his NDA
partners. I do not want to go on narrating his contradictions.
At one stage, he said that Shri. Advani, Dr Murli Manohar
Joshi, minister for human resource development, and Kumari
Uma Bharati had gone to Ayodhya to protect Babri Masjid.

I was shocked to hear it from the prime minister. He is a mature man and a senior-most leader. I do respect him. We were in jail during Emergency. Shri Atalji, Shri Advani and myself were all together. He was there for a short period and came to Delhi because of his ill health. He (Vajpayee) had the courage to tell the nation that these three leaders went to protect the mosque. If his intentions were true to his conscience, as he wants the country to believe, then why is there an attempt again to create problems in the same disputed place? . . . So, the hon. prime minister has to clarify the position in his reply. Otherwise, it is very difficult for us to trust the bona fides of the government.[28]

A couple of months before Godhra happened, there was an attack on the Orissa assembly by Bajrang Dal, Vishwa Hindu Parishad and Durga Vahini. Trident-wielding men rushed inside, indulged in vandalism for over thirty minutes, and had shouted 'Atal Bihari Vajpayee *zindabad*'. They beat up everybody who came in their way, including a BJD legislator, journalists and policemen. Pratap Sarangi, who was state unit Bajrang Dal president, was arrested on charges of rioting. In 1999, Australian missionary Graham Staines and his two children were also burnt alive in Orissa. Speaking on 18 March 2002 on the incident, Gowda had said: 'We cannot tolerate this situation. When you banned the SIMI (Students Islamic Movement of India), I issued a strong press note. I also wrote a letter to the prime minister. If you have banned the SIMI, why can you not ban the Bajrang Dal? If the prime minister is honest . . . if he is true to his conscience, he should take steps to ban this organization, which is going to be a threat to the democratic institutions.'[29] He was to similarly seek a ban on Bajrang Dal again in 2008 when church attacks took place in Mangalore. He had written to Manmohan Singh, who was then prime minister.

As one can see, Gowda was extremely blunt in exposing Vajpayee. In December 2002, he had also predicted Vajpayee's electoral fate two years in advance. In a discussion on problems faced by farmers,

he had said: 'I want to tell this government, please do not neglect
the remaining two years. It is a very important period for the NDA
government to revive itself. Otherwise, they will sink and somebody
else will sail.'[30] He had, in a way, predicted the fiasco of the 'India
Shining' campaign that was to be launched by the BJP during the
2004 elections.

In 2002, at the SPG raising day function, Gowda and Vajpayee
were sitting together. Advani was seated at a distance. They had a
candid moment. It was neither about ideology nor governance nor
was it about pure politics. There was camaraderie when Gowda
spoke to Vajpayee: 'There was a time in Bangalore when people
would throng to listen to you at the National College grounds.
What has happened to you now? You are not the same person. What
have you allowed to affect your personality? You are not the same
person.' Vajpayee dropped his guard: 'I do not know who my friend
is, and who my enemy is in my own party and government. I am very
confused.'[31]

The Consequence

If anybody thought there was no consequence to all the forthright
talk that Gowda was doing, and publicly embarrassing Vajpayee,
then that was a mistaken notion. Besides talking about the spread
of saffronization under the regime, Gowda had pursued corruption
charges against the NDA government, especially the distribution of
telecom licences and the purchase of Russian tanks for the army.
Anyway, Gowda wrote a letter marked 'Personal and Confidential'
on 20 January 2003. Its contents were telltale and the tone grim, but
there was ample caution too:

> On 23 December 2002 some CBI officers have collected the
> photostat copies of my income tax returns and also of my
> wife. They have also taken the photostat copies of the income
> tax returns of my four sons and two daughters who are living

separately. If the government has taken the decision to collect these photostat copies of the income tax returns I do not want to question the prerogative rights of the government as the CBI is working under prime minister. I do not know whether this has been done with your permission or not. What happened on 23rd is widely being discussed in the official quarters. This is for your kind information. I leave it at that. If you can kindly inform me a suitable time convenient to you, I will take that opportunity to meet you and discuss the matter further.[32]

It appears there was instant response to the letter from Vajpayee. On 22 January 2003, he wrote again: 'After your good self has gone through my letter dated 20.01.2003, you were kind enough to inform me that no such steps were taken by the CBI with regard to collecting photostat copies of income tax returns. You were also kind enough to inform me that you will ask the CBI director to meet me personally in this regard in Delhi on 26.01.2003. After your good self informed me about the factual position today, I am surprised to know that local CBI officer has addressed a letter on 21.01.2003 to chief commissioner of income tax, Karnataka to furnish all the IT details filed already. I am bringing the above developments to your kind notice.'[33]

This second letter pushed Vajpayee to pick up the phone and speak to Gowda, he mentioned the conversation in his letter of 26 January 2003. On that day, the CBI director had visited Gowda to assure him, personally, on the instructions of the prime minister, that the government was not embarking on a witch hunt against him. The ever-suspicious and cautious Gowda would not buy it outright but put things on record. He hinted politics but only hinted, did not elaborate:

I am grateful to you for your telephonic conversation with me after receiving my letter. The director of CBI met me as per your directions and explained to me about the position. I was

surprised to know from him that no CBI people have ever gone
to collect the income tax returns of mine, which have been
filed regularly by me and also my wife, sons and daughters,
as per the law. As per the income tax law, it is very clear that
nobody can take any documents of an assessee as he has been
given protection under the law to maintain the secrecy and the
confidentiality. It appears to me that my political rivals might
have taken this opportunity of collecting the photostat copies
of income tax returns with the connivance of some officials
of the income tax department. My request to your good self
is that the assesses of income tax returns in future should not
suffer by the illegal and immoral methods adopted by the
political rivals.[34]

Vajpayee personally wrote to Gowda and acknowledged the 26
January letter on 5 February 2003. He said he would further look
into the issues that had been raised. The letter was hand delivered to
his 5 Safdarjung Lane address in New Delhi.[35]

   In the context of income tax raids against the *Outlook* magazine,
and its proprietor Rajan Raheja, in May 2001, journalist Vinod
Mehta, in his memoirs, recounts a few meetings with people
at the top in the NDA government. He also meets Vajpayee,
his principal secretary Brajesh Mishra, and finance minister
Yashwant Sinha. He asks them to stop the harassment. But to
his surprise, both Vajpayee and Brajesh Mishra feign ignorance
and express surprise that *Outlook* was raided. They reiterate their
commitment to press freedom.[36] Later, Mehta recounted in an
off-the-record chat with seniors in his editorial team[37] that one of
the cabinet ministers had told him that Vajpayee does not take
criticism lightly. He gave vent to his frustration when he went
for a walk with Mishra every evening in his Race Course Road
residence. All action, or part-action, or non-action got decided
during the walk.

It was possible that Gowda's matter too was discussed in one such evening walk, and a half-threatening action was indicated. But, when it was brought up in writing, both the prime minister, and his CBI director feigned innocence and ignorance. Or perhaps, it was really a vague mischief mission about which Vajpayee had no idea.

21

Modi Focus and the Patel Backdrop

A few weeks after the results of the 2014 general elections were out, H.D. Deve Gowda went to 7 Race Course Road, the residence–office he had once occupied as prime minister, to meet its latest occupant. Gowda was a little hesitant as he stepped out of his car, but Narendra Modi was generous. He breezily rushed to the doorstep to receive him with a broad smile. His eagerness to welcome came across. Then, there was the warmth of a perfect namaste, all fingertips in alignment and with a gentle bow of the head; that was followed by a hug, and finally, there was a gripping handshake. Gowda was pleasantly surprised. As they moved inside, Modi cut the pace of his stride to match Gowda's step, and till they reached the chair in the drawing room, he continued to hold Gowda's hand.

As they settled down, Gowda pulled out a piece of paper from his pocket. There was a folder too with him, but this paper came from his pocket. He made a dramatic declaration: 'During the election campaign I had said that if you got a majority, I'll quit politics. You have now won a very handsome majority. I may have won my seat (from Hassan), but I will not enter the Parliament. I will resign. I will stand by my words.' The moment Gowda uttered this Modi stood up: 'What are you saying? For heaven's sake, please do not do something like that. Exchange of words happens during election rallies. You are one of the few senior people I look up to. I may have to consult you from time to time.' Gowda recalled Modi saying.[1]

Once the 'quitting' issue had been sorted out, they had a 'heart to heart exchange on personal matters'. One of the things that Modi was curious to know from Gowda was about his move to Delhi in 1996. 'You were doing wonderful work in Karnataka, why did you come to Delhi? Why? For the first time, you had got sixteen parliamentary seats in the state. You knew fully well the dirty politics of Delhi, in spite of it why did you come? You could have ruled Karnataka for twenty-five years. V.P. Singh had to leave the chair in thirteen months, Chandra Shekhar had to go in four months, Charan Singh was not even allowed to sit on Pandit Nehru's *gaddi*. They removed him within a month before he faced the Parliament. Knowing all this, why did you come to Delhi? Why did they remove you? Even for your entry into the Parliament they created so much of a problem. What sin have you committed?' Gowda recalled Modi's insistence for an answer.[2]

Gowda never revealed this exchange with Modi for a good four years. He spoke about it for the first time during the Karnataka assembly poll campaign in May 2018. He had brought it up when Modi had publicly defended him after Rahul Gandhi had attacked the Janata Dal (Secular) as the 'B team of BJP', thereby indirectly questioning the integrity of Gowda's leadership. Modi had chided Rahul Gandhi: 'I heard the Congress president speak at political rallies . . . the way he referred to respected Deve Gowdaji . . . is this your culture (sanskar)? This is arrogance . . . Your life (as Congress chief) has just begun. Deve Gowda is among the tallest leaders of the country. You are insulting him,' Modi had said.[3]

Thanking Modi with the usual caveats of the election season, Gowda had said: 'Before the 2014 elections, I had said I would resign my Lok Sabha membership if BJP gets a majority on its own. I decided to resign, but Modi persuaded me against doing so. He said the country needs the experience and services of senior leaders.'[4]

Gowda had timed the revelation so well that it had caused confusion in the state where a hung assembly was being predicted. Gowda had returned a compliment but had also ensured that it fully aided his game of brinkmanship. He had used it to fill up crevices and create fissures in the political atmosphere of the day. The local BJP leaders stopped attacking his party because they now knew their boss and Gowda had a relationship going. The Congress became cautious because it did not want an alliance to foster between the BJP and the JD(S). That was a classic Gowda checkmate, perfected over decades. Modi, too, perhaps praised Gowda to score a point against the Congress by further typecasting it as an arrogant party with an arrogant, self-serving dynasty. He had used Gowda, a self-made man, who held the highest office of the nation, to put down a 'novice' whose singular achievement was his providential birth. The two of the finest political minds seemed to be on a duet.

Something similar had happened on 18 May 2018, on Deve Gowda's birthday. Modi called up Gowda to wish him and told the media that he had done so.[5] This was so timed that it created a flutter in the media. JD(S) was in the process of forming a government in Karnataka, in alliance with the Congress, and Gowda's son, H.D. Kumaraswamy, was slated to take over as chief minister. The assembly results had been declared three days ago. The media, expectedly, went into a speculation overdrive, wondering if JD(S) would renege its promise to the Congress and go with the BJP, now that the prime minister was directly in touch with Gowda.

Returning to the resignation episode, even Gowda's closest aides did not know that he had offered to resign his parliamentary seat when he met Modi in 2014. One of the aides revealed: 'He carried a folder with him that day when he went to meet the prime minister. That contained papers on the Cauvery River and perhaps also on the Mahadayi River. He returned an empty folder when he came back. He had neither discussed his resignation nor had we typed it out for him to sign. He must have handwritten and placed it in his kurta pocket to maintain confidentiality. We were stunned when he revealed the true intent of his first meeting with Prime Minister Modi.'[6]

One can only guess why Gowda offered to resign his parliamentary seat in his meeting with Modi. He had far greater experience of politics than Modi to know that one usually does not transpose words uttered during a poll campaign into a post-election scenario when everything is generally forgiven. When everybody is busy moving on with the business of either sitting in the Treasury or the Opposition benches or forming alliances, campaign exchanges are conveniently forgotten. No one knew this pragmatism of politics better than Gowda, who had completed over 50 years in electoral politics in 2014. Yet, why did he offer to resign? Was it a gesture to break the ice between the two? Was it a momentary emotional expression? Was it done knowing fully well that it will never be accepted? After all, Modi was not the designated authority to accept Gowda's resignation. Was it about having a working relationship? Was it about protecting his party and his family? Was it an expression of empty intent, a test balloon of sorts, to gauge Modi's accommodation and flexibility? Or did he really think that he had embarrassed himself and his years of experience in politics? We will never know.

There was another thick layer of emotion to Gowda's resignation offer. When Gowda had challenged Modi in April 2014 by saying he would 'quit politics' if BJP got a majority, he had also given an extra twist by saying he would 'quit Karnataka' too. This was at a political meeting in Shimoga.[7] Modi, the BJP's prime ministerial candidate, had instantly responded the next day at a rally in Chikkaballapur. Modi picked up just the Karnataka bit to elaborate and showcase his humility and also showcase Gujarat, which was being constructed in the media as an ideal state. He had said: 'You are the former prime minister, and I am like your son. If it has become difficult for you to stay here, I pray, don't worry, I will extend all facilities in Gujarat for you. If you want to stay in an old age home, I will make all arrangements. If you want to take a home there, I'll find one. If you want to stay in a farmhouse that too is fine, and if you decide to stay with me, I will serve you more than your son. Please accept my invitation. I am ready to serve you.'[8] In the same breath, he had taken a swipe at the Gowda dynasty.

Gowda and Modi's strategies and utterances since 2014 have shadowed each other, and like fine players, they seem to have enjoyed every bit of the game.

Unexpected Praise

There may be many things that make Gowda unhappy about Modi, but there is one thing that makes him happy, which is the public recognition that Modi has given Gowda. 'No prime minister took my name in public after I stepped down in 1997. Vajpayee and Manmohan Singh did not. The Congress in general tried to ignore everybody outside the dynasty. But after 2014, Modi started taking my name. He started telling people that I was a senior leader, a tall leader, a farmer's leader, that I made it to the top, like him, on my own, and that I should be respected. He may have praised me to meet his ends and suit his election needs, but the fact is he did. Personally, he has always been very courteous. He has called me many times, received me many times at his home, and whenever we have sat down to talk, he listens. Yes, he is a good listener, but he never reacts. He will never react to anything— *mounam kalaham naasti* (a Sanskrit proverb that means, there will be no quarrel if one is silent). That is the one thing that he has cultivated. When I went to him in 2014 to resign, he treated me well. He was affectionate.'[9]

It may sound inappropriate, but Modi had mentioned the affection he showers on Gowda when he meets him, and that too in an election speech, in May 2018: 'I meet our former prime minister, Shriman Deve Gowdaji, whenever he comes to Delhi and seeks my time. That's not all. When he visits my home, I always go to his car to open the door to welcome him. And when he leaves, I go to the car to see him off. Politically he is our opponent, he criticizes me and votes against us in the Parliament. But Deve Gowdaji is among the greatest leaders, and I have no right to forget that. There will be differences in politics, but there are certain etiquettes in public life,' Modi had said.[10]

Gowda's general observation of Modi's deep urge to correct attitudes and history was accurate. In an interview in September 2016, Modi offered a rationale on why he had no time for the elite Lutyens's-Delhi crowd. He may be seen narrowly appropriating a larger argument for self-aggrandizement, but it was still insightful. He said: 'Look at history. Patel was always seen as a rural unsophisticate; nobody spoke of what Morarjibhai did but only discussed what he drank. None spoke of Deve Gowda's achievements as a farmer's son but only projected his slumber. They similarly made fun of Charan Singh, and in his time, Ambedkar was humiliated too.'[11] Modi had made a case for non-dynastic and non-Congress prime ministers and political stalwarts. It was a powerful message that he was sending across, urging people to look beyond the Congress, and beyond the dynasty.

Gowda was not aware of this interview. When he heard what Modi had said, he got into a long loop:

I will agree with the Modi argument. Other than the Congress dynasty, they do not want to take the names of anybody. Manmohan Singh served this country for ten years. Is his name anywhere? In the naming of all public programmes and public institutions, their imagination used to stop with a Gandhi name. Modi is trying to change all that. He has taken over the Nehru Memorial at Teen Murti and converted it into a museum for all prime ministers. That is a good thing. This is a big country, and as Thyagaraja said 'Endaromahanubhavulu', many great men have shaped this nation. How can modern history be built only around one surname and one family? My respect for Nehru and others from that family is there on one side, I would not deny that, but when it comes to the nation, we should acknowledge everybody's contribution. Congress started acknowledging other leaders who served their own party and the nation only when they feared that Modi and BJP would appropriate all of them. There should be genuine regard and respect; nothing should happen out of fear. Nobody becomes a prime minister just like that. Only a fool can be convinced that it happens like magic. You may be at the top for ten days, ten months or ten years, but it is not luck alone that takes you there. There is hard work, political moves, perseverance, and decades of waiting, and of course, there is the shower of God's grace. Getting there, I think, is the toughest, but surviving there is relatively easy. If you do not have a majority like Modi, you have to go on compromising. You will survive and float for a longer period. I chose not to do that.[12]

Gowda also revealed that Modi sought some kind of political alignment with him. At a NITI Aayog meeting in Delhi in early 2019, he had taken aside H.D. Kumaraswamy, Gowda's son and sitting Karnataka chief minister, and had apparently said: 'Your father is still addicted to Congress politics. He will not compromise with our politics. But the Congress wants to destroy you. You resign today, and you will take oath tomorrow with our support like Nitish Kumar. I will put you on the job for full five years.' That was around the time that Congress legislators were getting ready to cross over to the BJP and destabilize the coalition government. But Kumaraswamy had politely declined this offer: 'My son said I don't want to hurt my father at this age. He is suffering. My government may stay or go, at his advanced age, I can't hurt the feelings of my father.'[13] This was the same Kumaraswamy who had aligned with the BJP in 2006, against Gowda's wishes, but now he was not willing to cross the line. In fact, a day before Modi had praised Gowda in an election rally in 2018, the patriarch had declared in an interview that he would 'disown' his son if he aligned with the BJP after the assembly polls.[14]

The Opposition Game

When it comes to pure politics, Gowda and Modi are very refined players. Both think through their moves and spend considerable time fine-tuning the execution of their strategies. The manner with which they deal with their political opponents and also strike up friendships in the opposite camp are very similar. Their vindictiveness quotient may not be very different either. Perhaps there ends the similarity. While Modi is very articulate, very communicative, and in the eyes of many 'a demagogue', Gowda is at a totally different end in this department. He does not relish speaking much; his sentences are broken, he almost mumbles; rhetoric is not in his realm. There was a time very early in his career when he claims he was a forceful speaker, but there is neither a recording available nor is there a memory. He speaks straight and with data and documents, and that makes his communication bland and boring. In an old way, he believes that action should speak louder. He does not believe in publicizing his actions but wants them to be discovered. Actually he does not dwell on communication and publicity; therefore, chaos and confusion have reigned around his actions. However, Modi is no match to Gowda's thoroughness and engagement with big ideas. Gowda has areas of expertise like law, irrigation, agriculture, water disputes and general administration. Modi is, at best, a very vague generalist.

Ever since Modi came to power in 2014, Gowda has tried to maintain a decent relationship with him, like he has done with all prime ministers before and after him. He has, from time to time, written letters on subjects of public concern, but nothing really of significance. They were not like the letters he wrote to Vajpayee (Read the chapter 'Wrestling with Vajpayee and his mask'). There was an element of caution, too, because Modi did not reveal himself too much as a person, and Gowda could not really pierce through the enigma of his personality. In that sense, Modi was not like an old-world politician–colleague that Gowda had always demonstrated some finesse in handling. He met him privately half a dozen times[15] during his first term, but what was private there was very limited. As Gowda always said, 'He never reacted to anything. He listened, but you could not make out what was going on in his mind. No prime minister was like that.'

What Gowda perhaps meant was that there was no emotional crevice that could be exploited. There was no vulnerability that was confessed. Modi for Gowda was a strange kettle of fish as he had broken away from the familiar way of doing politics in India since Independence. He violated old lines and drew new boundaries. He poked and provoked everything, and his majority made the Opposition irrelevant. Yet, initially, Modi tried to keep senior people like Gowda and Sharad Pawar in good humour but once he was firmly in the saddle, he did not pay them much attention, except during political exigencies or to create a spectacle, like when Gowda was invited to be on the dais when the Goods and Services Tax regime was inaugurated in the Parliament at midnight.[16] Gowda, himself a consummate politician, often wondered what Modi was up to.

In 2018, around the time the Karnataka assembly elections were due, the status quo in the relationship was somewhat broken. Both sides told what they thought of each other in public. This continued till the 2019 parliamentary elections. As early as April 2019, Gowda had warned about Modi's intent to abrogate Article 370 if he came back to power. 'He is trying to make this a Hindu nation,'[17] he had said. In an interview, he had said Modi's economic and agricultural policy had totally failed.[18] And when it came to the general mood in the country, he had not minced words: 'Let me be very plain on this, the situation in the country is nothing but an undeclared Emergency.'[19]

In January 2019, when Modi had attacked his son-led Congress–JD(S) coalition government in Karnataka on the issue of farm loan waiver and called it a 'lollipop company', Gowda, usually restrained, got furious. He had not often been seen defending his son's administration in the media, but this time he took to Twitter. His comment sounded more like a warning:[20] 'I have been observing the taunting statements of PM Modi on Karnataka's crop loan waiver scheme. Dear PM, more than 60,000 farmers have already received money directly into their bank accounts. We are determined to keep our promise to the farmers and are acting on the same lines.' He also reminded Modi that if he was pointing a finger at his son's government, the other four were pointing at the PM himself. This was perhaps the first time that Gowda had used Twitter to counter criticism. Otherwise, his account is a boring journal of records, mostly meant for obituary and birthday notices, event attendance, and pictures of his official letters. Modi had earlier said: 'They gave lollipops to people in terms of assurances and promised loan waiver but only 800 people got their loans waived. How can you trust these lollipop companies?'

Earlier, Gowda had converted his son's swearing-in ceremony in the last week of May 2018 into the Opposition's show of strength against Narendra Modi. A report said:[21] 'He got CPM leaders Sitaram Yechury and Pinarayi Vijayan on the same stage as arch-rival Mamata Banerjee (Trinamool), with Mayawati (BSP) and Akhilesh Yadav (SP) reconstructing their *bua–bhatija* [aunt–nephew] roles. The array of leaders who stood with Kumaraswamy included Delhi CM Arvind Kejriwal, Andhra CM N. Chandrababu Naidu, NCP's Sharad Pawar, Sharad Yadav, RLD's Ajit Jogi, CPI's D. Raja, RJD's Tejaswi Yadav, Puducherry CM V. Narayanasamy and IUML MP P.K. Kunhalikutty.' Of course, Sonia Gandhi and Rahul Gandhi were present too.

At a similar joint Opposition rally that Mamata Banerjee had organized in Kolkata, Gowda had made concrete suggestions to defeat Modi in May 2019. It was reported[22] as follows:

The Janata Dal (Secular) supremo said a small group of senior leaders should be formed to decide on a roadmap on how they will ensure good governance. The herculean task of seat-sharing for the coming Lok Sabha elections has to be addressed to ensure a direct fight against the BJP, he said . . . A stable government is needed to build a strong nation, but after getting 282 seats in the 2014 elections, Narendra Modi instead of building a strong nation, wants to destroy the secular nature of the country and destroy all constitutional institutions . . . Stating that a question often asked is who would be the prime minister after Modi, he said the Opposition leaders must have confidence that they can give a stable government for five years. This must be ensured by the galaxy of leaders congregated at the rally. Modi claims that a coalition government is unstable and cannot achieve anything, but the Opposition has to show that it can give a stable government and develop the nation. Referring to the coalition government led by him between June 1996 and April 1997, he said it had sanctioned the Bogibeel bridge in Assam, which was inaugurated by Prime Minister Modi recently. Delhi Metro was also cleared by my government, thirty-six crore poor people were helped through rice, wheat and kerosene oil at subsidized prices, Gowda said, stressing that a coalition government can ensure development of people and the nation.

This was all a build up to the Lok Sabha elections. Somewhere deep inside Gowda's mind, with support from astrological calculations, he felt his 'phoenix' moment will arrive in May 2019 and he will be asked to steer the country out of Modi's mess. But, after Gowda lost the Lok Sabha election from Tumkur in May 2019, and the BJP got more seats than in 2014, things quietened a bit. The public transaction between the two was reduced to some routine letters and exchange of birthday wishes.

However, in private, Gowda was seething with anger. He thought 'nothing was going right' in the country. When the National Registry for Citizens (NRC) in Assam became contentious, and when the Citizenship Amendment Act (CAA) was passed, provoking widespread protests across the nation, Gowda contemplated and consulted his family and friends many times as to what his response should be. He wanted to protest, but his health was not cooperating. Right in the middle of the CAA protest, in November–December 2019, he had to be admitted to an ayurvedic facility in Kerala to treat his troublesome knee.[23] He also wanted to go to Kashmir and get detained. He even drafted a letter to the Lieutenant Governor of Jammu and Kashmir seeking permission to visit Srinagar. 'How can I let down my friend Farooq Abdullah? The people of Kashmir trusted me as prime minister. How can I let them down?' He had asked. He coordinated with Sharad Pawar and issued a statement[24] demanding the release of political detainees in Kashmir after Article 370 was abrogated, and a week later, Farooq Abdullah was freed.

He wanted to go the North-east and protest the NRC. He said: 'Manmohan Singh was sent to the Rajya Sabha for nearly thirty years from Assam. But he is not keeping well to go and protest. His nature is also very different. At least I should go and stand by the people of the North-east as a former prime minister. They have showered a lot of affection on me.'[25] After his election loss, he was constantly formulating a response to Modi. The fact that at eighty-seven he was now an elder in the nation's political arena made him feel that he had a duty to act.

He captured his mood and what was happening under Modi in a veiled manner when he went to Seoul for a peace meet in February 2020. When he spoke, the immediate past secretary-general of the United Nations, Ban Ki-moon, was on the dais, as well as sitting and former heads of state:

I have always believed that it is possible to see the universe in a grain of sand. This viewpoint that I developed was not acquired by learning. It was the cultural ethos that surrounded me. It was secular. Now, this worldview is being challenged. Sectarian violence is being stoked. Hate is fast becoming a byword for nationalism. It has become toxic. However, I am hugely relieved and happy that the youth across the globe are answering this challenge with great fortitude. In the Indian context, the young and the oppressed have made it a ritual to read the preamble of the Indian Constitution on the streets. The oppressed, whose hero is Dr B.R. Ambedkar, have become the primary custodians of the great liberal tome that guides our republic. There could not have been a better response and a better form of democratic resistance to what they feel is unjust. There is renewed hope for the Gandhian creed of non-violence and satyagraha.[26]

Unfortunately for him, as soon as he returned from Seoul, the COVID-19 pandemic struck, and he was forced to support Modi's efforts as a 'matter of principle' because the humanitarian crisis was unprecedented. He supported the 'Janata Curfew', he went with a mask to distribute ration kits to the needy, he contributed to the PM Cares fund,[27] and also wrote a long, four-page letter to Modi in mid-April on the distress of farmers.[28] The letter began by appreciating the measures Modi was contemplating and that he was 'constantly updating himself with the situation in the country'. But somewhere in the middle of the letter he became critical: 'For almost two months without any forethought and proper planning, lockdown was imposed in the country . . . Before imposing the lockdown, its impact on farmers, who are mostly small and marginal farmers, agricultural labourers and daily-wage workers should have been discussed in detail . . .' Then he lists what steps would have actually helped, and then ends with a diktat: 'When lockdown was announced none of us rushed to buy gold, land, car, expensive phone or clothes, but all of us rushed to buy fruits, vegetables, milk, rice, ragi and wheat. Farmers are the soul of the nation. Respect them.' The letter was a distillation of his common sense, concern, experience and expertise. It was like the dark filter coffee with milk that he drank four times a day. The milk and sugar reduced the bitterness of the brew. The letter was bitter-sweet.

The Past and Patel's Memory

It is not just events since 2014 that define the relationship between Gowda and Modi. It goes back to Modi's days as chief minister and the communal riots that spread from Godhra across all of Gujarat. He had then written very angry letters to Vajpayee, visited relief camps in Gujarat all alone, and was devastated by what he had seen. He also made long speeches and the harshest reference to Modi in the Parliament: 'On that day, the chief minister asked his establishment not to go to the rescue of the minorities. It is state-sponsored terrorism or it is goondaism or by whatever name you may call it,' he had said (read the chapter 'Wrestling with Vajpayee and his Mask').[29] For Gowda, Gujarat was the land of two great political figures he admired and identified with—Sardar Vallabhbhai Patel and Morarji Desai, whose mentee he thought he was (read the chapter 'Morarji: The Mentor and the Mantle'). Of course, there was Mahatma Gandhi too on a higher pedestal. But Modi and Godhra had disturbed the serenity of its landscape for him. When Gujarat was upturned by the Bhuj earthquake in January 2001, months before Modi was installed as chief minister, Gowda had felt compelled to help the home state of his ideal men. As a former prime minister, he had stepped out on the streets of Bangalore to collect around Rs 15 lakh, and had handed it over directly to Chief Minister Keshubhai Patel.[30]

After the Sardar Patel statute was inaugurated in October 2018, Gowda felt the urge to go and see it. He went uninvited in October 2019 and thought of it as a pilgrimage.[31] Being the politician that he was, he did not let go the opportunity to send a message across to Modi. He praised the Sardar statue but also recalled his long and loyal association to Gujarat. He spoke endlessly to all around him about how Gujarat had a deep emotional connect for him. He recalled how he had studied Sardar Patel's life when he was imprisoned during the Emergency. He analyzed the Kheda and Bardoli satyagrahas and how they shaped the personality of Patel and made him proximate to Mahatma Gandhi. He looked for details in Sardar's life that matched with his own: 'He was a farmers' leader too. He was a grassroots man who had complete control over the Congress organization. He was brilliant in organizing resources for the Congress party. He was not a great speechmaker, and was often misunderstood. His English was very functional too. He came from an ordinary family and worked very hard to rise up in life. He sacrificed a lot. He did not cross the line that the Mahatma drew.'[32]

When curiously asked about his reference to Patel's 'functional English', he said he had read it in a book long ago. One is not sure if it was an English book or a Kannada book that he had read about this. But, in Rajmohan Gandhi's biography of Patel, there is a tangential reference to the topic. Speaking about Patel's travel in the Tamil land in the early thirties with C. Rajagopalachari, Gandhi writes: 'Patel made speeches in English, "Occasional grammatical errors crept into this speech," but more striking was his frankness.' The reference in the biography to 'grammatical errors' was drawn from another book on Patel by Narhari Parikh.[33]

Shyamal Datta, the former director of the SPG responsible for the prime minister's security, recalled a reference to Patel's life that Gowda had made when his mother had passed away in August 1996.[34] Gowda was on a tour of Jammu and Kashmir when officials broke the news of his mother's passing away. They also suggested that the prime minister cancel his scheduled programmes and head straight to Bangalore. Gowda did not agree. He wanted all official work completed:

When we reached Jammu, I went inside his helicopter to express my condolences. Tears were rolling down his cheeks. He said certain things about his mother. He wept like a child. We decided that he should fly straight from Jammu to Bangalore and not stop in between at Delhi. During the flight, to my colleague, he made an anecdotal reference to Sardar Patel. He said, 'When Patel was in the middle of an argument in a court, a chit announcing the death of his wife was sent to him. He saw it, kept it in his pocket, and continued with the arguments. Only when his work was done did he attend to the bereavement in the family.' He was suggesting that he had only followed the Patel example. When we reached Bangalore, it was the middle of the night. From the airport, we drove down to Haradanahalli. We couldn't take a chopper because it was night. The entire village had assembled. Amidst the mourning, there was also a kind of celebration because the son had come home. For the first time, I saw a dead body seated on a chair. It was not lying on a cot or a stretcher. She was buried like that. There was a huge procession.

Interestingly, in November 2009, Gowda went to Matru Shradh Tirth Bindu Sarovar in Patel's Gujarat (in Siddhpur of Patan district) to perform the death rituals of his mother. He had said: 'Unfortunately, I was away from her when she died, so I always feel guilty for that. I was very close to her. When I became prime minister, she had lost her memory and was not able to understand anything. She never knew that her son had become prime minister. I believe in Indian mythological concept of *Matru Sanskar* (rituals for a parent). For a while, I wanted to come to Siddhpur to do *shradh* (homage ceremony) of my mother. Today I could fulfil my wish.' Gowda had said. During that trip, Modi had sent his health and tourism minister, Jaynarayan Vyas, to accompany Gowda.[35]

One of Gowda's old associates, Gitesh Shah, said during the October 2019 trip: 'When everybody had forgotten Patel, Gowdaji remembered him. On 31 October 1996, as prime minister, he landed in Ahmedabad, discussed with then chief minister Shankersinh Vaghela, and instantly decided to rename the airport as Sardar Vallabhbhai Patel International Airport.' In November 2018, Vaghela had clarified this when there was a claim being made that it was Keshubhai Patel and Vajpayee who had renamed the airport.[36] But Gowda offered an interesting twist to the tale. He said: 'After the announcement that the airport would be

named after Sardar Patel, a BJP delegation met me and gave me a
memorandum asking the airport to be named after Shyama Prasad
Mukherjee instead.' Was Modi part of the delegation? Perhaps, but
he could not confirm.[37]

When Gowda went to Gujarat as prime minister, he also
visited Karamsad, the place where Patel grew up and visited his
mud-brick family home that stood as a sad memorial for a great
man. He was the first prime minister to do so. During that visit,
when local people petitioned him for a grant to build a memorial
for the Sardar, he instantly sanctioned Rs 2 crore. 'I was surprised
that there was no proper memorial for Patel. His family home had
been preserved, but it hardly matched the stature of the man. I
thought of Patel before Modi thought of him,' Gowda claimed. By
the time the Patel memorial was ready to be inaugurated, Gowda
had stepped down as Prime Minister. Amrita Patel, the chairman
of the Patel Trust suggested that Prime Minister Vajpayee should
be invited to inaugurate it, and Gowda, who had made the initial
grant, should also be invited as the chief guest, but apparently
the Gujarat government was not keen on inviting Deve Gowda.
He recalled being told about this by people in the trust. 'Anyway,
I did not feel bad. I was happy that I had done my bit for the
Sardar,' Gowda said.[38]

In October 2019, when Gowda stood at the giant toes of the
Patel statue in his spartan white dhoti–kurta, the brown hue of
Patel's statue and Gowda's skin tone matched. They both looked as
brown as the soil. He toured the 'statue of unity' complex with onsite
engineers and asked them very technical questions on the statue's
ability to withstand the varying speed of wind and earthquake. In
the visitors' book, he said it was the 'greatest event' of his life to be at
the Sardar's feet. Patel was a Patidar, Gowda was a Vokkaliga. The
two communities had a lot in common, and both were primarily
associated with land and soil.

In November of 2018, Congress politician and former union
minister C.K. Jafar Sharief had organized the launch of a new

Urdu edition and discussion of Maulana Kalam Azad's book *India Wins Freedom*[39] at the Town Hall in Bangalore. He had invited Gowda to speak on the book. Gowda read the book thoroughly and made margin notes. He was deeply saddened by Azad's not so favourable account of Patel and the doubt he had placed on his secular character. Azad had examined Patel in the context of the Partition and the Delhi riots; he had mentioned his defiance of the Mahatma. Gowda did not know what to make of the book. He must have wondered if it was just one man's view. Until then, the Sardar was one flat narrative of adulation in Gowda's mind, but now he was being pushed to rethink; there was a counternarrative being offered. And it was happening when Modi had appropriated Patel. After a point, he did not allow the book to nag him any further. Sardar would remain tall in his mind. That is when he said he was 'much misunderstood like I have been misunderstood'. Anyway, the book launch and discussion never happened because Sharief, the organizer, died a couple of days before the function. Gowda was spared from stating his opinion.

After the Sardar statue complex, Gowda went around the Sardar Sarovar Dam, recalling technical details of the dam, the height of which he had helped decide as prime minister. He had not only negotiated and settled the height of the dam but had also restarted the work, braving protests. Modi, on 17 September 2019, his birthday, had visited the dam site to celebrate the water level reaching its highest capacity of 138.68 meters for the first time since the completion of the project. Gowda, who was there only a fortnight later, on 5 October 2019, thought he had a legitimate share in the celebrations. From the dam site, Gowda went straight to the Garudeshwar Dutta mandir nearby and offered prayers. Modi had done the same. 'Everybody had ignored Patel and Morarji, both great sons of Gujarat, I had a small role in reviving memory and interest in them. The other man from Gujarat who is not often remembered is Gulzarilal Nanda,' Gowda said.[40] In his Gujarat tour of October 2019, he had trailed Modi, and the political message it sent out was open to interpretation. He had offered a counter to Modi's politics of memories, memorials and monuments.

Kurien's Taj Mahal

Gowda had one other association with Gujarat. It was with Amul, Anand and Verghese Kurien. As prime minister, he had requested Kurien, known as the 'milkman of India', if he could set up a dairy cooperative in Karnataka that was similar to the one in Anand. It was actually his son, H.D. Revanna, who had insisted that Gowda speak to Kurien in this regard. Revanna had later done pioneering work as chairman of the Karnataka Milk Federation. When Gowda, as prime minister, visited Anand to inaugurate a new facility, he broached the subject with Kurien:

> I asked if he could build something similar in my home state? At first, he was curt. He said, 'A Taj Mahal cannot be replicated.' I did not say anything. I kept quiet. When the function was over, and I was about to board the aircraft, Kurien requested a couple of minutes time. I took him aside. He said, 'Sir, it appears I have hurt you.' I said, 'No, I am not upset. There may be practical difficulties in replicating this in another location. Other states may also pressure you. I can understand your mind. I will leave it to you if you want to try.' Then, he said, 'I cannot disappoint you, sir.' The rest is history. He sent his people, I gave full clearance, and we did not interfere one bit. Today the milk federation in Karnataka is a great institution.[41]

Before it became Modi's Gujarat (see chapter 'The Narmada and the Ganga'), it was the Mahatma's, Patel's and Morarji's Gujarat for Gowda, and that Gujarat shaped him in indirect yet incredible ways. His position appeared to be deceptively simple. He thought if Modi was honest and sincere to the memory of the great men from his home state, he would automatically take India to great heights. But the nagging question is how sincere he has been to their memory? And that sincerity is perhaps not judged by the height of a statue that one commissions. Gowda paid respects to the Patel statue. He was curious about it but not envious.

22

The Family, the Patriarch

It was a large family of six children—four sons and two daughters. The size of the family was nothing unusual for Deve Gowda and Chennamma's generation. Any rural, agricultural household in India at the time was large, and in the 1950s and 60s, when the Gowda family expanded, most of India lived in the villages.[1] Even though Gowda had become a legislator in 1962, the city remained distant and impersonal. Emotions and family resided in their village and the town nearby.

Schooling for all the six children happened in Holenarasipur town, and the family slowly started straddling between Hassan district and Bangalore only after Gowda became leader of the Opposition in 1972. Also, by then, the children's educational needs had grown. By the 1980s, all the children, except one son, eventually settled down in Bangalore, and that was after Gowda had become a minister in the state government.

Since education was accorded a high value by both Gowda and his wife, even amidst financial and political crises, they ensured that their children accessed higher education. The Gowda family is one of the most highly educated political families in Karnataka, although their unfashionable, rustic ways would easily mislead an onlooker.

Gowda's firstborn H.D. Balakrishna, passed his MSc in physics with a distinction and later joined the Karnataka Administrative Service. For a decade after obtaining his postgraduate degree, he had worked with the now-defunct New Government Electrical Factory (NGEF), which had German collaborators. H.D. Kumaraswamy, is a science graduate. H.D. Ramesh, the youngest son, is a successful radiologist. The eldest among the two daughters, H.D. Anasuya has a PhD in child development and built an independent career for herself. The youngest child, H.D. Shailaja, has a master's degree in communications and worked in a local daily for years before she gave it up to raise her family.

The only offspring of Gowda who did not take well to formal education was H.D. Revanna. He is a matriculate. Gowda's wife had pushed him hard as well, but he had dropped out. However, Revanna, who was originally seen as Gowda's political inheritor (before the emergence of H.D. Kumaraswamy in 2006) is reckoned as one of Karnataka's industrious power and public works ministers and is also credited with transforming the co-operative dairy sector in southern Karnataka. He is seen as someone who inherits Gowda's common sense and passion that borders on obsession for religious ceremonies and astrology. He became a legislator for the first time in 1994 from Holenarasipur. Gowda had handed over his home turf to him and shifted to Ramanagara, near Bangalore, which is now Kumaraswamy's constituency. Both Holenarasipur and Ramanagara have become family political boroughs.

Gowda chose his sons-in-law and daughters-in-law well. The pairings were all arranged within the Vokkaliga community and within their Gangatkar sub caste. None of Gowda's sons or daughters courted their spouses before marriage. Here again, education was a criterion, not wealth or political connections. Gowda's eldest son-in-law C. Manjunath is a renowned cardiologist with peer recognition for having developed unique surgical procedures. He is credited with transforming the Jayadeva Institute of Cardiovascular Sciences and Research in Bangalore as a public institution of excellence and service.

Apolitical to the bone, he has been preferred by all dispensations in Karnataka and feted by all regimes in Delhi. In political circles, it is said that Gowda's political graph may have fluctuated, but that of his surgeon son-in-law has remained steady. The other son-in-law, Dr H.S. Chandrashekar, is an orthopedic surgeon with international exposure. He headed the Sanjay Gandhi Institute of Trauma and Orthopedics in Bangalore. Among daughters-in-law, Kumaraswamy's wife, Anita, is an engineer and a legislator, and Ramesh's wife, Sowmya, is a doctor. Kavita, the eldest daughter-in-law is a graduate and Bhavani, Revanna's wife, has deepened the family's political links in Hassan district. In 2016, she became a Hassan zilla panchayat member.

There is an interesting story around how the family arranged the marriage of the eldest daughter Anasuya with C. Manjunath in 1982. This was the first wedding in the family. Since Manjunath was educationally at the top, he had many offers, including from the family of a prominent Hassan politician who was also a Congress minister. But Manjunath's family, from a village in Channarayapatna taluk of Hassan had preferred Deve Gowda's family. This was because in the 1970s, Gowda had made a name across the state. He was a kind of a star. He was seen as an uncompromising politician who had fought the Devaraj Urs government valiantly, gone to jail during the Emergency, and had resisted temptation from Indira Gandhi to join the Congress.

Manjunath recalled: 'When I told my future father-in-law that I would like to marry his daughter, he was obviously happy, but was surprised. He wanted to make sure I had made the decision for the right reasons. One day, he sat me next to him in his blue Ambassador car and drove it himself to Cubbon Park. Under a tree there, we had the most candid conversation. He said that he could be a pauper tomorrow or the chief minister of the state, nothing was guaranteed in politics, and I shouldn't be taken in by his current political status. He wanted me to be fully aware of what I was getting into. He also confessed that he could not afford a lavish wedding as he had only limited resources to spend—he had to dip into his insurance savings.

I had replied that I wanted to marry his daughter and not his political fame.'[2] The marriage took place at the modest Vokkaligara Sangha function hall in Bangalore, and the reception was held at the Gayana Samaja hall nearby. The marriage was not videographed, a trend that had picked up just then because Gowda thought it would suggest excess.[3] Chief Minister Gundu Rao and his wife had attended the wedding with other dignitaries.

Gowda has more details of what he thought was a 'blessed moment' when a bright young doctor with a promising future sought his daughter's hand:

> I spoke to him in Cubbon Park, but I wanted to be doubly sure. I gave his horoscope for study to an astrologer. He returned in a couple of days and said that there was a threat to the boy's life. I was disappointed to hear this because it was such a fine match. Where would I get a son-in-law like that? I decided to seek a second opinion from another astrologer in whom I placed greater faith. This astrologer came back when I had begun my dharna against the Gundu Rao government. He said, 'Your daughter is like my daughter, don't worry, go ahead and get her married, but ask her to perform some prayer rituals that I'll suggest. Whatever impediments there are will be overcome.' Years later, Manjunath met with an accident, but he escaped with minor injuries.[4]

Gowda's grandchildren have done well too. Among the nine, four are doctors training to be surgeons. In all, there are eight doctors and surgeons in a family of twenty-three members, and none of them needed Gowda's political clout to educationally advance themselves. Kumaraswamy's son, Nikhil Kumaraswamy, is into acting in Kannada movies, and Revanna's son, Prajwal Revanna, is already a member of Parliament from Hassan. Frugality, and sensitivity to public opinion, ended with the weddings that Gowda organized for his children. The weddings of his grandchildren have been garish, uninhibited spectacles that signalled the arrival of a new generation. Gowda's discomfort with the ways of the new generation of his family is palpable in the frugality of his words:

> People will always wonder where we get our money from. For fifteen years as a legislator, I used public transport. I could offer no great comfort to my children when they were growing up. Now, I try to tell them that if your children ask you for comfort, for instance, cars, do buy them by all means but don't splurge. Don't buy the most expensive brand and model. Buy something that will comfortably take them from point A to point B. I don't expect them to live like me, but I also realize that I do not have the power to influence their choices. My time has passed.[5]

From all accounts, more than Gowda, it was his wife, Chennamma, who ensured that the children took education seriously. Gowda hardly had time to focus on them. It was his wife who held the family together, raised the children, and given the precarious career of her husband, insisted that they all study, take up jobs and become independent. In her native wisdom, she always told the kids that 'wealth could be stolen, fame and popularity could be fleeting, but knowledge and education are forever', daughter Shailaja recalled.[6]

One is not sure when and where education as a value was implanted in Chennamma. But, to educate her children remained her singular purpose. Chennamma is also very devout and deeply ritualistic and keeps a punishing regimen of fasts. For a Vokkaliga woman, she is a strict vegetarian and has not considered even eggs in her diet. The daughter, Shailaja, said that the ritual element may have come from her days as a young wife in Holenarasipur where she was surrounded by priestly Brahmin households.[7] On Monday, 16 November 2020, the Deepavali day, an eighty-three-year-old Chennamma had not broken her fast till 3 p.m., because she had not been able to assemble 108 *bilva-patra* leaves (bael leaves, *aegle marmelos*) for her very defined pooja ritual.[8]

For a person at the bottom of the caste ladder in India, to be Brahminical is aspirational. It is seen as something that ensures social mobility and spiritual deliverance. Ritual and knowledge are seen as two conduits for this pole vault within the caste hierarchy. While democracy has ensured access to knowledge, ritual and food choices are largely by cultural assimilation. Gowda and Chennamma giving their children atypical Vokkaliga names like Balakrishna, Revanna, Kumaraswamy, Anasuya, Ramesh and Shailaja was also an indication of this aspirational element (see discussion on Vokkaliga names in the chapter on Gowda's childhood).

Nobody among the children or grandchildren took the 'Gowda' surname prominently. It could be seen as both a result of educational progress and what was called as 'Sanskritization' by M.N. Srinivas, an internationally renowned sociologist from the same princely Mysore region as Gowda.[9] This has somewhat been clear in Deve Gowda's mind too. He has had a greater affinity with Shankaracharya's Sringeri Math than with his own community's Adichunchanagiri Math. He once said: 'I was taken in by the culture and heritage of the Sringeri Math.'[10] Interestingly though, after Deve Gowda became prime minister the 'Gowda' surname acquired a new connotation, new pride, and revival of sorts within the Vokkaliga community. It coincided with the peak of the community's identity assertion that had been reignited in the 1980s.

When Revanna could not go far with education, the parents gave him charge of the family's agricultural lands in Paduvalahippe village. In his late teens, he also ran a flour mill in the village. Gowda had given away his tiny ancestral share of land in Haradanahalli to his brother and poorer cousins after he had made it as a legislator. Kumaraswamy, too, did not take up regular employment like his other brothers and sisters, but after his graduation took up civil contracts with the Bangalore municipal corporation. He soon moved to establishing a film distribution and production business. Before he made it big in politics, he was reasonably entrenched in the film industry.[11] He was first elected as a member of Parliament in 1996, but as a first-time legislator in 2004 assembly elections, he had broken away from his father and family to become the chief minister of the state. He was the outlier or rebel in the family. His enterprise and popularity as a politician had come as a complete surprise to Gowda, who thought he was grooming Revanna to take over his political mantle. However, the general opinion in political circles is that none of the children can beat Gowda's enterprise, innovation, organizing skills, risk-taking, grit, grasp, serious study, common sense, and parliamentary excellence as a politician. At least, not yet. This assessment does not hold true just in comparison with his family but also with all politicians of his generation. The simple proof of this is that he has never been politically irrelevant in Karnataka since he started out in 1962.

The world came to know of Gowda's large family, until then mostly hidden from the public eye, when he became prime minister. When Gowda went to the G-15 meeting in Harare, he took eight of his grandchildren, a daughter and two daughters-in-law, as well as his wife, in Air India One. That attracted an adverse press. The joke among journalists was that G-13 (Gowda's 13) was going to G-15. However, the family branched out from Harare to Johannesburg for a wildlife safari, and Gowda ensured he took care of their excursion bills personally. In fact, he not only paid the bills but also made it known that he had done so.[12]

The Extended Family

Gowda did not just have the responsibility of his children. He was entrusted with the responsibility of the extended family. His father, in his dying moments, in 1977, had told Gowda, 'Your uncles, brothers, sisters and cousins are not as bright and have not progressed as much as you have, so do take care of them.'[13] Gowda was then a legislator, and his means were limited. He had not accepted the perks of the Opposition leader. He was funding his political career with loans and was financially in bad shape.

Similarly, on his wife's side circumstances pushed him to accept the responsibility for his sister-in-law's family. When they were scouting for a groom for his sister-in-law, Savitramma, Gowda's father-in-law had plans to marry her off to a schoolteacher. But Gowda had suggested that she deserved better. Within three months of this conversation, the father-in-law had passed away. Being the eldest son-in-law, Gowda shouldered the responsibility of looking for a suitable groom. He suggested someone who had a diploma like him, but Chennamma hurriedly committed herself to another who had a postgraduate degree. She was keen that her sister married someone with a higher qualification, and that was an innocent, well-meaning ambition.

There is also an age-old custom in Karnataka that if there is a girl who has come of age, and the father passes away, she should be married off within a year of his death. This custom had also put the family in a race against time. Anyway, the marriage took place with a groom of Chennamma's choice, and they did well for a short period. But unfortunately, the brother-in-law developed cancer and passed away. He had left behind his wife and two girls. Gowda and his wife saw it as their responsibility to take care of Savitramma and raise the two girls. With six kids of their own, this became a larger family under a single roof.[14] It was Savitramma's house that Gowda had sold in the late 1970s to pay off his election debts, and the site that he had got her in return in Mysore had caused a furore in the mid-1980s when Hegde was chief minister (details in the earlier chapter on Hegde). Gowda did not have a large accommodation when the children were growing up. The boys, at times, slept in the car garage of a rented accommodation. They also had brief hostel stints. Gowda got a ministerial bungalow only in 1983 when he was nearly fifty, but his ministerial stints were not long, and he was never a squatter in government accommodation. He always vacated within seventy-two hours of losing power.[15]

Interestingly, Gowda never built a home for himself in Bangalore. The one he started in Sadashivanagar, on a plot allotted to him as a long-serving legislator, remained incomplete as he got into a financial crunch. Later, he gave the plot away to his four sons.[16] Therefore, between 1962 and 1972, when he was a legislator, he stayed in a room without an attached toilet in the general hostel, and the family was in Holenarasipur. As leader of the Opposition between 1972 and 1980, he stayed in a rented accommodation in Bangalore's Jayanagar locality. After 1978 though, he had mostly spent time in Paduvalahippe village tilling the lands. In 1983, he became a minister, and till about 1989, he stayed in the 3, Crescent Road bungalow in Bangalore. When he lost his ministership, he lived alone in a small house in lower Palace Orchards, and the wife and kids moved into son-in-law Manjunath's house. He continued in the two-bedroom house after he became an MP in 1991. It was in 1994, as chief minister that he again got a bungalow. In 1996, he moved to Delhi as prime minister. After he stepped down as PM, his Bangalore residence was his elder daughter Anasuya's home. In the last decade, he and his wife moved in with their younger daughter Shailaja.

In Delhi, Gowda has retained the 5 Safdarjung Lane bungalow since 1991, except for a short period when he was prime minister. During that period, S.R. Bommai, who was a minister in his cabinet, occupied the bungalow. He never desired a bigger type Lutyens bungalow that former prime ministers were eligible for. The fact that the house is astrologically sound is only a small reason. It has more to do with the absence of vanity. Montek Singh Ahluwalia recalled his meetings with Gowda in this house: 'He was living very modestly in Safdarjung Lane. It was a rather small house for a former prime minister. But he did not look uncomfortable at all.'[17]

Even in Bangalore, Gowda's living is unostentatious. He receives most of his guests and party workers in an extended part of his second-floor bedroom, which is filled with pictures and idols of gods, photographs of his parents and family, and a large television set. It doubles up as his study as well with books and documents neatly stacked in more than one corner, and also on a two-seater sofa. Plastic chairs are piled up in another corner and would be put on the floor depending on the number of visitors coming in, and also depending on whether Gowda wants to spend time with them or wants them packed off quickly. Gowda presides over his durbar in that bedroom seated behind a tiny desk, less than three feet in spread. The only luxury is a recliner with a floor lamp, where he stretches to read late at night or early in the morning. The house itself is built vertically on a tiny plot without a garden. It is on a narrow, thirty-feet lane in a middle-class locality called Padamanabhanagar. It is far removed from the city's central business district and was underdeveloped even when Gowda was chief minister.

Near-Death Experiences

Gowda had two near-death experiences. One had to do with his throat condition in the 1980s, and the other, due to a mental shock when his son H.D. Kumaraswamy rebelled and aligned with the BJP.

When Gowda was a minister in the Hegde government, around 1985, he started realizing that the air conditioning in the assembly was hurting him. He would always sit with his head wrapped in a shawl. There was pain in the ears and throat. Suddenly, his voice became shrill, and he started mumbling. He had always spoken with force and clarity. In fact, at the end of the 1970s, Morarji Desai had warned him that his vocal cords would be affected if he shouted while making public speeches. 'There is a microphone that amplifies your voice. Why do you need to shout?' he had asked.[18] Strangely, his throat problem coincided with his growing conflict with Ramakrishna Hegde. He also became a diabetic around 1985.[19] The sudden dip in his voice became the most pronounced manifestation of his poor health. Initially, people thought it was political stress and workload as a minister that was consuming him. That was true, but physiologically it was a nodule, a non-malignant growth in his throat that was touching the vocal cords.[20]

Gowda tried to ignore the throat condition for a few months, but by 1986 it became unbearable. He could not rest at night. He could only drift away into sleep for a couple of hours, only around 2 a.m. Until then, he would be awake trying to read or work on files or chat with somebody who would then be dropped home after Gowda fell asleep. Those days, he was the occupant of the 3 Crescent Road bungalow. To not disturb his wife with his insomnia, he had moved to a small room in the bungalow's compound outside the main living quarters. Perhaps Chennamma's impression of her husband altered at that stage, which she once wittily expressed: 'He does not sleep well, he does not stop thinking, and he does not smile easily.'[21] Gowda used to meet doctors and be constantly under medication, but it was not helping. At a point, a rumour spread that he was suffering from throat cancer. In fact, once, senior politician S. Bangarappa asked Gowda's private secretary, K.A. Thippeswamy, who played badminton at the secretariat club with him, if the rumour was true. Thippeswamy had gone home that day and made sure Gowda spoke to Bangarappa to dispel the falsehood. Thippeswamy also remembered that Gowda spoke for thirty long minutes at a stretch that day with Bangarappa. His staff thought that was a miracle.[22]

Seeing Gowda's condition, Chandra Shekhar, the Janata Party national president, made an appointment with Dr Hiranandani at the Jaslok Hospital in Bombay and insisted that Gowda go along with him. Dr Hiranandani had conducted a number of tests and told him that a fifteen-minute operation was necessary. The non-malignant growth in the throat which rubbed the vocal cords had caused a blood clot, he had said. The operation went off successfully but within a couple of minutes of gaining consciousness, Gowda had felt breathless and had banged the operation table to draw the attention of the doctors:

I opened my eyes on the operation table. I could see the lights and did a namaste to the doctors standing around by way of saying thank you. But I suddenly felt something dark taking over me. I hit the table to draw the attention of the doctors and passed out. Later, they told me a little thing they had used during the surgery had slipped in the windpipe, and the doctors sewing up had not noticed it. It was an accident. They had immediately opened up again and found it in a delicate position. They had removed it and restored me. Even if they had taken a few extra seconds to remove it, I would be dead. Dr Hiranandani said that if I had been shifted to the recovery room, they could not have saved me. Luckily, I was still on the operation table.[23]

While leaving for the operation from Bangalore, Gowda's astrologer had said that he should avoid an operation till the end of the month, that is for a fortnight. When Dr Hiranandani suggested an operation, Gowda honestly shared this input with him. But the doctor had asked Gowda if he trusted his astrologers so much? To which, Gowda had said: 'I am in your care. You take a call. I just shared what was told to me.'[24] Gowda recovered from pain and regained health, but he never got back the earlier quality of his voice. It remained feeble. Later, when newspapers cruelly wrote about Gowda's mumbling, he chose not to speak about his medical condition. That operation, anyway, had led to the blossoming of a friendship with Dr Hiranandani, and later, as prime minister, he had sent him as an envoy to begin talks with Pakistan (see chapter on Kashmir).

The second near-death incident in Gowda's life was in 2006, when his son, H.D. Kumaraswamy, rebelled and joined hands with the BJP to form a coalition government in Karnataka. Gowda had never approved the company that Kumaraswamy kept and his habits, but he had not expected him to walk away from him and the family. When that happened in January–February 2006, Manjunath, the son-in-law, recalled that Gowda's blood pressure was 240/140:

He started talking incoherently. He shouted in Kannada that it was the darkest day of his life. He ranted that he had engaged in secular politics all his life, had never compromised for the sake of power, but was now ruined. People outside may dismiss all this as a drama enacted by the family to grab power, but I speak as a doctor. He developed a persistent headache and I thought he would have a brain hemorrhage. We rushed him at 2 a.m. to Mallya hospital for a CT scan. The next sixty days, he went into clinical depression and hardly spoke. He would get agitated even if family members or nurses touched him. He would push them away. The only touch he did not resist was mine. To be honest, I was not hopeful of his recovery.[25]

Manjunath continued: 'During that sixty-day period, his shoulders drooped. His gait changed. He started bending while walking. He had an erect, confident posture earlier, and that was never recovered after this incident. That phase was a struggle both physically and psychologically.' Gowda too recalled: 'I told my elder son-in-law to do his duty, but my time was over. Once, I told him, "If Eshwara (the Almighty) calls me I will have to go. Don't waste your time standing here." He had walked away without saying anything.'[26]

As therapy and reconciliation, after a couple of months, the family arranged a meeting between the father and son:

One day my son, Kumaraswamy, suddenly arrived and stood before me. He said, 'I will resign today and go away to a faraway place' (Gowda remembers he used the word *deshantara*). Tears were rolling down my eyes. I said whatever I had created has been washed away. A seed of doubt has been sown in peoples' mind. 'Your resignation will not bring back anything. It will not return my peace. If I wanted to accept BJP's support, I could have accepted Vajpayee's offer in 1997 and continued as prime minister, but in fifty years of public life I had not wavered from the secular cause. Now that you have become chief minister, go and do good to people,' I said. I knew Kumaraswamy would never resign.

Thirteen years later, in 2019, when Gowda remembered the encounter with his son, he was standing near the Sardar Sarovar Dam, watching the Narmada fall from the crest gates and wash away emptiness that sat like an invisible fog. 'The sacred river is flowing here, and the lord knows what pain I went through then,' he remarked and added that if he had survived that moment in 2006, it was because God thought that his duties on earth were not over.[27] After this moment of divergence and reconciliation between the father and son, the popularity and realpolitik of Kumaraswamy largely sustained the party. He related better with the younger generation. Power at the top of the party was now shared. Gowda did not always have a veto. Manjunath remarked: 'If ideologically the two had moved forward together, it would have been a potent combination.'[28] What he meant was that his father-in-law was ideologically stubborn, while his brother-in-law was flexible. If both had been on the same side of the divide, they would have cornered a greater vote share and more seats for the party. Their political culture, perception of political exigencies and worldviews were vastly different. Gowda preferred the long-term game. He had waited for twenty-one years to become a minister, but Kumaraswamy, who had never been a minister, in his very first term as legislator became the chief minister.

When Kumaraswamy had struck a deal with the BJP and was yet to be sworn in as chief minister, Gowda with his eldest son Balakrishna and the second-born Revanna, had rushed to a temple near Chennai, with their family friend and astrologer, Ravinarayan. They desperately prayed to God there to nix Kumaraswamy's chances. It was an Amavasya (new moon night in the lunar calendar), and Gowda made a vow that if his wish was granted, he would come back for three consecutive Amavasyas to offer prayers.[29]

Dynasties are complex. The relationship between fathers and sons is complex, but then the world flattens these complexities to fancifully impose an interpretation that it deems convenient. When the time came in 2008, Gowda categorically told Kumaraswamy not to transfer power to B.S. Yediyurappa and the BJP. That was his way

484 Furrows in a Field

of getting back politically and recovering his lost political ground. But the same people who criticized Kumaraswamy for aligning with the BJP, criticized the Gowda family for reneging on the promise of transfer of power. They read it as a double fault. In the court of public opinion, the family and the party were ostracized for nearly a decade, till Kumaraswamy became chief minister again in 2018, this time with Congress' support and his father's complete blessings. In 1997, when Gujral had become prime minister, he had offered to take Kumaraswamy into his cabinet, but Gowda had refused and had also ensured that Kumaraswamy did not entertain the idea in his mind.[30]

The Acid Victim

Five years before this crisis related to Kumaraswamy, in 2001, there was another crisis of an entirely different magnitude that shocked the Gowda family. At the very Eshwara (Shiva) temple where Gowda's parents had prayed fervently before his birth in Haradanahalli, Gowda's wife Chennamma suffered an acid attack on 21 February 2001, the Mahashivaratri festival day. The attacker was Gowda's nephew Lokesh, his younger brother H.D. Basave Gowda's son. Bhavani, Gowda's daughter-in-law and Revanna's wife, was also attacked, but it was Chennamma who suffered grievous burn injuries.

According to eyewitnesses, quoted in news reports, the security personnel did not suspect Lokesh because he was a close relative.[31] In 2001, Chennamma was still protected by the elite SPG (prime ministers get SPG protection for five years after they step down). On the pretext of prostrating before the Nandi statue in the temple, he had suddenly fished out a container full of acid and poured it over Chennamma's head and tried to splash it on Bhavani. The two women were seated waiting for their turn to offer pooja as Lokesh's mother, Jayamma, was offering her prayers. The priests at the temple had told reporters that 'luckily Deve Gowda did not turn up for prayers, which he normally did not miss'.[32] However, villagers had contended that even if Gowda had come, he would not have been attacked as Lokesh's target was only his aunt and her daughter-in-law. Gowda himself had once said that the acid was meant for his son, Revanna.[33]

The incident was termed as a 'family feud' and the result of 'vengeance'.[34] It was said the family of Basave Gowda had remained poor even as elder brother Deve Gowda had reached the pinnacle of power in India, and that had led to bad blood between the two families, although not between the two brothers. The newspapers also reported, quoting villagers, that Gowda wanted to help the brother's family of six children, which included two mentally challenged nieces, but Chennamma and her daughter-in-law, Bhavani, had 'stonewalled' Gowda from being generous.[35]

Although politics was denied in this incident, initial reports did raise doubts about some local Congress leaders provoking Lokesh, and also helping him procure the acid for the murderous attack. Basave Gowda's family had shifted its political affiliations to the Congress a few years back, and some villagers opined that it had intensified the rivalry between the two families. In fact, Basave Gowda's wife, Jayamma, had contested the zilla panchayat elections on a Congress ticket the previous year and had attributed her defeat to Revanna.[36] Jayamma, however, condemned her son's action: 'We may not be on speaking terms, but had I known that my son would attack the family members of Deve Gowda, I would have locked him in a room before going to the temple.'[37]

The villagers had strongly disapproved of the crime Lokesh had committed and confirmed that Deve Gowda had left his ancestral property in Haradanahalli in the care of his brother's family. A Deve Gowda aide from his days as chief minister said it was untrue that his boss had looked away from his brother's family, totally. He had discreet ways and channels of extending help. B.L. Shankar, Gowda's parliamentary secretary as chief minister, too confirmed that Gowda never sent back his brother empty handed.[38] But whether cordiality existed between the two families is an altogether different question.

Gowda's nephew Lokesh was sentenced to eight years jail with a fine of Rs 11,500 by a local court in September 2002. The S.M. Krishna-led state government, with Mallikarjuna Kharge as home minister, had the very next day of the incident announced a judicial inquiry by a sitting high court judge.[39]

In a conversation in November 2020, Gowda's youngest daughter Shailaja said that the family had given up hope that Chennamma would survive the attack.[40] She had suffered over 70 per cent burns, and in the assessment of surgeon and son-in-law, Manjunath, there was less than 5 per cent chance of his mother-in-law's survival. 'She insisted that I shouldn't put her on a ventilator and if she eventually survived, it was due to her tremendous willpower. She was in Mallya hospital in Bangalore for over two months. There was an additional problem. She was a pure vegetarian and the food we gave with egg mixed in it had to be passed off as God's offerings (prasad). In fact, she ate only what was given as God's offerings and did not consume what she perceived as plain food.'[41] The family wondered if Chennamma should be taken abroad for plastic surgery, but they settled for Bangalore since they could access top professionals locally.

The manner in which Deve Gowda took this incident was astonishing. First, he thought of it as a result of a mistake he had committed in his past life and did not shave for a few days.[42] When the police statement had to be made, he requested his wife to just name the boy who had thrown the acid and nobody else. He did not want the family honour to be dragged around in the streets. Later too, he not only ensured the boy's jail term was commuted but also got him married. Nobody else in the family attended his wedding, though.[43] It was one of the most painful episodes of his life, but he had dealt with it as a family elder. Perhaps the promise he had made to his father during his dying moments must have played on him.

In a few years, the brother, Basave Gowda, developed cancer. He suffered for nearly six years, and when he reached his terminal stage, Deve Gowda had worked behind the scenes to get his nephew's sentence commuted. He did not want his brother to die without seeing his son.[44] Deve Gowda did not want to complicate his karma chart. The pardon and reconciliation were all deeply rooted in Deve Gowda's religious beliefs. During the terminal stage, the daughters also asked Chennamma if she would like to see the brother-in-law? She took some time to get back to them but agreed to visit him. The family ensured that there was no one else from Basave Gowda's family when she went to the hospital ward. The two did not exchange words, but tears rolled down the brother-in-law's cheeks.[45] When Basave Gowda was at the Kidwai Memorial Institute of Oncology in Bangalore, Deve Gowda had asked his aides in Delhi to be constantly in touch with the nurse in charge to get a regular update.[46] Gowda has not been reticent about this acid incident but has spoken about it publicly a number of times. The last time he reflected upon it was at a public function in November 2018 in Bangalore.[47]

Reluctant Patriarch

Deve Gowda is seen as an ageing patriarch in Indian politics. He presides over a powerful regional party and his large family. In the last two decades, his party workers have called him Appaji, meaning father. Until the end of 2000, he was only 'Gowdaru', but this shift to kinship address has happened quietly. Kannada matinee idol Rajkumar was similarly referred to as 'Annavaru', which meant elder brother or could even mean father because in the princely Mysore region 'Anna', 'Annaiah' and 'Aiyah' are terms used to address fathers or father-figures. Deve Gowda called his father Aiyah, and his children call him Anna. The stalwarts in the Dravidian movement like Annadurai, Karunanidhi, M.G. Ramachandran, J. Jayalalitha, all developed similar kinship relationships with their followers. In the North, Charan Singh and Devi Lal earned similar mass adulation, they became *tauu* or uncles. Gandhi and Ambedkar have been largely internalized in the Indian society through a kinship link. They have been gentle patriarchs of a large nation, keeping the conscience and consciousness of the masses. There is a benignness associated to their authority and command.

In the case of the patriarch, there is also a shade of the feudal that gets mixed up in the Indian context. There is absence of dialogue, lack of critical exchange, and limited emotional space. It is kept pretty simple—there is either surrender or rebellion. Gowda's patriarchy is far from this. He has never appeared authoritative. If anything, he has been a fine listener. He absorbs every single word, every sigh, and stores it in the deepest recesses of his mind to chew the emotional cud in solitary engagement. He may use his memory to build a cold and brutal political plan or to conditionally accommodate and forgive. In his long political life, people who have rebelled and issued the most vicious statements against him have come around to join hands, part again, and join again, or stay away completely. For this patriarch, there have been no permanent friends and permanent enemies, an archetype of a moral that has guided the most astute in Indian politics for a long time.

Inside the family, Manjunath, the son-in-law, said that Gowda does not operate like a patriarch: 'He has always advised his children never to take political shortcuts. With his sons, in general, he reluctantly advises them, but if they continue to argue, he withdraws. He also senses that if any of his sons do not visit him for ten days, then, whatever advice he has offered has not gone down well. He avoids a confrontation. He never categorically tells his children anything, even when they are wrong. He would rather not have a face-to-face confrontation with them. I have not seen him assert himself with his sons. With the daughters, he sees emotional anchorage.' Manjunath points out Chennamma is the one who has held things together in the family.[48] Is she then the matriarchal figure?

Epilogue
This Far and Further

This book has come this far. It has spanned and scanned over seventy years of Deve Gowda's life. His life and politics do not end at 2004, where this book stops being particular and specific. There is a lot to examine in the last fifteen years. There are also issues and events in the intervening period between 1997 (after he stepped down as prime minister) and 2000, which deserve greater scrutiny. Like for instance, he took on Prime Minister A.B. Vajpayee and Defence Minister George Fernandes in 1998–99 on the purchase of the T-72S and T-90 battle tanks, which also put him in conflict with a few senior personnel in the Indian army, especially Lt Gen. S.S. Mehta, the deputy chief of the Indian army.[1] Gowda wrote a series of letters[2] to Vajpayee on the subject but when they elicited no response, he went public. He had said that the deal to procure the tanks was happening in a 'hush-hush manner', and there were some 'unscrupulous elements' compromising national interest.[3] George Fernandes also went ballistic against Gowda, but since he was already caught in the controversy surrounding the dismissal of Indian Navy chief Admiral Vishnu Bhagwat, things did not go down well for him. Soon after, the Kargil war clouds had begun to gather. Congress president Sonia Gandhi and AIADMK leader Jayalalitha had stood by Gowda on the issue.[4]

This issue of the purchase of the battle tanks became so big that it even figured in the no-confidence debate against the Vajpayee government in April 1999. Some of Gowda's remarks against Lt Gen. S.S. Mehta were even expunged[5] from Lok Sabha records. George Fernandes in an interview to *India Today* had angrily said: 'If I had to make a choice between General Gowda and General Mehta, I won't take a second look at General Gowda. General Mehta has lived with tanks all his life. He and his men would have to fight, not Gowda's sons. We are playing with our men's lives. Gowda wanted a JPC (Joint Parliamentary Committee) on me. They should have a JPC on him if they wanted to have fun and games in security matters.' An infuriated Gowda had also sought the intervention of President K.R. Narayanan[6] on the issue.

In September 1998, Gowda had also fired the first salvo in what later came to be known as the telecom scam. His letter[7] to Vajpayee alleged: 'I have read in the recent press reports that there is a proposal to grant several reliefs to the cellular phone licensees . . . the above reliefs, I am told are being contemplated in view of the state of industry wherein, as expected, although the bidders won the licences bidding high licence fees outsmarting others, they are now looking for concessions on the very basis on which they won the licences . . . while on the one hand, the cellular operators have asked for reliefs, on the other they have merrily been divesting their shareholding in favour of foreign partners and even various infrastructure funds like AIF, AIG etc. with due government approval. Most of the current licence (holders) including BPL, Essar, Modi, Tata, JT Mobile, Hutchison Max have all sold equity at sizeable premium netting in private hands thousands of crores— DoT (Department of Telecommunication) has completely ignored these gains in evaluating their request.' It was a detailed six-page letter. His series of letters[8] continued to Vajpayee till February 1999.

The impact of Gowda's charges was seen in a confidential communication (the letter was labelled 'secret') between Jagmohan, the Union minister for communications, and Yashwant Sinha, the Union finance minister, where Jagmohan said: 'In connection with this case, a number of specific allegations have been made by Shri H.D. Deve Gowda and other senior members of Parliament and also in the two writ petitions filed in the Delhi High Court. These allegations, I find, have not so far been checked with the specificity they merit. I shall be grateful if you will kindly have these allegations checked from the finance ministry's agencies/organizations which may, directly or indirectly, be concerned with them.'[9] Vajpayee also called up Gowda to assure him that he was looking into the charges. In this telecom battle, Somnath Chatterjee, who was the chairman of the standing committee on communication, stood by Gowda.

Besides the big fights as prime minister, as well as before and later, there is one aspect that this book does not discuss. It has to do with Gowda as a local MLA and MP for nearly sixty years and the work he did for the constituencies he represented. Hassan and Holenarasipur are among the parliamentary and assembly constituencies respectively that have seen the finest development. In May 2009, *Outlook* in an article titled, 'A golden island of his own', wrote that the constituencies represented by Gowda and his family are among the 'best nurtured electoral regions in Karnataka', and his rivals in the Congress and BJP had conceded that if development alone were the criterion Gowda and his family could never be defeated for decades to come.[10] Although Gowda had embraced a larger national cause as prime minister with refined ease, Haradanahalli, Holenarasipur and Hassan, and of course Karnataka, never escaped him.

In the papers of S.S. Meenakshisundaram, joint secretary in Gowda's PMO, there is a neat handwritten seven-page note on the letterhead of the Calcutta Raj Bhavan, dated and signed by Gowda,[11] in which he lists the decisions that need to be taken with regard to Karnataka and Hassan. When he wrote the note, he was waiting for the British Prime Minister John Major to arrive. There is a similar handwritten note on the letterhead of the Hotel Imperial in Singapore[12] on the specific decisions to be taken in Karnataka on their return. This was from his time as chief minister. The local and the universal always blended without conflict in Gowda.

There has been a joke in circulation in Karnataka, which throws light on how Gowda operates with ease, and elan, at different levels as a politician. It goes: Gowda is a gram panchayat operative at the *hobli* (cluster of villages) level, a taluk level operative at the assembly level, a local member of Parliament at the district level, a state-level operative in Bangalore, the state capital, but once he reaches Delhi, he is a statesman. As mentioned earlier too in the book, his approach was about perceiving the world through a grain of sand.

The Struggle and the Compromise

After he had made his presence felt in Delhi and the Parliament in 1998–99 after he had stepped down as prime minister, he lost the 1999 general elections from Hassan. The Janata Dal had splintered, and his former colleagues like J.H. Patel had joined hands with George Fernandes to launch the Janata Dal (United). Ramakrishna Hegde had launched his own outfit, Lok Shakti, and aligned with the BJP to contest the polls. This had given the BJP a big electoral boost in Karnataka, as the splintered vote share of the Janata Dal mostly accrued to them, especially in north Karnataka. There is a carefully arranged silence in Karnataka on how a lifelong secular leader like Hegde, and a Lohia-socialist like Patel, capitulated to their lifelong opponents, the Jan Sangh/BJP, and the Hindutva forces.

Gowda did not sit quiet. He launched his own Janata Dal (Secular) with a symbol of a woman carrying sheaves of paddy on her head in 1999.[13] By 2004, he had ensured that his party became part of the government in Karnataka in alliance with the Congress. That was a herculean achievement given the unsuccessful history of regional parties in Karnataka till then. He did not have money during the 2004 elections to fund his party candidates, and some of his colleagues like Siddaramaiah did not cooperate.[14] He had taken a loan of Rs 3 crore from Baddi Chennappa by giving a post-dated cheque. Taking loans for elections and repaying them had anyway become a habit. It had become a kind of gamble since the 1980 general elections when to repay loans he had sold his widowed sister-in-law's property.[15] That was also the period that had signaled the end of his raw idealism.[16]

Politics had pushed him to be pragmatic. Since 2004, Gowda has ensured that the party has maintained an average 20 per cent vote share, which has kept him politically relevant even in 2021. After 2004, the party has been part of the government in Karnataka twice, once without Gowda's consent, when his son, H.D. Kumaraswamy walked away in 2006 and forged a twenty-month partnership with the BJP; however, in 2018, the coalition government formed with the Congress was under his supervision. His son's swearing-in ceremony as chief minister was converted into a rally of Opposition leaders from every corner of the country. This mega exercise of building the party from 1999 deserves a closer look.

After losing parliamentary elections in 1999, Gowda politically revived himself in 2002 in a by-poll from Kanakapura. He could not retain this seat in 2004 but regained Hassan since he had contested two seats during that election. His winning streak continued until he was defeated again in 2019 as an eighty-seven-year-old candidate. This time he had handed over the Hassan seat to his grandson, Prajwal Revanna, and had chosen to contest the Tumkur seat instead. But again, in 2020, he was sent back to the Rajya Sabha, the upper house of the Parliament after he was elected unopposed. The Congress and the BJP did not put up a candidate against him. He was eighty-eight and showed no signs of retiring. On the day he took oath as Rajya Sabha MP, on 20 September 2020, he delivered his nuanced reading and objection to the three controversial farm bills that were due to be passed.[17]

The struggle of party-building after 1999 pushed him into some compromises. He had to raise money and fund elections. He was alone now, and the buck stopped at this desk. There was neither a high command in Delhi nor multiple power centres across the nation. He was now what the media called a 'supremo'. A patriarchal figure for his party men. But whatever compromises he may have had to make was not exclusive to him and his party alone. All political parties engaged in them to survive in an electoral space that had become excessively competitive and had seen paradigm shifts with new interests entering the arena. For instance, in Karnataka, the mining and real estate lobby had captured all political parties. They altered the way politics was conducted and elections were fought.

The scandal years of Karnataka politics somewhat began around 2000, when a sleepy town like Bangalore transformed itself into a metropolis bursting at its seams. Bangalore became the information technology back office of the world, and the world spoke of being 'Bangalored'.[18] The capital city contributed to over 60 per cent of the state's revenue. Ambition and aspiration among politicians turned into greed. The candidates picked for upper house nominations by Gowda's party, as well as the Congress and the BJP, became controversial with each passing year as the accommodation of big businessmen and moneybags continued unabated. The Bellary mining scam involving the Reddy brothers of the BJP drew public attention first when Gowda's son was chief minister and later consumed the B.S. Yediyurappa government (the BJP's first state government in southern India). This, too, deserves separate attention.

To Gowda's credit, when it came to his core socio-political commitments, he remained faithful to his secular ideals. He was one political leader who did not hesitate to wear the skull cap and pray with members of the Muslim community in public during their festivals.[19] After 2014, when other non-BJP leaders in Karnataka baulked when it came to openly associating themselves with Muslims, and other minorities, for fear of losing the Hindu vote, Gowda did not succumb to the pressure Hindutva was applying. In 2018, Gowda's Janata Dal (Secular) could have had a more stable alliance with the BJP, but it was Gowda who put his foot down. Even later,

Modi had personally made an offer to Kumaraswamy to switch when similar switches were happening in many states across the nation.

However, as he endeavoured to keep his secular persona intact, there was a deepening of his party's caste identity politics. From 2005 on, with the expulsion of Siddaramaiah from the party, it was perceived as a party exclusively of Vokkaligas. Here again, Gowda's party was not the only one deepening its caste game. A national party like the BJP, too, allowed B.S. Yediyurappa to build a strong Lingayat identity for the party that led to rapid electoral gains. During this phase, the core Hindutva agenda and cultural nationalism of the BJP played second fiddle to Yediyurappa's caste engineering. Yediyurappa transformed himself into 'a Mandal politician with a Hindutva air cover'.[20]

In the last decade, the dynastic charge against the Janata Dal (Secular) has also sharpened. Again, this was not an exclusive ailment of Gowda's party but was a national phenomenon. As Gowda's two sons, two daughters-in-law, two grandsons and many first circle relatives dominated the party and the larger political space, the party began to look like it was increasingly under the thumb of one family. There is no doubt that Gowda would have been freer and more forceful if he did not have to ensure the political careers of his bloodline. But the dynastic argument is the same paradoxical one for all political dynasties—the parties hold together because the families act as glue, and without them, the parties may implode or splinter.

This paradox sniggers at democracy. It is difficult to imagine a Congress without the Nehru–Gandhis, the Shiv Sena without the Thackerays in Maharashtra, Uttar Pradesh and Bihar without the Yadav parties, Punjab without the Akali Dal of the Badals, Orissa's BJD without the Patnaiks, Tamil Nadu's DMK without the Karunanidhi family, Andhra Pradesh's Telugu Desam Party (TDP) and Yuvajana Sramika Rythu Congress Party (YSRP) without the N.T. Rama Rao and Y.S. Rajashekar Reddy families respectively, and Telangana's Telangana Rashtra Samithi (TRS) without the K. Chandrashekar Rao family among others. Political dynasties in

India have been mutating from generation to generation. In this context, the Gowdas are no different. Also, Indian democracy has shown that dynasties are not easily rejected by the electorates as much as they are by the intelligentsia. This political model has been challenged by Narendra Modi and the BJP for now, but it remains to be seen if the BJP will succeed in eliminating dynasties or create its own edition. When politics has become a heavy investment business, dynasties appear like promoters growing profits for their shareholders. Their desperate moves reflect more a survival game than an ideas game, or an ideology game. An extension of this book will need to examine all this carefully. Perhaps this book will need an update after a while when contemporary history appears less current.

Waiting and the Work Ethic

It is not just politics for which Deve Gowda's enthusiasm has remained intact as he approaches ninety. He has remained open to new ideas and learning as well. His reading is up to date, and the personal library is well maintained. He never reads fiction but engages with anything related to contemporary politics, economy, and agriculture. Biographies and memoirs, especially of those who he has known or worked with, land up on his table. He also has the habit of clipping and preserving book reviews. In fact, the first time he learnt that Isher Judge Ahluwalia, the wife of Montek Singh Ahluwalia, was not well was through a review of her memoir in an English daily.[21]

When the Galwan valley clash happened between Indian and Chinese troops, his table had a pile of books on China (*1962: The War That Wasn't*; *Watershed 1967: India's Forgotten Victory over China*; *Indo–China Boundary Problem: History and Diplomacy*) and also copies of agreements he had signed with China as prime minister. The result of this was a well-calibrated six-point statement on 19 June 2020, which said, among other things: 'In order to ensure that we do not escalate matters, I sincerely urge that nationalist rhetoric should be toned down. This is not the time for a language of provocation and revenge.' He also said: 'There is a feeling among our fellow citizens that we are engulfed by hostile nations. It is the duty of the political leadership to ensure that such anxiety is quelled with proper information. It is important to keep the nation informed at all times. Underplaying certain developments and overstating certain information may be a bad strategy in the long run.' Finally, he warned: 'The government should also not encourage reactionary language of economic boycott. Its implications are deep. We should be guided by pragmatism.'[22] In November 1996, when Gowda received Chinese President Jiang Zemin in New Delhi on a three-day visit, he had signed a pact on the 2800-mile Himalayan frontier between the two countries, which said that 'neither side shall use force against the other by any means or seek unilateral military support'.[23]

Similarly, when he was invited to the Sheikh Mujibur Rahman birth centenary in Bangladesh in 2020, he surrounded himself with books on that country and re-read the Farakka treaty that he had worked out and called up experts to understand if the treaty was still holding good in 2020. The trip was anyway postponed due to the COVID-19 pandemic. Gowda's reading has a specific purpose. It is to either understand something that is unfolding or to fix something. The concept of reading or doing anything for leisure or entertainment is an idea totally absent in his scheme. He has continued to deal with any issue that occupies his mind like a lawyer would with a case he has to fight in court. Besides these books, he reads his prayer books without fail each day after his bath. They are kept in a frail-looking bag and travel everywhere with him with his medicine pouch. Not to forget a session of yoga a few days a week under expert supervision. He ensures that the mind, body and soul are regularly nurtured.

Although he has not held executive power since he stepped down as prime minister, he has maintained enough goodwill and network across party lines to get things done. The number of letters he writes every week and follows them up with people on their progress is a habit that he formed very early as a politician. He still drafts his statements diligently and reads and re-reads them before they are released. He keeps a punishing ten-hour work schedule attending office in Bangalore and travelling frequently within the state, across India, and also internationally.

When the COVID-19 pandemic was just about spreading globally, in February 2020, he was in Seoul for a peace conference organized by an affiliate of the United Nations that was trying to get South Korea and North Korea to engage.[24] After his official engagements were over, he expressed interest in meeting young researchers from local universities to understand agriculture and infrastructure projects in the country. He had the longest discussion with a researcher working on plant genetics from Dongguk University on Korean rice varieties and rice products. In the middle of the discussion, he revealed that he had been to South Korea in 1974 on a study tour, and how as chief minister in 1996, the group housing scheme he had envisioned was inspired by the notes from his 70s Korean trip.[25] While in Seoul, he wanted to experience the high-speed train to Busan, and it took some effort for the Indian embassy staff to dissuade him from going to the city, which had become a COVID-19 hotspot by then. For the eight-hour-long flight back to New Delhi, he wanted to pick books. He pulled the deputy chief of mission in the Indian embassy to a bookshop and boarded the flight with a small haul. All through the flight, he was engrossed with Michael Breen's book: *The New Koreans: The Business, History and People of South Korea.*[26]

Gowda tries to keep himself ahead of the game, perhaps with the hope that his phoenix moment, as he had declared in April 1997 when he bowed out of the prime minister's office, may arrive any time. It is this work ethic and attitude, the gift of health, besides his political shrewdness that has kept him relevant to this day and is bound to do so till his last breath.

Acknowledgements

A well-crafted image in a poem by Kannada writer G.S. Shivarudrappa says that if one looks back, 'life is a mine filled with gemstones of indebtedness'. As this book project drew to a close, I was filled with nothing but indebtedness for people and contexts that I knew had facilitated my exploration, and also for those circumstances and people who had contributed to my progress without my knowledge. I thank both the known and the unknown.

First and foremost, to H.D. Deve Gowda himself, and to his phenomenal memory, I owe a huge debt. If he had not agreed to be interviewed for this book, it would have still been written but would not have been so richly illustrated. He, at times, saw his conversations with me as 'divinely arranged', so that he could reflect on the highs, lows, commissions and omissions of his long life in its final stretch. Therefore, as we sat down for long conversations, he sometimes addressed himself and sometimes his God too. He was certainly curious of what sense I was making of his life, but never once did he insist that I should show him the drafts or the final manuscript. I did not even share the title of the book with him. He was like an archivist of his life. He dispassionately provided material I sought to read and examine. If there are gaps in this book, it is not because he did not offer answers or explanations, but because I did not seek the material, and because I, as a biographer, chose to frame his life in a certain way.

* * *

My teacher Jeremy Seabrook has shaped me not just with his writings, but also with his humanity and empathy. He read through the entire manuscript, sent detailed comments and gave me the confidence to place the book before a larger audience. On my insistence, he also wrote a blurb for the book jacket. He is too modest to accept my reverence.

Chiranjiv Singh is an elder I have deeply respected and relied on. When I decided to do this book, he not only offered me perspective but introduced me to his friend and colleague S.S. Meenakshisundaram. The value that introduction added to this book is there for everybody to see. Singh also read the draft of the book and offered his comments. To speak of our relationship, I need to borrow the title of his own Kannada book: *Idu Yaava Janmada Maitri* (Is This a Relationship from Another Life?)

Ajith Pillai's friendship has not only sustained this book but also my journalism since 2004. He mentored my political writing in Vinod Mehta's *Outlook*. His rectitude and selflessness are uncommon and exemplary. Partha Chatterjee's friendship opened new worlds for me. For the time and trust he has bestowed on me, and on my writing, I am grateful.

I interviewed over eighty people for this book; some did it on record and some off the record. Among those who did on-record interviews S.S. Meenakshisundaram, B.L. Shankar, P.G.R. Sindhia and K.A. Thippeswamy, sat down with me for multiple sessions. I thank them for being generous with their time and for being wonderful hosts. Their understanding of Gowda, developed over the years, has richly informed this book. Meenakshisundaram not only spoke to me at length but also read through the drafts of some crucial chapters and made suggestions. He shared with me copies of the papers he had preserved from his time in the Prime Minister's Office. This book has hugely benefitted from his kindness and commitment to the legacy of Deve Gowda, whom he served in top roles.

Among those who gave me long interviews and shared their assessments of Deve Gowda were P. Chidambaram, Sitaram Yechury, Srikant Jena, Lt Gen. J.S. Dhillon, Montek Singh Ahluwalia, Shyamal Datta, S.M. Jaamdar, Mohan V. Katarki, Medha Patkar, Sunderlal Bahuguna, S.P. Shukla, C. Manjunath, Gitesh Shah, C.M. Ibrahim, M.P. Nadagouda, C.S. Dwarakanath, B. Parthasarathy, Ravindra Reshme, Mahadev Prakash and Ratnakar Rao. I sincerely thank each one of them.

Friends and colleagues Kiran Pasricha, N.R. Vishu Kumar, Mohan Kondajji, K.N. Shanth Kumar, V.S. Jayaschandran, Bhanu Prakash Chandra, D.S. Kishor, C.P. Nagaraja, Srinivas G. Kappanna, Varun Santosh, Chandersuta Dogra, D.K. Singh, Radhika Ramaseshan and Krishna Gowda responded earnestly to my request for help with either contacts, books, documents or photographs. My thanks are due to Pradeep Bahuguna and Niranjan Hiranandani, for promptly sending across material related to their illustrious fathers—Sunderlal Bahuguna and Dr L.H. Hiranandani, respectively.

My colleague and friend G. Mahantesh, with his journalistic enterprise, helped me source a few legislative and legal documents for the book. His help has been invaluable. Similarly, Puru S.B. Doddi has been a fine resource. Librarians and archivists at the Nehru Memorial Library and Museum in New Delhi, and the Karnataka Legislature Library—especially Kanakappa Nalavagal and T.R. Venkatramu—richly deserve my thanks. I also thank the long-time personal aides of Deve Gowda in Bangalore and New Delhi—A.G. Anjani Gowda, K.R. Shivakumar and B.R. Chandrasehkar—for helping me locate a few papers and photographs associated with their boss.

My friend and advocate B.T. Venkatesh patiently listened to, and passionately commented on, a few chapters I read aloud under a banyan tree at the National Gallery of Modern Art in Bangalore. The

others who listened to me read out tiny sections from the book were
Nidhi Nambiar, Poonam Sethi, Deepak Sethi and Veronica Bajpai.

Farooq Abdullah, Jairam Ramesh, Sugata Bose, Christophe
Jaffrelot and Saeed Naqvi—elders and scholars I respect—
read through this book and gave me quotes for the jacket. Their
endorsement has added immense value. I am indebted for the trust
they placed in my writing and for their generosity of spirit.

The person who made this book happen with her quiet
enthusiasm, diligence and positive energy is Milee Ashwarya of
Penguin Random House India. My heartfelt thanks to her and her
wonderful team. I need to make a special mention of Vineet Gill and
Shubhomoy Sikdar, who edited this book.

* * *

My family has been very supportive of this project. I start by thanking
the youngest first. When I refused to share with her my expensive
Bluetooth earphones, my seven-year-old daughter, Misuni, reasoned
that if she played her audiobook loudly, it would clash with my brain
waves, and I would end up writing, 'Deve Gowda was born into a
family of wizards, and went to the Hogwarts School of Witchcraft
and Wizardry'; so, I'd better hand over the earphones and stay
focused on my writing, which I did. Misuni, who is perennially on a
joyride of love and celebration, has taught me so much.

When I was writing this book, my son, Sumeru, besides
studying microorganisms, was busy consuming volume after volume
of *The Wheel of Time* by Robert Jordan—a series I was completely
unfamiliar with. He was reading the eleventh book when I completed
my book. I got him to read a few chapters I had written. He said it
was quite engrossing for a generation so removed from Gowda's time
and which was interested in politics in a very different way. Gowda's
elevation to the highest position in the land was like Jordan's fantasy
fiction, he remarked. Sumeru is the wisest person in our family. His
eclecticism and perseverance have baffled me.

This book is dedicated to my partner, Rosy. When she read the dedication she asked me furiously why, and how, I had quantified the song of the stars to just a hundred. I had to remind her that it was a line from her own poem, written in her past life and anthologized in her collection, *Manna Bisupu* (The Warmth of the Soil). I cannot ever quantify her love, support and friendship.

I am indebted to my mother, Saraswathy Raju, who taught me courage and discipline; and to my mother-in-law, Lucy Pereira, for her unspoken lessons in dignity and hope. For the warmth and engagement of Ruta Srinivasaraju, Sweatha Pawar, Viyata Ruta and Rakendu Ruta, who were busy saving democracy in the United States of America as I wrote this book, my abundant thanks. For J. Bhanumati's capacious heart and warmth, language is limiting. I miss my father, Chi. Srinivasaraju, the original 'Bookman Bold' of our family, who gave me a precious pair of lenses to view the world and left too soon. His serenity was unmatched.

This entire book was written in eleven months, when the COVID-19 pandemic took charge of the world. While the virus wreaked anxiety and suffering, it offered me seclusion to write. The suffering and seclusion have been terrible. No thanks for that. I hope I write my next book in relatively healthier and happier circumstances.

Notes

Chapter 1: The Beginnings and the Background

1. Haradanahalli village in Halekote Hobli (cluster of villages) had
    0824.5 acres of land. There were sixty-six houses and seventy-three
    households as per the 1951 census. The total population of the
    village was 430 in 1941 and 432 in 1951. In 1941, the village had
    forty-eight literates and by 1951, when Gowda had completed his
    matriculation and joined a diploma course, it had jumped to 129.
    However, only eighteen of the 129 were female literates. Most
    of the villagers engaged in agriculture and most of them were
    cultivating owners with only two tenant cultivators. Only eleven
    people were engaged in production other than cultivation. The
    census figures are taken from the *1951 Census Handbook: Hassan
    District*, printed in 1956.
2. *Lessons from history to combat Covid-19: The Influenza Pandemic
    of 1918*, by T.V. Sekhar, International Institute for Population
    Sciences, Mumbai, May 2020. Interestingly, the 1921 census
    figures for Hassan district records negative population growth for
    many taluks in the district. Alur taluk had 1163 persons less, Belur
    taluk had 2174 less, Arakalgud had 2170 people, Channarayapatna
    had 1532 people less, and Holenarasipur taluk, where Gowda's
    village was had 335 people. In fact, in the first fifty years of the

twentieth century, Alur and Belur taluk had seen negative growth in population for the first four decades. There may be many reasons for the negative growth, not disease and pandemic alone, but it is mentioned here to only offer a perspective. The census figures are taken from the *1951 Census Handbook: Hassan District*, printed in 1956.

3.   Eshwara temple, which was a tiny nondescript temple, has now become a mini complex with a tower and a cupola. It was renovated with funds donated by H.D. Deve Gowda's family after he became prime minister.

4.   *Kulla* in the name Kulla Iyengar means short-statured in Kannada. It cannot be his real name. But neither Gowda nor the villagers remember calling him anything else other than Kulla Iyengar. In spoken Kannada it would be shortened to 'Kul Iyengar'. The 'Iyengar' in the name was a marker of caste. They were Vaishnavite Brahmins and followers of Ramanujacharya's vishishtadvaita philosophy. Former Tamil Nadu chief minister J. Jayalalitha was not only an Iyengar, but her family also came from this part of the world: The Hassan–Melukote–Mandya region.

5.   Shraavana in the Hindu calendar is the fifth month of the year. Its corresponding slot in the Gregorian calendar would usually begin late-July and stretch across August. It heralds the arrival of the South–West monsoons. It is a holy month in the Hindu calendar.

6.   Author's interview with H.D. Deve Gowda, 15 September 2019.

7.   Gururaja Joshi, the father of the Hindustani music legend, Bhimsen Joshi, had retrospectively woven a conception myth for his son. Bhimsen Joshi was growing up in Dharwad district around the same time Deve Gowda was rising in Hassan district. When stardom had started chasing the son, the senior Joshi had written on the auspicious alignment of nature, love and blessings that had created his son's genius talent: 'In the light of my guru's philosophical instruction; the joy of my wife's company and due to the proximity of nature, our minds, which were stirred, attained a certain stillness. An unusual peace and serenity were established inside us. On the sandbanks of the Falgu river, our hearts met and felt the edge of eternity. Although the apparel was of *sringara* our souls were transferred onto the wings of divinity, and while they

rested on it, they viewed the world with a meditative glance. Why should one be surprised if this strange communion with truth and the ecstatic experience of beauty found expression in [Bhimsen's] music?' Gururaja Joshi's longish biographical essay on his son was published in Kannada in an anthology titled, *Nadedu Banda Daari*, Manohara Grantamala, Dharwad, 1961.

8. *Bharatada Pradani Deve Gowda*, by Konandur Venkatappa Gowda, Yashashvi Prakashana, 1997.

9. Ibid.

10. Author's interview with H.D. Deve Gowda, 20 December 2020.

11. Discussion with Kannada author and linguist C.P. Nagaraj on 28 January 2021.

12. Kannada-English Dictionary by Rev. F. Kittel, Mangalore Basel Mission Book & Tract Depository, 1894.

13. Reply to the motion on confidence, 11 April 1997, Lok Sabha debates.

14. 'When Earnestness Is Misspelt', by Sugata Srinivasaraju, *Mumbai Mirror*, 19 February 2020: https://mumbaimirror.indiatimes. com/opinion/columnists/when-earnestness-is-misspelt/amp_ articleshow/74197086.cms

15. Report of the committee appointed to consider steps necessary for the adequate representation of communities in the public service, Mysore government, July 1919. The committee comprised Leslie C. Miller, C. Srikantesvara Aiyar, H. Chennaiya, M. Basavaiya, Ghulam Ahmed Kalami, M. Muthanna and M.C. Ranga Iyengar.

16. Ibid.

17. Ibid.

18. Ibid.

19. *1600 Varshagala Vokkaligara Ithihasa*, by Dr B. Pandukumar, Vedavati Prakashana, 2007.

20. 'Seminaries of the oppressed' in *Keeping Faith with the Mother Tongue: The Anxieties of a Local Culture* by Sugata Srinivasaraju, Navakarnataka Publications, 2008.

21. Natha Panth was a socio-religious order from around the twelfth century. It combined ideas from Buddhism, Shaivism and Yoga traditions. Gorakhnath is considered to be the originator of the Nath Panth, and has indelible footprints in the Deccan region,

including Karnataka. The Adichunchanagiri Math has close ties with the Natha Sampradaya (tradition). Of the seventy-two pontiffs that the math has seen across centuries (list of pontiffs in *1600 Varshagala Vokkaligara Ithihasa*, by Dr B. Pandukumar, Vedavati Prakashana, 2007) seventy of them have the 'Nath' prefix attached to their name. It started with the third pontiff, who was called Sri Karmanatha. The first was, however, called Sri Adirudra and the second was Sri Siddhayogi. The current pontiff, the seventy-second is Sri Nirmalanandanatha Swamiji, a structural engineer who studied at the National Institute of Engineering, Mysore and Indian Institute of Technology, Madras. The exploration on the Adichunchangiri Math's connections with the Natha Panth increased after Yogi Adityanath became the chief minister of Uttar Pradesh in March 2017. Also see 'BJP eyes revival in Karnataka with Adityanath riding its campaign wagon,' by Nistula Hebbar, *The Hindu*, 10 March 2018: https://www.thehindu.com/elections/karnataka-2018/bjp-eyes-revival-in-karnataka-with-yogi-riding-its-campaign-wagon/article23036067.ece

22. 'New Shoots and Old Roots,' by Chiranjiv Singh, *Multiple City: Writings on Bangalore*, edited by Aditi De, Penguin Books India, New Delhi, 2008.
23. Author's interview with H.D. Deve Gowda, 15 September 2019.
24. Ibid.
25. Author's interview with H.D. Deve Gowda, 6 October 2019 and 20 December 2020.
26. Ibid.
27. Ibid.
28. Ibid.
29. Author's visit to Halekote government middle school on 30 January 2021.

Chapter 2: The Local World

1. Author's interview with H.D. Deve Gowda on 20 December 2020.
2. Ibid.
3. Ibid.

4. Author's visit to the Holenarasipur Municipal High School on 30 January 2021.
5. Author's interview with H.D. Deve Gowda on 20 December 2020.
6. Ibid.
7. Page 84, *1951 Census Handbook: Hassan District.* Preface by G. Nanjundaiah, census commissioner of Mysore. Census of India Archives.
8. 'Freedoms and Resistance', by Sugata Srinivasaraju, 15 August 2019, *New Indian Express*: https://www.newindianexpress.com/opinions/2019/aug/15/freedoms-and-resistance-2019242.html
9. Author's interview with H.D. Deve Gowda on 20 September 2020.
10. Ibid.
11. Page 64, diary entry for 14.4.1943, *Window on the Wall: Quit India Prison Diary of 19-Year-Old* by H.Y. Sharada Prasad, edited by Sugata Srinivasaraju, Navakarnataka, 2010.
12. Author's interview with H.D. Deve Gowda on 20 December 2020.
13. Ibid.
14. Author's visit to L.V. Polytechnic Institute in Hassan on 29 January 2021.
15. Author's interview with H.D. Deve Gowda on 20 December 2020.
16. Ibid.
17. Ibid.
18. Ibid.
19. Ibid.
20. Ibid.
21. Ibid.
22. Ibid.
23. Author's interview with H.D. Deve Gowda on 11 March 2020.

Chapter 3: The Grassroots Game

1. H.D. Deve Gowda in the talk show *Weekend with Ramesh*, episodes 21 and 22, season 3, Zee Kannada entertainment channel, 10 June and 11 June 2017.

2.   Villagers and friends in the talk show *Weekend with Ramesh*, episodes 21 and 22, season 3, Zee Kannada entertainment channel, 10 June and 11 June 2017.

3.   Ibid.

4.   Chapters 'Muttigehalli Patel Gowdaru' and 'Vivaha' in *Bharatada Pradhani Deve Gowdaru* by Konanduru Venkatappa Gowda, Yashasvi Prakashana, 1997.

5.   Author's interview with H.D. Deve Gowda on 20 January 2019.

6.   Author's conversation with H.D. Shailaja on 16 November 2020.

7.   Author's interview with H.D. Deve Gowda on 20 September 2020.

8.   H.D. Deve Gowda in the talk show *Weekend with Ramesh*, episodes 21 and 22, season 3, Zee Kannada entertainment channel, 10 June and 11 June 2017.

9.   Ibid.

10.   Ibid.

11.   Chapter 4, 'Rajakeeyadatta Seletha,' *Sadhaneya Shikararohana: Pradana Mantriyagi HD Deve Gowda Avara Sadhanegalu*, edited by Dr Pradhan Gurudutt and Dr C. Naganna, Sapna Book House, 2017.

12.   Author's interview with H.D. Deve Gowda on 15 September 2019.

13.   Author's interview with H.D. Deve Gowda on 15 September 2019.

14.   Chapter 4, 'Rajakeeyadatta Seletha,' *Sadhaneya Shikararohana: Pradana Mantriyagi H.D. Deve Gowda Avara Sadhanegalu*, edited by Dr Pradhan Gurudutt and Dr C. Naganna, Sapna Book House, 2017.

15.   Author's interview with H.D. Deve Gowda on 20 September 2020.

16.   Ibid.

17.   'Linguistic State and an Identity Debate' by Sugata Srinivasaraju, *Mumbai Mirror*, 11 November 2020: https://mumbaimirror.indiatimes.com/opinion/columnists/sugata-srinivasaraju/linguistic-state-and-an-identity-debate/amp_articleshow/79161879.cms

18.   Statistical reports, Election Commission of India.

19. Chapter 16, 'As chief minister of Mysore' in *BDJ: A Portrait of a Vice President* by S.R. Gunjal, Sterling Publishers, 1979.

20. Ibid.

21. Chapter 2, 'A heritage of poverty,' *in BDJ: A Portrait of a Vice President* by S.R. Gunjal, Sterling Publishers, 1979.

22. P. Lankesh had given him this name, and others too, in his satirical writings in *Lankesh Patrike*, the weekly tabloid he founded and edited.

23. Statistical reports, Election Commission of India.

24. Mysore State assembly debates, 3 April 1962.

25. Author's interview with H.D. Deve Gowda on 6 January 2021.

26. Ibid.

27. Ibid.

28. Ibid.

29. Author's interview with H.D. Deve Gowda on 20 December 2020.

30. Statistical reports, Election Commission of India.

31. Chapter 'As chief minister of Mysore' in *BDJ: A Portrait of a Vice President* by S.R. Gunjal, Sterling Publishers, 1979.

32. Author's interview with H.D. Deve Gowda on 25 August 2019.

33. Ibid.

34. Shimoga was the centre of socialist activity in the Mysore state. The Karnataka socialists were inspired by Ram Manohar Lohia. Besides, the Praja Socialist Party of Jayaprakash Narayan and J.B. Kripalani, which had a pan-Karnataka presence between 1962 and 1972, socialists won on tickets of three different mutating political formations as per Election Commission records—Socialist Party, Sanghata Socialist Party and Samyukta Socialist Party.

35. Author's interview with H.D. Deve Gowda on 27 July 2019.

36. Ibid.

37. 'Chronicle of a Defeat Foretold', book review by N. Kalyan Raman, *Open*, 12 February 2021: https://openthemagazine.com/lounge/books/chronicle-defeat-foretold/

38. 'Shantaveriya Ashanta Santa', a poem by Gopalakrishna Adiga first appeared in his poetry collection *Battalara Gange*. Included in his collected poetry *Adigara Samagra Sahitya - 1*, IBH Prakashana, 1987.

39.   'Why It Is Important to Remember Gopala Gowda in These
        Politically Unhinged Times in Karnataka', by Sugata Srinivasaraju,
        Indian Express, 27 July 2019: https://indianexpress.com/article/
        opinion/columns/karnataka-crisis-politics-assembly-speaker-flor-
        test-bjp-congress-jds-5855063/

Chapter 4: Devaraj Urs, Emergency and a Stormy Decade

1.   Part One, *Broadening and Deepening Democracy—Political Innovation
        in Karnataka* by E. Raghavan and James Manor, Routledge, 2009.
2.   The strength of the Karnataka legislative assembly went up to 224
        later.
3.   Statistical report on general election 1972 to the legislative
        assembly of Mysore, Election Commission of India.
4.   S. Bangarappa, M. Veerappa Moily, S.M. Krishna and Dharam
        Singh were all closely associated and groomed by Devaraj Urs.
        J.H. Patel, who was a socialist, headed Karnataka Kranti Ranga,
        a regional party that Urs set up after he quit the Congress.
        Siddaramaiah, who became chief minister in 2013, was also
        inspired by Urs. Mallikarjun Kharge, M.Y. Ghorpade and Abdul
        Nazirsab, who did not become chief ministers but had the
        potential, were also under his watch.
5.   Chiranjiv Singh's interview to author on 3 December 2020.
6.   'Nanna Hiriyanna' by H.D. Deve Gowda in *Namma Arasu*, edited
        by Basavaraju Megalkeri, Pallava Prakashana, 2020.
7.   Ibid.
8.   Author's interview with P.G.R. Sindhia on 5 August 2020.
9.   Ibid.
10.   'Nanna Hiriyanna' by H.D. Deve Gowda in *Namma Arasu*, edited
        by Basavaraju Megalkeri, Pallava Prakashana, 2020.
11.   Author's interview with H.D. Deve Gowda on 5 January 2020.
12.   Ibid.
13.   Ibid.
14.   Author's interview with Chiranjiv Singh on 3 December 2020.
15.   Author's interview with H.D. Deve Gowda on 27 July 2019. Also,
        in 'Nanna Hiriyanna' by H.D. Deve Gowda in *Namma Arasu*,
        edited by Basavaraju Megalkeri, Pallava Prakashana, 2020.

16. Ibid.
17. Ibid.
18. Ibid.
19. Ibid.
20. Author's interview with H.D. Deve Gowda on 27 July 2019.
21. Ibid.
22. Official resolution on naming the state as 'Karnataka', 27 July 1972, Mysore legislative assembly debates.
23. Discussion on transfer and promotion of officials, 6 July 1972, Mysore legislative assembly debates.
24. Ibid.
25. Ibid.
26. Author's interview with H.D. Deve Gowda on 9 January 2021.
27. *Part One, Broadening and Deepening Democracy: Political Innovation in Karnataka* by E. Raghavan and James Manor, Routledge, 2009.
28. Ibid.
29. Ibid.
30. Author's interview with H.D. Deve Gowda on 16 August 2020.
31. Author's interview with P.G.R. Sindhia on 5 August 2020.
32. Ibid.
33. Ibid.
34. Author's interview with H.D. Deve Gowda on 20 December 2020.
35. Author's interview with P.G.R. Sindhia on 5 August 2020.
36. 'Patrikegala Hogalike Tegalike' in *Bahuroopi Arasu* by Vaddarase Raghurama Shetty, Sapna Book House, 2000.
37. Author's interview with P.G.R. Sindhia on 5 August 2020.
38. Ibid.
39. Ibid.
40. Ibid.
41. S. Nijalingappa's letter to Chandra Shekhar, 30 January 1978, *Janata Party Papers*, Nehru Memorial Museum and Library (NMML) Archives, New Delhi.
42. Ibid.
43. H.D. Deve Gowda's letter to S. Nijalingappa, 5 January 1978, *Janata Party Papers*, NMML Archives, New Delhi.

44. H.D. Deve Gowda's letter to S. Nijalingappa, 11 January 1978, *Janata Party Papers*, NMML Archives, New Delhi.
45. Author's interview with P.G.R. Sindhia on 5 August 2020.
46. 'Nanna Hiriyanna' by H.D. Deve Gowda in *Namma Arasu*, edited by Basavaraju Megalkeri, Pallava Prakashana, 2020.
47. Ibid.
48. Author's interview with H.D. Deve Gowda on 6 October 2019.
49. Ibid. Gowda had developed a rapport with Charan Singh. In fact, he and his wife had stayed in Charan Singh's house for a night during one of their Delhi visits. He remembered that since he nor his wife knew Hindi, the conversations were clipped and in gestures. At least, Gowda could manage in English, but his wife was totally mute during the stay because her ability to communicate in English or Hindi with Charan Singh's wife and rest of the family was zero.
50. 'Grover Panel Indicts Urs', *Indian Express*, 10 May 1979: https://indianexpress.com/article/india/may-10-1979-forty-years-ago-urs-under-scanner-5720021/
51. H.D. Deve Gowda's speech: motion of confidence in the council of ministers, 12 June 1996, Lok Sabha debates, Lok Sabha Digital Library.
52. Author's interview with H.D. Deve Gowda on 20 October 2019.
53. Letter dated 9 November 1978. In Part Two, 'Politician,' *The Goenka Letters*, edited by T.J.S. George, East West Books, 2006.
54. 'Nanna Hiriyanna' by H.D. Deve Gowda in *Namma Arasu*, edited by Basavaraju Megalkeri, Pallava Prakashana, 2020.
55. Chiranjiv Singh's interview to the author on 3 December 2020.
56. 'Samyukta Karnatakavannu Ulisida Kathe' in *Bahuroopi Arasu* by Vaddarase Raghurama Shetty, Sapna Book House, 2000.
57. Author's interview with P.G.R. Sindhia on 5 August 2020.
58. Author's interview with B.L. Shankar on 30 May 2020.
59. *Pursuit of Law and Order*, the autobiography of IPS officer A.P. Durai, Notion Press, 2015.
60. Author's interview with H.D. Deve Gowda on 25 August 2019.
61. Report of the working of the Karnataka Pradesh Janata Party: 1981-83, date of report filed not mentioned, *Janata Party Papers*, NMML Archives, New Delhi.

Chapter 5: Morarji: The Mentor and the Mantle

1. 'Preface,' *The Story of My Life Volume One*, by Morarji Desai, 1974, Macmillan India.
2. Chapter 8, 'End of Government Service,' *The Story of My Life Volume One*, by Morarji Desai, 1974, Macmillan India.
3. Author's interview with H.D. Deve Gowda on 23 December 2018 and 15 September 2019.
4. Chapter 1, 'My Childhood', *The Story of My Life Volume One*, by Morarji Desai, 1974, Macmillan India.
5. Chapter 8, 'End of Government Service', *The Story of My Life Volume One*, by Morarji Desai, 1974, Macmillan India.
6. Author's interview with H.D. Deve Gowda on 23 December 2018 and 15 September 2019.
7. Ibid.
8. Ibid.
9. Ibid.
10. Narrated by Chiranjiv Singh, the then district collector of Mandya, to the author. He later became India's ambassador to UNESCO when Gowda became prime minister.
11. Letter from N. Balakrishnan, permanent secretary to Morarji Desai, to H.D. Deve Gowda, Karnataka state president, Janata Party dated 25 April 1979, *Janata Party Papers*, NMML, New Delhi.
12. Author's interview with H.D. Deve Gowda on 23 December 2018 and 15 September 2019.
13. Ibid.
14. Bapuji Educational Association was established in 1958 by a group of philanthropic personalities of Davangere to promote education in and around the Davangere district of the then Mysore state. JJM Medical College and Hospital of this Association was established in 1965. The administrative block of the college is now named after S. Nijalingappa. Source: www.jjmmc.org
15. Author's interview with H.D. Deve Gowda on 23 December 2018 and 15 September 2019.
16. Ibid.
17. Ibid.

18. Ibid.
19. Letter to Chandra Shekhar, president, All India Janata Party, from A. Ramachandra dated 7 January 1979, *Janata Party Papers*, NMML, New Delhi.
20. Letter to Morarji Desai, prime minister from A. Ramachandra received on 27 February 1979, *Janata Party Papers*, NMML, New Delhi.
21. Letter from H.D. Deve Gowda, Karnataka state president, Janata Party, to Ramakrishna Hegde, general secretary, All India Janata Party dated 11 September 1978, *Janata Party Papers*, NMML, New Delhi.
22. Chapter 32, 'Jawaharlal Nehru: In My View,' *The Story of My Life Volume Two*, by Morarji Desai, 1974, Macmillan India.
23. Chapter 41, 'Refutation of Allegations against my son Kantilal', *The Story of My Life Volume Two*, by Morarji Desai, 1974, Macmillan India.
24. Chapter 7, 'In the Panchamahals', *The Story of My Life Volume One*, by Morarji Desai, 1974, Macmillan India.
25. Chapter 3, 'In the UTC', *The Story of My Life Volume One*, by Morarji Desai, 1974, Macmillan India.
26. Author's interview with H.D. Deve Gowda on 23 December 2018 and 15 September 2019.
27. Ibid.
28. Chapter 4, 'Early Years in Public Life,' *Down Memory Lane: A Memoir*, by M.Y. Ghorpade, 2004, Penguin Enterprise.
29. 'During the Indira Gandhi Years' by H.Y. Sharada Prasad, *GP: The Man and His Work*, edited by H.Y. Sharada Prasad, 1998, New Age International (P) Limited Publishers.
30. Author's interview with H.D. Deve Gowda on 23 December 2018 and 15 September 2019.
31. Ibid.
32. Letter from S.R. Bommai, leader of the Opposition, Karnataka legislative assembly, to Morarji Desai, prime minister, dated 30 January 1979, *Janata Party Papers*, NMML, New Delhi.
33. Author's interview with H.D. Deve Gowda on 23 December 2018 and 15 September 2019.
34. Author's interview with P.G.R. Sindhia on 5 August 2020. Also, author's interview with K.A. Thippeswamy on 1 June 2020.

35. Press Information Bureau release, government of India, 28 February 1997.

Chapter 6: The Epic Battle with Ramakrishna Hegde

1. Author's interview with M.P. Nadagouda, former legislator and close associate of Ramakrishna Hegde on 6 November 2020.
2. Author's interview with B.L. Shankar on 30 May and 22 June 2020. Also 'Nanna Hiriyanna' by H.D. Deve Gowda in *Namma Arasu*, Pallava Prakashana, 2020.
3. 'Hegde Deve Gowda Yembha Karataka Dhamanakaru', by P. Lankesh, *Lankesh Patrike*, 26 June 1996.
4. 'Dynasty' in *Imaginary Homelands*, by Salman Rushdie, Granta Books, 1991.
5. Author's interview with H.D. Deve Gowda on 25 August 2019 and 5 October 2019.
6. Ibid.
7. Sociologist M.N. Srinivas spoke of 'Sanskritization' in the 1950s. This term is also read as 'Brahminization'. He propounded this theory in his DPhil thesis at Oxford University, and it spoke about a person from the lower castes imitating or adopting the customs, rites and beliefs of the Brahmins. For a critical understanding of M.N. Srinivas' idea, read the introduction and chapter two of *Debrahmanising History: Dominance and Resistance in Indian Society* by Braj Ranjan Mani, Manohar, 2018.
8. Author's interview with H.D. Deve Gowda on 25 August 2019 and 5 October 2019.
9. Ibid.
10. *Janata Party Papers*, NMML, New Delhi
11. Ibid.
12. Author's interview with B.L. Shankar on 30 May and 22 June 2020 and P.G.R. Sindhia on 5 August 2020.
13. Ibid.
14. Author's interview with H.D. Deve Gowda on 25 August 2019 and 5 October 2019.
15. Ibid.
16. Ibid.

17. Letter dated 29 January 1978 from Ramakrishna Hegde to H.D. Deve Gowda, *Janata Party Papers*, NMML, New Delhi.

18. Author's interview with H.D. Deve Gowda on 25 August 2019 and 5 October 2019.

19. Letter from S. Nijalingappa to Chandra Shekhar on 30 January 1978. Also, letter to Rabi Ray, L.K. Advani, Surendra Mohan on 25 January 1978, *Janata Party Papers*, NMML, New Delhi.

20. Author's interview with H.D. Deve Gowda on 25 August 2019 and 5 October 2019.

21. Ibid.

22. Author's interview with B.L. Shankar on 30 May and 22 June 2020. Also, author's interview with K.A. Thippeswamy on 29 May 2020.

23. Letter from N. Balakrishnan, permanent secretary, Janata Party to H.D. Deve Gowda on 16 March 1978, NMML, New Delhi.

24. Letter from Ramakrishna Hegde to Bisalhop Timmappa Hegde, president, Janata Party, Sirsi, north Kanara, on 4 March 1978, *Janata Party Papers*, NMML, New Delhi

25. Letter from Ramakrishna Hegde to Shri Aigal, president, Janata Party, Ankola and to Nagesh Shanbhag, president, Janata Party, Yellapur, north Kanara, on 4 March 1978, NMML, New Delhi.

26. Letter from Ramakrishna Hegde to K.S. Nagaratnamma on 9 March 1978, *Janata Party Papers*, NMML, New Delhi.

27. Letter from Y. Ramakrishna to Morarji Desai on 5 April 1978, *Janata Party Papers*, NMML, New Delhi.

28. Letter from Chandra Shekhar to H.D. Deve Gowda through N. Balakrishnan, permanent secretary, Janata Party, on 7 March 1978, *Janata Party Papers*, NMML, New Delhi.

29. Letter from G.S. Kulkarni, general secretary, Janata Party, Indi taluk to L.K. Advani on 30 March 1978, NMML, New Delhi.

30. Letter to H.D. Deve Gowda from Ramakrishna Hegde on 16 January 1978, *Janata Party Papers*, NMML, New Delhi.

31. Letter from L.K. Advani to G.S. Kulkarni on 6 April 1978, *Janata Party Papers*, NMML, New Delhi.

32. Letter from Veerendra Patil to I.C. Nagathan on 1 February 1978, *Janata Party Papers*, NMML, New Delhi.

33. Author's interview with H.D. Deve Gowda on 25 August 2019 and 5 October 2019.

34. Author's interview with B.L. Shankar on 30 May and 22 June 2020.

35. Ibid.

36. Ibid.

37. Ibid.

38. Ibid.

39. Ibid.

40. Part Three, *Broadening and Deepening Democracy: Political Innovation in Karnataka*, by E. Raghavan and James Manor, Routledge, 2009.

41. Author's interview with B.L. Shankar on 30 May and 22 June 2020.

42. Ibid.

43. Part Three, *Broadening and Deepening Democracy: Political Innovation in Karnataka*, by E. Raghavan and James Manor, Routledge, 2009.

44. Author's interview with B.L. Shankar on 30 May and 22 June 2020.

45. Author's interview with H.D. Deve Gowda.

46. Author's interview with K.A. Thippeswamy on 29 May 2020.

47. Author's interview with H.D. Deve Gowda.

48. L.C. Jain or Lakshmi Chand Jain (1925–2010) was a writer, activist, member of the planning commission, and India's ambassador to South Africa. He was deeply involved in the legislation to decentralize governance and create the panchayat raj system.

49. Author's interview with P.G.R. Sindhia on 5 August 2020.

50. Author's interview with H.D. Deve Gowda on 6 January 2021.

51. Ibid.

52. Author's interview with H.D. Deve Gowda on 25 August 2019 and 5 October 2019.

53. Ibid.

54. Ibid.

55. Part Three, *Broadening and Deepening Democracy: Political Innovation in Karnataka* by E. Raghavan and James Manor, Routledge, 2009.

56. Author's interview with H.D. Deve Gowda on 25 August 2019 and 5 October 2019.
57. Ibid.
58. Ibid.
59. *Lankesh Patrike*, edited by P. Lankesh.
60. Author's interview with H.D. Deve Gowda on 25 August 2019 and 5 October 2019.
61. 'Panchatara Patrakartara Drishtiyalli Arasu' in *Bahuroopi Arasu* by Vaddarase Raghurama Shetty, Sapna Book House, 2000.
62. Author's interview with P.G.R. Sindhia on 5 August 2020.
63. Author's interview with B.L. Shankar on 30 May and 22 June 2020.
64. Author's interview with K.A. Thippeswamy on 29 May 2020.
65. Author's interview with H.D. Deve Gowda on 11 March 2020.
66. *Sunday* magazine, 21–27 June 1987.
67. The limerick was written by IAS officer Chiranjiv Singh, then in charge of rural development, and passed on to fellow bureaucrat, P.J. Naik, who was then secretary of planning. Naik later became the CMD of Axis Bank and Singh became India's ambassador to UNESCO.
68. Ibid.
69. Ibid.
70. Ibid.
71. Ibid.
72. Ibid.
73. Part Three, *Broadening and Deepening Democracy: Political Innovation in Karnataka* by E. Raghavan and James Manor, Routledge, 2009.
74. Response of the Karnataka Lokayukta on 4 September 2020 to an RTI query by G. Mahantesh dated 6 August 2020. It said since the thirty-year-old report had not been digitized, they are finding it difficult to trace it.
75. Author's interview with K.A. Thippeswamy on 29 May 2020.
76. Author's interview with H.D. Deve Gowda on 11 March 2020.
77. Part Three, *Broadening and Deepening Democracy: Political Innovation in Karnataka* by E. Raghavan and James Manor, Routledge, 2009.

78. Author's interview with B.L. Shankar on 30 May and 22 June 2020.
79. H.D. Deve Gowda's letter to Ramakrishna Hegde on 28 March 1988.
80. H.D. Deve Gowda's letter to Ramakrishna Hegde on 29 March 1988.
81. H.D. Deve Gowda's letter to Ramakrishna Hegde on 19 April 1988.
82. Ibid.
83. Ibid.
84. Ibid.
85. Ibid.
86. Ibid.
87. Ibid.
88. Ramakrishna Hegde's letter to H.D. Deve Gowda on 20 April 1988.
89. Author's interview with Ravindra Reshme on 26 August 2020.
90. Ibid.
91. Ibid.
92. Ibid.
93. Report of the Justice Kuldip Singh Commission of Inquiry, June 1990.
94. Ibid.
95. Ibid.
96. 'More Law Cases Notably the Hegde Years,' *Evolving with Subramanian Swamy: A Roller Coaster Ride* by Roxna Swamy, self-published, 2017.
97. Source of the joke is Dr M.P. Nadagoudar, former MLC and Hegde camp follower. Narrated to the author on 19 March 2020.
98. 9 August 1988, Lok Sabha debates.
99. Ibid.
100. Ibid.
101. Ibid.
102. Author's interview with B.L. Shankar on 30 May and 22 June 2020.
103. Ibid.
104. Ibid.

105. Author's interview with H.D. Deve Gowda on 11 March 2020.
106. Ibid.
107. 'Former BJP MP's Books Charge PM Deve Gowda with Graft, Threaten to Sully His Reputation', by Stephen David, *India Today*, 31 December 1996: https://www.indiatoday.in/magazine/indiascope/story/19961231-former-bjp-mps-books-charge-pm-deve-gowda-with-graft-threaten-to-sully-his-reputation-834291-1996-12-31
108. Apparently, K. Venkatagiri Gowda had lobbied to become vice chancellor when Ramakrishna Hegde was chief minister. But he had been told by Jeevaraj Alva, who was in Hegde's inner circle that while Hegde preferred him, Deve Gowda had blocked his selection. This had made the professor embittered. Gowda, however, says that he was not in the first place aware of the professor's desire to be vice-chancellor, but Hegde and Alva had conveniently used his name to put the professor off the race so that they could push their own candidate at the time. Deve Gowda had learnt of this 'conspiracy' much later, after the damage had been inflicted.
109. *The King of Corruption and The Unmaking of India*, by K. Venkatagiri Gowda, self-published, October 1996.
110. Author's interview with H.D. Deve Gowda on 11 March 2020.
111. Ibid.
112. Ibid.
113. A death ritual among Hindu upper castes to ensure that the departed has enough nourishment during her or his final journey.
114. Author's interview with H.D. Deve Gowda on 11 March 2020.

Chapter 7: A Lonely Phase, Unpredicted

1.   Author's interview with K.R. Shivakumar on 7 April 2020.
2.   Author's interview with P.G.R. Sindhia on 5 August 2020.
3.   Statistical report on the general election, 1989 to the legislative assembly of Karnataka, Election Commission of India.
4.   Author's interview with B.L. Shankar on 30 May 2020 and K.A. Thippeswamy on 29 May 2020.
5.   Author's interview with B.L. Shankar on 30 May 2020.

6.   Author's interview with K.A. Thippeswamy on 29 May 2020.

7.   Author's interview with H.D. Deve Gowda on 20 October 2019.

8.   Author's interview with H.D. Deve Gowda on 25 August 2019.

9.   Author's interview with B.L. Shankar on 30 May 2020.

10.   Ibid.

11.   Author's interview with K.R. Shivakumar on 7 April 2020.

12.   Author's interview with H.D. Deve Gowda 20 October 2019.

13.   Author's interview with K.R. Shivakumar on 7 April 2020.

14.   Author's interview with P.G.R. Sindhia on 5 August 2020.

15.   Ibid.

16.   Author's interview with Gitesh Shah on 5 October 2019.

Chapter 8: Finally, in the Fifth Attempt, Mr Chief Minister

1.   When Devaraj Urs was transport minister in the Nijalingappa cabinet, Gowda as a Holenarasipur legislator went to him often seeking better bus connections between his constituency and Bangalore, the state capital.

2.   Hegde resigned in 1986 after the high court ruled against his government in the arrack bottling case. A confidential letter he had written to party president Chandra Shekhar, offering to resign, got leaked to the *Statesman* newspaper.

3.   'Nayakatvada Ayke Tanda Aatanka', in *Bharatada Pradhani Deve Gowda*, by Konanduru Venkatappa Gowda, Yashasvi Prakashana, 1997. Also, author's interview with H.D. Deve Gowda on 25 August 2019.

4.   Author's interview with H.D. Deve Gowda on 5 January 2020.

5.   Author's interviews with B.L. Shankar, P.G.R. Sindhia and M.P. Nadagoudar on 30 May 2020, 5 August 2020 and 26 February 2020 respectively.

6.   Author's interview with B.L. Shankar on 30 May 2020. Also, 'Nayakatvada Ayke Tanda Aatanka', in *Bharatada Pradhani Deve Gowda*, by Konanduru Venkatappa Gowda, Yashasvi Prakashana,1997.

7.   'Aanadada Galigeyalli Asantoshada Honalu,' in *Bharatada Pradhani Deve Gowda*, by Konanduru Venkatappa Gowda, Yashasvi Prakashana, 1997.

8.   Ibid.
9.   Ibid.
10. Ibid.
11. Ibid.
12. Author's interview with P.G.R. Sindhia on 5 August 2020.
13. Ibid.
14. Author's interview with S.S. Meenakshisundaram on 13 September 2019.
15. Ibid.
16. Ibid.
17. Ibid.
18. Author's interview with K.A. Thippeswamy on 29 May 2020.
19. Ibid.
20. Ibid.
21. Ibid.
22. 'SC glosses over vital facts in holding senior Karnataka bureaucrat J. Vasudevan guilty', by Manoj Mitta, 15 October 1995, *India Today*: https://www.indiatoday.in/magazine/special-report/story/19951015-sc-glosses-over-vital-facts-in-holding-senior-karnataka-bureaucrat-j.-vasudevan-guilty-807839-1995-10-15
23. 'Working with Sri. Deve Gowda,' by K. Padmanabhaiah, former home secretary, Government of India, an article written for an unpublished volume on H.D. Deve Gowda. Courtesy: office of H.D. Deve Gowda, New Delhi.
24. Author's interview with B.L. Shankar on 30 May 2020.
25. Author's interview with K.A. Thippeswamy on 29 May 2020.
26. Author's interview with H.D. Deve Gowda on 27 July 2019.
27. Author's interview with K.A. Thippeswamy on 29 May 2020.
28. Ibid.
29. 'Is "IT" All for Land?' by Sugata Srinivasaraju, 7 November 2005, *Outlook*: https://magazine.outlookindia.com/story/is-it-all-for-land/229158
30. 'How Many Shares?' by Sugata Srinivasaraju, 21 November 2005, Outlook: https://magazine.outlookindia.com/story/how-many-shares/229300
31. 'Infy Rules,' Bangalore Diary, by Krishna Prasad, 17 December 2001, Outlook: https://magazine.outlookindia.com/story/infy-rules/214026

32. 'Cyber Rajas,' Bangalore Diary, by Krishna Prasad, 28 March 2005, Outlook: https://magazine.outlookindia.com/story/cyber-rajas/226906

33. A booklet published by the legal cell, Janata Dal (Secular), Karnataka state unit, Bangalore, 2008.

34. 'Delhi Metro Rail Project (Modified Phase 1): The Unsaid Story Behind Its Financial Closure in September 1996', by N.P. Singh, former urban development secretary, Government of India, an article written for an unpublished volume on H.D. Deve Gowda. Courtesy: office of H.D. Deve Gowda, New Delhi

35. Ibid.

36. Author's interview with B.L. Shankar on 30 May 2020.

37. Author's interview with H.D. Deve Gowda on 16 August 2020.

38. Author's interview with K.A. Thippeswamy on 29 May 2020.

39. Ibid.

40. Author's interview with H.D. Deve Gowda on 27 July 2019.

41. Ibid.

42. Ibid.

43. 'Storm Rages over Cogentrix Project Coming up in Karnataka', by Stephen David, 15 August 1996, *India Today*: https://www.indiatoday.in/magazine/environment/story/19960815-storm-rages-over-cogentrix-project-coming-up-in-karnataka-833692-1996-08-15

44. Author's interview with P.G.R. Sindhia on 5 August 2020.

45. Author's interview with S.S. Meenakshisundaram on 23 September 2019.

46. Author's interview with C.S. Dwarakanath on 11 August 2020.

47. Ibid.

48. Ibid.

49. Ibid.

50. H.D. Deve Gowda's press statement on 1 September 2020.

51. Discussion on Constitution (Scheduled Tribes) Order (Second Amendment) Bill, 19 August 1991, Lok Sabha debates.

52. Author's interview with H.D. Deve Gowda on 6 January 2021.

53. 'Can Coalition Governments Give Good Governance', in *India at Turning Point: The Road to Good Governance*, by T.S.R. Subramanian, Rainlight Rupa, 2014.

54. Ibid.
55. Author's interview with H.D. Deve Gowda on 21 August 2019.
56. 'Dispute over the ownership leads BJP to build up Hubli Idgah Maidan issue in Karnataka', by Saritha Rai, 15 September 1994, *India Today*: https://www.indiatoday.in/magazine/indiascope/story/19940915-dispute-over-ownership-leads-bjp-to-build-up-idgah-maidan-issue-in-karnataka-810194-1994-09-15
57. Motion regarding expressing grave concern over the failure of administration in ensuring the security of minority community in various parts of the country, especially in Gujarat, 30 April 2002, Lok Sabha debates.
58. Author's interview with B.L. Shankar on 30 May 2020.
59. Ibid.
60. Author's interview with H.D. Deve Gowda on 25 August 2019.
61. Author's interview with S.S. Meenakshisundaram on 23 September 2019.
62. Ibid.
63. Jyoti Basu had termed his party the Communist Party of India (Marxist)'s decision to not allow him to accept the prime ministership of India in 1996 as a 'Himalayan blunder'.

Chapter 9: The Krishna and the Cauvery

1. *Naanu Kannambadi Katte: Heegondu Atmakate*, by P.V. Nanjaraj Urs, Abhiruchi Prakashana, 2017. This book delves into historical documents to argue that in the twenty-one-year history of the dam's construction, Visvesvaraya was only one among the eight chief engineers who had worked on it. The project existed before his time in office and after him, yet he is the only one who has captured popular imagination. Not even the Maharaja who commissioned the project.
2. Author's interview with S.M. Jaamdar on 21 March 2020.
3. Ibid.
4. Karnataka assembly debates, 19 April 1995.
5. Narration of H.D. Deve Gowda's life by Y.S.V. Datta. Select recordings were presented as a podcast series in The State, a Kannada digital news platform, now defunct.

6. Author's interview with S.M. Jaamdar on 21 March 2020.
7. Ibid.
8. Ibid.
9. Ibid.
10. Ibid.
11. Narration of H.D. Deve Gowda's life by Y.S.V. Datta. Select recordings were presented as a podcast series in The State, a Kannada digital news platform, now defunct.
12. Author's interview with S.M. Jaamdar on 21 March 2020.
13. Ibid.
14. Ibid.
15. Ibid.
16. Ibid.
17. Narration of H.D. Deve Gowda's life by Y.S.V. Datta. Select recordings were presented as a podcast series in The State, a Kannada digital news platform, now defunct.
18. Author's interview with H.D. Deve Gowda on 4 October 2020.
19. The Deve Gowda-led cabinet cleared the proposal on 8 November 1995. The government order was issued on 13 November 1995.
20. Author's interview with S.M. Jaamdar on 21 March 2020.
21. Ibid.
22. Author's interview with Mohan V. Katarki on 22 September 2020.
23. Author's interview with H.D. Deve Gowda on 4 October 2020.
24. Author's interview with S.M. Jaamdar on 21 March 2020.
25. Staff Appraisal Report (7406-IN), Upper Krishna (Phase 2) Irrigation Project, World Bank Report (7406-IN), 12 April 1989.
26. Recent Experience with Involuntary Resettlement, India—Upper Krishna (Karnataka and Maharashtra), operations evaluation team, World Bank Report (17542), 2 June 1998.
27. Ibid.
28. Author's interview with S.M. Jaamdar on 21 March 2020.
29. Ibid.
30. Karnataka assembly debates, 21 August 1974.
31. Author's interview with H.D. Deve Gowda on 4 October 2020.
32. The C.P. Ramaswami Aiyar Foundation website www.cprfoundation.org
33. Mysore legislative assembly debates, 31 March 1964.

34. Author's interview with H.D. Deve Gowda on 04 October 2020.
35. Author's interview with H.D. Deve Gowda on 27 July 2019.
36. Author's interview with Mohan V. Katarki on 22 September 2020.
37. Ibid.
38. Photographs of the posters put up in Madukur, Tiruvarur and Nagapattinam by K. Rajaraman, district youth Congress president Nagai Quaid-E-Milleth (Nagapattinam) are available in Deve Gowda's New Delhi office. There is no date on the poster nor is there a date mark on the photographs. They are mostly from 1995 as it says, 'Hearty Welcome to Prime Minister's Cauvery Expert Team'.
39. Author's interview with Mohan V. Katarki on 22 September 2020.
40. Motion of thanks to the President's address, Lok Sabha debates, 17 July 1991.
41. Ibid.
42. Author's interview with Mohan V. Katarki on 22 September 2020.
43. Ibid.
44. Ibid.
45. Ibid.
46. Ibid.
47. Author's interview with S.S. Meenakshisundaram on 23 September 2019.
48. Author's interview with Mohan V. Katarki on 22 September 2020.
49. Ibid.
50. Ibid.
51. Ibid.
52. Ibid.
53. Author's interview with H.D. Deve Gowda on 21 September 2020.
54. H.D. Deve Gowda's letter to Fali S. Nariman on 11 June 2020.
55. Fali S. Nariman's letter to H.D. Deve Gowda on 21 June 2020.
56. Author's interview with H.D. Deve Gowda on 6 October 2019.
57. Author's interview with S.M. Jaamdar on 21 March 2020.
58. Author's interview with Thippeswamy on 29 May 2020 and 1 June 2020.
59. Ibid.
60. Author's interview with H.D. Deve Gowda on 6 October 2019.

61. Author's interview with Thippeswamy on 29 May 2020 and 1 June 2020.
62. Ibid.
63. Author's interview with H.D. Deve Gowda on 4 October 2020.
64. Author's interview with Thippeswamy.
65. Author's interviews with H.D. Deve Gowda on 5 October 2019, and 4 and 5 October 2020.
66. Author's interview with H.D. Deve Gowda on 11 October 2020.

Chapter 10: Becoming Prime Minister and the Left Connection

1. Author's interview with S.S. Meenakshisundaram on 23 September 2019.
2. Ibid.
3. Author's interview with Sitaram Yechury on 24 September 2020.
4. Ibid.
5. Before Gowda, four prime ministers—Jawaharlal Nehru, Indira Gandhi, Morarji Desai and P.V. Narasimha Rao—were all Brahmins. Rajiv Gandhi was a Brahmin from his mother's side. Lal Bahadur Shastri was a Kayastha. V.P. Singh and Chandra Shekhar were Kshatriyas. Charan Singh was a Jat from western Uttar Pradesh. They are classified as Shudras, but there are conflicting scholarly views on their varna status. However, Charan Singh was part of the Arya Samaj, a Hindu reform movement led by Dayananda Saraswati. Gulzarilal Nanda, the interim prime minister twice, was from the Khatri community, which was into trading. In terms of their varna status they are either Kshatriyas or Vysyas. Deve Gowda from the peasant Vokkaliga community was unambiguously a Shudra.
6. Author's interview with H.D. Deve Gowda on 25 August 2019.
7. Ibid.
8. Transcript of the oral history interview with Jyoti Basu on 18 December 2001, in Kolkata, by Shikha Mukherjee and Usha Prasad, NMML, New Delhi.
9. Ibid.
10. Author's interview with H.D. Deve Gowda on 25 August 2019.
11. Author's interview with H.D. Deve Gowda on 5 October 2019.

12. Ibid.
13. Author's interview with Srikant Kumar Jena on 3 October 2020.
14. Author's interview with H.D. Deve Gowda on 20 October 2019.
15. Author's interview with H.D. Deve Gowda on 25 August 2019.

Chapter 11: Prime Minister's Office and the Circle of Trust

1. 'Eyes and Ears', by Javed M. Ansari, part of the *India Today* cover-story package, 16 August 1996: https://www.indiatoday.in/magazine/cover-story/story/19960815-eyes-and-ears-753596-1996-08-15
2. Author's interview with Chiranjiv Singh on 14 June 2020.
3. Author's interviews with H.D. Deve Gowda on 27 July 2019 and 21 August 2019.
4. Author's interview with Chiranjiv Singh on 14 June 2020.
5. Author's interview with Shyamal Datta on 23 May 2020.
6. Author's interview with P. Chidambaram on 9 February 2020.
7. 'Prime Minister's Office: Dynamics of an Institution', by Rajni Goyal, the *Indian Journal of Political Science*, Volume 62, Number 4, December 2001.
8. 'Cabinet Secretary: Reforms in Infrastructure', in *Journeys through Babudom and Netaland: Governance in India*, by T.S.R. Subramanian, Rupa, 2004.
9. Ibid.
10. Ibid.
11. Author's interview with S.S. Meenakshisundaram on 3 October 2019.
12. Ibid.
13. Author's interview with K.A. Thippeswamy on 1 June 2020.
14. Ibid.
15. Author's interview with S.S. Meenakshisundaram on 3 October 2019.
16. Ibid.
17. Author's interviews with H.D. Deve Gowda on 27 July 2019 and 21 August 2019.
18. Author's interview with S.S. Meenakshisundaram on 3 October 2019.

19. Author's interview with K.A. Thippeswamy on 1 June 2020.
20. Author's interview with S.S. Meenakshisundaram on 3 October 2019.
21. Ibid.
22. Ibid.
23. Ibid.
24. Ibid.
25. *With Four Prime Ministers: My PMO Journey*, by Jarnail Singh, Konark, 2020.
26. Author's interview with S.S. Meenakshisundaram on 3 October 2019.
27. Author's interviews with H.D. Deve Gowda on 27 July 2019 and 21 August 2019.
28. Author's interview with S.S. Meenakshisundaram on 3 October 2019.
29. Author's interviews with H.D. Deve Gowda on 27 July 2019 and 21 August 2019.
30. Author's interview with P.G.R. Sindhia on 5 August 2020.
31. Author's interview with S.S. Meenakshisundaram on 3 October 2019.
32. Author's interviews with S.S. Meenakshisundaram on 3 October 2019 and H.D. Deve Gowda on 27 July 2019 and 21 August 2019.
33. Fali Nariman's letter to H.D. Deve Gowda, dated 21 June 2020, H.D. Deve Gowda's private collection.
34. H.D. Deve Gowda's letter to Fali Nariman, dated 11 June 2020, H.D. Deve Gowda's private collection.
35. Author's interview with K.A. Thippeswamy on 1 June 2020.
36. Ibid.
37. Ibid.
38. Author's interview with S.S. Meenakshisundaram on 3 October 2019.
39. Ibid.
40. Ibid.
41. Ibid.
42. 'A Call from the Prime Minister's Office', in *With Four Prime Ministers: My PMO Journey*, by Jarnail Singh, Konark, 2020.

43. Author's interviews with H.D. Deve Gowda on 27 July 2019 and 21 August 2019.

44. 'Cabinet Secretary: Reforms in Infrastructure' in *Journeys through Babudom and Netaland: Governance in India*, by T.S.R. Subramanian, Rupa, 2004.

45. Author's interview with S.S. Meenakshisundaram on 3 October 2019.

46. Ibid.

47. Ibid.

48. 'Cabinet Secretary: Reforms in Infrastructure', in *Journeys through Babudom and Netaland: Governance in India*, by T.S.R. Subramanian, Rupa, 2004.

49. Author's interview with S.S. Meenakshisundaram on 3 October 2019.

50. 'Administrative Reforms', in *The Story of My Life, Volume Two*, by Morarji Desai, Macmillan India, 1974.

51. Author's interviews with H.D. Deve Gowda on 27 July 2019 and 21 August 2019.

52. Author's interview with P. Chidambaram on 9 February 2020.

53. Author's interview with Montek Singh Ahluwalia on 7 February 2020.

54. Author's interview with S.S. Meenakshisundaram on 3 October 2019.

55. Author's interviews with H.D. Deve Gowda on 27 July 2019 and 21 August 2019.

56. Author's interview with S.S. Meenakshisundaram on 3 October 2019.

57. Author's interview with K.A. Thippeswamy on 1 June 2020.

58. Author's interviews with H.D. Deve Gowda on 27 July 2019 and 21 August 2019.

59. Author's interview with Chiranjiv Singh on 14 June 2020.

60. Author's interview with H.D. Deve Gowda on 21 August 2019.

61. Ibid.

62. Ibid.

63. 'For over 2 Hrs, Scientists Tried to Persuade Me to Go in for Nuclear Test, I Said No: Deve Gowda', by Sebastian P.T., 5 January 2007, *Indian Express*: http://archive.indianexpress.com/

news/for-over-2-hrs-scientists-tried-to-persuade-me-to-go-in-for-nuclear-test-i-said-no-deve-gowda/20170/2

64. Discussion under Rule 193, 29 May 1998, Lok Sabha debates.
65. Motion of confidence in the council of ministers, 16 April 1999, Lok Sabha debates.
66. Author's interviews with H.D. Deve Gowda on 27 July 2019 and 21 August 2019.
67. Author's interview with Chiranjiv Singh on 14 June 2020.

Chapter 12: SPG and the Incognito Dream

1. Special Protection Group Act 1988, Government of India.
2. Author's interview with Shyamal Datta on 23 May 2020.
3. Author's interviews with Shyamal Datta on 23 May 2020 and Ratnakar Rao on 26 June 2020.
4. Author's interview with Shyamal Datta on 23 May 2020.
5. Ibid.
6. Ibid.
7. Ibid.
8. Ibid.
9. Ibid.
10. Ibid.
11. Ibid.
12. Ibid.

Chapter 13: Mission Kashmir and a Bullet-Proof Birth Chart

1. *Shabdavedi* is a Kannada action film made in 2000. It is directed by S. Narayan and produced by Sri Bhargavi Arts Combines.
2. 'Deve Gowda: A Workaholic and a Sensitive Man,' by Harinder Baweja and Javed Ansari, 15 August 1996, *India Today*: https://www.indiatoday.in/magazine/cover-story/story/19960815-deve-gowda-a-workaholic-and-a-sensitive-man-833722-1996-08-15
3. Author's interviews with H.D. Deve Gowda on 21 August 2019 and 29 September 2019.
4. Ibid.

5. Ibid.
6. Ibid.
7. Ibid.
8. Ibid.
9. Chapter 20, 'Elections at Last', *In the Service of the Nation: Reminiscences,* by K.V. Krishna Rao, 2001, Penguin Books India, New Delhi.
10. Author's interview with Shyamal Datta on 23 May 2020.
11. 'PM Deve Gowda Sets Tone for Revival of the Political Process in War-Weary Kashmir Valley', by Harinder Baweja, *India Today,* 31 July 1996: https://www.indiatoday.in/magazine/nation/story/19960731-pm-deve-gowda-sets-tone-for-revival-of-political-process-in-war-weary-kashmir-valley-833653-1996-07-31
12. Author's interviews with H.D. Deve Gowda on 21 August 2019 and 29 September 2019.
13. Ibid.
14. Ibid.
15. Author's interview with Montek Singh Ahluwalia on 7 February 2020.
16. Parliament debates, 2 August 1996.
17. Parliament debates, 23 July 1996.
18. Author's interviews with H.D. Deve Gowda on 21 August 2019 and 29 September 2019.
19. Parliament debates, 23 July 1996.
20. Author's interviews with H.D. Deve Gowda on 21 August 2019 and 29 September 2019.
21. Ibid.
22. Author's interview with Lieutenant General J.S. Dhillon on 4 December 2019.
23. Parliament debates, 2 August 1996.
24. Press Information Bureau archives.
25. Author's interviews with H.D. Deve Gowda on 21 August 2019 and 29 September 2019.
26. Chapter 20, 'Elections at Last', *In the Service of the Nation: Reminiscences,* by K.V. Krishna Rao, 2001, Penguin Books India, New Delhi.

27. Ibid.
28. Ibid.
29. Author's interviews with H.D. Deve Gowda on 21 August 2019 and 29 September 2019.
30. 'Kashmir's Peace Hopes Put to a Vote', Kenneth J. Cooper, 7 September 1996, *Washington Post*: https://www.washingtonpost.com/archive/politics/1996/09/07/kashmirs-peace-hopes-put-to-a-vote/66e2da16-3cb5-4bf3-ab8f-3cb00b8250e8/
31. Author's interview with Lieutenant General J.S. Dhillon on 4 December 2019.
32. Ibid.
33. Ibid.
34. 'Indigu Kaaduva Gowdara Kadhmira Karyasoochi', *Kannada Prabha*, 11 September 2016.
35. Ibid.
36. Ibid.
37. Ibid.
38. Author's interviews with H.D. Deve Gowda on 21 August 2019 and 29 September 2019.
39. 'A Peace Offering at Last', Ajith Pillai and Masood Hussain, 19 June 1996, *Outlook*: https://magazine.outlookindia.com/story/a-peace-offering-at-last/201573
40. 'Five out of Ten for Gowda', Vinod Mehta, 17 July 1996, Outlook: https://magazine.outlookindia.com/story/five-out-of-ten-for-gowda/201757
41. 'Kashmir's Peace Hopes Put to a Vote', Kenneth J. Cooper, 7 September 1996, *Washington Post*: https://www.washingtonpost.com/archive/politics/1996/09/07/kashmirs-peace-hopes-put-to-a-vote/66e2da16-3cb5-4bf3-ab8f-3cb00b8250e8/
42. Chapter 20, 'Elections at Last', *In the Service of the Nation: Reminiscences*, by K.V. Krishna Rao, 2001, Penguin Books India, New Delhi.
43. 'Amarnath Yatra Turned into a Seemingly Endless March of Death', by Sayantan Chakravarty and Harinder Baweja, 15 September 1996, *India Today*: https://www.indiatoday.in/magazine/nation/story/19960915-freak-weather-conditions-during-amarnath-yatra-claim-200-lives-834427-1996-09-15

44. Author's interviews with H.D. Deve Gowda on 21 August 2019 and 29 September 2019.
45. Ibid.
46. Ibid.
47. 'Dr L.H. Hiranandani', *Global Sindhis: Inheritors of the Indus Valley Civilisation*, by Ram S. Jawhrani, Sindhishaan, 2009.
48. Author's interviews with H.D. Deve Gowda on 21 August 2019 and 29 September 2019.
49. Chapter 4, 'Envoy, Crusader, Activist', *Born to Heal* by L.H. Hiranandani, 2004, Rupa & Co.
50. 'Dialogue with India will be top priority with my government', Sunil Narula interviews Nawaz Sharif, 19 February 1997, *Outlook*: https://magazine.outlookindia.com/story/dialogue-with-india-will-be-top-priority-with-my-government/203046
51. 'Five out of Ten for Gowda', Vinod Mehta, 17 July 1996, *Outlook*: https://magazine.outlookindia.com/story/five-out-of-ten-for-gowda/201757
52. Author's interview with Montek Singh Ahluwalia on 7 February 2020.
53. Motion of confidence, 11 April 1997, Lok Sabha debates.
54. Omar Abdullah tweet on 9 March 2019.
55. 'Deve Gowda Opposes Attempts to Scrap Article 370', 2 April 2019, *The Hindu*: https://www.thehindu.com/elections/lok-sabha-2019/deve-gowda-opposes-attempts-to-scrap-article-370/article26714731.ece
56. Chapter 12, 'Rajiv', *Durbar* by Tavleen Singh, 2012, Hachette India.
57. Keynote address at the World Peace Summit 2020 of the United Nations affiliated Universal Peace Federation, at Seoul, on 4 February 2020.

Chapter 14: Gowdanomics, Manmohanomics and Chidambaram's Debut

1. 'Reassessing Deve Gowda', by Vikas Kumar, 31 May 2018, *The Hindu*: https://www.thehindu.com/opinion/op-ed/reassessing-deve-gowda/article24039844.ece
2. Author's conversation with M.Y. Ghorpade in July 2010.

3. Author's interview with H.D. Deve Gowda on 9 November 2019.
4. Author's interview with Srikant Kumar Jena on 4 October 2020.
5. Author's interview with P. Chidambaram on 9 February 2020.
6. Discussion under Rule 193, Lok Sabha debates, 30 December 1993.
7. Author's interview with H.D. Deve Gowda on 9 November 2019.
8. Ibid.
9. Ibid.
10. Union budget speech 1996–97, Lok Sabha, 22 July 1996.
11. Ibid.
12. Author's interview with H.D. Deve Gowda on 9 November 2019.
13. Discussion on Finance Bill (No 2), Lok Sabha debates, 13 September 1991.
14. Author's interview with H.D. Deve Gowda on 9 November 2019.
15. Discussion on general budget 2002–3, Supplementary Demands for Grants, Lok Sabha debates, 20 March 2002.
16. Author's interview with H.D. Deve Gowda on 9 November 2019.
17. Union budget speech 1996–97, Lok Sabha, 22 July 1996.
18. Ibid.
19. Ibid.
20. Ibid.
21. Author's interview with H.D. Deve Gowda on 9 November 2019.
22. Union budget speech 1996–97, Lok Sabha, 22 July 1996.
23. Author's interview with B.L. Shankar on 22 June 2020.
24. Union budget speech 1997–98, Lok Sabha, 28 February 1997.
25. Author's interview with P. Chidambaram on 9 February 2020.
26. Ibid.
27. Union budget speech 1997–98, Lok Sabha, 28 February 1997.
28. Ibid.
29. Discussion on general budget 2002–3, Supplementary Demands for Grants, Lok Sabha debates, 20 March 2002.
30. Economic Survey 1997–98, government of India.
31. Author's interview with H.D. Deve Gowda on 9 November 2019.
32. Author's interview with P. Chidambaram on 9 February 2020.
33. Author's interview with S.S. Meenakshisundaram on 23 September 2019.
34. Author's interview with P. Chidambaram on 9 February 2020.

35. Author's interview with Montek Singh Ahluwalia on 7 February 2020.
36. Ibid.
37. Ibid.
38. Ibid.
39. Ibid.
40. Author's interview with H.D. Deve Gowda on 9 November 2019.
41. 'Minimum Support Price and Farmers' Income', *CUTS International*, 2015.
42. Author's interview with Montek Singh Ahluwalia on 7 February 2020.
43. Author's interview with Shyamal Datta on 23 May 2020.
44. Author's interview with Montek Singh Ahluwalia on 7 February 2020.
45. 'Prime Minister Deve Gowda Finally Leaves India Behind', by Sudeep Chakravarti, *India Today*, 28 February 1997: https://www.indiatoday.in/magazine/nation/story/19970228-prime-minister-deve-gowda-finally-leaves-karnataka-behind-830183-1997-02-28
46. 'Gowda scores for India', Vinod Mehta, *Outlook*, 19 February 1997: https://magazine.outlookindia.com/story/gowda-scores-for-india/203068
47. 'India: Confronting a strategic choice for growth', a presentation by Claude Smadja, managing director, World Economic Forum, at the 1996 India Economic Summit, New Delhi 27–29 October.
48. 'Last PM to go to Davos says Modi should not take all credit for India's progress', by Rohini Swamy, The Print, 24 January 2018: https://theprint.in/report/pm-davos-modi-credit-india-progress/31410/
49. Ibid.
50. Discussion on Finance Bill (No.2), Lok Sabha debates, 13 September 1991.
51. Discussion under Rule 193, Situation affecting Agriculture and Farmers interests due to increase in the prices of fertilizers and wheat import, Lok Sabha debates, 26 November 1992.
52. Debate on Ordinance and Gold Bonds (Immunities and Exemptions) Bill, Lok Sabha debates, 19 March 1993.
53. Discussion on budget, Lok Sabha debates, 22 April 1993.

54. Discussion under Rule 193, Lok Sabha debates, 30 December 1993.
55. Discussion on general budget 1994–95, Lok Sabha debates, 18 March 1994.
56. Ibid.
57. Motion of thanks on the President's address, Lok Sabha debates, 3 March 1994.
58. Discussion on general budget 2002–3, Supplementary Demands for Grants, Lok Sabha debates, 20 March 2002.
59. Discussion under Rule 193, Problems being faced by farmers in the country, Lok Sabha debates, 4 December 2002.
60. Discussion on general budget 2003–4, Demands for Supplementary Grants, Lok Sabha debates, 10 March 2003.
61. Discussion on general budget, Demands for Excess Grants, Lok Sabha debates, 20 July 2004.
62. Felicitations to Speaker, Lok Sabha debates, 4 June 2004.
63. Discussion under Rule 193, Lok Sabha debates, 8 December 1998.
64. Discussion on budget, Lok Sabha debates, 31 July 1991.
65. Discussion on budget, Lok Sabha debates, 1 August 1991.
66. *Walk the Talk* interview with Shekhar Gupta, March 2009, NDTV.
67. 'Neevu Deve Gowda Naati Maadidira', by Chiranjiv Singh, *Vijay Karnataka*, 25 October 2014.
68. *Yaava Janmada Maitri*, by Chiranjiv Singh *Navakarnataka*, 2019.
69. Author's interview with C.M. Ibrahim on 15 August 2020.
70. 'The Kulak's Last Sigh', by Anil Pandey, *Sunday Indian*, 29 May 2011: http://www.thesundayindian.com/en/story/the-kulak's-last-sigh/24/15185/
71. 'V P Singh Refuses to Criticise Gowda for Shielding Rao', *Business Standard*, 3 October 1996: https://www.business-standard.com/article/economy-policy/v-p-singh-refuses-to-criticise-gowda-for-shielding-rao-196100301160_1.html
72. *Sunday*, 1–7 September 1996, Volume 23, Issue 36.

Chapter 15: The Narmada and the Ganga

1. *Maneangaladalli Maatukathe* (courtyard conversations), a monthly public interaction organized with well-known personalities by

the Department of Information, Government of Karnataka, 17 November 2018.

2. 'PM Modi Performs Narmada Aarti at Sardar Sarovar Dam', *Economic Times*, 17 September 2019: https://economictimes. indiatimes.com/news/politics- and-nation/pm-modi-performs-narmada-aarti-at-sardar-sarovar-dam/articleshow/71163067.cms

3. 'Former PM H.D. Deve Gowda Visited the Statue of Unity in Gujarat', ANI, 5 October 2019: https://www.aninews.in/news/national/general-news/former-pm-hd-deve-gowda-visited-the-statue-of-unity-in-gujarat20191005134356/

4. Author's interview with H.D. Deve Gowda on 5 October 2019.

5. 'Dispute over Narmada Project Height Resolved for Now', by Uday Mahurkar, *India Today*, 15 August 1996: https://www.indiatoday. in/magazine/indiascope/story/19960815-dispute-over-narmada-project-height-resolved-for-now-833684-1996-08-15

6. Author's interview with H.D. Deve Gowda on 5 October 2019.

7. 'Dispute over Narmada project height resolved for now', by Uday Mahurkar, *India Today*, 15 August 1996: https://www.indiatoday. in/magazine/indiascope/story/19960815-dispute-over-narmada-project-height-resolved-for-now-833684-1996-08-15

8. Author's interview with H.D. Deve Gowda on 5 October 2019.

9. Discussion under Rule 153, 25 July 2002, Lok Sabha debates.

10. Author's interview with H.D. Deve Gowda on 5 October 2019.

11. Author's interview with Medha Patkar on 29 August 2020.

12. Ibid.

13. Ibid.

14. Author's interview with H.D. Deve Gowda on 6 October 2019.

15. Ibid.

16. Ibid.

17. Ibid.

18. Ibid.

19. Ibid.

20. Author's interview with V.K. Bodoni on 6 October 2019.

21. 'Project in Progress', by Sudha Mahalingam, *Frontline*, 6 June 1998: https://frontline.thehindu.com/environment/article30247590. ece/amp/

22. Ibid.

23. Author's interview with Sunderlal Bahuguna on 5 November 2019.
24. Ibid.
25. Department of Disaster Management, Government of Bihar: https://state.bihar.gov.in/disastermgmt/CitizenHome.html
26. 'Farakka Not to Blame for Bihar Floods: CWC', *Times of India*: https://timesofindia.indiatimes.com/city/patna/farakka-not-to-blame-for-bihar-floods-cwc/articleshow/57318767.cms
27. Author's interview with H.D. Deve Gowda.
28. Ibid.
29. Author's interview with Mohan V. Katarki on 22 September 2020.
30. Author's interview with H.D. Deve Gowda on 4 October 2020.
31. Kamran Reza Chowdhury interviews Ainun Nishat for www.thirdpole.net, reproduced in Firstpost: https://www.firstpost.com/long-reads/the-ganga-treaty-ainun-nishat-on-how-india-bangladesh-signed-a-historic-deal-5208161.html
32. Ibid.
33. Author's interview with Mohan V. Katarki on 22 September 2020.
34. Treaty between the Government of the People's Republic of Bangladesh and the Government of the Republic of India on sharing of the Ganga/Ganges waters at Farakka, signed on 12 December 1996.
35. 12 December 1996, Lok Sabha debates.
36. 'India and Bangladesh End Dispute on Ganges', *New York Times*, 13 December 1996: https://www.nytimes.com/1996/12/13/world/india-and-bangladesh-end-dispute-on-ganges.html
37. 'Bridge over Troubled Waters', by Tara Patel, *New Scientist*, 30 November 1996: https://www.newscientist.com/article/mg15220582-100-bridge-over-troubled-waters-india-and-bangladesh-have-quarrelled-over-rights-to-water-from-the-ganges-for-more-than-two-decades-can-they-finally-agree-a-deal-that-would-benefit-millions/
38. Ibid.
39. Ibid.
40. Author's interview with H.D. Deve Gowda on 4 October 2020.
41. Letter to H.D. Deve Gowda from Muhammad Imran, high commissioner of Bangladesh to India, no. 19.01.9101.203.44.061.17/543 dated 11 March 2020.

Chapter 16: On the Banks of the Brahmaputra

1. Author's interview with H.D. Deve Gowda on 1 September 2019.
2. Author's interview with K.A. Thippeswamy on 1 June 2020.
3. Author's interview with S.S. Meenakshisundaram on 3 October 2019.
4. Ibid.
5. Author's interview with H.D. Deve Gowda on 1 September 2019.
6. Ibid.
7. Ibid.
8. 'Getting to Know the North East', in *With Four Prime Ministers: My PMO Journey*, by Jarnail Singh, Konark, 2020.
9. Ibid.
10. Ibid.
11. Ibid.
12. Ibid.
13. Ibid.
14. Ibid.
15. Ibid.
16. Ibid.
17. Ibid.
18. Ibid.
19. Ibid.
20. 'Working with Sri. Deve Gowda', by K. Padmanabhaiah, an article written for an unpublished volume on H.D. Deve Gowda. Courtesy: Office of H.D. Deve Gowda, New Delhi.
21. H.D. Deve Gowda's statement on new initiatives for North-eastern region at a press conference in Guwahati on 27 October 1996.
22. Ibid.
23. Ibid.
24. Ibid.
25. 'Working with Sri. Deve Gowda', by K. Padmanabhaiah, an article written for an unpublished volume on H.D. Deve Gowda. Courtesy: office of H.D. Deve Gowda, New Delhi.
26. 'The NRC case: The Supreme Court's role', by V. Venkatesan, 25 September 2019, *Frontline*.

27. 'As on 09.12.97, Status of implementation of "New Initiatives for North Eastern Region" announced by Prime Minister on October 27, 1996', Prime Minister's Office.

28. *India's Northeast Resurgent: Ethnicity, Insurgency, Governance, Development*, by B.G. Verghese, Konark, 1996.

29. *Transforming the North East: Tackling Backlogs in Basic Minimum Services and Infrastructural Needs*, High Level Commission report to the prime minister, planning commission, government of India, March 7, 1997.

30. Ibid.

31. Ibid.

32. Ibid.

33. Ibid.

34. Author's interview with S.P. Shukla on 25 May 2020.

35. Ibid.

36. Ibid.

37. Ibid.

38. Ibid.

39. H.D. Deve Gowda's statement on new initiatives for the North-eastern region at a press conference in Guwahati on 27 October 1996.

40. 'Towards the Govt-Naga Peace Accord: Everything You Need to Know', by Samudra Gupta Kashyap, *Indian Express*, 4 August 2015: https://indianexpress.com/article/explained/simply-put-towards-accord-step-by-step/

41. Ibid.

42. Author's interview with H.D. Deve Gowda on 1 September 2019.

43. 'NSCN (K) Declared a Terrorist Organization,' *Indian Express*, 17 November 2015: https://indianexpress.com/article/india/india-news-india/nscn-k-declared-a-terrorist-organisation/

44. 'Deve Gowda Compliments Modi on Naga Peace Accord', *The Hindu*, 4 August 2015: https://www.thehindu.com/news/national/deve-gowda-compliments-modi-on-naga-peace-accord/article7499450.ece

45. 'Details of 2015 Naga Agreement Emerge', by Vijaita Singh, *The Hindu*, 19 July 2018: https://www.thehindu.com/news/

national/other-states/details-of-2015-naga-agreement-emerge/
article24464239.ece

46.　'PM Modi Has Mandated IB to Carry on Talks, Says NSCN-IM', by Abhishek Saha, *Indian Express*, 17 August 2020: https://
indianexpress.com/article/india/nscn-im-again-attacks-nagaland-governor-ravi-over-naga-peace-talks-6557528/

47.　Ibid.

48.　H.D. Deve Gowda's 'Statement on Negotiations with Nagas', 17
August 2020.

49.　'Deve Gowda's Efforts Changed Course of Naga Struggle from
War to Path of Peace: Naga Hoho', by Sumir Karmakar, *Deccan
Herald*, 18 August 2020: https://www.deccanherald.com/national/
east-and-northeast/deve-gowdas-efforts-changed-course-of-naga-struggle-from-war-to-path-of-peace-naga-hoho-874910.html

50.　'Naga Talks under Strain, Interlocutor Blasts State Govt, Vested
Interests', by Deeptiman Tiwary, *Indian Express,* 16 August 2020:
https://indianexpress.com/article/india/naga-talks-under-strain-interlocutor-blasts-state-govt-vested-interests-6556586/

51.　'Narendra Modi Inaugurates Bogibeel Bridge in Assam: 10 Things
to Know', *Mint*, 25 December 2018: https://www.livemint.com/
Politics/zMhowFzkONQkLllh9ycZtK/PM-Modi-inaugurates-Bogibeel-Indias-longest-railroad-brid.html

52.　'Aiyo Rama! Who Will Remember Me?: Deve Gowda on Being Left
out of Bogibeel Bridge Inaugural', *India Today*, 25 December 2015:
https://www.indiatoday.in/india/story/deve-gowda-on-being-left-out-of-bogibeel-bridge-inaugural-1417201-2018-12-25

53.　'Former PM H.D. Deve Gowda Offers Prayers at Kamakhya
Temple in Guwahati', ANI, 19 February 2019 (video).

54.　H.D. Deve Gowda's statement on Assam floods, 17 July 2020.

55.　Letter from Sarbananda Sonowal, Assam chief minister to H.D.
Deve Gowda, D.0. No. CMO. 1/2020/3034, Dispur, 18 July
2020.

Chapter 17: City of Intrigues and the September Shifts

1.　Author's interview with K.R. Shivakumar on 8 February 2020.

2.　Ibid.

3. Author's interview with K.R. Shivakumar on 8 February 2020.

4. Ibid.

5. Author's interviews with P. Chidambaram on 9 February 2020, with Shyamal Datta on 23 May 2020 and Srikant Kumar Jena on 3 October 2020.

6. Author's interview with S.S. Meenakshisundaram on 3 October 2019.

7. H.D. Deve Gowda's reply to the motion of confidence debate, 11 April 1997, Lok Sabha debates.

8. In his reply to the debate on the motion of confidence on 11 April 1997, Gowda mentions that Madhavrao Scindia had come to inform him when he decided to leave the United Front and rejoin the Congress and he had no problem with that. Scindia intervenes to say he met Gowda as a courtesy and not to seek permission. He was perhaps afraid that he would be misunderstood by his colleagues in the Congress. Gowda jogs Scindia's memory: 'Please go and join and strengthen the Congress party; I have no objection. Did I not say that?' To which Scindia agrees: 'I agree. You are absolutely right. When I informed you, you said: "Yes certainly."'

9. 'Delhi Metro Rail Project (Modified Phase 1): The Unsaid Story behind Its Financial Closure in September 1996', by N.P. Singh, former urban development secretary, Government of India—an article written for an unpublished volume on H.D. Deve Gowda. Courtesy: office of H.D. Deve Gowda, New Delhi.

10. Ibid.

11. Ibid.

12. Author's interview with K.A. Thippeswamy on 29 May 2020.

13. Author's interview with H.D. Deve Gowda on 27 July 2019.

14. Author's interview with C.M. Ibrahim on 15 August 2020.

15. Ibid.

16. Author's interview with H.D. Deve Gowda 20 December 2020.

17. 'Can Coalition Governments Give Good Governance?', in *India at Turning Point: The Road to Good Governance*, by T.S.R. Subramanian, Rainlight Rupa, 2014.

18. Author's interview with B.L. Shankar on 22 June 2020.

19. Author's interview with C.M. Ibrahim on 15 August 2020.

20. *Sunday* magazine, 1–7 September 1996, Volume 23, Issue 36.

21. 'The Kulak's Last Sigh', by Anil Pandey, *Sunday Indian*, 29 May 2011: http://www.thesundayindian.com/en/story/the-kulak's-last-sigh/24/15185/ and 'VP Singh Refuses to Criticise Gowda for Shielding Rao', *Business Standard*, 3 October1996: https://www.business-standard.com/article/economy-policy/v-p-singh-refuses-to-criticise-gowda-for- shielding-rao-196100301160_1.html

22. 'Democracy', in *The Idea of India* by Sunil Khilnani, Penguin Books India, New Delhi, 1998.

23. 'English in their Dhoti Creases', by Sugata Srinivasaraju, 22 July 2020, *Mumbai Mirror*: https://mumbaimirror.indiatimes.com/opinion/columnists/sugata-srinivasaraju/english-in-their-dhoti-creases/articleshow/77098226.cms

24. *Asian Englishes: Beyond the Canon*, by Braj Kachru, Hong Kong University Press, 2005.

25. *The Handbook of World Englishes*, Editors: Braj Kachru, Yamuna Kachru and Cecil Nelson, Wiley, 2006.

26. 'Minister Sans Any Powers', by Ranjith Bhushan, 26 March 1997, *Outlook*: https://magazine.outlookindia.com/story/minister-sans-any-powers/203273. Also, Karan Thapar's April 1997 interview: *In Focus, Home TV*.

27. 'Tiger Joginder', cover story in *Sunday* magazine, reported by Gauri Lankesh, Priya Sehgal, Anuja Pande and Aditi Phadnis, 1–7 September 1996.

28. Ibid.

29. Ibid.

30. *Inside CBI*, by Joginder Singh, Chandrika Publications, 1999.

31. Author's interview with H.D. Deve Gowda on 20 December 2020.

32. *Inside CBI*, by Joginder Singh, Chandrika Publications, 1999.

33. Ibid.

34. Motion of confidence, 15 July 1991, Lok Sabha debates.

35. *Inside CBI*, by Joginder Singh, Chandrika Publications, 1999.

36. Ibid.

37. Ibid.

38. Ibid.

39. Author's interview with H.D. Deve Gowda on 16 November 2020.

40. Author's interview with B.L. Shankar on 22 June 2020.
41. Author's interview with H.D. Deve Gowda on 20 December 2020. There is also the mention of this letter in his reply to the debate on the motion of confidence, on 11 April 1997, in Lok Sabha.
42. Author's interview with B.L. Shankar on 22 June 2020.
43. Ibid.
44. Ibid.
45. 'Why Sitaram Kesri Despises Deve Gowda', by George Iype, Rediff, April 1997: http://www.rediff.com/news/apr/04cong1.htm
46. Author's interview with P. Chidambaram on 9 February 2020.
47. 'Gowda Pulled Strings to Clear Ashok Jain's Travel Abroad', 26 June 1997, *Business Standard*: https://www.business-standard.com/article/economy-policy/gowda-pulled-strings-to-clear-ashok-jains-travel-abroad-197062601130_1.html
48. Author's interview with H.D. Deve Gowda on 16 November 2020.
49. 'Deepening Reforms', in *Portraits of Power: Half a Century of Being at Ringside* by N.K. Singh, pages 157–159, Rupa, 2020.
50. Author's interview with H.D. Deve Gowda on 16 November 2020.
51. Ashok Jain's interview to *Outlook* ('Kesri Is an Old Friend of the Family'), 16 July 1997: https://magazine.outlookindia.com/story/quotkesri-is-an-old-friend-of-the-familyquot/203860 and *India Today* ('I Have Not Even Met Gujral after He Became Prime Minister'), 7 July 1997: https://www.indiatoday.in/magazine/interview/story/19970707-i-have-not-even-met-gujral-after-he-became-prime-minister-says-ashok-jain-830301-1997-07-07
52. 'Kesri's Secret Account Abroad', by Virendra Kapoor, 1997, www.rediff.com: https://www.rediff.com/news/may/10buzz.htm
53. 'FERA charges against Times of India's proprietor become a political football', by Sumit Mitra, 7 July 1997, *India Today*: https://www.indiatoday.in/magazine/society-the-arts/media/story/19970707-a-b-vajpayee-accuse-i-k-gujral-of-shielding-tois-proprietor-ashok-jain-from-feras-case-830332-1997-07-07
54. George Fernandes' interview with Prem Panicker ('If my father is a rapist, I cannot, should not, defend him only because he is my father'),

28 February 1998, www.rediff.com: https://www.rediff.com/news/1998/feb/28george.htm

55. Ibid.
56. Author's interview with Srikant Kumar Jena on 3 October 2020.
57. Letters related to disciplinary action against C.M. Ibrahim in May–June 1979, *Janata Party Papers*, NMML, New Delhi.
58. 'Congress after Rajiv', in *The Coalition Years: 1996–2012*, by Pranab Mukherjee, Rupa, 2017.
59. Author's interview with Srikant Kumar Jena on 3 October 2020.
60. Author's interview with H.D. Deve Gowda on 25 August 2019.
61. 'Congress after Rajiv', in *The Coalition Years: 1996–2012*, by Pranab Mukherjee, Rupa, 2017.
62. Author's interview with H.D. Deve Gowda on 16 November 2020.
63. Author's interview with Srikant Kumar Jena on 3 October 2020.
64. 'Congress after Rajiv', in *The Coalition Years: 1996–2012*, by Pranab Mukherjee, Rupa, 2017.
65. Author's interview with B.L. Shankar on 22 June 2020.
66. Author's interview with Srikant Kumar Jena on 3 October 2020.
67. Author's interview with P. Chidambaram on 9 February 2020.
68. Author's interview with B.L. Shankar on 22 June 2020.

Chapter 18: How Many 'Brutuses', Sir?

1. Author's interview with H.D. Deve Gowda on 25 August 2019.
2. Ibid.
3. Harkishan Singh Surjeet, *Walk the Talk* interview with Shekar Gupta aired on NDTV, January 2004: https://youtu.be/Lb_FZlQOmn4
4. Author's interview with H.D. Deve Gowda on 25 August 2019.
5. Author's interview with Srikant Kumar Jena on 3 October 2020.
6. Author's interview with H.D. Deve Gowda on 25 August 2019.
7. Author's interview with Srikant Kumar Jena on 3 October 2020.
8. Author's interview with H.D. Deve Gowda on 25 August 2019.
9. Author's interview with P. Chidambaram 9 February 2020.
10. Author's interview with H.D. Deve Gowda on 25 August 2019.
11. Ibid.

12. Motion of confidence, 11 April 1997, Lok Sabha debates.
13. Author's interview with Srikant Kumar Jena on 3 October 2020.
14. Motion of confidence, 11 April 1997, Lok Sabha debates.
15. Transcript of the oral history interview with Jyoti Basu on 18 December 2001, in Kolkata, by Shikha Mukherjee and Usha Prasad, NMML, New Delhi.
16. 'Veteran Congressman Sitaram Kesri passes away' by Lakshmi Iyer, 6 November 2000, *India Today*: https://www.indiatoday.in/magazine/obituary/story/20001106-veteran-congressman-sitaram-kesri-passes-away-778366-2000-11-06
17. Ibid.
18. Karan Thapar's first interview for *In Focus* programme on Home TV was conducted within days of H.D. Deve Gowda stepping down as prime minister on 11 April 1997. The date stamp for the interview is not available, but the YouTube link is as follows: https://youtu.be/K46oOO-HEW4
19. Karan Thapar's second interview for *In Focus* programme on Home TV was conducted immediately after the I.K. Gujral government fell in March 1998. The date stamp for the interview is not available, but the YouTube link is as follows: https://youtu.be/oRxgCdJoUfo
20. Author's interview with H.D. Deve Gowda on 25 August 2019.

Chapter 19: Tryst with the Congress Dynasty

1. 'PM in conversation with H.K. Dua, senior journalist and political commentator'. Telecast on 8 July 1996. Transcript: Press Information Bureau, government of India.
2. Chapter 15 to 18, *Bharatada Pradani Deve Gowda*, by Konandur Venkatappa, Yashasvi Prakashana, 1997.
3. Ibid.
4. Author's interviews with H.D. Deve Gowda on 15 September 2019 and 29 September 2019.
5. Ibid.
6. Initiating motion of confidence. Lok Sabha debates, 11 June 1996.
7. Reply to the debate on the motion of confidence. Lok Sabha debates, 12 June 1996.

8.   Author's interviews with H.D. Deve Gowda on 15 September 2019 and 29 September 2019.

9.   Civic reception in honour of Dr. Nelson Mandela—prime minister's speech, 28 March 1997, Press Information Bureau, Government of India.

10.   'Prime Minister stresses need to strengthen and democratise UN'—NAM ministerial conference inauguration on 7 April 1997, Press Information Bureau, Government of India.

11.   Reply to the debate on the motion of confidence. Lok Sabha debates, 12 June 1996.

12.   Golden jubilee celebrations of the constitution of the Constituent Assembly, 9 December 1996.

13.   Statue of Jawaharlal Nehru unveiled in Moscow—PM's tribute on the occasion, 26 March 1997, Press Information Bureau, Government of India.

14.   Author's interviews with H.D. Deve Gowda on 15 September 2019 and 29 September 2019.

15.   'CM Must Bear Loss like Indira Did', 2 August 2016, *Coastal Digest*: http://www.coastaldigest.com/news/89637-cm-must-bear-the-loss-like-indira-did-gowda

16.   'Did Vajpayee Refer to Indira as Durga Avatar', 27 February 2016, *Deccan Herald*: https://www.deccanherald.com/content/531303/did-vajpayee-refer-indira-durga.html and 'Vajpayee Praised Indira Gandhi for 1971 War Victory: Rajnath Singh to Opposition', 29 April 2019, *Financial Express*: https://www.financialexpress.com/elections/atal-bihari-vajpayee-praised-indira-gandhi-for-1971-war-victory-rajnath-singh-to-opposition/1562939/

17.   Author's interviews with H.D. Deve Gowda on 15 September 2019 and 29 September 2019.

18.   Letter from H.D. Deve Gowda, Karnataka state president, Janata Party, to Chandra Shekhar, president, All India Janata Party dated 11 April 1978, *Janata Party Papers*, NMML, New Delhi.

19.   Letter from H.D. Deve Gowda, Karnataka state president, Janata Party, to Chandra Shekhar, president, All India Janata Party dated 11 April 1978, *Janata Party Papers*, NMML, New Delhi.

20.   Author's interviews with H.D. Deve Gowda on 15 September 2019 and 29 September 2019.

21. Ibid.
22. Ibid.
23. Ibid.
24. Ibid.
25. Ibid.
26. Ibid.
27. Ibid.
28. Ibid.
29. Ibid.
30. Ibid.
31. Author's interview with Margaret Alva on 16 April 2020.
32. Author's interviews with H.D. Deve Gowda on 15 September 2019 and 29 September 2019.
33. Author's interview with B.L. Shankar on 30 May 2020.
34. Author's interviews with H.D. Deve Gowda on 15 September 2019 and 29 September 2019.
35. Speech during motion of confidence. Lok Sabha debates, 16 April 1999.
36. 'Behind Bofors' in *Inside CBI* by Joginder Singh, Chandrika Publications, 1999.
37. 'JD(S) is BJP's B Team: Expect More Strikes from Rahul Gandhi', by Sowmya Aji, 25 March 2018, *Economic Times*: https://economictimes.indiatimes.com/news/politics-and-nation/jds-is-bjps-b-team-expect-more-strikes-from-rahul-gandhi/articleshow/63456475.cms
38. 'Modi Attacks Rahul for Insulting Deve Gowda', 1 May 2018, *Hindu Business Line*: https://www.thehindubusinessline.com/news/national/modi-attacks-rahul-for-insulting-deve-gowda/article23739336.ece
39. 'If Rahul Gandhi Becomes Prime Minister, I Will Be by His Side, Says H.D. Deve Gowda', 19 April 2019, www.scroll.com: https://scroll.in/latest/920614/if-rahul-gandhi-becomes-prime-minister-i-will-be-by-his-side-says-hd-deve-gowda
40. 'Rajya Sabha Elections: HD Deve Gowda's Exclusive Interview with TOI', by B.V. Shiva Shankar, 10 June 2020, *Times of India*: https://timesofindia.indiatimes.com/city/bengaluru/rajya-sabha-elections-hd-deve-gowdas-exclusive-interview-with-toi/articleshow/76298402.cms

Chapter 20: Wrestling with Vajpayee and His Mask

1. H.D. Deve Gowda lost the Hassan parliamentary seat in the 1999 general election. He was re-elected in a by-poll held in February 2002 from the Kanakapura parliamentary seat in Karnataka following the death of M.V. Chandrashekar Murthy, a Congress MP and former Union minister.

2. H.Y. Sharada Prasad, well-known as Indira Gandhi's confidante and information adviser, told the author in a private conversation in 2004 that if only his boss had Deve Gowda's understanding of the law, which came from the practical experience of litigating at all levels of Indian judiciary, she would have never imposed the Emergency.

3. Motion of thanks to the President's address, 17 July 1991, Lok Sabha debates.

4. Author's interview with H.D. Deve Gowda, 25 August 2019.

5. Discussion on motion regarding expressing grave concern over the failure of administration in ensuring security of minority community in various parts of the country, especially in Gujarat, 30 April 2002, Lok Sabha debates.

6. Raised to charge the government with directly or indirectly abetting the disruption of communal harmony in the country, 2 December 1998, Lok Sabha debates.

7. Motion of confidence, 11 June 1996, Lok Sabha debates.

8. Reply to the debate on motion of confidence, 12 June 1996, Lok Sabha debates.

9. Ibid.

10. Ibid.

11. Ibid.

12. Ibid.

13. Ibid.

14. In the 1998 parliamentary elections, the Janata Dal numbers were reduced to just six. In the 1999 general elections, there was no single entity called Janata Dal.

15. Janata Dal started to splinter into many regional parties across India immediately after the fall of the United Front government. The disintegration started in 1998 and was complete by 2000. Deve Gowda's own Janata Dal (Secular) was formed in 1999.

16. Regarding situation arising out of reported death of three farmers in police firing at Munderva Sugar Mill in Basti district, Uttar Pradesh, 12 December 2002, Lok Sabha debates.
17. Raised to charge the government with directly or indirectly abetting the disruption of communal harmony in the country, 2 December 1998, Lok Sabha debates.
18. Motion of confidence, 16 April 1999, Lok Sabha debates.
19. Ibid.
20. H.D. Deve Gowda's letter to Prime Minister A.B. Vajpayee, 6 March 2002, H.D. Deve Gowda papers (private).
21. H.D. Deve Gowda's letter to Prime Minister A.B. Vajpayee, 10 March 2002, H.D. Deve Gowda papers (private).
22. Discussion regarding Godhra killings and subsequent violence on Gujarat, 11 March 2002, Lok Sabha debates.
23. Discussion on motion of thanks to the President's address, 16 March 2002, Lok Sabha debates.
24. Author's interview with H.D. Deve Gowda on 5 October 2019.
25. Discussion on motion regarding expressing grave concern over the failure of administration in ensuring security of minority community in various parts of the country, especially in Gujarat, 30 April 2002, Lok Sabha debates.
26. Ibid.
27. Discussion regarding Ayodhya issue raised by Mulayam Singh Yadav, 27 February 2003, Lok Sabha debates.
28. Motion of thanks on the President's address, 16 March 2002, Lok Sabha debates.
29. Regarding incidents of violence and acts of vandalism in the precincts of Orissa legislative assembly, 18 March 2002, Lok Sabha debates.
30. Discussion regarding problems being faced by farmers in the country, 4 December 2002, Lok Sabha debates.
31. Author's interview with H.D. Deve Gowda on 3 June 2020.
32. H.D. Deve Gowda's letter to Prime Minister A.B. Vajpayee, 20 January 2003, H.D. Deve Gowda papers (private).
33. H.D. Deve Gowda's letter to Prime Minister A.B. Vajpayee, 22 January 2003, H.D. Deve Gowda papers (private).

34. H.D. Deve Gowda's letter to Prime Minister A.B. Vajpayee, 26 January 2003, H.D. Deve Gowda papers (private).
35. Letter from Prime Minister A.B. Vajpayee to H.D. Deve Gowda, 5 February 2003, H.D. Deve Gowda papers (private).
36. Section 4: 'Interesting Times', pages 199–206, *Lucknow Boy: A Memoir*, by Vinod Mehta, Penguin Books India, New Delhi, 2011.
37. Recounted to the author by Ajith Pillai, who was on the senior editorial team of *Outlook* magazine. Pillai wrote and coordinated the two cover stories on Vajpayee's PMO ('Rigging the PMO' 5 March 2001, and 'PM's Achilles Heel' 26 March 2001), which led to the raids on the magazine and its proprietor.

Chapter 21: Modi Focus and the Patel Backdrop

1. Author's interview with H.D. Deve Gowda on 5 October 2019.
2. Ibid.
3. 'PM Modi Warms up to JD(S), Chastises Rahul Gandhi for Insulting Tallest Leader Deve Gowda', 1 May 2018, www.news18.com: https://www.news18.com/news/politics/pm-modi-warms-up-to-jds-chastises-rahul-gandhi-for-insulting-tallest-leader-deve-gowda-1735201.html
4. 'HD Deve Gowda Commends PM Modi, Says Continued in Lok Sabha Only Because of Him', 3 May 2018, www.swarajyamag.com: https://swarajyamag.com/insta/hd-deve-gowda-commends-pm-modi-says-continued-in-lok-sabha-only-because-of-him
5. 'Amid Karnataka Drama PM Modi Calls JD(S) Chief Deve Gowda', 18 May 2018, *Statesman*: https://www.thestatesman.com/india/amid-karnataka-drama-pm-modi-calls-jds-chief-deve-gowda-1502637561.html
6. Author's interview with a former aide of H.D. Deve Gowda who chose to remain anonymous.
7. 'Modi Replies, Says Deve Gowda Welcome in Gujarat', 13 April 2014, *Outlook*: https://www.outlookindia.com/newswire/story/modi-replies-says-deve-gowda-welcome-in-gujarat/836988
8. Ibid.
9. Author's interview with H.D. Deve Gowda on 5 October 2019.

10. 'Modi Discovers Respect for Deve Gowda', 2 May 2018, *Telegraph*: https://www.telegraphindia.com/india/modi-discovers-respect-for-deve-gowda/cid/1343717

11. 'Sardar Patel, Morarji Desai and H D Deve Gowda Were Not Accepted by Lutyens's Delhi', https://youtu.be/iSH8WXPP2fI

12. Author's interview with H.D. Deve Gowda on 5 October 2019.

13. Ibid.

14. 'Will Disown Son if He Backs BJP: Deve Gowda on Karnataka Elections', https://www.youtube.com/watch?v=t385OXDL1sc

15. 'Offered to Quit as MP in 2014 after PM Modi Won, But . . . Deve Gowda', 14 February 2019, www.catchnews.com: http://www.catchnews.com/politics-news/offered-to-quit-as-mp-in-2014-after-pm-modi-won-but-hd-deve-gowda-149127.html

16. 'Former PM Deve Gowda Breaks Ranks with Opposition to Attend Midnight Event', 30 June 2017, *Financial Express*: https://www.financialexpress.com/india-news/gst-rollout-former-pm-deve-gowda-breaks-ranks-with-opposition-to-attend-midnight-event/741903/

17. 'Deve Gowda Opposes Attempts to Scrap Article 370', 2 April 2019, *The Hindu*: https://www.thehindu.com/elections/loksabha-2019/deve-gowda-opposes-attempts-to-scrap-article-370/article26714731.ece

18. 'Deve Gowda: There is an Undeclared Emergency in the Country', 23 April 2019, *Hindu Business Line*: https://www.thehindubusinessline.com/news/national/deve-gowda-there-is-an-undeclared-emergency-in-the-country/article26924387.ece

19. Ibid.

20. 'Deve Gowda Hits Back at PM over Lollipop Company Remark', 3 January 2019, *India Today*: https://www.indiatoday.in/india/story/deve-gowda-hits-back-at-pm-modi-over-his-lollipop-company-remark-1422858-2019-01-03

21. 'Kumaraswamy Swearing-in Turns into a Show of Strength for Opposition', 24 May 2018, *Economic Times*: https://economictimes.indiatimes.com/news/politics-and-nation/kumaraswamy-swearing-in-turns-into-show-of-strength-for-opposition/articleshow/64297718.cms?from=mdr

22. 'At Mamata Banerjee's Kolkata Rally Deve Gowda's Solution on Herculean Seat-Sharing Task', 19 January 2019, www.news18.com: https://www.news18.com/news/politics/at-mamata-banerjees-kolkata-rally-deve-gowdas-solution-on-herculean-seat-sharing-task-2007509.html

23. H.D. Deve Gowda testimonial on the Arya Vaidyasala website: https://www.aryavaidyasala.com/avs-in-news.php

24. 'Opposition Demands Immediate Release of Political Detainees in Kashmir', 9 March 2020, *The Hindu*: https://www.thehindu.com/news/national/opposition-demands-immediate-release-of-political-detainees-in-kashmir/article31023534.ece

25. Author's interview with H.D. Deve Gowda on 11 March 2020.

26. Keynote address delivered in Seoul on 4 February 2020 at the General Assembly of International Summit Council for Peace, organized by Universal Peace Federation, a United Nations-affiliated organization.

27. Prime Minister Narendra Modi's letter to H.D. Deve Gowda dated 29 April 2020, thanking him for his contribution to PM Cares fund.

28. H.D. Deve Gowda's letter to Prime Minister Narendra Modi dated 13 April 2020.

29. Discussion on motion of thanks to the President's address, 16 March 2002, Lok Sabha debates.

30. Bhuj earthquake happened on 26 January 2002. It killed nearly 20,000 people in India and Pakistan and injured over 1,50,000.

31. 'PM Expresses Happiness over Deve Gowda's Visit to Statue of Unity, Gowda Praises Modi for Constructing Tallest Statue', 14 October 2019, *Times of India*: https://timesofindia.indiatimes.com/india/pm-expresses-happiness-over-deve-gowdas-visit-to-statue-of-unity-gowda-praises-modi-for-constructing-tallest-statue/articleshow/71582009.cms

32. 'All Men Brown as Soil', by Sugata Srinivasaraju, 30 October 2019, *Mumbai Mirror*: https://mumbaimirror.indiatimes.com/opinion/columnists/all-men-brown-as-soil/articleshow/71811782.cms

33. Page 179, Section Four: '1929–34 Prisoner' in *Patel: A Life*, by Rajmohan Gandhi, Navajivan Publishing House, 1991.

34. Author's interview with Shyamal Datta on 22 May 2020.

35. 'Gowda Performs Matru Shradh at Siddpur', 5 November 2009, *DNA*: https://www.dnaindia.com/india/report-gowda-performs-matru-shradh-in-siddhpur-1307406

36. 'Ahmedabad Airport Was Named after Sardar Vallabhbhai Patel in My Rule: Shankersinh Vaghela', 5 November 2018, *Indian Express*: https://indianexpress.com/article/cities/ahmedabad/ahmedabad-airport-was-named-after-sardar-vallabhbhai-patel-in-my-rule-shankersinh-vaghela-5433990/

37. 'All Men Brown as Soil', by Sugata Srinivasaraju, 30 October 2019, *Mumbai Mirror*: https://mumbaimirror.indiatimes.com/opinion/columnists/all-men-brown-as-soil/articleshow/71811782.cms

38. Author's interview with H.D. Deve Gowda on 5 October 2019.

39. *India Wins Freedom*, by Maulana Abul Kalam Azad, Orient Blackswan, 2019.

40. 'All Men Brown as Soil', by Sugata Srinivasaraju, 30 October 2019, *Mumbai Mirror*: https://mumbaimirror.indiatimes.com/opinion/columnists/all-men-brown-as-soil/articleshow/71811782.cms

41. Author's interview with H.D. Deve Gowda on 5 October 2019.

Chapter 22: The Family, the Patriarch

1. In 1951, India's total population was 36,10,88,090, of which rural population was 29,86,44,381 and urban population 6,24,43,709. In 1961, the total population was 43,92,34,771, of which rural was 36,02,98,168 and urban 7,89,36,603. Source: https://censusindia.gov.in/Census_Data_2001/India_at_glance/variation.aspx

2. Author's interview with C. Manjunath on 7 January 2021.

3. Ibid.

4. Author's conversation with H.D. Deve Gowda on 7 January 2021.

5. Author's interview with H.D. Deve Gowda on 20 October 2019.

6. Author's conversation with H.D. Shailaja on 16 November 2020.

7. Ibid.

8. Author's lunch meeting with H.D. Deve Gowda on 16 November 2020.

9. Sociologist M.N. Srinivas spoke of 'Sanskritization' in the 1950s. This term is also read as 'Brahminization.' He propounded this theory in his D.Phil thesis at Oxford University, and it spoke about

a person from the lower castes imitating or adopting the customs, rites and beliefs of the Brahmins. For a critical understanding of M.N. Srinivas' idea, read the introduction and chapter two of *Debrahmanising History: Dominance and Resistance in Indian Society* by Braj Ranjan Mani, Manohar, 2018.

10. Author's interview with H.D. Deve Gowda on 27 July 2019.
11. Author's interview with K.A. Thippeswamy on 22 December 2020.
12. 'G-15 Summit: Family Goes Holidaying while Deve Gowda Wins Some Instant Friends', by Harinder Baweja , 30 November 1996, *India Today*: https://www.indiatoday.in/magazine/diplomacy/story/19961130-g-15-summit-family-goes-holidaying-while-deve-gowda-wins-some-instant-friends-834137-1996-11-30. (Deve Gowda had instructed his private assistant K.R. Shivakumar to keep all the personal bills safely so that it could be made public if the media created a controversy—author's interview with K.R. Shivakumar on 8 Feburary 2020 revealed this.)
13. Author's interview with H.D. Deve Gowda on 5 January 2020.
14. Ibid.
15. Author's interview with K.A. Thippeswamy on 22 December 2020.
16. Author's interview with H.D. Deve Gowda on 5 January 2020.
17. Author's interview with Montek Singh Ahluwalia on 7 February 2020.
18. Author's interview with H.D. Deve Gowda on 15 September 2019.
19. Author's interview with C. Manjunath on 7 January 2021.
20. Ibid.
21. Chennamma in the talk show *Weekend with Ramesh*, episodes 21 and 22, season 3, Zee Kannada entertainment channel, 10 June and 11 June 2017.
22. Author's interview with K.A. Thippeswamy on 22 December 2020.
23. Author's interview with H.D. Deve Gowda on 20 October 2019.
24. Ibid.
25. Author's interview with C. Manjunath on 7 January 2021.
26. Author's interview with H.D. Deve Gowda on 5 October 2019.

27. Author's interview with C. Manjunath on 7 January 2021.
28. Eldest son H.D. Balakrishna Gowda in the talk show *Weekend with Ramesh*, episodes 21 and 22, season 3, Zee Kannada entertainment channel, 10 June and 11 June 2017.
29. Ibid.
30. H.D. Deve Gowda in the talk show *Weekend with Ramesh*, episodes 21 and 22, season 3, Zee Kannada entertainment channel, 10 June and 11 June 2017.
31. Author's interview with K.R. Shivakumar on 8 February 2020.
32. 'Lokesh Had Brought a Slur on the Village', UNI report in rediff. com, 26 February 2001: https://www.rediff.com/news/2001/feb/26gowda.htm
33. Ibid.
34. 'Family Feud Suspected behind Acid Attack', by M.B. Maramkal, *Times of India*, 23 February 2001: https://m.timesofindia.com/family-feud-suspected-behind-acid-attack/articleshow/22360002.cms
35. Ibid.
36. 'Lokesh Had Brought a Slur on the Village,' UNI report in rediff. com, 26 February 2001: https://www.rediff.com/news/2001/feb/26gowda.htm
37. Ibid.
38. Author's interview with B.L. Shankar on 30 May 2020.
39. 'Acid Case: Deve Gowda's Nephew Gets 8-Year Jail Term', *Times of India*, 30 September 2002: https://m.timesofindia.com/city/bengaluru/acid-case-deve-gowdas-nephew-gets-8-year-jail-term/articleshow/23794619.cms Also, 'Acid Attack on Gowda's Wife: Judicial Probe Ordered', Zee News, 22 February 2001: https://zeenews.india.com/home/acid-attack-on-gowdas-wife-judicial-probe-ordered_8916.html
40. H.D. Deve Gowda in the talk show *Weekend with Ramesh*, episodes 21 and 22, season 3, Zee Kannada entertainment channel, 10 June and 11 June 2017.
41. Author's interview with C. Manjunath on 7 January 2021.
42. Ibid.
43. Ibid.
44. Author's conversation with H.D. Shailaja on 16 November 2020.

45. Ibid.
46. Author's interview with K.R. Shivakumar on 8 February 2020.
47. Maneangaladalli Maatukathe (courtyard conversations), a monthly public interaction organized with well-known personalities by the department of Kannada and culture, government of Karnataka. H.D. Deve Gowda participated in this on 17 November 2018.
48. Author's interview with C. Manjunath on 7 January 2021.

Epilogue: This Far and Further

1. 'Generals Angry with Gowda: Fernandes', *Asian Age*, 19 April 1999.
2. H.D. Deve Gowda's letter to Atal Bihari Vajpayee on 22 March 2000 refers to earlier letters. In fact, it starts by saying: 'You will recall my earlier letters to you in respect of procurement of T-90 tank.' In a press release Gowda issued on 4 January 1999, he refers to letters dated 8 November 1998 and 10 December 1998. H.D. Deve Gowda papers (private).
3. H.D. Deve Gowda's press release dated 4 January 1999. H.D. Deve Gowda papers (private).
4. 'Collision Course', by Raj Chengappa and Manoj Joshi, *India Today*, 12 April 1999: https://www.indiatoday.in/magazine/cover-story/story/19990412-opposition-uses-bhagwat-issue-to-launch-full-scale-offensive-to-bring-down-bjp-led-govt-780635-1999-04-12
5. 'Gowda's Statements Against Mehta to Be Expunged in LS', by Gaurav Sawant, *Indian Express*, 8 May 1999. Gowda quotes this story in his letter to Lok Sabha Speaker G.M.C. Balayogi on 19 April 1999. H.D. Deve Gowda papers (private).
6. K.R. Narayanan in his letter dated 5 May 1999 refers to H.D. Deve Gowda's letter of 3 May 1999 and says he is sending it to the prime minister: 'I am sending a copy to the Prime Minister specifically making a reference to your suggestion for a comparative trial of the tanks in peak summer conditions.' H.D. Deve Gowda papers (private).
7. H.D. Deve Gowda letter to Atal Bihari Vajpayee dated 5 September 1998. In H.D. Deve Gowda papers (private).

8.   H.D. Deve Gowda letters to Atal Bihari Vajpayee dated 15 September 1998, 8 October 1998 and 2 February 1999. H.D. Deve Gowda papers (private).

9.   Jagmohan's undated letter to Yashwant Sinha marked 'secret'. In the letter, Jagmohan's opening para said: 'You are, I understand seized of the problems pertaining to non-recovery of huge amounts of licence fees from operators of cellular phones and basic services. The matter was last considered by the cabinet on September 16, 1998.'

10. 'A Golden Island of His Own', by Sugata Srinivasaraju, *Outlook*, 4 May 2009: https://magazine.outlookindia.com/story/a-golden-island-of-his-own/240366

11. A handwritten, signed note by H.D. Deve Gowda, titled 'Important decision to be taken by GOI', dated January 1997 on the letterhead of Raj Bhavan, Calcutta. S.S. Meenakshisundaram papers (private).

12. A handwritten, undated, unsigned note on the letterhead of the Hotel Imperial, Singapore has fourteen points on various development projects on page one and seven points on page two. The second page is headlined 'Programme to be announced and implementation.' S.S. Meenakshisundaram papers (private).

13. There was an interesting tweet on 29 January 2021 by the handle @GoofySufi, which claimed that Janata Dal (Secular) was the only party in the world whose symbol was a woman farmer. The author has not been able to verify this.

14. Author's interview with H.D. Deve Gowda on 20 October 2019.

15. Author's interview with H.D. Deve Gowda on 5 January 2020.

16. Ibid.

17. H.D. Deve Gowda's speech on the farm bills on 20 September 2020 placed on record in the Rajya Sabha as he could not complete his speech due to pandemonium in the house. Posted on his Twitter account the same day.

18. On www.urbandictionary.com, one of the descriptions for 'Bangalored' reads: 'You are Bangalored when you get fired from your job because it was outsourced to an offshore company. The name derives from the city of Bangalore, India, where a lot of IT jobs in the US are being outsourced.'

19. A tweet from H.D. Deve Gowda's handle on 30 October 2020 said he attended a prayer meeting with 'Muslim friends' in Sira, Tumkur district. An accompanying picture showed him wearing a skull cap.

20. 'Yediyurappa Is a Chief Minister with Nine Lives', by Sugata Srinivasaraju, *Mumbai Mirror*, 6 January 2021: https://timesofindia.indiatimes.com/india/yediyurappa-is-a-chief-minister-with-nine-lives/articleshow/80119790.cms

21. 'A Life Apart', review by Omkar Goswami of *Breaking Through: A Memoir* by Isher Judge Ahluwalia, *Indian Express*, 30 August 2020: https://indianexpress.com/article/books-and-literature/the-personal-and-the-public-coalesce-in-isher-judge-ahluwalias-memoir-6574883/

22. H.D. Deve Gowda's statement on India and China border dispute dated 19 June 2020. Posted on his Twitter account the same day.

23. 'China, India Sign Agreement to Ease Border Dispute', CNN.com, 29 November 1996.

24. World Summit 2020, Universal Peace Federation held between February 3 and 9, 2020 at Seoul, South Korea. H.D. Deve Gowda attended the conference between February 2 and 5, 2020.

25. Notes of D.S. Kishor, department of life sciences, College of Life Science and Biotechnology, Dongguk University.

26. *The New Koreans: The Business, History and People of South Korea* by Michael Breen, Penguin Random House, 2017.